ACTS

ACTS

A Commentary for Biblical Preaching and Teaching

JOHN D. HARVEY

DAVID GENTINO

Acts: A Commentary for Biblical Preaching and Teaching

© 2023 by John D. Harvey & David Gentino

Published by Kregel Ministry, an imprint of Kregel Publications, 2450 Oak Industrial Dr. NE, Grand Rapids, MI 49505-6020.

Unless otherwise indicated, the translation of the Scripture portions used throughout the commentary is the authors' own English rendering of the original biblical languages.

Scripture quotations marked ESV are taken from The Holy Bible, English Standard Version. Copyright © 2001 by Crossway Bibles, a publishing ministry of Good News Publishers.

Scripture quotations marked NASB are taken from the New American Standard Bible® (NASB), Copyright © 1960, 1962, 1963, 1968, 1971, 1972, 1973, 1975, 1977, 1995 by The Lockman Foundation. Used by permission. www.Lockman.org

Scripture quotations marked NLT are taken from the Holy Bible, New Living Translation, copyright © 1996, 2004, 2015 by Tyndale House Foundation. Used by permission of Tyndale House Publishers, Inc., Carol Stream, Illinois 60188. All rights reserved.

Scripture quotations marked NIV are taken from the Holy Bible, New International Version®, NIV®. Copyright © 1973, 1978, 1984, 2011 by Biblica, Inc.™ Used by permission of Zondervan. All rights reserved worldwide. www.zondervan.com

Scripture quotations marked NRSV are taken from the Holy Bible, Revised Standard Version, copyright © 1946, 1952, and 1971 National Council of the Churches of Christ in the United States of America. Used by permission. All rights reserved worldwide.

Italics in Scripture quotations indicate emphasis added by the authors.

The Hebrew font, NewJerusalemU, and the Greek font, GraecaU, are available from www.linguistsoftware.com/lgku.htm, +1-425-775-1130.

All photos are under Creative Commons licensing, and contributors are indicated in the captions of the photos.

ISBN 978-0-8254-5829-3

Printed in Colombia

23 24 25 26 27 / 5 4 3 2 1

Contents

Publisher's Preface to the Series / 7

Preface to Acts / 9

Exegetical Author's Acknowledgments / 10

Preaching Author's Acknowledgments / 11

Overview of All Preaching Passages / 13

Abbreviations / 51

Introduction to Acts / 57

JERUSALEM (1:1–8:3)

The Promises Leading to Pentecost (1:1–11) / 75

The Preparation for Pentecost (1:12–26) / 85

The Power of Pentecost (2:1–40) / 95

The Early Church's Common Life (2:41–47) / 109

The Church's First Healing (3:1–26) / 117

The Church's First Opposition (4:1–31) / 129

The Church's Benevolence (4:32–37) / 141

The Church's Integrity (5:1–11) / 149

The Church's Impact (5:12–16) / 157

The Church's Unwavering Witness (5:17–42) / 163

The Church's First Problem (6:1–7) / 175

The Church's First Martyr (6:8–8:3) / 185

JUDEA, SAMARIA, AND SYRIA (8:4–12:25)

Philip's Witness in Samaria (8:4–25) / 203

Philip's Witness to an Ethiopian (8:26–40) / 215

Jesus's Appearance to and Confirmation of Saul (9:1–19a) / 225

Saul's Witness in Damascus and Jerusalem (9:19b–31) / 237

Peter's Witness in Coastal Judea (9:32–43) / 247

Peter's Witness to a Godfearer (10:1–48) / 255

Defense of Peter's Witness to the Gentiles (11:1–18) / 271

Bold Witness in Syrian Antioch (11:19–30) / 279

Opposition from Herod Agrippa I (12:1–25) / 289

CYPRUS, GALATIA, AND THE JERUSALEM COUNCIL (13:1–15:35)

Witness on Cyprus (13:1–12) / 303

Witness in Pisidian Antioch (13:13–52) / 311

Further Witness in South Galatia (14:1–28) / 323

The Jerusalem Council (15:1–35) / 335

MACEDONIA AND ACHAIA (15:36–18:17)

The Road to Europe (15:36–16:10) / 351

Witness in Philippi (16:11–40) / 359

Witness in Thessalonica and Berea (17:1–15) / 373

Witness in Athens (17:16–34) / 383

Witness in Corinth (18:1–17) / 395

ASIA (18:18–20:38)

Early Events in Ephesus (18:18–28) / 407

Witness in Ephesus (19:1–22) / 417

Trouble in Ephesus (19:23–40) / 429

Concluding the Mission in Europe (20:1–12) / 439

Concluding the Mission in Asia (20:13–38) / 447

JERUSALEM AND CAESAREA (21:1–26:32)

Journey to Jerusalem (21:1–14) / 461

Paul's Arrival in Jerusalem and the Elders' Proposal (21:15–26) / 469

Defense Before the Mob (21:27–22:29) / 479

Defense Before the Sanhedrin (22:30–23:11) / 493

Transfer to Caesarea Maritima (23:12–35) / 501

Defense Before Felix (24:1–27) / 511

Defense Before Festus (25:1–12) / 523

Defense Before Herod Agrippa II (25:13–26:32) / 531

MALTA AND ROME (27:1–28:31)

Storm and Shipwreck (27:1–44) / 549

Witness on Malta (28:1–10) / 563

Witness in Rome (28:11–31) / 569

References / 579

PUBLISHER'S PREFACE TO THE SERIES

Since words were first uttered, people have struggled to understand one another and to know the main meaning in any verbal exchange.

The answer to what God is talking about must be understood in every context and generation; that is why Kerux (KAY-rukes) emphasizes text-based truths and bridges from the context of the original hearers and readers to the twenty-first-century world. Kerux values the message of the text, thus its name taken from the Greek *kērux*, a messenger or herald who announced the proclamations of a ruler or magistrate.

Biblical authors trumpeted all kinds of important messages in very specific situations, but a big biblical idea, grasped in its original setting and place, can transcend time. This specific, big biblical idea taken from the biblical passage embodies a single concept that transcends time and bridges the gap between the author's contemporary context and the reader's world. How do the prophets perceive the writings of Moses? How does the writer of Hebrews make sense of the Old Testament? How does Clement in his second epistle, which may be the earliest sermon known outside the New Testament, adapt verses from Isaiah and also ones from the Gospels? Or what about Luther's bold use of Romans 1:17? How does Jonathan Edwards allude to Genesis 19? Who can forget Martin Luther King Jr.'s "I Have a Dream" speech and his appropriation of Amos 5:24: "No, no, we are not satisfied, and we will not be satisfied until 'justice rolls down like waters, and righteousness like a mighty stream'"? How does a preacher in your local church today apply the words of Hosea in a meaningful and life-transforming way?

WHAT IS PRIME IN GOD'S MIND, AND HOW IS THAT EXPRESSED TO A GIVEN GENERATION IN THE UNITS OF THOUGHT THROUGHOUT THE BIBLE?

Answering those questions is what Kerux authors do. Based on the popular "big idea" preaching model, Kerux commentaries uniquely combine the insights of experienced Bible exegetes (trained in interpretation) and homileticians (trained in preaching). Their collaboration provides for every Bible book:

- A detailed introduction and outline
- A summary of all preaching sections with their primary exegetical, theological, and preaching ideas
- Preaching pointers that join the original context with the contemporary one
- Insights from the Hebrew and Greek text
- A thorough exposition of the text
- Sidebars of pertinent information for further background
- Appropriate charts and photographs
- A theological focus to passages

- A contemporary big idea for every preaching unit
- Present-day meaning, validity, and application of a main idea
- Creative presentations for each primary idea
- Key questions about the text for study groups

Many thanks to Jim Weaver, Kregel's former acquisitions editor, who conceived of this commentary series and further developed it with the team of Jeffrey D. Arthurs, Robert B. Chisholm, David M. Howard Jr., Darrell L. Bock, Roy E. Ciampa, and Michael J. Wilkins. We also recognize with gratitude the significant contributions of Dennis Hillman, Fred Mabie, Paul Hillman, Herbert W. Bateman IV, and Shawn Vander Lugt who have been instrumental in the development of the series. Finally, gratitude is extended to the two authors for each Kerux volume; the outside reviewers, editors, and proofreaders; and Kregel staff who suggested numerous improvements.

—Kregel Publications

PREFACE TO ACTS

Think of everything we would be missing if the book of Acts were absent from the New Testament canon. When we want to learn about the beginning of the early church, the growth of the early church, the community life of the early church, or the preaching of the early church, we visit the book of Acts. When we want to learn about the essentials of the gospel message, the power of the name of Jesus, the way in which God works among his people, or the ministry of the Holy Spirit, we visit the book of Acts. When we want to learn about how Jesus's disciples crossed ethnic and cultural boundaries; confronted competing religious systems; persevered in the face of religious, economic, and civil opposition; or defended their faith before those in authority, we visit the book of Acts.

We visit the book of Acts so frequently because Luke tells the story of events that interest us and are important to us, and he does it brilliantly. He combines historical details, theological themes, and missional strategies within the narrative framework of a single volume. The multifaceted allure of Acts grows out of Luke's multiple purposes in writing. Historically, Acts provides an account of the origin and growth of Christianity. Theologically, Acts portrays God in action through his people. Evangelistically, Acts presents Jesus as the one who brings salvation to both Jew and Gentile. Apologetically, Acts defends Christianity in the face of religious and civil opposition. Missiologically, Acts provides models for crossing new geographical and cultural thresholds with the gospel. Those multiple purposes and the way in which Luke pursues them lead us on a rich journey as we follow Jesus's disciples from Jerusalem, throughout Judea, Samaria, and Syria, into Cyprus, Galatia, Macedonia, Achaia, and Asia, back to Jerusalem and Caesarea, and eventually across the Mediterranean to Malta and Rome. It is a journey well worth taking.

EXEGETICAL AUTHOR'S ACKNOWLEDGMENTS

This book is dedicated to the memory of Dr. William J. Larkin, Jr.,
teacher, mentor, colleague, and friend,
who was a far more accomplished Luke-Acts scholar than I will ever be.

For many years I would say that everything I knew about the book of Acts, I learned from Bill Larkin. His course on Acts in Historical, Theological, and Missiological Perspective was a mainstay of our seminary's curriculum. I had an opportunity to take the course with Bill while I was working as a faculty assistant, and later, I had the privilege of teaching the course whsile Bill was on sabbatical. His careful, interdisciplinary approach to the book became formative for the way I view and teach Acts, whether on our main campus in Columbia, South Carolina, or at our site in Korntal, Germany. Anyone who knew Bill will no doubt recognize echoes of his work in not a few places.

I would never have been so bold as to take on a commentary on Acts without Bill's mentoring. I would never have had the opportunity to work on this commentary without Herb Bateman's willingness to add me to the Kerux team. I would never have been able to commit to the project without David Gentino agreeing to assume the role of homiletical author. I would never have survived the editing process without Shawn Vander Lugt's patient guidance. Each of these individuals has been essential to seeing this project through to its conclusion.

The process of writing a commentary necessarily involves interacting with the work of scholars who have already made the same journey. As a result, an exegetical author stands on the shoulders of giants. In addition to Bill Larkin, there are now many others to whom I am indebted. I have learned far more from them than I have contributed to the study of Acts. If this volume proves to be helpful to those who consult it, then God has been gracious indeed.

—John D. Harvey

PREACHING AUTHOR'S ACKNOWLEDGMENTS

To my family,
To my local church family,
To my global church family—we have
enjoyed this unhindered gospel together.

Because I am a fumbling missionary, church planter, now pastor, the book of Acts has never been far from my imagination. At times I have read it wrongly as an impossible standard, a wistful wish for an ancient church that got everything right. But the more I read and study, the more Jesus thunders on every page. His "absence" in his ascension is a marvelous and powerful presence then and now.

Our family has lived out these pages of Acts within Jesus's church. We have read and talked about them together. We printed copies of Acts in a half dozen languages and studied them with a group of seekers in our flat in South Asia. We turned to them again when we gathered a core group to plant Columbia Presbyterian Church here in South Carolina. We have returned to this book when we tearfully commissioned church planters and missionaries from our midst. These are to us the true continuation of Jesus's doing and teaching onward to the ends of the earth.

The homiletical contributions found here are jumping-off points for teachers in varied contexts. I preached Acts to our church on the heels of writing this commentary and found myself making changes to fit our setting. The apostles would have expected as much.

I am indebted to John D. Harvey for his invitation to join him in this project. I have learned much from him in these pages. I am thankful to the wonderful Kerux team. I am deeply grateful to my precious family—Julie, Judah, Amelie, Gabriel, Noah—and to my dear church family Cola Pres for giving time, space, prayers, and encouragement. To God be the glory.

—David Gentino

OVERVIEW OF ALL PREACHING PASSAGES

Acts 1:1–11

EXEGETICAL IDEA
During the forty days from the resurrection to the ascension, Jesus reminded the apostles of the Father's promise, he commanded them to rely on the Spirit's power, and two angels challenged them to expect the Son's return.

THEOLOGICAL FOCUS
Jesus sets the parameters and provides the resources for his followers to extend his ministry to the end of the earth.

PREACHING IDEA
Jesus's directives determine our direction.

PREACHING POINTERS
Have you ever faced a situation that appeared impossible? You can respond to that sort of situation in one of two ways. You can tremble in despair, or you can trust in God. Jesus's disciples must have felt as though they were facing an impossible situation at the beginning of Acts. Jesus was getting ready to leave them (again). He had told them multiple times that they were to reach the entire world with the gospel, but there were only 120 of them, they had no "leader," and the environment was as hostile as anyone could imagine. With Luke's original readers, we need to understand that Jesus speaks into impossible situations to give us the encouragement we need. If we do, we will follow his instructions and trust in his promises regardless of how impossible the situation might appear to be.

People today should be able to relate to the desire to know what the future holds and to the role of witnesses who testify to the truth of statements and/or events. They should also be familiar with teachers instructing a group over an extended period of time, as Jesus did with his disciples. The events described in Acts 1:1–11 correct any suggestion that Jesus's ministry ended when he ascended, or that his followers can engage in ministry in their own power. They commend trust in God's promises and resources, hope in Jesus's return, and commit to the task Jesus has assigned. They remind us that Jesus's directives—his instructions and his promises—determine the direction of our ministries.

Acts 1:12–26

EXEGETICAL IDEA
While they waited for the promise of the Holy Spirit, Jesus's followers restored the integrity of apostolic leadership by engaging in united prayer, looking to inspired Scripture for direction, and trusting in God to identify the person of his choosing.

THEOLOGICAL FOCUS
Engaging in mission requires a leadership team that is intact, qualified, and set apart by God.

PREACHING IDEA
God's mission requires leadership that is unified, qualified, and sanctified.

PREACHING POINTERS
A well-known leadership axiom reminds us that although we can go faster alone, we can go farther as part of a team. What do you do, though, when the team has been fractured, whether through sin, interpersonal conflict, or death? That was the challenge the eleven remaining apostles faced after Judas Iscariot's apostasy and suicide. Their task of continuing Jesus's ministry to the Jews first required a twelfth member for their leadership team. It was crucial that they fill that vacancy with the right person. With Luke's original readers, we need to understand the importance of following the guiding principles the apostles used to restore and preserve the integrity of their leadership team by filling the vacancy with the individual God intended. If we do, we will ensure that we are prepared to engage in the mission he has given us.

People today should be able to relate to the need to replace someone who has left a position or role, whether voluntarily or involuntarily. They should also be able to relate to the practice of finding qualified candidates to fill the resulting vacancy. The apostles' actions in Acts 1:12–26 correct any suggestion that a leadership failure can go unanswered or that preserving the integrity of a leadership team is unimportant. The passage commends commitment to the important guiding principles of devotion to prayer, reliance on Scripture, and trust in God's choice. Adhering to those principles produces a prepared leadership team that is unified, qualified, and set apart by God for the task he has given that team.

Acts 2:1–40

EXEGETICAL IDEA
The Spirit's coming at Pentecost created initial confusion, provided an opportunity for Peter to preach the gospel, and resulted in the conversion of three thousand individuals.

THEOLOGICAL FOCUS
The Holy Spirit opens doors for witness, empowers believers for witness, and brings conviction through God's Word in witness.

PREACHING IDEA
Pentecost power sets the pattern for the church's advance.

PREACHING POINTERS
How does any movement begin, whether social, political, or religious? Origins are important, and Larkin notes, "a people reinvigorates itself by drawing comfort and challenge from the

way it was in the beginning" (1995, 48). How did the early church grow from 120 members meeting in an upstairs room in Jerusalem to a major religious movement that would eventually reach the capital of the Roman Empire? With Luke's original readers, we need to understand how God ordered the events surrounding the birth of the Christian movement and mission. In particular, we need to understand the role the Holy Spirit played—and should continue to play—in the church's witness and mission.

People today should be able to relate to the confusion that might arise when something out of the ordinary happens, whether in their own lives or in the lives of others. They should also be familiar with public speeches and assemblies of people from different countries; both converge whenever the general assembly of the United Nations meets. Followers of Jesus can readily relate to incorrect perceptions about Christianity and possible mockery by nonbelievers. The confusion and different conclusions of the listeners present at Pentecost correct the suggestion that the miraculous is adequate for men and women to come to faith, because the events of that morning required interpretation from Scripture. The account of the events at Pentecost commends recognition of the opportunities God provides for witness, reliance on the Holy Spirit for power in witness, and the resource of God's Word in witness. It also provides insight into the roles God's Spirit, God's Word, and God's people have as the church's mission advances.

Acts 2:41–47

EXEGETICAL IDEA
Devotion, generosity, close relationships, a good reputation, and continuing numerical growth characterized the common life of the Jerusalem church.

THEOLOGICAL FOCUS
Adopting the attitudes and activities of the NT church fosters spiritual growth and missional impact.

PREACHING IDEA
Church life fuels church growth, both spiritual and numerical.

PREACHING POINTERS
How does an organization deal with success? Success can lead to stress as it stretches and challenges existing systems, practices, and relationships. An organization's willingness to adapt and change as necessary can make the difference between continued growth, inertia, or decline. How did the Jerusalem church deal with the sudden, unexpected, explosive growth that followed Peter's Pentecost speech? With Luke's original readers, we need to understand how to live out an authentic relationship with Christ and other believers in a growing community of like-minded disciples. How can the contemporary church experience the same spiritual and numerical growth that the early church did?

People today should be able to relate to multiple ideas in the passage, including enjoying time with others, meeting the needs of the financially disadvantaged, and having a good reputation within the larger community. Followers of Jesus should connect with the concepts of teaching, prayer, and worship. The vibrant community life of the Jerusalem church corrects the idea that following Jesus is a purely individual activity. In fact, being a disciple involves participating actively in the common life of the body of Christ. Luke's account commends the importance of the shared life among believers that brings praise to God, meets the needs among its members, enjoys a good reputation among those outside the congregation, and attracts others to faith in Christ. As Christians, we need to understand how the early church lived out their new commitment to Christ so that we will embrace the devotion, care, intimacy, and witness that characterized NT church life.

Acts 3:1–26

EXEGETICAL IDEA
The healing of a lame man in the temple precincts provided Peter with an opportunity to preach about faith in Jesus, repentance, and judgment to the crowd that gathered.

THEOLOGICAL FOCUS
The proper response to Jesus's working through his witnesses is to turn from sin to God and experience the end-time blessings the OT promises.

PREACHING IDEA
The truth about Jesus demands a decision.

PREACHING POINTERS
It is impossible to remain neutral on the question of who Jesus is. When you face the truth about him, how will you respond? Will you reject him or accept him? How would the residents of Jerusalem respond when faced with the truth about Jesus? Peter's second sermon called them to make a decision about him and recognize the consequences of their decision. With Luke's original readers, we need to understand the seriousness of responding properly to the truth about Jesus and his continuing work through his followers, and we need to understand that the decision we make about him has eternal consequences.

People today should be able to relate to multiple facets of Acts 3:1–26. Most understand the challenges imposed by physical limitations. Many have experienced someone asking them for money. Local church leaders often find themselves answering requests for financial assistance from individuals in need. Joy at recovery from a serious illness is a common emotion, and questions often arise about miraculous recoveries from illness. Misperceptions of public figures are common, and actions based on ignorance abound. The passage corrects any suggestion that the natural laws of the universe limit God, or that human power or piety play any role in miraculous occurrences. It also corrects the ideas that Jesus is just another religious figure and that status as God's people comes from religious or ethnic heritage. The account commends an honest self-appraisal of our own spiritual condition, a willingness to turn from sin to God, an accurate understanding of who Jesus is, and confidence in the promises of Scripture. It also reinforces the importance of making the right decision about Jesus.

Acts 4:1–31

EXEGETICAL IDEA
The healing and sermon in the temple precincts lead to arrest, examination, warning, release, and united prayer for continuing bold witness.

THEOLOGICAL FOCUS
God sustains and empowers his people when they encounter opposition.

PREACHING IDEA
Human opposition opens divine doors of opportunity.

PREACHING POINTERS
If something is truly important, it is seldom easy. When Jesus promised to build his church, he did not promise that it would be an easy process. In fact, he told his disciples repeatedly that they would encounter opposition. Sometimes, the opposition would come from religious authorities; at other times, it would come from civil authorities; at still other times, it would come from members of their own families. Whatever the source, opposition would come, just as it came to the Jerusalem church in Acts 4. The healing of the lame man at the Beautiful Gate and Peter's sermon in Solomon's Portico led both to salvation of the powerless multitudes and to opposition from the powerful few. With Luke's original readers, we need to know how Jesus's early disciples responded when they encountered opposition, and we need to understand that opposition opens doors of opportunity to trust God, rely on the Holy Spirit, and witness boldly for Jesus.

People today should be able to relate to several elements of Luke's account in Acts 4:1–31. Religious persecution occurs in various forms around the world. Arrests and trials feature prominently in news stories. Warnings and threats of various sorts are common occurrences. Christians are familiar with prayer meetings, including meetings called to address special needs. The passage corrects the idea that Christians will never encounter opposition, or that such opposition is somehow outside of God's control. It also corrects the suggestion that effective witness requires formal education or training. It provides balance to a rigid interpretation of Romans 13:1–7 that might advocate for absolute obedience to authority regardless of the circumstances or demands. The account commends trust in God's providence, reliance on the Holy Spirit when facing difficult circumstances, and the importance of prayer.

Acts 4:32–37

EXEGETICAL IDEA
In a context of grace, unity, witness, and sharing, Barnabas is a positive example of the community's practice of caring for the impoverished.

THEOLOGICAL FOCUS
The Lord's grace unites his people to engage in powerful witness to those outside the church and generous care for those inside the church.

PREACHING IDEA
God's great grace produces great results.

PREACHING POINTERS
Where does money fit into the church's mission? In particular, how should the church view material need? How should it respond when its members encounter financial hardship? The Jerusalem church not only faced opposition from the religious leaders; its members were also isolated from the social support system of both the temple and the synagogues. As a result, many of the disciples were facing financial hardship. The apostles had witnessed boldly to Jesus and his resurrection and had taken an uncompromising stand for him in the face of opposition. The community had experienced great grace. How would that grace show itself when some of the disciples were impoverished? Barnabas, the son of encouragement, gave Jesus's followers a model of what it means not only to witness boldly but also to give generously.

People today should be able to relate to the idea of people in financial need, the process of selling property, and the practice of giving to those who are in need. The example of Barnabas's generosity corrects the idea that living the Christian life is a purely spiritual endeavor with no material component, as well as the idea that God's people cannot ignore the financial needs of others. Luke's account commends a commitment to holistic ministry that includes addressing material issues, being willing to put the needs of others above personal gain, and sharing voluntarily and generously to meet the needs of others. As Jesus's disciples, we need to understand that God's grace unites us for witness and mutual care, so that we will respond with generous sharing to meet the needs of others within his body.

Acts 5:1–11

EXEGETICAL IDEA
Ananias and Sapphira's act of counterfeit generosity constituted a sin against God and resulted in divine judgment.

THEOLOGICAL FOCUS
Because God holds his people accountable to a divine standard of integrity, he will take any action necessary to preserve the purity and peace of his church.

PREACHING IDEA
No one lies to God and lives.

PREACHING POINTERS
We can probably all identify with the shock of having someone we know die suddenly—especially when the death is unexpected. Imagine the trauma that would ensue when two members of a church, a husband and wife, fall dead in public in exactly the same way within three hours of each other. Several questions arise naturally, including: What is God doing? Why did they die? Did they do something to incur God's judgment? Are the rest of us in danger of the same fate? Barnabas's example of genuine benevolence gave the Jerusalem church a model of grace-filled generosity. What did the first-century disciples learn from Ananias and Sapphira's

fate following their act of false benevolence? What can the contemporary church learn about God's presence among, and standards for, his people?

People today should be able to relate to multiple ideas in this passage, including financial irregularities, the desire to look good in front of others, lying to cover up what they have done wrong, and unexpected deaths of relatives or friends. The negative example of Ananias and Sapphira corrects any suggestion that it is possible to hide attitudes or actions from God, that a relationship with God is limited to spiritual aspects of life, or that God overlooks sin. Luke's account commends living with integrity, honoring God in every aspect of life, respecting his holiness, and cultivating a sense of his presence with his people. As Christ's followers we must understand that he holds us accountable for our attitudes and actions, so that we will honor him in every area of our lives.

Acts 5:12–16

EXEGETICAL IDEA
Working through the apostles, God enhanced the church's reputation, added to the number of believers, and extended the mission to the towns surrounding Jerusalem.

THEOLOGICAL FOCUS
When God is at work through his people, the church grows spiritually, numerically, and missionally.

PREACHING IDEA
When God is at work, people will notice.

PREACHING POINTERS
Do people outside the church pay attention to what God is doing inside the church? When something special happens, people notice. Although their responses might differ, they will respond. When God is working among his people, men and women around them notice. They might be alarmed, or they might be attracted, but they notice. When the Holy Spirit was at work among the early disciples, the residents of Jerusalem responded with excitement and hope. That response, however, did not stop with the residents of the city. Reports of what God was doing spread to the towns around Jerusalem. With Luke's original readers, we need to realize that God's mission advances as he works through his people. We also need to live expectantly, looking for him to work in his church and make a difference in the world.

People today should be able to relate to the attention that accompanies extraordinary events, whether those events are positive or negative. Everyone talks about them and has strong feelings about them. If they are positive, they generate excitement and hope, just as the events in Jerusalem did. Luke's account of those events corrects any suggestion that those outside the church have no interest in what God is doing. His account also commends dependence on God to advance his purposes and the expectation that he will fulfill those purposes. As his people, we must understand that his mission advances as he works through his people—and that as he does, people will notice.

Acts 5:17–42

EXEGETICAL IDEA
The apostles respond to a second arrest with unshakeable resolve, unquenchable joy, and unwavering witness.

THEOLOGICAL FOCUS
The proper response to opposition is to stay faithful to the mission Jesus has given his church.

PREACHING IDEA
Remain steadfast in success or in suffering.

PREACHING POINTERS
Everyone enjoys success, at least when it is their own success. When it is someone else's success, however, it can breed other emotions, including jealousy and anger. By any measure, the early church in Jerusalem was experiencing success. The group was growing both numerically and spiritually. It was growing in influence and in impact. The high priest and his associates, however, saw that success as a threat to their authority. As the church's influence expanded, the leaders' opposition escalated. With Luke's original readers, we need to know that there is more than one side to success, including the potential for opposition and suffering, and we need to understand that Jesus expects us to remain faithful to the mission he has given us, regardless of the circumstances.

People today should be able to relate to the idea that success can breed negative feelings, including jealousy and anger. They most likely are familiar with judicial processes that include arrest, detention, hearing, verdict, and punishment. The idea of witnesses should also be familiar, whether as part of the judicial process or in other contexts. The passage corrects suggestions that opposition is a reason to stop sharing the gospel, that followers of Jesus must obey established authority under all circumstances, or that suffering for Jesus's sake is a reason for shame. It commends resolve, joy, and perseverance in the face of opposition and/ or suffering.

Acts 6:1–7

EXEGETICAL IDEA
The church commissions seven men to address an oversight in the care of widows, while the apostles focus on their primary ministry, and the number of disciples continues to grow.

THEOLOGICAL FOCUS
In meeting the challenges of ministry, God's people must set clear priorities, share leadership responsibilities, and maintain proper balance between mercy and mission.

PREACHING IDEA
Match calling with the need to balance mercy and mission.

PREACHING POINTERS

Have you ever found yourself facing a choice between equally important needs? You set out the pros and cons and find that your lists are the same length. What should you do? You could choose to ignore both needs. You could focus on one and ignore the other. You could do both poorly. You long to find a way to do both well. If there is a way, what is it? The early church faced exactly that sort of problem when a complaint arose about the treatment of the widows in the Jerusalem congregation. How would they handle a problem that seemed to pit mercy against mission? The solution was to match calling with need. The result was continued numerical growth as well as a model for how congregations can identify emerging leaders to meet the ever-changing demands of ministry.

People today should be able to relate to multiple concepts in the passage, including the challenges widows face, perceived unequal care of minority groups, and tensions that can arise between cultural groups. They should also be able to relate to establishing qualifications for selecting individuals for a role or position, setting priorities for different roles, and division of labor to meet needs. The passage corrects any notion that material needs are unimportant or that giving attention to needs within a congregation somehow restricts the potential for church growth. Luke's account commends a commitment to shared ministry, to balancing the competing needs created by ministry, and to matching calling to ministry need. As Christ's people encounter needs that arise within their congregations today, they need to follow the early church's example of adaptability and flexibility, while keeping their focus on the mission he has given them.

Acts 6:8–8:3

EXEGETICAL IDEA

Stephen's witness to Hellenistic Jews leads to his arrest, his speech before the Sanhedrin, his death by stoning, and persecution that scatters the Jerusalem church.

THEOLOGICAL FOCUS

God is faithful to provide the faith, grace, wisdom, and power his witnesses need as they are faithful to the mission he has given them, even if that mission leads to their deaths.

PREACHING IDEA

God is always faithful to his faithful witnesses.

PREACHING POINTERS

What does it mean to be a faithful witness for Christ? When we encounter resistance to the gospel, how can we overcome it? When we are falsely accused, how should we answer? When opposition turns violent, even deadly, how should we respond? Stephen faced each of these challenges in his public ministry. Luke's account of Stephen's ministry, speech, and death by stoning provide an example of what it means to trust God and be a faithful witness, even to the point of death. With Luke's original readers we need to know that we can trust God to be faithful to us as we are faithful witnesses for him.

People today should be able to relate to seeing accounts of mob violence, sometimes related to religious persecution. They should also be able to relate to people arguing over religion and to people making false accusations against their opponents. This passage corrects any notion that there is discontinuity between Judaism and Christianity when, in fact, Christianity is the fulfillment of God's covenant promises to Israel. It also corrects any misguided impression that God fails to notice when people ignore or reject his message or messengers. Stephen's faithful witness commends dependence on the Holy Spirit, trust in God who is faithful to his promises, and forgiveness of those who sin against Jesus and his followers. As his followers, we must understand that Jesus expects us to be faithful witnesses for him and to trust him to provide the resources we need to fulfill the mission to which he calls us, regardless of the consequences.

Acts 8:4–25

EXEGETICAL IDEA
Philip's evangelistic ministry demonstrated to the Samaritans that the gospel was superior to magic and opened the door for the Holy Spirit to incorporate them into the church.

THEOLOGICAL FOCUS
The gospel is superior to competing religious systems, excludes other forms of spirituality, and accepts on an equal basis all who respond in faith.

PREACHING IDEA
The gospel is both exclusive and inclusive.

PREACHING POINTERS
Can something be both exclusive and inclusive? Will one concern conflict with the other? What should we exclude from the church? Whom should we include in the church? Stephen's evangelistic ministry in Samaria raises these questions and more as he crosses boundaries of geography, history, culture, and religion, and as Peter and John investigate the reports they receive of the results of his ministry. Although the Jews considered them "half-breeds" at best, the Samaritans were the people group closest to the Jews in history, culture, and religion. What would happen when the message of the Messiah encountered the syncretism of the Samaritans? Would the church accept the Samaritans despite their differences? Luke's account of the gospel coming to Samaria highlights both the exclusive nature of the claims of Christianity and its inclusive embrace of all who respond to the good news in faith.

From this passage, people today should be able to relate to fascination with magic, the supernatural, and events that are novel. They should able to relate to rejoicing over unexpected recovery from illness or physical disability. Attempts to purchase influence or prominence appear far too frequently in the news. This passage corrects multiple attitudes, including the idea that all religions are equal, the suggestion that it is possible to combine the gospel with other forms of spirituality, fascination with the occult, and attempts to hide a sinful heart attitude from God. It commends faithful proclamation of the truth of God's Word, the response of faith to the gospel, acceptance of other people groups as part of the church, and the willingness to examine our heart attitudes and change them to align with God's way of thinking.

Acts 8:26–40

EXEGETICAL IDEA

Following divine directions, Philip preached the gospel to an Ethiopian official whom he baptized, and then continued evangelizing coastal Judea.

THEOLOGICAL FOCUS

God guides his witnesses to individuals who are prepared to hear and respond to the gospel.

PREACHING IDEA

Divine appointments create gospel opportunities.

PREACHING POINTERS

Are there such things as "chance encounters"? When we find ourselves seated next to someone new on a train or in an airplane, how should we view the situation? When our travel plans suddenly change, does it bother us or excite us? Our answers to those questions probably depend on our understanding of God's providence. Philip's experience on the road to Gaza suggests that we should hold our plans loosely, be open to what God might be doing, and be ready to make the most of the evangelistic opportunities that might present themselves. With Luke's original readers, we need to understand that God is at work in the hearts of "seekers" and will take whatever actions might be necessary to get the gospel to them, including arranging divine appointments that create opportunities for his witnesses to share the good news.

People today should be able to relate to the ideas of surprise encounters, meeting new people while they are traveling, sudden changes in travel plans, meeting prominent individuals, and needing assistance in understanding unclear information. This passage corrects several ideas: that men or women of high social status have no interest in spiritual matters, that individuals have little value in God's eyes, that people can find their own way to Jesus, or that there is such a thing as a "chance encounter." It commends openness to spiritual truth, obedience to divine guidance, sensitivity to the spiritual condition of others, the ability to contextualize passages from any portion of Scripture to listeners' needs, and the ability to adapt evangelistic methods to the need of the moment. Philip's encounter with the Ethiopian embodies Peter's injunction always to be "ready to make a defense to everyone who asks you to give an account for the hope that is in you" (1 Peter 3:15).

Acts 9:1–19a

EXEGETICAL IDEA

Jesus appears to Saul on the road to Damascus and sends Ananias to confirm Saul's incorporation into "the Way."

THEOLOGICAL FOCUS

God's sovereign intervention results in the total transformation of every life he touches.

PREACHING IDEA
Only Jesus can transform an adversary into an advocate.

PREACHING POINTERS
Have you ever known anyone who thought he or she was doing what was right when it was totally wrong? Perhaps you know someone whose behavior was self-destructive, although he or she was unable or unwilling to acknowledge it. One way to address such a situation is to hold an "intervention," a carefully planned course of action designed to confront that person and put him or her on the right track. In Acts 9:1–19a, we find what might be the ultimate divine intervention as Jesus appeared to Saul on the road to Damascus in all his heavenly glory and confronted him with the shocking truth that what he thought was helping God's cause was actually opposing God's purposes. In so doing, he transformed Saul from a vessel destined for destruction into a vessel destined for glory.

People today should be able to relate to individuals making radical changes of direction in their lives. They might know about the circumstances or experiences that led to such changes. They might even be aware of the practice of holding an "intervention" to confront a loved one about the consequences of his or her self-destructive behavior. This passage corrects the ideas that there might be people who are beyond God's reach, or that God never intervenes in the lives of individuals. It also corrects the ideas that God has no interest in the sufferings of his followers, or that following Jesus makes a person immune from suffering. It commends an attitude of openness to what God is doing; the expectation that God will work in the lives of those around us; obedience to his instructions or commands; and the willingness to welcome, care for, and support every person God brings to himself. It is a testimony to the truth that God can and will intervene in the lives of even his most dedicated opponents, if it suits his purposes to do so.

Acts 9:19b–31

EXEGETICAL IDEA
Saul's early ministry in Damascus and Jerusalem included acceptance by the church, preaching in the synagogues, opposition from the Jews, and escape from opponents.

THEOLOGICAL FOCUS
A new disciple's willingness to connect to the body of Christ, witness in the name of Christ, and endure suffering for the cause of Christ attests to the depth of his or her relationship with Christ.

PREACHING IDEA
Genuine faith in Christ yields genuine fruit for Christ.

PREACHING POINTERS
How can we know that a person's profession of faith is genuine? Are there indicators that can help us as we work to integrate a new believer into a local church? Should we insist on a probationary period to evaluate the depth of his or her commitment? If ever there was situation that would seem to require caution, it was Saul's. He was a notorious persecutor of the church who

had come to Damascus to continue his activities. He had no doubt arrested, imprisoned, and interrogated many members of the Jerusalem church. Yet there he was in both cities professing to follow the very name he had persecuted. What did he do to demonstrate that his commitment to Christ was genuine? He immediately sought to connect to the body of Christ both in Damascus and in Jerusalem. Once he was connected, he engaged actively in the life and the witness of the congregation, and he demonstrated significant growth in areas of his giftedness and calling. When opposition arose, he was willing to suffer for the cause of Christ. His example demonstrates the truth that genuine faith yields genuine fruit.

People today should be able to relate to skepticism that might arise about a person who makes a sudden and radical change in his or her attitude, action, or lifestyle. They can probably also relate to someone serving as a sponsor to introduce someone new to a group. Dramatic escapes or rescues from danger occur frequently, whether in the news, in books, or in movies. The passage corrects several possible wrong attitudes, including any suggestion that someone who comes to Christ can continue living "life as usual," that new disciples have no need of connecting with the body of Christ, or that it is necessary to make certain new disciples are "ready" before permitting them to engage in ministry. It commends the importance of helping new believers connect with a local congregation, allowing new believers to engage early and often in the active life and ministry of a congregation, and providing mutual support and assistance to members of the congregation who might be facing difficulties or be in trouble.

Acts 9:32–43

EXEGETICAL IDEA
Miraculous works that resulted in widespread conversions characterized Peter's witness in Lydda and Joppa.

THEOLOGICAL FOCUS
Jesus exercises his power through his witnesses to advance his mission according to his sovereign will.

PREACHING IDEA
Jesus uses his power to build his church.

PREACHING POINTERS
What determines when God chooses to transcend the laws of nature? Why does he choose to act miraculously in some circumstances but not in others? How do miraculous works relate to the proclamation of the gospel message and the advance of the Christian mission? Peter's witness in coastal Judea raises these questions and more. His healing of paralyzed Aeneas and his raising of lifeless Dorcas demonstrated Jesus's power, sent shock waves throughout the region, and resulted in widespread conversions as Jesus worked through his witness to heal and to save. As the gospel spread outward geographically and ethnically from Jerusalem, Jesus continued to use his apostolic witnesses according to his sovereign will to accomplish his kingdom purposes as they depended on him to exercise his power, authenticate their witness, and advance his mission.

People today should be able to relate to individuals who suffer from prolonged illness or paralysis, grief over the loss of a loved one, and the sense of helplessness that can arise from such situations. They should also be able to relate to the rapid spread of reports about dramatic news such as the events in Lydda and Joppa. The passage corrects suggestions that there are no such things as miracles, that God does not intervene in human affairs, or that any situation is beyond hope of God's help. It commends trusting in and depending on God, turning to him for help in desperate circumstances, and responding in faith when he does the unexpected. As his people, we need to understand that Jesus uses whomever he wishes in whatever circumstances he wishes to accomplish whatever he wishes, in order to advance mission in whatever way he wishes.

Acts 10:1–48

EXEGETICAL IDEA
God uses divine guidance, christocentric proclamation, and Holy Spirit confirmation to overcome Peter's prejudice and bring forgiveness to Cornelius and his household.

THEOLOGICAL FOCUS
The impartial God uses the "more light" principle to bring the truth about Jesus, the Lord and judge of all, to responsive seekers from every people group.

PREACHING IDEA
God gives us the light we need to save us and sanctify us.

PREACHING POINTERS
How does God help us overcome our ethnic/religious/social prejudices? How does he orchestrate events to get the gospel to genuine seekers from people groups who have never heard the good news about Jesus? Luke's account of Peter's divinely orchestrated appointment with Cornelius illustrates the answers to both questions and highlights two complementary themes: the impartiality of God and the universality of the gospel. As God leads Peter step by step to acknowledge that he welcomes individuals from every people group, he also leads Cornelius step by step to accept Jesus as the Lord of all and the judge of the living and dead. What ties together the experiences of Peter and Cornelius is the principle that God gives more light to men and women who respond to the light they have. Luke's narrative recounts the parallel journeys of two men who are obedient to the light God gives them and, as a result, reach the different but important goals he has for each of them.

There are elements of the passage that people today might find strange, such as seeing angels, hearing heavenly voices, and concern about strict dietary rules. Nevertheless, they should be able to relate to ethnic/religious/social differences as well as to the idea of religious piety expressed by prayer and good works. The passage corrects the idea that God makes distinctions between people because of ethnicity, religious heritage, or social status. Instead, as the old hymn says, "at the foot of the cross, everyone stands the same." The passage also corrects any suggestion that good works alone are all that God requires of a person. Otherwise, Cornelius would have had no need to summon Peter to hear the words that God had commanded him to speak. Positively, the passage commends the attitudes of being open to the truth, being responsive to the light God provides, and being willing to obey divine guidance immediately. If we adopt those attitudes, we can be confident that God will bring us to the place where he wants us to be, whether it is to an acknowledgement of God's impartial stance toward humankind or to an acceptance of Jesus's universal lordship.

Acts 11:1–18

EXEGETICAL IDEA
In response to concerns from some of the disciples, Peter reports on what God accomplished in Caesarea, resulting in praise from the church.

THEOLOGICAL FOCUS
God expects us to praise him when he works in unexpected ways, not criticize the means he uses to accomplish his purposes.

PREACHING IDEA
Focus on what God does, not on how he does it.

PREACHING POINTERS
Are you guilty of putting God in a box? In his classic book *Your God Is Too Small*, J. B. Phillips writes that we are crippled by limited concepts of God. One of those limited concepts is "God-in-a-Box"—a God whom we have "captured and tamed and trained to [our] own liking" and have "forced into little man-made boxes with neat labels upon them" (1961, 37). That is exactly what we do when we expect God to act according to our expectations, prejudices, or traditions. When he dares to act counter to those expectations, prejudices, or traditions, we become confused, uncomfortable, and even angry. Yet, we cannot put the God of the Bible in a box. He does what he does in the way he chooses for the reasons he knows are best. Never was that truth more evident than in the events that led Peter to share the gospel with Cornelius and his household. Because Peter's actions ran counter to centuries of Jewish tradition, a segment of the disciples took exception to what he had done. In response, Peter reported that God had directed every step along his way. Instead of looking in the rearview mirror at the way Judaism had always done things, the church needed to look forward to what Jesus was doing to make it possible for repentance to be preached in his name to all the nations (Luke 24:47).

People today should be able to relate to being criticized for their actions. Members of churches or individuals engaged in Christian leadership can also relate to disputes over ministry-related decisions or activities. The passage corrects the practices of criticizing others for their ministry activities, resisting what God might be doing when it runs contrary to our expectations, or perpetuating divisions within the body of Christ. It commends openness to God's leading, willingness to confront our prejudices, acceptance of others who are different from us, and praise for God's work in saving others. As his followers, we must understand that God expects us to praise him when he works in unexpected ways, not criticize the people or the means he uses to accomplish his purposes. Instead, we should focus on him and the results he produces.

Acts 11:19–30

EXEGETICAL IDEA
The church in Antioch was planted by bold witnesses, nurtured by gifted leaders, characterized by explosive growth, and committed to the welfare of God's people.

THEOLOGICAL FOCUS
God is at work to build his church in every geographical location and in every cultural context.

PREACHING IDEA
When you see God moving, get on board.

PREACHING POINTERS
"Watch to see where God is working and join him in his work." That axiom is one of Henry Blackaby's best-known quotations. Acts 11 suggests a similar principle guided Barnabas's life. It is a reasonable inference that he observed God at work among the first disciples and joined them in their commitment to Jesus. As a member of the Jerusalem church, he saw God moving to meet the needs of others and became an example of Christian generosity. As a member of the Jerusalem church, he also heard reports of Saul's conversion and evangelistic effectiveness and took the initiative in introducing him to the apostles. When the Jerusalem church heard reports of what God was doing in Antioch and sent him to that city as its representative, he saw the grace of God at work, rejoiced, encouraged the new disciples, and recruited Saul to provide additional leadership for the new congregation. Later, he would respond to the Holy Spirit's direction by becoming one of the first missionaries commissioned by the church in Antioch. God was moving in Antioch, Barnabas saw it, and he got on board. Are we willing to do the same?

People today can relate to large crowds and popular movements. The Billy Graham crusades of the twentieth century drew huge crowds; public demonstrations of the twenty-first century provide more recent examples. They should also be able to relate to reports of widespread food shortages and solicitation for funds to feed the hungry. The passage corrects any suggestion that evangelistic efforts should be limited by ethnicity, that a single leader can "do it all," or that individual congregations stand alone with no connection to other groups of believers. It commends faithful witness to all people and groups, the importance of gifted leadership for congregational nurture, the importance of balancing edification and evangelization in ministry, generosity toward others who are in need, and promoting unity and connectedness between local congregations. As Jesus's disciples, we need to understand that God is at work to build his church, and we must be willing to join him in what he is doing.

Acts 12:1–25

EXEGETICAL IDEA
God responded to Herod Agrippa's persecution of the Jerusalem church by miraculously delivering Peter from prison and striking down Herod in judgment.

THEOLOGICAL FOCUS
Although Christ's disciples will encounter persecution, God will protect his people, punish their persecutors, and prevail over opposition.

PREACHING IDEA
Kings might persecute, but God always prevails.

PREACHING POINTERS
No one can oppose God and win. Previous kings had tried. Previous kings had failed. Pharaoh thought he could keep the Israelites in Egypt; he lost his army in the Red Sea (Exodus 14). Saul did his best to kill David; he lost his kingdom, his sons, and his life (1 Samuel 31). Nebuchadnezzar claimed the sovereignty that belonged to God alone; he lost his mind and ended up eating grass like a cow (Daniel 4). It makes you wonder what Herod Agrippa I was thinking when he executed the apostle James and arrested the apostle Peter. As much as we might tend to focus on Peter and his miraculous escape from prison, the main characters in Acts 12 are the king of Judea and the King of the universe, and Herod's futile attempt to oppose what God was doing through the Jerusalem church is the focus of the chapter. Herod let his arrogance, pride, and political ambition get in the way of a proper perspective on the God of heaven who removes and establishes kings (Dan. 2:21). He thought he could oppose God, and he ended up eaten by worms. In the most drastic way possible, he learned the lesson we all need to remember: kings might persecute, but God always prevails.

People today should be familiar with individuals being arrested and held in jail as well as with the frantic search that follows when someone escapes from jail or prison. They might also be aware of religious persecution from civil authorities in other countries and the need for missionaries to leave a country to avoid trouble. The passage corrects an attitude of pride or self-glorification. It also corrects any idea that it might be possible to oppose God and be successful. It commends trust in God's care, the importance of prayer, humility in recognizing God's rule, and the wisdom of withdrawing from danger when necessary. As Jesus's disciples, we need to understand that God continues to care for his people so that we will remain steadfast in the face of opposition, will continue in prayer, and will trust God to work in the face of seemingly impossible circumstances.

Acts 13:1–12

EXEGETICAL IDEA
Sent out by the Holy Spirit and the church in Antioch, Barnabas and Saul preach the gospel in the synagogues on the island of Cyprus and see the Roman proconsul respond in faith to God's word despite spiritual opposition.

THEOLOGICAL FOCUS
God's word has the power to defeat those who oppose it and deliver those who are open to it.

PREACHING IDEA
God's word confounds the resistant and convinces the receptive.

PREACHING POINTERS

When a public figure does something unusual or unexpected it makes news, whether that individual is involved in politics, entertainment, sports, or another area. When he or she shows interest in spiritual things, it turns heads. The response must have been the same in the first century, and when Luke's readers discovered that a Roman proconsul had believed the gospel, it must have caught their attention. Adding to their interest would have been the spiritual confrontation between Saul/Paul and the proconsul's court astrologer, especially when they heard that the result of the confrontation was the magician losing his sight. The contrasts between the proconsul and his astrologer included their character, their responsiveness to the gospel, and the outcomes of their interaction with Barnabas and Saul. The contrast makes it clear that different individuals respond to the gospel in different ways, require different styles of ministry, and arrive at different spiritual outcomes.

People today should be able to relate to men and women responding in different ways to an idea or concept, and they most likely can relate to someone seeking to oppose a course of action. They should also be familiar with hearing about important people making news and being amazed at an unexpected turn of events. The passage corrects suggestions that there is a single response to the gospel, that there is a single ministry approach to dealing with people, or that it is possible to oppose God without any consequences. It commends being open to the message of God's word, rejecting other spiritual options, and being sensitive to the Holy Spirit and his leading. The objectives in preaching this passage should be to challenge believers to have confidence in the enabling of the Holy Spirit and the power of the gospel and to encourage nonbelievers to respond in faith to the message of the gospel.

Acts 13:13–52

EXEGETICAL IDEA

Paul and Barnabas's ministry in Pisidian Antioch began with preaching in the synagogue, resulted in conversions followed by Jewish opposition, and led them to shift their focus to the Gentiles.

THEOLOGICAL FOCUS

The gospel message and mandate do not change, even if the mission strategy must.

PREACHING IDEA

Mission must be adaptable in its approach but consistent in its message.

PREACHING POINTERS

Have you ever faced the need to change direction—whether in your own life or in ministry? How did you decide which direction to take? What was negotiable? What was nonnegotiable? What did you continue? What did you discontinue? Why? That was the challenge Paul and Barnabas faced during their ministry in Pisidian Antioch. They were following their usual strategy, and everything seemed to be going well, with conversions among both Jews and Gentiles. Then, things went off the rails when Jews in the city stirred up prominent civic leaders to begin a persecution against the missionaries. How did they respond? What aspects of their ministry changed? What aspects remained constant? What lessons can we learn from their approach? A look at Acts 13:13–52 helps us with the answers to those questions.

People today should be able to relate to individuals who are invited to speak in public settings, opportunities provided by receptive audiences, and divisions over religious differences. They should also be able to relate to people becoming jealous over the success of others and to people seeking the support of prominent members of society. The passage corrects any suggestion that the Jews are somehow irrelevant to God's plan, or that a witness to the Gentiles is somehow a change in direction to that plan. It also corrects the idea that it is wrong to change ministry strategy or that it is necessary to pursue a particular strategy indefinitely if it is not productive. The passage commends the ability to contextualize the gospel message to different audiences, the ability to apply Scripture to the circumstances of ministry, and the ability to discern when changes in ministry strategy might be needed because of complications and/or challenges. Overall, the passage commends the need to understand that the gospel message and mandate do not change even if the mission strategy must and to adopt an approach to ministry that is adaptable but consistent with a mission God has launched.

Acts 14:1–28

EXEGETICAL IDEA
Paul and Barnabas's witness in the cities of South Galatia resulted in numerous conversions, encountered active opposition, strengthened the new churches, and concluded with a return to Syrian Antioch.

THEOLOGICAL FOCUS
God's grace opens doors for his witnesses to fulfill the work he has given them despite the tribulations they might experience.

PREACHING IDEA
God's work triumphs over tribulations.

PREACHING POINTERS
Are you an optimist or a pessimist? Do you see the proverbial glass as half-full or half-empty? Paul and Barnabas must have been God-oriented optimists, because they were able to focus on the good news of what God was doing despite the difficulties they faced. A superficial look at Acts 14 might lead some to see all the problems the missionaries faced, including opposition from Jews, Gentiles, and civil authorities; divided public opinion; misunderstanding of their message; mob violence; and—in Paul's case—stoning. Yet, when they reported to the church in Syrian Antioch about their ministry in Cyprus and South Galatia, where did they focus? They gathered the church together and described everything God had accomplished with them and how he had opened a door of faith for the Gentiles. They clearly understood that God's work triumphs over (and through) tribulations.

People today should be able to relate to multiple aspects of the Acts 14:1–28, including people with serious physical or health issues, quick shifts in public opinion, and a mob mentality. Paul and Barnabas's experiences epitomize the saying "trouble follows him" as the Jews followed them from Pisidian Antioch to Iconium to Lystra. They can probably also relate to the idea of reporting on progress at the end of an assigned task or project. The passage corrects any inclination to ascribe supernatural powers to human beings as well as the tendency to adopt incorrect views of God. It also corrects the idea that violence can stop the progress of the gospel or an approach to ministry that suggests evangelism alone is the mission of the church. It commends persevering in the face of opposition, depending on God and his working, being able to address wrong ideas about God, knowing how to care for new believers, and being accountable in ministry. The objective in communicating the passage is to help listeners understand that tribulations might arise but God's triumph is certain, so that they will learn to see the doors he opens instead of the difficulties they face.

Acts 15:1–35

EXEGETICAL IDEA
The Jerusalem Council resolved a dispute over whether it was necessary to circumcise Gentile disciples by reviewing the history of the mission to the Gentiles, applying OT prophecy to the situation, and establishing guidelines that would facilitate table fellowship between Jews and Gentiles.

THEOLOGICAL FOCUS
A balanced approach to mission maintains a commitment to essential doctrines, recognizes cultural differences, and respects personal convictions in secondary matters of faith and practice.

PREACHING IDEA
Wise counsel guards the truth without binding the conscience.

PREACHING POINTERS
"In essentials unity, in nonessentials liberty, and in all things charity." This saying seems particularly applicable to the decision of the Jerusalem Council in Acts 15. How should the church balance commitment to essential doctrines, recognition of cultural differences, and respect for personal convictions in secondary matters of faith and practice? That was the challenge the early church faced when certain law-observant Jewish members advocated requiring circumcision of the large number of Gentile disciples who were entering the church through the missionary work of Paul and Barnabas. The decision they reached and the way in which they reached it reminds us that we must interpret what God is doing in light of Scripture, so that we are careful to guard the truth without binding the conscience.

People today can relate to church conferences, debates over religious practices, or reaching a compromise to preserve unity. They should also be able to relate to taking an issue to a higher court, appealing to precedent, documenting a decision in writing, and rejoicing over a favorable decision. The passage corrects imposing cultural values or practices on others, being dogmatic on nonessentials, putting God to the test by questioning what he is doing, or suggesting that religious practices must supplement faith in order for a person or a group to gain salvation. It commends recognizing and respecting God's working, respecting cultural differences, turning to Scripture for guidance in decision-making, seeking resolutions that maintain unity, and being willing to limit personal liberty out of respect for the convictions of others. The objective in communicating the passage should be to help listeners understand that their identity in Christ supersedes their cultural identity so that they will learn to balance a commitment to truth with respect for their brothers and sisters in Christ.

Acts 15:36–16:10

EXEGETICAL IDEA
The process that led Paul to minister in Europe involved resolving interpersonal differences, addressing cultural considerations, and following the Holy Spirit's guidance.

THEOLOGICAL IDEA
Taking the gospel to new frontiers requires discernment in order to maintain team unity, to be culturally sensitive, and to follow the Spirit's guidance.

PREACHING IDEA
The progress of God's gospel demands discernment by God's people.

PREACHING POINTERS
Christian ministry is not easy; it can be a minefield with multiple opportunities to step in the wrong place. Paul and Barnabas discovered that interpersonal issues could threaten team unity. Paul had to make a tough decision about how to be culturally sensitive. As Paul and Silas traveled together, they repeatedly encountered closed doors. In each instance, God's witnesses needed discernment and the Holy Spirit's guidance to navigate the process of taking the gospel to new frontiers. With the original readers of Acts, we need to understand how God works to take the gospel to new frontiers, and we need to know how to make the right choices along the way.

People today should be able to identify with the potential pitfalls of ministry, because those issues echo everyday life in general—disagreements with coworkers and unexpected changes in plans are just two examples. In that regard, the account of how God expanded the scope of the church's outreach to Gentile Europe corrects any notion that ministry is simple or easy. At the same time, this passage commends the virtues of discernment, perseverance, and obedience, as Paul and his missionary team follow the Holy Spirit's leading to new avenues of outreach. It reminds us that the progress of God's gospel demands discernment by God's people.

Acts 16:11–40

EXEGETICAL IDEA
God uses Paul and Silas's witness in Philippi to open the hearts of a Godfearing woman and a jailer to the gospel, to cast a demon out of a slave girl, and to establish the legitimacy of the newly planted church.

THEOLOGICAL IDEA
The preaching of the gospel disrupts the religious, spiritual, economic, personal, and civic lives of the individuals who encounter it.

PREACHING IDEA
The gospel changes everything.

PREACHING POINTERS
Whether through firsthand experience or through secondhand news reports, everyone understands the disruption a major earthquake can create. Earthquakes were common in the Eastern Mediterranean, and the ancient Greeks considered them to be the expression of "the earthshaker" Poseidon's anger (Homer, *Il.* 20.57–58). When Paul arrived in Philippi, the gospel hit the city like a 9.0 magnitude earthquake—both literally and in every other way. The gospel touched—and disrupted—the lives of everyone in the city. With the original readers of Acts, we need to understand that God's working through the gospel touches every aspect of life and culture.

People today can easily relate to the disruptions of life, whether religious, spiritual, economic, personal, or civic. It is rare for an installment of the evening news to end without at least some mention of one or more such events. The account of Paul and Silas's ministry in Philippi corrects any idea that the gospel leaves other aspects of life and culture untouched. It commends the responses of saving faith and shared life in response to God's working. It reminds us that we should expect the gospel to "shake up" our own lives and the lives of those around us, because wherever it is preached, the gospel changes everything

Acts 17:1–15

EXEGETICAL IDEA
The gospel's advance in Macedonia continued in the synagogues of Thessalonica and Berea, involving careful argument from and study of the Old Testament, resulting in positive responses among Jews and Gentiles, and leading to persistent opposition from zealous Jews.

THEOLOGICAL FOCUS
Effective preaching of the gospel includes engagement, explanation, and exposition, while appropriate receptivity to the gospel manifests itself in openness, eagerness, and thoroughness.

PREACHING IDEA
Proper presentation of the gospel encourages careful consideration of its claims.

PREACHING POINTERS
Although we live in an increasingly post-Christian society, many men and women retain a degree of biblical preunderstanding. The teachings of the OT were foreign to the Greco-Roman citizens of Macedonia, but God had planted Jewish synagogues throughout the empire in accordance with his plan to use Israel as a light to the nations (Isa. 42:6; 49:6). The men and women who worshipped in those synagogues possessed a high degree of biblical

preunderstanding and represented potentially receptive audiences for the gospel. With Luke's original readers, we need to understand how to present the gospel effectively to listeners with a biblical preunderstanding, and we need to be able to recognize open-minded receptivity to the gospel when we encounter it.

People today should be able to relate to the suggestion that they be open to ideas that run counter to their preconceptions. The call for "tolerance" is widespread in contemporary society. The accounts of Paul and Silas's ministry in Thessalonica and Berea correct any notions that the gospel will always produce a positive response, all Jews are hostile to the gospel, or civil authorities will always respond benevolently when acting in response to charges against God's witnesses. The accounts commend both a commitment to presenting the gospel carefully and an attitude of open-minded receptivity to truth. It reminds us that proper presentation of the gospel encourages careful consideration of its claims.

Acts 17:16–34

EXEGETICAL IDEA
Paul's ministry in Athens began with teaching in the synagogue and marketplace, culminated with a speech before the council of the city, and produced mixed results.

THEOLOGICAL FOCUS
Scripture's truth about God's acts of creation and providence offers a foundation to contextualize the gospel for those who lack a biblical preunderstanding.

PREACHING IDEA
The truth of Scripture challenges the dogmas of human philosophies.

PREACHING POINTERS
Because we live in an increasingly post-Christian society, it becomes increasingly important for us to know how to contextualize the message of God's love and forgiveness for men and women who lack a biblical preunderstanding. Ancient Athens provided the perfect setting for Paul to engage the prominent philosophical thinking of his day. His speech before the Areopagus Council offers one example of how to present the gospel to such an audience. With Luke's original readers, we need to understand that Scripture challenges the dogmas of human philosophies, but it is still possible to interact with postmodern thinkers in a manner that is both scriptural and respectful.

People today should be able to relate to having an interest in "something new." The prospect of Apple releasing a new iPhone or the opening of a new episode in a popular movie franchise is enough to send users/followers into a frenzy. The account of Paul's ministry in Athens corrects multiple ideas—that the world simply "happened," that pantheism and deism are plausible explanations for God's relationship to his creation, that there is no purpose to life, and that there is no possibility of knowing God. The same account commends a proper understanding of God's works of creation, providence, and judgment as well as the need for men and women to repent of their wrong concepts of who God is and how he acts.

Acts 18:1–17

EXEGETICAL IDEA
During Paul's bivocational and full-time ministry in Corinth, fellow believers helped him, God reassured him, and the Roman proconsul vindicated him.

THEOLOGICAL IDEA
God uses ordinary and extraordinary means to assure and guide his obedient witness in the face of financial need, religious opposition, and legal challenge.

PREACHING IDEA
God gives us what we need, to do what he asks us to do.

PREACHING POINTERS
At some point, every individual, family, congregation, or ministry experiences need. The need might be financial, physical, spiritual, or legal. Sometimes the needs occur sequentially; other times they occur simultaneously. Whatever the nature or timing of the needs, they are opportunities for God to act to meet them. He might meet them in ways we expect, or his provision might be totally unexpected. During his ministry in Corinth, Paul experienced a variety of needs. In each instance, God provided the resources Paul needed to witness faithfully for the Lord Jesus. His experience reminds us that God gives us what we need, so that we can do what he asks us to do.

People today should be able to relate to experiencing financial need and/or uncertainty, working for a living, being encouraged by friends or colleagues, and being involved in legal proceedings. The account of Paul's ministry in Corinth corrects suggestions that religion—including missionary activity—is illicit or illegal, or that the state has authority over church affairs. The same account commends trust in God's promises and guidance as well as faithfulness in witness despite difficult circumstances. It reinforces the theological truth that God uses both ordinary and extraordinary means to advance his kingdom purposes.

Acts 18:18–28

EXEGETICAL IDEA
Paul's initial witness, Apollos's apologetic ministry, and Priscilla and Aquila's continuing care laid the foundation for Ephesus to become the center of gospel outreach in Asia.

THEOLOGICAL IDEA
God uses a variety of people, each with different giftings, to advance his purposes.

PREACHING IDEA
It takes a team to do God's tasks.

PREACHING POINTERS
Hillary Clinton's 1996 book *It Takes a Village* brought to prominence the African proverb that says, "It takes a village to raise a child." The proverb captures the idea that an entire community

of people must participate if children are to grow up in a healthy environment. The same principle applies to the growth of works that God begins. In his sovereign working he used Paul, Apollos, Priscilla, and Aquila to begin a work in Ephesus that would ultimately make an impact throughout western Asia Minor. With Luke's original readers, we need to understand that God uses different people in different ways to accomplish his kingdom purposes. If we do, we will be intentional about looking for our roles in what God is doing and will fill those roles as he empowers us to do so.

People today should be able to relate to multiple elements from this passage, including overseas travel, eloquent speakers, and working with coaches. Men and women who are familiar with mission work can most likely relate to the ideas of a "vision trip" to explore a possible future area for ministry and of a "home ministry assignment" after a term on the mission field. The accounts of Paul's and Apollos's ministries in Ephesus correct the ideas that "lone ranger" ministry is a valid option and that there is no need to learn from others. The accounts commend the values of trust in God's will and teachability as well as the practice of private correction when a fellow believer is in error. They remind us that—because God uses different people in different ways—it takes a team to do God's tasks.

Acts 19:1–22

EXEGETICAL IDEA
During Paul's extended ministry in Ephesus, the gospel spread to Jews and Greeks throughout the province of Asia as he proclaimed the kingdom of God and performed works of power.

THEOLOGICAL FOCUS
Opening new frontiers for the gospel requires God's witness to address other theological systems, proclaim the good news about Jesus, rely on divine empowerment, and be sensitive to the Spirit's leading.

PREACHING IDEA
The church advances when God's power accompanies gospel proclamation.

PREACHING POINTERS
What does it take to open new areas for the gospel? Should we expect to see God perform signs and wonders? What is the relationship between supernatural demonstrations of God's working and the preaching of the gospel? How should we go about evangelizing the cities where we live? As we seek to obey Jesus's commission to be his witnesses, what strategies might we need to use, and how can we keep them in proper balance? Luke's account of Paul's ministry in Ephesus points the way to answers by presenting the key elements of his missionary activity. He was working not only in an area where Jesus's name had not been named but also in one of the major metropolitan centers of the empire. As the result of his extended work in the city, all the inhabitants of the province of Asia had the opportunity to hear the good news about Jesus. The objective in communicating the passage should be to help listeners understand the strategic ingredients of gospel ministry so that they will be bold in proclaiming Jesus and faithful in relying on God for his enabling and leading.

People today should be able to relate to encountering people who misunderstand what God expects of them, combine different religious systems, or attempt to appropriate supernatural power for their own purposes. They can certainly relate to making travel plans, and they might have heard about instances of book burning. This passage corrects any suggestion that a partial understanding of the gospel is adequate, that it is possible to mix other religious systems with biblical truth, that Jesus's name is simply a magical formula, or that involvement with the occult is appropriate for Jesus's followers. It commends a commitment to upholding orthodox doctrine, to teaching biblical truth faithfully and consistently, to relying on divine enabling and leading, and to being willing to acknowledge and confess sin. It reinforces the theological truth that the church advances when God's power accompanies gospel proclamation.

Acts 19:23–40

EXEGETICAL IDEA
As Paul prepares to leave for Macedonia, an angry crowd gathers in the city's amphitheater to protest the impact of his ministry on the economy, prestige, and religion of Ephesus.

THEOLOGICAL FOCUS
Although the gospel challenges multiple aspects of a culture, it poses no threat to public order.

PREACHING IDEA
Law-abiding witness can capture a city for Christ.

PREACHING POINTERS
What impact does the peaceful proclamation of the gospel have on the life of a city? Does the gospel pose a threat to the local economy, to local religion, or to the local civic life? What can we learn about those questions from the events that occurred near the close of Paul's ministry in Ephesus? Luke's account of those events sheds light on the way in which opportunists can turn personal interests into public protest, uninformed bystanders can become an irrational mob, innocent parties can be falsely accused, and well-reasoned counsel can defuse a potentially dangerous situation. It also establishes the truth that although Christianity challenges multiple aspects of culture, it poses no threat to established civil law and order. The objective in communicating the passage should be to help listeners understand that ministering peacefully within the established civil order allows Jesus's followers to make a multidimensional impact on a city and its surrounding region.

People today should be able to relate to the emotional response that results when something they hold dear is threatened, whether it is their financial livelihood, their public reputation, or their cherished beliefs. They might well have observed or experienced the confusion that can result when a public demonstration goes out of control. They should also be able to relate to the fear of official intervention or retaliation that widespread public disorder might provoke. This passage corrects the ideas that extralegal action is an appropriate response to an area of concern or that unthinking participation in public protest is wise. It also corrects any suggestion that Christianity is a threat to public order. In fact, the passage teaches the opposite: Christianity might threaten financial and/or religious special interests, but it does not threaten the established civil order. The passage commends discerning assessment of inflammatory claims, prudent restraint in volatile situations, and proper respect for the judicial process. It suggests that persuasion is more effective than protest.

Acts 20:1–12

EXEGETICAL IDEA
Paul concludes his missionary work in Europe by revisiting and encouraging the churches in Macedonia, Achaia, and Troas.

THEOLOGICAL FOCUS
Local bodies of believers require regular care and support.

PREACHING IDEA
Local congregations need loving care.

PREACHING POINTERS
What do young children and new churches have in common? They both need loving care if they are to develop according to God's design. If parents fail to care for their children well, those children will, in all probability, fail to develop physically, mentally, and/or emotionally. In the same way, if a new church is neglected, it will fail to develop into the sort of body Paul describes in Ephesians 4:1–16: united, speaking the truth in love, maturing, functioning according to the giftedness of its members, growing both spiritually and numerically. Paul understood that the new churches he planted needed regular care and support. Accordingly, his established practice was to revisit those churches and encourage them to persevere in their faith. Acts 20:1–12 describes one of those return trips—this time to visit the churches he had planted in Europe—and underscores the importance of and the means for providing ongoing support and care for believers in local congregations. The objective in communicating the passage should be to help listeners understand that local bodies of believers require regular care and support, so that they will intentionally invest themselves in encouraging other believers through their time, teaching, conversation, and compassion.

People today should be able to relate to visiting churches to which they have previous connections, house group meetings, and people who have the gift of encouragement. They can most likely also relate to listening to long-winded speakers and the experience of getting drowsy while listening to those speakers. The passage, like others before it, both corrects the idea that it is possible to engage in "lone ranger" ministry and commends the value of a working with a team in ministry. Similarly, it both corrects any suggestion that local congregations can stand entirely on their own and commends interdependence among congregations. It also commends the ministry of encouragement and trust in God to do "the impossible." It reinforces the importance of the continuing care and support of congregations and the members of those congregations.

Acts 20:13–38

EXEGETICAL IDEA

In his farewell to the Ephesian elders, Paul reminds them of his past ministry among them and prepares them for his future ministry without him.

THEOLOGICAL FOCUS

Responsible leaders learn from the example of those who ministered to them, pay close attention to themselves and their flock, and rely on the God who gives his word of grace to them all.

PREACHING IDEA

Responsible leaders learn from the past and look to the future.

PREACHING POINTERS

What qualities should characterize responsible leaders? How should they view those who have gone before them? How should they view themselves and those they are leading? Where should they turn for the resources they need as they engage in their work? Those questions become particularly acute when a group faces a transition in leadership. During his three years in Ephesus, Paul had invested himself deeply in the new church—working night and day, facing trials and tribulations, teaching the gospel comprehensively. Now, he was on his way to Jerusalem and fully expected that he would never see the disciples or their leaders again. What could he tell them that would prepare them for their work in his absence? In his farewell speech in Miletus, he spoke to the elders to remind them (and us) of his past ministry among them and to instruct them (and us) about the role and responsibility of leaders as they face both external and internal threats to the well-being of the congregation.

People today should be able to relate to transitions in leadership, tearful farewells that include parting words, role models, internal and external threats, and the desire to finish a task well. The passage corrects any suggestion that leadership is easy or a potential source of material gain. It also corrects the idea that it is possible to take time off from the responsibilities of being a leader or that personal well-being provides an "out" from those responsibilities. The passage commends both the example a leader sets for others and the benefits of paying attention to that example. It also commends the qualities of humility, care for others, perseverance, alertness, courage, and commitment. The objective in communicating the passage should be to help listeners understand the role and responsibility of congregational leaders, so that leaders will fulfill their appointed ministry and members of the congregation will give them the respect they deserve (1 Tim. 5:17–20).

Acts 21:1–14

EXEGETICAL IDEA

As he travels from Miletus to Caesarea, Paul affirms his commitment to follow the Spirit's leading despite repeated attempts to dissuade him from going to Jerusalem.

THEOLOGICAL FOCUS

Following God's will involves remaining steadfast in the face of potentially dangerous circumstances.

PREACHING IDEA

Our commitment to Jesus determines our course of action.

PREACHING POINTERS

How do you respond when you are convinced that you understand the direction in which God is leading you, and everyone else disagrees? How do you evaluate apparently contradictory advice? Do you continue when you know for certain there is danger ahead, or do you let self-interest determine your direction? Paul had to wrestle with those and other questions as he traveled from Europe to Jerusalem. He heard the Holy Spirit speak to him repeatedly about his destination and what awaited him there. His traveling companions, however, interpreted the information differently and did their best to dissuade him from going to Jerusalem. What kept Paul going? How did he remain steadfast in the face of potentially dangerous circumstances? He knew the mission to which Jesus had called him, and like Jesus, he was willing to submit to the task God had for him regardless of the consequences. His commitment to Jesus determined his course of action.

People today should be able to relate to being committed to completing a task—perhaps despite the consequences—and attempts to dissuade someone from a course of action. They should also be able to relate to traveling, visiting friends, and saying farewell to others. The passage corrects any suggestion that majority opinion is always correct or that self-interest should determine a person's actions. It commends discernment of and commitment to God's will; obedience to and alignment with divine guidance; and fellowship, love, and hospitality among Jesus's disciples. The objective in communicating the passage should be to help listeners understand the importance of discerning and submitting to God's will regardless of the consequences, so that they will follow it steadfastly in the face of well-intentioned counsel, opposition, and potential danger.

Acts 21:15–26

EXEGETICAL IDEA

Upon arriving in Jerusalem, Paul received a warm welcome, reported on his ministry activities, and agreed to a proposal from the elders in the hope of alleviating the tension his arrival might cause.

THEOLOGICAL FOCUS

The peace of the church rests on the willingness to accept others with different values and forego personal liberty without compromising the truth of the gospel.

PREACHING IDEA

The pursuit of peace in Christ's church requires flexibility without compromise.

PREACHING POINTERS

One of the ministerial vows in a certain denomination calls the candidate for ordination to "maintain the truths of the gospel and the purity and peace and unity of the church" (PCA *Book of Church Order* 21-5). Did you catch the two guardrails in that vow? On one side of the road are the truths of the gospel and the purity of the church. On the other side of the road are the peace and unity of the church. It can be challenging to stay between those guardrails, can't it? If we go too far in the pursuit of peace, we run the risk of compromising the truth. If we insist on certain nonessential practices as the primary means of preserving the purity of the church, we run the risk of destroying the unity of the body. How do we maintain the proper balance? Paul and the Jerusalem elders faced precisely that challenge in Acts 21:15–26. On the one hand, Paul was known to preach a law-free gospel to the Gentiles. On the other hand, Jewish believers in the Jerusalem church were zealous to uphold the law. How did Paul and the Jerusalem elders resolve the tension?

People today should be able to relate to hearing reports about what God is doing in the ministries of others, to being zealous about something they consider important, or to being concerned about potential differences among friends and/or colleagues. The passage corrects the ideas that certain ways of expressing personal piety are absolute, that individual liberty is more important than the common good, or that accepting un-substantiated reports about other believers is appropriate. It commends the importance of being committed to unity, being willing to be flexible on nonessentials, and being intentional about resolving conflict within the body of Christ. The objective should be to help listeners understand that the truth of the gospel and the peace of the church are more important than personal preferences, so they will accept others who hold values different from their own and commit to acting in ways that will promote the edification of other believers, the progress of the gospel, and the glory of God.

Acts 21:27–22:29

EXEGETICAL IDEA

Learning of an uproar in the temple precincts, a Roman commander acts to restore order and, as a result, delivers Paul from a violent death at the hands of a Jewish mob.

THEOLOGICAL FOCUS

God sometimes uses unexpected means to protect his witnesses in the face of injustice.

PREACHING IDEA

God can open doors of deliverance in unexpected directions.

PREACHING POINTERS

There is a story about a man who is trapped on the roof of his house during a flood. Because he is waiting for God to rescue him, he declines help from someone in a rowboat, someone in a motorboat, and someone in a helicopter. Eventually, the waters rise over his head, and he drowns. When the man gets to heaven and asks God why he did not rescue him, God reminds the man that he had sent two boats and a helicopter to rescue him! What's the point? Sometimes God's deliverance can come from sources other than those we might expect. That was Paul's experience when a Jewish mob attacked him in the temple and tried to kill him. In the middle of the uproar, a Roman commander and his soldiers intervened to restore order and, in so doing, delivered Paul from a violent death. The events Luke narrates in Acts 21:27–22:29 remind us that God can open doors of deliverance in unexpected directions.

People today should be able to relate to large group gatherings that turn violent, confusion over the causes of public unrest, or intervention by government authorities to address civil disorder. They should also be able to relate to potential miscarriages of justice and individuals attempting to defend themselves against legal charges. The passage corrects any attitude that gives preference to traditionalism over truth, that believes violence is an appropriate solution to a problem, or that views properly constituted authorities as always hostile to Christianity. It commends willingness to accept truth, trust in God's working to protect his people, and readiness "always to make a defense to everyone who asks you to give an account for the hope that is in you" (1 Peter 3:15). The objective in communicating the passage should be to help listeners understand that God can use secular authorities to protect his witnesses, so that they will be alert to doors of deliverance that God might open for them and will trust him to protect them from persecution by whatever means he might choose.

Acts 22:30–23:11

EXEGETICAL IDEA
Paul's defense before the Sanhedrin responded to the charges against him, defined the central theological issue of the gospel, and resulted in assurance from the Lord Jesus.

THEOLOGICAL FOCUS
Remaining faithful to the task God has assigned honors him and results in his assurance.

PREACHING IDEA
If you take a stand for Jesus by his power, he will stand by you.

PREACHING POINTERS
How do you know when you have effectively accomplished an assigned task? Do you measure success by faithfulness, completion, or positive results? What measure does God use? Can failure in our eyes be success in God's eyes? Paul's experience before the Sanhedrin suggests that the answer to the last question is a resounding "yes." On the face of it, Paul's defense before the council was a failure. The high priest ordered him punished. The members of the council rebuked him for losing his temper. The council discussion deteriorated into a theological free-for-all. The Roman commander ordered him returned to custody in the Antonia Fortress. Had he failed in the task assigned to him? If he had any doubts, Jesus's appearance and words put them to rest. As he had been faithful to the task God had assigned to him in Jerusalem, God would be faithful to enable Paul to fulfill the same task when he reached Rome.

People today should be able to relate to fact-finding investigations that sometimes involve emergency meetings, divisions over religious beliefs, and legal irregularities. The passage corrects hypocritical behavior or suggestions that it is acceptable to act contrary to established legal standards. It also corrects the belief that it is always possible to receive a fair hearing and the idea that a negative response is necessarily failure. It commends remaining faithful in difficult circumstances, discernment to know what topics to pursue with an audience, and trust in God's sovereign working. The objective in communicating the passage should be to help listeners understand that although telling the truth might not persuade opponents, it honors Jesus and results in his approval, so that they will remain steadfast in their testimony for him and trust in his sovereign care.

Acts 23:12–35

EXEGETICAL IDEA
When he receives a report about a Jewish conspiracy to kill Paul, the Roman commander transfers him to the governor's custody in Caesarea.

THEOLOGICAL FOCUS
God can and will use human agency to protect his people, but they must act wisely in response to the opportunities he provides.

PREACHING IDEA
Trust God's providential working, but act wisely while he works.

PREACHING POINTERS
Alexander Graham Bell said, "When one door closes, another opens." It is important to remember that God closes doors and opens windows to establish his purposes. The theological idea that lies behind the saying is the doctrine of God's providence, which the Westminster Shorter Catechism defines as "his most wise, and powerful preserving and governing of all his creatures, and all their actions." That is, God is continually at work to accomplish his purposes in the world. The version of the saying that applies most directly to Paul's situation in Acts 23:12–35, though, comes from Jeannette Walls: "When God closes a door, he opens a window . . . but it is up to you to find it." Jesus had promised Paul that he would reach Rome, but he was in custody in Jerusalem. The door that led to Rome seemed shut. Then, his nephew became aware of a Jewish plot to kill Paul. Paul found an open window in that news as he connected his nephew with the Roman commander, who arranged for his transfer to Caesarea. Paul's experience reminds us that God can and will use human agency to protect his people, but they must act wisely in response to the opportunities he provides.

People today should be able to relate to multiple details from the passage, including conspiracies among religious extremists, potential ambushes that call for protective details, insider information that comes from confidential sources, reports to superiors or supervisors, and spinning information to put yourself in the best possible light. The passage corrects using violence to solve problems, thinking that human actions can upset God's plans, and taking no action in the face of trouble. It commends using discernment in asking for help, being concerned for those in your care, acting promptly on information, and being faithful in acting on orders and information. The objective in communicating the passage should be to help listeners understand, on the one hand, that God can and will use human agency as part of his providential working, and on the other hand, that he expects his people to act wisely when he opens windows for them to ask for help.

Acts 24:1–27

EXEGETICAL IDEA
During his two years of imprisonment in Caesarea, Paul defended himself against Jewish accusations while also declaring the gospel to the Roman governor.

THEOLOGICAL FOCUS
Jesus's faithful witnesses are able not only to refute false charges effectively but also to present the gospel boldly before whatever audience they might face.

PREACHING IDEA
The best defense is a good offense.

PREACHING POINTERS
"The best defense is a good offense" is an axiom that applies to multiple areas of human endeavor, including sports, military combat, and business. In law, it refers to defense counsel's strategy of attacking the prosecution's case to persuade the jury that there is reasonable doubt about the defendant's guilt. It can also apply to the defense of the gospel, as Paul's appearance before Felix, the Roman governor of Judea, demonstrates. Facing formal legal accusations presented before the governor by a polished professional advocate, Paul effectively refuted those accusations, proved that there was no legal case against him, and boldly proclaimed the gospel to the governor, both during the legal proceedings and during frequent personal conversations with Felix and his wife, Drusilla. He turned the defense of his activities on behalf of Jesus into a proclamation of the good news about Jesus by applying the axiom that the best defense is a good offense.

People today can relate to various aspects of judicial proceedings, including prosecutors, defendants, adjourning the proceedings while waiting for additional evidence or witnesses, and delayed verdicts. They should also relate to trying to decide between two choices, attempting to gain favor with others, and the potential for securing financial gain through unscrupulous means. The passage corrects attempts to manipulate the judicial process for personal gain, any tendency to think that Christians must passively accept false charges against them, and the idea that it is possible to accept only part of the gospel message. It commends holding fast to the truth in the face of lies, making an active defense against false charges, seizing the opportunities God provides to present the gospel, and maintaining a faithful witness in the face of difficult circumstances. The objective in communicating the passage should be to help listeners understand that it is possible both to refute false charges effectively and to present the gospel boldly before authority figures, so that they will stand boldly for truth and the gospel regardless of the audiences they might face.

Acts 25:1–12

EXEGETICAL IDEA

After the new Roman governor denies a Jewish request for a change of venue to Jerusalem, Paul appears before Festus in Caesarea, defends himself against Jewish charges, and appeals to his right as a Roman citizen to present his case before Caesar in Rome.

THEOLOGICAL FOCUS

Wise witnesses use every legitimate means available to them to meet the challenges before them and fulfill the mission entrusted to them.

PREACHING IDEA

Trust God's providential means to accomplish his providential purposes.

PREACHING POINTERS

"Desperate times call for desperate measures." That saying traces its roots to the ancient Greek physician Hippocrates, who originally wrote that "extreme diseases must have extreme remedies." What he meant was that, sometimes, what might seem to be the last resort is the right one for the circumstances you are facing. You can see that idea at work in Paul's defense speeches in Acts 22–25. Before the Jewish mob in the temple, Paul emphasized his continuity with his Jewish heritage. Before the Sanhedrin, he focused on a point of doctrine. Before Felix, he refuted, point by point, the Jewish charges and demonstrated that there was no case against him. Before Festus—facing a choice between Roman execution or Jewish assassination—he appealed to Caesar as a last resort that stopped the judicial process, protected him from a Jewish ambush, and ensured that he would travel to Rome. He understood that desperate times call for desperate measures, and by appealing to Caesar he relied on the rule of civil law as one of the means God has ordained to accomplish his purposes.

People today should be able to relate to the judicial aspects of the passage—following legal procedures, requests to change the venue of trials, hung juries that cannot decide whether to convict or acquit, and appealing a verdict. They should also be able to relate both to political intrigue and favors and to using the legal system to gain an advantage. The passage corrects the practice of seeking to manipulate the judicial system and trading impartial decisions for political expediency. It commends knowing and making wise use of legal rights, relying on the rule of law, and being committed to the task God has assigned. The objective in communicating the passage should be to help listeners understand that God expects his witnesses to use every legitimate means available to them to meet the challenges before them, including trusting in his providential means to accomplish his providential purposes.

Acts 25:13–26:32

EXEGETICAL IDEA

Paul's defense before King Herod Agrippa II had the goal of helping Festus determine what to write to Caesar, focused on Jesus as the fulfillment of the OT promise of the resurrection, and convinced the king that Paul was innocent of all charges.

THEOLOGICAL FOCUS
The gospel message fulfills the OT promises, focuses on the risen Jesus, offers universal blessing, is true and reasonable, and poses no threat to civil authority.

PREACHING IDEA
The gospel proclaims Messiah, not madness or mayhem.

PREACHING POINTERS
Do some people who hear the message of the gospel consider it madness? Or is the message that Jesus rose from the dead true and reasonable? The answer to all three of those questions is a resounding "Yes!" It is entirely possible that at some point in our lives each of us has encountered someone who has considered incredible the basic message of the gospel that Jesus died, was buried, rose after three days, and appeared to his followers (1 Cor. 15:3–8). The idea of someone rising from the dead differs so drastically from our normal way of thinking that some people might consider it to be insane. Festus, the Roman governor of Judea, certainly did. When Paul concluded the account of his life, conversion, commission, and ministry in Acts 26, Festus responded in a loud voice, "Paul, you are out of your mind! Your great learning is driving you mad." Paul's response was, "I am not out of my mind, but I am speaking words that are true and reasonable." Paul's experience on the road to Damascus changed his thinking, his theology, and his life's work. He had met the risen Jesus and he knew that the gospel proclaims Messiah, not madness or mayhem.

People today should be able to relate to making a presentation, having others challenge their thinking or beliefs, and seeking to be faithful in completing a task assigned to them. The passage corrects the idea that the gospel is foolish or accepted only by ignorant people, the idea that the ministry of the gospel oversteps established legal boundaries, and the idea that the state has jurisdiction over matters of faith or religious practice. It commends bold proclamation of the gospel in the face of potentially intimidating or hostile audiences, faithful obedience to an assigned task regardless of the personal consequences, and willingness to accept the truth, even if doing so involves changing beliefs or practices. The objective in communicating the passage should be to help listeners accurately understand the nature and message of the gospel so that they will proclaim it boldly before whatever audience God gives them.

Acts 27:1–44

EXEGETICAL IDEA
Paul's sea voyage to Rome began with travel against contrary winds, continued with a violent storm, ended in a shipwreck, and gave Paul opportunities to speak words of encouragement to his fellow travelers based on God's promise of deliverance.

THEOLOGICAL FOCUS
God's protection from danger provides opportunities to point others to him.

PREACHING IDEA
God's protection should prompt our proclamation.

PREACHING POINTERS

"God moves in a mysterious way, his wonders to perform. He plants his footsteps in the sea, and rides upon the storm." Was William Cowper (1731–1800) thinking of Acts 27 when he wrote that hymn? One thing is certain: we can all relate to the power of God that storms reveal. Some people might talk about the power of "Mother Nature," but God is the true power behind any storm. In fact, storms are simply one facet of God's providential governing of his creation. Storms—natural or spiritual—are also one of the means God uses to accomplish his purposes in and for his people. The divine reassurance he offers in the midst of those storms is another. When a violent storm swept down from the mountains of Crete and blew Paul and his traveling companions across the Mediterranean Sea to run aground fourteen days later on the island of Malta, they were never outside God's will or outside his protection. The angelic reassurance Paul received in the midst of the storm led him to encourage the crew and other passengers to trust in God's protection and deliverance. Confidence in God's protection from danger prompted Paul to point others to him as well.

People today should be able to relate to travel and decisions related to travel, as well as to severe weather and storms. They should also be able to relate to anxiety created by danger, seemingly hopeless circumstances, and the positive effects of encouragement in those circumstances. The passage corrects putting profit ahead of prudence, thinking that a majority opinion is necessarily always the best one, viewing any situation as hopeless in God's providential control, and failing to look for the potentially positive side of dangerous situations. The passage commends trusting in God's protection, heeding wise counsel, caring about the safety of others, encouraging others in dangerous situations, and speaking up for God in those situations. The objective in communicating the passage should be to help listeners understand that they can trust God to protect them from danger, so that they will look for opportunities to share their trust in him with others.

Acts 28:1–10

EXEGETICAL IDEA

Paul's ministry on Malta included humble service to his fellow travelers, divine protection from snakebite, and compassionate healing of those who were ill.

THEOLOGICAL FOCUS

God's providence opens doors for ministry to those in need.

PREACHING IDEA

We should seize the opportunity to serve those who suffer.

PREACHING POINTERS

Carpe diem! The admonition of the ancient Roman poet Horace to "seize the day" has found its way into popular culture at various times, including the title of Saul Bellow's 1956 novel *Seize the Day*, and Robin Williams's exhortation to his students in the 1989 movie *Dead Poets Society*. The apostle Paul articulated the same idea in Colossians 4:5. The kjv translated his words in that verse as "redeeming the time," which sounds a bit like time management. The nasb and other versions capture the sense more clearly as "making the most of the opportunity," which fits well in the immediate context of Paul's prayer request that he would know how to share the gospel while he was in Roman custody. Making the most of the opportunity must have been a ministry axiom for Paul. Wherever he was, whoever was around, whatever the circumstances might be, he looked for the opportunities he could seize to minister to others. You can see him implementing that axiom during his brief period of ministry on the island of Malta in Acts 28:1–10. Through shipwreck, snakebite, and a father's sickness, God providentially opened the doors for Paul to minister to those in need. When God opened the doors, Paul walked through them and engaged in a ministry of service to his fellow travelers and a ministry of healing to the Maltese people.

In this passage, people today should be able to relate to the discomfort caused by rain and cold as well as the relief gathering around a warm fire gives. The passage corrects a fatalistic view of divine judgment for wrongdoing, the idea that people will necessarily interpret the miraculous correctly, and the idea that the agent God chooses to use is the true source of the healing. The passage commends trust in God's protection, trust in God to heal, and trust in God to open doors for ministry. It also commends an attitude that is alert to those in need and is willing to serve those in need humbly. The objective in communicating the passage should be to help listeners understand that wherever God's providence places them, there are opportunities to minister for him, so that they will seize the opportunities before them to serve others who are in need.

Acts 28:11–31

EXEGETICAL IDEA
Paul's witness in Rome began with a warm welcome by Christians, included two meetings with the members of the Jewish community, and continued for two years during which he preached the kingdom of God and taught about Jesus to anyone who visited him in his rented quarters.

THEOLOGICAL FOCUS
God continues to extend his mission to all who seek him, regardless of locale, listeners, or apparent limitations.

PREACHING IDEA
The end of the book is not the end of the story.

PREACHING POINTERS
"Are we there yet?" Have you ever been on a long trip and heard this plaintive question come from the back seat of the car: "Are we there yet?" Although we might agree intellectually with musician Michael Card that there is "joy in the journey," most of us are far more focused on the destination; and when the journey gets long, we wonder when we will ever arrive. Perhaps Luke's original readers were wondering whether Paul would ever reach Rome. After all, he had been talking about it for at least three years. Imprisonment, judicial trials, storm at sea, shipwreck, snakebite, three months on Malta—he had endured all of those experiences since Jesus told him that he would bear witness in Rome. In Acts 28, Paul reached the capital of the empire.

He was finally there! Yet Luke leaves his readers hanging about what ultimately happened to Paul, because the end of the book is not the end of the story. His account of Paul's witness in Rome reminds us that God continues to extend his mission to all who seek him, regardless of locale, listeners, or apparent limitations. Acts is not a biography of the apostle Paul; it is an account of Jesus's faithful followers, whom he commissioned and empowered to be his witnesses to the ends of the earth. Are we there yet?

People today should be able to relate to people who are spiritually blind, deaf, or hard-hearted; to meeting with civic leaders; and to someone being placed under house arrest. The passage corrects the attitudes of giving credence to unsubstantiated reports or prejudging new ideas uncritically. It also commends being open to the truth, trusting God to open doors for witness, and being willing to engage others with the gospel as long as they are willing to listen. The objective in communicating the passage should be to help listeners understand that God is in charge of his ongoing mission and its progress, so that they will be faithful in carrying out the commission he has given them.

ABBREVIATIONS

GENERAL ABBREVIATIONS

A.D.	In the year of our Lord (*anno Domini*)
B.C.	Before Christ
LXX	Septuagint
NT	New Testament
OT	Old Testament

TECHNICAL ABBREVIATIONS

ca.	circa
cf.	*confer,* compare
ed.	edition/editor
e.g.	*exemplum gratia,* for example
etc.	and so forth, and the rest (*et cetera*)
i.e.	*id est,* that is
s.v.	*sub verbo,* under the word
vol(s).	volume(s)

BIBLICAL

Old Testament

Gen.	Genesis
Exod.	Exodus
Lev.	Leviticus
Num.	Numbers
Deut.	Deuteronomy
Josh.	Joshua
Judg.	Judges
Ruth	Ruth
1 Sam.	1 Samuel
2 Sam.	2 Samuel
1 Kings	1 Kings
2 Kings	2 Kings
1 Chron.	1 Chronicles
2 Chron.	2 Chronicles
Ezra	Ezra
Neh.	Nehemiah
Esther	Esther
Job	Job
Ps./Pss.	Psalm(s)
Prov.	Proverbs

Old Testament (cont)

Eccl.	Ecclesiastes
Song	Song of Songs
Isa.	Isaiah
Jer.	Jeremiah
Lam.	Lamentations
Ezek.	Ezekiel
Dan.	Daniel
Hos.	Hosea
Joel	Joel
Amos	Amos
Obad.	Obadiah
Jonah	Jonah
Mic.	Micah
Nah.	Nahum
Hab.	Habakkuk
Zeph.	Zephaniah
Hag.	Haggai
Zech.	Zechariah
Mal.	Malachi

New Testament

Matt.	Matthew
Mark	Mark
Luke	Luke
John	John
Acts	Acts
Rom.	Romans
1 Cor.	1 Corinthians
2 Cor.	2 Corinthians
Gal.	Galatians
Eph.	Ephesians
Phil.	Philippians
Col.	Colossians
1 Thess.	1 Thessalonians
2 Thess.	2 Thessalonians

New Testament (cont)

1 Tim.	1 Timothy
2 Tim.	2 Timothy
Titus	Titus
Philem.	Philemon
Heb.	Hebrews
James	James
1 Peter	1 Peter
2 Peter	2 Peter
1 John	1 John
2 John	2 John
3 John	3 John
Jude	Jude
Rev.	Revelation

EXTRABIBLICAL SOURCES

Jewish Apocrypha and Pseudepigrapha

1 Macc.	1 Maccabees
2 Macc.	2 Maccabees
3 Macc.	3 Maccabees
4 Macc.	4 Maccabees
Tob.	Tobit

Mishnah (Rabbinic Works)

m. Naz.	Nazir
m. Ohol.	Oholot
m. Sanh.	Sanhedrin
m. Sotah	Sotah

Apostolic Fathers

Barn.	Epistle of Barnabas
Did.	Didache
Herm. *Mand.*	Shepherd of Hermas, *Mandate*
Herm. *Sim.*	Shepherd of Hermas, *Similitude*
Herm. *Vis.*	Shepherd of Hermas, *Vision*

Classical and Ancient Writers (Greek and Latin Works)

Appian	*Bell. civ.*	*Civil Wars (Bella Civia)*
Cicero	*Pis.*	*Against Piso (In Pisonem)*
	Verr.	*Against Verres (In Verrem)*
Clement of Alexandria	*Strom.*	*Miscellanies (Stromata)*
Demosthenes	*Macart.*	*Against Macartatus (Contra Macartatum)*
Eusebius	*Hist. eccl.*	*Ecclesiastical History (Historia ecclesiastica)*

Herodotus	*Hist.*	*Histories (Historiae)*
Hesiod	*Op.*	*Works and Days (Opera et dies)*
Hippocrates	*Morb.*	*Diseases (De morbis)*
Homer	*Il.*	*Iliad (Ilias)*
	Od.	*Odyssey (Odyssea)*
Irenaeus	*Haer.*	*Against Heresies (Adversus haereses)*
Jerome	*Vir. ill.*	*On Illustrious Men (De viris illustribus)*
John Chrysostom	*Hom. Act.*	*Homilies on Acts (Homiliae in Acta apostolorum)*
Josephus	*A.J.*	*Jewish Antiquities (Antiquitates judaicae)*
	B.J.	*Jewish War (Bellum judaicum)*
	Vita	*Life (Vita)*
Justin Martyr	*1 Apol.*	*First Apology (Apologia i)*
	2 Apol.	*Second Apology (Apologia ii)*
Justinian	*Cod.*	*Justinian Code (Codex Justinianus)*
Origen	*Comm. Rom.*	*Commentary on Romans (Commentarii in Romanos)*
Ovid	*Her.*	*The Heroines (Heroides)*
	Metam.	*Metamorphoses (Metamorphoses)*
Philo	*Legat.*	*On the Embassy to Gaius (Legatio ad Gaium)*
Pliny	*Nat.*	*Natural History (Naturalis historia)*
Polybius	*Hist.*	*Histories (Historiae)*
Suetonius	*Claud.*	*Life of Claudius (Divus Claudius)*
Strabo	*Geogr.*	*Geography (Geographica)*
Tacitus	*Ann.*	*Annals (Annales)*
	Hist.	*Histories (Historiae)*
Tertullian	*Marc.*	*Against Marcion (Adversus Marcionem)*
	Mart.	*To the Martyrs (Ad martyras)*
Xenophon	*Hell.*	*Hellenica (Hellenica)*

PERIODICALS

HJ	*Heythrop Journal*
HUCA	*Hebrew Union College Annual*
JETS	*Journal of the Evangelical Theological Society*
JSNT	*Journal for the Study of the New Testament*
JTS	*Journal of Theological Studies*
NTS	*New Testament Studies*
PJT	*Pharos Journal of Theology*
TynBul	*Tyndale Bulletin*
VE	*Verbum et Ecclesia*

SERIES

AB	Anchor (Yale) Bible
AcBib	Academia Biblica

ANTC	Abingdon New Testament Commentaries
BECNT	Baker Exegetical Commentary on the New Testament
BHGNT	Baylor Handbook to the Greek New Testament
EBC	Expositor's Bible Commentary
HNTE	Handbooks for New Testament Exegesis
ICC	International Critical Commentary
IVPNTC	InterVarsity Press New Testament Commentary
JSNTSup	Journal for the Study of the New Testament Supplement Series
NAC	New American Commentary
NIBC	New International Bible Commentary
NICNT	New International Commentary on the New Testament
NIGTC	New International Greek Testament Commentary
NovTSup	Novum Testamentum Supplement
PNTC	Pillar New Testament Commentary
SBLMS	Society of Biblical Literature Monograph Series
SNTW	Studies in the New Testament and Its World
SP	Sacra Pagina
TNTC	Tyndale New Testament Commentary
WBC	Word Biblical Commentary
WUNT	Wissenschaftliche Unterschungen zum Neuen Testament
ZECNT	Zondervan Exegetical Commentary on the New Testament

REFERENCES

BDAG	Danker, Frederick W., Walter Bauer, William F. Arndt, and F. Wilbur Gingrich. *Greek-English Lexicon of the New Testament and Other Early Christian Literature*. 3rd ed. Chicago: University of Chicago Press, 2000.
DPL	Hawthorne, Gerald F., Ralph P. Martin, and Daniel G. Reid, eds. *Dictionary of Paul and his Letters*. Downers Grove, IL: InterVarsity Press, 1993.
GGBB	Wallace, Daniel B. *Greek Grammar beyond the Basics*. Grand Rapids: Zondervan, 1996.
LSJ	Liddell, Henry George, Robert Scott, and Henry Stuart Jones. *A Greek-English Lexicon*. 9th ed with revised supplement. Oxford: Clarendon, 1996.
L&N	Louw, Johannes P., and Eugene A. Nida, eds. *Greek-English Lexicon of the New Testament: Based on Semantic Domains*. 2nd ed. New York: United Bible Societies, 1989.
NewDocs	Horsley, Greg H. R., and Stephen Llewelyn, eds. *New Documents Illustrating Early Christianity*. Grand Rapids: Eerdmans, 1981–.
OCD	Hornblower, Simon, and Anthony Spawforth, eds. *The Oxford Classical Dictionary*. 4th ed. Oxford: Oxford University Press, 2012.
TCGNT	Metzger, Bruce M., ed. *A Textual Commentary on the Greek New Testament*. 2nd ed. New York: United Bible Societies, 1994.
TDB	Elwell, Walter A., and Philip W. Comfort, eds. *Tyndale Bible Dictionary*. Carol Stream, IL: Tyndale, 2001.

TDNT   Kittel, Gerhard, and Gerhard Friedrich, eds. *Theological Dictionary of the New Testament*. Translated by Geoffrey W. Bromiley. 10 vols. Grand Rapids: Eerdmans, 1964–1976.

BIBLE TRANSLATIONS

ASV	American Standard Version
CEV	Contemporary English Version
CSB	Christian Standard Bible
GNB	Good News Bible
ERV	Easy-to-Read Version
ESV	English Standard Version
KJV	King James Version
LEB	Lexham English Bible
NASB	New American Standard Bible
NEB	New English Bible
NET	New English Translation
NIV	New International Version
NJB	New Jerusalem Bible
NKJV	New King James Version
NLT	New Living Translation
NRSV	New Revised Standard Version
RSV	Revised Standard Version
TNT	The New Translation of the Epistles

INTRODUCTION TO ACTS

OVERVIEW OF ACTS

Author: Luke, a traveling companion of the apostle Paul

Place of Origin: Luke most likely wrote Acts as the second volume of his double work either during or shortly after Paul's house arrest in Rome.

Date: A.D. 60–75

Occasion for Writing: Questions arose from different sources about Christianity's relationship to Judaism, people from non-Jewish ethnic groups, and Roman civil authority.

Readers: Luke wrote to Theophilus and other middle-class, urban, educated Gentiles in Rome and the cities where Paul planted churches during his Aegean mission.

Genre: Historical monograph

Purposes: Luke wrote with multiple purposes: to provide an account of the origin and spread of Christianity, to present God in action as Jesus's disciples fulfilled the commission he gave them, to present Jesus as Messiah and the source of salvation for all people groups, to address objections to and accusations against the Christian movement, to validate the Gentile mission, and to provide models for public proclamation and defense.

AUTHORSHIP OF ACTS

Although the canonical books entitled "The Gospel according to Luke" (ΚΑΤΑ ΛΟΥΚΑΝ) and "The Acts of the Apostles" (ΠΡΑΞΕΙΣ ΑΠΟΣΤΟΛΩΝ) are formally anonymous, Eckhard Schnabel notes, "It can be reasonably assumed that the early church knew . . . the authors of these long books" (2012, 21). It is also logical to conclude that Theophilus (Θεόφιλε), to whom both books are dedicated (Luke 1:3; Acts 1:1), knew who the author was (Köstenberger, Kellum, and Quarles 2016, 308). In addition to their common audiences, many commentators recognize similarities between Luke and Acts in interest, language, and style (Larkin 1995, 17). Further, the author of Acts explicitly refers to "the first account" (τὸν πρῶτον λόγον) Theophilus had received, and F. F. Bruce suggests that Luke-Acts was originally intended as a single book that was produced in two volumes because it was too long for one scroll (1988, 3). These considerations, therefore, suggest that it is logical to view Luke-Acts as the literary product of a single author.

The so-called "we" passages (Acts 16:10–17; 20:5–15; 21:1–18; 27:1–28:16) provide the primary internal evidence from Acts itself and suggest that the author accompanied Paul on at least some of his travels; see the discussion of those passages below. Since it would be unusual for the author to refer to himself using both first-person and third-person language, it is possible to eliminate Silas (Acts 16:19), Sopater, Aristarchus, Secundus, Gaius, Timothy, Tychicus, and Trophimus (Acts 20:4) from consideration. Other coworkers Paul mentions in his letters include Epaphroditus (Phil. 2:25), Crescens (Col. 4:10), Titus (Col. 4:10), Jesus Justus (Col. 4:11), Epaphras (Col. 4:12; Philem. 23), Mark (Philem. 24), and Demas (Philem. 24). Andreas Köstenberger, Scott Kellum, and Charles Quarles discuss reasons to rule out the latter set of individuals (2016, 310–11). Paul also mentions Luke, who of his named companions seems to be the most likely option, since he was present during one of Paul's imprisonments (Col. 4:14; Philem. 24).

External evidence consistently connects Luke's name with both the gospel and Acts. The manuscript P⁷⁵ (ca. A.D. 175–225) was the first extant document that attached the superscription εὐαγγέλιον κατὰ Λουκᾶν to the third gospel. Irenaeus (A.D. 130–200) wrote, "Luke, the follower of Paul, set down in a book the gospel proclaimed by him" (*Haer.* 3.1.1). The Anti-Marcionite Prologue (A.D. 160–180) states, "Luke is an Antiochean Syrian, a doctor by trade; he was a disciple of the apostles, having followed Paul until has death . . . and afterward the same Luke wrote the Acts of the Apostles." The Muratorian Canon (A.D. 180–200) states, "The Acts of all the apostles were written in one book. Luke compiled for 'Most Excellent Theophilus' the several things that were done in his presence." Clement of Alexandria (*Strom.* 5.12), Tertullian (*Marc.* 4.2), Eusebius (*Hist. eccl.* 3.4.1), and Jerome (*Vir. ill.* 7) all attribute Acts to Luke.

Both internal and external evidence, therefore, suggest that Luke was the author of both the gospel according to Luke and the Acts of the Apostles. Craig Keener suggests that Luke was an ethnic Gentile, who "was probably at least a Godfearer before becoming a Christian" and "traced his spiritual heritage to the Hellenist Jewish Christian movement of Acts 6" (2012, 405). Whether he was a "doctor by trade," as the Anti-Marcionite Prologue records, is an open question.

DATE OF WRITING

Suggested dates for Acts range from as early as A.D. 60 until as late as A.D. 120. Keener concludes that dating the book as late as the early second century "hardly seems likely" (2012, 395). If the author was, in fact, one of Paul's companions, a reasonable span would begin with the final events of the book and would end with that individual's death (Larkin 1995, 18)—in other words, A.D. 60–95. Within that span, commentators hold three general positions. Richard Longenecker (1981, 235–38) represents those who affirm an early date (A.D. 60–70). Bruce (1990, 12–18) represents those who affirm a middle date (A.D. 70–85). C. K. Barrett (1998, xlii) represents those who affirm a late date (A.D. 85–95).

Two of the main arguments offered for a middle or late date are that Luke was dependent on Mark's gospel in writing his own and that Luke's accounts of Jesus's statements during the passion week presuppose the fall of Jerusalem (Luke 19:41–44; 21:20–24). Schnabel adequately refutes both of these arguments (2012, 27–28). Although he affirms a middle date, David Peterson notes, "a good case can be made for a date as early as A.D. 62–64" and gives four reasons for his statement (2009, 5). Schnabel adds a fifth reason (2012, 28). First, Luke shows no knowledge of Paul's letters. Second, Luke portrays Judaism as a legal religion. Third, Luke omits any reference to Nero's persecution. Fourth, Luke omits any mention of Paul's imprisonment. Fifth, Luke does not mention either the Jewish revolt that began in A.D. 66 or the destruction of Jerusalem in A.D. 70.

Although it is logical to conclude that Luke wrote Acts soon after he completed his first volume, there is no certain way of dating when the gospel reached its final form. Although

Keener affirms a middle date, he observes that correspondence with first-century historical events as well as the local charges leveled against Paul both reflect early memory of the events Luke describes (2012, 384). An agreed-upon conclusion as to whether Luke wrote his two volumes before or after the fall of Jerusalem is beyond reach. It is probably best, therefore, to suggest a date for the double work of Luke-Acts within the period of A.D. 60–75.

St. Luke by Giorgio Vasari. Public domain.

PLACE OF ORIGIN, DESTINATION, AND READERS

Regarding the place of origin, Barrett writes, "almost any guess will do" (1998, xliii). Darrell Bock lists suggestions by others as Achaia, Caesarea, Corinth, Ephesus, and Rome (2007, 27). If Luke wrote Acts during or shortly after Paul's two years in his rented quarters (Acts 28:30–31), Rome would be a logical place of origin as well as a possible destination, since Luke addresses both the gospel and Acts to Theophilus (Luke 1:3; Acts 1:1). Keener suggests that, in addition to an audience in Rome, Luke might have written for the churches planted during Paul's Aegean mission (2012, 429).

The fact that Luke addresses Theophilus as "most excellent" (κράτιστε) in the gospel suggests that he was most likely a high government official (Luke 1:3; cf. Acts 24:3; 26:25). The comment that he was writing in order that Theophilus might have "accurate information" (ἀσφάλειαν) about what he had been taught suggests that Theophilus was receptive to the gospel but had questions (Luke 1:4). Luke's larger audience was most likely middle class (Larkin 1995, 19), urban, Greek, and educated (Keener 2012, 426), and with a knowledge of the eastern empire (Longenecker 1981, 217).

OCCASION AND PURPOSES FOR WRITING

If Acts originated from the period between A.D. 60 and A.D. 75, Luke's readers would have heard its message amid "strong dissenting voices" (Larkin 1995, 19). Unbelieving Jews viewed the new Christian movement as a threat to their temple, Torah, and tradition. Some within the movement itself had reservations about how Gentiles should become members. There were stories from cities across the empire—including Rome—where disturbances connected with the preaching of the gospel had occurred. Luke's readers were most likely either new disciples or seekers who were receptive to the gospel, but they would have had questions. They would have benefited from knowing "the exact truth" about the matters in which they had been orally instructed (Luke 1:4, NASB).

Because the occasion for Luke's two-volume work was multifaceted, commentators have suggested multiple purposes for Acts. Keener, however, notes, "rarely do writers . . . have only a single agenda in mind when producing a literary work" (2012, 436). In the case of Acts, it is probably most helpful to think in terms of a cluster of purposes. Historically, Acts provides an account of the origin and spread of Christianity from Jerusalem to Rome (Stott 1990, 21–25). Theologically, Acts presents God—particularly the Holy Spirit—in action as Jesus's followers fulfill the mission he gave them (Bock 2007, 23–24). Evangelistically, Acts presents Jesus as the Messiah promised to the Jews and the one who would bring salvation to the Gentiles (Larkin 1995, 19–20). Apologetically, Acts addresses questions about Jewish opposition

to Christianity and accusations that the movement posed a threat to the order of the Roman Empire (Peterson 2009, 36–39). Missiologically, Acts validates the Gentile mission and provides models for confronting other religions and crossing cultural boundaries (Schnabel 2012, 36–38).

GENRE

Scholarly suggestions for defining the genre of Acts abound. They include travel narrative (Knox 1948), epic (Bonz 2000), novel (Pervo 1987), biography (Talbert 1974), and historical monograph (Palmer 1993). The question is complicated by the fact that Luke wrote two volumes. Charles Talbert suggests that biography applies to both volumes, specifically that Luke-Acts is a "succession narrative" in which short biographies of successors follow a longer biography of the founder of a philosophical school (1984, 1–3). David Turner also concludes that

both volumes fit the genre of biography and views Acts as "a quasi-biography of the church" (2019, 35). Although biography fits Luke's gospel well (Aune 1987, 64), Keener notes, "the genre that scholars most commonly propose for Acts is some form of ancient historiography" (2012, 90).

David Aune identifies three general categories of ancient historiography: Greco-Roman, Israelite, and Hellenistic Jewish (1987, 84–109). Subsets of Greco-Roman historical writings include mythography, ethnography, chronography, historical monograph, local history, general history, and antiquarian history. The three main Israelite historical/narrative compositions are the biblical books of Genesis–Deuteronomy, Joshua–2 Kings, and 1 Chronicles–Nehemiah. The primary Hellenistic Jewish historical works are 1 Maccabees, 2 Maccabees, and the writings of Josephus.

Keener follows George Sterling in viewing Acts as apologetic history (2012, 115; cf. Sterling 1992). Aune concludes that Acts is "a popular 'general history' written by an amateur Hellenistic historian with credentials in Greek rhetoric" (1987, 77). Ben Witherington concludes that Acts "follows no one model" and aligns with Greco-Roman historical works in its form, method, and arrangement, with Hellenistic Jewish historical works in its content and apologetic aims, and with Israelite historical works in its echoes of the OT and its emphasis on fulfillment (1998, 39). Given the variety of conclusions scholars draw from the available data, such a nuanced approach seems reasonable.

TEXT

Bruce Metzger notes that the text of Acts circulated in two "quite distinct" forms: the Alexandrian and Western. He further notes that the primary witnesses to the Alexandrian text are the papyri P[45] and P[75], the uncials ℵ, A, B, D, and Ψ, and the minuscules 33, 81, 104, 326, and 1175, while the primary witnesses to the Western text are the papyri P[29], P[38], and P[48], and the uncial D (*TCGNT*, 222). For Acts, the most important Western manuscript is a bilingual Greek-Latin text known as Codex Bezae (D), which includes the Gospels and Acts and dates from the fifth century.

In general, UBS[5] follows the Alexandrian text, but the Western text—which circulated in Italy, Gaul, and North Africa—is of interest for several reasons. Although Codex Bezae lacks 8:29–10:14; 22:10–20; 22:29–28:31, the extant portions are more than eight hundred words longer than the corresponding Alexandrian portions (Schnabel 2012, 41). That additional length reflects the fact that the Western text tends to smooth out grammatical difficulties; clarify ambiguous theological points; and add historical, biographical, and geographical details (Larkin 1995, 23). In the Western text, Metzger writes, "Words, clauses, and even whole sentences are freely changed, omitted, or inserted. Sometimes the motive appears to have been harmonization, while at other times it was the enrichment of the narrative by the addition of traditional or apocryphal material" (*TCGNT*, 6*). The commentary sections will note Western readings that inform the discussion of the text.

SOURCES

Luke referred to information that others had "handed down" (Luke 1:2), and many commentators go to some length to identify the specific sources for passages within Acts (e.g., Barrett 1994, 1998). In contrast, Jacques Dupont concludes that the author of Acts "is not satisfied with transcribing his sources, he rewrites the text by putting the imprint of his vocabulary and his style everywhere," which makes it impossible to define any specific sources that Luke used (1964, 166). William Larkin, however, notes, "for every section of Acts . . . there are identifiable personal acquaintances of Luke who were eyewitnesses to the events recounted" (1995, 21). His summary is the starting point for the following table.

Barnabas	1:1–5:42; 9:26–31; 11:19–30; 13:1–15:41
Mark (including from Peter)	1:1–5:42; 9:32–11:18; 12:1–25; 13:1–12
Philip	6:1–15; 8:4–40; 21:7–14
Paul	7:1–8:3; 9:1–31; 11:25–30; 13:1–28:31
Luke himself ("we" passages)	16:10–17; 20:5–15; 21:1–18; 27:1–28:16

HISTORICAL RELIABILITY

Peterson notes that a number of scholars have expressed concerns about aspects of Luke's reliability as a historian, including his use of sources, his portrayal of Paul, and his theological agenda (2009, 23). The discussion above addressed Luke's possible sources, and the discussion below will address the relationship between Acts and Paul's letters. Keener has an extended discussion of ancient historiography, in which he notes that ancient historical writers were interested in both the accuracy of their historical information and the artistry of their rhetorical presentation (2012, 117). An author's concern to convey a particular perspective on history did not necessarily lead to a distortion of the historical events recounted.

Larkin provides three helpful questions that may be used to evaluate the historical reliability of a narrative (1995, 21). First, "Did [the author] have access to the events reported, so that he had the capacity to write reliable history?" As noted in the table under Sources above, Luke had access to eyewitnesses for every section of his narrative. Second, "Did [the author] write an account that is in any way self-contradictory?" Suggested discrepancies, for example, between Luke's three accounts of Saul's Damascus road experience (9:3–18; 22:6–16; 26:12–18) reflect different emphases related to the audiences rather than historical contradictions. Third, "[Did the author's account] conflict with other witnesses to the events or other ancient evidence?" Keener presents a detailed discussion of correspondences between Acts and the events of the Paul's life

and ministry (2012, 237–50), and Colin Hemer presents an extended list of correspondences between Acts and extrabiblical historical evidence (1987, 101–243). When measured against these three standards, therefore, Luke proves to be a reliable historian.

THE SPEECHES

Speeches comprise approximately one-third of the content of Acts (Bock 2007, 20;

Conversion of St. Paul by Domenico Morelli.
Public domain.

Peterson 2009, 28). Luke includes six brief speeches by non-Christians: Gamaliel (5:33–39), Demetrius the silversmith (19:25–27), the town clerk of Ephesus (19:35–40), Tertullius (24:28), and Festus (25:14–21; 25:24–27). He also includes twenty-two speeches of varying lengths by major figures in the early church.

Text	Speaker	Location	Audience	Purpose	Type
1:16–22	Peter	Jerusalem	Disciples	Executive	Deliberative
2:14–31	Peter	Jerusalem	Jews	Evangelistic	Deliberative
3:12–26	Peter	Jerusalem	Jews	Evangelistic	Deliberative
4:8–12	Peter	Jerusalem	Sanhedrin	Apologetic	Forensic
5:29–32	Peter	Jerusalem	Sanhedrin	Apologetic	Forensic
7:2–53	Stephen	Jerusalem	Sanhedrin	Apologetic	Forensic
10:34–43	Peter	Caesarea	Gentiles	Evangelistic	Deliberative
11:4–17	Peter	Jerusalem	Disciples	Executive	Deliberative
13:16–41	Paul	Pisidian Antioch	Jews	Evangelistic	Deliberative
14:15–17	Paul	Lystra	Gentiles	Evangelistic	Deliberative
15:7–11	Peter	Jerusalem	Disciples	Executive	Deliberative
15:13–21	James	Jerusalem	Disciples	Executive	Deliberative
17:22–31	Paul	Athens	Areopagites	Evangelistic	Deliberative
20:17–35	Paul	Miletus	Ephesian elders	Hortatory	Deliberative
22:1–21	Paul	Jerusalem	Jews	Apologetic	Forensic
23:1–6	Paul	Jerusalem	Sanhedrin	Apologetic	Forensic
24:10–21	Paul	Caesarea	Felix	Apologetic	Forensic
25:8–11	Paul	Caesarea	Festus	Apologetic	Forensic
26:2–23	Paul	Caesarea	Agrippa II	Apologetic	Forensic
27:21–26	Paul	Ship	Passengers	Hortatory	Deliberative
28:17–20	Paul	Rome	Jews	Apologetic	Forensic
28:23–28	Paul	Rome	Jews	Evangelistic	Deliberative

The speeches have been critiqued as too short, too similar, and too Lukan to be authentic. I. Howard Marshall describes and refutes four common arguments that the speeches reflect a theological outlook that is later than the events described (1980, 40). On one hand, Keener writes, "virtually no scholars . . . argue that the speeches are verbatim" (2012, 309). On the other hand, Larkin writes, "there is still no impediment to taking the speeches as containing . . . the substance of what was said on the occasion" (1995, 23). Luke had access to eyewitness sources, and he had adequate time to become familiar with the nature of apostolic preaching, decision-making, and defense. It seems reasonable to conclude that the speeches he included were in keeping with what the speakers were likely to have said on the occasions and in the contexts described.

The extent of the content in Acts that is devoted to speeches serves to hold the readers' attention, provide a theological explanation and defense of the gospel, and present a model for witness. Keener notes that direct address in ancient writings held readers' attention more effectively than indirect discourse did, and that it was common for ancient narratives to include interrupted speeches because it reproduced "the realism of the ancient rhetorical situation" (2012, 269). The evangelistic speeches commended the teaching of the apostles, and the apologetic speeches commended the legitimacy of the movement. The evangelistic speeches in particular provided a model for witness by consistently incorporating essential elements of the gospel that have their origin in Jesus's postresurrection teaching (Luke 24:44–49).

Basis	According to Scripture	Luke 24:44–45
Events	Christ must suffer	Luke 24:46a
	Christ must rise	Luke 24:46b
Call	Repentance	Luke 24:47
Benefits	Promise of forgiveness	Luke 24:47
	Promise of blessing	Luke 24:49

THE "WE" PASSAGES

A special feature of Acts is a series of four passages where the author writes in the first-person plural. Scholars commonly refer to them as the "we" passages. Until the early nineteenth century, commentators followed Irenaeus's example in viewing these passages as a reference to "Luke . . . inseparable from Paul, and his fellow-laborer in the gospel" (*Haer.* 1:14.1).

Acts 16:10–17	Travel from Troas to Philippi via Neapolis
Acts 20:5–15	Travel from Philippi to Miletus via Troas
Acts 21:1–18	Travel from Miletus to Jerusalem via Caesarea
Acts 27:1–28:16	Travel from Caesarea to Rome via Malta

Since 1800, three alternate approaches have emerged. Vernon Robbins represents a group of scholars who take a comparative literary approach and argue that the "we" passages reflect a common literary convention associated with travel by sea (1978, 215–42). The evidence he uses to support his argument, though, involves both travel on land and by sea and implies that first-person narrative relates more closely to firsthand participation in the events recounted than to literary convention.

Ernst Haenchen represents a group of scholars who take a redaction-critical approach and argue that the final redactor of Acts inserted "we" to lend eyewitness support to the narrative (1971, 85). The fact that the author never identifies who "we" are, however, seems to run counter to a concern for eyewitness support.

Other scholars take a source-critical approach and propose that the degree of detail and accuracy in the "we" passages reflects a written source (perhaps from Timothy?) that the author of Acts chose to preserve in his finished work. There is no precedent, however, "for an historian reproducing someone else's 'we' source without giving notice to the reader and without transposing the first persons into thirds" (Hansen 1967, 169).

An approach that views the "we" passages as reflecting the author's participation in the events narrated, however, is the simplest and most obvious. It has exegetical support from Luke 1:1–4, which allows for eyewitness reporting of some of the events by the author. It has historical support from the general setting of Acts 27–28 (Hemer 1985, 109). It has literary support in the unity of the book, the unforced quality of the first-person narration, and the immediacy of the information included.

THE RELATIONSHIP TO PAUL'S LETTERS

There are notable differences between the portrayals of Paul in Acts and in his letters. Acts describes Paul as an apostle only twice (14:4, 14); in his letters, Paul makes frequent mention of his apostleship (Rom. 1:1; 1 Cor. 15:8–9; Gal. 1:1, 11–12). In Acts, Paul is an impressive public speaker (9:22, 29), who writes no letters; in his letters, he is an impressive letter writer but a weak speaker (2 Cor. 10:10). In Acts, Paul is a man of power (13:9–11; 14:8–10; 16:16–18; 19:11); in his letters, he is a man who boasts in his weaknesses (2 Cor. 12:9–10) and only speaks about what Christ has done through him (Rom. 15:18–19). In Acts, Paul practices Jewish piety (18:18; 21:23–26) to the point of having Timothy circumcised (16:3); in his letters, he rejects it (Col. 2:16–17) and makes a point of the fact that Titus was not compelled to be circumcised (Gal. 2:3). Marshall notes, however, "The differences between Luke's account of Paul and the picture we get from Paul's own writings are basically due to the different purposes of the two writers" (1980, 43). In effect, Luke portrays Paul's work as a missionary who planted churches, while Paul's letters reflect his pastoral care for the churches he planted.

In contrast, Keener has an extended discussion of the correspondences between Luke's account of Paul in Acts and details gleaned from Paul's letters (2012, 237–49). Similarly, Bruce comments, "Data about Paul in Acts and the letters agree well enough, without being forced into harmonizing conformity" (1990, 47). There are at least eight points of contact between the two portrayals of Paul. In both, he was a Pharisee (Acts 23:6; Phil. 3:5) and a persecutor of the church (Acts 8:3; 9:1–2; Gal. 1:13; Phil. 3:6). In both, the scope of his mission work extended from Jerusalem to the Adriatic (Acts 9–20; Rom. 15:19) and his mission strategy was to go first to the Jews, then to the Gentiles (Acts 13:44–47; Rom. 1:6; 2:9). In both, he supported himself bivocationally when necessary (Acts 18:3; 20:34; 1 Cor. 4:12; 1 Thess. 2:4; 2 Thess. 3:7–10) and encountered severe Jewish opposition (Acts 17:5–9, 13; 1 Thess. 2:14–16). The list of his sufferings in 2 Corinthians 11:23–27 echoes his experiences in Acts (14:19), and his sermon in Pisidian Antioch (Acts 13:38–39) echoes his exposition in Romans 8:1–4. There is, in fact, more agreement than disagreement between the two portrayals of Paul, his life, and his ministry, and it is possible to construct a fairly complete outline of Paul's ministry from the two sources.

OUTLINE OF PAUL'S MINISTRY

Luke's record of Paul's ministry in Acts begins with his vision on the Damascus road, consists of six periods, and ends with his arrival in Rome. Evidence from Paul's letters corresponds to five of those periods. The following table summarizes the data from both sources. (See Harvey 2012, 54–71 for a detailed analysis.)

Damascus and Arabia (A.D. 34–37)		
Acts 9:1–22	Damascus	Gal. 1:17
---	Arabia	Gal. 1:17
Acts 9:23–25	Damascus	Gal. 1:17; 2 Cor. 11:32–33
Acts 9:26–29	Jerusalem	Gal. 1:18–19
Syria and Cilicia (A.D. 37–48)		
Acts 9:30; 11:25	Syria and Cilicia	Gal. 1:21
Acts 11:26	Antioch	---
Acts 11:27–30	Jerusalem	Gal. 2:1–10
Acts 12:25–13:3	Antioch	Gal. 2:11–14
Cyprus and Galatia (A.D. 48–50)		
Acts 13:4–12	Cyprus	---
Acts 13:13–14:25	South Galatia	---
Acts 14:26–28	Antioch	---
Acts 15:1–29	Jerusalem	---
Acts 15:30–35	Antioch	---

Macedonia and Achaia (A.D. 50–53)		
Acts 15:36–41	Syria and Cilicia	---
Acts 16:1–10	Derbe to Troas	---
Acts 16:11–40	Philippi	1 Thess. 2:2
Acts 17:1–9	Thessalonica	1 Thess. 2:2; Phil. 4:15–16
Acts 17:10–14	Berea	---
Acts 17:15–34	Athens	1 Thess. 3:1
Acts 18:1–18	Corinth	2 Cor. 11:7–9
Acts 18:19–21	Ephesus	---
Acts 18:22	Caesarea to Antioch	---
Ephesus and Corinth (A.D. 53–57)		
Acts 19:1–40	Ephesus	1 Cor. 16:8
---	Troas	2 Cor. 2:12
Acts 20:1	Macedonia	2 Cor. 2:13; 7:5
Acts 20:2	Corinth	1 Cor. 16:5 (planned)
Acts 20:7–12	Troas	---
Acts 20:13–38	Miletus	---
Acts 21:1–16	Miletus to Caesarea	---
Imprisonment (A.D. 57–63)		
Acts 22:17–23:30	Jerusalem	Rom. 15:25 (planned)
Acts 23:31–26:32	Caesarea	---
Acts 28:1–10	Malta	---
Acts 28:11–28:31	Rome	Eph. 3:1; 4:22; Col. 4:18; Phil 1:13–14

PAUL'S VISITS TO JERUSALEM

In Acts, Luke mentions five visits Paul made to Jerusalem. In his letters, Paul describes three visits. Most scholars agree that Acts 9:26–27 aligns with Galatians 1:18–21 and Acts 21:15–17 aligns with Romans 15:25–32. They disagree on whether the visit Paul describes in Galatians 2:1–10 relates to the visit Luke records in Acts 11:27–30 or the visit he records in Acts 15:1–29.

The former understanding is often linked to a South Galatia destination for Paul's letter to those congregations, while the latter understanding is often linked to a North Galatia destination. John Knox, followed by some scholars, takes a drastically different approach in which he concludes that Paul made only three visits to Jerusalem and raises questions about Luke's historical accuracy (2000, 43–52).

Date	Acts	Paul	Knox
A.D. 34	"Acquaintance" Visit (9:26–27)	Galatians 1:18–21	Luke accurately places the acquaintance visit here (Gal. 1:18–21; cf. Acts 9:26–27).
A.D. 46	"Famine" Visit (11:29–30)	Galatians 2:1–10 (South Galatia theory)	Luke mistakenly describes the collection visit here as a "peace offering" prior to the Judaizing issue being settled.
A.D. 48	"Conference" Visit (15:1–29)	Galatians 2:1–10 (North Galatia theory)	Luke mistakenly describes the conference visit here because he believed the Judaizing issue was settled early.
A.D. 52	"Vow" Visit (18:22)		The conference visit (Gal. 2:1–10) actually occurs here, but Luke describes it in Acts 15:1–29.
A.D. 57	"Collection" Visit (21:15–17)	Romans 15:25–32	The collection visit (Rom. 15:25–32) actually occurs here, but Luke describes it in Acts 11:29–30.

Central to the discussion is the relationship of Acts 11 and 15 to Galatians 2. The two primary solutions are (1) that Acts 11 describes the Galatians 2 visit, or (2) that Acts 15 describes the Galatians 2 visit. The arguments for and against each position have been summarized well by others and are fairly well balanced on both sides.

David Williams argues against equating Galatians 2 with Acts 11 for six reasons: (1) the apostles are mentioned in Galatians 2 but not in Acts 11; (2) Titus is mentioned in Galatians 2 but not in Acts 11; (3) the controversy in Galatians 2 related to table fellowship rather than to circumcision; (4) the commendation of Barnabas and Paul in Galatians 2 seems unlikely before their ministry in Acts 13–14; (5) it is difficult to reconcile the three- and fourteen-year periods.

mentioned in Galatians 1 and 2 with the timing of the visit mentioned in Acts 11; and (6) Paul is subordinate to Barnabas in Acts 11 but not in Galatians 2 (1989, 257–58). On the other hand, Schnabel notes five arguments in support of equating Galatians 2 with Acts 11: (1) both passages describe the visit to Jerusalem as Paul's second; (2) both passages relate the visit as the result of a revelation; (3) both passages mention material needs in Judea; (4) both passages mention the Gentile mission; and (5) the apostles are not mentioned in Acts 11 because the leadership of the Jerusalem church had already changed (2004, 988–89).

Marshall argues against equating Galatians 2 with Acts 15 for four reasons: (1) Galatians 2 describes a private meeting, while Acts 15 describes a public meeting; (2) Galatians 2 says nothing about the decree and letter that were the outcome of Acts 15; (3) the controversy in Galatians 2 seems unlikely if it occurred after Acts 15; and (4) Galatians 2 says specifically that it describes Paul's second visit (1980, 244). On the other hand, Barrett notes four similarities between Galatians 2 and Acts 15: (1) others accompany Paul and Barnabas in both passages; (2) both passages mention Paul meeting with the apostles; (3) the apostles accept Paul and Barnabas as colleagues in both passages; and (4) both passages address table fellowship as an important issue (1998, 711).

The position adopted in this commentary is (1) that Galatians 2:1–10 describes the "famine visit" of Acts 11; (2) Galatians 2:11–14 describes an incident that took place in Antioch during the "long time" mentioned in Acts 14:27–28; (3) Paul wrote his letter to the Galatians prior to the events of Acts 15 (ca. A.D. 48), perhaps while he was on his trip to the Jerusalem consultation; (4) Paul addressed his letter to the churches he and Barnabas had planted in South Galatia during the missionary activity Luke describes in Acts 13–14; (5) Paul does not mention the "conference visit" of Acts 15 or the "vow visit" of Acts 18 in his letters; and (6) Romans 15:25–32 describes the anticipated "collection visit" of Acts 21.

NORMATIVE CONTENT IN BIBLICAL NARRATIVE

The book of Acts offers an exciting look at the beliefs and behaviors of the early church. Luke's narrative, however, naturally raises questions about the extent to which the contemporary church may adopt those beliefs and behaviors as normative. Nine questions can assist in determining normative content found in NT narrative in general and in Acts in particular (Harvey 2015, 89–96).

First, does the author limit the belief or behavior in the immediate context? Scripture can limit a belief or a behavior by directing a teaching to a specific individual or group. For example,

Peter limits his statement that the promise of the Holy Spirit is "for you and for your children and for all who are far off" by adding the clause "as many as the Lord will call to himself" (2:39). Forgiveness of sins is normative, but only for a certain group of people. Peter's statement does not support a belief in universal salvation.

Second, does the author provide a positive or negative comment on the belief or behavior? A negative example is Peter's rebuke of the attempt by Simon Magus to purchase the gift of bestowing the Holy Spirit (8:20–23), which clearly rejects such behavior as normative for believers. A positive example is Dorcas, whose generosity Luke commends both explicitly with his description of her in Acts 9:36 and implicitly in his comment about the widows showing Peter all the tunics and garments she had made.

Third, does the author incorporate the belief or behavior into an authoritative preaching or teaching section? As eyewitnesses to Jesus's life, death, resurrection, and ascension, the Twelve were authoritative spokesmen for him. When, in his Pentecost sermon, Peter called his listeners to "repent and . . . be baptized in the name of the Lord Jesus Christ" and followed that call with the promise that they would "receive the gift of Holy Spirit" (2:38), he affirmed the doctrines of repentance and the Spirit's indwelling as well as the practice of baptism.

Fourth, does the author provide a narrative clue to the importance of the belief or behavior? For example, Luke uses the phrases "filled with the Spirit" and "full of the Spirit" to designate what an individual says or does as authoritative and, therefore, normative. When he adds the statement that Barnabas was "a good man, full of the Holy Spirit and of faith" in Acts 11:24, he points to the elements of Barnabas's ministry as applicable for all believers today.

Fifth, does the author connect the belief or behavior to a key theme that runs throughout the book? For example, one of the key themes in Acts is "salvation" (twenty-four occurrences). By tracing the theme of salvation through the book, it becomes clear that the Lord saves (2:21) through grace (15:11) based on faith in Jesus (16:31). The belief derived from these passages, therefore, is normative.

Sixth, does the author use Scripture to explain or clarify the belief or behavior? In other words, does Luke cite the OT to explain or justify a teaching or action? For example, James uses Amos 9:11–12 to validate his proposal that the Jerusalem Council adopt an eschatological model of bringing Gentiles into the church apart from circumcision (15:13–21).

Seventh, does the author place the belief or behavior in a context that indicates its importance? A case in point is Luke's use of summary statements at various points in his narrative. When such a summary statement comments on a belief or behavior in the context that precedes it, the statement suggests that the belief or behavior is normative. For example, the summary statement in Acts 6:7 highlights the positive results that stemmed from the choosing of the Seven in Acts 6:1–6

Eighth, does the author use the belief or behavior to illustrate an underlying teaching found elsewhere in Scripture? One example is the way in which Peter and John's Spirit-filled response before the Sanhedrin in Acts 4:5–12 illustrates Jesus's teaching in Luke 12:11–12. The Spirit gave his followers the words to speak when they stood before religious authorities. Their dependence on the Spirit is normative because it illustrates Jesus's clear teaching.

Ninth, does the author present the belief or behavior as part of a consistently repeated pattern? For example, on the one hand, the lack of a consistent pattern of the Spirit's coming on people in Acts argues against a specific sequence of events as normative for all believers. On the other hand, God's giving of the Spirit to the Samaritans (8:5–17), Cornelius's household (10:34–48), and twelve men in Ephesus (19:2–6) suggests that supernatural spiritual manifestations might accompany the initial incorporation of new people groups into the church.

THEOLOGICAL EMPHASES

Not surprisingly, given the scope of the book, scholars arrive at different conclusions about the main contours of the "theology" of Acts. Rather than following standard systematic theology categories (e.g., theology proper, Christology, soteriology, eschatology), it is more natural to approach the book from the perspective of biblical theology and examine key themes that run throughout the book. Even so, the suggested theological themes scholars highlight can vary significantly. In their work on the theology of Acts, for example, Marshall and Peterson (1998) group essays from twenty-three contributors under three main categories: The Salvation of God, The Call of God, and The Renewing Work of God. In his subsequent commentary, Peterson devotes sixty-four pages to ten major themes in Acts, most of which diverge from the earlier work (2009, 33–97). The following synopsis seeks to gather multiple themes under four overarching theological emphases.

God is at work through the Holy Spirit to fulfill the promises of his Word. As Keener notes, "there is not a pericope that, in light of the whole work that forms its context, fails to exude this concern [for God]" (2012, 493). In particular, Luke highlights divine necessity by using the impersonal verb $\delta\epsilon\hat{\iota}$ sixteen times (1:16, 21; 3:21; 4:12), divine activity by the repeated use of the divine passive (2:40; 3:7, 19; 4:12), and divine agency by the using the phrase $\dot{\upsilon}\pi\grave{\diamond}$ $\tauo\hat{\upsilon}$ $\theta\epsilono\hat{\upsilon}$ to denote God as the ultimate actor (10:41, 42; 26:6). It is the Holy Spirit, however, whom Luke mentions fifty-seven times in the narrative and who fills Jesus's disciples for ministry (4:8, 31; 5:32; 6:3, 10; 7:55; 11:28; 13:9; 21:11), guides them (8:29, 39; 10:19; 16:6, 7; 19:21), and comforts them (9:31). The Spirit comes upon the 120 (2:1–5), the Samaritans (8:14–17), the members of Cornelius's household (10:44–48), and the twelve men in Ephesus (19:1–7) to confirm each group as part of the church, and he is the epitome of God's faithfulness in fulfilling the promises of his word. The verb $\pi\lambda\eta\rho\acuteo\omega$ ("fulfill") occurs nine times, and the noun ἐπαγγελία ("promise") occurs eight times. The phrase ὁ λόγος τοῦ θεοῦ ("the Word of God") occurs eleven times, and the noun γραφή ("writing") occurs eight times with the sense of "Scripture(s)."

Jesus is the Messiah and Savior for every people group. The name of Jesus (ὄνομα τοῦ Ἰησοῦ) and equivalent phrases occur thirty-one times in Acts with two senses—Jesus as an object of faith (2:21; 3:16; 4:12; 9:14, 21; 10:43; 22:16) and Jesus as a source of authority (3:6; 4:7, 10, 30; 16:18; 19:13). The title Messiah (Χριστός) occurs twenty-seven times, and cognate words related to salvation (σῴζω, σωτήρ, σωτηρία) occur twenty-four times. The concept of Messiah would have connected naturally to Jewish audiences, while the concept of salvation would have been familiar to Gentile audiences. The offer of salvation includes a call to repentance (μετανοέω/μετάνοια, eleven times) and expects a response of faith (πίστις/πιστεύω, fifty-seven times). One of the benefits of salvation is forgiveness of sins (ἄφεσις ἁμαρτιῶν, five times), and Jesus's witnesses are to preach that benefit among all the nations (10:35; 14:16; cf. Luke 24:47), even to the ends of the earth (1:8). Luke's consistent reports of the gospel crossing cultural boundaries demonstrate the universal scope of the gospel (6:8–15; 8:4–24, 25–40; 10:1–48; 11:19–26; 13:4–12, 44–51; 14:8–18; 16:14–34; 28:1–10). The repeated mention of "nations/Gentiles (ἔθνος, forty-three times) highlights it. The discussion after Cornelius's conversion validates it (11:1–18). The decision of the Jerusalem Council ratifies it (15:1–35).

The gospel advances through apostolic proclamation and demonstrations of divine power. As eyewitnesses to Jesus's life from his baptism to his ascension (1:21–22), the apostles (ἀπόστολος, twenty-eight times) are the guarantors of the church's message, and their evangelistic speeches in Acts provide important models for apostolic proclamation of the gospel (2:14–21; 3:12–26; 10:34–43; 13:16–41; 14:15–17; 17:22–31). The speeches are contextualized for their audiences,

but they include several common elements that should be considered essentials of the gospel. The historical events described were foretold in Scripture and focus on the fact that Messiah must suffer and rise. The witness issues a call to repentance, offers forgiveness of sins, and promises blessing from God (Luke 24:44–49). The primary means of communicating those essentials is through preaching (κηρύσσω, nine times), proclamation (ἀπαγγέλλω, thirteen times), and witness (μαρτυρέω/διαμαρτύρομαι, fifteen times). Demonstrations of divine power, however, often accompany apostolic proclamation. Luke mentions signs (σημεῖα, ten times), wonders (τέρατα, eight times), and works of power (δυνάμεις, two times) most frequently when the gospel moves into new territory (8:4–8; 9:32–43; 13:8–11; 14:8–10; 16:16–18; 19:11–20; 28:1–10), although they also occur in the early days of the Jerusalem church (3:1–10; 5:12–16; 6:8–10). In both settings, they serve to attract listeners and to authenticate the messenger who must interpret their significance.

Church life and growth occurs in a context of opposition. One of Luke's purposes is to provide an account of the origin and spread of the Christian movement. It is logical, therefore, that he would include an account of the birth of the new church at Pentecost (2:1–40). In addition to that account, he includes multiple snapshots of NT church life (1:12–26; 2:41–47; 4:23–37; 5:12–16; 6:1–7; 11:19–26; 20:7–12; 21:7–14) that help his readers understand the practical outworking of the gospel message in the lives of Jesus's followers. Especially in the account of the Jerusalem church, Luke interweaves his snapshots of church life with accounts of opposition. Opposition comes in a variety of forms and from a variety of sources, including religious (4:1–22; 5:17–42; 6:8–15; 7:54–8:3; 13:44–52; 14:19–23; 17:5–9, 13; 18:12–17; 21:27–23:10; 28:23–28), civil (12:1–24; 16:19–24; 19:23–41), and spiritual (8:9–13; 13:8–11; 16:16–18; 19:11–20). Despite opposition, however, the church does more than merely exist; it "grows" (αὐξάνω, 6:7; 12:24;

19:20) and "multiplies" ($\pi\lambda\eta\theta\acute{\nu}\nu\omega$, 6:1, 7; 9:31; 12:24), as Luke's repeated summary statements make clear (2:41; 4:4; 5:14; 6:1; 9:31; 11:26; 12:24; 14:1; 16:5; 19:20). In fact, it is part of God's plan ($\delta\epsilon\hat{\iota}$) that his people enter his kingdom through many tribulations (14:22)

OUTLINE

The book of Acts consists of seven major divisions that may be preached in forty-six sermons.

JERUSALEM (1:1–8:3)

- The Promises Leading to Pentecost (1:1–11)
- The Preparation for Pentecost (1:12–26)
- The Power of Pentecost (2:1–40)
- The Early Church's Common Life (2:41–47)
- The Church's First Healing (3:1–26)
- The Church's First Opposition (4:1–31)
- The Church's Benevolence (4:32–37)
- The Church's Integrity (5:1–11)
- The Church's Impact (5:12–16)
- The Church's Unwavering Witness (5:17–42)
- The Church's First Problem (6:1–7)
- The Church's First Martyr (6:8–8:3)

JUDEA, SAMARIA, AND SYRIA (8:4–12:25)

- Philip's Witness in Samaria (8:4–25)
- Philip's Witness to an Ethiopian (8:26–40)
- Jesus's Appearance to and Confirmation of Saul (9:1–19a)
- Paul's Witness in Damascus and Jerusalem (9:19b–31)
- Peter's Witness in Coastal Judea (9:32–43)
- Peter's Witness to a Godfearer (10:1–48)
- Defense of Peter's Witness to the Gentiles (11:1–18)
- Bold Witness in Syrian Antioch (11:19–30)
- Opposition from Herod Agrippa I (12:1–25)

CYPRUS, GALATIA, AND THE JERUSALEM COUNCIL (13:1–15:35)

- Witness on Cyprus (13:1–12)
- Witness in Pisidian Antioch (13:13–52)
- Further Witness in South Galatia (14:1–28)
- The Jerusalem Council (15:1–35)

MACEDONIA AND ACHAIA (15:36–18:17)

- The Road to Europe (15:36–16:10)
- Witness in Philippi (16:11–40)
- Witness in Thessalonica and Berea (17:1–15)
- Witness in Athens (17:16–34)
- Witness in Corinth (18:1–17)

ASIA (18:18–20:38)

- Early Events in Ephesus (18:18–28)
- Witness in Ephesus (19:1–22)
- Trouble in Ephesus (19:23–40)
- Concluding the Mission in Europe (20:1–12)
- Concluding the Mission in Asia (20:13–38)

JERUSALEM AND CAESAREA (21:1–26:32)

- Journey to Jerusalem (21:1–14)
- Paul's Arrival in Jerusalem and the Elders' Proposal (21:15–26)
- Defense Before the Mob (21:37–22:29)
- Defense Before the Sanhedrin (22:30–23:11)
- Transfer to Caesarea Maritima (23:12–35)
- Defense Before Felix (24:1–27)
- Defense Before Festus (25:1–12)
- Defense Before Herod Agrippa II (25:13–26:32)

MALTA AND ROME (27:1–28:31)

- Storm and Shipwreck (27:1–44)
- Witness on Malta (28:1–10)
- Witness in Rome (28:11–31)

JERUSALEM (ACTS 1:1–8:3)

Luke's gospel closes with Jesus's resurrection (24:1–12), his appearances to his followers (24:13–49), and his ascension (24:50–53). Acts begins with an overlapping summary of Jesus's teaching during his appearances (1:1–5), his command-promise related to the coming of the Holy Spirit (1:6–8), and his ascension (1:9–11). That introduction launches Luke's account of the early days of the Christian movement and its witness in Jerusalem and the cities in the immediate vicinity. The first division of his account weaves together the themes of early church life (1:12–26; 2:42–3:10; 4:23–5:11; 6:1–7), active witness (2:1–41; 3:11–4:4; 5:12–16; 6:8–15), and religious opposition to the gospel (4:5–22; 5:17–42; 7:1–8:3). Luke punctuates the account with comments highlighting the explosive growth of the new Christian community (2:41; 4:4; 5:14; 6:7). The events Luke describes cover approximately two years, from the middle of A.D. 30 through the middle of A.D. 32.

30	Summer		Pentecost (2:1–41)
	Fall		Temple healing (3:1–4:4)
31	Winter		First arrest (4:5–31)
	Spring	Jerusalem (1:1–8:3)	Ananias and Sapphira (5:1–11)
	Summer		
	Fall		Second arrest (5:17–42)
32	Winter		Widows' complaint (6:1–7)
	Spring		Stephen's martyrdom (6:8–8:3)

This first division consists of twelve preaching sections. The first two sections recount the events related to Jesus's ascension (1:1–11) and its aftermath (1:12–26). The third and fourth sections describe the coming of the Holy Spirit at Pentecost (2:1–40) and the early church's post-Pentecost community life (2:41–47). The fifth and sixth sections record the first miracle the apostles performed (3:1–26) and the religious opposition that arose in response to the public preaching of the gospel (4:1–31). The seventh and eighth sections describe Barnabas's example of caring within the new community (4:32–37) followed by Ananias and Sapphira's attempt to imitate Barnabas's action while succumbing to their own greed (5:1–11). The ninth and tenth sections record the local and regional impact of the early church (5:12–16) as well as the renewed religious opposition that followed (5:17–42). The eleventh and twelfth sections narrate the way in which the church resolved the problem that arose related to the distribution of food to widows within the community (6:1–7) as well as the ministry and martyrdom of Stephen, who was one of the seven men chosen to distribute food to the widows (6:8–8:3).

Acts 1:1–11

EXEGETICAL IDEA

During the forty days from the resurrection to the ascension, Jesus reminded the apostles of the Father's promise, he commanded them to rely on the Spirit's power, and two angels challenged them to expect the Son's return.

THEOLOGICAL FOCUS

Jesus sets the parameters and provides the resources for his followers to extend his ministry to the end of the earth.

PREACHING IDEA

Jesus's directives determine our direction.

PREACHING POINTERS

Have you ever faced a situation that appeared impossible? You can respond to that sort of situation in one of two ways. You can tremble in despair, or you can trust in God. Jesus's disciples must have felt as though they were facing an impossible situation at the beginning of Acts. Jesus was getting ready to leave them (again). He had told them multiple times that they were to reach the entire world with the gospel, but there were only 120 of them, they had no "leader," and the environment was as hostile as anyone could imagine. With Luke's original readers, we need to understand that Jesus speaks into impossible situations to give us the encouragement we need. If we do, we will follow his instructions and trust in his promises regardless of how impossible the situation might appear to be.

People today should be able to relate to the desire to know what the future holds and to the role of witnesses who testify to the truth of statements and/or events. They should also be familiar with teachers instructing a group over an extended period of time, as Jesus did with his disciples. The events described in Acts 1:1–11 correct any suggestion that Jesus's ministry ended when he ascended, or that his followers can engage in ministry in their own power. They commend trust in God's promises and resources, hope in Jesus's return, and commit to the task Jesus has assigned. They remind us that Jesus's directives—his instructions and his promises—determine the direction of our ministries.

THE PROMISES LEADING TO PENTECOST (1:1–11)

LITERARY STRUCTURE AND THEMES (1:1–11)

The passage consists of two paragraphs (1:1–5; 1:6–11), each with two subsections. The first paragraph combines a brief "resumptive preface" (1:1–2; cf. Longenecker 1981, 252) with a concise summary of Jesus's postresurrection ministry (1:3–5). Luke frequently uses the combination οἱ μὲν οὖν to begin a new section of his narrative (1:6; cf. 2:41; 8:4, 25; 11:19; 15:30; 23:31). The second paragraph combines Jesus's final instructions to his followers (1:6–8) with an account of his ascension (1:9–11). Peterson notes four literary forms that align well with the four subsections: prologue, appearance narrative, farewell scene, and assumption narrative (2009, 99). Mentions of Jesus's ascension in verse 2 (ἀνελήμφθη) and verse 11 (ἀναλημφθείς) form an *inclusio* that frames the passage.

- ***Preface (1:1–2)***
- ***The Reminder of the Father's Promise (1:3–5)***
- ***The Promise of the Spirit's Power (1:6–8)***
- ***The Prospect of the Son's Return (1:9–11)***

EXPOSITION (1:1–11)

After a brief preface in which he links the present work to his former work (1:1–2), Luke introduces his new account by summarizing four aspects of Jesus's postresurrection activities. To those four aspects, he adds a commissioning scene (1:6–8) that also "serves as the theme, setting the stage for all that follows in Acts" (Longenecker 1981, 256).

	Luke 24:13–53	Acts 1:3–11
Appearances	24:13–43	1:3a
Instruction	24:44–48	1:3b
Promise of the Spirit	24:49	1:4–5
Commissioning	--	1:6–8
Ascension	24:50–53	1:9–11

In addition to the sequence of events narrated, there are multiple connections between the two works. Points of verbal correspondence include πάσχω (Luke 24:26; Acts 1:1), μάρτυρες (Luke 24:48; Acts 1:8), ἐπαγγελία (Luke 24:49; Acts 1:4), and δύναμις (Luke 24:49; Acts 1:8). Items of conceptual correspondence include Jerusalem as the epicenter of coming events (Luke 24:47; Acts 1:8) and the instruction to wait in the city (Luke 24:29; Acts 1:4).

Barrett includes verses 13–14 with the

introduction and identifies seven functions of the section (1994, 63), while Schnabel lists seven aims (2012, 63–64). An edited composite list that applies to 1:1–11 is:

- to establish continuity with the gospel of Luke
- to underline the central role of the apostles
- to emphasize the work of the Holy Spirit
- to highlight the global scope of the church's work (end of the earth)
- to fix the temporal scope of the church's work (ascension to return)

Preface (1:1–2)

Luke's present work continues his previous account of the actions and teachings of Jesus's earthly ministry.

1:1–2. Theophilus (ὦ Θεόφιλε) is the same individual to whom the "earlier work" (NJB, τὸν πρῶτον λόγον) was dedicated (Luke 1:3), although Luke omits the polite address of the gospel (κράτιστε) here. That earlier work concerned "all things . . . that Jesus began both to do and to teach" (περὶ πάντων . . . ὧν ὁ Ἰησοῦς ποιεῖν τε καὶ διδάσκειν), specifically during the timeframe leading to his ascension (ἄχρι ἧς ἡμέρας . . . ἀνελήμφθη). During that timeframe, he "gave orders" (ἐντειλάμενος) through the Holy Spirit (διὰ πνεύματος ἁγίου) to the apostles whom he had chosen (τοῖς ἀποστόλοις . . . οὓς ἐξελέξατο).

These verses serve four functions. They establish Acts as a sequel to Luke's gospel. They highlight the role of the Holy Spirit in Jesus's earthly ministry. They identify the apostles as the chosen recipients of Jesus's instruction. They point to "the continuing work of Jesus through the Holy Spirit in the ministry of the Twelve and other believers such as Stephen, Philip, and Paul" (Schnabel 2012, 70).

Apostle

The word "apostle" (ἀπόστολος) occurs twenty-eight times in Acts. All but two occurrences (14:4, 14) refer to the Twelve—eleven of the original disciples (1:13) plus Matthias as Judas's replacement (1:26)—who had accompanied Jesus from John's baptism until Jesus's ascension (1:21–22). Their primary role was to bear witness to Jesus's resurrection (1:22; cf. 2:22–36; 3:12–16; 4:8–12, 33; 5:29–32). Their apostleship was a ministry (1:25) that included teaching (2:42; 6:4), prayer (6:4), distributing financial resources to those in need (4:35–37), exercising discipline within the Christian community (5:1–11), and laying hands on the group of seven who were responsible to distribute food to widows (6:6). Signs and wonders authenticated their ministry (2:43; 5:12). They also served as gatekeepers who confirmed the progress of the gospel in Samaria (8:14–18), to Paul after his Damascus road vision (9:27–28), to Cornelius in Caesarea (11:1–18), and in Antioch, where Barnabas served as their representative (11:22–24). Together with the elders of the Jerusalem church, the apostles superintended the decision-making process of the Jerusalem Council (15:1–11) and endorsed the letter that documented the council's decision (15:22–29; cf. 16:4).

The Reminder of the Father's Promise (1:3–5)

During the forty days following his resurrection, Jesus appeared to the apostles, instructed them about the kingdom of God, commanded them to remain in Jerusalem, and reminded them to expect the promised Holy Spirit.

1:3. Simon Kistemaker lists ten postresurrection appearances (1991, 48). Luke provides five details about those appearances. They followed Jesus's passion (μετὰ τὸ παθεῖν αὐτόν). They consisted of Jesus presenting himself to the apostles (οἷς παρέστησεν ἑαυτόν). They took place over a period of forty days (δι' ἡμερῶν τεσσεράκοντα). They were accompanied by "many convincing and decisive proofs" (ἐν πολλοῖς τεκμηρίοις; cf. BDAG s.v. "τεκμήριον" 994). They provided Jesus with the opportunity to teach the disciples about the kingdom of God (λέγων τὰ περὶ τῆς βασιλείας τοῦ θεοῦ). Just as Jesus's burial confirmed his death, his appearances confirmed his resurrection.

> ### The Kingdom of God
>
> The kingdom of God (ἡ βασιλεία τοῦ θεοῦ) is God's dynamic reign rather than a geographical entity. James Dunn prefers "God's rule as king" (1996, 7). The exact phrase occurs thirty-two times in Luke's gospel and six times in Acts. The variants "his kingdom," "your kingdom," "my kingdom," and "the kingdom" occur an additional seven times in the gospel and twice in Acts. The kingdom is pictured as a banquet (Luke 13:28–29; 14:15; 22:16, 18, 30) that has no end (Luke 1:33) and for which it is worth leaving everything behind (Luke 9:62; 18:29). Jesus's followers are to seek it (Luke 12:31) and pray for its coming (Luke 11:2). They enter it as children (Luke 18:16–17) through many tribulations (Acts 14:22). It is "near" (Luke 10:9, 11; 21:31) and is present wherever Jesus is present (Luke 11:20; 17:21). When it comes, it does not come with observable signs (Luke 17:20). Above all, the kingdom is a message that is to be preached (Luke 4:43; 8:1; 9:2, 60; 16:16; Acts 8:12; 20:25; 28:31), spoken (Luke 9:11), taught (Acts 1:3; 28:31), and used to persuade (Acts 19:8; 28:23). Its content is "the things about the Lord Jesus Christ" (τὰ περὶ τοῦ κυρίου Ἰησοῦ Χριστοῦ; Acts 28:31). Barrett views it as "a general term covering the whole of the Christian proclamation" (1994, 70). Matthew's use of "the kingdom of the heavens" (ἡ βασιλεία τῶν οὐρανῶν) defers to Jewish sensibilities and denotes the same concept as "the kingdom of God" (Bruce 1990, 100).

1:4–5. On one particular occasion, while he was eating together (συναλιζόμενος) with them,

Jesus gave the apostles a specific command (παρήγγειλεν αὐτοῖς) not to leave Jerusalem (ἀπὸ Ἰεροσολύμα μὴ χωρίζεσθαι) but instead, to wait for the promise of the Father (ἀλλὰ περιμένειν τὴν ἐπαγγελίαν τοῦ πατρός). They had recently heard this promise from Jesus himself (ἣν ἠκούσατέ μου), when he had told them that he would also be instrumental in fulfilling it (Luke 24:49). They had first heard the promise from John the Baptist, who connected it with the coming Messiah, characterized it as "baptism," and declared that it was superior to his own baptism (Luke 3:16). This baptism "by the Holy Spirit" (ἐν πνεύματι ἁγίῳ) would take place "before long" (οὐ μετὰ πολλὰς ταύτας ἡμέρας; cf. Bock 2007, 55), as the subsequent narrative confirms. Schnabel goes to some length to translate baptism as "immersion" (2012, 74–75 and throughout his commentary), although he argues that the significance of the promise is the "overwhelming" character of the cleansing, salvation, and empowerment for witness that results. The most common OT image is that of God "pouring out" his Spirit.

> ### The Promise of the Holy Spirit
>
> Jesus mentions the Holy Spirit three times during his postresurrection appearances (Luke 24:49; Acts 1:4–5, 8). In two of them, he mentions "the promise of my Father," alluding to OT passages that promise a pouring out God's Spirit on Israel (Isa. 32:15; 44:3; 59:21; Ezek. 11:19; 36:26–27; 37:14; 39:29: Zech. 12:10). Specifically, the promise relates to the permanent internal administration of the new covenant (Jer. 31:33–34). In Isaiah, the Lord promises, "My Spirit which is upon you . . . shall not depart from [you]" (Isa. 59:21). In Ezekiel, he promises, "I will put my Spirit within you" (Ezek. 36:26–27; 37:14). Joel 2:28–32 (3:1–5 MT) provides the most familiar statement of the promise:
>
> I will pour out my Spirit on all mankind.
> Your sons and daughters will prophesy,
> your old men will dream dreams,

> your young men will see visions.
> Even on the male and female servants I
> will pour out my Spirit in those days.
>
> Adding that passage to Isaiah 32:15; 44:3; Ezekiel 39:29; and Zechariah 12:10 "highlight[s] four key aspects of the Old Testament promise regarding the Spirit. The Spirit's ministry will be internal. The Spirit's ministry will be permanent. The Spirit's ministry will be widespread. The Spirit's ministry will result in 'prophecy' and 'witness'" (Harvey 2008, 107). Jesus specifies the "witness" aspect of the promise in Acts 1:8. Further, Joel's prophecy extends the promise to "all people" without distinction of ethnicity, gender, age, or socioeconomic level.

The Promise of the Spirit's Power (1:6–8)

Rather than focusing on the timing of the kingdom's restoration, the apostles are to focus on being Spirit-empowered witnesses for Jesus.

1:6. Immediately before his ascension, while they were gathered together (συνελθόντες), the apostles were repeatedly asking (ἠρώτων) Jesus whether the time when he would restore the kingdom was near (εἰ ἐν τῷ χρόνῳ τούτῳ ἀποκαθιστάνεις τὴν βασιλείαν τῷ Ἰσραήλ;). The combination of Jesus's teaching on the kingdom of God (1:3) and the promise of the Holy Spirit's coming (1:4–5) led Jesus's followers to expect that the time must be close when he would restore the kingdom to Israel. The OT had promised that God would bring Israel back to their own country (Jer. 16:15; Hos. 11:11), so that they could live in the land (Jer. 28:3; 50:19; Ezek. 34:26–28), where they would increase in number (Ezek. 36:11, 37). At that time, the nations would be humbled (Ezek. 36:6), and their kingdoms would be given to Israel (Dan. 7:27). David's kingdom would be restored (Amos 9:11–15)—a kingdom without an end (Dan. 2:44; 7:14)—and God would pour out his Spirit upon his people (Ezek. 36:27; 39:29). Further, the topic of the kingdom had arisen multiple times during Jesus's preresurrection ministry (Luke 12:32; 19:11–27; 21:24; 22:24, 29–30).

1:7–8. Jesus did not reject the idea of restoring the kingdom to Israel, but he redirected the apostles' focus. They should not focus on the "times or seasons" because the Father had set the timing by his own authority (ὁ πατὴρ ἔθετο ἐν τῇ ἰδίᾳ ἐξουσίᾳ). Instead (ἀλλά), they should focus on the task Jesus had for them—to be his witnesses to the ends of the earth. Martin Culy and Mikael Parsons note that χρόνους ἢ καιρούς are synonyms with little significant difference in meaning (2003, 8). The apostles' task involved a specific role, relied on a special source of enabling, and had a global scope. The role was to be witnesses (ἔσεσθέ μου μάρτυρες) who both belonged to Jesus (possessive genitive) and bore witness to him (objective genitive). Their source of enabling was power they would receive after the Holy Spirit came upon them (λήμψεσθε δύναμιν ἐπελθόντος τοῦ ἁγίου πνεύματος ἐφ' ὑμᾶς). The scope would begin in Jerusalem (ἐν Ἰερουσαλήμ), expand through all Judea and Samaria (ἐν πάσῃ τῇ Ἰουδαίᾳ καὶ Σαμαρείᾳ), and reach to the end of the earth (ἕως ἐσχάτου τῆς γῆς). Larkin characterizes Jesus's words as a "command-promise," which the church carries out and for which God gives the impetus and direction (1995, 41). Bock notes that "The church does not *have* a mission; it is to be missional and *is* a mission" (2007, 66; emphasis original).

Readers have long recognized that Acts 1:8 provides a basic outline for the book. The geographic boundaries the gospel will cross are frequently noted. The gospel will also cross ethnic thresholds in ever-expanding circles (Larkin 1995, 42). Finally, David Pao suggests that the verse reflects a three-stage theopolitic program of the new era in which the early Christian community becomes the heir to God's promise of restoration to Israel (2000, 91–101).

	Geographic	Ethnic	Theopolitic
Acts 1–7	Jerusalem	Hebrew-speaking Jews (Acts 3–5)	Dawn of salvation upon Israel (Isa. 40:1–5)
		Greek-speaking Jews (Acts 6–7)	
Acts 8–12	Judea and Samaria	Samaritans (Acts 8:1–25)	Reconstitution and reunification of Israel (Isa. 43:1–7)
		Proselyte (Acts 8:26–40)	
		Godfearing Gentiles (Acts 10:1–11:18)	
Acts 13–28	End of the Earth	Pagan Gentiles (Acts 13–14)	Inclusion of the Gentiles within the people of God (Isa. 49:1–7)
		Greeks (Acts 16–20)	
		Romans (Acts 27–28)	

Although Jesus did not specifically mention Galilee, Herod Agrippa I had integrated that region into Judea (cf. 9:31). Schnabel notes that, in the first century, ancient literature variously defined "the end of the earth" (ἐσχάτου τῆς γῆς) as Britannia, Spain, Gaul, or Germania in the west; Scythia or the Arctic in the north; Ethiopia or Sudan in the south; and India or China in the east (2012, 79–80). The phrase is most likely an echo of Isaiah's statement, "I will also make you a light for the Gentiles that my salvation may reach to the ends of the earth" (Isa. 49:6).

> **"You will be my witnesses."**
> A "witness" (μάρτυς) is someone who testifies to legal matters (7:58) or affirms the truth about someone or something (6:3; 10:22; 15:8; 22:12). Jesus's command-promise to his disciples that they would be his witnesses (1:8) echoes God's statement through Isaiah to Israel: "You are my witnesses" (Isa. 43:10, 12; 44:8). In Isaiah and Acts, the designation "my witnesses" highlights both the source of the witnesses' authority and the content of their message. In Acts, the word applies to the twelve apostles, whose credentials are that they were with Jesus from the time of John's baptism until Jesus's ascension (1:21–22), and to Paul, whom Jesus commissioned directly (26:16–18). They were to be witnesses for Jesus (22:15) and his cause (23:11). Their message was to be about Jesus (22:18) and all he had done (10:39). Specifically, they were to be witnesses that "the Christ should suffer and rise again from the dead the third day, and that forgiveness of sins was to be proclaimed in his name to all nations, beginning from Jerusalem" (Luke 24:46–48; cf. Acts 2:32; 3:15; 5:32; 10:41; 13:31). Schnabel notes that their testimony "help[s] to establish the facts on which others can rely" (2012, 78).

The Prospect of the Son's Return (1:9–11)

Jesus's ascension marks the end of his earthly ministry, confirms his heavenly exaltation, and calls the apostles to look for his return.

1:9. Luke recounts Jesus's visible, bodily ascension in a single sentence, introduced by two circumstances. It took place after Jesus had spoken the words recorded in verses 7–8 (ταῦτα εἰπών) and while the apostles were looking at him (βλεπόντων αὐτῶν). The ascension itself involved a cloud "envelop[ing] him from underneath and [taking] him out of their sight" (Bock 2007, 67; ἐπήρθη καὶ . . . ὑπέλαβεν αὐτὸν ἀπὸ τῶν ὀφθαλμῶν αὐτῶν). Old Testament accounts of individuals being "taken up," including Enoch (Gen. 5:24), Moses (Deut. 34:9), and Elijah (2 Kings 2:9–22), provide the background for the event. The genitive absolute (βλεπόντων αὐτῶν) establishes the apostles as eyewitnesses to the event. Scholars variously understand the cloud (νεφέλη) as a reflection of God's Shekinah glory (Bruce 1990, 104; cf. Luke 9:31), a foreshadowing of Jesus's return (Larkin 1995, 43; cf. Luke 21:27), or a natural phenomenon (Schnabel 2012, 80). The details of the scene distinguish it from earlier disappearances (cf. Luke 24:31) and establish the finality of his departure (Bruce 1990, 103). Peterson appropriately notes that Jesus's ascension "was not the beginning of his heavenly exaltation. It was the ultimate confirmation of the status that had been his from the moment of his resurrection" (2009, 115).

1:10–11. As the apostles continued gazing upward (ὡς ἀτενίζοντες ἦσαν εἰς τὸν οὐρανόν), two men stood beside them (ἄνδρες δύο παρειστήκεισαν) and spoke to them (καὶ εἶπαν). The angels asked the apostles why they kept on trying to watch Jesus's departure (τί ἑστήκατε ἐμβλέποντες εἰς τὸν οὐρανόν;). Instead, they should now look for his return, since he would come back in the same manner as they saw him departing into heaven (οὕτως ἐλευσεται ὃν τρόπον ἐθεάσασθε αὐτον πορευόμενωον εἰς τὸν οὐρανόν). The fact that there were two men reflects the OT

requirement that two witnesses were needed to confirm evidence (Deut. 19:15). That they were dressed "in dazzling raiment" (Bruce 1990, 104; ἐν ἐσθήσεσι λευκαῖς) identifies them as angels (cf. Luke 24:4; Acts 10:3, 30). The phrase "into heaven" (εἰς τὸν οὐρανόν) occurs four times but should not be understood in a spatial sense. Instead, it points to the position of authority Jesus was about to assume at the Father's right hand (2:33; 7:55). As Jesus's burial confirmed his death and his postresurrection appearances confirmed his resurrection, so his ascension confirms the promise of his visible, bodily return.

THEOLOGICAL FOCUS

The narratival function of Acts 1:1–11 is to link Acts to Luke's gospel. The passage creates continuity between what Jesus "began to do and teach" during his earthly ministry and what the apostles continued to do and teach after he ascended to the Father's right hand. The passage also introduces major themes of the book, including the role of the apostles as witnesses to Jesus's earthly ministry, the empowerment of the Holy Spirit, the worldwide proclamation of the gospel, and Jesus as the ascended Lord. Commentators widely acknowledge that Acts 1:8 provides a basic outline for the book, both geographically and cross-culturally.

Theologically, Acts 1:1–11 places Jesus's teachings and promises at the center of the church's mission. Those directives establish the nature of the church's task, they set out the geographical and temporal scope of that task, and they explain the source of enabling on which the church must rely as it engages in that task. Further, Jesus's appearances confirm his resurrection, and his ascension confirms the promise of his return. Those events establish the apostles as eyewitnesses to Jesus's life and ministry, divinely appointed guarantors of Jesus's teaching, and gatekeepers of entry into the kingdom of God.

PREACHING AND TEACHING STRATEGIES

Exegetical/Theological Synthesis

Luke's first-century readers would want to know what Jesus told the apostles about his plans for them to continue his earthly ministry in his absence. They were facing a seemingly impossible task. To prepare them for that task, Jesus instructed the apostles regarding the kingdom of God, commanded them to wait in Jerusalem for the Father's promise, commissioned them as his witnesses who would receive the Holy Spirit's power, and established the finality of his departure by ascending to the Father's right hand. With the original readers, the twenty-first-century audience shares the need to understand the nature, scope, and resources available to them as they engage in the task Jesus has given them. His instructions and promises to the apostles provide encouragement for the task before them as well as the direction they need to join effectively in that task.

Preaching/Teaching Idea

Jesus's directives determine our direction.

Contemporary Connections

What does it mean?

A lot is happening in a few verses. First, this preaching section begins, overflows with, and ends with the glorious, risen, soon-to-be-ascended, Spirit-promising, commission-charging Son of God—Jesus himself. Luke lingers with Jesus. He repeats material from the conclusion of his gospel, which ties his works together, but it also gives us more of Jesus. For Luke to say that his gospel was "all that Jesus began to do and teach" (1:1) is to imply that Acts is all that Jesus continues to do and teach through his Spirit in his church. Second, the passage establishes the big themes of the book. It reiterates Jesus's resurrection (1:3) and tells the story of his ascension (1:6–11). Jesus's risen, reigning

presence will bear on the story at every turn. In the prologue, Jesus promises to send the Holy Spirit to empower the work (1:5, 8). He will animate all that is good and Christ-centered in the expanding mission. Finally, the Great Commission call is here—to be witnesses in a centrifugal spread outward from Jerusalem (1:8). The book of Acts, in turn, follows this outline of Jerusalem, Judea and Samaria, and to the ends of the earth. Jesus's directives—clearly communicated to his followers—grow out of his person and work and establish our direction forward.

Is it true?

Jesus's directives might well determine our direction, but his directives come tenderly to those who are so easily *mis*directed. Luke lingers, but so does Jesus. Jesus "delays" his ascension in order to spend forty days with his disciples. He has already been with them a thousand days, but now he adds forty more. By painstakingly proving his resurrection, he presumes that his disciples are prone to doubt. By carefully teaching them about the kingdom of God, he presumes that his disciples are prone to misunderstand. Yet, the disciples still struggle. First, they once again press Jesus for details about the restoration of Israel. Jesus redirects them to their task. Second, two angels catch them gawking toward heaven. The angels redirect them with the encouragement that Jesus will indeed return from that dimension in due time.

These beginnings are not promising. We might have been expecting more in the first chapter of Acts after where we have been in the Gospels. The messengers could well fumble the message. Jesus's witnesses take detours, but that fact makes the passage even more important and encouraging. Jesus knew about these threats and attended to them. Jesus himself will be no more absent in the book of Acts than he was in the OT. His Holy Spirit is there too, both while he taught (1:2) and after he departed (1:8). We have this Jesus-attending, God-breathed commission so that we can return to it repeatedly. When we lose our way, Jesus's directives remain to guide us.

Now what?
By way of application, if this Great Commission feels like a new legal burden that is too much to bear, something is wrong. We are missing the good news that we claim to believe. Jesus's work precedes his commission. His resurrection won what we proclaim: forgiveness of sins, the gift of the Spirit, and deliverance from this generation (cf. 2:38–40). The first principle for a Great Commission disciple to remember is that we must not focus on what we do for God, but on what he has first done for us.

The tenderness of Jesus in this passage is captivating. There is no bait and switch between the Jesus of Luke and the Jesus of Acts. He is the same Son, proclaiming the same good news and welcoming new members into the same kingdom. These scenes of our risen Lord in Scripture inspire his people today, as does his reigning presence with us now. *That* reality is good news, and it makes our witness compelling. We have peace with God, and we invite the nations to do the same.

Once we are secure in who we are, Jesus charges us with what we are to do. Jesus charges the church to bear witness to his death and resurrection, by the power of his Holy Spirit, to the ends of the earth. Every disciple receives these marching orders. Every disciple has a role in this great task. Every disciple prays, gives, goes, sends, supports, receives as the Lord equips and leads, so that each man, woman, and child has an opportunity to hear and respond to the reality of Jesus.

Creativity in Presentation
Famous last words are fascinating, controversial, and much debated. They are also memorable. German composer Beethoven might have said, "Friends, applaud; the comedy is finished." As he went to the electric chair, convicted murdered James Donald French reportedly said to the press, "Hey fellas! How about this for a headline for tomorrow's paper? 'French Fries'!" There are also touching thoughts shared about goodbyes. A. A. Milne, author of *Winnie-the-Pooh*, wrote, "How lucky I am to have something that makes saying goodbye so hard." There are also excruciating farewell words. In Broadway's *Hamilton*, Aaron Burr says of his parents, "My mother was a genius. My father commanded respect. When they died, they left no instructions—just a legacy to protect."

Speaking last lines at death or when departing wonderfully focuses the mind. What is most important? What captures where we have been? What hopes do we have in where we are going? Jesus's final scene with his apostles is a farewell without a goodbye, a departure with a promised presence.

A creative presentation builds this heightened tension at the end of one era and the beginning of another. It gets inside the apostles' minds and hearts and the anxiety they surely suffered in these days. No wonder Jesus had to prove his resurrection repeatedly, had to add forty days of teaching to the previous three years, and had to redirect their attention away from the timing of Israel's restoration to the task in front of them. The disciples were a mix of fear, doubt, and confusion. Jesus met them where they were and led them through their muddled state to bring them to his final words.

Lean in for these last words. They give clear guidance in the direction he sends us and give a clear promise in the power he gives to us. In the first, we are witnesses. We testify to the life, death, resurrection, and ascension of Jesus for the forgiveness of sins and peace with God, as the disciples' sermons in Acts demonstrate. In the second, we receive power from the Holy Spirit. Jesus does not leave us to ourselves; he had promised that his departure spelled the Spirit's arrival (John 16:7).

The book of Acts will go on to tell the beginning of this tale of ever-expanding, Spirit-filled witness. It will come with great and grave cost. It will require all the church's hands on deck. It will create conflict with friends. It will be tempting at every turn to change the commission into something else—something more accessible and achievable, something that costs less. A conclusion of an opening presentation of Acts and a preparation of what will come fittingly centers on Jesus. We witness to the one who graciously presents himself alive to us, tenderly teaches us, encourages and assures us, and then points us to the world to bring many others to enjoy this same Jesus. Jesus's directives determine our direction.

- The person of Jesus (1:1–5).

- The work of Jesus (1:3, 9–11).

- The directives of Jesus (1:8).

DISCUSSION QUESTIONS

1. What points of continuity did Luke establish between the events he records in Luke 24:13–53 and those he records in Acts 1:1–11? What function do those elements play in linking his two works?

2. What key thematic elements did Luke include in Acts 1:1–11 that would prepare his readers for the account as a whole?

3. What did Jesus actually teach about the kingdom of God during his earthly ministry? How did his followers misunderstand what he taught?

4. What OT background can you identify for Jesus's teaching that the preaching of the gospel would extend to the ends of the earth?

5. Why is the account of Jesus's ascension important? What truths does it teach about his return?

Acts 1:12–26

EXEGETICAL IDEA
While they waited for the promise of the Holy Spirit, Jesus's followers restored the integrity of apostolic leadership by engaging in united prayer, looking to inspired Scripture for direction, and trusting in God to identify the person of his choosing.

THEOLOGICAL FOCUS
Engaging in mission requires a leadership team that is intact, qualified, and set apart by God.

PREACHING IDEA
God's mission requires leadership that is unified, qualified, and sanctified.

PREACHING POINTERS
A well-known leadership axiom reminds us that although we can go faster alone, we can go farther as part of a team. What do you do, though, when the team has been fractured, whether through sin, interpersonal conflict, or death? That was the challenge the eleven remaining apostles faced after Judas Iscariot's apostasy and suicide. Their task of continuing Jesus's ministry to the Jews first required a twelfth member for their leadership team. It was crucial that they fill that vacancy with the right person. With Luke's original readers, we need to understand the importance of following the guiding principles the apostles used to restore and preserve the integrity of their leadership team by filling the vacancy with the individual God intended. If we do, we will ensure that we are prepared to engage in the mission he has given us.

People today should be able to relate to the need to replace someone who has left a position or role, whether voluntarily or involuntarily. They should also be able to relate to the practice of finding qualified candidates to fill the resulting vacancy. The apostles' actions in Acts 1:12–26 correct any suggestion that a leadership failure can go unanswered or that preserving the integrity of a leadership team is unimportant. The passage commends commitment to the important guiding principles of devotion to prayer, reliance on Scripture, and trust in God's choice. Adhering to those principles produces a prepared leadership team that is unified, qualified, and set apart by God for the task he has given that team.

THE PREPARATION FOR PENTECOST (1:12–26)

LITERARY STRUCTURE AND THEMES (1:12–26)

The passage consists of three sections. The temporal marker τότε ("then") introduces the first section (1:12–14), which describes the apostles' return to Jerusalem following Jesus's ascension. The continuative conjunction καί ("and") introduces both the second and third sections and ties the three sections together into a single narrative episode. The second section (1:15–22) recounts Peter's proposal for replacing Judas as the twelfth apostle and, because of its length and central placement, is the focus of the passage. The third section (1:23–26) records the implementation and results of that proposal.

- ***Devotion to Prayer (1:12–14)***
- ***Direction from Scripture (1:15–22)***
- ***Trust in God's Choice (1:23–26)***

EXPOSITION (1:12–26)

Immediately before his ascension, Jesus had instructed the apostles to return to Jerusalem and wait for the coming of the promised Holy Spirit (1:4–8). Acts 1:12–26 describes the disciples' activities during the ten days between the ascension and Pentecost of A.D. 30. Joining with a group of faithful women and other disciples who numbered approximately 120, the eleven apostles devoted themselves to persistent, united prayer (1:12–14), and filled the vacancy in their leadership that had resulted from Judas Iscariot's apostasy (1:15–26). As Luke recounts the events of those ten days, three guiding principles emerged that run throughout the first division of Acts (1:1–8:3) and regulate the early church's life.

Devotion to prayer (1:12–14) became a hallmark of the Jerusalem church in its common life (2:42–47), its decision-making (6:1–7), and its response to opposition (4:23–31). Guidance from Scripture (1:15–22) became central to the church's public proclamation of the gospel (2:14–36; 3:11–26), its defense before the religious authorities (4:8–12), and its prayer life (4:23–31). Trust in God's choice to restore the integrity of apostolic leadership (1:23–26) allowed the apostles to function as a team as they participated in the church's common life (2:42–47), administered the distribution of material goods (4:32–37), exercised discipline (5:1–11), faced opposition (5:12–32), and resolved congregational problems (6:1–7). Adopting and adhering to these guiding principles prepared the church for the mission on which they were about to embark. Larkin comments, "Luke's report of the disciples' activities as they waited for the Spirit's promised coming at Pentecost gives a pattern we would do well to emulate if we would prepare for an outpouring of the Spirit in revival" (1995, 44).

Devotion to Prayer (1:12–14)

After Jesus's ascension, the apostles obediently returned to Jerusalem, where they joined other disciples in devoting themselves to prayer.

1:12–14. Obedient to Jesus's instructions (1:4), the disciples returned to Jerusalem (ὑπέστρεψαν εἰς Ἰερουσαλήμ), a Sabbath day's journey (σαββάτου ἔχον ὁδόν) from the site of the ascension on the Mount of Olives (ἀπὸ ὄρους τοῦ καλουμένου Ἐλαιῶνος). In Jerusalem, the eleven original apostles entered "the upper room where they were staying" (τὸ ὑπερῷον . . . οὗ ἦσαν καταμένοντες). In the upstairs room, the apostles joined a group of women (σὺν γυναιξίν)—most likely the same female disciples who had followed Jesus throughout his ministry (Luke 8:1–3; 23:55; 24:10)—as well as Mary, Jesus's mother (Μαριὰμ τῇ μητρὶ τοῦ Ἰησοῦ), and his brothers (καὶ τοῖς ἀδελφοῖς αὐτοῦ). Together, this group engaged in prayer (τῇ προσευχῇ).

Although some locate the room in the house of Mary, the mother of John Mark (Acts 12:12), it is more likely the room where they had celebrated the Passover with Jesus (Luke 22:11–12)—a room designated as a "guest room" (κατάλυμα) or a "great upstairs room" (ἀνάγαιον μέγα). Prayer is a repeated theme in Acts (2:42; 6:4, 6; 12:5, 12; 13:3; 14:23; 16:25). Luke describes the church's upper room prayer as repeated (present tense), devoted (προσκαρτεροῦντες; 2:42, 46; 6:4), and united in purpose (ὁμοθυμαδόν; 2:46; 4:24; 5:12; 15:25). While they waited for the promise of the Father (1:4), it was only natural for Jesus's followers to unite in earnest prayer. Schnabel comments, "Before believers do anything else, they call on God, whether with praise or petition, thanksgiving or intercession, as they utterly depend on God in whose sovereignty they trust" (2012, 84).

TEXTUAL ANALYSIS: "a Sabbath day's journey"
The phrase "a Sabbath day's journey" (σαββάτου ἔχον ὁδόν) describes distance rather than timing, because forty days after the resurrection would have been a Friday. The standard measure of such a journey was two thousand cubits (m. Soṭah 5.3), which equals 1.2 kilometers or 0.75 miles, the distance to the crest of the Mount of Olives. Although Luke 24:50 mentions Bethany as the site of the ascension, that town was on the eastern side of the Mount, about two miles distant (John 11:18). The NIV and CSB resolve the apparent discrepancy by translating the phrase in the gospel (ἕως πρὸς Βηθανίαν) as "to the vicinity of Bethany."

The Eleven Original Apostles

The list of apostles in Acts 1:13 matches the earlier list in Luke 6:14–16 with the natural omission of Judas Iscariot and three differences in order. Andrew and John change places, and Thomas moves ahead of Bartholomew and Matthew. Luke most likely moved John forward because of his prominence and close association with Peter in the early events recorded in Acts (3:1, 3, 4, 11; 4:13, 19; 8:14). Peter was a fisherman from Bethsaida (John 1:44), who wrote two letters to churches in what is now northern Turkey (1–2 Peter); tradition suggests that he ministered in Turkey, Iraq, and Rome. John was also a fisherman from Bethsaida (John 1:44), who wrote a gospel (John), three letters (1–3 John), and an apocalypse (Revelation); tradition connects him to the church in Ephesus. James was John's brother (Matt. 4:21), who was designated "the Great"; he served the Jerusalem church and suffered martyrdom under Herod Agrippa I (Acts 12:2). Andrew was Peter's brother and a fisherman (Matt. 4:18), whom tradition records as ministering around the Black Sea in Ukraine, Georgia, and southern Russia. Philip was also from Bethsaida (John 1:44); tradition suggests that he ministered among Greek-speaking peoples in central Turkey. Thomas was another Galilean fisherman (John 21:2), whom tradition records as ministering in Iran and India. Bartholomew is commonly identified with Nathanael from Bethsaida (John 1:44); according to tradition, he ministered south of the Caspian Sea in Azerbaijan, Iran, and Turkmenistan with Matthew, the former tax collector (Matt. 9:9) and author of the first gospel (Matthew). James, the son of Alphaeus, was designated "the Less" to distinguish him from James the son of Zebedee; tradition records that he was the first bishop of Syria. Simon "the Zealot" was most likely a former member of the "Canaanaean" party that advocated active resistance against the Romans (Mark 3:18); according to tradition, he and Joseph of Arimathea traveled from Egypt, across northern Africa, through Spain, and into the British Isles. Judas, the son of James, who is commonly identified with Thaddaeus (Matt. 10:3), was the son of James the Great and the grandson of Zebedee; tradition suggests that he ministered south of the Caspian Sea with Bartholomew and Matthew.

Direction from Scripture (1:15–22)

Peter sets out scriptural rationale and qualifications for filling the vacancy left by Judas Iscariot's defection and death in order to restore the full number of apostles.

1:15. Although the phrase "in those days" (ἐν ταῖς ἡμέραις ταύταις) often signals a major break in the narrative (Bruce 1990, 108; cf. 6:1; 11:27), Luke uses καί ("and") to connect Peter's remarks closely to what precedes. When the group (ὄχλος) of "about 120" (ὡσεὶ ἑκατὸν εἴκοσι) was "in the same place" (ἐπὶ τὸ αὐτό), Peter arose to address the pressing issue before them: the need to fill the leadership void caused by Judas Iscariot's defection and death. The "days" in question were the ten days between Jesus's ascension and Pentecost. It is possible that the number 120 reflects the minimum number of individuals needed to establish a community with its own council (Marshall 1980, 64), although Schnabel views the idea as unconvincing because it is only approximate (2012, 95).

1:16–17. Peter's starting point was the "divine necessity of Judas's apostasy" (Larkin 1995, 45). The present circumstances, in fact, had arisen because "it was necessary for the Scripture to be fulfilled" (ἔδει πληρωθῆναι τὴν γραφήν). Through David, the Holy Spirit had predicted (προεῖπεν τὸ πνεῦμα τὸ ἅγιον διὰ στόματος Δαυίδ) concerning Judas (περὶ Ἰούδα) what would take place. Judas was able to act as a guide who led those who arrested Jesus (τοῦ γενομένου ὁδηγοῦ τοῖς συλλαβοῦσιν Ἰησοῦν; cf. Luke 22:47–48), because he had been counted among the apostles (κατηριθμημένος ἦν ἐν ἡμῖν; cf. Luke 6:13–16) and had been an active participant in ministry with them (ἔλαχεν τὸν κλῆρον τῆς διακονίας ταύτης; cf. Luke 9:1–6).

1:18–19. In these verses, Luke inserts parenthetical background "for the benefit of the reader" (Bruce 1990, 109), since the events were already "known to all who were living in Jerusalem" (γνωστὸν . . . πᾶσι τοῖς κατοικοῦσιν Ἰερουσαλήμ). They recount what happened to Judas Iscariot after Jesus's arrest and explain why his place among the apostles was vacant. Luke describes the following sequence of events: Judas received money for betraying Jesus. With the money (ἐκ μισθοῦ τῆς ἀδικίας) he purchased a field (ἐκτήσατο χωρίον) that became known as "Field of Blood" (Χωρίον Αἵματος). He then "fell headlong" (πρηνὴς γενόμενος) and "burst open in the middle" (ἐλάκησεν μέσος), so that "all his bowels poured out" (ἐξεχύθη πάντα τὰ σπλάγχνα αὐτοῦ).

Luke's account presents several apparent contradictions with Matthew's account (Matt. 27:1–10) because Luke focuses on Judas, while Matthew focuses on the Jewish leaders (Schnabel 2012, 98). In Luke's account, Judas purchased the field with the money he received and then hanged himself. In Matthew's account, Judas felt remorse, returned the money to the leaders, and hanged himself. The leaders then purchased the field as a burial place for strangers. Marshall suggests the following concise explanation: (1) Judas hanged himself, the rope broke, and his body ruptured from the fall; (2) functionally, the leaders were the agents through whom Judas purchased the field; (3) the priests purchased the field where Judas died (1980, 65).

1:20. Peter continued by explaining specifically what Scripture had foretold about Judas. First, Psalm 69:25 made it clear that Judas's place among the twelve would become vacant. Judas's death fulfilled that prophecy.

Second, Psalm 109:8 made it equally clear that another would fill his place. The group could now address that issue by appointing a successor. Since Jesus used Psalm 69, as well as other psalms, to comment on aspects of his own life (John 2:17; 15:25), it was natural for the early church to do the same (Rom. 11:9–10; Rom. 15:3 for Paul's uses of the psalm). As David suffered at the hands of a false companion (Ps. 41:9; John 13:18), so Jesus—"the eschatological Son of David" (Peterson 2009, 123)—suffered at the hands of one he had chosen to be part of his inner circle. It was only just for the betrayer's place to become deserted (γενηθήτω ἡ ἔπαυλις αὐτοῦ ἔρημος; Ps. 69:25). Similarly, it was only just to execute judgment on the betrayer by giving his place of service to another (τὴν ἐπισκοπὴν αὐτοῦ λαβέτω ἕτερος; Ps. 109:8).

1:21–22. Again invoking divine necessity (δεῖ οὖν), Peter called upon the group to fill the role of a witness to Jesus's resurrection (μάρτυρα τῆς ἀναστάσεως αὐτοῦ) along with the other eleven apostles (σὺν ἡμῖν). The individual to fill the role had to meet two qualifications. First, he must have traveled with the other apostles (τῶν συνελθόντων ἡμῖν ἀνδρῶν). Second, he must have been present for the entirety of their time with Jesus (ἐν παντὶ χρόνῳ ᾧ εἰσῆλθεν καὶ ἐξῆλθεν ἐφ' ἡμᾶς)—beginning from John the Baptist's ministry (ἀρξάμενος ἀπὸ τοῦ βαπτίσματος Ἰωάννου) until the day of Jesus's ascension (ἕως τῆς ἡμέρας ἧς ἀνελήμφθη ἀφ' ἡμῶν). Only an individual who met both qualifications would be able to testify to the facts of Jesus's life, ministry, death, resurrection, and ascension. Such an individual would also be able to guarantee that the early church's message accurately preserved the teaching they had received from Jesus. From the perspective of being a witness to Israel, it was also important that there be twelve apostles, so that the early church could "represent itself

to the Jewish nation as the culmination of Israel's hope and the true people of Israel's Messiah" (Longenecker 1981, 265).

Trust in God's Choice (1:23–26)

The group identifies two candidates, commits the matter to God in prayer, and accepts the Lord's choice of Matthias to become the twelfth apostle.

1:23. Either the apostles or the entire group then put forward (ἔστησαν) two candidates who met the requirements: Joseph Barsabbas, whose Roman name was Justus, and Matthias. Peterson suggests that the absence of any recorded verbal response to Peter's proposal reflects "complete agreement" by the group (2009, 127). Although Scripture records no additional information about either man, Joseph might have been a brother of Judas Barsabbas, who accompanied Paul, Barnabas, and Silas to Syrian Antioch after the Jerusalem Council (15:22, 30–33). Tradition reports that Matthias was a missionary to Ethiopia.

1:24–25. Following their practice of praying before they did anything else (cf. 1:14), the group asked for divine guidance. Their prayer reflected their confidence that the Lord Jesus (κύριε), who "knows the hearts of all men" (καρδιογνῶστα πάντων), would make his guidance clearly known (ἀνάδειξον), and would choose the individual he had in mind (ὅν ἐξελέξω). Just as he had chosen the other eleven apostles (1:2), Jesus would now choose one of these two candidates (ἐκ τούτων τῶν δύο ἕνα) to take "the place of ministry consisting of apostleship" (Barrett 1994, 103; τὸν τόπον τῆς διακονίας καὶ ἀποστολῆς) from which Judas Iscariot had turned away (ἀφ' ἧς παρέβη Ἰούδας). In a play on words, Luke notes that Judas had left his honorable "place" (τόπον) as an apostle to go to "his own place" (πορευθῆναι εἰς τὸν τόπον τὸν ἴδιον)—a place of dishonor and judgment.

1:26. Following established OT practice, the group cast lots to determine God's will in the matter (ἔδωκαν κλήρους), and the lot fell upon Matthias (ἔπεσεν ὁ κλῆρος ἐπὶ Ματθίαν). The group then enrolled (συγκατεψυθίσθη) him with the other eleven apostles (μετὰ τῶν ἕνδεκα ἀποστόλων). The twin facts that Matthias is never mentioned beyond this account and that Luke later designates Paul as an apostle (14:4, 14) has led some to suggest that the early church erred in choosing Matthias as the twelfth apostle. Several factors weigh against that suggestion. First, the group followed a process that a repeated pattern in Acts will establish as normative (see 6:1–7). Second, Luke includes no negative evaluation of either the process or the result. Third, of the original eleven apostles, only Peter (fifty-four times), John (seven times), and James (once) are mentioned beyond this account. Luke's intent appears to be to highlight Peter's role in reaching primarily Jewish contexts in Jerusalem, Judea, and Samaria, followed by Paul's role in carrying the gospel to largely Gentile contexts beyond those boundaries. Fourth, the church needed to fill Judas's place in order to represent itself to the Jewish nation. In contrast, Paul's call was to be an apostle to the Gentiles (9:15; 22:21; Gal. 2:2). Fifth, Paul does not meet the requirements set out in verses 21–22. Although he met the resurrected Jesus on the road to Damascus, he did not accompany the other apostles throughout the course of Jesus's ministry. Sixth, Paul himself acknowledged that his apostleship, although equal with that of the Twelve, was different (1 Cor. 15:8).

The Jewish practice was to write names on stones or other objects, place the stones in a container with an opening large enough for one stone, shake the container, and turn it upside down; the stone that fell out determined the issue in question (Josephus, *A.J.* 6.62). Throughout their history, the Jews cast lots for a variety of purposes: determining the scapegoat for the Day of Atonement (Lev. 16:8); dividing the land among the twelve tribes (Num. 26:55; Josh. 18:6, 10); settling priests among the different tribes (1 Chron. 6:65); determining guilty parties (Josh. 7:14; 1 Sam. 14:40–42); selecting participants for military action (Judg. 20:9); selecting Saul as their first king (1 Sam. 10:20–21); determining assignments for priests, musicians, and gatekeepers (1 Chron. 14:5; 25:8, 13–14); determining which returned exiles would live in Jerusalem (Neh. 11:1); and determining the order of priestly service in the temple (Luke 1:8–9). The lot "put an end to contention" (Prov. 18:18), because the Lord decided the outcome (Prov. 16:33). The apostles, therefore, were not wrong to cast lots to identify Judas's replacement (Larkin 1995, 47). It was a divinely sanctioned manner of determining God's will (Schnabel 2012, 102–3), and Luke included the practice in his narrative with no negative evaluation. It is worth noting, however, that the lack of any repeated pattern in Acts of the early church continuing to cast lots excludes the practice as normative for the contemporary church.

THEOLOGICAL FOCUS

The narratival function of Acts 1:12–26 is to provide insight into the disciples' activities during the ten days between Jesus's ascension and Pentecost. For the first time, they were truly on their own. Jesus had given them no indication of how long that would be the case, and he had given them no detailed instructions on what to do while they waited. How would the disciples respond to what Jesus had taught them during his postresurrection appearances? How would they address Judas Iscariot's apostasy? What guiding principles would they follow as they waited for God to show them their next steps? Luke's account of the disciples' activities as they waited for the promised coming of the Holy Spirit answers those questions.

Theologically, Acts 1:12–26 is about the importance of restoring and preserving the integrity of the apostolic leadership team as preparation for Pentecost. Schnabel correctly notes that "the passage is not about apostasy and suicide, or decision making, or the radical nature of forgiveness" (2012, 104). Nor is it about whether the apostles were wrong to fill Judas's vacancy with Matthias instead of Paul or were wrong to cast lots to identify Matthias as the twelfth apostle. Peterson notes, "the unfinished list of apostles in 1:13 shows [that] the circle of the Twelve had been broken" (2009, 119). Further, "the apostle's leadership qualification was in serious question because of their association with Judas—the apostle who betrayed Jesus" (Estrada 2004, 231). Luke's account of the apostles' actions between Jesus's ascension and Pentecost highlights the divine necessity of events, the way in which those events fulfilled prophecy, the apostles' qualifications as witnesses to the entirety of Jesus's earthly ministry, and the Lord Jesus as the one who appointed each of the twelve apostles. The passage, therefore, serves an apologetic function that prepares the readers for the central role the apostles will play as divine witnesses in Jerusalem, Judea, and Samaria (Peterson 2009, 120).

PREACHING AND TEACHING STRATEGIES

Exegetical/Theological Synthesis
Luke's first-century readers would want to know how Jesus's followers responded to the apostasy of Judas Iscariot—one of the original apostles Jesus himself had chosen. The remaining eleven apostles addressed the challenge before them by engaging in united prayer, looking to inspired Scripture for direction, and trusting in God to identify the person of his choosing. The result was a leadership team intact, qualified, and set apart by God. With the original readers, the twenty-first-century audience shares the need to understand how to respond to leadership failures and the vacancies those failures create. From the perspective of a calling to a vocational ministry role, Longenecker suggests that the appropriate process "entails (1) evaluating personal qualifications, (2) earnest prayer, and (3) appointment by Christ himself" (1981, 266). The apostles' approach provides a model for the congregation or ministry that would seek to ensure that it has in place a leadership team prepared for the mission the Lord Jesus has for it.

Preaching/Teaching Idea
God's mission requires leadership that is unified, qualified, and sanctified.

Contemporary Connections

What does it mean?
A lot happens during the powerful ten-day interlude between Jesus's Great Commission for worldwide evangelization and the Holy Spirit's supernatural empowering for the task. The bookends of the Son and the Spirit underscore the fragility and neediness of the very human team preparing for their assignment. Without sound leadership, humanly speaking, this first thrust of missionary work would fail. What this first-ever Christian leadership team does during this week and a half together both *proves* and *feeds* their unity and quality. The elements of prayer, Scripture, and trust are front and center. The apostles and the company of disciples both devote themselves to prayer (1:14) and pray for guidance in a particular situation (1:24). They look to Scripture to guide them, expecting help from it and applying it to their situation (1:16–20). Finally, they trust God to lead them by appointing the right apostle (1:24–25). These fledgling habits will only grow within this

leadership team. These elements are essential markers of a leadership that is unified, qualified, and sanctified.

Is it true?
The picture forming behind these practices is one of absolute dependence. Prayer, Scripture, and trust are habits of the needy, not the self-satisfied. They are the physician's prescription not for the healthy, but for the sick; not for the self-righteous, but for the sinner. They are for leadership teams who seek God to do far and above the sum of human talent in the room.

Even more importantly, prayer, Scripture, and trust are learned habits. They are habits the disciples first saw in Jesus. See how Jesus prayed! He started and ended his ministry in prayer, taught and modeled prayer, sneaked away for all-night prayer meetings with his Father in the mountains, prayed before choosing the disciples, and prayed before facing the cross. See how Jesus handled the Scriptures! He fought the devil with Deuteronomy, preached his identity in Isaiah, cried bitter tears from the Psalms. See how Jesus trusted God in all things! He matched his life to the Father's will, his days to the Father's timing, his movement from town to town for the Father's mission, his ultimate sacrifice to the Father's will. These practices were not lost on the disciples. They saw, learned, and imitated the Master.

These learned habits made the apostolic leadership team into a group that was unified by their dependence on God, not disunified because of independent egos. It made them into a group that was qualified by their daily reliance on God, not disqualified by burnout or moral failure from relying on themselves. It made them into a group that was set apart for God's work, not seeking to build their own kingdoms. In short, it prepared them for the mission ahead.

Now what?
Every Christian leadership team should take note: on the heels of the greatest ministry assignment ever given, the disciples' first response is surprising and sadly countercultural to the way many churches and Christian organizations run. Before reaching for the whiteboard or the budget spreadsheet, assigning roles, or drawing up workflow charts, the disciples *prayed*. Their prayer was not the perfunctory premeeting warm-up prayer to grease the wheels for hours of talk, the "cut flower prayers" Eugene Peterson decries. They "with one accord were devoting themselves to prayer" (1:14). It was repeated prayer, passionately devoted prayer, and united in purpose prayer. The leadership pursued Scripture and trust in the same way.

Eyes on prayer, Scripture, and divine trust have a way of distracting eyes from the normal gaze of Christian and non-Christian leadership alike: ego. Prayer makes little room for prejudice; Scripture crowds out self; trust cannot coexist with territorialism. Taking cues from the disciples, who took their cues from Jesus, invites us into supernatural possibilities for leadership united around God's purposes for our teams and the missions they represent. May our Christian leaders do the same!

Creativity in Presentation
There is an old joke you might have heard. A ship finds a Baptist stranded alone on an uninhabited island (enter the cantankerous denomination of your choosing). He gives his rescuers a tour of how he lived before they came. There are three grass huts. He tells them proudly, "This hut is where I live. This hut is where I go to church." Curious, the rescuers ask about the third hut. "Oh," the man answered. "That's where I used to go to church."

It is funny but sad. We Christians divide too easily. We throw ego behind nuances in mission, subtle doctrinal differences, leadership personalities, and watch churches, organizations, and teams dissolve. The leading cause of missionary attrition year after year is division in the Christian teams on the field.

The modern reader braces for that kind of fallout in the opening scenes of Acts. Jesus is "gone." The apostles must fill a critical role. A twelfth apostle is not just an even number. The newly appointed apostle will represent the Jewish nation itself and will sit on the twelfth throne (Luke 22:30). When the congregation puts Joseph and Matthias forward, we cringe. We know how the process usually goes. People pick favorites, feelings get hurt, words are said that cannot be unsaid. Before you know it, we have opposing denominations in Jerusalem. The "I follow Joseph" church cannot seem to find any common ground with the "I follow Matthias" group. If we need a NT example, all we need to do is look at 1 Corinthians 1:10–17.

A creative presentation of this text builds this tension to the breaking point. By exploring what is at stake, what personalities are involved, how easy it would be to divide, we end up feeling the mirror glare of our own sinful tendencies here. It could be the same song, different verse. We desperately need the very Christ we are to preach. Fortunately for us, he is here. Miracle of miracles, God tends to this fledgling body by his means of grace, prayer, Scripture, and trust. What felt like certain division becomes a shining Ebenezer of God-wrought unity.

Reginald Rose wrote a teleplay-turned-film called *Twelve Angry Men*. Twelve New York City jurors were set to deliberate the case of a young man accused of murdering his father. When juror number eight holds out against the eleven clamoring for *guilty*, fireworks fly. How precious it is in our passage to see not twelve angry men, but twelve humble apostles, claimed and shaped by God to do his work.

God's mission requires leadership that is unified, qualified, and sanctified.

- The church gathers (1:12–14).

- The church addresses a potentially divisive problem (1:15–22).

- God leads the church to a unifying solution (1:23–26).

DISCUSSION QUESTIONS

1. What does it mean to "devote yourself continually to prayer with one mind" (1:14)? How would that practice look in your own life and in the life of the congregation of which you are a part?

2. Why is it significant that Jesus's brothers had joined the group of disciples who met in the upstairs room (1:14; cf. John 7:1–13)?

3. How do you explain Peter's application of Psalms 69 and 109 to the apostles' situation (1:16, 20)? What does his practice teach about the way in which the apostles used the OT?

4. Why was it important that the disciples had clear qualifications for the candidates they put forward to replace Judas (1:21–22)? How did those qualifications ensure the accuracy of the early church's gospel witness?

5. Why was it important for the ministry of the early church that there be twelve apostles? What implications for leadership in the contemporary church can you draw from their joint ministry?

Acts 2:1–40

EXEGETICAL IDEA
The Spirit's coming at Pentecost created initial confusion, provided an opportunity for Peter to preach the gospel, and resulted in the conversion of three thousand individuals.

THEOLOGICAL FOCUS
The Holy Spirit opens doors for witness, empowers believers for witness, and brings conviction through God's Word in witness.

PREACHING IDEA
Pentecost power sets the pattern for the church's advance.

PREACHING POINTERS
How does any movement begin, whether social, political, or religious? Origins are important, and Larkin notes, "a people reinvigorates itself by drawing comfort and challenge from the way it was in the beginning" (1995, 48). How did the early church grow from 120 members meeting in an upstairs room in Jerusalem to a major religious movement that would eventually reach the capital of the Roman Empire? With Luke's original readers, we need to understand how God ordered the events surrounding the birth of the Christian movement and mission. In particular, we need to understand the role the Holy Spirit played—and should continue to play—in the church's witness and mission.

People today should be able to relate to the confusion that might arise when something out of the ordinary happens, whether in their own lives or in the lives of others. They should also be familiar with public speeches and assemblies of people from different countries; both converge whenever the general assembly of the United Nations meets. Followers of Jesus can readily relate to incorrect perceptions about Christianity and possible mockery by nonbelievers. The confusion and different conclusions of the listeners present at Pentecost correct the suggestion that the miraculous is adequate for men and women to come to faith, because the events of that morning required interpretation from Scripture. The account of the events at Pentecost commends recognition of the opportunities God provides for witness, reliance on the Holy Spirit for power in witness, and the resource of God's Word in witness. It also provides insight into the roles God's Spirit, God's Word, and God's people have as the church's mission advances.

THE POWER OF PENTECOST (2:1–40)

LITERARY STRUCTURE AND THEMES (2:1–40)

The passage consists of three sections. The first section describes the pouring out of the Holy Spirit (2:1–13). It divides into two paragraphs: the events surrounding the Spirit's coming (2:1–4) and the confusion created by those events (2:5–13). The second section records Peter's speech to the assembled multitude (2:14–36). It divides into three paragraphs, each beginning with direct address to the listeners and concluding with OT support.

Peter's Pentecost Speech (2:14–36)	
Introduction: The Coming of the Holy Spirit (2:14–21)	
Address (2:14)	"Men of Judea and all who live in Jerusalem"
Claim (2:14–16)	The events of the morning fulfilled what Joel predicted.
OT Support (2:17–21)	Joel 2:28–32
Argument #1: The Resurrection of the Crucified Jesus (2:22–28)	
Address (2:22)	"Men of Israel"
Claim (2:22–24)	God raised Jesus from the dead.
OT Support (2:25–28)	Psalm 16:8–11
Argument #2: The Exaltation of the Risen Jesus (2:29–35)	
Address (2:29)	"Brothers"
Claim (2:29–33)	God exalted Jesus and gave him the gift of the Spirit.
OT Support (2:34–35)	Psalm 110:1
Conclusion: God has enthroned Jesus as Lord and Messiah (2:36)	

The third section describes the multitude's response to the speech (2:37–40), including their request for guidance (2:37), and Peter's call for repentance (2:38–40).

- ***The Divine Initiative (2:1–4)***
- ***The Initial Confusion (2:5–13)***
- ***The Coming of the Holy Spirit (2:14–21)***
- ***The Resurrection of the Crucified Jesus (2:22–28)***
- ***The Exaltation of the Risen Jesus (2:29–36)***
- ***The Informed Response (2:37–40)***

EXPOSITION (2:1–40)

In fulfillment of God's OT promise (Isa. 32:15; 44:3; 59:21; Ezek. 11:19; 36:26–27; 37:14; 39:29; Joel 2:28–32; Zech. 12:10) and Jesus's promise immediately before his ascension (Acts 1:6–8), the Holy Spirit filled the disciples on the day of Pentecost and enabled them to testify to God's wonders in known languages that were not their own (2:1–4). To dispel the resulting confusion (2:5–13), Peter preached the early church's first sermon and called the listeners to repent, be baptized, and receive the Holy Spirit (2:14–40). Luke records the results in the next paragraph (2:41–47).

The centerpiece of the passage is Peter's speech that incorporates the essentials of the gospel the apostles received from Jesus (Luke 24:44–48).

- The salvation plan set out in Scripture (Luke 24:44; Acts 2:16–21, 25–28, 31)
- The salvation events of Jesus's death and resurrection (Luke 24:46; Acts 2:22–24, 32)
- The salvation call to repentance (Luke 24:47; Acts 2:38)
- The salvation promise of forgiveness of sins (Luke 24:47; Acts 2:38)
- The universal scope of the salvation offer (Luke 24:47; Acts 2:39)

Taking 2:41–42 into account, the passage also suggests a sixfold pattern for witness by the early church.

- God acts (2:1–4)
- The listeners respond with interest (2:5–13)
- The witness explains from Scripture (2:14–36)
- The listeners respond with understanding (2:37)
- The witness calls for a decision (2:38–40)
- The listeners respond with commitment (2:41–42)

The premise underlying Peter's sermon was that the last days had arrived (2:17). Accordingly, he incorporated into his sermon five key events the OT predicted would characterize the last days.

- The Spirit's coming (2:17–18; cf. Isa. 32:15; 44:3; Ezek. 36:26–27; 37:14; 39:29; Zech. 12:10)
- Messiah's ability to perform signs and wonders (2:22; cf. Isa. 35:5–6)
- Messiah's death (2:23; cf. Isa. 53:4–12)
- The resurrection of the dead (2:24; cf. Job 19:23–27; Isa. 26:19; Dan. 12:2)
- Messiah's ascension and enthronement at God's right hand (2:33–35; cf. Ps. 68:18; Dan. 7:13–14).

The evidence that these events occurred at Pentecost and during Jesus's life and ministry furnished conclusive proof that Jesus was the Messiah (2:36) and that Peter's listeners should call on him for salvation (2:38–40). The passage also reinforces the principle that miraculous events are unclear without scriptural interpretation.

The Divine Initiative (2:1–4)

On the day of Pentecost, the Holy Spirit fills the disciples and enables them to speak languages they had not previously learned.

2:1. Luke marks the completion of the period since the Passover (Bruce 1990, 113) by introducing the next event with the infinitival phrase "when the day of Pentecost arrived" (ἐν τῷ συμπλυροῦσθαι τὴν ἡμέραν τῆς πεντηκοστῆς). Peterson notes the echo of Luke 9:51 (ἐν τῷ συμπληροῦσθαι τὰς ἡμέρας τῆς ἀναλήμψεως αὐτου) and suggests that Luke is presenting "a new stage in the outworking of God's purposes" (2009, 131). The "all" (πάντες) who were together in the assembly (ὁμοῦ ἐπὶ τὸ αὐτό) were either the twelve apostles or the whole group of believers. Culy and Parsons note three arguments in favor of the first option (2003, 23). Bock (2007, 94) and Schnabel (2012, 113), however, conclude that Luke was referring to the 120 mentioned in 1:15.

Pentecost

Pentecost was the last of four celebrations on the Jewish calendar between March/April and June. The third, First Fruits, celebrated the beginning of the barley harvest; the fourth, Weeks, celebrated the beginning of the wheat harvest. In later Judaism, the Feast of Weeks became known as Pentecost ("fiftieth") because the Jews were to "count fifty days to the day after the seventh Sabbath" following Passover (Lev. 23:16).

Celebration	Hebrew Calendar	Scripture Reference
Passover	14th day 1st month (Nisan)	Lev. 23:5 Num. 28:16; Deut. 16:1–8
Unleavened Bread	15th–22nd day 1st month (Nisan)	Lev. 23:6–8 Exod. 28:15; Num. 28:17–25
First Fruits	16th day 1st month (Nisan)	Lev. 23:9–14 Exod. 23:16a
Weeks	6th day 3rd month (Sivan)	Lev. 23:15–21 Exod. 23:16b; Num. 28:26–31; Deut. 16:9–12

Larkin notes that scholars have connected Pentecost with the renewal of the covenant, the giving of the law, and the reversal of Babel. He continues by noting that the idea of covenant renewal is not developed and that Peter's speech lacks allusions to Sinai or the law (1995, 48). Marshall concludes that there is no evidence for the reversal of Babel and that the association with the giving of the law was a later tradition (1980, 68). It might be suggestive that the verb Luke uses in Acts 2:6 for the multitude being "thrown into confusion" (συνεχύθη) is cognate with the name the LXX gives to "Babel" (Σύγχυσις) in Genesis 11:9.

2:2–3. "Suddenly" (ἄφνω) there was a "noise" (ἦχος) like "the roaring of a mighty windstorm" (NLT, φερομένης πνοῆς βιαίας). Luke describes its supernatural source as "from heaven" (ἐκ τοῦ οὐρανοῦ) and its volume as filling "the whole house where they were staying" (ὅλον τὸν οἶκον οὗ ἦσαν καθήμενοι). A visible phenomenon accompanied the audible, when "what looked like tongues of fire that spread out" (GNB, διαμεριζόμενοι γλῶσσαι ὡσει πυρός) appeared and "touched each person there" (GNB, ἐκάθισεν ἐφ' ἕνα ἕκαστον αὐτῶν). The idea of a violent wind is closest to Ezekiel 13:13 (πνοὴν μετὰ θυμοῦ) and suggests the power of God's presence (2 Sam. 22:16; 1 Kings 19:11; Job 37:10). By using πνοή rather than πνεῦμα, Luke makes it clear that he is describing the Spirit's coming rather than the Spirit himself. Fire is commonly connected with God's presence (Exod. 3:2; 13:21; 19:18; Isa. 66:15), and John the Baptist linked the coming of the Holy Spirit with fire (Luke 3:16).

The Pentecost by Juan Bautista Maino. Public domain.

Bock concludes, "the image of fire points to the association of heavenly glory in the presence of the Spirit as well as a theophany" (2007, 98).

TEXTUAL ANALYSIS: "tongues of fire that spread out"
The clause ὤφθησαν αὐτοῖς διαμεριζόμενοι γλῶσσαι ὡσεὶ πυρὸς καὶ ἐκάθισεν ἐφ' ἕνα ἕκαστον αὐτῶν is difficult for a number of reasons. First, does the participle διαμεριζόμενοι function as attendant circumstance or attributively? NJB opts for attendant circumstance modifying ἐκάθισεν and translates as "separated and came to rest." Culy and Parson, however, note that participles of attendant circumstance are usually aorist when they modify an aorist verb (2003, 24). Second, how is διαμερίζω best understood? BDAG notes that the verb has a range of meaning that encompasses (1) to divide into separate parts, (2) to distribute objects to a series of persons, or (3) to be divided into opposing units (BDAG s.v. "διαμερίζω" 233). The NKJV, NRSV, and ESV follow the first nuance and translate as "divided tongues." The NASB, NIV, and CSB follow the second nuance and translate as "tongues . . . that separated/spread out." Third, why is ἐκάθισεν singular? (The Western text reads ἐκάθισαν.) The most likely answer is that Luke was describing a phenomenon that distributed itself to multiple individuals. A translation that captures the sense would be "tongues of fire that were distributing themselves appeared to them, and a tongue settled on each one of them."

2:4. Accompanying the outward visible sign was "an inward invisible reality" (Marshall 1980, 69) that Luke describes as the entire group being filled with the Holy Spirit (ἐπλήσθησαν πάντες πνεύματος ἁγίου). That filling became evident to others when the group began speaking in other tongues (ἤρξαντο λαλεῖν ἑτέραις γλώσσαις). The subsequent context makes it clear that the "other tongues" were languages that the speakers had not previously learned but were intelligible to others (cf. 2:6–8, 11).

These tongues were a sustained—although not necessarily permanent—gift (ἐδίδου) from the Spirit that made it possible for the speakers to express themselves clearly and in a way that others could understand (ἀποφθέγγεσθαι). The content of their Spirit-enabled speech was "the mighty deeds of God" (2:11).

Filled with the Spirit

In Luke-Acts, Luke uses the verb "fill" (πίμπλημι) eight times and the adjective "full" (πλήρης) five times in connection with the Holy Spirit. In each instance, "Spirit" (πνεῦμα) occurs in the genitive case—which Daniel Wallace identifies as a genitive of context (*GGBB*, 94)—and suggests the translations "filled with" and "full of" the Holy Spirit. The phrase describes three different experiences: initial reception, continuing condition, and special enabling. Although Luke uses "filled with the Spirit" once to refer to Paul's initial reception of the Spirit (Acts 9:17), other verbs include "baptize" (Acts 1:5; 11:16), "pour out" (2:17; 10:45), and "receive" (10:47). Elsewhere, Luke describes Jesus (Luke 4:1), Stephen (Acts 6:3, 5; 7:55), and Barnabas (Acts 11:24) as "full of the Spirit." John the Baptist was "filled with the Spirit from his mother's womb" (Luke 1:15); Barnabas and Paul were also "filled with joy and the Holy Spirit" (Acts 13:52). Each of these occurrences describes a continuing condition that goes beyond an initial reception of the Spirit. Finally, Elizabeth (Luke 1:41), Zacharias (Luke 1:67), Peter (Acts 4:8), Paul (Acts 13:9), and all the disciples in Jerusalem (Acts 2:4; 4:31) were filled with the Spirit in situations that required special enabling for prophecy or witness. The three experiences occur in Jesus's ministry. The Spirit descended on him at his baptism (Luke 3:22). Immediately after his baptism, he was full of the Spirit (Luke 4:1). In Nazareth, the Spirit of the Lord was upon him when he preached his synagogue sermon (Luke 4:18). It might be helpful, therefore, to refer to the initial reception as "baptized by the Spirit" (Acts 1:5), the continuing condition as "filled with the Spirit" (cf. Eph 5:18), and the special enabling as "anointed by the Spirit" (Luke 4:18; Acts 10:38).

Other Tongues

"Tongue" (γλῶσσα) occurs fifty-one times in the NT. Fifteen times it refers to the physical organ of speech (e.g., Luke 1:64; 16:24; Acts 2:26), and seven times in Revelation it is part of the all-inclusive phrase "every tribe and tongue and people and nation" (Rev. 5:9; 7:9; 10:11; 11:9; 13:7; 14:6; 17:15). In Acts 2:3, it describes the visionary experience of the Holy Spirit's coming at Pentecost. In the remaining twenty-eight occurrences, it denotes speech or language. In a few of those occurrences, there is an explanatory word—"new tongues" (Mark 16:17), "kinds of tongues" (1 Cor. 12:10, 28), "interpretation of tongues" (1 Cor. 12:10), and "other tongues" (Acts 2:4; 1 Cor. 14:21; cf. Isa. 28:11). Since the latter phrase occurs in both Acts and 1 Corinthians, the question arises as to whether the two phenomena are similar or different. In Acts, the phenomenon is connected with prophecy (Acts 2:17–18), but in 1 Corinthians it is distinguished from prophesying (1 Cor. 14:1–5). Further, the tongues in Acts 2 are known languages (2:11; cf. 2:8) that are intelligible to others, and Peter's account of his encounter with Cornelius connects the tongues in Acts 10 and 19 with those in Acts 2 (11:17; cf. 10:46; 19:6). In contrast, the tongues in 1 Corinthians 12–14 require "two steps (utterance and interpretation) . . . for understanding" (Bock 2007, 99). The two phenomena, therefore, are different.

The Initial Confusion (2:5–13)

When the amazed multitudes hear the disciples speaking, their confusion about what they are hearing leads them to different conclusions.

2:5–6. Luke now changes his focus from the disciples to those who heard them speaking. He describes the hearers as "Jews dwelling in Jerusalem" (εἰς Ἰερουσαλὴμ κατοικοῦντες Ἰουδαῖοι), who were "devout men" (ἄνδρες εὐλαβεῖς) "from every nation under heaven" (ἀπὸ παντὸς ἔθνους τῶν ὑπὸ τὸν οὐρανόν). When the sound of the disciples' speech occurred (γενομένης τῆς φωνῆς ταύτης), this diverse multitude (τὸ πλῆθος) gathered in confusion (συνῆλθεν καὶ συνεχύθη), because they were each hearing in their own dialect (τῇ ἰδίᾳ διαλέκτῳ) what the disciples were saying. Pilgrims from outside Palestine increased the population of Jerusalem to over one million during the celebration of Pentecost (Schnabel 2012, 116), but the use of "living" (κατοικοῦντες) suggests that the hearers were currently residents (2:5; cf. 1:20; 7:2, 4, 48; 9:22; 11:29; 13:27; 17:24, 26; 22:12). An exception is the explicit mention of Jews and proselytes "visiting" (ἐπιδημοῦντες) from Rome (2:10; cf. 17:21). Most likely, those present had immigrated to Palestine from the Diaspora and were living in Jerusalem at that time (Longenecker 1981, 272).

2:7–8. By doubling the hearers' response (ἐξίσταντο καὶ ἐθαύμαζον), Luke highlights their amazement; Culy and Parsons suggest "they were completely astounded" (2003, 27). Their amazement grew out the fact that all the speakers were Galileans (ἅπαντες οὗτοι εἰσιν οἱ λαλοῦντες Γαλιλαῖοι). Yet, each person present (ἕκαστος) kept on hearing (ἀκούομεν) in his or her native dialect (τῇ ἰδίᾳ διαλέκτῳ ἡμῶν ἐν ᾗ ἐγεννήθημεν) what the disciples were saying. The imperfect tense of both ἐξίσταντο and ἐθαύμαζον points to an ongoing state of mind, and the present tense of ἀκούομεν highlights the fact that the disciples' inspired speech continued for some time. It might have been that the peculiarities of Galilean speech were noticeable even as the disciples spoke other languages (Bruce 1990, 116), or it might have been that the degree of education expected of Galileans

contributed to the crowd's amazement (Barrett 1994, 120). Dunn highlights "the antithesis between the small regional beginnings of the Nazarene movement and the world-wide outreach about to be foreshadowed" (1996, 27).

2:9–11. The hearers represented fifteen different countries of origin. The geographical movement is from beyond the eastern border of the empire (Parthia, Media, Elam) westward to the Fertile Crescent (Mesopotamia, Judea) and Asia Minor (Cappadocia, Pontus, Asia, Phrygia, Pamphylia), then south to northern Africa (Egypt, Libya/Cyrene) and westward again to Italy (Rome), with Crete and Arabia appended. Each of these regions had substantial Jewish populations, and their diversity highlights the diverse languages that the disciples spoke by the Spirit's filling. What the disciples were speaking (λαλούντων αὐτῶν) were "the wonderful things God has done" (NLT, τὰ μεγαλεῖα τοῦ θεοῦ).

2:12–13. Luke again highlights the hearers' continuing confusion by describing them as being both astounded (ἐξίσταντο) and confounded (διηπόρουν). It is little wonder that their evaluations differed. One part of the multitude acknowledged their inability to understand what was going on and kept on asking one another "What does this mean?" (τί θέλει τοῦτο εἶναι). Another part of the multitude dismissed what they were hearing and mockingly (διαχλευάζοντες) kept on saying "They are filled with new wine" (γλεύκους μεμεστωμένοι εἰσίν). Larkin pointedly asks, "How should we respond to the working of the Spirit in our midst?" He then answers his own question: "We must avoid the mockery of the scoffer who explains everything in empirical terms. We must be open to a divinely given explanation" (1995, 52). Peter is about to provide that explanation.

The Coming of the Holy Spirit (2:14–21)

Peter explains that what the crowd hears is the result of God pouring out the Holy Spirit as

Joel prophesied would take place in the last days.

2:14–16. As he had done previously (1:15), Peter assumed the role of spokesperson for the Twelve (σὺν τοῖς ἕνδεκα) by standing up (σταθείς), raising his voice (ἐπῆρεν τὴν φωνήν), and beginning to speak (ἀπεφθέγξατο) to the crowd. The verb ἀποφθέγγομαι describes the disciples' speaking in tongues in 2:4 and Paul's speaking words of truth and sound judgment to Agrippa in 26:25. In the LXX, it denotes inspired speech (Ezek. 13:11; Mic. 5:1; Zech. 10:2). Peter began his first of three proofs with direct address to the crowds—"Judean men and all who are living in Jerusalem" (ἄνδρες Ἰουδαῖοι καὶ οἱ κατοικοῦντες Ἰερουσαλὴμ πάντες)—and called them to pay close attention (ἐνωτίσασθε) to the words he was about to speak (τὰ ῥήματά μου). The explanation for what they were hearing was not, as some of them supposed (ὡς ὑμεῖς ὑπολαμβάνετε), that the speakers were intoxicated (οὐ . . . οὗτοι μεθύουσιν), because it was only 9:00 a.m. (ἔστιν ὥρα τρίτη τῆς ἡμέρας). Instead, what they were observing (τοῦτο) was what God had spoken through the OT prophet Joel (τὸ εἰρημένον διὰ τοῦ προφήτου Ἰωήλ)—the coming of the Holy Spirit of prophecy.

2:17–21. Peter quotes Joel 2:28–32 in its entirety and adds a few clarifying phrases. The prophecy supports his claim that these events mark the Holy Spirit's coming. Peter replaces Joel's original "after these things" (μετὰ ταῦτα) with "in the last days" (ἐν ταῖς ἐσχάταις ἡμέραις) to make it clear that these events signal "the start of the decisive eras of fulfillment" (Bock 2007, 112) and adds "says God" (λέγει ὁ θεός) to identify the ultimate source of the prophecy. In 2:33, Peter will make it clear that Jesus, who is seated at the Father's right hand, pours out the Spirit (ἐκχεῶ ἀπὸ τοῦ πνεύματος).

The promise of the Spirit's coming affects all humankind (ἐπὶ πᾶσαν σάρκα), transcends gender distinction (υἱοι . . . θυγατέρες), age

difference (νεανίσκοι . . . πρεσβύτερποι), and social status (δούλους . . . δούλας) differences, and results in prophesying (προφητεύσουσιν). Wonders in heaven (τέρατα ἐν τῷ οὐρανῳ) and signs on earth (σημεῖα ἐπὶ τῆς γῆς) will accompany the ultimate eschatological event—"the great and glorious day of the Lord" (ἡμέραν κυρίου τὴν μεγάλην καὶ ἐπιφανῆ). The magnitude of these events should remind everyone that "whoever calls upon the name of the Lord will be saved" (ὅς ἂν ἐπικαλέσηται τὸ ὄνομα κυρίου σωθήσεται), and Peter applies that call to salvation at the end of his sermon (2:40).

> ### The Fulfillment of Joel 2:28–32
>
> The fact that Peter quoted Joel 2:28–32 in its entirety presents an interpretive challenge. The fulfillment of the Spirit's coming is clear (2:17–18), but how should we understand the fulfillment of the signs and wonders Joel includes (2:19–20)? Four understandings have been suggested. The first is that there was no fulfillment at Pentecost. Peter simply applied the prophecy to the events of Pentecost because of one point of similarity: the pouring out of the Spirit (Ice 1994, 40–41). The fulfillment, therefore, lies entirely in the future (Bock 2007, 116–17; Marshall 1980, 74). The second is that the events of the fifty days from Jesus's crucifixion to Pentecost completely fulfill the prophecy (Bruce 1988, 62). The third is that Joel 2 is a unitary prophecy with multiple (both near and far) references—Pentecost and the future (Kaiser 1989, 123–24). The fourth is that the prophecy is an example of split reference (cf. McQuilkin 2009, 297–98). This last approach comes in several forms. Daniel Treier's is the most complex in that he assigns the pouring out of the Spirit (2:17–18) to Pentecost, the earthly signs and wonders (2:19) to Jesus's ministry, and the heavenly signs and wonders (2:20) to the future (1997, 21). Similarly, Schnabel assigns the signs and wonders on earth and in the sky (2:19a) to Jesus's ministry, death,

and ascension and the blood, fire, columns of smoke, and signs in the heavens (2:19b–20) to the future (2012, 138–39). Although seldom adopted by scholars, split reference that assigns verses 17–18 to Pentecost and verses 19–20 to the future seems most natural given the eschatological imagery of judgment in verse 19 (Keener 2012, 918–19) and the allusion to Joel 2:20 in Revelation 6:12. Peterson suggests that, taken as a whole, the prophecy refers to the entire period of "the last days," which would relate well to Peter's addition (ἐν ταῖς ἐσχάταις ἡμέραις) in verse 17 (2009, 143).

The Resurrection of the Crucified Jesus (2:22–28)

Peter continues by adding three "last days" signs connected to Jesus's life and ministry: his miracles, his death, and his resurrection.

2:22–24. Although the Spirit's coming was the most recent sign of the last days to occur (2:17), it was actually the fifth in a series of OT signs that surrounded the life and ministry of Jesus the Nazarene (Ἰησοῦν τὸν Ναζωραῖον). Peter, therefore, called his listeners to hear what else he had to say (ἄνδρες Ἰσραηλῖται, ἀκούσατε τοὺς λόγους τούτους). Chronologically, the first sign included the miraculous deeds (δανάμεσι καὶ τέρασι καὶ σημείοις; cf. Luke 7:18–23; Isa. 35:5–6) that God did through Jesus (οἷς ἐποίησεν δι' αὐτοῦ ὁ θεός) and by which he attested (ἀποδεδειγμένον) that Jesus was the one who was coming. The second sign was Jesus's death by crucifixion (προσπήξαντες ἀνείλατε; cf. Luke 23:32–38; Ps. 22:18; Isa. 53:4–12), which took place according to God's "fixed intention and foreknowledge" (τῇ ὡρισμένῃ βουλῇ καὶ προγνώσει; Culy and Parsons 2003, 30) through the hands of lawless men (διὰ χειρὸς ἀνόμων). The third and most important sign was God's act of raising Jesus (ὃν ὁ θεὸς ἀνέστησεν; cf. Luke 24:1–12; Job 19:23–27; Isa. 26:19), by which he destroyed the pains of death (λύσας τὰς ὠδῖνας τοῦ θανάτου) and demonstrated that Jesus could not be held by it (οὐκ ἦν δυνατὸν κρατεῖσθαι αὐτὸν ὑπ' αὐτοῦ).

2:25–28. Just as Peter quoted Joel 2:28–32 to support his claim that the events of the morning fulfilled the predicted coming of the Holy Spirit, so he quoted David's testimony (Δαυὶδ λέγει) in Psalm 16:8–11 to support his claim that God raised Jesus from the dead. References to God's presence bracket the quotation (2:25, 28; προορώμην τὸν κύριον ἐνώπιον μου . . . πληρώσεις με εὐφροσύνης μετὰ τοῦ προσώπου σου). The quotation itself focuses on the hope the psalmist has (2:26b; ἡ σάρξ μου κατασκηνώσει ἐπ' ἐλπίδι) because he knows God will not abandon his soul to Hades (2:27a; οὐκ ἐγκαταλείψεις τὴν ψυχήν μου εἰς ᾄδην) or allow him to experience corruption (2:27b; οὐδὲ δώσεις τὸν ὅσιόν σου ἰδεῖν διαφθοράν). The psalm supports the expectation of the resurrection, and the fact that David is the speaker allows Peter to make the natural connection to Jesus, who is the Son of David. The fact that God raised Jesus and delivered him from death provides the third sign of the last days. Further, as Schnabel concludes, "Since what happened to Jesus fits what David prophesied in the psalm, Jesus must be the Messiah" (2012, 145). Bock has an extended discussion of the wording of the quotation, which agrees exactly with the LXX but differs from the MT in six respects (2007, 138).

The Exaltation of the Risen Jesus (2:29–36)

Peter concludes by proclaiming that Jesus's ascension, enthronement at the Father's right hand, and pouring out of the Holy Spirit demonstrates that he is both Lord and Christ.

2:29–31. A third instance of direct address (ἄνδρες ἀδελφοί) introduces the next step in Peter's argument. Having introduced Psalm 16 as referring to the resurrection, Peter used David's role as a prophet (2:29–31) to connect

Jesus's resurrection to his exaltation, which was the fourth sign of the last days, and back to the fifth sign and starting point of his speech: the coming of the Spirit (2:32–35). He could confidently say (ἐξὸν εἰπεῖν μετὰ παρρησίας) that Psalm 16 could not refer to David, since David died (ἐτελεύτησεν), was buried (ἐτάφη), and his tomb was still among them (τὸ μνῆμα αὐτοῦ ἔστιν ἐν ἡμῖν ἄχρι τῆς ἡμέρας ταύτης). Because David was a prophet (προφήτης ὑπάρχων) and because he knew God's promise to him (Ps. 132:11; cf. 2 Sam. 7:12–13), he knew that God had sworn an oath (ὅρκῳ ὤμοσεν αὐτῷ) that one of his descendants (ἐκ καρποῦ τῆς ὀσφύος αὐτοῦ) would sit on his throne (καθίσαι ἐπὶ τὸν θρόνον αὐτοῦ). Psalm 16, therefore, referred to the resurrection of the Messiah (ἐλάλησεν περὶ τῆς ἀναστάσεως τοῦ Χριστοῦ).

2:32–35. The disciples were all witnesses (πάντες ἡμεῖς ἐσμεν μάρτυρες) to the fact that God raised this Jesus (τοῦτον τὸν Ἰησοῦν ἀνέστησεν ὁ θεός). Although Peter did not highlight the fact that they also witnessed Jesus's ascension to the right hand of the Father, the ascension and enthronement of "this Jesus" is the next step in his argument. As the logical sequel (οὖν) to his resurrection, God exalted Jesus to his right hand (τῇ δεξιᾷ τοῦ θεοῦ ὑψωθεὶς) and gave him the promise of the Holy Spirit (τὴν ἐπαγγελίαν τοῦ πνεύματος τοῦ ἁγίου λαβὼν παρά τοῦ πατρός). Jesus then poured out the sign they were seeing and hearing (ἐξέχεεν τοῦτο ὃ ὑμεῖς καὶ βλέπετε καὶ ἀκούετε) that morning. Psalm 110:1 demonstrated that David also foresaw Messiah's exaltation, but it was equally clear that Psalm 110 could not refer to David, since he did not ascend into heaven (οὐ Δαυὶδ ἀνέβη εἰς τοὺς οὐρανούς). The quotation follows the LXX exactly and provides OT support for the claims that Jesus was of higher rank than David (τῷ κυρίῳ μου), was seated at God's right hand (κάθου ἐκ δεξιῶν μου), and was given authority over his enemies (θῶ τοὺς ἐχθρούς σου ὑποπόδιον τῶν ποδῶν σου).

2:36. The inescapable conclusion (ἀσφαλῶς οὖν) for all the house of Israel (πᾶς οἶκος Ἰσραήλ) to draw from Jesus's resurrection, exaltation, and sending of the Spirit was that God enthroned this Jesus, whom his listeners crucified (ὃν ὑμεῖς ἐσταυρώσατε), as both Lord and Christ (καὶ κύριον . . . καὶ χριστόν). Regarding the title Messiah, Longenecker notes, "In Jewish thought, no one has a right to the title till he has accomplished the work of the Messiah" (1981, 280). Peter had now demonstrated that Jesus, on the basis of God's working through him, had accomplished the work of Messiah—specifically, miraculous works (2:22), death (2:23), resurrection (2:24, 32), enthronement (2:34–35), and sending of the Spirit (2:17, 33). God could therefore award Jesus the titles of "Lord" and "Messiah" (2:36). As "Lord," he is the one on whom men and women may call for salvation (2:21; cf. 2:40).

The Informed Response (2:37–40)

When the listeners respond to his speech with a request for spiritual guidance, Peter issues a call to repent, be baptized, and receive the gift of the Holy Spirit, resulting in the conversion of three thousand individuals.

2:37. In contrast to their initial confused response (2:12–13), Peter's listeners were "stabbed in the heart" (Culy and Parsons 2003, 43, κατενύγησαν τὴν καρδίαν) and asked Peter and the rest of the apostles (Πέτρον καὶ τοὺς λοιποὺς ἀποστόλους) what they should do (τί ποιήσωμεν;). Their question arose from "the conviction of guilt that leads to repentance" (Bruce 1990, 129), as they realized they had crucified the very Messiah for whom they had been looking (cf. 2:36). Later accusations that listeners had killed Jesus (5:33) and the prophets (7:54) elicited similar emotional reactions (διεπρίοντο; "they were cut to the quick") but a different volitional response: the desire to kill the speakers. The Pentecost crowd's question acknowledged their spiritual need in the same way the crowds who went out to see John the Baptist had (Luke 3:10, 12, 14) and the Philippian jailer would (Acts 16:30).

2:38. In response to their question, Peter called his listeners to repent (μετανοήσατε), be baptized in Jesus's name (βαπτισθήτε . . . ἐπὶ τῷ ὀνόματι Ἰησοῦ Χριστοῦ), experience the forgiveness of sins (εἰς ἄφεσιν τῶν ἁμαρτιῶν), and receive the gift of the Holy Spirit (λήμψεσθε τὴν δωρεὰν τοῦ ἁγίου πνεύματος). Repentance is both the content of the gospel (Luke 24:47) and the proper response to it (Luke 5:32), as Keener notes (2012, 974). It involves a change in direction of life (Marshall 1980, 80). For these particular listeners, that change involved confessing the sin of involvement in Jesus's death, feeling sorrow for rejecting Jesus, changing their attitude concerning Jesus, and accepting Jesus as Messiah (Schnabel 2012, 161). Baptism was not a means of salvation but, rather, a demonstration of repentance. Baptism "in Jesus's name" distinguished it from other forms of baptism (e.g., pagan, Jewish proselyte, John the Baptist's) and involved submitting to his authority, acknowledging his claims, subscribing to his teaching, engaging in his service, and relying on his merits (Larkin 1995, 59). Forgiveness of sins would release them from the legal and moral obligations imposed by sin as well as from its consequences (Schnabel 2012, 164). It was the message Jesus commissioned his disciples to proclaim (Luke 24:47) and the message they faithfully shared (Acts 3:19; 5:31; 13:38). The gift of the Holy Spirit was "the mark of all people who repent and acknowledge that Jesus is the crucified, risen, and exalted Messiah and Lord" (Schnabel 2012, 165), as Luke makes clear throughout Acts (8:14; 10:46; 11:15; 15:8; 19:6).

2:39. Peter continued by explaining (γάρ) that the promise of the gospel extended "across time and space, generations and cultures" (Larkin 1995, 59). He included four groups: "to you" (ὑμῖν), "to your children" (τοῖς τέκνοις ὑμῶν), "to all who are far off" (πᾶσιν τοῖς εἰς μακράν), and "as many as the Lord our God shall call to himself" (ὅσους ἂν προσκαλέσηται κύριος ὁ θεὸς ἡμῶν). The first two groups were the immediate listeners and future generations of Israelites. The third group was Diaspora Jews (Peterson 2009, 157) or Gentiles (Bruce 1990, 130). Isaiah 57:19 and Acts 22:21 seem to support the latter suggestion. An alternate understanding is that Peter was referring to Diaspora Jews, but that Luke understood the reference to include the Gentiles as well (Longenecker 1981, 286; cf. Bock 2007, 145; Keener 2012, 987). Including the fourth group echoed Joel 2:32 ("even among the survivors whom the Lord calls") and brought Peter's argument back to where it had begun in verses 17–21. It also highlighted God's direction and the delicate balance between human responsibility (2:21) and divine sovereignty (2:39).

2:40. Luke notes that Peter continued to address his listeners "with many other words" (ἑτέροις λόγοις πλείοσιν) of testimony (διεμαρτύρατο) and persuasion (παρεκάλει), but he skips additional content and moves directly to Peter's final appeal (Keener 2012, 984). Using a divine passive, Peter called his listeners to "be saved" (σώθητε) "from this perverse generation" (ἀπὸ τῆς γενεᾶς τῆς σκολιᾶς ταύτης). Jesus himself had described the generation among whom he had ministered as "perverse" (Luke 9:41), Dunn notes the possible echo of Deuteronomy 32:5 and Psalm 78:8 (1996, 34), and Larkin suggests that the use of the phrase intensifies Peter's call to repentance by identifying his listeners with the rebellious wilderness generation (1995, 60). In 2:41–47, Luke records the response to Peter's appeal.

THEOLOGICAL FOCUS

The narratival function of Acts 2:1–40 is to begin the account of Jesus's followers as witnesses in Jerusalem (2:1–8:3). Jesus had commanded his followers to return to Jerusalem and wait for the gift of the Spirit the Father had promised (1:1–11). While they waited, they had restored the integrity of the apostolic leadership team as preparation for Pentecost (1:12–26). What would happen next? How would Jesus fulfill his promise that the Holy Spirit would come upon them? How would they fulfill their role as Jesus's witnesses? Luke's account of the events on the day of Pentecost answers those questions and places the Holy Spirit front and center as the person of the Trinity who will lead and empower the church as it engages in its mission in Jerusalem, in all Judea and Samaria, and to the ends of the earth.

Theologically, Acts 2:1–40 presents three paradigms related to the progress of the church's mission and witness. The sequence of events on the day of Pentecost establishes a pattern for gospel witness that appears multiple times in Acts: God acts, the listeners respond with interest, the witness explains from Scripture, the listeners respond with understanding, and the witness calls for a decision. Peter's speech provides the first of multiple examples of the essentials that should be included when preaching the gospel: the OT foundation, the centrality of Jesus's death and resurrection, the importance of a call to repentance, the promise of forgiveness of sins, and the universal scope of the gospel offer. Undergirding the events Luke records is the work of the Holy Spirit as he opens doors for witness, empowers believers for witness, and brings conviction through God's Word in witness. In so doing, the passage sets the pattern for the church's advance, both in the first century and in the twenty-first century.

PREACHING AND TEACHING STRATEGIES

Exegetical/Theological Synthesis
Theophilus and Luke's other first-century readers would have wanted to know how the early church grew from 120 members meeting in an upstairs room in Jerusalem to a major religious movement that would eventually reach the capital of the Roman Empire. Jesus had promised that his followers would receive power when the Holy Spirit would come upon them and that they would be his witnesses beginning in Jerusalem. The events at Pentecost were the fulfillment of that promise, and the result was the first mass ingathering of converts to the new movement. With the original readers, the twenty-first-century audience shares the need to understand how God orchestrated the events surrounding the birth of the Christian movement and mission. In particular, it needs to understand the role the Holy Spirit played in the church's witness and mission. The events at Pentecost make it clear that the Holy Spirit opens doors for witness, empowers believers for witness, and brings conviction through God's Word in witness. If the contemporary church hopes to experience growth similar to that of the early church, it will do well to remember that it accomplishes its mission only by relying on the Spirit's empowerment.

Preaching/Teaching Idea
Pentecost power sets the pattern for the church's advance.

Contemporary Connections

What does it mean?
The Pentecost pattern, repeated in Acts, highlights the Spirit's role and the Spirit's message. With respect to his role, as promised just ten days prior, the Holy Spirit provides real power toward fulfilling Jesus's commission. First, he opened the door for an evangelistic opportunity. It was providential that his arrival coincided with a mass, multicultural gathering on the disciples' front doorstep. The gift of foreign languages is not a random miracle. The Spirit orchestrated everything—crowd, loud sound, languages. Second, the Spirit empowered the disciples, chiefly Peter, to speak boldly to a crowd that had already killed and would soon

kill again. He brought remembrance of God's Word to Peter, even a passage about himself, and the elements of the gospel message. Finally, the Holy Spirit brought supernatural and immediate conviction to several thousand from the crowd in a single day.

Pentecost shows us not only the Holy Spirit's role but also his saving message of the gospel. The preachers in Acts will follow this outline consistently. It starts with an OT foundation—this time Joel and two psalms. Peter highlights the centrality of Jesus's death and resurrection (2:23–24, 31–32). The invitation is to repent and be baptized (2:38). The unmerited gift is forgiveness of sins and the promise of the Holy Spirit (2:38). Peter makes clear this gospel is available to everyone—the hearers, coming generations, Jews and Gentiles, and everyone whom God calls to himself (2:39).

Is it true?
One of the most compelling apologetics for Christianity is that a ragtag group of Galileans, following a publicly executed rabbi, launched from an upper room, found their way to the global Roman Empire stage, virtually overnight. Men like the apostle Peter, who just weeks before denied Jesus to save his skin, were ready to face death to testify to their teacher's resurrection. There is not a natural explanation. It is supernatural. The Holy Spirit accomplished what no movement could dream.

Just as the apostolic team had learned their leadership habits from Jesus in the previous section, now they take their missionary cues from his playbook. They had seen Jesus regularly use the OT Scriptures to point to himself—reading Isaiah in the synagogue, stumping religious leaders with the Psalms, and teaching from Moses and the Prophets on the road to Emmaus. They had heard Jesus prophesy his death as central to God's work. They had heard his predecessor, John the Baptist, and then Jesus himself call for repentance and promise forgiveness of sins. No wonder Luke says that his

first book, the gospel of Luke, was "all that Jesus began to do and to teach" (Acts 1:1). The presumption is that this second book will be all that Jesus continues to do and teach. His presence in these pages is palpable.

Now what?
Saving souls is simple, but it is not easy. A child can understand what is at stake, but it will take the Triune God to make it so. Generations of controversy surrounding revivals, reformations, awakenings, second works of the Spirit, baptismal regeneration, cold Calvinism, hot-seat Arminianism, seeker-sensitive services, altar calls, and repeated invitations to ask Jesus into our hearts at the conclusion of every summer camp have muddied the waters considerably. Add to that our anxiety to seek the new, the cutting-edge, the memorable, the relevant, and it is no wonder that our theology and methodology for Great Commission conversions are strained and powerless.

We desperately need a God-centered approach to evangelism today. A God-centered approach relies on God's Spirit to open *his* doors, open *our* mouths, and open *their* hearts. A God-centered approach sticks to his fundamental message: that forgiveness, cleansing, and the Spirit's empowerment to change are found in the crucified, resurrected, ascended Lord Jesus. A God-centered approach seeks this means and this message in bold faith and expectation to "everyone whom the Lord our God calls to himself" (2:39). Such an approach might not sell books or church-growth webinars, but it worked pretty well at Pentecost. By God's design, it is still working today.

Creativity in Presentation
An out-of-the-box presentation of such a long passage could be to tell the story of Pentecost from the perspective of a Jerusalem resident. Such an approach would set the stage to give background details on the hearers' worldview, the surprise and confusion of the first gathering,

the clarity and content of Peter's sermon, and the Holy Spirit's miraculous conviction. It has the clear narrative arc of a well-told story. Such a sermon could use first-person narrative: "I was in Jerusalem getting ready for the Feast of Weeks with my family"; or it could use third-person narrative: "Imagine a first-century Parthian Jew living in Jerusalem."

The audience appears to be residents of Jerusalem (2:5). They were a diverse group, representing at least fifteen named nations. They were celebrating Pentecost that late spring/early summer at the beginning of the wheat harvest. The city was crowded with pilgrims from abroad. Jesus's public and controversial crucifixion had just happened not two months ago. Since then, there were disturbing rumors that his Galilean followers stole his body.

Dramatically, the sound of a mighty wind gathered a massive crowd. Imagine the shock of coming together and each person hearing someone speaking in his or her own language. The text's description of the hearers as "bewildered," "amazed," "astonished," and "perplexed" capture that well.

There are a lot of moving parts in Peter's sermon. By capturing his speech from the perspective of the hearer, the preacher has the ability to distill the main points. The message was grounded in the Hebrew Scriptures and was not a novelty. It placed Jesus's death and resurrection at the center. It called everyone to repent of sin and receive forgiveness, and Peter offered those blessings to everyone.

In portraying the crowds' informed response, describe how it looks and feels to be "cut to the heart" by God's Spirit. What is the difference between fearfully hedging our bets with Christianity and responding with genuine heartfelt conversion? What immediate assurances and promises did Peter give these new converts? The beauty of preaching a sermon on a sermon resides in the prayerful

expectation that God will bear fruit today as he did on that Pentecost morning. Pentecost power sets the pattern for the church's advance.

- The church advances: The Holy Spirit opens mouths and doors (2:1–13 and 14–36).

- The church advances: The Holy Spirit opens hearts (2:37–40).

DISCUSSION QUESTIONS

1. What is the role of the miraculous in the advance of the gospel? How do miracles relate to the proclamation of God's Word?

2. In what ways does Peter's speech connect the gospel to the teaching of the OT as well as to the circumstances of his listeners? How does his speech inform the evangelistic and missionary peaching of the contemporary church?

3. Why does Peter call for repentance and baptism but not for faith? Does his understanding of conversion differ from Paul's? Why or why not? Does his invitation establish baptism as essential for salvation? Why or why not?

4. In what way(s) is the working of the Holy Spirit at Pentecost both similar to and different from his working in the OT?

5. In what way(s) is the work of the Holy Spirit critical to the church accomplishing its mission? What implications for the contemporary church can you draw from the events of the early church's beginning at Pentecost?

Acts 2:41–47

EXEGETICAL IDEA
Devotion, generosity, close relationships, a good reputation, and continuing numerical growth characterized the common life of the Jerusalem church.

THEOLOGICAL FOCUS
Adopting the attitudes and activities of the NT church fosters spiritual growth and missional impact.

PREACHING IDEA
Church life fuels church growth, both spiritual and numerical.

PREACHING POINTERS
How does an organization deal with success? Success can lead to stress as it stretches and challenges existing systems, practices, and relationships. An organization's willingness to adapt and change as necessary can make the difference between continued growth, inertia, or decline. How did the Jerusalem church deal with the sudden, unexpected, explosive growth that followed Peter's Pentecost speech? With Luke's original readers, we need to understand how to live out an authentic relationship with Christ and other believers in a growing community of like-minded disciples. How can the contemporary church experience the same spiritual and numerical growth that the early church did?

People today should be able to relate to multiple ideas in the passage, including enjoying time with others, meeting the needs of the financially disadvantaged, and having a good reputation within the larger community. Followers of Jesus should connect with the concepts of teaching, prayer, and worship. The vibrant community life of the Jerusalem church corrects the idea that following Jesus is a purely individual activity. In fact, being a disciple involves participating actively in the common life of the body of Christ. Luke's account commends the importance of the shared life among believers that brings praise to God, meets the needs among its members, enjoys a good reputation among those outside the congregation, and attracts others to faith in Christ. As Christians, we need to understand how the early church lived out their new commitment to Christ so that we will embrace the devotion, care, intimacy, and witness that characterized NT church life.

THE EARLY CHURCH'S COMMON LIFE
(2:41–47)

LITERARY STRUCTURE AND THEMES (2:41–47)

Commentators differ on where this summary passage begins. Barrett, Bruce, Peterson, and Keener place the break at verse 41 (cf. NLT). Longenecker, Larkin, Bock, and Schnabel place the break at verse 42 (cf. NET, NIV, CSB, ESV, NEB, NJB). Marshall places the break at verse 43, as does UBS⁵ (cf. GNB, NASB, NRSV). Since Luke uses μὲν οὖν with plural substantival participles elsewhere to introduce new paragraphs (8:4; 11:19; 13:4), it seems logical to see verse 41 as marking the transition. Supporting that decision is the *inclusio* created by the occurrences of προστίθημι in verse 41 (προσετέθησαν) and verse 47 (προσετίθει).

Talbert (2005, 33) and Keener (2012, 991) propose chiastic structures for the paragraph, but both base their suggestions on general topics they see within the paragraph. A more objective control for identifying such structures, however, is the repetition of words or phrases. In this paragraph, προστίθημι occurs in verses 41 and 47, προσκαρτερέω occurs in verses 42 and 46, and κλάσις/κλάω + ἄρτος also occurs in verses 42 and 46. Further, the phrase καθ' ἡμέραν brackets verses 46–47. These features suggest an ABA′ structure for the paragraph:

A Addition leading to devotion (2:41–42)
B Impact on outsiders and insiders (2:43–45)
A′ Devotion leading to addition (2:46–47)

This passage is one of three summaries in 2:1–8:3 that describe the community life of the Jerusalem church. The summary passage of 5:12–16 describes the impact of "signs and wonders" (τέρατα καὶ σημεῖα) in more detail (2:43), and 4:32–37 describes the practice of "having all things in common" (εἶχον ἅπαντα κοινά) in more detail (2:44–45). In addition, 3:11–25 provides an example of the apostles' teaching (2:42), and 4:23–31 provides an example of the church's prayer life (2:42).

- ***Addition Leading to Devotion (2:41–42)***
- ***Impact on Outsiders and Insiders (2:43–45)***
- ***Devotion Leading to Addition (2:46–47)***

EXPOSITION (2:41–47)

The immediate result of Peter's Pentecost speech (2:14–40) was the conversion of three thousand new disciples. Before describing further expansion of the Christian mission, Luke includes a summary passage that describes key aspects of the believers' lives in Jerusalem. Schnabel identifies five purposes for the summaries. Historically, they report what happened in the early church. Literarily, they indicate the passage of time in the narrative. Theologically, they reinforce the continued presence of God's power in the community. Ecclesiologically, they outline the essential characteristics of the early Christian community. Missiologically, they record the continued growth and expansion of the church (2012, 175). This first summary passage identifies four essential aspects of early church life: instruction, fellowship, shared meals, and prayer (2:41–42). It describes the impact of God's working within the early church: awe among outsiders and generous sharing among insiders (2:43–45). It records the results for the

Christian mission: praise to God, respect from the people of Jerusalem, and continued conversion growth (2:46–47). Luke's concluding comment establishes the activities recorded in the paragraph as normative for NT church life. Luke describes selected aspects of that church life in more detail in subsequent preaching units.

Addition Leading to Devotion (2:41–42)

Peter's speech leads to the conversion of three thousand new disciples, who devote themselves to instruction, fellowship, shared meals, and prayer.

2:41. In response to Peter's appeal at the end of his speech (2:38–40), "about three thousand souls" (ψυχαὶ ὡσεὶ τρισχίλιαι) received his word (οἱ ἀποδεξάμενοι τὸν λόγον αὐτοῦ), were baptized (ἐβαπτίσθησαν), and were added (προσετέθησαν) to the number of the disciples. "Souls" is a synecdoche for the whole person. "The word" has a prominent place in the subsequent narrative as it "grows" (6:7; 12:24), "multiplies" (12:24), "spreads" (13:49), "grows strong" (19:20), and as groups "receive" it (11:1). As noted in 2:38, baptism was not a means of salvation but evidence of having received the word. The reference to large numbers of men and women "being added" to the Jerusalem church is the first of five in the early chapters of Luke's narrative (2:47; 5:14; 6:7; 9:31; 12:24).

2:42. The new converts engaged in the community life of the Jerusalem disciples by "persistently devoting themselves" (ἦσαν προσκαρτεροῦντες; cf. Schnabel 2012, 42) to four essential activities. The first activity was "the apostles' teaching" (τῇ διδαχῇ τῶν ἀποστόλων). Bruce notes that the disciples would have considered the teaching authoritative "because it was delivered as the 'teaching of the Lord through the twelve apostles'" (1990, 131). The noun "teaching" (διδαχή) occurs three other times in Acts (5:28; 13:12; 17:19), and the verb (διδάσκω) occurs seventeen times.

In 4:2, Luke links the verb with "proclaiming" (διὰ τὸ διδάσκειν . . . καὶ καταγγέλλειν), and in 5:42, he links it with "preaching the good news" (διδάσκοντες καὶ εὐαγγελιζόμενοι). Later, "teaching" describes Paul's proclamation to Sergius Paulus on Cyprus (13:12) as well as his evangelistic preaching in the Athenian marketplace (17:19). These occurrences support Barrett's contention that the apostles' teaching "cannot be sharply or consistently distinguished from their preaching" (1994, 163) and Larkin's conclusion that their teaching included both evangelism and edification (1995, 61). The apostles taught "in Jesus's name" (4:18; cf. 3:6, 16; 4:7, 10, 12, 17), proclaimed "the resurrection from the dead in Jesus" when they taught (4:2), and "filled Jerusalem with their teaching" (5:25).

The second activity was "fellowship" (τῇ κονωνίᾳ). The noun occurs only in this verse of Acts, although the adjective "common" (κοινός) occurs in 2:44 and 4:32. Paul used the noun to denote both charitable contribution to material needs (Rom. 12:13; 15:26; 2 Cor. 8:4; 9:13) and close association with someone or something (1 Cor. 1:9; 10:16; 2 Cor. 1:7; 6:14; 13:13; Gal. 2:9; Phil. 1:5; 3:10). Since the term occurs with three other general terms, it is probably best to understand the latter, broader sense for the noun here and the former, narrower sense for the adjective in 2:44 and 4:32. Culy and Parsons suggest that the term refers to "a general sense of close fellowship" (2003, 46). Barrett writes, "the meaning is that they continued in faithful adherence to the newly formed community of those who had accepted the messiahship of Jesus and the belief that God's salvation of his people was being put into effect through him" (1994, 164).

The third activity was "the breaking of bread" (τῇ κλάσει τοῦ ἄρτου). The phrase occurs four other times in Acts (2:46; 20:7, 11; 27:35), each with the most natural sense of "shared meals" (Dunn 1996, 42). The same sense is most appropriate for two of the three occurrences in Luke's gospel (24:30, 35) as well. Similar wording in Luke 22:19 (λαβὼν ἄρτον εὐχαριστήσας ἔκλασεν καὶ ἔδωκεν αὐτοῖς) and 1 Corinthians 11:24–25, however, leads Marshall (1981, 82), Bruce (1990, 132), Barrett (1994, 164), and Keener (2012, 1003) to see at least an allusion to the celebration of the Lord's Supper. It seems most natural, however, to understand the phrase as referring to ordinary meals the disciples shared in their homes for three reasons. First, the phrase occurs in a list of general terms. Second, the broader sense of the phrase appears to be in view in 2:46 (Bock 2007, 150). Third, the church's adoption of the term "breaking of bread" as a title for the Lord's Supper is not formally attested until the second century (Peterson 2009, 161)

The fourth activity was "prayers" (ταῖς προσευχαῖς). The noun "prayer" (προσευχή) occurs four other times in Acts in connection with the life of the early church (1:4; 3:1; 6:4; 12:5), and the verb (προσεύχομαι) occurs sixteen times. The apostles considered the ministry of prayer to have the same priority as the ministry of the Word (6:4). Prayer—in conjunction with fasting (13:3; 14:23)—was an integral part of the decision-making process, including the process for selecting Judas's replacement (1:24), choosing qualified individuals to care for the needs of the widows (6:6), appointing missionaries (13:3), and appointing elders (14:23). Paul (9:11–12; 22:17), Peter (10:9; 11:15), and Cornelius (10:30) all experienced visions while they were praying. Prayer accompanied the laying on of hands for healing (9:40; 28:8) and receiving the Holy Spirit (8:15). The church prayed in the face of opposition (4:23–31) and imprisonment (12:5, 12; 16:25). In this context, the term most likely refers both to private and communal prayers (Schnabel 2012, 179).

Impact on Outsiders and Insiders (2:43–45)

God's working within the community of disciples leads to a continuing state of awe among nonbelievers and the regular practice of generosity among believers.

2:43. God's working within the community of disciples had an impact both on those outside it and on those within it. Luke first relates the impact on the former group: "awe was upon every soul" (ἐγίνετο δὲ πάσῃ ψυχῇ φόβος). The sense of awe arose from the "many signs and wonders" (πολλὰ τέρατα καὶ σημεῖα) that God was doing "through the apostles" (διὰ τῶν ἀποστόλων). The imperfect tense of ἐγίνετο highlights the continuing state that existed. Peterson notes that "every soul" is "a hyperbolic way of referring to nonbelievers in Jerusalem" and stands in contrast to "all the believers" in verse 44 (2009, 162). In Acts, φόβος can denote "awe" (9:31; 19:17) or "fright" (5:5, 11; 10:4; 24:25). The former is preferable, and NET translates the noun as "reverential awe."

The phrase "signs and wonders" echoes Joel's prophecy (2:19) and Peter's statement about Jesus (2:22). They were "evidence of God's presence with his people" (Longenecker 1981, 290), as is also the case in 5:12–16. Elsewhere in Acts, Stephen (6:8), Phillip (8:6, 13), Paul, and Barnabas (14:3; 15:12) performed signs and wonders as the gospel crossed significant cultural thresholds. The disciples' prayer in 4:30 makes it clear that the signs and wonders took place "through the name of your holy servant Jesus" (διὰ τοῦ ὀνόματος τοῦ ἁγίου παιδός σου Ἰησοῦ).

Luke provides an example of God's supernatural working through the apostles in the next paragraph (3:1–10).

2:44–45. Next, Luke turns to the impact on "all the believers" (πάντες οἱ πιστεύοντες) in the entire assembly (ἐπὶ τὸ αὐτό). The aspect of community life that Luke chooses to highlight is the regular practice of generosity among the members, who "were having all things in common" (εἶχον ἅπαντα κοινά). He provides a fuller account in 4:32–37. The imperfect tense of εἶχον in verse 44 along with the imperfect tenses of ἐπίπρασκον and διεμέριζον in verse 45 describe an established practice (Longenecker 1981, 291). The adjective κοινός occurs five times in Acts, twice with the sense "common" (2:44; 4:32; cf. Titus 1:4; Jude 3) and three times with the sense "unclean" (10:14, 28; 11:8; cf. Mark 7:2, 5; Rom. 14:14 [three times]; Heb. 10:29; Rev. 21:27).

> *TEXTUAL ANALYSIS: "the entire assembly"*
> The phrase ἐπὶ τὸ αὐτό occurs five times in Acts *(1:15; 2:1, 44, 47; 4:26)* and poses an interpretive challenge. In 2:44 and 47, Culy and Parsons choose "in the same place" (2003, 47–48); Bock decides on "together" (2007, 152); Schnabel views the phrase as synonymous with ὁμοθυμαδόν and concludes that it designates unity rather than location (2012, 181). For the occurrence in 1:15, Bruce suggests "in full assembly" (1990, 108); in 2:47, NLT translates the phrase as "to their fellowship"; in 4:26, the phrase occurs in a quotation of Psalm 2:2 with the verb συνάγω and reflects LXX usage (cf. 2 Sam. 10:15; Mic. 2:12). The closest NT parallels are 1 Corinthians 11:20 and 14:23, where the phrase occurs with συνέρχομαι and refers to ἡ ἐκκλησία (cf. 1 Cor. 11:18). From these considerations, Barrett concludes that the phrase "is technical . . . signifies the union of the Christian body . . . [and] can be rendered by some such phrase as *in church*" (1994, 173; emphasis original). It is best to understand the phrase as referring to the entire group of disciples in Jerusalem, whether gathered together or scattered throughout the city.

Periodically, the disciples would sell (ἐπίπρασκον, iterative imperfect) their real estate (τὰ κτήματα) and other possessions (τὰς ὑπάρξεις) and distribute (διεμέριζον, iterative imperfect) the proceeds to whoever might be having a need (πᾶσιν καθότι ἄν τις χρείαν εἶχεν). In their active care for those in need, the disciples were adhering to OT law (Deut. 15:4–5), demonstrating the fruit of their repentance as John the Baptist had taught (Luke 3:7–14), and following Jesus's instructions to give generously to the poor (Luke 6:30–36; cf. 12:33–34; 14:33; 18:22). A variant in the Western text that

reads "as many as were having properties or possessions" (ὅσοι κτήματα εἶχον ἢ ὑπάρξεις) is an assimilation to 4:32, but the implication of the latter verse is that not every member of the community owned property to sell (cf. Barrett 1994, 169). There is nothing in the text to suggest that members of the community were required to sell their property or possessions, and the contrast between Barnabas's generosity (4:32–37) and Ananias and Sapphira's greed (5:1–11) leads Marshall to the conclusion "that the selling of one's goods was a voluntary matter." He continues, "each person held his goods at the disposal of the others whenever the need arose" (1980, 84)

Devotion Leading to Addition (2:46–47)

The disciples' daily activities in the temple and in homes result in praise to God, respect from outsiders, and continued conversion growth.

2:46–47. In addition to the periodic selling of possessions to meet financial needs, the disciples' devotion (προσκαρτεροῦντες) also included daily activities (καθ' ἡμέραν) that epitomized their unity (ὁμοθυμαδόν). Those daily activities took place both in the temple (ἐν τῷ ἱερῷ) and in various houses (κατ' οἶκον; cf. Barrett 1994, 170). The disciples also met in houses (κατ' οἶκον), where they regularly shared meals (κλῶντες . . . ἄρτον μετελάμβανον τροφῆς). Their life together overflowed with extreme joy (ἐν ἀγαλλιάσει) and heartfelt sincerity (ἀφελότητι καρδίας). As a result, God received praise (αἰνοῦντες τὸν θεόν), and the disciples experienced a good reputation among those outside the Christian community (ἔχοντες χάριν πρὸς ὅλον τὸν λαόν).

Both 3:11 and 5:12 identify Solomon's Portico (ἐν τῇ Στοᾷ Σολομῶντος) as the temple venue where the disciples met. Luke does not specify the temple-related activities, but 3:1 suggests that the disciples observed the regular Jewish hours of prayer, and 5:12 suggests that they met frequently in the temple precincts for other activities. Larkin describes the atmosphere surrounding the community as "constant intimacy, exultant joy . . . transparency of relationship . . . a gracious witness to the people" (1995, 62). Luke adds his stamp of approval to this description of the Jerusalem church's community life by noting that the Lord (ὁ κύριος) continued adding (προσετίθει) to the assembly (ἐπὶ τὸ αὐτο) every day (καθ' ἡμέραν) those who were being saved (τοὺς σῳζομένους).

THEOLOGICAL FOCUS

The narratival function of Acts 2:41–47 is to build a bridge from the events of the day of Pentecost to the next set of events in Luke's account of the expansion of the early Christian mission (Marshall 1980, 83). This summary paragraph provides insight into the daily life of the new community and introduces aspects of Jerusalem church life that are described in greater detail until the members of the community are scattered as a result of the persecution following Stephen's martyrdom (3:1–8:3). What impact would the addition of three thousand new converts have on the community of disciples? Would they remain true to Jesus's teaching? Would it dilute the close fellowship they had enjoyed since Jesus's ascension? How would they address needs that might arise? How would they live out the piety as Jewish-background followers of Christ? How would other Jews in Jerusalem view them? In seven short verses, Luke begins to answer all of these questions.

Theologically, Acts 2:41–47 establishes essential elements of NT church life as normative. Those elements include teaching, fellowship, private and corporate prayer, care for one another, large- and small-group meetings, and worship. It also demonstrates the impact that results when God is at work in a like-minded body of disciples. When followers of Jesus embrace the devotion, care, and intimacy that characterized the Jerusalem church, and when they allow God to be at work in their midst, the result is sustained spiritual and numerical

growth that results in praise to God and favor in the eyes of the community at large. John Stott characterizes the Jerusalem church using four adjectives: learning, loving, worshipping, and evangelistic (1990, 82–87). Bock concludes that Acts 2:41–47 portrays the church as "a place of spiritual growth and spiritual praise, a place that is relational enough to meet needs, engage the culture, and share Christ" (2007, 155).

PREACHING AND TEACHING STRATEGIES

Exegetical/Theological Synthesis

Luke's first-century readers would have wanted to know how the original group of 120 disciples responded to the addition of three thousand new converts to the Christian community in Jerusalem. The disciples responded by incorporating those converts into the new community with unwavering devotion, compassionate care, heartfelt sincerity, and joyful worship. The result was praise to God, favor in the eyes of those outside the community, and steady conversion growth. With the original audience, the twenty-first-century audience shares the need to appreciate and appropriate the essential elements of NT church life that will enable local congregations to experience significant spiritual and numerical growth like that of the Jerusalem church. Luke's account introduces those elements and establishes them as normative for congregations across time, space, and culture.

Preaching/Teaching Idea

Church life fuels church growth, both spiritual and numerical.

Contemporary Connections

What does it mean?
After a wild, watershed moment in the life of the church, Luke settles us into the earliest routine of the body. In line with the Great Commission recorded in Matthew's gospel, now that the

apostles have made born-again disciples of the nations present in Jerusalem and baptized them, it is time to teach them to observe all that Jesus commanded. That process distills into four activities that produce many fruits.

Church life consisted of, first, the apostles' teaching, which presumably sounded much like Peter's—exegesis of the OT through the lens of Jesus's death and resurrection (4:2). It probably included a blend of both building up the body and evangelizing seekers. Second, the church fellowshipped with one another and gave generously to those in need. Third, underscoring the nature of her fellowship, the church was hospitable to her members and ate meals together. Fourth, the disciples continued praying as they had in the upper room.

The fruit of these four simple practices abounds. Luke reports reverential awe toward God, open hands with possessions, open doors with friendliness, daily community, happy and worshipful hearts, and a strong reputation among outsiders. Significantly, more and more friends came to faith daily.

Is it true?

In the earliest days, when the church numbered 120 members and was waiting for the Holy Spirit, they were already "devoting" themselves to prayer (1:14) and the Word (1:16–20). Now with the Spirit's presence, and a few thousand friends added to her ranks, they added to their devotion both fellowship and the breaking of bread. The upper room became many rooms throughout the city. What started as a shared love for the Lord with all their heart, mind, soul, and strength, immediately expanded to loving neighbors like themselves. Love for God and for others are worth more than whole burnt offerings and sacrifices (Mark 12:28–34); on these attitudes the Law and Prophets depend (Matt. 22:34–40), and together they constitute life that is worth living (Luke 10:25–28).

These post-Pentecost days of routines also tell the story of the relationship between the extraordinary and the ordinary. Pentecost was fantastic; post-Pentecost was familiar. What began with rushing wind, fire, and mass conversions settled into daily practices around teaching, friendship, food, and prayer, all in customary settings like houses and the temple. As much as we might like to stay on the Mount of Transfiguration, there is work to do in the valley. There was only one Pentecost, but there is daily opportunity for this new, post-Pentecost work.

Now what?

The first-century church's spiritual and numerical growth ought to bring real conviction to the twenty-first-century church. The church today has slipped its moorings and is adrift on the sea of a consumeristic culture. We can become so eager to provide what our membership expects that we have little time to devote ourselves to the church life God desires. We run ourselves ragged staffing programs, events, concerts, content, streaming services, and Sunday experiences that we cannot bear to add one more task to our plate—even if it is the main thing. Before the church became a storefront, a show, a therapy lounge, or a corporation, she was a gathering of the unlikeliest of people. Those people met under the banner of Jesus's death and resurrection and lived out that reality publicly and privately, in word, prayer, friendship, and hospitality. They were so Spirit-filled and vital that they were in awe of God. It was so generous and outward-focused that physical and spiritual needs were met. It was so warm and attractive that new friends were added daily. We have much to learn, much to change, much to reform. Approaching this passage with humble hearts goes a long way toward becoming who we were meant to be as the church.

Creativity in Presentation

My local oil change garage boasts a twenty-three-point inspection on each car they service, from fluids, to wiper blades, to brakes. I have seen competitors hasten to make theirs a twenty-four- or twenty-nine-point inspection; the most I have ever seen is a 150-point inspection. At that point, I am not even sure there is anything left to inspect. Regardless of the number of points involved, the idea is the same: make sure the different functions of the car are working at their optimal level. Our passage can serve in this way for our church. Acts 2 is a four-point inspection to see if these functions are operating at their God-inspired level. Work point-by-point through the text and the church context, evaluating each sign of health.

The early disciples "devoted themselves to the apostles' teaching" and repeatedly grounded themselves in Scripture and in its prophetic revelation of Jesus as Christ and Lord. Is our church rooted in the Bible? How well do we read and study individually on our own, together with our families, and as a church body? Does God's Word guide all we do? The early disciples "devoted themselves to . . . fellowship" and engaged in authentic life-giving community together. Their commitment to one another led to radical examples of generosity to the neediest among them. How well do I know my fellow members—their joys, struggles, fears, gifts? How well do I love them? When is the last time I saw a need in our church body and responded with generosity that cost me something?

The early disciples "devoted themselves . . . to the breaking of bread." At the very least, they ate together. It seems likely that they also celebrated the Lord's Supper together. Luke goes on to say that at these dinner tables "they received food with glad and generous hearts" (2:46). Who sits around my dinner table night after night? Are they only my family, only my closest friends, only people with whom I already have a lot in common? Finally, the early disciples "devoted themselves . . . [to] prayers" to maintain a vital, communal connection with God. The church prayed when things were small, tough, and bleak in chapter 1. In chapter 2, they prayed as things were exciting, growing, and hopeful. The ministry context might change, but the prayers do

not. Are we a praying people? Do we set aside time personally and corporately to pray? These four activities are not God's burdens; they are his blessings. These "inspection points" should not expose and discourage us; they should show us what we are missing if we neglect them.

By God's design, this kind of church life fuels spiritual and numerical growth.

- God gives the church numerical growth (2:41, 47).

- God gives the church spiritual growth (2:42–47).

DISCUSSION QUESTIONS

1. What challenges does sudden and substantial growth create for a local congregation? Where are the stress points?

2. How can a local congregation keep teaching, fellowship, shared meals, and prayer in proper balance? What practical steps can it implement to do so?

3. How does the early church's approach to material possessions relate to Jesus's teaching on that topic? Does their practice provide grounds for advocating "Christian communism"? Why or why not?

4. How does active participation in the life of a local congregation promote spiritual growth among its members? How does it contribute to the congregation's witness for Christ?

5. Should the contemporary church expect the sort of exponential numerical growth the early church experienced? Why or why not? What can a congregation do to foster conversion growth rather than transfer growth?

Acts 3:1–26

EXEGETICAL IDEA
The healing of a lame man in the temple precincts provided Peter with an opportunity to preach about faith in Jesus, repentance, and judgment to the crowd that gathered.

THEOLOGICAL FOCUS
The proper response to Jesus's working through his witnesses is to turn from sin to God and experience the end-time blessings the OT promises.

PREACHING IDEA
The truth about Jesus demands a decision.

PREACHING POINTERS
It is impossible to remain neutral on the question of who Jesus is. When you face the truth about him, how will you respond? Will you reject him or accept him? How would the residents of Jerusalem respond when faced with the truth about Jesus? Peter's second sermon called them to make a decision about him and recognize the consequences of their decision. With Luke's original readers, we need to understand the seriousness of responding properly to the truth about Jesus and his continuing work through his followers, and we need to understand that the decision we make about him has eternal consequences.

People today should be able to relate to multiple facets of Acts 3:1–26. Most understand the challenges imposed by physical limitations. Many have experienced someone asking them for money. Local church leaders often find themselves answering requests for financial assistance from individuals in need. Joy at recovery from a serious illness is a common emotion, and questions often arise about miraculous recoveries from illness. Misperceptions of public figures are common, and actions based on ignorance abound. The passage corrects any suggestion that the natural laws of the universe limit God, or that human power or piety play any role in miraculous occurrences. It also corrects the ideas that Jesus is just another religious figure and that status as God's people comes from religious or ethnic heritage. The account commends an honest self-appraisal of our own spiritual condition, a willingness to turn from sin to God, an accurate understanding of who Jesus is, and confidence in the promises of Scripture. It also reinforces the importance of making the right decision about Jesus.

THE CHURCH'S FIRST HEALING (3:1–26)

LITERARY STRUCTURE AND THEMES (3:1–26)

The passage follows a sequence similar to chapter 2, with a narrative section (3:1–10; cf. 2:1–13) leading to a sermon (3:11–26; cf. 2:14–40). The following table highlights the parallel structure.

Pentecost	Sequence of Events	Temple Healing
2:1–4	God acts	3:1–8
2:5–13	Listeners respond with interest	3:9–10
2:14–40	The witness interprets	3:11–26
2:41	The gospel advances	4:4

The narrative section follows the general pattern of biblical narrative. Verses 1–3 set the *context*, using verbs in the imperfect tense to highlight the severity of the lame man's situation ($\dot{\alpha}\nu\acute{\epsilon}\beta\alpha\iota\nu\sigma\nu$ . . . $\dot{\epsilon}\beta\alpha\sigma\tau\acute{\alpha}\zeta\epsilon\tau\sigma$ . . . $\dot{\epsilon}\tau\acute{\iota}\theta\sigma\nu\nu$ . . . $\dot{\eta}\rho\acute{\omega}\tau\alpha$). Verses 4–5 recount the *rising action* involving Peter, using verbs in the aorist tense. The account reaches its *climax* in verse 6, where Peter pronounces the healing, and verbs in the present tense highlight the immediacy of the action ($\dot{\upsilon}\pi\acute{\alpha}\rho\chi\epsilon\iota$ . . . $\acute{\epsilon}\chi\omega$ . . . $\delta\acute{\iota}\delta\omega\mu\iota$ . . . $\pi\epsilon\rho\iota\pi\alpha\tau\epsilon\iota$). Verses 7–8 recount the *falling action* of the man's response, using verbs in the aorist tense. Verses 9–10 describe the *conclusion* of the episode, with the crowd's amazed response at the lasting results of the healing. Luke highlights those results by using the perfect tense ($\sigma\upsilon\mu\beta\epsilon\beta\eta\kappa\acute{\sigma}\tau\iota$).

After a transitional sentence (3:11), the sermon divides into three parts: (1) an apologetic explanation that Jesus healed the lame man in response to faith (3:12–16); (2) an evangelistic appeal to repent, turn to God, and experience the blessings the prophets promised (3:17–21); (3) an urgent warning that failure to respond would carry dire consequences (3:22–26). Direct address introduces the first two sections (3:12, 17). Occurrences of the verb $\dot{\alpha}\nu\acute{\iota}\sigma\tau\eta\mu\iota$ frame the third section (3:22, 26). References to God's servant frame the sermon as a whole (3:13, 26).

- ***Healing the Lame Man (3:1–10)***
- ***Explaining the Miracle (3:11–16)***
- ***Calling for Repentance (3:17–21)***
- ***Warning of Judgment (3:22–26)***

EXPOSITION (3:1–26)

Following the summary paragraph that describes the community life of the Jerusalem church (2:41–47), Luke introduces the first of six detailed accounts (3:1–26: 4:1–31; 5:1–11; 5:17–42; 6:1–7; 6:8–8:3) that alternate with two additional summary paragraphs (4:32–37; 5:12–16) and provide closer looks at the experiences of the early disciples. The current episode illustrates their continuing involvement at the temple (cf. 2:46), the wonders and signs that were taking place through the apostles (cf. 2:43), and the favor the disciples were having with all the people (cf. 2:47). A subsequent comment in 4:4 highlights the way in which the Lord was adding to the number of the disciples daily (cf. 2:47). As was true in his Pentecost sermon, Peter's apostolic teaching included key essentials of the gospel in the sermon that followed the healing of the lame man (cf. 2:42). Jesus himself had delivered those essentials to the apostles immediately before he ascended (Luke 24:44–49).

	Luke 24:44–49	Acts 2:14–41	Acts 3:11–26
According to Scripture	24:44–45	2:16–21, 25–28, 30–31, 34–35	3:18, 21, 22–25
Christ must suffer	24:46a	2:23	3:13b–15a, 18
Christ must rise	24:46b	2:24–32	3:15
Call to repentance	24:47	2:38a	3:19a
Promise of forgiveness	24:47	2:38b	3:19b
Promise of blessing	24:49	2:38c–39	3:19c–21

Peter again connected the events leading up to the healing as well as the healing itself to the last days (3:24; cf. 2:17). The Law and Prophets had predicted those events, including the fact that God would bring on the scene of history a Messiah who would fulfill the promises of God's covenant with Israel (3:18, 21, 22–25). Jesus was that Servant/Righteous One/Author of Life/Prophet/Seed of Abraham. Although the people and their leaders denied him and put him to death out of ignorance (3:13b–15a, 17), God had preselected Jesus as Messiah (3:20), raised him from the dead (3:16), and glorified him (3:13). It was faith in Jesus that made the healing possible (3:6, 16) and promised forgiveness of sins, times of refreshing, and the restoration of all things (3:19–21). If the people would turn to him, he would bless them and turn them from their evil ways (3:26). If not, he would utterly cut them off from being his covenant people (3:21).

Healing the Lame Man (3:1–10)

As Peter and John are entering the temple, Jesus's authority enables them to heal a man who has been lame from his birth.

3:1–3. In accordance with the disciples' practice of meeting daily in the temple (cf. 2:46), Peter and John were in the process of "going up" (ἀνέβαινον) to the temple when the next recorded episode in the life of the new community of disciples occurred. Luke notes the time as "at the hour of prayer" (ἐπὶ τὴν ὥραν τῆς προσευχῆς), specifically "the ninth" (τὴν ἐνάτην), which places the incident at three in the afternoon. Bruce notes that the stated hours of prayer were at daybreak, at the time of the afternoon sacrifice (3:00 p.m.), and at sunset (1990, 136). The ninth hour, therefore, was a natural time for large numbers of pious Jews to come to the temple and for the poor to expect them to show compassion by giving alms (cf. Tob. 4:6–11).

One such individual (τις ἀνήρ), who had been lame from birth (χωλὸς ἐκ κοιλίας μητρὸς αὐτοῦ ὑπάρχων), was carried (ἐβαστάζετο) and laid (ἐτίθουν) every day (καθ᾽ ἡμέραν) at one of the temple gates (πρὸς τὴν θύραν τοῦ ἱεροῦ). Since lameness excluded individuals from entering God's presence (Lev. 21:17–20), the man was there in order to ask for alms (αἰτεῖν ἐλεημοσύνην) from those who were entering (παρὰ τῶν εἰσπορευομένων). When he saw that Peter and John were about to enter (ἰδὼν Πέτρον καὶ Ἰωάννην μέλλοντας εἰσιέναι), it was natural for him to begin asking them for alms (ἠρώτα ἐλεημοσύνην λαβεῖν).

3:4–6. As Paul would do later in Lystra (14:9), Peter "fixed his gaze" (ἀτενίσας) upon the lame man. Was he able, as Paul was, to see that the lame man had the faith to be healed? Peter then commanded the man to give them his attention (βλέψον εἰς ἡμᾶς). Bock notes, "seeking the man's attention tells him that a response is coming, but it will not be what he expects" (2007, 161). Because he was expecting to receive something from them (προσδοκῶν τι παρ'

Saints Peter and John Healing the Lame Man by Nicolas Poussin. Public domain.

αὐτῶν λαβεῖν), the man began "looking at them eagerly" (NLT, ἐπεῖχεν). Peter's next words to the man are the high point of the paragraph (Schnabel 2012, 191). The NLT renders them as

> I don't have any silver or gold for you.
> But I'll give you what I have.
> In the name of Jesus Christ the Nazarene,
> get up and walk!

In contrast to the financial gift the man thought he needed because of his disability, Peter offered him the gift that he really needed: perfect health instead of his disability (3:16; cf. 4:10).

195). In Jesus's name (i.e., under his authority) his followers baptize (2:38; 10:48; 19:5); perform miracles (3:6; 4:7, 10, 30; 16:18; 19:13); and speak, preach, or teach (4:17, 18; 5:28, 40; 8:12; 9:27, 28). The emphasis on the miraculous is clearly in view in 3:1–10, but it is important to note that "healing does not take place because the right formula is pronounced, but because Jesus is acknowledged as the only source of help and salvation" (Peterson 2009, 169).

3:7–8. As proof of the healing, Peter took hold of the man (πιάσας αὐτον) by the right hand (τῆς δεξιᾶς χειρός) and raised him (ἤγειρεν αὐτόν). The healing was immediate (παραχρῆμα) and complete—both his feet (αἱ βάσεις αὐτοῦ) and his ankles (τὰ σφυδρά) were strengthened (ἐστερεώθησαν; divine passive). The man "jumped to his feet" (Culy and Parsons 2003, 53; ἐξαλλόμενος), "stood upright" (NASB, ἔστη), and began walking (περιεπάτει, inceptive imperfect). Then, he did what he had never been able to do: he entered the temple (εἰσῆλθεν εἰς τὸ ἱερόν). His entrance, however, was no ordinary entrance. Not only was he walking (περιπατῶν); he was leaping (ἁλλόμενος) and praising God (αἰνῶν τὸν θεόν).

The use of ἅλλομαι both here and in 14:10 echoes Isaiah 35:6, where the prophet includes "the lame will leap like a deer" (LXX, ἀλεῖται ὡς ἔλαφος ὁ χωλός) in his description of the messianic age (Larkin 1995, 65). The kingdom that had arrived with Jesus continued to invade time and space through the ministry of the apostles. Marshall comments, "The main point in the story is the continuing power of the name of Jesus to perform the same gracious and healing acts which were signs in the Gospels of the coming of the kingdom or rule of God" (1980, 86).

3:9–10. Schnabel notes that Hippocrates listed lameness among the conditions that permanently disabled a person (*Morb.* 1.1), and

therefore, the lame man would have been regarded as a hopeless case (2012, 197). When "all the people" (πᾶς ὁ λαός) who were present at the temple saw the man walking and praising God, "it began to dawn on them" (Culy and Parsons 2003, 53; ἐπεγίνωσκον) that he was the man whom they had previously seen sitting and begging every day outside the gate. As a result, they were filled with wonder and amazement (ἐπλήσηησαν θάμβος καὶ ἐκστάσεως), because of what had happened (ἐπὶ τῷ συμβεβηκότι) to the man.

Culy and Parsons note that the doublet θάμβος καὶ ἐκστάσεως emphasizes the crowd's "utter amazement" (2003, 54). The perfect tense of συμβεβηκότι highlights the lasting effects of the healing. As was true of the miracle of "other tongues" in the previous chapter, however, amazement at God's miraculous working was not faith. The miracle of healing still needed interpretation and a call for a decision. Larkin notes, "Witnessing miracles may contribute to a person's embrace of faith, but it cannot produce faith. That is why God's Word must now be preached" (1995, 66). Peter was up to the occasion.

Explaining the Miracle (3:11–16)
When he sees the crowd's amazement, Peter explains that Jesus healed the lame man in response to faith.

3:11–12a. Luke notes that the scene of the action shifted from the Beautiful Gate to Solomon's Portico (ἐπὶ τῇ στοᾷ τῇ καλουμένη Σολομῶντος), where Jesus had previously walked and taught (John 10:22), and where his followers subsequently met (5:12). The crowd's great surprise (ἔκθαμβοι) continued as they saw the former beggar clinging (κρατοῦντος) to Peter and John, and they ran together (συνέδραμεν) to where the apostles were (πρὸς αὐτούς). Once again, God had gathered an attentive audience for witness (cf. 2:12–13).

When he saw the audience, Peter seized the opportunity to address the people (ὁ Πέτρος ἀπεκρίνατο πρὸς τὸν λαόν). Barrett explains the use of ἀπεκρίνατο as Peter "answering the question implied by the crowd's amazement and mistaken supposition regarding the cause of the cure" (1994, 192).

Solomon's Portico

According to Josephus, Solomon's Portico was 650 feet long and 50 feet deep, had a double row of columns, and was located along the eastern side of the temple (*A.J.* 20.9.7; *B.J.* 5.5.1). A portico (στοά) was "the general purpose building of the Greeks. It offered shelter from sun, wind, and rain. It could be used as council-chamber or court-house, market-hall or class-room; and also for informal conversation" (*OCD*, 1016). The exact location in Herod's temple is uncertain. Acts 3:8 implies that Solomon's Portico was inside the temple (εἰσῆλθεν σὺν αὐτοῖς εἰς τὸ ἱερόν), which would place the location along the eastern side of the Court of the Women. A variant reading for Acts 3:11 in the Western text, however, has Peter and John leaving the temple before the crowd gathered (ἐκπορευομένου δὲ τοῦ Πέτρου καὶ Ἰωάννου), which would place the location along the eastern side of the Court of the Gentiles. Commentators strongly favor the latter location (Bock 2007, 167; Bruce 1990, 139; Larkin 1995, 66; Marshall 1980, 90; Peterson 2009, 172; Schnabel 2012, 183).

3:12b. As he did on the day of Pentecost (2:14), Peter addressed the crowd directly: "Men of Israel!" (Ἄνδρες Ἰσραηλῖται; cf. 2:22).

Also as he did on the day of Pentecost (2:15), Peter began by correcting the crowd's wrong understanding. Culy and Parsons note that his two questions (τί θαυμάζετε . . . τί ἀτενίζετε;) carry the force of rebukes: "You should not be surprised! You should not be staring at us!" (2003, 55). The crowd inferred

that Peter and John had caused the man to walk (πεποιηκόσιν τοῦ περιπατεῖν) either because they possessed special power (δυνάμει) or because they were so godly (εὐσεβείᾳ) that God had responded to their prayers in a special way (Marshall 1980, 90). The answer, however, was that God had been at work through Jesus, as Peter would soon make clear.

3:13–15. Before he presented the correct explanation for the miracle, Peter provided a christological perspective on the events that had led up to it. Just as the crowds now reached the wrong conclusion about the miracle, they had previously reached the wrong conclusion about Jesus. They had handed him over to Pilate (παρεδώκατε), they had denied him despite Pilate's decision to release him (ἠρνήσασθε κατὰ πρόσωπον Πιλάτου κρίναντος ἐκείνου ἀπολύειν), they had denied him by asking that Barabbas be given to them instead (ἠρνήσασθε καὶ ᾐτήσασθε ἄνδρα φονέα χαρισθῆναι ὑμῖν), and they had caused his death (ἀπεκτείνατε). They had failed to understand that Jesus was God's servant (τὸν παῖδα αὐτοῦ), the holy and righteous one (τὸν ἅγιον καὶ δίκαιον), and the author of life (τὸν ἀρχηγὸν τῆς ζωῆς), whom God glorified (ἐδόξασεν) by raising him from the dead (ὃν ὁ θεὸς ἤγειρεν ἐκ νεκρῶν).

Christological Titles in Peter's Sermon

Bock writes that "this speech is one of the most christologically rich addresses in Acts" (2005, 165). Three titles occur in 3:13–15; three more occur in later verses. There is general agreement that when Peter speaks of God glorifying "his servant, Jesus" (τὸν παῖδα αὐτοῦ Ἰησοῦν) in 3:13, he is invoking the OT servant figure of Isaiah 42:1–4 and 52:13–53:12 (Barrett 1994, 194). The same title also occurs in 4:27 and 4:30. Schnabel traces the parallels between Jesus and the servant (2012, 209).

	Jesus	Servant
Suffering/death	Acts 3:13–15, 18	Isa. 53:2–10
Resurrection/ glorification	Acts 3:15	Isa. 52:13
Forgiveness/ atonement	Acts 3:19–20	Isa. 53:5

The second title is "the righteous one" (τὸν δίκαιον) in 3:14, which both Bruce (1990, 141) and Bock (2007, 171) note was a messianic description in Judaism (2 Sam. 23:3; Isa. 53:1, 11; Zech. 9:9). The same title occurs in Acts 7:52 and 22:14. The third title is "the author of life" (τὸν ἀρχηγόν τῆς ζωῆς) in 3:15. The noun ἀρχηγός can carry three senses (BDAG s.v. "ἀρχηγός" 138): one who has a prominent position (leader), one who begins or originates (founder), and one who begins something that is the first in a series (pioneer). Peter applies the title to Jesus a second time in 5:31 with the sense of "leader." The author of Hebrews applies it to Jesus with the sense of "founder" (Heb. 2:10; 12:2). Although a different word occurs in Hebrews 6:20, that verse captures the idea of Jesus as our "pioneer." The fourth title is "his Messiah" (τὸν Χριστὸν αὐτοῦ) in 3:18, which occurs seven other times in its absolute form in Acts (2:31, 36; 4:26; 8:5; 9:22; 17:3; 26:23). Of particular interest are 4:26, which quotes Psalm 2 and is best translated "his anointed one," and 17:3, which speaks of Messiah suffering and uses wording similar to Peter's (τὸν Χριστὸν ἔδει παθεῖν). The fifth title is a "prophet" (προφήτην) like Moses in 3:22 (cf. 7:37). That title clearly had messianic overtones in the apostles' time (Luke 7:16; 24:19; John 1:21, 25; 6:14). The sixth title, although not directly applied to Jesus, is Abraham's seed (ἐν τῷ σπέρματί σου) in 3:25, a connection that Paul makes explicit in Galatians 3:16. About Peter's use of Genesis 22:18 here, Longenecker comments, "Peter proclaims that the promise to Abraham also has its ultimate fulfillment in Christ" (1981, 299).

3:16. Having established the historical and theological context, Peter moved to the ultimate explanation for the miracle. Although the syntax of the sentence is "awkward" (Peterson 2009, 176), Peter's point is clear: Jesus healed the man in response to faith. The faith came through Jesus (ἡ πίστις ἡ δι᾽ αὐτοῦ), who was also the object of faith (ἐπὶ τῇ πίστει τοῦ ὀνόματος αὐτοῦ). The evidence was that this man (τοῦτον), whom they could see (ὃν θεωρεῖτε), stood before all of them (ἀπέναντι πάντων ὑμῶν) in perfect health (τὴν ὁλοκληρίαν ταύτην). Culy and Parsons translate ἐπὶ τῇ πίστει as "in response to faith" (2003, 57); τοῦ ὀνόματος is an objective genitive (Bruce 1990, 142). As in verse 6, "his name" (τὸ ὄνομα αὐτοῦ) is a metonymy that is associated with Jesus and his authority. Schnabel notes, "The focus on Jesus's name and on faith implies an appeal to the audience. Peter challenges them to come to faith in Jesus . . . this appeal becomes explicit in vv. 17–21" (2012, 212).

Calling for Repentance (3:17–21)

Peter invites the crowd to turn from sin and turn to God, so that they can experience the blessings the prophets promised.

3:17–18. The combination of "and now" (καὶ νῦν) plus direct address (ἀδελφοί) marks a new section of Peter's speech, as he moved from an apologetic explanation of the healing to an evangelistic invitation based on the evidence he has provided. The use of "brothers" addressed his audience as fellow Jews rather than as fellow Christ-followers (cf. 2:29; contrast 1:16). Peter characterized what they had done previously (ἐπράξατε), as well as the actions of their leaders (ὥσπερ καὶ οἱ ἄρχοντες ὑμῶν), as taking place out of ignorance (κατὰ ἄγνοιαν). Schnabel writes, "their rejection of Jesus and of his message was not based on a genuine understanding of who he really was and how his message was an integral part of God's plan of salvation" (2012, 212). Although they acted in ignorance,

God used their actions to fulfill his plan in the way he intended (ὁ θεὸς … ἐπλήρωσεν οὕτως). God had "preannounced" the events of that plan through his prophets (ἃ προκατήγγειλεν διὰ στόματος πάντων τῶν προφητῶν), specifically that "his Christ would suffer" (παθεῖν τὸν Χριστὸν αὐτοῦ).

TEXTUAL ANALYSIS: "through the mouth of all his prophets"
Did Peter engage in hyperbole when he said that "all" the OT prophets (διὰ στόματος πάντων τῶν προφητῶν) predicted Jesus's suffering (Marshall 1980, 93), or was that phraseology simply another way of referring to the OT as a whole? Larkin notes that Jesus's suffering is mentioned by three of the major prophets (Isaiah, Jeremiah, Daniel) as well as by Zechariah, who is one of the minor prophets (1995, 68), and Peterson notes similar occurrences in the book of Psalms (2009, 179). Jesus himself said that the Law of Moses, the Prophets, and the Psalms all wrote that the Christ would suffer and rise (Luke 24:44–47; cf. Luke 24:25, 27). Rather than viewing the phrase as hyperbole, it seems more natural to understand it as referring to the many places in which the OT predicted Messiah's suffering.

3:19–21. Because the crowd had acted out of ignorance, there was still hope for them. So, Peter issued a two-part invitation and extended a three-part promise. As the logical response to the truth about Jesus that Peter has just presented (οὖν), they needed to turn from sin (μετανοήσατε; cf. 2:38; 8:22; 17:30) and turn to God (ἐπιστρέψατε; cf. 9:35; 11:21; 14:15; 15:19). Both verbs are aorist imperatives that call for immediate, decisive action (cf. 26:20). Elsewhere in Luke-Acts, repentance (μετάνοια/ μετανοέω) leads to forgiveness of sins (Luke 3:3; 24:47; Acts 2:38; 5:31) and is demonstrated through action (Luke 3:8). Ἐπιστρέφω denotes "a radical reorientation of life, turning back to God to seek reconciliation and express obedience" (Peterson 2009, 179).

If they would respond to the invitation, Peter extended the promise of three blessings. First, their sins would be "wiped away" (εἰς τὸ ἐξαλειφθῆναι ὑμῶν τὰς ἁμαρτίας). Bock writes that ἐξαλείφω describes an obliteration that leaves no trace (2007, 175). In this context, the promise is the complete forgiveness of sins by God (divine passive). Second, "seasons of refreshing" (καιροὶ ἀναψύξεως) would come. In this context, the promise is the experience of spiritual refreshment (Bock 2007, 176; Larkin 1995, 68). Schnabel suggests that this second promise might well correlate with the ministry of the Holy Spirit in the present time (2012, 215). Third, God would send to them Jesus, his "preselected Messiah" (τὸν προκεχειρισμένον … Χριστόν), who will bring about the "restoration of all things" (ἀποκαταστάσεως πάντων). In this context, the promise is the perfect restoration of God's intended order on earth at Jesus's return, just as God spoke through the prophets (ἐλάλησεν ὁ θεὸς διὰ στόματος τῶν … προφητῶν). Until that return, "heaven holds Jesus at God's right side" (Bock 2007, 177; ὃν δεῖ οὐρανόν δέξασθαι). It is possible, therefore, to see a Trinitarian framework to the promises— forgiveness by the Father, refreshing by the Spirit, and restoration by the Son.

Warning of Judgment (3:22–26)

Peter urges the crowd to respond in obedience to Jesus, God's prophet and servant, or be excluded from God's covenant people.

3:22–26. Having already invoked the prophets twice in the preceding section (3:18, 21), Peter next moved to specific OT evidence that supported his call to action. Uses of ἀνίστημι (ἀναστήσει in v. 22 and ἀναστήσας in v. 26) frame the section, with the sense of "to bring on the stage of human history" (Larkin 1995, 69; Marshall 1980, 96). Longenecker notes that Peter defined his argument against the context of three great Jewish leaders—Moses, David, and Abraham—(1981, 298), and Schnabel notes that Peter invoked both the Law and the Prophets in support of his argument (2012, 218).

The logic of Peter's argument moved through four steps, with the application included in a combined quotation from Deuteronomy 18:19 and Leviticus 23:29. First, Moses spoke of a prophetic figure whom God would bring on the stage of human history (3:22; προφήτην ὑμῖν ἀναστήσει κύριος ὁ θεός). Second, all the prophets beginning with Samuel (πάντες οἱ προφῆται ἀπὸ Σαμουήλ) announced the events of "these days" (3:24; κατήγγειλαν τὰς ἡμέρας ταύτας). Third, the promises Peter invoked were intended for his listeners as the sons of the prophets and the sons of the covenant (3:25; ὑμεῖς ἐστε οἱ υἱοὶ τῶν προπητῶν καὶ τῆς διαθήκης). Fourth, God raised up and sent his servant (ἀναστήσας ὁ θεὸς τὸν παῖδα αὐτοῦ ἀπέστειλεν), Jesus, to bless them by turning each one of them from their evil ways (3:26; εὐλογοῦντα ὑμᾶς ἐν τῷ ἀποστρέθειν ἕκαστον ἀπὸ τῶν πονηριῶν ὑμῶν).

It was, therefore, essential for his listeners to "hear" Jesus (αὐτοῦ ἀκούσεσθε). Otherwise, they would be cut off (ἐξολεθρευθήσεται) from God's people (3:23). Ἀκούσεσθε is an imperatival future that issues a command the listeners are obligated to obey (Schnabel 2012, 218). Ἐξολεθρευθήσεται denotes "to eliminate by destruction, *destroy utterly*" (BDAG s.v. "ἐξολεθρεύω" 351; emphasis original) and points to the totality of the judgment that failure to respond brings (Bock 2007, 179). Τὰς ἡμέρας ταύτας refers to the end-time events they were experiencing—including Jesus's resurrection, his ascension, and the Spirit's coming (Barrett 1994, 211). With rhetorical polish, Peter concluded his message by returning to the idea of God's servant. Jesus, the servant who healed the lame man (3:13), was also the servant God had sent to turn Israel from its evil ways (3:26).

THEOLOGICAL FOCUS

The narratival function of Acts 3:1–26 is to illustrate the impact Jesus's miraculous working through his followers had on the residents of Jerusalem. As a result of the Holy Spirit's coming at Pentecost and Peter's first sermon on that summer morning, the community of disciples had exploded from 120 to more than three thousand (2:1–40). Their common life was characterized by instruction, fellowship, shared meals, and prayer (2:42), as well as wonders and signs that made a significant impact within the city (2:43). What sort of wonders and signs occurred, how did the residents of Jerusalem respond, and how did the disciples explain those events? Luke records the events surrounding the miraculous healing of a man who had been lame from birth as a specific example of how God used that healing to accelerate the growth of the Jerusalem church.

Theologically, Acts 3:1–26 provides a detailed presentation of the apostolic teaching about Jesus and sets out the consequences of possible responses to the truth about him. As Bock notes, the passage combines Christology, soteriology, and eschatology (2007, 182). The christological truth about Jesus is that he is God's servant, the righteous one, the author of life, the Messiah, the prophet whom Moses had promised, and the seed of Abraham. The soteriological truth about Jesus is that by dying, rising, and ascending he makes it possible for God to blot out our sins and turn us from our evil ways. The eschatological truth about Jesus is that he has inaugurated the last days in which the Holy Spirit provides refreshing for our souls, while Jesus waits in heaven to come again and restore perfectly God's intended order on earth. Two contrasting responses to that truth lead to drastically different consequences. On the one hand, ignorance and rejection result in final judgment. On the other hand, repentance and faith result in abundant blessing. The truth about Jesus demands a decision and makes an eternal difference.

PREACHING AND TEACHING STRATEGIES

Exegetical/Theological Synthesis

Luke's first-century readers would have wanted to know more about how Jesus continued to work through his followers. How would the other residents of Jerusalem respond to what he was doing? How would his followers take advantage of the opportunity for witness that his working presented? Luke's account of the healing of the lame man and Peter's subsequent sermon answers both questions. As was true at Pentecost, Jesus's miraculous working again attracted the amazed attention of the crowds and opened the door for witness. Peter seized the opportunity; presented the truth about faith in Jesus, repentance, and judgment; and called for a response from his listeners. With the original audience, the twenty-first-century audience shares the need to recognize and respond to Messiah Jesus, who is—in the words of A. B. Simpson's "fourfold gospel"—savior (3:19), sanctifier (3:26), healer (3:16), and coming king (3:21). They also need to understand that neutrality is impossible and that their response makes an eternal difference. To be specific, the proper response to Jesus's working through his witnesses is to turn from sin to God and experience the end-time blessings the OT promises.

Preaching/Teaching Idea

The truth about Jesus demands a decision.

Contemporary Connections

What does it mean?

There are two components to this text's teaching idea: the truth about Jesus and the decision he demands. Once again, the truth about Jesus is front and center. Peter's sermon is dripping with Jesus. The miraculous healing, like all miracles, was important inasmuch as it attested to the reality of Jesus (cf. 2:22). As shown above, both of Peter's sermons in Acts 2 and 3 reflect Jesus's

teaching in Luke 24. All three passages give scriptural proof of Jesus, speak of Jesus's suffering and death, and testify to Jesus's resurrection. To the weight of truth about Jesus, Peter adds six wonderful titles for Jesus. The sermon never strays from its focus on Jesus—and for good reason. It is the reality of Jesus prophesied, come, crucified, resurrected, reigning, and coming again that turns Peter's words from a history lesson to a galvanizing call to respond. The explanation for the miracle and the one behind the miracle turns into a direct evangelistic appeal to the crowd (3:17–21) and an urgent warning if they do not (3:22–26). There are no neutral observers in the crowd who can "unsee" a lame man healed or "unhear" the call of Jesus to follow. As the writer to the Hebrews pleads, "Today, if you hear his voice, do not harden your hearts as in the rebellion" (Heb. 3:15).

Is it true?

In a sense, this healing "invaded" the community, shook up an unsuspecting audience, and pressed them for radical change as soon as possible. For all their lives, it was business as usual: get up, work, head to the temple, give alms to the lame, pray, work, sleep, repeat. No one asked for a change in that routine, *not even the man born lame*. It was wholly outside their wildest imagination that things could be different. When Peter and John spoke "in the name of Jesus Christ of Nazareth," healed a hopeless disability, and pointed the crowd to the source, everything changed. It upturned money-changing tables in the hearts of every person there that day. They would leave changed. They would leave either running toward Jesus or running away from him.

There is a nugget of tremendous gospel symbolism here in the story. This unnamed man was born lame and had lived that way for more than forty years (4:22). For his entire life, he could not participate in traditional temple worship (cf. Lev. 21:17–20). He watched "daily" (3:2) as friends, family, and neighbors entered the temple before God, while he waited outside. Jesus changed that. The finished work of Jesus, the power in his name, the servants he commissioned to testify to him now greeted this man, witnessed to him, and healed him. He was then able to do what he had never done physically or spiritually in this way: he approached the throne of God. He rushed into the brick-and-mortar temple on earth even as he drew near with confidence to the heavenly throne of grace (cf. Heb. 4:16).

Now what?

Our postmodern culture resists any claim to absolute truth in the spiritual realm. It is anathema to tell others that their feelings about god or gods are wrong. We vehemently protect the code "to live and let live" and are ready to shout down any opposition. Sadly, this tendency pervades the church too. We have heard Christians dismiss evangelism and missions simply stating, "We have our religion, let them have theirs." It shocks our postmodern sensibilities to listen in to Peter and John so passionately plead with this crowd to repent and turn lest they perish.

Do I believe the truth about Jesus? Do I believe that the truth about him demands an eternal decision to resist or to follow? The enormous suffering to follow in the pages of Acts and early church history, inflicted upon men and women who were faithful to preach this truth, makes little sense outside the desperate reality of Jesus. For Peter and John to interrupt a pious temple crowd known to demand the death of rebels, to identify themselves with one such rebel Jesus not two months crucified, and to press for a decision to follow him, will only possibly make sense if what they are saying is true.

Creativity in Presentation

Do not let the opening act upstage the main event. Many bands have made the embarrassing mistake of inviting a superior performer to open and warm up the crowd, only to have the opening act outshine them. Think about Garth Brooks as the lead for the Judds or Rage Against the Machine for U2. The up-and-coming Led Zeppelin was so popular and powerful that headlining bands simply stopped showing up to play after them. There is a way in our minds and in our sermons to let the healing upstage the Healer—to make more of the healing of a man born lame than the pronouncement of forgiveness of sins. Jesus made this point himself when he healed the paralytic in Matthew 9.

A creative presentation of this text might include a dramatic telling of the healing. Describe the midafternoon gathering at the temple of Jews to pray and the needy to beg. There is compassion in Peter and John stopping and engaging the lame man. They learned well from Jesus. The healing is so miraculous that it seems to surprise Luke himself in retelling it. He tells us three times that this forty-plus-year-old man is now actually walking for the first time.

The healing is the opener. There is actually greater news in store than a miraculous healing. We must make as much of Jesus as Peter does. One way is to show the core elements of the gospel story that are now being repeated for a third time—first in Luke 24, then in Acts 2, and now in Acts 3. Another approach would be to savor the six christological titles of Jesus that Peter mentioned: God's servant, the righteous one, the author of life, Messiah, prophet, and Abraham's seed. Each title gives us a nuanced perspective on how marvelous Jesus is.

It would be hard to resist ending with the symbolism of this man healed physically and spiritually. As mentioned above, he was experiencing physically in his proximity outside the temple what everyone experiences spiritually outside fellowship with God. His physical healing allowed him for the first time ever to "Enter his gates with thanksgiving, and his courts with praise" (Ps. 100:4). His spiritual healing in conversion allowed him to do the same.

The truth about Jesus demands a decision.

- The truth about Jesus (3:1–16).

- The decision over Jesus (3:17–26).

DISCUSSION QUESTIONS

1. Taken in isolation, do Peter's words to the lame man suggest that Jesus's followers should not be concerned with the physical and material needs of those around them? What passages elsewhere in Acts might provide complementary evidence?

2. Based on the events recounted in Acts 3, what are the marks of an authentic NT healing miracle? Should the contemporary church expect to see Jesus perform similar miracles through his followers?

3. What elements does Peter's second sermon have in common with his first? What elements are omitted? What elements are added?

4. Does Peter's sermon suggest that ignorance is an acceptable reason for rejecting Jesus? If so, is it better not to share the gospel and leave people in their ignorance? If not, why does Peter seem to excuse his listeners for their ignorance?

5. Why does Peter focus on his listeners as sons of the prophets and sons of the covenant? Why are the teachings of the Law and the Prophets particularly important in that respect? How can contemporary witnesses contextualize Peter's approach when sharing the gospel with others?

Acts 4:1–31

EXEGETICAL IDEA

The healing and sermon in the temple precincts lead to arrest, examination, warning, release, and united prayer for continuing bold witness.

THEOLOGICAL FOCUS

God sustains and empowers his people when they encounter opposition.

PREACHING IDEA

Human opposition opens divine doors of opportunity.

PREACHING POINTERS

If something is truly important, it is seldom easy. When Jesus promised to build his church, he did not promise that it would be an easy process. In fact, he told his disciples repeatedly that they would encounter opposition. Sometimes, the opposition would come from religious authorities; at other times, it would come from civil authorities; at still other times, it would come from members of their own families. Whatever the source, opposition would come, just as it came to the Jerusalem church in Acts 4. The healing of the lame man at the Beautiful Gate and Peter's sermon in Solomon's Portico led both to salvation of the powerless multitudes and to opposition from the powerful few. With Luke's original readers, we need to know how Jesus's early disciples responded when they encountered opposition, and we need to understand that opposition opens doors of opportunity to trust God, rely on the Holy Spirit, and witness boldly for Jesus.

People today should be able to relate to several elements of Luke's account in Acts 4:1–31. Religious persecution occurs in various forms around the world. Arrests and trials feature prominently in news stories. Warnings and threats of various sorts are common occurrences. Christians are familiar with prayer meetings, including meetings called to address special needs. The passage corrects the idea that Christians will never encounter opposition, or that such opposition is somehow outside of God's control. It also corrects the suggestion that effective witness requires formal education or training. It provides balance to a rigid interpretation of Romans 13:1–7 that might advocate for absolute obedience to authority regardless of the circumstances or demands. The account commends trust in God's providence, reliance on the Holy Spirit when facing difficult circumstances, and the importance of prayer.

THE CHURCH'S FIRST OPPOSITION (4:1–31)

LITERARY STRUCTURE AND THEMES (4:1–31)

The passage narrates the events that follow the healing of the lame man and Peter's subsequent sermon (3:1–26). Those events unfold in four scenes. First, members of the priestly establishment arrest Peter and John and take them into custody overnight (4:1–4). Second, the Jewish ruling council examines the apostles, who respond with a clear witness for Jesus (4:5–12). Third, unable to refute the apostles' explanation of the miracle, the council warns the apostles not to continue teaching in Jesus's name and releases them (4:13–22). Both the second and third scenes include segments of dialogue between the council members and the apostles. Barrett suggests that the passage reaches its climax in verses 19–20 with the apostles' bold declaration that they must obey God rather than the council (1994, 218). Finally, when the apostles report to the Christian community, God answers their prayer for bold witness with a fresh filling of the Holy Spirit (4:23–31). The fourth scene concludes not only the opposition episode of 4:1–22 but also the events of 3:1–4:31 as a whole.

- *Arrest and Confinement (4:1–4)*
- *Examination and Defense (4:5–12)*
- *Warning and Release (4:13–22)*
- *Report and Prayer (4:23–31)*

EXPOSITION (4:1–31)

Just as Peter's sermon at Solomon's Portico followed closely on the healing of the lame man, so the events of Acts 4 followed closely on his sermon and introduced a new aspect of the Jerusalem church's experience: opposition from the Jewish authorities. Several repeated motifs underline the close connection between chapters 3 and 4: the name of Jesus (3:6, 16; 4:7, 10, 12, 17, 18, 31), Jesus as God's servant (3:13, 26; 4:27, 30) and Messiah (3:18, 20; 4:27), the evidence of the healing sign (3:9–12, 16; 4:10, 14, 22), and the elements of the apostolic witness (3:13–21; 4:8–12). Following Joachim Jeremias, Longenecker notes that Jewish legal procedure required a warning to individuals without rabbinic training before punishing them (1981, 300). The examination before the Jewish ruling council in chapter 4 constituted the warning phase, while the second arrest in chapter 5 would be the punishment stage when, after Gamaliel argued against killing the apostles, the council ordered them to be beaten (cf. 5:33–40).

The backdrop for the episode was Jesus's promise that he would give his followers words and wisdom to speak when brought before opponents for his sake (Luke 21:12–15). In response to the threats of the council at their first hearing, the apostles and the disciples responded with bold proclamation (4:8–12), fixed purpose (4:19–20), and united prayer (4:24–30). Their prayer was rooted in God's sovereign control over creation and its inhabitants (4:24b), the widespread opposition to God and his Messiah that would arise (4:25–26), and the circumstances they were experiencing in Jerusalem (4:27–28). God answered their prayers by manifesting his presence with them, filling them with the Holy Spirit, and granting them boldness for continuing witness (4:31). As Larkin writes, "The messengers are unstoppable. The mission continues with divine momentum" (1995, 81).

Arrest and Confinement (4:1–4)

Alarmed by the apostles' teaching in the temple precincts, members of the priestly establishment arrest Peter and John and take them into custody until the next day.

4:1–2. The genitive absolute Luke uses to begin the paragraph (λαλούντων αὐτῶν πρὸς τὸν λαόν) can be understood in either of two ways. Culy and Parsons suggest that the Jewish leaders interrupted Peter (2003, 64; cf. Bock 2007, 186; Peterson 2009, 187). Barrett argues that Peter had finished his speech and John had joined in conversation with the crowds (1994, 218). In either case, there is a close connection to the preceding action. Members of the priestly establishment approached Peter and John. The verb ἐπέστησαν suggests hostile intent (Schnabel 2012, 233).

They acted because they could no longer put up with the apostles' actions (διαπονούμενοι; cf. 16:18; Barrett 1994, 219). From their perspective, the problem was threefold. First, Peter and John were teaching the people within the temple precincts (διὰ τὸ διδάσκειν αὐτοὺς τὸν λαόν), which usurped the priests' role (Peterson 2009, 187). Second, the apostles were doing so based on the authority of Jesus (καταγγέλλειν ἐν τῷ Ἰησοῦ), whom the leaders had recently condemned to death (Schnabel 2012, 234). Third, they were proclaiming the resurrection from the dead (τὴν ἀνάστασιν τὴν ἐκ νεκρῶν), which was contrary to Sadducean orthodoxy (Longenecker 1981, 302).

4:3–4. The temple guard arrested (ἐπέβαλον αὐτοῖς τὰς χεῖρας) Peter and John. Because it was already evening (ἦν ἑσπέρα ἤδη), they took the apostles into custody (ἔθεντο εἰς τήρησιν) until the next day (εἰς τὴν αὔριον). The response of many (πολλοί) in the crowd stood in sharp contrast to the response of the priestly establishment, however. They heard the word (ἀκουσάντων τὸ λόγον), and about five thousand believed (ἐπίστευσαν; cf. 2:44) it. Luke does not record either the charges against the apostles or the location where they were held.

Both the "word" (6:7; 8:4, 14, 25; 10:44; 11:1, 19; 12:24; 13:5, 7, 26, 44, 46, 48, 49; 14:25; 15:5, 35, 36; 16:6, 32; 17:11, 13; 18:11; 19:10, 20; 20:35) and those who "believe" (8:12–13; 9:42; 11:21; 13:12, 48–49; 14:1; 15:7; 17:12, 34; 18:8, 27; 19:2, 4) become key themes in the rest of Acts.

Commentators differ on the best understanding of the number Luke mentions (ἐγενήθη ὁ ἀριθμὸς τῶν ἀνδρῶν ὡς χιλιάδες πέντε). Does the number describe five thousand new converts (Bock 2007, 188), or does it describe growth from three thousand to five thousand disciples (Larkin 1995, 72)? Does the number include men only (Barrett 1994, 222), or does it include both men and women (Peterson 2009, 188)? Uses of ἀριθμός in 6:7 and 16:5 suggest that Luke most likely intended Theophilus to understand "total number." Where Luke describes both males and females, he uses the construction ἄνδρες τε καὶ γυναῖκες (5:14; 8:12; 17:12).

The Jerusalem Opposition

Luke introduces the Jewish opposition in Jerusalem in three verses. Members of the priestly establishment appear in 4:1. The priests (οἱ ἱερεῖς) were Levites who were responsible for the temple ritual (Josephus, *B.J.* 2.15.4). The captain of the temple guard (ὁ στρατηγὸς τοῦ ἱεροῦ) was a high-ranking Levite who commanded the police force responsible for maintaining order in the temple precincts (Josephus, *A.J.* 20.6.2). The Sadducees (οἱ Σαδδουκαῖοι) were members of the priestly aristocracy who viewed only the Mosaic Law as authoritative and denied the resurrection (Josephus, *B.J.* 2.8.14; *A.J.* 13.5.9; 13.10.6; 18.1.4). The members of the ruling council appear in Acts 4:5. That ruling council was the Sanhedrin (τό Συνέδριον) and had jurisdiction over noncapital cases. It consisted of the chief priest, who presided (Josephus, *A.J.* 20.9.1), and seventy other members (Josephus, *A.J.* 14.9.4) from three groups. The rulers (οἱ ἄρχοντες) were members of the high priestly family (Josephus, *B.J.* 2.14.8); the elders (οἱ πρεσβύτεροι) were powerful lay leaders (Josephus, *B.J.* 2.15.2; 2.17.3); the scribes (οἱ γραμματεῖς) were professional teachers and interpreters of the OT Scriptures (Josephus, *B.J.* 6.5.3). Individuals of special prominence from the high priestly family (ἐκ γένους ἀρχιερατικοῦ) appear in Acts 4:6. Annas (Ἄννας) had been the high priest from A.D. 6–15 (Josephus, *A.J.* 18.2.1; 20.9.2). Caiaphas (Καϊάφας) was Annas's son-in-law and the high priest from A.D. 18–36 (Josephus, *A.J.* 18.2.2; 18.4.3). John (Ἰωάννης) was most likely Jonathan, Annas's son, who would become the high priest from A.D. 36–37 (Josephus, *A.J.* 18.4.3). Alexander (Ἀλέξανδρος) is unknown.

Examination and Defense (4:5–12)

In response to questioning by the ruling council, the apostles affirm that healing and salvation are available only in Jesus's name.

4:5–7. On the next day (ἐπὶ τὴν αὔριον), the ruling council—chaired by the high priest and consisting of seventy additional members from the high-priestly family, the elders of the people, and the professional teachers of the OT law—convened to examine the apostles. The council caused the apostles to stand (στήσαντες αὐτούς) in the open center space of the semicircle (ἐν τῷ μέσῳ) and began the process of examining them (ἐπυνθάνοντο, inceptive imperfect). The issue before the council was the miraculous healing that had occurred on the previous day, and they asked what they perceived to be the crucial question about the miracle: "By what power or by what name did you do this?" (ἐν ποίᾳ δυνάμει ἢ ἐν ποίῳ ὀνόματι ἐποιήσατε τοῦτο ὑμεῖς;).

There were similar councils in other cities of Israel, but in Jerusalem (ἐν Ἰερουσαλήμ), the council met in a hall in the temple precincts and sat in a semicircle facing the high priest (m. Sanh. 4:3). The council was "charged with distinguishing between truth and error

in the Jewish religion" (Larkin 1995, 72). The council's explicit question echoed the crowd's implied question (3:12), focused on the apostles' claim that it was Jesus's name that made the healing possible (3:10, 16), and raised the priestly establishment's central concern: the source of the authority (ἐν ποίῳ ὀνόματι) that was the basis for their actions. "Name" (ὄνομα) was, again, a metonymy for authority and, so, linked "the effect of the miracle-working power (δύναμις) with a particular person whose name was invoked during the healing" (Schnabel 2021, 237). In response to their question, Peter would fulfill Jesus's promise of Spirit-empowered witness for the third time (cf. Acts 1:8).

4:8–9. Luke specifically highlights the fact that Peter's answer to the council's question was a result of the Spirit's filling (πλησθεὶς πνεύματος ἁγίου). It is the second of eight mentions of the Spirit's filling in Acts (2:4; 4:31; 6:3, 5; 7:55; 9:17; 11:24; 13:9). The subtext is Jesus's promise that he would give his followers words and wisdom to speak when brought before opponents for his sake (Luke 21:12–15). After a polite address (ἄρχοντες τοῦ λαοῦ καὶ πρεσβύτεροι), Peter began "by reframing the council's question" (Larkin 1995, 73). He replaced their neutral "this thing" (τοῦτο) with the positive "concerning a good deed done to a crippled man" (ἐπὶ εὐεργεσίᾳ ἀνθρώπου ἀσθενοῦς), which echoed Jesus's question about another good deed done on behalf of another crippled person (Luke 6:9). Peter also described the good deed in terms of deliverance from a desperate physical condition (ἐν τίνι οὗτος σέσωται), which echoed Jesus's description as well (ψυχὴν σῶσαι ἢ ἀπολέσαι) and began a wordplay he would complete in verse 12 (ἐν ᾧ δεῖ σωθῆναι ἡμᾶς).

4:10. If it is true that the good deed was the reason they were being examined (εἰ ἡμεῖς σήμερον ἀνακρινόμεθα), it was imperative that both the council and all the people of Israel know the answer (γνωστὸν ἔστω πᾶσιν ὑμῖν καὶ παντὶ τῷ λαῷ Ἰσραήλ). The answer is clear: the man was healed "by means of the name of Jesus Christ the Nazarene" (ἐν τῷ ὀνόματι Ἰησοῦ Χριστοῦ τοῦ Ναζωραίου). It is by this means (ἐν τούτῳ) that the man stood before them in good health (οὗτος παρέστηκεν ἐνώπιον ὑμῶν ὑγιής). The perfect tense of παρέστηκεν highlights the permanent state of the man's healing. To that declaration, Peter adds the "kerygmatic core" of the apostolic witness (Dunn 1996, 53), including Messiah's suffering (4:10; cf. 2:23; 3:18) and resurrection (4:10; cf. 2:24; 3:15), the support of the OT Scriptures (4:11; cf. 2:17–21, 3:22–25), and the promise of divine blessing (4:12; cf. 2:38–39; 3:19–21).

4:11–12. The OT support comes from Psalm 118:22, a verse Jesus himself cited to underline the seriousness of rejecting him when he was questioned about the authority he had to teach the people in the temple (Luke 20:1–2, 17–18). The promised blessing was salvation (σωτηρία), a key idea in Acts (σωτηρία occurs six times; σῴζω occurs thirteen times; σωτήρ occurs twice). In verse 9, salvation referred to deliverance from a desperate physical condition; in verse 12, it refers to deliverance from a desperate spiritual condition. In both cases, salvation was available only through the stone they had previously rejected (οὐκ ἔστιν ἐν ἄλλῳ οὐδενὶ ἡ σωτηρία).

Peter's concluding statement highlighted Jesus as the exclusive source of salvation in three ways. First, "no other name under heaven" (οὐδὲ ὄνομά ἐστιν ὑπὸ τὸν οὐρανόν) rules out any other religious system as offering a possible way of salvation. Second, the divine passive of "that has been given to human being" (τὸ δεδομένον ἐν ἀνθρώποις) emphasizes the one true God as the source of salvation. Third, "by which it is necessary to be saved" (ἐν ᾧ δεῖ σωθῆναι) underlines God's sovereign stipulation that salvation is available only by faith in Jesus.

Warning and Release (4:13–22)

After the ruling council warns them to stop teaching in Jesus's name, the apostles declare that they must obey God rather than men.

4:13–14. Peter's answer to the council's question forced them to grapple with four factors. The apostles spoke with confidence (τὴν τοῦ Πέτρου παρρησίαν καὶ Ἰωάννου). They had no formal theological training (καταλαβόμενοι ὅτι ἄνθρωποι ἀγράμματοί εἰσιν καὶ ἰδιῶται). They had spent time with Jesus (ἐπεγίνωσκόν αὐτοὺς ὅτι σὺν τῷ Ἰησοῦ ἦσαν). The healed man stood before them (τὸν ἄνθρωπον βλέποντες σὺν αὐτοῖς ἑστῶτα τὸν τεθεραπευμένον). In the face of the evidence, "they could find no answer" (NJB, οὐδὲν εἶχον ἀντειπεῖν).

For Luke, παρρησία ("confidence" or "boldness") describes "the prophetic compulsion and divine enabling to speak the truth about God" (Peterson 2009, 194). That enabling will appear again in 4:31 as a product of the Spirit's filling, and it repeatedly describes Paul's proclamation (9:27, 28; 13:46; 14:3; 18:26; 19:8; 26:26; 28:31). The combination of ἀγράμματοί . . . καὶ ἰδιῶται describes the apostles as untrained laymen who would not be expected to carry on a sustained theological discussion (Longenecker 1981, 306). Ἀγράμματος describes a person "who has not acquired a formal education" (L&N §27.23), and ἰδιώτης describes a person "who has not acquired systematic information or expertise in [a] field of knowledge or activity" (L&N §27.26). Although Jesus had no formal training, he had been widely acknowledged as "Teacher" (Luke 7:40; 9:38; 10:25; 11:45; 12:13; 18:18; 19:39; 20:21, 28, 39; 21:7), and he had clearly prepared the apostles well for their mission. The perfect tense of τεθεραπευμένον again reinforces the accomplished fact of the healing. The reasons the council members could find no answer became clear in their private deliberations.

4:15–17. The council dismissed the apostles from the meeting room (κελεύσαντες δὲ αὐτοὺς ἔξω τοῦ συνεδρίου ἀπελθεῖν) and began an extended time of debate (συνέβαλλον πρὸς ἀλλήλους). They found themselves facing a dilemma and asking, "What shall we do with these men?" (τί ποιήσωμεν τοῖς ἀνθρώποις τούτοις;). On the one hand, they could not deny (οὐ δυνάμεθα ἀρνεῖσθαι) that an "extraordinary sign" (γνωστὸν σημεῖον) had taken place through the apostles (γέγονεν δι' αὐτῶν). That fact was obvious (φανερόν) to all the residents of Jerusalem (πᾶσιν τοῖς κατοικοῦσιν Ἰερουσαλήμ).

Elsewhere, σημεῖον denotes a miraculous act that authenticates a messenger God has sent (Luke 11:16, 29; Acts 2:22; 6:8; 8:13; 14:3). Clearly, the council members were unwilling to view the healing in that way. On the other hand, they did not want this new teaching to spread any further among the people (ἵνα μὴ ἐπὶ πλεῖον διανεμηθῇ εἰς τὸν λαόν). Judicially, there was no reason to convict the apostles; politically, there was every reason to acquit them (Larkin 1995, 77). They chose, however, to follow a middle course (Schnabel 2012, 215) and warn the apostles "to speak no more to any man in this name" (NASB, μηκέτι λαλεῖν ἐπὶ τῷ ὀνόματι τούτῳ μηδενὶ ἀνθρώπων). The verb translated "let us warn" (ἀπειλησώμεθα) carries the sense of threatening someone with something (BDAG s.v. "ἀπειλέω" 100).

Luke provides no explanation of how he knew the details of the closed deliberations. Bock lists Paul, Nicodemus, and Joseph of Arimathea as potential sources suggested by others (2007, 197). Marshall notes that, regardless of the source(s), the council's remarks when the apostles return reflect the deliberations that took place while they were absent (1980, 102).

4:18–20. The council members recalled the apostles (καλέσαντες αὐτούς) and announced their verdict: Peter and John were "not to speak or teach at all in the name of Jesus" (τὸ καθόλου μὴ φθέγγεσθαι μηδὲ διδάσκειν ἐπὶ τῷ ὀνόματι τοῦ Ἰησοῦ). Καθόλου carries the sense of "under no condition" (Culy and Parsons 2003, 72). Peter and John's response included an implicit request and an explicit rejection. Their request for the council to reverse its decision was worded as a rhetorical question: "Do you think God wants us to obey you rather than him?" (NLT, εἰ δίκαιόν ἐστιν ἐνώπιον τοῦ θεοῦ ὑμῶν ἀκούειν μᾶλλον ἢ τοῦ θεοῦ:). Their rejection of the decision was worded as statement of conscience: "We cannot stop telling about everything we have seen and heard" (NLT, οὐ δυνάμεθα ἡμεῖς ἃ εἴδαμεν καὶ ἠκούσαμεν μὴ λαλεῖν).

Bruce notes that by using μή with the present infinitives (φθέγγεσθαι and διδάσκειν) the council issued a command "to stop doing something they had already begun to do" (1990, 155). Ἡμεῖς in the apostles' response is emphatic. Their words might be paraphrased as "You must make your own decision about whom to obey. As for us, though, we must by all means keep on speaking about what we have seen and heard." In other words, they must be faithful to the role Jesus has given them as his eyewitnesses (Luke 24:48; Acts 1:8), even if they must disobey the religious leadership to do so. As Marshall notes, the apostles' answer makes explicit the limitation that is implicit in Romans 13: Jesus's followers must obey established governing authorities until those authorities demand that God's people do something contrary to God's will (1980, 102).

4:21–22. The council concluded that they should reinforce their threats (προσαπειλησάμενοι) against the apostles and release (ἀπέλυσαν) them, for three reasons. First, their examination had found no basis to punish Peter and John (μηδὲν εὑρίσκοντες τὸ πῶς κολάσωνται αὐτούς). Second, the people ascribed the healing to God (πάντες ἐδόξαζον τὸν θεὸν ἐπὶ τῷ γεγονότι). Third, there was no denying that a miraculous sign of healing had occurred (γεγόνει τὸ σημεῖον τοῦτο τῆς ἰάσεως). As Larkin notes, the release "[shows] for the first time what Luke will contend consistently: Christianity is both innocent before the state and triumphant when its enemies seek to use state authority to hinder its advance" (1995, 78).

Report and Prayer (4:23–31)

When Peter and John report on their hearing before the council, the disciples pray for boldness in witness and are filled with the Holy Spirit.

4:23–24a. After the council released them (ἀπολυθέντες), Peter and John returned "to their own" (πρὸς τοὺς ἰδίους) and reported on all that the council members said (ὅσα . . . οἱ ἀρχιερεῖς καὶ οἱ πρεσβύτεροι εἶπαν). Bock notes that Luke does not specify the identity of the group to which the apostles reported (2007, 203), and commentators reach different conclusions. Barrett thinks it was the other ten apostles (1994, 243). Marshall (1961, 104) and Larkin (1995, 78) argue for the original 120 disciples. Following Irenaeus (*Haer.* 3.12.5), Barrett concludes that it was the entire community of five thousand-plus (1994, 242). Schnabel addresses one objection to a large group by noting that they could have met at Solomon's Portico as 5:12 later records (2012, 254).

The group's response was united prayer (ἦραν φωνὴν πρὸς τὸν θεόν), which Luke describes using the adverb ὁμοθυμαδόν (cf. 1:14; 2:46; 5:12; 15:25). Bock suggests that the singular φωνήν indicates one person praying for the whole community (2007, 203). Their prayer began with a confession of God's absolute sovereignty and authority. The noun δεσπότης, with which the prayer addressed God, describes an individual who has legal control and authority over one or more subjects, and the cognate verb (δεσπόζω) describes having complete power over someone or something

(BDAG s.v. "δεσπόζω" 219). The prayer goes on to include three specific aspects of God's sovereign control over events.

4:24b. First, God is the one who created heaven, earth, sea, and everything in them (ὁ ποιήσας τὸν οὐρανὸν καὶ τὴν γῆν καὶ τὴν θάλασσαν καὶ πάντα τὰ ἐν αὐτοῖς). The description of God as creator (ὁ ποιήσας) echoed Psalm 146:6 (145:6 LXX). Paul would use the same description in his preaching (Acts 14:15; 17:24). Peterson notes that, in Psalm 146, the truth that God is creator is part of "the basis for confidence in God's ability to help his people when they are oppressed" (2009, 199). It was, therefore, particularly pertinent for the disciples who were facing opposition in Jerusalem.

4:25–26. Second, God is the one who foresaw the opposition that David described in Psalm 2 (ὁ τοῦ πατρὸς ἡμῶν διὰ πνεύματος ἁγίου στόματος Δαυὶδ παιδός σου εἰπών). David listed four sources of opposition: the nations who rage (ἐφρύαξαν ἔθνη), the peoples who devise futile things (λαοὶ ἐμελέτησαν κενά), the kings of the earth who approach with hostile intent (παρέστησαν οἱ βασιλεῖς τῆς γῆς), and the rulers who gather in assembly (οἱ ἄρχοντες συνήχθησαν ἐπὶ τὸ αὐτό). They opposed the Lord and his Messiah (κατὰ τοῦ κυρίου καὶ κατὰ τοῦ Χριστοῦ αὐτοῦ). The disciples, therefore, should not be surprised that acting in the name of Jesus would arouse opposition from all sides.

TEXTUAL ANALYSIS: "the one who spoke, through the Holy Spirit, by means of the mouth of our father, David, your servant"
The syntax of Acts 4:25 is notoriously complex. The substantival participle ὁ . . . εἰπών frames the clause and stands in apposition to the pronoun σύ in verse 24. The prepositional phrase διὰ πνεύματος ἁγίου specifies the secondary agent. The genitive noun στόματος denotes the means of speaking. The genitive phrase τοῦ πατρὸς ἡμῶν

is a possessive genitive. The indeclinable noun Δαυὶδ is a genitive that stands in apposition to πατρός. The genitive phrase παιδός σου stands in apposition to David.

4:27–28. Third, God is the one who predetermined the opposition Jesus's followers were facing in Jerusalem (ἐν τῇ πόλει ταύτῃ) and who was using it for his purposes (ποιῆσαι ὅσα ἡ χείρ σου καὶ ἡ βουλή σου προώρισεν γενέσθαι). The noun βουλή describes something that has been intended and planned (L&N §30.57; cf. 2:23; 5:38; 13:36; 20:27), and the verb προορίζω denotes the act of deciding on something beforehand (BDAG s.v. "προορίζω" 873; cf. Rom. 8:29–30; 1 Cor. 2:7; Eph. 1:5, 11). Specifically, the prayer equated Herod with the "kings" of Psalm 2, Pilate with the "rulers," the Gentiles with the "nations," and the residents of Jerusalem with the "peoples." Their opposition was directed against Jesus, who is God's "holy servant" (τὸν ἅγιον παῖδά σου) whom he anointed (ὃν ἔχρισας). Both descriptions echoed two of the christological emphases in Peter's sermon (servant in 3:13, 26 and Messiah in 3:18, 20). Through it all, the disciples could be confident that God would use the schemes of those who oppose his Messiah to accomplish his own plans.

4:29–30. The prayer then moved to the disciples' petitions (καὶ τὰ νῦν, κύριε), which God answered immediately and emphatically. They made three requests. They prayed that God would take note of the council's threats (ἔπιδε ἐπὶ τὰς ἀπειλὰς αὐτῶν; cf. 4:17, 21). They prayed that he would give them boldness for witness (δὸς τοῖς δούλοις σου μετὰ παρρησίας πάσης λαλεῖν τὸν λόγον σου; cf. 4:13). They prayed that he would show his power by performing healings, signs, and wonders (ἐν τῷ τὴν χεῖρά σου ἐκτείνειν σε εἰς ἴασιν καὶ σημεῖα καὶ τέρατα; cf. 4:16, 22) through the name of Jesus (διὰ τοῦ ὀνόματος Ἰησοῦ; cf. 3:6, 16; 4:7, 10, 12, 17, 18), God's servant (τοῦ ἁγίου παιδός σου; cf. 3:13, 26).

4:31. God answered with three signs while the disciples were still in the process of praying (δεηθέντων αὐτῶν). First, he shook the place where they were gathered (ἐσαλεύθη ὁ τόπος ἐν ᾧ ἦσαν συνηγμένοι), which Marshall notes was an OT sign of God's presence (1980, 107; cf. Exod. 19:18; Isa. 6:4). Second, the Spirit filled all of them (ἐπλήσθησαν ἅπαντες τοῦ ἁγίου πνεύματος; cf. 4:8). Third, they began speaking God's Word with boldness (ἐλάλουν τὸν λόγον τοῦ θεοῦ μετὰ παρρησίας; cf. 4:13). Bock summarizes, "In sum, this prayer is an expression of complete dependence on God, a recognition of his sovereignty, a call for God's justice and oversight in the midst of opposition, for an enablement for mission, and for the working of his power to show that God is behind the preaching of the name of Jesus in healing and signs" (2007, 210).

THEOLOGICAL FOCUS

The narratival function of Acts 4:1–31 is to introduce the opposition to the gospel that arose in Jerusalem, the way in which the disciples responded to that opposition, and the way in which God sustained them in the face of opposition. The healing of the lame man resulted in amazement among the crowds (3:10) and continued numerical growth among those who responded in faith to Peter's message (4:4). The people were responsive, but how would the religious leaders react to the explosive growth of this new movement? More importantly, how would the members of the new community respond if those leaders opposed the message Jesus had commissioned them to proclaim? Luke records the circumstances surrounding the first opposition to the Christian mission and the implications for the progress of that mission.

Theologically, Acts 4:1–31 lifts the curtain on opposition to the Christian mission. The Jewish religious leaders felt threatened because the apostles were usurping the priests' role of teaching people within the temple precincts, were claiming authority in Jesus's name, and were proclaiming a doctrine that they considered heretical. Faced with the evidence of the apostles' boldness despite their lack of formal rabbinic training and the healed man who stood before them, the leaders had no answer. Judicially, there was no reason to convict the apostles; they were innocent, just as Jesus had been. Politically, there was every reason to acquit them, but the leaders feared the spread of their teaching. So, the leaders chose to threaten the apostles and release them. The leaders failed to realize, however, that God not only foresaw their opposition to the Messiah and his followers, but that he also used it to accomplish his predetermined plan. Jesus's followers should expect to encounter opposition, while being confident of God's control of events and his provision of the resources they need to carry out his mission.

PREACHING AND TEACHING STRATEGIES

Exegetical/Theological Synthesis
Luke's first-century readers would have wanted to know how the disciples responded when they encountered opposition in Jerusalem, the headquarters of the Jewish religion. How would the religious establishment react to the growing Christian mission? How would the disciples respond if that reaction turned out to be negative? How would opposition affect the movement's progress? Luke's account of the apostles' first arrest, questioning, and release answers each of those questions. More opposition would follow, but this first episode set the pattern for subsequent encounters. Confident in God's absolute sovereign control of events, the disciples would proclaim the name of Jesus boldly, remain steadfast in their commitment to the mission Jesus had given them, and unite in prayer that God would enable his servants to do his will. With the original audience, the twenty-first-century audience shares the need to know that God is in control and provides the resources they need when they encounter opposition. They need to

realize that opposition opens doors of opportunity—the opportunity to witness boldly by the power of the Holy Spirit, the opportunity to stand firmly for Jesus, and the opportunity to trust in God's sovereign control.

Preaching/Teaching Idea
Human opposition opens divine doors of opportunity.

Contemporary Connections

What does it mean?
The first show of force against the Great Commission in Acts is an impressive warning shot. The Jewish leadership arrays priests, the captain of the temple guard, Sadducees, rulers, elders, scribes, and the high priest's family against Peter and John. The disciples and their converts would have highly regarded these men. Together they expressed annoyance (4:2) and suspicion (4:7), and they were determined to stop the spread of this message (4:17). For men who "had nothing to say in opposition" to the credibility of the healing (4:14), they had a lot to say about stopping further talk of the divine healer. Perhaps an arrest, a night in jail, a trial, and further threats and warnings would silence Jesus's followers. Human opposition, however, opens divine doors of opportunity. The show of force backfired. All that saber-rattling sounded the alarm for the seriousness of what was at stake. The group of believers responded by praying fervently to a God who is used to being opposed by his fallen creation. God answered the believers' prayers, filled them afresh with his Spirit, and emboldened them to evangelize. Now, however, they were doing their commission work with a renewed sense of what was at stake and a joint dependency on God to provide. The opposition actually reinvigorated the work.

Is it true?
Why was there such vehement opposition to a pair of "uneducated, common men" performing

a miraculous deed to deliver someone in suffering? It was because, in truth, the issue was not with the healing but with the healer. Had Peter and John healed this man and slipped quietly on with their day, there would have been no issue. As soon as they began "proclaiming in Jesus the resurrection from the dead," though, they found themselves in custody.

Peter's Spirit-filled defense before these rulers only prodded this sore spot further. The rulers cannot even bring themselves to say the name *Jesus*. They asked about "what name" (4:7) and warn against speaking "this name" (4:17), but Peter filled in the blank: "Jesus Christ of Nazareth." The rulers referred to what happened to the lame man as "this thing" (4:7), but again, Peter filled in the blank: "a good deed done to a crippled man" (4:9). There was more. Peter left no doubt that God's Christ suffered rejection and crucifixion at the hands of these men (4:10–11), that there was indeed a resurrection from the dead (4:2), and that Jesus was the sole means of God's salvation for humanity (4:12). His answer was nothing less than a complete reimagining of God's means of deliverance. What Peter happily shared as a declaration of peace, these rulers could only hear as a declaration of war.

Sadly, the prayer meeting that followed revealed these dynamics in stark terms. In a dark twist, the cry of Psalm 2 against raging Gentiles applied perfectly to raging Jewish leaders (4:25). These rulers had gravely "gathered together against your holy servant Jesus," joining the ranks of Herod and Pontius Pilate (4:27). By praying these dynamics aloud, the believing community was able to see the opposition more clearly. Their request was to face threats with courage, and that was exactly what the Holy Spirit did.

Now what?

Today's era of Western Christianity and mission enjoys a safety not shared by brothers and sisters around the world today or throughout the history of the church. It is true that the message of absolute truth and salvific exclusivity is growing more offensive by the day, but even the most outspoken Bible-thumpers will not be spending a night in jail anytime soon. In God's perfect hand that predestines what takes place (4:28), the Western church will experience these remaining daylight hours of peace before the night of persecution that will surely come. If the onset of opposition challenged the early church to witness with Spirit-filled boldness, what hope is there to rouse a sleepy church that is enjoying its security?

It helps to see in our passage that the opposition started by speaking honest words about Jesus. In that regard, the church shares the same fate around the world and throughout history. The opposition might look and feel different, and it might vary by degree, by pain, or by cost, but it will universally move to silence any speaking of "this name." Where we as the church feel intimidated, inadequate, and ill equipped to "speak [God's] word with boldness" (4:29), we join King David and the early church in this prayer to meet rage with resistance, to meet threats with courage.

Creativity in Presentation

Taylor Branch's Pulitzer Prize-winning history *Parting the Waters* tells the story of the civil rights movement in the 1950s and 1960s. It reads like a novel, as he describes the chaos that ensued when young people, black and white, boarded Greyhound buses to test federal desegregation laws in hotspots in the South and became known as the Freedom Riders. By its bloody end, a handful of people had the attention of the nation—local authorities, law enforcement, mobs, marshals, the attorney general, and the president himself. Their prophetic performance lit a match to the tinderbox of race relations in America.

There are other examples of how seemingly small acts of resistance or protest gained enormous attention. Whether or not they wanted to, Peter and John found themselves facing that same notoriety. A miracle and a sermon on a lazy weekday afternoon turned Jewish leadership on its head and landed the apostles in front of the highest authority of the temple. The audacity of bringing Jesus, the true tabernacle of God in flesh, into the fading form of the temple almost got the disciples killed. New wine burst old wineskins. Very soon, red would run.

One creative angle to this story would be to contrast the disciples' side with the rulers' side. Luke gives us a rare glimpse inside the inner difficulties of the rulers. The rulers and the disciples came from two different worlds, with different vocabularies, and different expectations. Their goals could not have been more different. Even so, as the disciples' prayer made clear, the fight was with opposition to Jesus, not with flesh and blood. God's answer to their prayer was supernatural, courageous witness to all peoples.

Human opposition opens divine doors of opportunity.

- Human rulers resist and oppose (4:1–22).

- God opens doors of opportunity (4:23–31).

DISCUSSION QUESTIONS

1. Why does the gospel pose a threat to those in positions of religious authority and/or power? What are some of the beliefs and practices that it challenges?

2. What truths are central to a faithful proclamation of the gospel? How does Peter incorporate and contextualize those truths in the apostles' defense before the Sanhedrin?

3. Is there a contradiction between Peter and John's answer to the Sanhedrin (4:19–20) and Paul's teaching on obeying the governing authorities in Romans 13? If not, why not? How can followers of Christ keep the two teachings in balance?

4. Why is the truth that God is creator a basis for confidence when his people are facing opposition?

5. Why did the Jerusalem church ask God both to give them boldness in witness and to demonstrate his power through signs and wonders?

Acts 4:32–37

EXEGETICAL IDEA

In a context of grace, unity, witness, and sharing, Barnabas is a positive example of the community's practice of caring for the impoverished.

THEOLOGICAL FOCUS

The Lord's grace unites his people to engage in powerful witness to those outside the church and generous care for those inside the church.

PREACHING IDEA

God's great grace produces great results.

PREACHING POINTERS

Where does money fit into the church's mission? In particular, how should the church view material need? How should it respond when its members encounter financial hardship? The Jerusalem church not only faced opposition from the religious leaders; its members were also isolated from the social support system of both the temple and the synagogues. As a result, many of the disciples were facing financial hardship. The apostles had witnessed boldly to Jesus and his resurrection and had taken an uncompromising stand for him in the face of opposition. The community had experienced great grace. How would that grace show itself when some of the disciples were impoverished? Barnabas, the son of encouragement, gave Jesus's followers a model of what it means not only to witness boldly but also to give generously.

People today should be able to relate to the idea of people in financial need, the process of selling property, and the practice of giving to those who are in need. The example of Barnabas's generosity corrects the idea that living the Christian life is a purely spiritual endeavor with no material component, as well as the idea that God's people cannot ignore the financial needs of others. Luke's account commends a commitment to holistic ministry that includes addressing material issues, being willing to put the needs of others above personal gain, and sharing voluntarily and generously to meet the needs of others. As Jesus's disciples, we need to understand that God's grace unites us for witness and mutual care, so that we will respond with generous sharing to meet the needs of others within his body.

THE CHURCH'S BENEVOLENCE (ACTS 4:32–37)

LITERARY STRUCTURE AND THEMES (4:32–37)

This passage is the second of three summaries in 2:1–8:3 that describe the community life of the Jerusalem church. The first passage (2:41–47) described essential aspects of the early church's common life, and the impact that common life had on those both inside and outside the community of disciples. The third passage (5:12–16) will describe the impact of signs and wonders (cf. 2:43). The current passage (4:32–37) describes the practice of having all things in common (cf. 2:44–45) and divides into three parts, with each part providing more detail than the one that precedes it. The first part (4:32–33) highlights four characteristics of the growing Christian community. The second part (4:34–35) focuses on one of those characteristics: the way in which "they shared everything they had" (NLT, 4:33). The third part (4:36–37) presents Barnabas as "Exhibit A" of their generosity (cf. Longenecker 1981, 312).

- *The Community Context of Benevolence (4:32–33)*
- *The Church's Practice of Benevolence (4:34–35)*
- *Barnabas's Example of Benevolence (4:36–37)*

EXPOSITION (4:32–37)

Opposition had a beneficial effect on the community of disciples. It not only strengthened their resolve to continue speaking out in Jesus's name (4:18–20), but it also drove them to turn to God for his help (4:23–30). His answer was a fresh filling of the Holy Spirit (4:31) as evidence that his grace was upon them (4:33). Luke now inserts a summary passage that provides a second snapshot of the early church's common life, with particular focus on one of the essentials he had identified earlier: generous sharing among the disciples (cf. 2:44–45). Luke sets their sharing in the context of the disciples' community life (4:32–33), provides the details of the process by which the community met financial needs (4:34–35) and includes the positive example of Barnabas (4:36–37). In so doing, Luke highlights the way in which conflict with the Jewish religious establishment contributed to the spiritual growth of the Christian community (Schnabel 2012, 268). God's great grace (4:33b) moved the disciples to engage in powerful witness to the resurrection (4:33a) and mutual care for one another (4:32, 34–37).

The Community Context of Benevolence (4:32–33)

Great grace, deep unity, powerful witness, and generous sharing characterize the growing community of disciples.

4:32–33. Luke highlights the explosive growth of the Christian movement (cf. 2:41; 4:4) by describing it as "the multitude of those who believed" (τοῦ πλήθους τῶν πιστευσάντων). In the context of that growth, the multitude exhibited four characteristics. The first characteristics was their deep unity (cf. 1:14; 2:46; 5:12). Culy and Parsons take καρδία καὶ ψυχή as the subject of the first clause and μία as the predicate adjective and translate "the heart and soul of the whole group of believers was one" (τοῦ πλήθους τῶν πιστευσάντων ἦν καρδία καὶ ψυχὴ μία), which emphasizes the depth of the group's unity (2003, 80–81). The second characteristic was their generous sharing. Their perspective on possessions was that "none of them said that any of their belongings were their own" (GNB, οὐδὲ εἷς τι τῶν ὑπαρχόντων αὐτῷ ἔλεγεν ἴδιον εἶναι). Instead (ἀλλ᾽), "they all shared with one another everything they had" (GNB, ἦν αὐτοῖς πάντα κοινά), which repeats Luke's earlier description in 2:44. Together, the two contrasting clauses provide the topic statement that the remainder of the paragraph will develop.

The third characteristic of the community was the apostles' powerful witness. They were "giving witness" (ἀπεδίδουν τὸ μαρτύριον) "with great power" (δυνάμει μεγάλῃ) to Jesus's resurrection (τῆς ἀναστάσεως τοῦ κυρίου Ἰησοῦ), as Luke had just recorded in 3:1–4:31. The fourth characteristic was, in fact, the source of the other three. It was God's "great grace" (χάρις μεγάλη) that was upon all of them (ἐπὶ πάντας αὐτούς). In this context, χάρις was not favor with those outside the community as in 2:47. Instead, it denotes "divine aid bestowed in unusual measure" (Barrett 1994, 254) that showed itself in various ways and, here, was the source of unity, sharing, and witness. Elsewhere in Acts, χάρις is the source of power for signs and wonders (6:8), the basis for commissioning to ministry (14:26; 15:40), and the means by which men and women believe (18:27).

The Church's Practice of Benevolence (4:34–35)

The apostles implement the practice of benevolence by distributing voluntary contributions according to needs within the community.

4:34–35. The background for the community's practice of benevolence was the OT teaching on caring for the poor and needy (Deut. 15:7–11) and Jesus's teaching on the proper use of wealth (Luke 12:22–34; 18:18–30). When Luke writes, "there was not a needy person among them" (οὐδὲ ἐνδεής τις ἦν ἐν αὐτοῖς), he echoes Deuteronomy 15:4 (LXX, οὐκ ἔσται ἐν σοὶ ἐνδεής). The adjective ἐνδεής carries the sense of "impoverished" (Schnabel 2012, 271). The

description of the disciples' selling (πωλοῦντες) and the apostles' distributing (διεδίδετο) echo Jesus's challenge to the rich young ruler to "sell [πώλησον] all that you possess, and distribute [διάδος] it to the poor" (Luke 18:22).

The process the community followed in distributing their benevolent support included three steps. First, those members who owned property would sell it (ὅσοι κτήτορες χωρίων ἢ οἰκιῶν ὑπῆρχον, πωλοῦντες). Then, they would bring the proceeds (ἔφερον τὰς τιμὰς τῶν πιπρασκομένων) and lay them at the apostles' feet (ἐτίθουν παρὰ τοὺς πόδας τῶν ἀποστόλων). Finally, the apostles would distribute those proceeds to members who were having need (διεδίδετο ἑκάστῳ καθότι ἄν τις χρείαν εἶχεν). The repeated use of finite verbs in the imperfect tense and participles in the present tense points to a regular, most likely iterative, practice. Longenecker suggests the sense of "from time to time" (1981, 311). Bock describes it as a "gradual liquidation of assets" (2007, 215). The practice was voluntary (cf. 5:4) and based on need (4:35). Laying the proceeds at the apostles' feet acknowledged their full authority over the funds.

Barnabas's Example of Benevolence (4:36–37)

Barnabas's actions are a positive example of the community's benevolence.

4:36–37. To conclude his summary passage, Luke introduces an individual who provided a positive example of the community practice he has been describing and who will become a key "bridge person" through much of his narrative (Dunn 1996, 60; Larkin 1995, 83). His given name was Joseph (Ἰωσήφ), but the apostles gave him the name by which history remembers him: Barnabas (Βαρναβᾶς). Ethnically, he was a Jew; culturally, he was a Hellenist from Cyprus (Κύπριος τῷ γένει); vocationally, he was a Levite (Λευίτης), although it does not appear that he carried out functions in the temple. In

OT times, Levites did not own property (Num. 18:20; Deut. 10:9). By the first century, however, the practice had changed (Josephus, *Vita* 13–15), and Barnabas owned a piece of land (ὑπάρχοντος αὐτῷ ἀγροῦ), whether in Cyprus or in Jerusalem is not clear. Aware of a financial need in the community, Barnabas followed the church's practice of benevolence; he sold the piece of land (πωλήσας), brought the proceeds of the sale to the apostles (ἤνεγκεν τὸ χρῆμα), and laid those proceeds at their feet (ἔθηκεν παρὰ τοὺς πόδας τῶν ἀποστόλων) for them to distribute as they saw fit. In so doing, he lived up to his name as "son of encouragement" (υἱὸς παρακλήσεως). Schnabel concludes, "In the historical context of the Jerusalem church, we can assume that [Barnabas] served as a role model for perhaps 8,000 believers" (2012, 273).

Joseph, Named Barnabas

Luke introduces Joseph in Acts 4:36–37. He was a Levite who was born in Cyprus. The Jerusalem apostles called him Barnabas (4:36), perhaps to distinguish him from others with the same name in the community (cf. 1:23). There has been extended discussion of the etymology of the name Barnabas (Βαρναβᾶς) and why Luke writes that it was interpreted "son of encouragement" (υἱὸς παρακλήσεως), with different scholars reaching different conclusions (Barrett 1994, 258; Larkin 1995, 84). The remainder of the book, however, makes it clear that the interpretation is particularly apt, as Luke portrays him in six different roles. In Jerusalem, Barnabas was both a model of generosity (4:36–37) and a sponsor who introduced Paul to the apostles (9:26–27). When the apostles sent Barnabas as their representative to check on the new work in Antioch, he validated that work, recruited Paul as a coworker, helped carry the famine relief to Jerusalem, and served as one of the congregation's prophets/teachers (11:22–30; cf. 12:25; 13:1). Sent out by the Holy Spirit with Paul, he served as an apostolic church-planting missionary in his native Cyprus and in southern Galatia (13:1–14:28). With Paul, Barnabas served as a commissioner representing the church in Antioch at the Jerusalem Council (15:1–35). After his split with Paul, Barnabas was a mentor to his cousin, John Mark, and helped him overcome his initial ministry failure (15:36–39; cf. 13:13). As Bock writes, "[Barnabas] is surely one of Luke's heroes" (2007, 216).

THEOLOGICAL FOCUS

The narratival function of Acts 4:32–37 is to begin a series of three short accounts of the early church's life before returning to the theme of opposition in 5:17–42. After the extended account of the lame man's healing, Peter's second sermon, the religious establishment's opposition, and the church's united prayer, this paragraph describes the way in which the community of disciples cared for one another in a context of religious opposition and financial hardship. In addition to the religious opposition of the establishment leaders, who imposed economic and social sanctions, the disciples in Jerusalem faced famine and limited employment opportunities (Longenecker 1981, 310). How would they respond to the challenge? Luke's summary passage makes it clear that opposition and hardship deepened the disciples' commitment to their mission and to one another.

Theologically, Acts 4:32–37 provides a model of holistic ministry—ministry that balances mission toward outsiders with mutual care for insiders—in a setting of opposition and hardship, with a special focus on generous giving to assist needy members of the church. The passage provides a framework for Christian benevolence. The context of that benevolence is corporate unity (4:32). The source is God's grace (4:33). The method is voluntary contribution (4:34). The motive is the alleviation of need (4:35). Barnabas provides a concrete model of benevolence (4:36–37), not only for the Jerusalem church of the first century but also for the churches of today. Later, the church in Antioch would follow the same practice of caring for the needs of the believers in Jerusalem (Acts 11:27–30), and Paul would organize a contribution from the Gentile churches he had planted, also for the church in Jerusalem (Rom. 15:25–28).

PREACHING AND TEACHING STRATEGIES

Exegetical/Theological Synthesis
Luke's first-century readers would have wanted to know how the early disciples responded to opposition and hardship. He had already provided an extended account of the apostles' bold witness in the face of opposition from the priestly establishment (4:1–22). God had responded by filling the disciples with the Holy Spirit for continued bold witness (4:23–31, 33b). As further evidence of his great grace, God granted them unity so strong that they shared what they owned with one another. The way in which they lived out that unity provides a model of how God expects his people to care for one another when members of their body are facing financial hardship. With the original audience, the twenty-first-century audience has the privilege of following Barnabas's example by responding to God's grace with selfless generosity toward those in need. Luke's account reminds us that God's grace unites his people to engage in powerful witness to those outside the church and generous care for those inside the church.

Preaching/Teaching Idea
God's great grace produces great results.

Contemporary Connections

What does it mean?
Because they were fully grounded in the gospel, the "testimony to the resurrection of the Lord Jesus" filled this fledgling Christian community with God's "great grace" (4:33). How could it not? Luke has already shown in sermons and community life the great grace in store for God's people—forgiveness of sins, the gift of the Holy Spirit, salvation from this crooked generation, a new family eating meals together, signs and wonders, times of refreshing, new access to God, and God's ear in time of persecution. Grace abounds full, wild, and free. Grace, however, is not stagnant. We must not collect it and keep it to ourselves like day-old manna. We receive grace freely, and we must give it freely (Matt. 10:8). At the end of Acts 4, the community is bulging at the seams with grace to give each other. Luke highlights four facets of grace in this little summary: supernatural single-minded unity, countercultural generosity of material provision, divinely empowered witness, and even greater experience of divine favor.

Is it true?
The early church's care for the poor was not an original idea; nor was this care an optional appendage she might take or leave with her newfound faith. No, generosity from God's people for the needy is as old as the OT, springing from his character of grace into a people of grace. Deuteronomy 15:11 says simply, "Therefore I command you, 'You shall open wide your hand to your brother, to the needy and to the poor, in your land.'" This statement precedes a litany of commands for tithes, alms, leaving corners of one's crops, paying fair and prompt wages, and the year of Jubilee.

Jesus took these laws to heart, preaching on radical generosity to the poor, spending a good portion of his ministry among the marginalized and poor, and entrusting communal funds to Judas, in part for giving gifts to the poor. The church comes by its generosity honestly. It is no wonder Luke paid particular attention to Jesus's words about the poor in his gospel and now repeatedly shows in Acts the example of the early church caring for the poor.

The apostle Paul will go on to speak of the gospel itself as Christ giving his wealth to us in our poverty. He says, "For you know the grace of our Lord Jesus Christ, that though he was rich, yet for your sake he became poor, so that you by his poverty might become rich" (2 Cor. 8:9). Paul uses this blessed truth as motivation to respond to Jesus's generosity to us with open-handed material generosity to others. Truly, the great grace of the gospel leads us toward great grace with each other.

Now what?
Churches today tend to favor piety or social action, theology or activity. Those who emphasize piety and theology can be guilty of a purely personal spirituality. The caricature of them is a gnostic, hyperindividualistic retreat from the world into a prayer closet. Those who emphasize social action and activity can be guilty of a purely horizontal religiosity. The caricature of them is a liberal movement, shallow on doctrine, squeamish over evangelism and conversion, but deep on addressing felt needs. It can be hard to find common ground.

Imagine members of the early church trying to separate what God had joined. Imagine one group, eager to hear the apostles' teaching but unmoved to share with the needy. They would be content to let the other half of the church sell property and give generously to ease the needs of others. Meanwhile, imagine the other group, busy serving the community but unconcerned with apostolic teaching. They would be content to let the other half of the church study Scripture and teach it to others. How divisive and undeveloped this body of believers would be. How far apart their different trajectories would take them.

Our passage reorients us to the early days of the church in Jerusalem, when these twin movements coexisted happily—sinfully, awkwardly, in need of extra care for sure—but together. Like the other summary passages, we hold this early church body up to our existing local church body and wonder aloud together whether God's great grace in our midst leads us to each of these elements of unity, sharing, and witness. If not, we have deep, hard changes ahead of us, and we will be looking for the Barnabas in our midst to help show us the way.

Creativity in Presentation
Apostolic preaching then and today finds its fullest grounding in the gospel. We preach Christ crucified, risen, saving, and now animating every aspect of our lives with precious grace. Some passages are harder to draw a straight line between Jesus and the moral commands in the text. This passage is not one of them. God's great grace to the church sparks her generous grace to each other. To miss the line between Jesus and generosity is to miss the line between the sun and a sweltering day.

A creative, albeit far-reaching, approach to this sermon might be to build the connection between the gospel and generosity in the Bible from the OT, to the rich young ruler, to Jesus, to the early church. First, places like Deuteronomy 15 show that generosity is in God's heart, and his commands reflect his generosity. God gave generously to Israel, so that she, in turn, could give generously to others. Second, the story of the rich young ruler in Luke 18 is our story. We resist God's way, grasp at our own, make idols of his gifts, and if left to ourselves would hang on to them kicking and screaming to hell. Indeed, Jesus said it is hard for rich people, pretty people, successful people, or self-loving people to enter the kingdom of God. Without Jesus, it is impossible.

Third, God so loved the world that his rich son Jesus made himself poor, so that his poverty would bring us eternal wealth (2 Corinthians 8). Jesus did what the law, weakened by greedy flesh, could not do. He has made us inheritors of his great grace. Fourth, that great grace fills us to overflowing in this new life in Christ. Where the rich young ruler could not bring himself to *sell* and *distribute*, this young church, by God's grace, *sells* and *distributes* (same words here as in Luke 18).

How great is the grace of the gospel! God *forgives* our greediness in the death of his Son. Now, God *frees* us from a life bound to greediness in the resurrected new life in his Son. The hymn writer Bart Millard got it exactly right when he penned these lyrics:

> Grace, grace, God's grace
> Grace that will pardon and cleanse within
> Grace, grace, God's grace
> Grace that is greater than all our sin

Truly, God's great grace produces great results.

- God's great grace (4:33).

- God's gracious results (4:32–37).

DISCUSSION QUESTIONS

1. How are unity, witness, and benevolence outward manifestations of God's grace?

2. Is the practice of benevolence that Luke describes in Acts 4:32–37 normative for all believers in all ages? Why or why not?

3. What qualities define the early church's practice of benevolence?

4. What standard(s) should govern who receives benevolent support? How much? How often? In what circumstances?

5. How can the contemporary church follow the early church's model of benevolence?

Acts 5:1–11

EXEGETICAL IDEA

Ananias and Sapphira's act of counterfeit generosity constituted a sin against God and resulted in divine judgment.

THEOLOGICAL FOCUS

Because God holds his people accountable to a divine standard of integrity, he will take any action necessary to preserve the purity and peace of his church.

PREACHING IDEA

No one lies to God and lives.

PREACHING POINTERS

We can probably all identify with the shock of having someone we know die suddenly—especially when the death is unexpected. Imagine the trauma that would ensue when two members of a church, a husband and wife, fall dead in public in exactly the same way within three hours of each other. Several questions arise naturally, including: What is God doing? Why did they die? Did they do something to incur God's judgment? Are the rest of us in danger of the same fate? Barnabas's example of genuine benevolence gave the Jerusalem church a model of grace-filled generosity. What did the first-century disciples learn from Ananias and Sapphira's fate following their act of false benevolence? What can the contemporary church learn about God's presence among, and standards for, his people?

People today should be able to relate to multiple ideas in this passage, including financial irregularities, the desire to look good in front of others, lying to cover up what they have done wrong, and unexpected deaths of relatives or friends. The negative example of Ananias and Sapphira corrects any suggestion that it is possible to hide attitudes or actions from God, that a relationship with God is limited to spiritual aspects of life, or that God overlooks sin. Luke's account commends living with integrity, honoring God in every aspect of life, respecting his holiness, and cultivating a sense of his presence with his people. As Christ's followers we must understand that he holds us accountable for our attitudes and actions, so that we will honor him in every area of our lives.

THE CHURCH'S INTEGRITY (5:1–11)

LITERARY STRUCTURE AND THEMES (5:1–11)

The passage consists of two brief narratives (5:1–6, 7–11), in what Bock describes as a "mirror structure" (2007, 219). Both the sequence of actions and repeated vocabulary hold the two paragraphs together, as the following chart makes clear.

	5:1–6			5:7–11	
5:1–2	Ananias acts with Sapphira knowing (συνειδυίης καὶ τῆς γυναικός)	Setting	Sapphira arrives without knowing (ἡ γυνὴ αὐτοῦ μὴ εἰδυῖα)		5:7
5:3–4	Ananias lies to the Holy Spirit (ψεύσασθαί σε τὸ πνεῦμα τὸ ἅγιον)	Interaction with Peter	Sapphira tests the Spirit of the Lord (πειράσαι τὸ πνεῦμα κυρίου)		5:8–9
5:5–6	Death, great fear, burial (ἐξέψυξεν . . . ἐγένετο φόβος μέγας . . . ἔθαψαν)	Result	Death, burial, great fear (ἐξέψυξεν . . . ἔθαψαν . . . ἐγένετο φόβος μέγας)		5:10–11

- ***Ananias's Cover-Up (5:1–6)***
- ***Sapphira's Complicity (5:7–11)***

EXPOSITION (5:1–11)

Closely connected with Barnabas's positive example of generosity (4:32–36)—but in sharp contrast to it—was Ananias and Sapphira's negative example of greed. Dunn describes the passage as "one of the most unnerving episodes in the whole of the New Testament" and "a profoundly shocking picture" (1996, 62). Ananias and Sapphira followed the same form of benevolence Barnabas modeled, but they failed to exhibit the same integrity he possessed. They let their desire to look good in the eyes of others override their willingness to adhere to God's standard for their attitudes and actions, and their sin led to divine judgment that demonstrated God's presence and work among his people.

Ananias's Cover-Up (5:1–6)

God strikes down Ananias for the sin of lying to the Holy Spirit about his professed generosity.

5:1–2. Luke has already established the three-step process by which the early church distributed benevolent support to the needy, first by summarizing it in general (4:34–35), then by recounting Barnabas's specific example (4:36–36). Ananias and Sapphira followed that process: they sold property (ἐπώλησεν κτῆμα), they brought the proceeds to the community (ἐνέγκας), and they placed those proceeds at the apostles' feet (παρὰ τοὺς πόδας τῶν ἀποστόλων ἔθηκεν). There were, however, two significant differences—one in their attitude, the other in their action. First, they agreed (cf. συνεφωνήθη in 5:9) to "misappropriate funds for their own benefit" (L&N §57.246; ἐνοσφίσατο ἀπὸ τῆς τιμῆς). Second, they only brought a portion of the proceeds (μέρος τι) to the apostles. Although Ananias is the primary actor in the first half of the account, it is clear that he and Sapphira conspired, because he sold the property "with, Sapphira, his wife" (σὺν Σαπφίρῃ τῇ γυναικὶ αὐτοῦ), and he perpetrated the fraud "with his wife's consent" (NLT, συνειδυίης καὶ τῆς γυναικός). They acted together, and God would judge them for their joint action.

5:3–4. With prophetic insight (Peterson 2009, 209), Peter asked Ananias three questions that exposed his spiritual motivation, his financial prerogatives, and his personal accountability. The motivation for his action was spiritual and came from Satan, who "filled [his] heart" (τί ἐπλήρωσεν ὁ Σατανᾶς τὴν καρδίαν σου), with two results—one temporal and one spiritual. Ananias kept back part of the price from the sale of the land (νοσφίσασθαι ἀπὸ τῆς τιμῆς τοῦ χωρίου); more significantly, he lied to the Holy Spirit (ψεύσασθαί σε τὸ πνεῦμα τὸ ἅγιον). The decision he made, though, was entirely his. Financially, as long the property remained unsold, it was his (μένον σοὶ ἔμενεν); after he sold it, the money he received was in his control (πραθὲν ἐν τῇ σῇ ἐξουσίᾳ ὑπῆρχεν). Ultimately, Ananias was personally accountable (middle voice) for putting this deed in his own heart (ἔθου ἐν τῇ καρδίᾳ σου τὸ πρᾶγμα τοῦτο). Satan had suggested the idea, but Ananias adopted it as his own. The conclusion was inescapable: he did not lie to men but to God (οὐκ ἐψεύσω ἀνθρώποις ἀλλὰ τῷ θεῷ).

Satan

"Satan" is the transliteration of the Greek proper noun ὁ Σατανᾶς, which is itself a loanword from Hebrew. In the OT, it is a general term for an adversary (1 Kings 11:14; Ps. 109:6) but also describes a personal spiritual being who accuses (Job 1:6–13) and tempts (1 Chron. 21:1). The word occurs thirty-six times in the NT, of which seven occurrences are in Luke-Acts. The other word the NT uses frequently to describe the same personal spiritual being is ὁ διάβολος (seven times in Luke-Acts, twenty-seven times in the rest of the NT). Other titles include "the evil one" (1 John 2:13, 14; 3:12; 5:18, 19), "the ruler of this age" (1 Cor. 2:6, 8; 2 Cor. 4:4), and "the father of lies" (John 8:44). His dominion is one of darkness (Acts 26:18), and he exercises his power by oppressing individuals (Luke 13:16; Acts 10:38). He is the enemy of righteousness, who opposes God and his purposes (Acts 13:10) and takes away God's word when it is sown in people's hearts (Luke 8:12). He tested Jesus in the wilderness (Luke 4:1–13), entered Judas to prompt the betrayal of Jesus (Luke 22:3; cf. John 13:27), and "sifted" Peter in his threefold denial of Jesus (Luke 22:31). His attack on the community of disciples through Ananias (Acts 5:3) was merely the latest campaign in his continuing war against God's mission (cf. Rev. 12:7–9)—a war he can never win (Luke 10:18; cf. Rom. 16:20).

5:5–6. As soon as Ananias heard Peter's words (ἀκούων δὲ ὁ Ἀνανίας τοὺς λόγους τούτους), he "fell down and died" (Culy and Parsons 2003, 87; πεσὼν ἐξέψυξεν). As a result, great fear came upon everyone who heard about the death (ἐγένετο φόβος μέγας ἐπὶ πάντας τοὺς ἀκούοντας). After members of the community wrapped him up (συνέστειλαν αὐτόν), certain younger men carried him out (ἐξενέγκαντες), and buried (ἔθαψαν) him. The verb ἐκψύχω is rare, but when it occurs, it describes a person who is struck down by divine judgment (12:23; cf. Judg. 4:21). Despite suggestions that Ananias died from shock or other natural causes (Marshall 1980, 112), his cause of death is most naturally understood as "death at the hands of heaven" (Larkin 1995, 86; cf. Lev. 10:1–7; 22:9). In this context, φόβος denotes dread in response to the supernatural rather than reverence for God (Barrett 1994, 268). The verb συσστέλλω means to "wrap up in preparation for removal" (L&N, §79.119) and, in this context, implies preparation for burial. The "younger men" (οἱ νεώτεροι) who performed the tasks are not otherwise identified, and as Marshall notes, there is no particular need to suggest that Luke is identifying a specific church office or role (1980, 112).

Sapphira's Complicity (5:7–11)

God strikes down Sapphira for her part in the sin of testing the Holy Spirit.

5:7–9. After an interval of about three hours (ὡς ὡρῶν τριῶν διάστημα), Sapphira arrived on the scene. She had no prior knowledge of what had happened to her husband (μὴ εἰδυῖα τὸ γεγονός). As he had done with her husband, Peter asked two questions that exposed her complicity in the sin. First, he gave Sapphira the opportunity to set the record straight about the price for which they sold the land (εἰ τοσούτου τὸ χωρίον ἀπέδοσθε;). Then, he gave her the opportunity to admit that she and Ananias had conspired to test the Holy Spirit (τί ὅτι συνεφωνήθη ὑμῖν πειράσαι τὸ πνεῦμα κυρίου;). Finally, again with prophetic insight, Peter announced her impending judgment by declaring that the same young men who had buried her husband would carry her out as well (οἱ πόδες τῶν θαψάντων τὸν ἄνδρα σου ἐπὶ τῇ θύρᾳ καὶ ἐξοίσουσίν σε). Marshall notes that critics have considered Sapphira's ignorance unlikely (1980, 113), but Bock addresses the objection by noting the selective nature of the narrative and the circumstances of Ananias's death resulting from

divine judgment (2007, 225). The idea of putting God to the test echoes Israel's actions in the wilderness (Num. 14:20–23; Deut. 6:16; Ps. 95:7–11). "Feet" is a synecdoche for the young men, and "at the door" portrays their readiness to act.

5:10–11. As was the case with her husband, Sapphira "immediately fell down at the apostles' feet and died" (ἔπεσεν παραχρῆμα πρὸς τοὺς πόδας αὐτοῦ καὶ ἐξέψυξεν). The young men came in (εἰσελθόντες οἱ νεανίσκοι), found her dead (εὗρον αὐτὴν νεκράν), carried her out (ἐξενέγκαντες), and buried her with her husband (ἔθαψαν πρὸς τὸν ἄνδρα αὐτῆς). The result was, again, "great fear" (φόβος μέγας) that extended to both the community of disciples (ἐφ' ὅλην τὴν ἐκκλησίαν) and to everyone who heard about the events (ἐπὶ πάντας τοὺς ἀκούοντας ταῦτα). There is a hint of irony in the fact that where she fell is where she and Ananias should have demonstrated their recognition of God's authority over their attitudes and actions. The experience of great fear here echoes the experience of great grace in 4:33. Repeating the phrase at the end of the episode (5:5) both emphasizes it and prepares the way for the reaction of the residents of Jerusalem and its surrounding cities in the next summary statement (5:12–16).

The Death of Sapphira
by Nicolas Poussin. Public domain.

> ### ἐκκλησία
>
> The word ἐκκλησία occurs 114 times in the NT. The most common translation is "church," and the word refers to the community of God's people 109 times. The popular explanation that the word means "the 'called out people'" should be abandoned once for all, resting as it does on a false derivation of meaning from etymology" (Marshall 1980, 114; cf. Schnabel 2012, 289). In classical Greek, the word designated the political assembly of a city (Bruce 1990, 166). In the LXX, the word sometimes described the sacred meetings of Israel's religious community (Deut. 9:10; 18:16; 23:1; 31:30). Ἐκκλησία occurs twenty-three times in Acts, with three occurrences parallel to the classical Greek use (19:32, 39, 41) and one parallel to the LXX use (7:38). Nineteen times it refers to the community of God's people, with the first occurrence in 5:11 designating the group that had previously been called "brothers" (1:15) and "believers" (2:44). In Luke's narrative as a whole, ἐκκλησία denotes both local communities of those who profess faith in Christ (8:1; 11:26; 13:1) and the collection of those communities regionally (9:31) and worldwide (20:28). It denotes the people Christ was gathering through the preaching of the gospel, empowering through the work of the Holy Spirit, and holding accountable to his standard of integrity. Larkin suggests that "to find [ἐκκλησία] at the climax of [5:1–11] only heightens the seriousness of Ananias and Sapphira's sin and gives explicit justification for the severity of their punishment" (1995, 87).

THEOLOGICAL FOCUS

The narratival function of Acts 5:1–11 is to describe another significant aspect of early church life while connecting two of Luke's summary passages. He had previously depicted the community of believers as characterized by great grace that resulted in powerful witness and generous sharing (4:32–37). He would subsequently depict it as also characterized by great power that resulted in many signs and wonders (5:12–16). In both summary passages, he highlighted the disciples' deep unity (4:32; 5:12). By succumbing to Satan's influence, Ananias and Sapphira's actions placed that unity in jeopardy. How would God maintain the unity and integrity of the community he was gathering? What impact would his actions have on that community? Luke's two brief narratives describing Ananias and Sapphira's sin and judgment make it clear that God the Holy Spirit is present among his people, knows everything they do, and acts to maintain the purity and peace of his church.

Theologically, Acts 5:1–11 serves several purposes related to the spiritual life of the Christian community. It reveals Satan's continuing opposition to what Jesus began to do and teach. Satan had previously attacked Jesus, Judas, and Peter; now he shifted his attention from the leadership of the movement to its members. It reminds that human beings are responsible for their sin. Satan might have suggested the idea of withholding some of the proceeds from the sale of property, but Ananias had adopted the action as his own, and Sapphira was in full agreement. It reinforces the Holy Spirit's presence and activity in the community of Jesus's followers. Ananias's sin of lying was not a sin against men but against the Spirit; Sapphira's complicity in the sin was an act of testing the Spirit. It reminds us that God sets high standards for his people and expects them to live up to those standards. Barnabas observed those standards and became a model for the community; Ananias and Sapphira violated those standards and became a warning for it. This latter reminder is the primary lesson to draw from the passage: God holds his people accountable to a divine standard of integrity. Just as it had been important to maintain the integrity of the apostolic team (1:12–26), it was equally important to maintain the integrity of the community of disciples the apostles led.

PREACHING AND TEACHING STRATEGIES

Exegetical/Theological Synthesis

Luke's first-century readers would have wanted to know whether the corporate life of the early church was as idyllic as the preceding summary passages suggested. He had depicted the community of disciples as committed, caring, sincere, and devout (2:42–47). Although there was opposition from outsiders (4:1–31), the community continued to grow, and the disciples continued to exhibit great grace, deep unity, powerful witness, and selfless generosity (4:32–37). The disciples, however, still lived in a fallen world, and this time the threat came from inside. Luke's account of the events surrounding the deaths of Ananias and Sapphira reveals the continuing spiritual conflict the church faces. Satan is still active. Human beings are still sinful. All sin is still against God, who is still holy and still judges it. One significant difference is the presence of the Holy Spirit among Christ's people. As Barrett writes, "the Spirit so completely and radically dwells in the church as to be the one who experiences what is done to it" (1994, 266). The Spirit's experience of Ananias and Sapphira's attitudes and actions resulted in summary divine judgment that served as a warning for the rest of the disciples: "God deals with sin, especially church members' deceit and lack of integrity" (Larkin 1995, 84). With the original audience, the twenty-first-century audience shares the need to understand that God holds his people accountable for their attitudes and actions and will take whatever actions might be necessary to preserve the purity and peace of his church.

Preaching/Teaching Idea

No one lies to God and lives.

Contemporary Connections

What does it mean?

Acts opens with a flurry of Spirit-filled activity and growth. Thousands of souls joined God's community inspiring presumably hundreds of transactions of selling possessions and property and entrusting the proceeds to the apostles' care to help the neediest among them. A lot of money changed hands, and it would soon overwhelm the apostles (cf. 6:1–7). In the midst of the dizzying exchange of goods and funds, however, God's Spirit was present in every moment—guiding, directing, fulfilling, or judging. Barnabas gave out of God's great grace; Ananias and Sapphira resisted God and gave for self-righteousness's sake.

The Holy Spirit's intimate presence here, even in a financial exchange buried among many happening weekly or daily, is evident in the text. Peter tells Ananias that his supposed little white lie of the sale price of his land was no less than siding with Satan and seeking to deceive God to his face. Selling the land in the first place was not the issue; the couple could have kept it. Giving only a portion of the proceeds of the land was not the issue either; they could have given a portion of it toward this mercy work. The issue was that Ananias and Sapphira agreed to sell the land and kept part of the proceeds, but sought to deceive Peter and the apostles into thinking that they, like Barnabas and others before him, were giving the full sale price away. They wanted to appear more generous than they actually were.

If left to their own resources, the plan would probably have fooled the apostles. Ananias and Sapphira would have gotten away with the double "gain" of a reputation in the church for generosity and secret cultivating of private greed. The apostles were not the only ones in the room, though. God's Spirit was there, as everywhere, weighing the thoughts and intentions of the heart (cf. Heb. 4:12–13).

Is it true?
There are haunting echoes in this passage of another couple, another temptation, another fall from God's blessed community. Satan tempted Adam and Eve to disobey God and choose self over obedience. When God confronted them in their sin, they faced death and lost the purity of what God had made. Now, all these millennia later, Ananias and Sapphira came on the scene in the setting of the Jerusalem church. Although the early disciples were certainly not sinless like Adam and Eve, Luke had highlighted the purity and unity of the church from the beginning of his narrative. Suddenly, the harmony came to a screeching halt. Together, Ananias and Sapphira sided with Satan and broke communion with God and the church. Unlike Adam and Eve's delayed death sentence, they died instantly.

More significant than their similarity to Adam and Eve is the text's portrayal of their dissimilarity to Barnabas. When the two acts of giving are set side by side, they are strikingly different. Barnabas was moved by God's great gospel grace, a grace as lavish as the giving of his son and as far-reaching as radical generosity one to another, even to newly met strangers. This act, no doubt, helped earn him the title "son of encouragement" as a blessing to the body. Ananias and Sapphira's motivations were sinister. They wanted what Barnabas had without giving up what Barnabas gave. They wanted a reputation for generosity without the pinch of generosity. In short, they wanted the attention for serving God and the benefits of serving Mammon. God was not fooled in the least. He gave *great grace* where the church was flourishing in life-giving generosity. Now he allowed *great fear* where the church might be tempted to follow in these footsteps of self-serving greed. In doing so he proves himself ever-present, faithfully guarding his flock.

Now what?
This passage hits a little too close to home for comfort. Every Christian who has spent any time in a church community knows the pull of wanting others to think better of us than we really are. It is an odd paradox. We came to faith in the first place by trusting the good news preached in the early pages of Acts: repenting and believing, finding salvation in no other name but Jesus, receiving his forgiveness of sins, and being joined to him. Although we joyfully came with no claim to a righteousness of our own, now that we are here, there is a temptation to add our good works to that righteousness. Ananias and Sapphira had all they needed in Christ. They were clothed in his righteousness and enjoyed perfect standing with God. They had God's perfect credit to their name. Why would they grasp for cheap credit with others?

We might ask, but we know the answer. It plays out in our walk constantly. Jesus wisely warned his disciples to "beware of practicing your righteousness before other people in order to be seen by them" (Matt. 6:1). His first example was giving to the needy. If we are going to walk this costly road of discipleship, we reason, we might as well get credit from each other for it. Jesus, however, entices us with something better than the applause of those around us: "your Father who sees in secret will reward you" (Matt. 6:4). That promise gives us the positive motivation we need, and if we need negative motivation, our passage provides it. God sees; God knows; God weighs the things that we might use to fool one another. They do not fool God. He does not sit idly by. There are times and places where his arm is swift and just to purify his people. Like Nadab and Abihu, Achan, and Ananias and Sapphira, we risk a terrifying end when we put him to the test.

Creativity in Presentation
Yeast is a powerful leavening agent. When you add a teaspoon of yeast to a pound of flour and the right amount of water, that yeast goes to

work in the dough. Yeast breaks down starch molecules, digests its simple sugars, and produces thousands of carbon dioxide bubbles throughout the entire batch of dough. Once leavened, the mixture cannot return to plain flour and water. The yeast is there to stay.

No wonder Jesus and Paul found a striking illustration in leaven. If the leaven is good, it is welcome within the bread. If the leaven were poison, though, such spreading would be disastrous to everything. Jesus warned his disciples, "Watch and beware of the leaven of the Pharisees and Sadducees" (Matt. 16:6). Paul pleads with the Corinthians, "Your boasting is not good. Do you not know that a little leaven leavens the whole lump? Cleanse out the old leaven that you may be a new lump, as you really are unleavened" (1 Cor. 5:6–7). A little false teaching left unchecked, or a little sexual immorality left unaddressed, could spread like poisonous leaven to infect the entire body.

The health of the body of Christ was at stake in Jerusalem. The fledgling church has seen widespread, Spirit-filled success. They had enjoyed mass conversions, powerful teaching, and beautiful community. It should have come as no surprise that Satan was lurking nearby—as he was with Jesus, Peter, and Judas. He was picking at the edges. He was testing where to infect the dough with fast-spreading leaven. If he could get the church's eyes off the risen Savior and his righteousness, and onto herself and her righteousness, then toxic pride, competition, posturing for recognition, boasting in good deeds, and seeking each other's applause would poison the entire community.

Fortunately, God's Spirit protected God's church to preserve God's glory. There is much to expound here: the Holy Spirit's presence, why lying to each other is really lying to God, and the seriousness of putting God to the test. Preachers can easily fall into the trap of cleaning up stories to make God look agreeable, but removing potential offense is not Luke's aim in this passage, and it should not be ours. God sees and judges the heart. That truth is good news for a church that longs to be pure and unified in him.

No one lies to God and lives.

- Ananias and Sapphira sin (5:1–4, 7–9).

- God responds (5:5–6, 10).

- The church reacts (5:11).

DISCUSSION QUESTIONS

1. What do you think motivated Ananias and Sapphira to act as they did? What was inappropriate about the way in which they handled their finances?

2. What influence does Satan have over the actions of individuals? Why are those individuals—not Satan—accountable for their own actions?

3. What does it mean "to put God to the test"? What are some examples from Scripture of individuals who tested God? Why did he not judge all of them immediately as he judged Ananias and Sapphira?

4. To what extent should we expect God to administer his divine judgment in the lives of his people? What means might he choose to use?

5. Were Ananias and Sapphira regenerate followers of Christ or unregenerate sympathizers to the new movement? What evidence would you provide to support your conclusion?

Acts 5:12–16

EXEGETICAL IDEA
Working through the apostles, God enhanced the church's reputation, added to the number of believers, and extended the mission to the towns surrounding Jerusalem.

THEOLOGICAL FOCUS
When God is at work through his people, the church grows spiritually, numerically, and missionally.

PREACHING IDEA
When God is at work, people will notice.

PREACHING POINTERS
Do people outside the church pay attention to what God is doing inside the church? When something special happens, people notice. Although their responses might differ, they will respond. When God is working among his people, men and women around them notice. They might be alarmed, or they might be attracted, but they notice. When the Holy Spirit was at work among the early disciples, the residents of Jerusalem responded with excitement and hope. That response, however, did not stop with the residents of the city. Reports of what God was doing spread to the towns around Jerusalem. With Luke's original readers, we need to realize that God's mission advances as he works through his people. We also need to live expectantly, looking for him to work in his church and make a difference in the world.

People today should be able to relate to the attention that accompanies extraordinary events, whether those events are positive or negative. Everyone talks about them and has strong feelings about them. If they are positive, they generate excitement and hope, just as the events in Jerusalem did. Luke's account of those events corrects any suggestion that those outside the church have no interest in what God is doing. His account also commends dependence on God to advance his purposes and the expectation that he will fulfill those purposes. As his people, we must understand that his mission advances as he works through his people—and that as he does, people will notice.

THE CHURCH'S IMPACT (5:12–16)

LITERARY STRUCTURE AND THEMES (5:12–16)

According to the segmentation in UBS[5], the paragraph consists of four sentences (5:12a, 12b–13, 14–15, 16). Some commentators view the paragraph as disjointed, reflecting Luke's use of different sources (Marshall 1980, 114), with 5:12a and 5:15–16 focused on the apostles' miracle working and 5:12b–14 focused on the disciples' continued unity and numerical growth. The KJV reflects that perspective by setting off 5:12b–14 as a parenthetical statement. The more natural approach is to take verses 12–13 as a picture of the community's spiritual growth, to take verses 14–15 as a picture of its local impact, and to take verse 16 as a picture of its regional impact.

- ***Mixed Reactions to the Miraculous (5:12–13)***
- ***From Local to Regional Impact (5:14–16)***

EXPOSITION (5:12–16)

This passage is Luke's final summary passage describing the community life of the Jerusalem church. The first (2:41–47) presented the most comprehensive picture, including the practice of "having all things in common" (εἶχον ἄπαντα κοινά) among insiders (2:44–46) and the impact of "signs and wonders" (τέρατα καὶ σημεῖα) on outsiders (2:47). The second provided more details about the church's sharing among insiders (4:32–37). This third summary provides more details about the church's impact on outsiders (5:12–16), and echoes both Jesus's earlier healing ministry in Capernaum (Luke 4:31–44) and Paul's later healing ministry in Ephesus (19:11–12). It moves from God's supernatural power at work through the apostles, to the mixed reactions of the residents of Jerusalem, to the impact of the new movement as it extended to the surrounding towns of Judea.

Mixed Reactions to the Miraculous (5:12–13)

Signs, wonders, and unity among the disciples lead to fear and respect from the people of Jerusalem.

5:12. As the Spirit worked through Peter to speak prophetically into Ananias and Sapphira's complicity, so he worked through all the apostles to perform signs and wonders (σημεῖα καὶ τέρατα πολλά) among the people. In addition, Luke notes the continued unity of the people (ἦσαν ὁμοθυμαδὸν ἅπαντες) and their continued practice of meeting publicly at Solomon's Portico (ἐν τῇ Στοᾷ Σολομῶντος). The imperfect tense of the verb (ἐγίνετο, iterative imperfect) highlights the repeated occurrence of the signs and wonders. The phrase "through the hands of the apostles" (διὰ τῶν χειρῶν τῶν ἀποστόλων) is a synecdoche for the apostles themselves, rather than a reference to laying on hands as part of a healing practice (Schnabel 2012, 291). The phrase "among the people" (ἐν τῷ λαῷ) highlights the public nature of the miracles.

5:13. As is consistently the case in Acts, the miraculous produced mixed reactions. On the one hand, great fear came upon all those who had heard about Ananias's and Sapphira's demise (cf. 5:11), so that those outside the community were reluctant to associate with the disciples (τῶν λοιπῶν οὐδεὶς ἐτόλμα κολλᾶσθαι αὐτοῖς). On the other hand, those same crowds held the members of the community in great esteem (ἐμεγάλυνεν αὐτοὺς ὁ λαός) because they recognized the divine power that was at work through them (5:12). "The rest" (τῶν λοιπῶν) most likely refers to other worshippers in the temple. Elsewhere in Luke-Acts, μεγαλύνω is the appropriate response to God's great works (Luke 1:46, 58; Acts 10:46; 19:17).

> *TEXTUAL ANALYSIS: "None of the rest dared to associate with them."*
> The identity of τῶν λοιπῶν ("the rest") is actually part of a larger question regarding the identities of the three groups mentioned in the passage: "all" (5:12b), "the rest" (5:13a), and "the people" (5:13b). Suggestions for the first group include the apostles (Bock 2007, 231), the apostles and all the disciples (Barrett 1994, 274), and the apostles and some of the disciples (Polhill 1992, 163). Suggestions for the second group include all the disciples (Bock), a number of timid disciples (Polhill), nonbelieving Jews (Larkin 1995, 89), and the residents of Jerusalem (Bruce 1990, 167). Most commentators agree that the third group designates the general populace of Jerusalem, although Longenecker is more specific in suggesting responsive Jews (as opposed to nonresponsive Jews designated by "the rest"; 1981, 317). Elsewhere in Acts, the use of ὁμοθυμαδόν refers to the entire group of disciples (1:14; 2:1, 46; 4:24; 15:25) and supports the understanding of "all" in 5:12b as describing the members of the entire community. Ὁ λαός regularly refers to the residents of Jerusalem in general (2:47; 3:9, 11, 12; 4:1, 10, 17, 21). One possible solution to the identity of "the rest" is that they were other worshippers in the temple precincts who were present when the disciples were gathered in Solomon's Portico (5:12b). If so, they comprised a subset of "the people" who resided in Jerusalem. The opposition of the religious hierarchy (4:1–22) might have made many who were otherwise sympathetic to the movement reluctant to associate with the disciples when they were meeting in Solomon's Portico.

From Local to Regional Impact (5:14–16)

God continues to use the ministry of the apostles to grow the church numerically and extend its ministry geographically.

5:14. Despite the reluctance of other worshippers to associate with the disciples when they were in the temple precincts, God continued to use the ministry of the apostles. God kept on adding (προσετίθεντο; imperfect and divine passive) new believers in the Lord (πιστεύοντες τῷ κυρίῳ) in increasing numbers (μᾶλλον). The numbers were so great that Luke describes them as "crowds of both men and women" (πλήθη ἀνδρῶν τε καὶ γυναικῶν). As a result (ὥστε), the impact of the new movement spread beyond the temple precincts, first to the streets of Jerusalem, then to the towns surrounding the city.

5:15. In Jerusalem, the residents kept on bringing out (ἐκφέρειν) those who were sick (τοὺς ἀσθενεῖς) into the streets (εἰς τὰς πλατείας) and placing them on small beds and on mattresses (τιθέναι ἐπὶ κλιναρίων καὶ κραβάττων). Their hope was that, when Peter passed by (ἵνα ἐρχομένου Πέτρου), his shadow might fall on some of them (κἂν ἡ σκιὰ ἐπισκιάσῃ τινὶ αὐτῶν). The πλατείαι were the broad main streets of the city (Barrett 1994, 276). Κἂν (crasis of καὶ ἄν) plus the subjunctive (ἐπισκιάσῃ) marks the contingent nature of the people's hope. Schnabel notes that there are no exact parallels to the expectation that a shadow would heal (2012, 293), although the response to Paul's ministry in Ephesus reflects similar expectations (19:11–12). Luke does not state definitively that such healing actually occurred, but as Bock notes, "the crowd's expectation shows the attention the apostolic work has drawn and the excitement it has created" (2007, 232).

5:16. The attention and excitement extended beyond Jerusalem to crowds from the surrounding towns (τὸ πλῆθος τῶν πέριξ πόλεων Ἰερουσαλήμ). They were bringing people who were sick and troubled by unclean spirits (φέροντες ἀσθενεῖς καὶ ὀχλουμένους ὑπὸ πνευμάτων ἀκαθάρτων) to the apostles, and all of those who were brought were being healed (οἵτινες ἐθεραπεύοντο ἅπαντες). Bock notes,

"Luke does not make a distinction between towns and cities in using the word πόλις" (2007, 233). Elsewhere, the noun refers to the town of Bethlehem (Luke 2:4). Most commentators conclude that the crowds from the surrounding towns traveled to Jerusalem (Peterson 2009, 216), although Schnabel suggests that the apostles began visiting the towns of Judea as Jesus had trained them to do (2012, 293; cf. Luke 10:1–12). Regardless, the gospel was growing numerically (5:14) and spreading geographically (5:16). In its next advance, the church would cross the cultural threshold of witness to Hellenistic Jews living in Jerusalem (6:1–15).

THEOLOGICAL FOCUS

The narratival function of Acts 5:12–16 is to set the stage for the renewed opposition the church would encounter in 5:17–42. The growing popularity and influence of the new movement filled the Jewish religious leaders with jealousy (5:17), to the point where they felt they must act (Marshall 1980, 114). God was clearly at work through the disciples—especially the apostles—not only through their words but also through their works. Previously, the leaders were concerned about the apostles' teaching in the temple (4:1–7). Now, the apostles' influence extended to the streets of the city and to the towns surrounding the city, as crowds of people were joining the new community and were bringing the sick and demon-possessed to the apostles for help. Far from being intimidated by the religious council's threats, the disciples remained committed to caring for one another, to maintaining God's standards for his people, and to making a difference in the lives of those around them. Luke's summary passage makes it clear that God was at work, and the religious leaders had good reason to be concerned.

Theologically, Acts 5:12–16 highlights the truth that God was at work to advance his mission. The LEB captures the idea well by translating three key verbs in the imperfect tense as divine passives. In verse 12, "many signs and wonders were being performed" through the hands of the apostles. In verse 14, "even more believers were being added." In verse 16, the sick and demon-possessed "were all being healed." Just as he was at work to maintain the purity and peace of his church, he was also at work to fulfill its mission. The disciples might have been the intermediate agents of his activity (διὰ τῶν χειρῶν τῶν ἀποστόλων), but God was the ultimate agent. God was at work, and the people in and around Jerusalem paid attention. As reports about what he was doing spread, excitement and hope also spread. As a result, the church grew spiritually, numerically, and missionally.

PREACHING AND TEACHING STRATEGIES

Exegetical/Theological Synthesis

Luke's first-century readers would have wanted to know how the Jerusalem "man in the street" would have viewed the events surrounding the new Christian movement. The number of disciples had passed five thousand, and more converts were joining on a regular basis. The religious hierarchy had publicly arrested and released the movement's leaders, and now, there were reports that two of the members had dropped dead in one of their meetings. What did people outside the movement think about it? How would they respond to what they had seen and heard? Would they be alarmed or attracted? Luke's third summary passage says that people responded in multiple ways. Some were afraid to associate with the disciples; others praised them. Some decided to follow Jesus; others hoped—perhaps superstitiously—for miraculous healing. The lives of the early Christians captured the attention of the people around them, and they looked to the disciples with hope to find answers to their problems. With the original audience, the twenty-first-century audience shares the need to realize that when God is at work among his people, the potential exists for a widespread positive response from those around them. For that reason, they should live expectantly, looking for him to work in the church and make a difference in the world.

Preaching/Teaching Idea
When God is at work, people will notice.

Contemporary Connections

What does it mean?
The church's supernatural, Spirit-filled witness was like a pot full of boiling water with the lid on. It was "contained" for a short season in and around the temple, but now it spilled out into the streets, grabbing the attention of bystanders and compelling their response. The visibility of God's work moved outward from Solomon's Portico at the temple complex (5:12), into Jerusalem's wide main streets lined with the sick on mats (5:15), and out to the surrounding towns of Judea where more come to seek Jesus's healing power (5:16). God was certainly at work, but the people's notice took many forms. Some, sadly, were resolved to notice from afar. They esteemed the workers, the message, and the divine power present, but they were too afraid to join the disciples. Perhaps they feared the religious leaders' persecution, feared the God who struck Ananias and Sapphira dead, or closer to home, feared the disruption to their family or their way of life. Others who took notice were certainly eager for healing and exorcism, but their interest in the healer behind the healing had not yet emerged. Even so, there was a great, growing crowd of men and women who noticed, responded, and joined the Lord.

Is it true?
The centrifugal movement of the gospel in an ever-expanding area around Jerusalem clearly shows the early fulfillment of Jesus's commission in Acts 1:8. Jesus called for witnesses "in Jerusalem and in all Judea and Samaria, and to the end of the earth." Our text checks the Jerusalem box and rests its pencil on the Judea box. The Spirit is moving Jesus's gospel outward and expanding Jesus's kingdom. As long as Jesus is at the helm, the ends of the earth are inevitable.

The supernatural signs and wonders show that Jesus is certainly at the helm. There is a sense of déjà vu here. The apostles' ministry looks a lot like Jesus's ministry. Crowds of oppressed and possessed Israelites are pressing in, friends are carrying mats and cots, and unauthorized individuals are teaching in the temple to the chagrin of religious leaders. The same activities had happened just months ago—but now, where Jesus stood bodily, the apostles stand. His ministry is their ministry; his feet are their feet; his hands are their hands. The church embodies Jesus and acts in Jesus's name, all to receive friends into fellowship with Jesus.

Now what?
Churches today tend to subscribe either to an attractional model or to a missional model. An attractional model seeks to attract people, typically to the church's seeker-sensitive worship service, as a means of evangelism. A missional model works to move outward to reach people where they live, work, and play as a means of evangelism. Both models have strengths and weaknesses, and the text supports both approaches at their best. These summaries of church life paint a compelling picture of life in Jesus that is so supernatural, so divinely infused, so attractive, that unbelievers are enthralled. They want what the church has, and they come looking. Verses 12–14 portray an attractional church at its best. It is a church that draws people in and sees them "added to the Lord" to enjoy what it treasures most. The church, however, cannot stay within its four walls—even the borrowed walls of the temple—and be faithful to its commission. It

must move outward. Verses 15–16 portray the missional church at its best as it takes to the streets and greets those from the surrounding region. It will only grow. What started as a trickle from Jerusalem outward will expand overnight to a torrent of saints sent to the furthest reaches of the empire with the gospel.

Creativity in Presentation

There are two ways to keep cattle on a ranch. One is to build a fence around the perimeter. The other is to dig a well at the center. The first approach prohibits cattle from leaving. The second compels cattle to stay. There is no need to wonder which option the cattle would prefer. These summaries of Jerusalem church life in 2:41–47, 4:32–37, and 5:12–16 are like deep, life-giving wells that draw the multitudes from far and wide—men and women, rich and poor, Hebrew and Hellenist—to drink living water that quenches eternal thirst. Jesus is that attractive and compelling. God's power is that supreme over all other elements. We see heart-deep desire to move toward Jesus in this text.

A creative, faithful message might begin by digging this well. We are five chapters into Acts, and there are many enthralling truths about this God in three persons offering this gospel of repentance and grace. Everything in these chapters is fair game in this sermon, because the news spread by word of mouth and attracted the crowds. The church needed no television advertising or billboards, because the lives and testimonies of those being changed were enough to excite the curiosity and desire of a nation. What were people in Jerusalem and these Judean towns hearing that made them come?

Noticing Jesus, coming to receive something from Jesus, and even hanging around where people are discussing Jesus is not enough, though. Jesus himself warned of superficial discipleship in John 6, when he challenged the people for following him because he offered free food (John 6:26). Our text portrays crowds, not converts. Interest in novelty is not new life; to esteem Jesus highly is not to believe in him. The sermon's application might walk through *positive* responses to Jesus that are not *saving* responses to Jesus. This difference is critical. God forbid that there might be those in the crowd of our hearers who are holding Jesus in high esteem, but dare not lay down their life, take up their cross, and join him. For those who do, our text says, they are doing more than joining to a movement. They are doing more than just joining the church; the Scriptures say they are "being added to the Lord" (5:14). They have found the well. May they never be thirsty again.

When God's grace is at work, needy people will notice.

- God is graciously at work (5:12).

- The neediest souls notice and respond (5:13–16).

DISCUSSION QUESTIONS

1. What role did the miraculous play in the life of the early church? How did signs and wonders relate to the growth of the church?

2. What role should the contemporary church expect signs and wonders to play in congregational life?

3. Why was it significant that the disciples continued to use Solomon's Portico in the temple for their gatherings?

4. What did the practice of carrying people into the streets, in hope that Peter's shadow would fall on them, suggest about the spiritual mindset of the residents of Jerusalem?

5. How can contemporary congregations make the same sort of local and regional impact that the Jerusalem church did?

Acts 5:17–42

EXEGETICAL IDEA

The apostles respond to a second arrest with unshakeable resolve, unquenchable joy, and unwavering witness.

THEOLOGICAL FOCUS

The proper response to opposition is to stay faithful to the mission Jesus has given his church.

PREACHING IDEA

Remain steadfast in success or in suffering.

PREACHING POINTERS

Everyone enjoys success, at least when it is their own success. When it is someone else's success, however, it can breed other emotions, including jealousy and anger. By any measure, the early church in Jerusalem was experiencing success. The group was growing both numerically and spiritually. It was growing in influence and in impact. The high priest and his associates, however, saw that success as a threat to their authority. As the church's influence expanded, the leaders' opposition escalated. With Luke's original readers, we need to know that there is more than one side to success, including the potential for opposition and suffering, and we need to understand that Jesus expects us to remain faithful to the mission he has given us, regardless of the circumstances.

People today should be able to relate to the idea that success can breed negative feelings, including jealousy and anger. They most likely are familiar with judicial processes that include arrest, detention, hearing, verdict, and punishment. The idea of witnesses should also be familiar, whether as part of the judicial process or in other contexts. The passage corrects suggestions that opposition is a reason to stop sharing the gospel, that followers of Jesus must obey established authority under all circumstances, or that suffering for Jesus's sake is a reason for shame. It commends resolve, joy, and perseverance in the face of opposition and/or suffering.

THE CHURCH'S UNWAVERING WITNESS (5:17–42)

LITERARY STRUCTURE AND THEMES (5:17–42)

The passage follows the common pattern for narrative passages. The apostles' second arrest at the hands of the religious leaders sets the *context* (5:17–18). The apostles' release, preaching, and rearrest provide the *rising action* (5:19–26). The apostles' second examination and defense before the council constitute the *climax* (5:27–32). Gamaliel's counsel and the council's decision provide the *falling action* (5:33–40). The apostles' joyful response and their renewed witness in the temple and from house to house are the *conclusion* to the narrative (5:41–42).

- *Second Arrest and Confinement (5:17–18)*
- *Release, Preaching, and Rearrest (5:19–26)*
- *Second Examination and Defense (5:27–32)*
- *Gamaliel's Counsel and a Decision (5:33–40)*
- *Renewed Witness in the Temple (5:41–42)*

EXPOSITION (5:17–42)

Prompted by the growing popularity and influence of the new Christian movement, both in Jerusalem and in the surrounding towns, the Jewish religious leaders renewed their opposition to it. The basic sequence of events is similar to the first incident (4:1–22)—arrest, questioning, decision, and release—with the addition of the apostles' miraculous release, preaching, and rearrest (5:19–26). Barrett itemizes the differences between the two episodes (1994, 281) and demonstrates that this passage is not a doublet of the first. Instead, it represents a second phase in the leaders' increasingly determined opposition to the movement.

In the first phase, the Jewish leaders warned Peter and John to stop preaching (4:1–22). In this second phase, the opposition intensifies, and they beat all the apostles (5:17–42). In the third phase, the opposition will escalate to the point of stoning Stephen and persecuting the entire church (7:1–8:3). As Dunn notes, this passage "sharpen[s] the sense of conflict between the apostles and their opponents and focus[es] that opposition in the high priest and his entourage" (1996, 67). The apostles' defense before the council repeated their commitment to obey God rather than men (5:29; cf. 4:19–20), laid the responsibility for Jesus's death at the leaders' feet (5:30; cf. 4:10), and provided "a concise summary of the primitive kerygma" (Bruce 1990, 172), as they once again contextualized the essentials of the gospel (5:30–32; cf. 4:8–12).

According to Scripture	5:30a	("the God of our fathers")
Christ must suffer	5:30b	("you put to death by hanging him on a cross")
Christ must rise	5:30a	("raised Jesus")
Call to repentance	5:31d	("to grant repentance to Israel")
Promise of forgiveness	5:31d	("and forgiveness of sins")
Promise of blessing	5:32b	("the Holy Spirit, whom God has given")

Second Arrest and Confinement (5:17–18)

The religious leaders arrest the apostles publicly a second time and place them in prison.

5:17–18. Filled with zeal (ἐπλήσθησαν ζήλου), the high priest and all the Sadducees (ὁ ἀρχιερεὺς καὶ πάντες οἱ σὺν αὐτῷ, ἡ οὖσα αἵρεσις τῶν Σαδδουκαίων) decided to act against the apostles by arresting them and putting them in public custody (ἔθεντο αὐτοὺς ἐν τηρήσει δημοσίᾳ). In contrast to the disciples who were filled with the Holy Spirit (4:31), the religious leaders were filled with "zeal" (ζῆλος), a word that can denote either religious zeal or sinful jealousy and frequently describes the Jewish reaction to the gospel (13:45; 17:5; cf. Rom. 10:19; 11:11). Larkin notes that zeal can easily devolve into jealousy, when it is not combined with knowledge (1995, 91; cf. Rom 10:2).

Although Luke describes the Sadducees as a "sect" (αἵρεσις), the word denotes "a group that holds tenets distinctive to it" (Schnabel 2012, 305), and elsewhere refers to a religious "party" (15:5; 24:5, 14; 26:5), including Christians (28:22). Culy and Parsons note that "rose up" (e.g., NASB, ἀναστάς) should probably not be taken literally (2003, 93), and Schnabel suggests the sense of "took action'" (2012, 305). To "lay hands on" is a metonymy for the act of arresting the apostles (e.g., NIV). Luke uses the dative adjective δημοσίᾳ adverbially to mean "publicly" (Barrett 1994, 283), which Culy and Parsons suggest implies public shaming of the apostles (2003, 94).

Release, Preaching, and Rearrest (5:19–26)

After an angel releases them, the apostles resume their public preaching, but the captain of the temple returns them to the council.

5:19–21a. During the night (διὰ νυκτός), an angel of the Lord (ἄγγελος δὲ κυρίου) opened the doors of the prison (ἤνοιξε τὰς θύρας τῆς φυλακῆς), led the apostles out (ἐξαγαγών), and gave them instructions on what to do. They were to go, stand in the temple precincts, and speak to all the people. Obedient to the angel's instructions, they entered (εἰσῆλθον) the temple (εἰς τὸ ἱερόν) at daybreak (ὑπὸ τὸν ὄρθρον) and began to teach (ἐδίδασκον, ingressive imperfect). This supernatural release is the first of three "door-miracles" in Acts (Longenecker 1981, 319; cf. 12:6–11; 16:26–30).

In spite of the Greek word order, English versions consistently take "in the temple" (ἐν τῷ ἱερῷ) with "stand" (σταθέντες; e.g., CSB), and Longenecker suggests that the participle carries the idea of "dogged steadfastness" (1981, 319). "The people" (τῷ λαῷ) had consistently been receptive to the apostles' message, in contrast to the religious leaders who had imprisoned them. The present imperative of λαλεῖτε is best understood as iterative with the idea of "speak continuously" (*GGBB*, 521). Their message was to be "all the words of this life" (πάντα τὰ ῥήματα τῆς ζωῆς ταύτης), which is "the life made possible by the saving work of Jesus" (Peterson 2009, 219). Schnabel suggests that the phrase implies that the apostles were "not to hold anything back" (2012, 307).

Angel of the Lord

Angels appear frequently in Luke's two-volume work. They announced Jesus's birth (Luke 2:13–15); they announced his resurrection (Luke 24:4–7, 23); and they will accompany his return in glory (Luke 9:26). The angel Gabriel announced John's birth to Zacharias (Luke 1:8–23) and Jesus's birth to Mary (Luke 1:26–38; 2:21). The most frequently appearing angelic figure is variously designated as "an angel of the Lord" (Luke 2:9), "an angel from heaven" (Luke 22:43), "an angel of God" (Acts 10:3), or "a holy angel" (Acts 10:22). In Acts, this figure performs miraculous deeds—including releasing the apostles from prison (5:19), releasing Peter from prison (12:7–11), and striking Herod with a fatal ailment (12:23)—and brings instructions to the apostles (5:20), Philip (8:26), Cornelius (10:1–8; 11:13), and Paul (27:23).

This angel, however, is distinct from God, who sends him (12:11). As Peterson notes, he is *"an* angel of the Lord" not *"the* angel of the Lord" (2009, 218; emphasis original). When an angel of the Lord appears in Acts, therefore, he is neither a theophany (contrast Exod. 3:1–9 where the angel who speaks to Moses is "the Lord" in v. 7) nor a christophany (Bock 2007, 239, who notes that Luke always mentions Jesus when he is present). He is an agent of divine intervention whom God sends to accomplish an assigned task. In Acts 5:19–20, that task is to release the apostles and give them instructions on how to proceed in the face of this new phase of opposition from the religious leaders.

5:21b–23. When the high priest and his associates (ὁ ἀρχιερεὺς καὶ οἱ σὺν αὐτῷ) arrived at the council hall, they called together (συνεκάλεσαν) the ruling council and sent (ἀπέστειλαν) to the prison in order for the apostles to be brought before them (ἀχθῆναι αὐτούς). Bock interprets "the Sanhedrin and all the council of the sons of Israel" (τὸ συνέδριον καὶ πᾶσαν τὴν γερουσίαν τῶν υἱῶν Ἰσραήλ) as a hendiadys in which συνέδριον and γερουσία refer to the same body and concludes that "every available leader at every level is present" (2007, 240). Luke refers to τήρησις in 5:18, δεσμωτήριον in 5:21 and 5:23, and φυλακή in 5:22 and 5:25. Τήρησις is best understood as "custody"; φυλακή is the more common word for "jail" or "prison," but it does not differ significantly from δεσμωτήριον.

When the officers (οἱ παραγενόμενοι ὑπηρέται) arrived, though, they did not find the apostles in the prison (οὐχ εὗρον αὐτοὺς ἐν τῇ φυλακῇ). In this context, οἱ ὑπηρέται ("assistants") is best understood to refer to members of the temple guard (Barrett 1994, 286). They returned (ἀναστρέψαντες) to the council and reported (ἀπήγγειλαν) what they had found (εὕρομεν). The prison was "securely locked" (NLT, δεσμωτήριον κεκλεισμένον ἐν πάσῃ ἀσφαλείᾳ), and the guards were standing at their posts beside the doors (τοὺς φύλακας ἑστῶτας ἐπὶ τῶν θυρῶν), but there was no one inside (ἔσω οὐδένα εὕρομεν). Luke does not explain how the guards were unaware of the escape. Marshall suggests that the angel rendered them unconscious (1980, 118); Schnabel suggests that the angel blinded them (2012, 308).

5:24–26. When the captain of the temple and the chief priests (ὁ στρατηγὸς τοῦ ἱεροῦ καὶ οἱ ἀρχιερεῖς) heard the report (ἤκουσαν τοὺς λόγους τούτους), they were thrown into a state of ongoing confusion (διηπόρουν, inceptive imperfect) over the events that left them wondering "what this might be" (LEB, τί ἂν γένοιτο τοῦτο). Elsewhere, Luke uses διαπορέω ("to be confused") when individuals encounter the supernatural (Larkin 1995, 92; cf. Luke 9:7; Acts 2:12; 10:17).

While they were still confused, someone whom Luke does not identify (τις) arrived (παραγενόμενος) and brought them unexpected news (ἀπήγγειλεν αὐτοῖς). The men whom the leaders had put in the prison (οἱ ἄνδρες οὓς ἔθεσθε ἐν τῇ φυλακῇ) were now standing in the temple precincts (εἰσὶν ἐν τῷ ἱερῷ ἑστῶτες) and were in the process of teaching the people (διδάσκοντες τὸν λαόν)—just as the angel had commanded them (5:20). The captain of the temple and his officers (ὁ στρατηγὸς σὺν τοῖς ὑπηρέταις) then successfully accomplished what the officers alone had been unable do: they brought (ἦγεν) the apostles before the council. Because they were afraid that the people might stone them (ἐφοβοῦντο τὸν λαόν, μὴ λιθασθῶσιν), though, they were careful not to use any force (μετὰ βίας). The apostles did not resist, which Marshall notes is characteristic of the disciples whenever they were arrested (1980, 119).

Second Examination and Defense (5:27–32)
In response to the high priest's questioning, the apostles reaffirm their obedience to God and the message he has given them.

5:27–28. The captain and his officers brought (ἀγαγόντες) the apostles into the council chamber and caused them to stand (αὐτοὺς ἔστησαν) "before the council" (GNB, ἐν τῷ συνεδρίῳ). Most likely, as before, the apostles stood in the open center space created by the semicircle where the council members sat (4:7). The high priest himself conducted the examination (ἐπηρώτησεν αὐτοὺς ὁ ἀρχιερεύς), which highlights the seriousness of the hearing (Schnabel 2012, 309). His examination included a rebuke and two accusations.

First, he reminded the apostles that the council had previously instructed them (παραγγελίᾳ παρηγγείλαμεν ὑμῖν) to stop teaching on the authority of Jesus's name (μὴ διδάσκειν ἐπὶ τῷ ὀνόματι τούτῳ; cf. 4:18). Παραγγελίᾳ παρηγγείλαμεν "suggests a Semitic construction, either a translation of or an imitation of a Hebrew infinitive absolute" (Barrett 1994, 288). The NLT translates the idea as "we gave you strict orders." Μὴ διδάσκειν is indirect discourse and equivalent to μή plus the present imperative to command the apostles to stop an activity that was already in progress (*GGBB*, 724). Ἐπὶ τῷ ὀνόματι τούτῳ could indicate either the content of their teaching ("about this name") or the authority for their teaching ("on the basis of this name").

Then, he accused the apostles of doing exactly the opposite of what they had been commanded. Rather than stopping, they had filled Jerusalem full of their teaching (πεπληρώκατε τὴν Ἰερουσαλὴμ τῆς διδαχῆς ὑμῶν). The consummative perfect of πεπληρώκατε emphasizes the leaders' evaluation of the current situation in Jerusalem: the city has been filled with the apostles' teaching (genitive of content). In fact, their teaching had even begun to overflow into the surrounding towns (5:16).

Finally, he accused the apostles of intending to make the leaders guilty of Jesus's death (βούλεσθε ἐπαγαγεῖν ἐφ' ἡμᾶς τὸ αἷμα τοῦ ἀνθρώπου τούτου). The use of βούλεσθε points to an ongoing (present tense) deliberate plan on the apostle's part, at least from the leaders' perspective. To "bring blood on" someone is to blame that person for another's death (2 Sam. 1:16; Ezek. 18:13; Hos. 12:14). Ironically, his statement echoed the crowd's response to Pilate when he declared Jesus innocent: "His blood be on us and on our children" (Matt. 27:25). Schnabel notes that although the apostles had indeed been ascribing responsibility for Jesus's death to the leaders (2:23, 36; 3:13–15, 17; 4:10–11, 27), they attributed it to ignorance (3:17) and had not expressed a desire for revenge (2012, 311).

5:29–32. With Peter acting as the primary spokesperson (ἀποκριθεὶς Πέτρος), the apostles responded (οἱ ἀπόστολοι εἶπαν) and reiterated their previous commitment to obey God rather than men (πειθαρχεῖν δεῖ θεῷ μᾶλλον ἢ ἀνθρώποις; cf. 4:19–20). The verb πειθαρχέω frames verses 29–32 and clarifies the basic issue as obedience. Obedience to God includes not only the apostles' faithfulness to their mission (5:29) but also the leaders' response to the apostles' message (5:31)—the apostles proved to be obedient; the leaders did not.

Peter continued by summarizing recent events. The God of their fathers raised up Jesus (ἤγειρεν Ἰησοῦν), but the leaders (ὑμεῖς) killed (διεχειρίσασθε) him by hanging him on a tree (κρεμάσαντες ἐπὶ ξύλου). The mention of "the God of our fathers" (ὁ θεὸς τῶν πατέρων ἡμῶν) made it clear that the events "belong to the history of salvation that God initiated with his revelation to Abraham, Isaac, Jacob, Moses, David, and the other prophets" (Schnabel 2012, 311). Johannes Louw and Eugene Nida suggest "to lay hands on someone and kill" for διαχειρίζομαι (L&N §20.62). "Hanging someone on a tree" (κρεμάσαντες ἐπὶ ξύλου) is idiomatic for crucifixion (Culy and Parsons 2003, 100) and alludes to the curse in Deuteronomy 21:22–23 (cf. Gal. 3:13).

This Jesus (τοῦτον) whom they had killed was in fact leader (ἀρχηγόν; cf. 3:15) and savior (σωτῆρα; cf. 4:12), and God had exalted him to his right hand (ὕψωσεν τῇ δεξιᾷ αὐτοῦ; cf. 2:33). The purpose of that exaltation was to give (δοῦναι, infinitive of purpose) repentance (μετάνοιαν; cf. 2:38; 3:19) and forgiveness of sins (ἄφεσιν ἁμαρτιῶν; cf. 2:38) to Israel (τῷ Ἰσραήλ). Jesus was not a threat to Israel, as its leaders supposed; he was a potential source of blessing. The apostles were faithful and obedient witnesses of these events (ἡμεῖς ἐσμεν μάρτυρες τῶν ῥημάτων τούτων), as was the Holy Spirit (καὶ τὸ πνεῦμα τὸ ἅγιον), whom God would give to those who would obey him (ὃ ἔδωκεν ὁ θεὸς τοῖς πειθαρχοῦσιν αὐτῷ) by responding to the gospel message. The Holy Spirit was both the second witness needed to confirm a testimony (cf. Deut. 17:6; 19:15) and a second promise of blessing who would accompany the forgiveness of sins.

TEXTUAL ANALYSIS: "God . . . raised up Jesus"
Although the verb ἐγείρω commonly refers to God raising Jesus from the dead (3:15; 4:10; 10:40; 13:30, 37; 26:8), Larkin argues for "to bring on the stage of human history," based on the verb's placement at the beginning of Peter's description of salvation events (1994, 94). To this point in Luke's narrative, however, ἀνίστημι has denoted the latter idea (3:22, 26). Barrett's analysis is helpful: if ὕψωσεν τῇ δεξιᾷ αὐτοῦ refers to Jesus's postresurrection exaltation (which seems likely), ἤγειρεν more naturally refers to the

resurrection (1994, 289). Since Larkin was part of the translation team for Acts, it is interesting that NLT translates verse 30 as "The God of our ancestors raised Jesus from the dead, after you killed him by hanging him on a cross."

Gamaliel's Counsel and a Decision (5:33–40)

Heeding Gamaliel's counsel to proceed with caution, the religious leaders beat, warn, and release the apostles.

5:33–34. When they heard the apostles' response (ἀκούσαντες), the members of the council became infuriated (διεπρίοντο) and began planning to kill them (ἐβουλεύοντο ἀνελεῖν αὐτούς). The verb διαπρίω has the literal meaning of "to saw through," but in this context, Bock suggests "to split open in rage" (2007, 249). The members of the council had reached the point of murderous fury. They would act on that fury when they stoned Stephen (7:54), but in this instance, a Pharisee by the name of Gamaliel (Φαρισαῖος ὀνόματι Γαμαλιήλ) forestalled them. He asked the guards to put the apostles outside for a little while (ἔξω βραχὺ τοὺς ἀνθρώπους ποιῆσαι) so that the council could go into executive session and consider his counsel.

A Pharisee by the Name of Gamaliel
The Talmud mentions Gamaliel the Elder (also Gamaliel I) twenty-eight times, and he is the only rabbi Luke mentions in Acts (Bock 2007, 249). He lived from ca. A.D. 20 until ca. A.D. 50, was the grandson of Hillel the Elder, and was Paul's teacher (Acts 22:3). Luke describes him as a member of the Sanhedrin (τις ἐν τῷ συνεδρίῳ), a teacher of the law (νομοδιδάσκαλος), respected by the people (τίμιος παντὶ τῷ λαῷ), and a Pharisee (Φαρισαῖος). Josephus includes the Pharisees as one of the four main Jewish parties, along with the Sadducees, the Essenes, and the Zealots (Josephus, *B.J.* 2.8.14; *A.J.*

13.5.9; 18.1.3). The Pharisees came from diverse backgrounds, were devoted to the study of the law—including oral tradition—and applied the law to every aspect of life (Peterson 2009, 224). Theologically, they believed in the sovereignty of God, the existence of angels and demons, the resurrection, and the afterlife (Mason 2003, 786). Luke later notes that some of the Pharisees believed (Acts 15:5), and when Paul stood before the council, his appeal to the resurrection created a dissension between the Pharisees and the Sadducees (Acts 23:6–10).

5:35–37. Gamaliel's brief speech is an example of deliberative rhetoric, designed to dissuade the council from the action they were contemplating. It consists of three parts: a one-sentence *propositio* introduced his advice (5:35), a *confirmatio* set out two historical examples as proof that supported his advice (5:36–37), and a concluding *peroratio* appealed to their emotions by suggesting that they might be found to be opposing God (θεομάχοι) if they did not follow his advice (5:38–39a). He began by addressing them as "men of Israel" (ἄνδρες Ἰσραηλῖται; cf. 2:22) and advising them to "think before [they] act on [their] emotions" (Bock 2007, 250).

His first historical example (πρὸ γὰρ τούτων τῶν ἡμερῶν) was Theudas, who persuaded (ἐπείθοντο αὐτῷ) about four hundred men to follow him (ᾧ προσεκλίθη ἀνδρῶν ἀριθμὸς ὡς τετρακοσίων). Ultimately, he was killed (ἀνῃρέθη), his followers were scattered (διελύθησαν), and the movement came to nothing (ἐγένοντο εἰς οὐδέν). The second historical example was Judas the Galilean (ὁ Γαλιλαῖος), who led people after him in revolt (ἀπέστησεν λαὸν ὀπίσω αὐτοῦ) in the days of the census (ἐν ταῖς ἡμέραις τῆς ἀπογραφῆς). Ultimately, he perished (ἀπώλετο) and his followers were scattered (διεσκορπίσθησαν). Larkin suggests that Gamaliel's logic is "that as these movements died with the death of the leader . . . Christianity too will soon die out, for its leader is now dead" (1995, 96).

Theudas and Judas

In support of his counsel to exercise care regarding the apostles, Gamaliel cites two revolutionary movements, the first led by Theudas (5:36), the second led by Judas (5:37). Barrett notes, "the identification and date of Judas are not in doubt" (1994, 294). He was Judas of Gamala in Gaulanitis, who led a protest against taxation in Judea ca. A.D. 6 and, as a result, launched the Zealot movement (Josephus, *B.J.* 2.8.1). The identity of Theudas, however, has prompted considerable scholarly discussion, including suggestions by some that it is "the most atrocious historical blunder in Acts" (Longenecker 1981, 322, who subsequently refutes that suggestion). The problem is that Josephus mentions a Theudas, who led a revolt ca. A.D. 44–46 when Fadus was procurator (*A.J.* 20.5.1), but Gamaliel was speaking ca. A.D. 31 and placed Theudas *before* Judas. Barrett believes "the simple solution" is that Luke made a mistake, because he was either confused or unaware of the true date of Theudas's uprising (1994, 296). Other commentators, however, conclude that Gamaliel was referring to a different, earlier Theudas (Larkin 1995, 97; Longenecker 1981, 323; Marshall 1980, 122; Peterson 2009, 225; Schnabel 2012, 315). Bruce offers three arguments in support of the latter conclusion: (1) Luke is a credible historian; (2) Theudas was a common contraction of Theodurus, Theodotus, or Theodosius; and (3) there were many uprisings after Herod the Great died in 4 B.C. (1990, 176). Regarding Bruce's third point, Josephus writes, perhaps with some hyperbole, "at this time [of Herod's death] there were ten thousand other disorders in Judea" (*A.J.* 17.10.4). The number of Jewish revolutionary movements during the time of Roman occupation, therefore, allows for the conclusion that the events to which Gamaliel referred occurred in the sequence he indicated sometime between 4 B.C. and A.D. 6.

5:38–39a. Gamaliel introduced the concluding application of his argument with the phrase καὶ τὰ νῦν ("so in the present case," ESV). His advice was clear: "Stay away from these men and leave them alone" (NET, ἀπόστητε ἀπὸ τῶν ἀνθρώπων τούτων καὶ ἄφετε αὐτούς). As his two examples suggested, "if they are planning and doing these things merely on their own" (NLT, ἐὰν ᾖ ἐξ ἀνθρώπων ἡ βουλὴ αὕτη ἢ τὸ ἔργον τοῦτο), it was logical to conclude that the current movement would come to nothing (καταλυθήσεται). Further, the danger in opposing the movement was twofold: if it had its source in God (εἰ ἐκ θεοῦ ἐστιν) the council would not be able to stop the apostles (οὐ δυνήσεσθε καταλῦσαι αὐτούς), and they would run the risk of opposing God (μήποτε καὶ θεομάχοι εὑρεθῆτε).

Does Gamaliel's use of different conditional constructions in verses 38 and 39 suggest that he views the second explanation as more likely? The first construction is a third-class condition (ἐὰν ᾖ ἐξ ἀνθρώπων) that can indicate a present general condition, a hypothetical situation, or a more probable future occurrence (*GGBB*, 696). The second construction is a first-class condition (εἰ ἐκ θεοῦ ἐστιν) that assumes the truth of the condition for the sake of argument. Culy and Parsons suggest that "the shift in construction is a rhetorical device that simply lends force to Gamaliel's injunction to leave the men alone" (2003, 105). Bruce notes that "the interplay of conditional constructions belongs to Luke's Gr[eek], not to Gamaliel's Aram[aic]" (1990, 178). The combination, therefore, does not necessarily indicate that Gamaliel believed the new Christian movement had God as its source, although it might possibly express Luke's assessment of the situation (Marshall 1980, 123).

5:39b–40. Gamaliel's counsel was pragmatic rather than pro-Christian (Schnabel 2012, 317);

it did not take the apostles' charges against the leaders seriously (Peterson 2009, 294); and it substituted procrastination for a decision about the gospel (Larkin 1995, 97). Nevertheless, it persuaded the council (ἐπείσθησαν αὐτῷ), who summoned the apostles (προσκαλεσάμενοι τοὺς ἀποστόλους), beat them (δείραντες), commanded them to stop speaking in Jesus's name (παρήγγειλαν μὴ λαλεῖν ἐπὶ τῷ ὀνόματι τοῦ Ἰησοῦ), and released them (ἀπέλυσαν). Luke uses a general term for beating (δέρω), and many commentators conclude that the apostles were flogged thirty-nine times (Bock 2007, 252; Marshall 1980, 123; Peterson 2009, 227). It is possible, however, that they might have received a lesser punishment (Bruce 1988, 117). Regardless, they had disobeyed the council's previous warning (4:18), and they were now liable to punishment. The council's command to the apostles was precisely what it had been previously: they were to stop speaking in Jesus's name.

Renewed Witness in the Temple (5:41–42)
Rejoicing in the opportunity to suffer for Jesus's sake, the apostles continue proclaiming him as the Messiah.

5:41–42. The apostles responded to the council's decision with joy and resolve as they continued the mission Jesus had given them. As they left the council (ἐπορεύοντο . . . ἀπὸ προσώπου τοῦ συνεδρίου), they rejoiced (χαίροντες) because (ὅτι) they had been counted worthy (κατηξιώθησαν) to suffer dishonor (ἀτιμασθῆναι) on behalf of Jesus's name (ὑπὲρ τοῦ ὀνόματος). The participle χαίροντες is adverbial of manner; the present tense highlights the ongoing nature of their joyful attitude. Bock notes that "the phrase 'counted worthy to suffer dishonor' is an oxymoron," because in a culture that valued honor above shame, being beaten would normally be a cause for shame (2007, 252). The apostles, however, viewed their punishment as a badge of honor and a reason for rejoicing, because it meant they were identified with Jesus.

Consequently, every day (πᾶσάν ἡμέραν)—both in the temple (ἐν τῷ ἱερῷ) and from house to house (κατ᾽ οἶκον)—they disobeyed the council's command and continued teaching and preaching (οὐκ ἐπαύοντο διδάσκοντες καὶ εὐαγγελιζόμενοι) the message that "the Messiah was Jesus" (τὸν Χριστόν ᾽Ιησοῦν). The frequency and venues of their ministry echo Luke's initial summary passage (2:41–47). Peterson notes that verse 42 is the first of fifteen times that εὐαγγελίζομαι occurs in Acts, and that the verb becomes a key description of the early church's witness (2009, 228). The content of that witness was τὸν Χριστόν ᾽Ιησοῦν, which is best understood as a construction where the infinitive εἶναι is implied and the article marks the subject (cf. 18:5). In the face of intensified opposition, the apostles intensified their own activitiy by repeatedly proclaiming that Jesus was the fulfillment of the OT messianic promises.

THEOLOGICAL FOCUS

The narratival function of Acts 5:17–42 is to close Luke's account of the disciples' witness to Hebrew-speaking Jews in Jerusalem (2:1–5:42). That account has included examples of the apostolic witness (2:1–40; 3:1–26), snapshots of the disciples' community life (2:41–47; 4:23–31, 32–37; 5:12–16), and their response to opposition from the Jewish religious leaders (4:1–22; 5:17–42). Each of those aspects appears in the passage. The apostles' response to the high priest's question both affirms their commitment to their mission and contextualizes the essentials of the gospel (5:29–32). The events following their release echo elements of both early church life and apostolic preaching (5:41–42). The focus of the passage is the second phase of the leaders' opposition. It lays the foundation for the cultural and geographic expansion that will take place in subsequent events: Stephen's witness to the Hellenistic Jews in Jerusalem (6:1–13), his trial and martyrdom (7:1–60), and

the persecution following his death that will scatter the disciples throughout the regions of Judea and Samaria (8:1–3). Through it all, the disciples remained faithful to the mission Jesus gave his church: to be his witnesses beginning in Jerusalem (5:42).

Theologically, Acts 5:17–42 calls God's people to stay faithful to the mission he has given them. By any measure, the early church in Jerusalem was experiencing success. The disciples were seeing numerical growth, spiritual revival, popular approval, and regional influence. Success, however, can lead to suffering. The success of the church in Jerusalem and the surrounding towns filled the religious leaders with jealousy and led them to arrest the apostles a second time. During both arrests, the apostles remained steadfast in their witness. When the council questioned them the first time, they unapologetically preached the gospel to the council (4:8–12). When the council warned and released them the first time, they kept on preaching the gospel with boldness (4:31). When the leaders arrested them the second time, they followed the instructions of the angel who released them and kept on preaching the gospel (5:21). When the council questioned them again, they unapologetically preached the gospel to the council (5:29–32). When they were beaten, commanded to stop preaching Jesus, and released again, they kept on preaching the gospel (5:42). Neither success nor suffering diverted the apostles from their mission as witnesses to Jesus's death and resurrection (5:32). In the same manner, Jesus expects his people to stay faithful to the mission has given them—to be his witnesses in Jerusalem, in all Judea and Samaria, and to the ends of the earth.

PREACHING AND TEACHING STRATEGIES

Exegetical/Theological Synthesis

Luke's first-century readers would have wanted to know how the Jewish religious establishment responded to the increasing popularity and influence of the growing Christian movement. Not only were the apostles teaching regularly in the temple, but the crowds were also coming to them for help in the streets of Jerusalem and from the surrounding towns. As far as the leaders were concerned, the apostles had filled Jerusalem with their teaching and had accused the leaders of killing Jesus. Would the leaders respond obediently to the truth about Jesus, or would they escalate their opposition to him? Would the apostles be obedient to God, or would they succumb to pressure from the authorities? What would be the outcome of the success the early church was experiencing? With the original audience, the twenty-first-century audience shares the need to know that there is more than one side to success. It can produce public esteem, official opposition, or both at the same time. For the apostles, success included the indignity of being publicly arrested and privately beaten because they were preaching in Jesus's name. If success can lead to suffering, what should our strategy be? The apostles' example gives us the answer: we should stay faithful to the mission Jesus has given us.

Preaching/Teaching Idea

Remain steadfast in success and in suffering.

Contemporary Connections

What does it mean?

Things were heating up in Jerusalem. Just a few short months after Jesus's crucifixion, there was murderous fury in the air once again. In the last chapter, the religious leaders brought the apostles in for the first time to size them up and intimidate them. Failing to silence them, this second arrest led to jail, a warning, and a beating with a clear desire to do worse given any excuse. The costliness of following Jesus was becoming more apparent. It would not be all breaking bread, shared possessions, and happy fellowship with new friends. Some would bleed.

The call on every Christian is to remain steadfast in success and in suffering, all in service to Jesus. Peter and the apostles reiterated that to which every believer is bound—the core tenets that make steadfastness in the face of opposition essential. The God of Scripture delivered Jesus to be crucified, raised, and ascended, so that he might offer repentance, forgiveness, and his Spirit to all who believe (5:29–32). If the message is true, if the impulse for obedience and witness comes from the triune creating and delivering God himself, then no human authority, even credentialed religious authority, can stand between a born-again believer and resolute submission to her God, whatever the cost.

Is it true?

Many of the ideas in this passage are backward from the world's perspective but straightforward from God's perspective. First, the religious leaders had the message of Jesus backward. They complained to the apostles, "You intend to bring this man's blood upon us" (5:28). The irony is that they thought the apostles intended to make them look guilty before the people. They saw it as a threat. Meanwhile, the apostles meant it as a blessing. If they would own the charge of the sin that required Jesus's sacrificial death, they would find God's gift of forgiveness. Bringing this man's blood upon someone in personal guilt would open the door to bring this man's blood upon someone in washing that very guilt away.

Second, the religious leaders presumed that they were *defending* God by opposing man, but in reality they were *offending* God by opposing these men sent in God's name. They presumed to know God, but they were actually forbidding these men to do what God's angel specifically called them to do. Even though Gamaliel pointed out this terrifying possibility, by beating the apostles and charging them not to speak of Jesus these leaders placed themselves among the very opposition to God they thought they were avoiding.

Third, what the religious leaders meant for shame in arresting, beating, and warning the apostles, God's leaders received as just the opposite—a high honor in service of their master, further invigorating their work for him. Ultimately, steadfastness and even joy in suffering is only possible in God's upside-down kingdom, where Jesus's blood is welcome, civil disobedience may be obedience, and enduring shame is truly an honor.

Now what?
The great, insidious enemy of the church is not persecution but comfort, not want but plenty, not beatings and arrests but being ignored. It might be difficult for the church in free countries today to imagine the constant anxiety of imminent persecution at any moment in the apostles' day. Our persecutions will be light in comparison. Even so, the same truths that formed the core of the apostles' trial testimony, and the same truths that showed the religious leaders to be backward in their assumptions, propel us forward in obedience to Christ. If the God of Scripture truly delivered Jesus over to death and glory to offer terms of peace, we are compelled to follow. If in God's kingdom, Jesus's blood upon us is good, opposing his people is opposing him, and shame is honor, we are compelled to follow. Come comfort or persecution, come success or trials, we walk with the early church in the footsteps of Jesus, steadfast in his Spirit, for the sake of his name and fame.

Creativity in Presentation
"What's in a name?" Juliet complains in Shakespeare's *Romeo and Juliet*. "That which we call a *rose* by any other name would smell as sweet," she continues. Were her beloved Romeo not of the family enemy Montagues, he would be eligible. He happened to be a Montague, though, and was decidedly not eligible. Apparently, there is a lot in a name.

The same truth applies to our passage. The religious leaders were furious that Christians were filling Jerusalem with "*this* name" with a message about "*this* man's blood" (5:28). This unmentionable name is the sticking point. To the apostles, "there is no other name" in which to find salvation (4:12) and it would be a great honor "to suffer for the name" (5:41). The Sadducees demanded them "not to speak in the name of Jesus" (5:40). Apparently, there is a lot in a name.

One creative approach to preaching this section and building to steadfast suffering in Jesus's name would be to unpack the upside-down ways the kingdom of God operates in this passage. As noted above, the apostles and the religious leaders could not have thought more differently about the message, the messengers, and the means. To the religious leaders, the message of guilt for Jesus's death seemed like a curse; to the disciples it was the first step to God's greatest blessing. To the religious leaders, they were opposing a manmade movement; to the disciples they were opposing God. To the religious leaders, beating the disciples would shame them; but to the disciples, shame in Jesus's name was a great honor. The two sides could not have understood what was happening more differently. Only one side was squarely within God's will. Only God could give eyes to see reality. That warning is, essentially, what Gamaliel told his fellow leaders.

In 1945, a group of Army Rangers and Filipino guerilla fighters sneaked thirty miles behind Japanese enemy lines to rescue five hundred American prisoners of war at Cabanatuan. Captured at the Battle of Bataan, these prisoners had endured unspeakable suffering in the Bataan Death March and nearly three years of imprisonment in harsh conditions. When the surprise raid came, the prisoners had been imprisoned so long they could not recognize the new uniforms of fellow American soldiers. Fearing a Japanese trick, some resisted and even fought back against rescue. So it is in our text. Without divine eyes to see truth from error, light from darkness, honor from shame, the upside-down kingdom of a crucified Savior looks like bad news to be resisted and opposed, not good news to be embraced. Opposing the messenger is tantamount to opposing God, while those who shamefully resisted and were persecuted end up divinely honored. But as for us, we remain steadfast in success or in suffering.

- Our messengers: Being beaten in Jesus's name is not a shame but an honor (5:17–26, 41).

- Our message: Jesus's death is not a curse but a blessing (5:27–32).

- Our means: This movement is not man's but God's (5:33–42).

DISCUSSION QUESTIONS

1. What charges did the high priest level against the apostles? How did the apostles answer those charges?

2. Why did the apostles focus on "obedience" in their defense before the council?

3. Why did the council members react so strongly to the apostles' answer, to the point of wanting to kill them?

4. How would you evaluate Gamaliel's counsel? Would you characterize it as wise, pragmatic, fatalistic, or something else entirely?

5. Why were the disciples able to rejoice despite being beaten?

Acts 6:1–7

EXEGETICAL IDEA

The church commissions seven men to address an oversight in the care of widows, while the apostles focus on their primary ministry, and the number of disciples continues to grow.

THEOLOGICAL FOCUS

In meeting the challenges of ministry, God's people must set clear priorities, share leadership responsibilities, and maintain proper balance between mercy and mission.

PREACHING IDEA

Match calling with the need to balance mercy and mission.

PREACHING POINTERS

Have you ever found yourself facing a choice between equally important needs? You set out the pros and cons and find that your lists are the same length. What should you do? You could choose to ignore both needs. You could focus on one and ignore the other. You could do both poorly. You long to find a way to do both well. If there is a way, what is it? The early church faced exactly that sort of problem when a complaint arose about the treatment of the widows in the Jerusalem congregation. How would they handle a problem that seemed to pit mercy against mission? The solution was to match calling with need. The result was continued numerical growth as well as a model for how congregations can identify emerging leaders to meet the ever-changing demands of ministry.

People today should be able to relate to multiple concepts in the passage, including the challenges widows face, perceived unequal care of minority groups, and tensions that can arise between cultural groups. They should also be able to relate to establishing qualifications for selecting individuals for a role or position, setting priorities for different roles, and division of labor to meet needs. The passage corrects any notion that material needs are unimportant or that giving attention to needs within a congregation somehow restricts the potential for church growth. Luke's account commends a commitment to shared ministry, to balancing the competing needs created by ministry, and to matching calling to ministry need. As Christ's people encounter needs that arise within their congregations today, they need to follow the early church's example of adaptability and flexibility, while keeping their focus on the mission he has given them.

THE CHURCH'S FIRST PROBLEM (6:1–7)

LITERARY STRUCTURE AND THEMES (6:1–7)

The passage follows the form of an "appointment history" (Talbert 2005, 73–75; cf. Bock 2007, 256) that also occurs in the OT (Gen. 41:25–45; Exod. 18:13–26; Num. 11:10–24; 27:12–23; Deut. 1:9–18). The basic form consists of three parts: (1) stating a problem; (2) proposing a solution, including qualifications; and (3) making the selection. The following table highlights the common structure of two OT accounts in Numbers and two NT accounts in Acts.

	Seventy Elders (Num. 11:10–25)	Joshua (Num. 27:12–23)	Matthias (Acts 1:15–26)	The Seven (Acts 6:1–6)
Problem	11:10–16	27:12–14	1:15–20	6:1
Solution	11:17–23	27:15–21	1:21–22	6:2–4
Selection	11:24–25	27:22–23	1:23–26	6:5–6

In Acts 6:7, Luke adds the first of several "progress reports" that appear throughout the remainder of the book (9:31; 12:24; 16:5; 19:20; 28:31; cf. Bruce 1990, 185). That report also indicates Luke's commendation of the way in which the early church solved the problem before it and, therefore, suggests that at least some aspects of their actions are normative for the contemporary church (Harvey 2015, 92; Larkin 1995, 17). The repetition of the verb πληθύνω (6:1, 7) forms an *inclusio* that frames the passage, and the cognate noun πλῆθος (6:2, 5) serves as a link-word within the passage. Culy and Parsons note that the conjunctions καὶ . . . καὶ . . . τε in verses 5–7 tie the progress report to the appointment history as part of a single incident that is preliminary to 6:8–8:3 (2003, 110).

- ***The Problem (6:1)***
- ***The Proposed Solution (6:2–4)***
- ***The Selection (6:5–6)***
- ***The Result (6:7)***

EXPOSITION (6:1–7)

Since Pentecost, the early church had seen consistent numerical growth—from 120 (1:15) to more than three thousand (2:41), to more than five thousand (4:4), to a "multitude" of men and women (5:14). The disciples had found favor with the residents of Jerusalem (2:42), who held them in high esteem (5:13), and they were making an impact in the towns surrounding the city (5:16). Luke, however, does not idealize his account. Not everything had gone smoothly. The priestly establishment's opposition had challenged their witness (4:1–31) and their obedience (5:17–42). Ananias and Saphhira's greed had challenged their integrity (5:1–11). Next, an issue related to the care of widows within the church would challenge their unity and would put competing demands on their leadership team (6:1–7).

So far, the disciples had balanced "mission" (4:23–41) and "mercy" (4:42–47) well. Now, the growth of the mission created an administrative snag that threatened to divide the congregation along cultural lines, as the Hellenistic disciples raised a complaint against the Hebraic disciples. For the apostles, that complaint created competing demands between the ministry of service to the congregation (mercy) and the ministry of evangelism to the community (mission). Both ministries were important, and both areas needed attention. For the apostles, assuming responsibility for serving the widows would divert them from their primary focus on the Word of God and prayer. The solution was not an expansion of the apostolic group but the selection of a second group of leaders with exceptional character, exemplary piety, and excellent judgment who could focus on the new need. The selection process they followed was similar to the one used to replace Judas (1:15–26), but the qualifications were different because the roles were different. By instituting a system of shared ministry that matched calling to need, the church in Jerusalem set apart a new group of leaders, met the needs of the congregation, and facilitated its evangelistic mission.

The Problem (6:1)

The growth of the Jerusalem church creates an issue related to the care of widows.

6:1. "Now in those days" (ἐν δὲ ταῖς ἡμέραις ταύταις) shifts the narrative to a new incident that took place within the same general time-frame as the second arrest and release of the apostles. Rather than opposition slowing the growth of the movement, however, Luke notes that the number of disciples kept on multiplying (πληθυνόντων τῶν μαθητῶν). The grumbling that arose (ἐγένετο γογγυσμός) related to an inequity in the care of the widows (αἱ χῆραι) within the community. Specifically, the Hellenistic disciples (τῶν Ἑλληνιστῶν) were concerned that the widows from their house churches "were being overlooked" (NIV, παρεθεωροῦντο) by the Hebraic disciples (τοὺς Ἑβραίους) in the daily ministry (ἐν τῇ διακονίᾳ τῇ καθημερινῇ).

The present tense of πληθυνόντων highlights continuing growth over time, and this verse is the first occurrence of μαθηταί in Acts, although the noun occurs repeatedly in Luke's gospel (6:1; 7:11, 18; 8:9, 22) and multiple times in Acts (6:2, 7; 9:19, 25, 26, 38; 13:52; 14:28). The imperfect tense of παρεθεωροῦντο suggests that the neglect had been an issue for some time. Widows were particularly vulnerable members of first-century society (Barrett 1994, 306), and the OT gave special attention to their care, along with orphans and aliens (Exod. 22:21–24; Deut. 14:28–31; 24:17–22; 26:12; Isa. 1:17, 23; 10:2; Jer. 7:6; 22:3; Ezek. 22:7; Mal. 3:5). The "daily ministry" reflects the Jewish custom of distributing food every day to the casual poor, as well as food and clothing every week to the poor of the community (Barrett 1994, 310). Bock suggests that the assistance might also have included money as necessary (2007, 257). Schnabel notes that the issue was not one of sin or of theological difference but of unintentional omission (2012, 300).

the two groups attended different synagogues (Peterson 2009, 231), and Dunn sees the subsequent putting forward of seven candidates as pointing to the existence of seven Greek-speaking house churches in the Jerusalem church (1996, 84). Regardless, the Hellenistic disciples would become instrumental in taking the gospel beyond the limits of Jerusalem to Samaria (8:4–24), the Ethiopian (8:26–39), the cities along the Judean coast (8:40), and Antioch (11:19–26).

The Proposed Solution (6:2–4)

The apostles propose a solution to address the issue.

6:2. When the issue came to their attention, the apostles called together (προσκαλεσάμενοι) the disciples and proposed a solution. Luke designates the apostles as "the Twelve" (οἱ δώδεκα) for the only time in Acts, although he previously used "the eleven apostles " (τῶν ἕνδεκα ἀποστόλων) prior to Matthias's appointment (1:26) and "Peter with the eleven" (ὁ Πέτρος σὺν τοῖς ἕνδεκα) at Pentecost (2:14). He describes the assembled members of the community as "the multitude" (τὸ πλῆθος) of the disciples (4:32; 5:14; 6:5; 15:12, 30), highlighting the extensive numerical growth of the church. He uses the same word elsewhere to describe especially large groups, including the angels who announced Jesus's birth (Luke 2:13), the crowds that followed Jesus (Luke 6:17), the Jews present at Pentecost (Acts 2:6), and the crowds from the towns surrounding Jerusalem (Acts 5:16).

The apostles began by noting a complication. If they were to assume direct responsibility for the daily service, it would divert them from their primary responsibility—the ministry of the Word of God (τὸν λόγον τοῦ θεοῦ). It would not be appropriate for them to leave that ministry behind (καταλείψαντας) in order to add another. The apostles described the daily service as διακονεῖν τραπέζαις. English versions usually translate the phrase "to serve tables" (e.g., ESV), although Bruce argues that it can have a financial sense (1990, 182; contra Barrett 1994, 311). Luke uses "the Word" as shorthand for the gospel, including verse 7, where it is "the Word" that grows while the number of disciples multiplies (4:4, 31; 8:4, 14, 25; 10:44; 11:1, 19; 13:5, 7, 46, 48; 14:25; 15:7, 36; 16:6, 32; 17:11; 18:11; 19:10). Although the adjective ἀρεστός sometimes has the sense of "pleasing (12:3), in this context, it is better understood as "desirable" (e.g., NASB) or "appropriate" (Peterson 2009, 203). Bock notes that the apostles made "a priority choice about observing the call of God" (2007, 259).

6:3. The solution engaged the members of the community in the decision-making process. The disciples were to select (ἐπισκέψασθε) seven men, whom the apostles would put in charge (καταστήσομεν) of the task. In addition to being part of the community (ἐξ ὑμῶν) the candidates should meet three criteria. They should be "well-spoken of" (μαρτυρουμένους; cf. 16:2), which points to their reputation both within the congregation and within the community at large (cf. 1 Tim. 3:7). They should be "full of the Spirit" (πλήρεις πνεύματος; cf. 11:24), which points to their Christian character as reflected by the presence of the fruit of the Holy Spirit (cf. Gal. 5:22–23). They should be full of "wisdom" (σοφίας; cf. 6:10), which points to their ability to make good administrative decisions (cf. Luke 12:41–48). Larkin captures the last three qualifications as "moral, spiritual, practical" (1995, 101).

There is no certain explanation for why the apostles set the number at seven. Josephus writes that Moses instructed the Israelites to appoint seven judges in each city (*A.J.* 4.8.14). Joseph Fitzmyer suggests that seven was an odd number that would be important if decisions came to a vote (1998, 349). Dunn suggests that seven reflects the number of Hellenistic house churches in Jerusalem (1996, 84). The most natural reading is that the seven men were to be from the congregation as a whole, although Longenecker notes that ἐξ ὑμῶν might refer to the Hellenistic segment of the congregation (1981, 330).

6:4. The solution also allowed the apostles to maintain their focus on the ministry to which God had called them. While the Seven would focus on the ministry of service to meet the material needs of the congregation, the Twelve would focus on the ministry of the Word (τῇ διακονίᾳ τοῦ λόγου) and on prayer (τῇ προσευχῇ) to meet the spiritual needs of the community. As the disciples devoted themselves to the apostles' teaching (2:42), so the apostles devoted themselves (προσκαρτερήσομεν) to their teaching ministry with persistence and perseverance (BDAG s.v. "προσκαρτερέω" 2, 881). "Prayer" might refer to united prayer in decision-making (1:24–25), regular prayer in house groups (2:42), daily prayer in the temple (3:1), focused prayer for effective witness (4:23–31), or most likely, all of the above. Regardless, the apostles understood that "prayer is essential to the church's vitality and advance" (Larkin 1995, 100).

The Selection (6:5–6)

The disciples identify seven candidates whom the apostles set apart for the task.

6:5. Luke uses a wordplay to introduce the congregation's response to the apostles' proposal. For the apostles to add the ministry of service to their ministry of the word would not have been "pleasing" (οὐκ ἀρεστόν), but the suggestion that others assume the task "pleased" (ἤρεσεν) the entire group (ἐνώπιον παντὸς τοῦ πλήθους). They implemented the solution by choosing (ἐξελέξαντο) seven men, although Luke does not describe the means used to select them. As Longenecker notes, "the apostles made the proposal; the community made the decision" (1981, 331).

Stephen's name occurs first, most likely because of his prominence in subsequent events (6:8–8:3). Luke describes him as a man who is "full faith and the Holy Spirit" (πλήρης πίστεως καὶ πνεύματος ἁγίου), and both qualities will be on full display beginning in 6:8. Philip's name is second, and he will take up Stephen's work of crossing cultural thresholds with the gospel (8:4–40). Luke later notes that Philip was known as "the evangelist" (21:8), and the fact that the Twelve laid hands on the Seven (6:6) indicates that he is a different individual from the apostle with the same name.

All the names are common Greek names (Barrett 1994, 315), and Longenecker cautions against drawing conclusions based on the names (1981, 331). Marshall, however, suggests that they were unlikely names for individuals born in Palestine (1980, 127). The fact that Luke describes Nicolas as a proselyte from Antioch (προσήλυτον) identifies him as a Gentile convert to Judaism and suggests that the other six were born Jews. Connecting Nicolas to Antioch (Ἀντιοχέα) identifies him as from the Diaspora, although it says nothing about the place of origin for the other six. It is at least possible that the Seven were part of the Hellenistic portion of the congregation to meet a need related to the Hellenistic widows.

The Seven

Beyond Stephen and Philip, traditions regarding the other five men listed in Acts 6:5 vary. The Greek Orthodox Church and the Roman Catholic Church celebrate Prochorus, Nicanor, Timon, and Parmenas as saints on a single feast day. Bruce notes that Prochorus appears in tradition as an attendant to the apostle John, the author of the *Acts of John*, and the bishop of Nicomedia in Bithynia (1990, 184). According to one tradition, Nicanor served as a missionary in his homeland of Cyprus, where he died. Timon reportedly served as the bishop of Bostra in Arabia, where he suffered martyrdom by fire. Parmenas reportedly died in Philippi after serving as a missionary in Asia Minor and Macedonia. Although Ireneaus (*Haer.* 1.26.3) and Eusebius (*Hist.* 3.29.1–3) identified Nicolas as the founder of the Nicolaitans (cf. Rev. 2:6, 15), Clement of Alexandria minimized the connection (*Strom.* 2.20.118). Witherington rejects the suggestion (1998, 250). The early identification, however, is most likely the reason the Greek Orthodox and Roman Catholic churches do not recognize Nicolas as a saint along with the other six men appointed in Acts 6.

6:6. Having selected seven "outstanding candidates" (Peterson 2009, 233), the disciples caused them to stand before the apostles (ἔστησαν ἐνώπιον τῶν ἀποστόλων), who prayed (προσευξάμενοι) and laid hands on them (ἐπέθηκαν αὐτοῖς τὰς χεῖρας). Although some commentators have suggested that the members of the congregation laid hands on the men (Barrett 1994, 315), it is more natural to understand that role as the apostles' (Larkin 1995, 101).

Laying on hands was an established OT practice of delegating authority (Num. 27:15–23; Deut. 34:9). In the NT, the practice is also connected with receiving the Holy Spirit (Acts 8:17), healing (Acts 9:17), setting apart for missionary work (Acts 13:3), baptizing (Acts 19:6), and bestowing spiritual gifts (1 Tim. 4:14; 2 Tim. 1:6). In this context, the action describes a setting apart rather than an ordination (Peterson 2009, 235). Schnabel concludes that "the laying on of hands signifies the apostles' recognition of the men's endowment with the Holy Spirit, their appointment as representatives of the community of believers, and the expectation that God will bless them in their role" (2012, 335).

As will become especially clear in the cases of Stephen and Philip, these men filled other roles as well. Marshall notes, "[Luke] does not disguise the fact that they were spiritual leaders and evangelists" (1980, 125). Although the office of deacon (διάκονοι) existed by the time Paul wrote his letter to the Philippians (Phil. 1:1) and his first letter to Timothy (1 Tim. 3:7),

it is anachronistic to view this episode as the origin of that office. As Bock observes, "the title is never used of the group, nor is there evidence that these men do all the things that deacons do" (2007, 262). It might be better to view them as members of the first mercy ministry team.

The Result (6:7)
As a result, the community of believers continues to grow numerically.

6:7. Luke concludes with a report that both explicitly emphasizes the continuing growth of the church and implicitly commends the way in which the group addressed the problem that arose from that growth. He uses three imperfect tense verbs to describe the way the word of the Lord kept on growing (ὁ λόγος τοῦ θεοῦ ηὔξανεν), the way the number of disciples kept on multiplying (ἐπληθύνετο ὁ ἀριθμὸς τῶν μαθητῶν), and the way a great crowd of priests kept on becoming obedient to the faith (πολύς ὄχλος τῶν ἱερέων ὑπήκουον τῇ πίστει). See "the Word of God" in 6:2. The idea of that word "growing" occurs again in similar reports later in Acts (αὐξάνω in 12:24; 19:20; cf. Luke 8:5–14), as does "multiplying" (πληθύνω in 9:31; 12:24), which also forms an *inclusio* with 6:1.

Although the subsequent narrative will continue tracing the expansion of the mission to Greek-speaking Jews in Jerusalem, the "great crowd of priests" testifies to the continuing growth of the mission to the Hebrew-speaking residents of the city. For Larkin, "the response of the priesthood reflects the total triumph of the church's mission . . . no segment of Jewish society was beyond the reach of the gospel" (1995, 102). Paul viewed "obedience that consists in faith" (ὑπακοή πίστεως) as the objective of his ministry (Rom. 1:5; 16:26). By including this positive progress report, Luke puts his stamp of approval on the church's solution of balancing the ministry of serving those inside the congregation with the mission of reaching those outside the congregation.

THEOLOGICAL FOCUS

Narratively, Acts 6:1–7 presents a final account of the community life of the Jerusalem church as it faces another challenge—this time, to its internal unity. The passage provides a model for balancing internal care with external outreach and for setting apart leaders to meet unanticipated needs. It also serves as a bridge from the early church's witness to Hebraic Jews (3:1–5:42) to its witness to Hellenistic Jews (6:8–8:3) and introduces a new group of leaders who will cross both geographical boundaries and cultural thresholds. That group of seven includes Stephen, who will debate members of the synagogue of the freedmen; and Philip, who will introduce the Samaritans and the Ethiopian to the gospel and will preach among the coastal cities of Judea. Others, scattered by the persecution that follows Stephen's martyrdom, will preach the gospel to Greeks in Antioch. The mission in Jerusalem is nearly complete; the mission to Judea, Samaria, and beyond is nearly ready to begin. What remains is the account of Stephen's martyrdom and the persecution that will follow it.

Theologically, Acts 6:1–7 provides a blueprint for dealing with the complex challenges that can arise in congregational life. The problem the Jerusalem congregation faced was multifaceted. It arose out of the increasing size of the community of disciples; it highlighted the cultural diversity within that community; it stressed the capacity of the existing leaders; and it raised competing ministry needs. How did they address the challenge? They identified the problem and the implications connected with it (6:1–2). They set clear priorities that would maintain a balance between mercy and mission (6:3–4). They established moral, spiritual, and practical qualifications that allowed them to identify emerging leaders who would share ministry responsibilities with the existing leaders (6:3). They involved the members of the congregation in the decision-making process (6:5). They publicly set apart the individuals appointed to the task (6:6). As a result, not only was the problem within the congregation resolved, but the mission to those outside the congregation continued to grow.

PREACHING AND TEACHING STRATEGIES

Exegetical/Theological Synthesis

Luke's first-century readers would have wanted to know how the early church dealt with internal problems that might have arisen. The apostles had been arrested, questioned, beaten, and commanded to stop preaching the gospel, but they remained faithful to the mission Jesus had entrusted to them (5:17–42), and the number of disciples continued to multiply. They had successfully dealt with a threat to the integrity of the congregation (5:1–11). Now, a threat to the unity of the congregation arose. They met that threat by commissioning seven men to address the immediate issue, while allowing the apostles to remain focused on their primary responsibilities. God gave them the wisdom and grace to institute a system of shared ministry that matched calling to need, addressed the internal issue, and continued the external mission. With the original audience, the twenty-first-century audience has the opportunity to adopt the early church's example of Spirit-filled problem-solving by following the principles and process recorded in Acts 6:1–7. Luke's account of the church's first problem reminds us that matching calling with need makes it possible to balance mercy and mission.

Preaching/Teaching Idea

Match calling with the need to balance mercy and mission.

Contemporary Connections

What does it mean?
Two essential elements of Christian ministry, mercy and mission, pressed for more attention

until things came to a head. The Great Commission church immediately adopted the Jewish practice of daily food distribution to the poor, with a special eye to widows and presumably orphans and aliens. This practice fit God's desire for his people as expressed throughout the OT. Intentionally or unintentionally, however, the daily distribution was overlooking a minority group: Hellenistic widows, most likely Greek-speaking or culturally Greek Jews. Just like the decision of Matthias over Joseph to replace Judas, this conflict could have easily pitted two groups against each other, potentially splitting them. Wisely, though, the Twelve gathered the whole body, identified the problem while underscoring the need to maintain both mercy and mission, proposed a solution, and pleased the entire group with the results. Seven Spirit-filled men emerged, who were probably culturally closer to those neglected widows, and took the burden of mercy from the leaders leading in mission. The callings matched the needs. Mercy and mission could bloom once again.

Is it true?
It is beautiful to witness the nonnegotiables of the early church. When pressed to skimp on Word and prayer mission on the one hand or mercy on the other hand, the church refused. Both ministries were essential to a fully orbed embodiment of Jesus's call. It would have been tempting. On the one hand, the apostles could have preached less and given more attention to doing mercy well. That solution might have made the Hellenists happy in the short run. On the other hand, they could have chalked up the neglect as unintentional and part of the cost of a fast-growing evangelistic ministry. There were simply too few hands to do it perfectly. The Hebrews might not have cared much. The leadership did neither. Either quick fix would have created a movement that would drift from God's intention for this body. Both gospel proclamation and generous mercy are part of God's kingdom work. The disciples had seen

this balance in their OT Scriptures; they had seen it in Jesus who prayed and preached while healing and keeping a money bag for the poor. Now they do likewise, and the fruit of their obedience were newly installed Spirit-filled leaders and more conversion growth.

Now what?
It would be anachronistic to squeeze today's unique racial tensions in America into this story with a very different setting. Nevertheless, the themes ring true. There were probably two versions of what was going on depending on where you were sitting. The minority group was feeling slighted; the majority group was thinking it was not that big a deal. To watch wise, tender leadership in the midst of a sticky situation is inspiring. We too need vision that puts gifted leaders in places that meet the essential ministries of the church. If a congregation is drifting toward all mercy and no mission, she needs godly leaders to take the helm of prayer and Word. If a congregation prides itself as a teaching church and a bastion of truth but has no care for the least of these, she needs godly leaders to trumpet mercy and justice. The care they take is noteworthy. Daily food distribution was not an "administrivial" chore. The church needed men of faith and good repute from the neglected community who were in-step with the Spirit. The mercy team would go on to include the church's first martyr and a gifted cross-cultural evangelist. Godly, gifted leadership today recognizes godly, gifted leadership for the needs at hand.

Creativity in Presentation

A speaker once decried the sad truth that most Christian workers stay closest to where there are already many laborers, while few workers go to where there are few laborers. To illustrate the point, he asked a group from the audience to lift a large log at the front of the venue. They spread out evenly out and lifted it easily. Then he asked four-fifths of the group to move to one end and one-fifth to move to the other end. Of course, the poor volunteers with a fifth of the help struggled to hold their side while the other group only needed one hand. The balance was off, and without correction, the few doing the most work would not last. In an informal setting this picture could be recreated (with less liability insurance) by simply giving the group many items to hold and asking the few to hold more and more. In our passage, the few are doing too much. Without more hands evenly distributed over what is most important, something must drop.

A creative presentation might set up this dilemma and consider the options available one by one to see if they fit. The first option is to choose mercy over mission. After all, the squeaky wheel gets the grease. If the mercy department is causing the most problems and threatening the most division, maybe that was where the apostles should spend their time this season. Of course, the Great Commission pleads otherwise. This scenario is the place to underscore how vital it is for the church to maintain this call. The second option is to choose mission over mercy. The short-term benefits include an immediate stop to the complaint. But much like flustered parents with children, if they cannot agree where to put their attention, no one benefits. The scenario is the place to underscore just why the early church saw this issue as vital, and why she invested such enormous resources in mercy. It would be possible to illustrate these options from the OT, from Jesus's ministry, and through the great summary statements so far.

Wisely, the early church chose a third option. They protected godly leadership in mission by empowering godly leadership in

mercy. If this passage does not describe the office of deacon proper, it is a sneak preview. The offices of elder and deacon work hand in hand to lead the church in her vital roles, both to the lost and to the hurting. By matching calling with need they balanced mercy and mission.

- A problem of need arises (6:1).

- A solution of calling is reached (6:2–6).

- God blesses the new direction (6:7).

DISCUSSION QUESTIONS

1. Is it possible for a church to grow too rapidly or too extensively? What sort of challenges can arise when a congregation experiences rapid growth?

2. How can ethnic and/or cultural differences contribute to issues that arise within a congregation? What are appropriate ways to address those differences?

3. Why is a combination of moral, spiritual, and practical qualities important in identifying candidates for ministry roles?

4. How does involving members of a congregation in the decision-making process contribute to buy-in of the final decision?

5. Does implementing biblical principles in congregational life ensure numerical growth? Why or why not?

Acts 6:8–8:3

EXEGETICAL IDEA

Stephen's witness to Hellenistic Jews leads to his arrest, his speech before the Sanhedrin, his death by stoning, and persecution that scatters the Jerusalem church.

THEOLOGICAL FOCUS

God is faithful to provide the faith, grace, wisdom, and power his witnesses need as they are faithful to the mission he has given them, even if that mission leads to their deaths.

PREACHING IDEA

God is always faithful to his faithful witnesses.

PREACHING POINTERS

What does it mean to be a faithful witness for Christ? When we encounter resistance to the gospel, how can we overcome it? When we are falsely accused, how should we answer? When opposition turns violent, even deadly, how should we respond? Stephen faced each of these challenges in his public ministry. Luke's account of Stephen's ministry, speech, and death by stoning provide an example of what it means to trust God and be a faithful witness, even to the point of death. With Luke's original readers we need to know that we can trust God to be faithful to us as we are faithful witnesses for him.

People today should be able to relate to seeing accounts of mob violence, sometimes related to religious persecution. They should also be able to relate to people arguing over religion and to people making false accusations against their opponents. This passage corrects any notion that there is discontinuity between Judaism and Christianity when, in fact, Christianity is the fulfillment of God's covenant promises to Israel. It also corrects any misguided impression that God fails to notice when people ignore or reject his message or messengers. Stephen's faithful witness commends dependence on the Holy Spirit, trust in God who is faithful to his promises, and forgiveness of those who sin against Jesus and his followers. As his followers, we must understand that Jesus expects us to be faithful witnesses for him and to trust him to provide the resources we need to fulfill the mission to which he calls us, regardless of the consequences.

THE CHURCH'S FIRST MARTYR (6:8–8:3)

LITERARY STRUCTURE AND THEMES (6:8–8:3)

The passage presents an account of Stephen's public ministry and divides into four sections. A narrative section recounts his witness among Hellenistic Jews and his subsequent arrest (6:8–15). An extended speech before the Sanhedrin provides a selective review of Israel's history (7:1–53). Another narrative section recounts Stephen's death by stoning (7:54–60). A brief transitional narrative—framed by references to Saul—records Stephen's burial and introduces the persecution that dispersed the Jerusalem church into the regions of Judea and Samaria (8:1–3).

- ***Stephen's Ministry and Arrest (6:8–15)***
- ***Stephen's Speech Before the Council (7:1–53)***
- ***Stephen's Death by Stoning (7:54–60)***
- ***Persecution and Scattering of the Jerusalem Church (8:1–3)***

EXPOSITION (6:8–8:3)

Stephen's ministry extended far beyond the work of serving widows (6:1–7). The wisdom, faith, grace, and power the Holy Spirit bestowed on him (6:3, 5, 8) made him a powerful witness in deed and word as he led the way in taking the gospel across the cultural threshold from Hebraic Jews to his fellow Hellenistic Jews in the synagogue of the freedmen (6:8–9). Because those he debated were unable to refute Stephen's arguments, they instituted a whispering campaign against him, fueled by the testimony of false witnesses (6:10–11). They ultimately brought Stephen before the ruling council, where the high priest demanded that he respond to the accusations against him (6:12–7:1).

The centerpiece of the passage is Stephen's speech in response to the high priest's questioning (7:2–53). Bock suggests an outline based on Greco-Roman rhetoric (2007, 275), but as Heinz-Werner Neudorfer argues, the speech is more closely aligned with OT historical reviews (1998, 276). Dunn notes that historical reviews can serve a variety of functions, including defining identity, encouraging penitence, reinforcing the interpretation of the law, and encouraging trust in God's purpose (1996, 89). The closest parallel is Ezekiel 20, where the prophet uses such a review to rebuke Israel for their disloyalty and disobedience. The most natural outline, therefore, follows the periods in Israel's history—God's dealings with Abraham (7:2–8), the patriarchs' move to Egypt (7:9–16), the exodus and wilderness wanderings (7:17–43), the settlement and united monarchy (7:44–50)—followed by a polemical application that draws parallels between Israel's past and its present (7:51–53).

Stephen's point is that just as their fathers rejected God's servants as his messengers (Joseph, Moses, the prophets) and God himself as the proper object of worship, so they were rejecting Jesus who was a prophet like Moses (7:37)—and the Righteous One whom God had exalted to his right hand (7:55–56). In so doing, they failed to hear the Holy Spirit (7:51) and failed to keep the law (7:53). In reviewing Israel's history, Stephen also exposed the unsubstantiated nature of the charges leveled against him (6:11–14) by using Torah as story to demonstrate that his perspective on God (7:2–16), Moses (7:17–43), and the temple (7:44–50) are, without a doubt, grounded in the OT Law and Prophets. Missiologically, the speech makes it clear that God is not restricted to one land or building (Bruce 1988, 130), that God's people are resident aliens (Hertig 2004, 76–81), and that God is constantly at work to fulfill his covenant with Abraham (Barrett 1994, 337).

The prophetic indictment at the end of his speech angered Stephen's listeners (7:51–54), but his report of seeing Jesus standing at God's right hand pushed them over the edge (7:55–56). They dragged him outside the city and stoned him, while he prayed for Jesus to receive his spirit and forgive those who were killing him (7:57–60). In the aftermath of his death, devout men buried and mourned Stephen (8:2), while Saul took the lead in a persecution that scattered the Jerusalem church throughout the regions of Judea and Samaria (8:1, 3).

Stephen's Ministry and Arrest (6:8–15)
Stephen's Spirit-filled witness leads to his arrest and questioning before the Sanhedrin.

6:8–10. Although the disciples initially chose Stephen as one of the seven men to supervise the daily distribution to the Hellenistic widows within the congregation, God's plan for him extended well beyond that task. He soon began performing great wonders and signs in public (ἐποίει τέρατα καὶ σημεῖα μεγάλα ἐν τῷ λαῷ), and he soon engaged in witness to other Hellenistic Jews. As Larkin notes, Stephen's ministry involved both deed and word (1995, 103) and was, therefore, parallel to the ministry of the apostles (2:42–43; 3:1–26; 5:12, 42). His ministry in deed was characterized by grace and power (χάριτος καὶ δυνάμεως), and his ministry in word was characterized by Spirit-inspired wisdom (τῇ σοφίᾳ καὶ τῷ πνεύματι; cf. NEB). In that regard, his ministry was also reminiscent of Paul's, who attributed his entire ministry to the working of Christ and the Holy Spirit (Rom. 15:18–19).

Stephen soon encountered opposition from members of Hellenistic Jewish residents of the city, whom Luke describes as members of the synagogue of the freedmen. Scholars differ on whether Luke refers to one or more synagogues, with suggestions ranging from one to five (Bock 2007, 270). The singular form of "synagogue" (ἐκ τῆς συναγωγῆς) is at least suggestive that there was a single synagogue comprised of freed Jewish slaves (Λιβερτίνων), who had migrated to Jerusalem from North Africa (Κυρηναίων καὶ Ἀλεξανδρέων) and from Asia Minor (Κιλικίας καὶ Ἀσίας). They were soon actively debating with Stephen (συζητοῦντες τῷ Στεφάνῳ), but they were unable to withstand his Spirit-inspired wisdom (οὐκ ἴσχυον ἀντιστῆναι τῇ σοφίᾳ καὶ τῷ πνεύματι ᾧ ἐλάλει). The present and imperfect tenses suggest that the debate continued for an extended period.

> **Synagogue of the Freedmen**
> The origin of the Jewish synagogue dates at least to the Persian period, or perhaps to the Babylonian exile (Bruce 1990, 186). Its primary functions were the reading and exposition of the OT Scriptures, accompanied by prayer and instruction. Synagogues also served as centers of community life, including the distribution of charitable funds. The leader of a synagogue was the ἀρχισυνάγωγος (Luke 8:49; 13:14; Acts 13:15; 18:8, 17). The social term Λιβερτῖνος in Acts 6:9 is a loanword from the Latin *libertinus* that applied to freed slaves. It might refer to descendants of Jews whom Pompey sent to Rome as slaves and who were later freed (Bock 2007, 270; cf. Philo, *Legat.* 155). The four terms that follow denote different geographical regions: Cyrene and Alexandria in North Africa and Cilicia and Asia in Asia Minor. The exact number of synagogues to which Luke refers is uncertain (Schnabel 2012, 345). Bruce, Dunn, and Peterson argue for one (Bruce 1990, 186; Dunn 1996, 86; Peterson 2009, 239). Barrett and Marshall argue for two (Barrett 1994, 323; Marshall 1980, 129). Larkin argues for five (1995, 103). Regardless of the number, Stephen's debate partners were Diaspora Jews who had settled in Jerusalem and were eager to demonstrate the same level of spiritual commitment as Jews born in Palestine.

6:11–14. Diaspora Jews who settled in Jerusalem did so, in part, to be near the temple as the center of Jewish worship (Dunn 1996, 86). They also tended to be zealous to demonstrate their orthodoxy and to protect themselves from any perception of liberalism (Longenecker 1981, 336). Unable to prevail in public debate, Stephen's opponents resorted to a less direct approach—they began a "whisper campaign" (Schnabel 2012, 347) and "secretly induced" (NASB, ὑπέβαλον) men to make accusations against him. Luke records those accusations three times in slightly different ways:

	Torah	Temple
6:11	Blasphemous words against Moses ῥήματα βλάσφημα εἰς Μωϋσῆν	Blasphemous words against God ῥήματα βλάσφημα εἰς τὸν θεόν
6:13	Words against the law ῥήματα κατὰ τοῦ νόμου	Words against this holy place ῥήματα κατὰ τοῦ τόπου τοῦ ἁγίου τούτου
6:14	Change the customs Moses delivered ἀλλάξει τὰ ἔθη ἃ παρέδωκεν Μωϋσῆς	Destroy this place καταλύσει τὸν τόπον τοῦτον

These charges were serious, and the double occurrence of "we have heard" (ἀκηκόαμεν) in verses 11 and 14 implies that the accusers had heard the statements repeatedly over a period of time (iterative perfect), as does "he is always talking" (GNB, οὐ παύεται λαλῶν) in verse 13. At this point in Jewish history, "blasphemous words" (ῥήματα βλάσφημα) included "any slanderous or scurrilous word spoken against humankind or God or anything associated with his majesty and power" (Larkin 1994, 104). The reference to "this Nazarene Jesus" (Ἰησοῦς ὁ Ναζωραῖος οὗτος) in verse 14 makes it clear that "Jesus stood at the heart of Stephen's message" (Dunn 1996, 87). The claim that Jesus said he would destroy the temple, however, was "a subtle and deadly misrepresentation of what was intended" (Longenecker 1981, 336), because John's gospel makes it clear that Jesus was speaking of the temple of his body that would be raised from the dead (John 2:21). Although he predicted the destruction of the temple (Luke 21:5), Jesus never advocated its destruction. Nor did he advocate changing the OT law. Rather, he explicitly stated that he came to fulfill it (Matt. 5:17).

The accusers stirred up (συνεκίνησαν) the people, the elders, and the scribes (τὸν λαὸν καὶ τοὺς πρεσβυτέρους καὶ τοὺς γραμματεῖς); confronted (ἐπιστάντες) Stephen; seized him by force (συνήρπασαν); led him to the Sanhedrin (ἤγαγον εἰς τὸ συνέδριον); and put forward false witnesses (ἔστησάν μάρτυρας ψευδεῖς). Barrett describes the work of the accusers as "a large-scale rabble-rousing activity" (1994, 326). The participation of "the people" (τὸν λαόν) represented a major shift in public opinion, since the residents of Jerusalem had previously been favorably disposed toward the disciples (2:47; 5:13–15). The OT specifically prohibited bearing false witness (Exod. 20:16; Deut. 19:16–18), and by characterizing the witnesses in that way, Luke portrays them "as unreliable and offensive to God" (Peterson 2009, 242).

6:15. In contrast to the false witnesses, when all those seated in the council (πάντες οἱ καθεζόμενοι ἐν τῷ συνεδρίῳ) looked intently (ἀτενίσαντες) at Stephen, they saw something very different. The NET notes that the description of Stephen's face as "like the face of an angel" (ὡσεὶ πρόσωπον ἀγγέλου) presents him as having "the appearance of a supernatural, heavenly messenger." The allusion might be to angels (Ezek. 8:2; Dan. 10:5–6), to Moses's glowing face (Exod. 24:29–35), or to Jesus's appearance at his transfiguration (Luke 9:29). Regardless, his appearance was evidence of someone who had an intimate relationship with and spoke for God. Larkin describes Stephen as "so full of the Spirit, so full of wisdom, faith, grace, and power . . . that the glory of God shines from his face" (1994, 105).

Stephen's Speech Before the Council (7:1–53)

Stephen uses a review of Israel's history to challenge his listeners not to resist the Holy Spirit as their fathers consistently had.

7:1–8. In response to the high priest's question, "Are these accusations true?" (NLT, εἰ ταῦτα οὕτως ἔχει;), Stephen began a selective reading of Israel's history with Abraham. Far from speaking blasphemous words against God (6:11), Stephen recognized and honored him as "the God of glory" (ὁ θεὸς τῆς δόξης; cf. 7:55), who graciously revealed himself to Abraham on four occasions. He called Abraham out of Ur of the Chaldees in Mesopotamia (7:2–4a; cf. Gen. 12:1–3). He promised Abraham's descendants an inheritance in the land of Canaan (7:4b–5; cf. Gen. 13:14–18). He foretold the sojourn of those descendants in Egypt and their deliverance from their suffering (7:6–7; cf. Gen. 15:12–16). He gave Abraham the covenant of circumcision (7:8; cf. Gen. 17:10–14). Stephen's account not only honored God as the God of glory; it also portrayed him as the God who reveals himself to his people, who takes the initiative in his dealing with them, who calls them to obedience, who delivers them from suffering, and who is faithful to his covenant promises.

Three potential chronological issues arise in 7:1–8. First, Stephen stated that God called Abraham before he moved to Haran (7:2). His statement agrees with Genesis 15:7 and Nehemiah 9:7 and means that the call recorded in Genesis 12:1–3 looked back to the period described in Genesis 11:27–32. Placing the account of Abraham's call at the beginning of Genesis 12 allowed it to introduce the Abraham narrative of 12:1–25:11. Second, Stephen stated that Abraham left Haran after his father died (7:4). His statement agrees with Genesis 12:4 and suggests that Abraham was born when Terah was 130 and lived in his father's house for seventy-five years (Gen. 12:4) until his father died at the age of 205 (Gen. 11:32). Listing Abraham first in Genesis 11:26 looked ahead to his prominence in the subsequent narrative (cf. Larkin 1995, 106; contra Barrett 1994, 342). Third, Stephen stated that Abraham's descendants would live as aliens for four hundred years (7:6). His statement agrees with Genesis 15:13, but it conflicts with Exodus 12:40 and Galatians 3:17, which both set the length of the sojourn at 430 years. Bruce notes that the rabbis counted four hundred years from the birth of Isaac until the exodus, but they counted 430 years from Abraham's arrival in Canaan to the giving of the law (1988, 135). Most commentators take four hundred as a rounded number (Schnabel 2012, 368).

7:9–16. From God's promise to Abraham, Stephen moved forward approximately two hundred years to God's preservation through Joseph (Larkin 1995, 105), as he superintended three pivotal episodes in the lives of the patriarchs. He rescued Joseph from his afflictions and made him governor over Egypt after his brothers had rejected him (7:9–10; cf. Gen. 37:1–36; 44:1–53). He delivered Jacob and his extended family from famine by preparing a place for them in Egypt (7:11–14; cf. Gen. 41:53–46:27). He returned Jacob and the patriarchs to Canaan for burial (7:15–16; cf. Gen. 48:1–50:13). This section of his speech continued Stephen's honoring of the God who fulfilled prophecy, was present with Joseph, delivered him from affliction, vindicated and elevated him to a place of prominence, protected Jacob and the patriarchs from harm, and nurtured their faith in his promise that they would ultimately possess the land of Canaan as he had declared.

Two potential historical issues arise in 7:9–16. First, Stephen stated that Jacob and his relatives numbered seventy-five people (7:14). His statement agrees with the LXX of Genesis 46:27 and Exodus 1:5, but it disagrees with the MT of Genesis 46:27, Exodus 1:5, and Deuteronomy 10:22. The difference relates to how many of Joseph's sons are included (Stott 1990, 133), and Marshall observes that the larger number is best understood as "the total of Jacob's descendants who went down into Egypt or were born there" (1980, 138). Second, Stephen stated that Jacob and his sons were buried in the tomb Abraham purchased in Shechem (7:16). His statement agrees with Genesis 23:16, which records Abraham purchasing a cave to serve as a tomb for Sarah, as well as with Genesis 49:29–32 and 50:13, which record Jacob being buried in that tomb. It disagrees with Genesis 33:18–19, which records Jacob purchasing the property in Shechem, and Joshua 24:32, which records Joseph's bones being buried in that location. Stott solves the problem by suggesting that Jacob bought the property in Shechem in Abraham's name, who was still alive at the time (1990, 134). Other commentators suggest that Stephen telescoped Genesis 49:29–32 (Jacob buried on the property Abraham purchased) and Genesis 50:13 (Joseph and his brothers buried on the property Jacob purchased; Bruce 1990, 196). Regardless, as Bock concludes, "Stephen's key point is that burial took place in the promised land . . . and the move was an act of faith that God would keep his word" (2007, 289).

7:17–22. Next, Stephen moved forward approximately two hundred years to the life and ministry of Moses. Far from speaking blasphemous words against Moses (6:11), Stephen used the largest portion of his speech to honor Moses, the Law, and the customs he had handed down, beginning with Moses's early years in Egypt set in their theological and historical context (Peterson 2009, 253). God's prophecy/promise to Abraham in Genesis 15 set the stage for Israel's future and included seven events. First, Abraham's descendants would become as numerous as the stars of heaven (15:5). Second, they would be strangers in a land that was not theirs (15:13a). Third, they would be enslaved and oppressed (15:13b). Fourth, God would judge the nation that enslaved them (15:14a). Fifth, they would come out of that land with many possessions (15:14b). Sixth, they would return to the land of the Amorites (15:16). Seventh, they would possess that land (15:18–21).

Stephen's narrative included the first three of those events, as the people grew and multiplied during their sojourn in Egypt (7:17; cf. Exod. 1:1–7) and Pharaoh mistreated them and forced them to expose their infants (7:18–19; cf. Exod. 1:8–22). Stephen then introduced Moses, who would be Israel's deliverer and lawgiver, describing his birth, upbringing, and education (7:20–22; cf. Exod. 2:1–10). By including these events in his historical review, Stephen highlighted God's fulfillment of prophecy, his faithfulness to his promise to Abraham, his protection of Moses, and his preparation of Moses. He also implied parallels to Jesus who, like Moses, was born at a key point in time (ἐν ᾧ καιρῷ; 7:20; cf. Luke 2:1–2), was characterized by wisdom (ἐν πάσῃ σοφίᾳ; 7:22; cf. Luke 2:40, 52), and was powerful in words and works (δυνατὸς ἐν λόγοις καὶ ἔργοις; 7:22; cf. Luke 24:19).

7:23–29. Moving forward to the time when Moses was forty years old, Stephen recounted the events that led to Moses's exile in Midian (Exod. 2:11–22). When Moses saw an Egyptian mistreating a Hebrew, he intervened, struck the Egyptian, and killed him. The next day, when he intervened in a dispute between two Hebrews, one of them made it clear that he knew what Moses had done, prompting Moses to flee to Midian.

Four phrases in verses 23–25 highlight the fact that God raised up Moses as his appointed deliverer. The events happened after the time of forty years "was fulfilled" (ἐπληροῦτο), which aligns with Luke's sense of divine timing (Luke 9:51; 21:24; Acts 2:1; 7:30). The idea of Moses "visiting" (ἐπισκέψασθαι) his brothers echoes God's visits to his people (Luke 1:68, 78; 7:16; Acts 15:14). That idea "entered his heart" (LEB, ἀνέβη ἐπὶ τὴν καρδίαν αὐτοῦ), which suggests that God planted it there (Marshall 1980, 140). Moses supposed that his Hebrew brothers would recognize that God was "giving salvation" (δίδωσιν σωτηρίαν) through his hand, which would, in fact, happen when God judged the Egyptians and brought Abraham's descendants out of that land (cf. 7:7).

These same events also returned to a theme that Stephen had first introduced in connection with Joseph: the rejection of God's messenger by those who should be looking for him (Barrett 1994, 358). Joseph's brothers were jealous of him (ζηλώσαντες τὸν Ἰωσήφ) and sold him into Egypt (7:9). The Israelites "did not understand" (οὐ συνῆκαν) Moses's mission (7:25) and "pushed him away" (ἀπώσατο αὐτόν) so that he fled to Midian (7:27). Subsequently, they would deny him (7:35) and would choose not to obey him (7:39). In the same way, Stephen would charge his listeners with rejecting Jesus by betraying and murdering him (7:52).

7:30–34. Next, Stephen moved forward another forty years to the end of Moses's time in Midian and recounted the occasion when God sent Moses back to Egypt (Exod. 3:1–10). At the burning bush, God revealed himself as the God of Abraham, Isaac, and Jacob and declared that he had seen the oppression of his people, had heard their groaning, had come down to rescue them, and was sending Moses back to Egypt. The passage clearly established Moses as the messenger sent by God to deliver his people (ἀποστείλω σε εἰς Αἴγυπτον). The statement that forty years "were fulfilled" (πληρωθέντων ἐτῶν τεσσαράκοντα) again emphasized God's sovereign timing.

By identifying himself as "the God of your fathers" (ὁ θεὸς τῶν πατέρων σου) and "the God of Abraham, Isaac, and Jacob" (ὁ θεὸς Ἀβραὰμ καὶ Ἰσαὰκ καὶ Ἰακώβ), God established the continuity of his actions with his covenant promises (Larkin 1995, 113). As Barrett notes, "The same God was at work through the whole of the OT tradition, notwithstanding the patriarch's treatment of Joseph and the Israelites' rejection of Moses" (1994, 361). God expressed his concern for his people by seeing their cruel suffering (εἶδον τὴν κάκωσιν τοῦ λαοῦ μου) and hearing their groaning (τοῦ στεναγμοῦ αὐτῶν ἤκουσα). He demonstrated his faithfulness to his promises by coming down to rescue them (κατέβην ἐξελέσθαι αὐτούς). By commanding Moses to remove his sandals (λῦσον τὸ ὑπόδημα τῶν ποδῶν σου, ὁ γὰρ τόπος ἐφ' ᾧ ἕστηκας γῆ ἁγία ἐστίν), he made it clear that "there is holy ground outside the holy land" (Stott 1990, 137).

7:35–38. After recounting Moses's commissioning, Stephen departed from his historical review and shifted to a more kerygmatic style in which he used the demonstrative pronoun οὗτος five times to highlight important facts about Moses. Stating those facts in the way he did again demonstrated that, far from speaking blasphemous words against Moses (6:11), Stephen held him in highest regard. God sent "this Moses" to be both a ruler and a redeemer (ὁ θεὸς καὶ ἄρχοντα καὶ λυτρωτὴν ἀπέσταλκεν). "This Moses" led the people out (ἐξήγαγεν αὐτούς), while doing wonders and signs (ποιήσας τέρατα καὶ σημεῖα) in Egypt (Exodus 7–11), in the Red Sea (Exodus 14), and during the forty years in the wilderness (Numbers 1–36). "This Moses" was the prophetic prototype of the Messiah whom God would raise up from among their brothers (προφήτην ὑμῖν ἀναστήσει ὁ θεὸς ἐκ τῶν ἀδελφῶν ὑμῶν ὡς ἐμέ; cf. Deut. 18:15). "This Moses" received and passed on the living oracles of God at Sinai (ἐδέξατο λόγια ζῶντα δοῦναι ἡμῖν; cf. Exodus 19–24)—a statement that reflects not only Stephen's esteem for Moses but also his esteem for God's law. As Bruce summarizes, "Under [Moses's] leadership, the people had experienced the redemptive power of God; they received the revelation of God; they enjoyed the presence of God" (1990, 202). "This Moses," however, was also the one whom the people renounced (ὃν ἠρνήσαντο), just as Joseph's brothers had rejected him (7:9) and just as Stephen's listeners had rejected Jesus (7:52). As he had done previously (7:17–22), Stephen also implied parallels to Jesus who, like Moses, was sent (Luke 4:18, 43; Acts 3:26), was a redeemer (Luke 1:68; 2:38; 24:21), performed signs and wonders (Acts 2:22), was a prophet (Acts 3:19–22), and was rejected (Acts 3:13–14; 4:11). In Bruce's opinion, "The implied parallel with the recent refusal of Jesus is too plain to require elaboration" (1988, 142).

7:39–43. Despite the fact that Moses was God's appointed ruler, redeemer, miracle worker, prophet, and lawgiver, Stephen continued, their fathers were unwilling to be obedient to Moses's leadership (ᾧ οὐκ ἠθέλησαν ὑπήκοοι γενέσθαι οἱ πατέρες ἡμῶν) and "pushed him aside" (ἀπώσαντο) a second time (cf. 7:27). As an example, he returned to his historical review and recounted the golden calf incident (Exod.

32:1–6). The people rejected Moses (7:39–40) and, in so doing, rejected God and his law by offering sacrifices to the golden calf (7:41). In response, God judged them by "handing them over" (παρέδωκεν αὐτούς; cf. Rom. 1:24, 26, 28) to wholesale idolatry (7:42–43).

Citing Amos 5:25–27 (LXX), Stephen added that, approximately seven hundred years later, the prophet referred to this particular incident as the first act in a story of "constant disobedience that Israel . . . manifested throughout its history" (Barrett 1994, 370). In so doing, Stephen established a pattern of Israel's idolatry leading to God's judgment (Bock 2007, 300). As the people of Moses's generation rejected his message and died without entering the land, so the people of Amos's generation rejected his message and were taken out of the land. He also continued to build his case. The problem was not with God's messengers; the problem was with the people who rejected those messengers. The patriarchs who received God's promises rejected Joseph; the generation who experienced God's deliverance rejected Moses; the people who possessed God's land rejected the prophets.

7:44–50. Although Israel had rejected God and his law by worshipping the golden calf, God gave them the tabernacle and the temple. Stephen next turned to those structures and made it clear that, far from speaking words against the temple (6:13), he esteemed both the tabernacle and the temple as God's appointed settings for true worship. God showed Moses the plan for the tabernacle in the wilderness (7:44; cf. Exodus 25–27), they brought it into the land during the conquest under Joshua (7:45a; cf. Josh. 18:1), and it continued to be the focus of Israel's worship until David's days (7:45b; cf. 2 Sam. 6:17). When David asked permission to build a more permanent structure, his plan found favor in God's sight (7:46; cf. 2 Sam. 7:1–17), but God designated Solomon as the one who would build it (7:47; cf. 2 Kings 5–8). God designed the tabernacle and sanctioned the temple, but Stephen also made it clear that "the Most High" (ὁ ὕψιστος) could not be contained in a manmade structure (7:48–50; cf. Isa. 66:1–2). In so doing, he emphasized God's transcendence and sovereign rule (Schnabel 2012, 385).

The question of Stephen's attitude toward the temple arises in 7:44–50. Dunn argues that since the OT used the phrase "made with hands" (χειροποιήτοις) to refer to idols (e.g., Lev. 26:1, 30; Isa. 28:18: 10:11), Stephen denounced the temple as an idol when he referred to it in that way (1996, 97). Bruce argues that Stephen's brief reference to the temple "expresses plain disapproval" (1988, 149). Similarly, Longenecker concludes that Stephen's brevity reflects a "pejorative attitude" (1981, 346). Peterson rejects both suggestions (2009, 263), and Schnabel offers five reasons that Stephen's words are not a critique of the temple (2012, 385). Stott's conclusion seems to be on target: "[Stephen] expresses neither a preference for the tabernacle nor a distaste for the temple . . . [his] point is not that it was wrong to construct either the tabernacle or the temple, but that they should never have regarded it in any literal sense as God's home" (1990, 138). Throughout his speech, Stephen consistently showed respect for the topics he had been accused of disparaging—God, Moses, the law, and the temple—and pointed out the way in which "the fathers" rejected and/or misunderstood God, his messengers, and his institutions. His next words would drive home that indictment.

7:51–53. Stephen then made "a sharp shift in [his] rhetorical approach" (Culy and Parsons 2003, 142) from historical review to prophetic indictment. He had been accused of speaking against God, Moses, the law, and the temple (6:11, 13–14), but throughout his speech he had demonstrated his respect for God and his covenant of circumcision (7:2–8), God and his providential protection (7:9–16), Moses (7:17–37),

the law (7:38–43), the tabernacle (7:44–45), and the temple (7:46–50). Witherington writes, "Stephen's speech is not Law or temple critical, it is people critical" (1998, 275). Longenecker agrees, "As Stephen recounts the history of Israel, it is a litany of sin, rebellion, and rejection of God's purposes" (1981, 347).

His indictment applied the historical survey to his listeners: as their fathers were, so were they also (ὡς οἱ πατέρες ὑμῶν καὶ ὑμεῖς). They were unyielding (σκληροτράχηλοι; cf. Exod. 33:3, 5; 34:9; Deut. 9:6, 13; 31:27), unfaithful (ἀπερίτμητοι καρδίαις; cf. Lev. 26:41; Deut. 10:16; Jer. 9:26), and unresponsive (ἀπερίτμητοι τοῖς ὠσίν; cf. Jer. 6:10). They always (ἀεί) stifled the Spirit (τῷ πνεύματι τῷ ἁγίῳ ἀντιπίπτετε; cf. Isa. 63:10–14), persecuted the prophets (τίνα τῶν προφητῶν οὐκ ἐδίωξαν; cf. Luke 11:49–51), murdered the Messiah (τοῦ δικαίου οὗ νῦν ὑμεῖς προδόται καὶ φονεῖς ἐγένεσθε; cf. Acts 3:14–15), and transgressed the Torah (τὸν νόμον . . . οὐκ ἐφυλάξατε; cf. Acts 15:10). Their rejection of Stephen's Spirit-filled witness (6:3, 5, 10; 7:55) was consistent with Israel's repeated rejection of God and his purposes.

Stephen's Death by Stoning (7:54–60)

Enraged by Stephen's indictment, his listeners drag him outside the city and stone him.

7:54–56. When they heard Stephen's indictment (ἀκούοντες ταῦτα), his listeners "began to feel increasingly angry" (Barrett 1994, 382). Their anger had an inward component, as their hearts began to be ripped open (διεπρίοντο ταῖς καρδίαις αὐτῶν; cf. 5:33), and an outward component, as they began gnashing their teeth at him (ἔβρυχον τοὺς ὀδόντας ἐπ᾿ αὐτόν). His listeners were full of rage, but Stephen was filled with the Holy Spirit (ὑπάρχων δὲ πλήρης πνεύματος ἁγίου; cf. 6:3, 5, 8, 10) and experienced a vision of the heavenly glory that was awaiting him. In his vision, he saw the heavens standing open (τοὺς οὐρανοὺς διηνοιγμένους), God in his shekinah glory (δόξαν θεοῦ), and

Jesus at God's right hand (Ἰησοῦν ἑστῶτα ἐκ δεξιῶν τοῦ θεοῦ). Not only did Stephen see the vision—he also told his listeners about it. By calling Jesus "the Son of Man" (τὸν υἱὸν τοῦ ἀνθρώπου), Stephen identified him as the messianic figure of Daniel 7:13–14 and echoed his self-identification before the same Sanhedrin (Luke 22:66–70). By placing Jesus at God's right hand, Stephen confirmed his resurrection, exaltation, and transcendent authority (2:32–36; 3:13–15; 5:30–31). Although Stephen's words traced Israel's history, Israel's Messiah stood at the center of his witness (6:14).

> ### The Son of Man at God's Right Hand
>
> Although it is more common for the NT to describe Jesus as sitting at God's right hand (Luke 22:69; Col. 3:1; Heb. 1:13; 8:1; 10:12), Stephen saw him standing (ἑστῶτα ἐκ δεξιῶν τοῦ θεοῦ; cf. 7:55–56). Barrett lists eleven suggested explanations for why Jesus is standing rather than sitting, including to worship as the angels do, to minister as a priest does, to help Stephen, to intercede for Stephen, to witness against Stephen's accusers, and to welcome Stephen. He ultimately concludes that Jesus rises to come to Stephen at his death (1994, 384–85). The most common explanations are that Jesus has risen to plead Stephen's case (Bruce 1988, 156; Longenecker 1981, 350; Marshall 1980, 149; Stott 1990, 141), and that Jesus has risen to judge Stephen's accusers (Bock 2007, 311; Peterson 2009, 267; Schnabel 2012, 390). Larkin, however, argues that the issue is position rather than posture: "Stephen is emphatically confessing Jesus's transcendent place in heaven" (1995, 121). His conclusion aligns well with Peter's speeches that emphasize Jesus's vindication as "exalted to the right hand of God" (τῇ δεξιᾷ τοῦ θεοῦ ὑψωθείς; cf. 2:33; 5:31).

7:57–58. Stephen's description of his vision was too much for his listeners. They cried out loudly (κράξαντες φωνῇ μεγάλῃ), covered their ears (συνέσχον τὰ ὦτα αὐτῶν), rushed at him with one purpose in mind (ὥρμησαν ὁμοθυμαδὸν ἐπ᾽ αὐτόν), dragged him outside the city (ἐκβαλόντες ἔξω τῆς πόλεως), and began stoning him (ἐλιθοβόλουν, inceptive imperfect). The act of covering their ears reflected their conviction that Stephen was guilty of blasphemy, but it also confirmed his earlier accusation that they were unresponsive to God's truth (7:51).

The Mishnah set out the process for execution by stoning (m. Sanh. 6:1–4). The guilty person was to be stripped, taken to a place far from the court, and thrown down from a height. A witness first dropped a stone on the head; then another dropped a stone on the heart. If the person still lived, then all Israel stoned him or her. Barrett notes, however, that only taking Stephen out of the city corresponded to the usual process (1994, 386). Luke makes a point of reporting that the witnesses laid their outer garments at the feet of Saul, and so introduces a key figure in the narrative that will follow.

Commentators have differing opinions on the question of whether the stoning was legal. Marshall views it as "a spontaneous act of mob violence" (1980, 148). Larkin concludes that it was "a true execution after a Jewish trial" (1995, 122). Schnabel characterizes it as "an act of establishment violence" (2012, 391). The legality of the act is secondary to the fact that the stoning was the next step in the increasingly violent opposition the early church faced. That opposition had escalated from threatening (4:21) to beating (5:40) to stoning (7:58–59), and it would immediately lead to widespread persecution (8:1).

7:59–60. The stoning continued for an extended period of time (ἐλιθοβόλουν, progressive imperfect). While it continued, Stephen was praying (ἐπικαλούμενον). His prayers included two petitions: "Lord Jesus, receive my spirit" (Κύριε Ἰησοῦ, δέξαι τὸ πνεῦμά μου), and "Lord, do not hold this sin against them" (Κύριε, μὴ στήσῃς αὐτοῖς ταύτην τὴν ἁμαρτίαν). His final prayers echoed Jesus's final prayers, just as his death followed the pattern of Jesus's death. The Sanhedrin tried him (6:12; cf. Luke 22:66–71), and false witnesses accused him (6:13–14; cf. Luke 23:1–2). He was identified with the exalted Son of Man (7:56; cf. Luke 22:69) and entrusted to God's care (7:59; cf. Luke 23:46). He prayed for his accusers (7:60; cf. Luke 23:34), and godly men buried him (8:2; cf. Luke 24:50–53). Peterson writes, "Stephen's death is . . . the inevitable outcome of his courageous testimony to Christ . . . he dies expressing faith in Christ and love for his enemies" (2009, 269).

The Stoning of Saint Stephen by Anthony van Dyck. Public domain.

Persecution and Scattering of the Jerusalem Church (8:1–3)

Widespread persecution, aggressively promoted by Saul, scatters the disciples throughout the regions of Judea and Samaria.

8:1–3. Having introduced him as the one at whose feet the witnesses against Stephen laid their garments (7:58), Luke adds that Saul "was approving of" (συνευδοκῶν) Stephen's killing (τῇ ἀναιρέσει αὐτοῦ; cf. Bock 2007, 316), and that he was instrumental in the persecution that followed Stephen's death. His activities frame the paragraph, as Luke further describes Saul as "ravaging" the church (ἐλυμαίνετο τὴν ἐκκλησίαν), entering "house after house" (κατὰ τοὺς οἴκους εἰσπορευόμενος), "dragging away" both men and women (σύρων τε ἄνδρας καὶ γυναῖκας), and handing them over to imprisonment (παρεδίδου εἰς φυλακήν). The imperfect tenses of the verbs highlight his repeated activity over time. "On that day" (ἐν ἐκείνῃ τῇ ἡμέρᾳ) suggests that Stephen's death ignited the great persecution (διωγμὸς μέγας) that arose against the church in Jerusalem (ἐπὶ τὴν ἐκκλησίαν τὴν ἐν Ἰεροσολύμοις). As a result, all were scattered (διεσπάρησα) throughout the regions of Judea and Samaria, with the exception of the apostles (πλὴν τῶν ἀποστόλων). Meanwhile, devout men buried (συνεκόμισαν) and mourned (ἐποίησαν κοπετὸν μέγαν) Stephen.

Three questions arise from Luke's brief account. First, did "all" (πάντες) the disciples leave Jerusalem? Later events make it clear that at least some disciples remained in Jerusalem (9:26; 11:29; 12:1), and Bock regards "all" as hyperbolic for "many" (2007, 318). The most frequent suggestion is that it refers to the Hellenistic segment of the church (Bruce 1988, 162; Dunn 1996, 104), although Schnabel assesses that explanation as "historically unlikely" (2012, 394). Second, why did the apostles remain in Jerusalem? The most frequent suggestion, again, is that the persecution focused on Hellenistic disciples (Bock 2007, 318; Marshall 1980, 151). Based on Acts 2–5, however, Witherington suggests that the residents held the apostles in such high regard that they were protected (1998, 278), and Stott concludes that the apostles saw it as their duty to remain in the city (1990, 145). Third, who were the "devout men" (ἄνδρες εὐλαβεῖς) who buried Stephen? The most frequent suggestion is that they were non-Christian Jews who were open to the gospel (Longenecker 1981, 350; Peterson 2009, 276). Larkin, however, suggests that they were Hebraic disciples who remained in Jerusalem (1995, 124), and Marshall notes that in 22:12 Paul referred to Ananias, the disciple in Damascus who laid hands on him, as "devout by the standard of the law" (1980, 152). Regardless of the answers to these three questions, Luke's point appears to be that great persecution led to great dispersion that, in turn, led to great evangelism (Stott 1990, 145), as the gospel began to move outward from Jerusalem to Judea and Samaria in fulfillment of Jesus's promise/command (1:8).

THEOLOGICAL FOCUS

Narratively, Acts 6:8–8:3 closes Luke's account of the Jerusalem church that began with Jesus's ascension and the day of Pentecost. It brings to a climax the opposition the church faced and introduces Paul as the leading figure in the persecution that follows. It also serves as a transitional passage as the church's witness expands missionally, culturally, and geographically. Missionally, the appointment of the seven (6:1–7) introduced a new group of leaders within the church who now take center stage as witnesses for Christ. Culturally, Stephen crosses the threshold from Hebraic Jews to Hellenistic Jews (6:8–15), while Philip will be instrumental in evangelizing both the Samaritans and the Ethiopian. Geographically, the persecution that followed Stephen's death scattered the disciples into Judea and Samaria (8:1–3) in line with Jesus's promise/command (1:8).

Theologically, Acts 6:8–8:3 highlights the multifaceted work of the Holy Spirit, the new movement's continuity with and respect for its Jewish origins, Jesus as the fulfillment of God's covenant promises, humankind's resistance to God's revelation, and its rejection of his appointed messengers. Luke makes a point of emphasizing the Holy Spirit's work in Stephen's ministry as he supplied Stephen with the wisdom and faith to serve (6:1–7), the grace and power to witness (6:8–15), and the steadfastness and assurance to remain faithful to the end (7:54–60). Stephen's review of Israel's history honored major Jewish figures and institutions and presented Jesus as both the climax of God's revelation and the fulfillment of his promises. Running throughout that review was the theme of Israel's failure to recognize and respond to God's messengers as they faithfully announced the coming of Jesus, the Righteous One. Stephen's indictment of his listeners serves to remind Luke's readers that they resist the work of the Holy Spirit and the truth about Jesus at their peril.

PREACHING AND TEACHING STRATEGIES

Exegetical/Theological Synthesis

Luke's first-century readers would have wanted to know the depth of the disciples' commitment to the mission Jesus had given them. They had been faithful in the face of threats and beatings. How would they respond when the opposition turned violent, even deadly? What does it mean to be a faithful witness for Christ? Luke's account of Stephen's ministry, speech, and death by stoning provides a model of what it meant to be a witness who was willing to die for his faith. His example highlights six traits of a faithful witness as he relied on the Holy Spirit, honored God as the God of glory, pointed his listeners to Jesus, called for a decision, forgave his accusers, and trusted himself to God's care. In response, God was faithful to provide the wisdom, power, grace, and faith Stephen needed to fulfill the mission Jesus had given him. With the original audience, the twenty-first-century audience shares the need to rely on God and his provision as they seek to be faithful witnesses for him.

Preaching/Teaching Idea

God is always faithful to his faithful witnesses.

Contemporary Connections

What does it mean?

Stephen was a witness full of grace and power, active in word and deed, and with a message that no one was able to withstand. His power was not the power of Stephen the man, but of Stephen the son, redeemed in Christ and filled by his Spirit. God so filled his witness that to resist Stephen's message was to resist the Holy Spirit (7:51).

The church had set Stephen apart to do mercy ministry among Hellenistic widows. By speaking often and loudly about Jesus wherever he went, however, he soon found himself on the cultural fault line of Hellenistic Jews incensed by his message. Because they were not able to refute him to his face, they trumped up false charges that Stephen spoke against God—specifically the Torah and the temple: God's law and his dwelling place.

Stephen's lengthy sermonic response was brilliant. He turned the tables on his hearers, vigorously sided with God, and esteemed his Torah and his temple. He concluded by accusing his accusers, who rejected God, his Torah, his temple, and his messengers, even as those messengers pled for change. Stephen was Spirit-filled; his audience was rage-filled. They rushed him and stoned him to death, covering their ears from the very message that could have saved them from eternal death.

Is it true?

The crux of the Hellenistic Jews' disagreement with Stephen was a matter of who was telling the story of the Scriptures rightly. Were the members of the synagogue of the freedmen right? If Jesus of Nazareth stood against temple and Torah, his teaching was tantamount to standing against God (6:13–14). Was Stephen interpreting his Bible rightly in claiming that Jesus of Nazareth is the culmination of a long line of prophets—indeed *the* prophet (7:37), fulfilling Torah and temple? Pilate and Gamaliel had faced a similar decision (5:33–39). Were they opposing man or God? The stakes could not have been higher.

Whatever reservations their leaders might have had, the crowd did not share them. The crowd might have observed the Torah outwardly, but inwardly they rejected it. They might have taken great pride in the temple, but they had murdered the one who "templed" among them. They might have claimed to serve God, but their stiff-necked resistance said otherwise. They might have fancied themselves in league with the faithful prophets of old, but sadly they proved themselves to be, in every way, like their fathers who killed the prophets. Jesus had warned his disciples, "the hour is coming when whoever kills you will think he is offering service to God" (John 16:2). The opposition had started with threats, beatings, and imprisonment. Now, the fateful hour of death had come.

Now what?

God will be faithful to his faithful witnesses. Fortunately for us, Paul writes to Timothy, "If we are faithless, he remains faithful—for he cannot deny himself" (2 Tim. 2:13). This truth is God's *comfort.* His staying hand makes it possible for Stephen and us to endure the *cost* of witness. Consider the ways in which God helped Stephen and helps us now. God filled him with his Holy Spirit (6:5) who exudes "grace and power" (6:8). He gives us this same Spirit, this same grace and power. God filled Stephen with words to say at this kangaroo court, just as he promised (Luke 12:11–12). This promise is ours too. Miraculously, God gave Stephen the gift of forgiveness toward his enemies (7:60). Raging hatred and bitterness did not poison the final moments of his earthly life. God's forgiveness coursed through Stephen, just as he offers to do with us toward those who persecute us. Finally and supremely, God gave Stephen and gives us himself in his Son. Jesus stood at God's right hand ready to receive Stephen (7:56). He now sits at God's right hand to intercede for us (Heb. 1:13; 8:1; 10:12). It is true that there is a cost to being a faithful witness. Stephen paid the ultimate price in the world's eyes. God might call some of us to do the same, but we will all suffer. These light, momentary afflictions of witness or obedience cannot compare to the surpassing glory of God's faithfulness.

Creativity in Presentation

This unit is challenging to preach because of its breadth and depth. Stephen is meeting Jews who are well versed in their OT and is seeking to prove points with which modern Gentiles do not readily identify. It would be daunting to teach verse-by-verse here. Another difficulty is that the bulk of the preaching lies before and after Stephen's sermon rather than in the fifty-two verses of the sermon itself. It is important, therefore, not to lose sight of God's faithfulness to Stephen, to his message, and to us.

One creative way of organizing the sermon might be to paint the picture of a courtroom scene. An informal teaching setting could actually act this out. Although the details are different from what we might observe today, all the elements are present: defendant (Stephen), plaintiff (religious leaders), witnesses (Hellenistic Jews), and the judge and jury (the council). The charge is that Stephen is blaspheming God by denigrating his Torah and temple. Stephen, who is representing himself, pleads "not guilty" and presents his compelling defense. Of course, like any good made-for-television courtroom drama, the action behind the scenes is as intriguing as the action in the court. Here, the faithful God of Abraham, Joseph, Moses, David, Solomon— Stephen's own roll call of deceased witnesses— holds Stephen steady in his darkest hour. He is always faithful to his faithful servants.

As the stones landed heavily, Stephen's final words were heavenly. In begging God to forgive his murderers, he showed more concern for the guilty who were living than for his own innocence as he was dying. A long line of martyrs after Stephen would share this Spirit-filled desire. One such instance occurred in 1536, when the king of England arrested and imprisoned William Tyndale for speaking out against his marriage annulment. A tribunal convicted Tyndale of heresy, commanded his execution by strangulation, and ordered his body to be burned at the stake. Reportedly, his final words were, "Lord, open the king of England's eyes." Indeed, the martyr is in good and faithful hands. The persecutor needs prayer the most.

God is always faithful to his faithful witnesses.

- God is faithful to his message (6:8–7:53).

- God is faithful to his messenger (7:54–8:3).

DISCUSSION QUESTIONS

1. What does Stephen's experience teach about the ways in which the Holy Spirit empowers for ministry?

2. What does Stephen's experience teach about how to deal with false accusations from opponents?

3. What does Stephen's speech teach about God's faithfulness to his promises and the way in which he vindicates his witnesses?

4. How does Stephen's trial and death echo the pattern of Jesus's trial and death?

5. How does Stephen's death illustrate Tertullian's statement that "the blood of martyrs is the seed of the Church"? What are some other examples—either historical or contemporary—of that statement?

JUDEA, SAMARIA, AND SYRIA (ACTS 8:4–12:25)

Jesus's promise/command was that his disciples would be his witnesses in Jerusalem, and in all Judea and Samaria, and even to the remotest part of the earth (1:8). The coming of the Spirit at Pentecost launched the first phase of the mission in the city of Jerusalem and the villages surrounding it. The persecution that followed Stephen's martyrdom provided the impetus for the next phase, as the disciples were scattered throughout all the regions of Judea and Samaria (8:2). The second division of Acts documents the movement of the church outward from Jerusalem in concentric circles both geographically and culturally. In chapter 8, Philip crosses cultural thresholds to the "half-breed" Samaritans and an Ethiopian adherent to Judaism. In chapter 9, Luke records the conversion of Saul, who would become instrumental in the mission to the Gentiles. In chapters 10 and 11, the gospel moves to the Gentiles—first, through Peter's witness to the Godfearing Cornelius, then, through the witness of unnamed disciples from Cyprus and Cyrene to pagan Gentiles in Syrian Antioch, the third-largest city in the empire.

	Geographic Region	Text Section	People Group	Missionaries
Acts 3–7	Jerusalem	Acts 3:1–5:42	Hebrew-speaking Jews	Peter and John
		Acts 6:1–7:60	Greek-speaking Jews	Stephen
Acts 8–11	Judea, Samaria, and Syria	Acts 8:4–25	Samaritans	Philip
		Acts 8:26–40	Ethiopian (adherent)	Philip
		Acts 10:1–11:18	Cornelius (Godfearer)	Peter
		Acts 11:19–30	Gentiles	Barnabas

Several important themes run throughout the section. Coincident with the crossing of cultural thresholds is the overcoming of prejudices about other ethnic and cultural groups. In order to overcome those prejudices, God repeatedly takes the initiative to push his witnesses out of their comfort zones. In order to persuade the church that he is working where his people might not expect him to be, God uses a variety of means to confirm that he is at work, including outward manifestations of the coming of the Holy Spirit, specific instructions from the Spirit, angelic visits, heavenly visions, and the validation of trusted representatives. The events recounted most likely cover the period of A.D. 32–46.

32	Judea and Samaria (8:4–40)	Samaritans (8:4–25) Ethiopian (8:26–40)	Paul in Jerusalem
	Damascus (9:1–22)	Damascus road vision (9:3–9)	Paul in Arabia 32–34 (Gal. 1:17)
33			
34	Damascus (9:23–25)	Paul escapes Aretas (9:23–25)	
	Jerusalem (9:26–31)	Paul meets the apostles (9:26–29) Paul sent to Tarsus (9:30)	Paul in Syria and Cilicia 34–42 (Gal. 1:21)
35–40	Lydda and Joppa (9:36–43)	Aeneas and Dorcas (9:36–43)	
	Caesarea (10:1–48)	Cornelius converted (10:1–48)	
	Jerusalem (11:1–18)	Peter reports (11:1–18)	
41	Jerusalem (12:1–19)	James martyred (12:2) Peter imprisoned (12:3–19)	
42	Syrian Antioch (11:19–26)	Barnabas arrives (11:22–24) Paul arrives (11:25–26)	
43			Paul in Syrian Antioch 42–46
44	Caesarea (12:20–24)	Herod's death (12:20–24)	
45			
46	Jerusalem	Famine relief visit (11:27–30)	
	Syrian Antioch (12:25)	Barnabas and Paul return (12:25)	

Homiletically, the second division consists of nine preaching sections. The first and second sections describe Philip's witness in Samaria (8:4–25) and to an Ethiopian adherent (8:26–40). The third and fourth sections recount Paul's conversion (9:1–19a) and his initial activities as a witness in Damascus and Jerusalem (9:19b–31). The fifth, sixth, and seventh sections record Peter's witness in coastal Judea (9:32–43), his witness to the Godfearing Cornelius (10:1–48), and his report on the Gentile mission before the church in Jerusalem (11:1–18). The eighth section describes the witness among the Gentiles in Antioch that resulted in the church being planted in the capital of the province of Syria (11:19–30). The ninth section closes the first phase of the mission in Jerusalem as the church endures opposition from Herod Agrippa I (12:1–25).

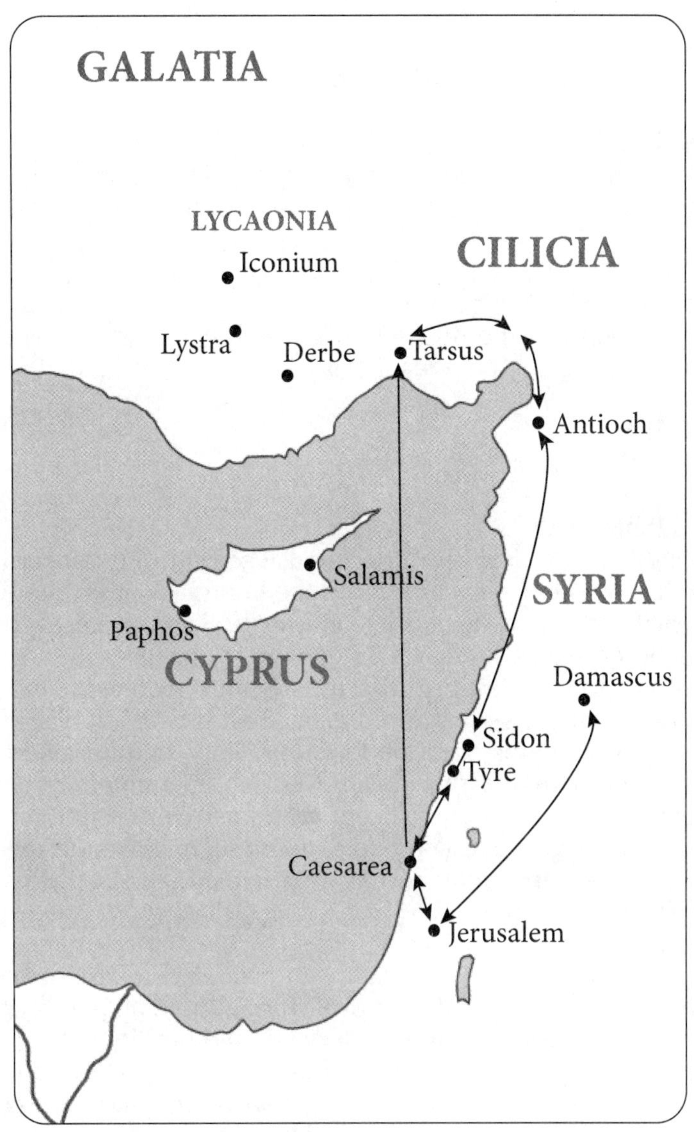

Paul's Early Travels

Acts 8:4–25

EXEGETICAL IDEA

Philip's evangelistic ministry demonstrated to the Samaritans that the gospel was superior to magic and opened the door for the Holy Spirit to incorporate them into the church.

THEOLOGICAL FOCUS

The gospel is superior to competing religious systems, excludes other forms of spirituality, and accepts on an equal basis all who respond in faith.

PREACHING IDEA

The gospel is both exclusive and inclusive.

PREACHING POINTERS

Can something be both exclusive and inclusive? Will one concern conflict with the other? What should we exclude from the church? Whom should we include in the church? Stephen's evangelistic ministry in Samaria raises these questions and more as he crosses boundaries of geography, history, culture, and religion, and as Peter and John investigate the reports they receive of the results of his ministry. Although the Jews considered them "half-breeds" at best, the Samaritans were the people group closest to the Jews in history, culture, and religion. What would happen when the message of the Messiah encountered the syncretism of the Samaritans? Would the church accept the Samaritans despite their differences? Luke's account of the gospel coming to Samaria highlights both the exclusive nature of the claims of Christianity and its inclusive embrace of all who respond to the good news in faith.

From this passage, people today should be able to relate to fascination with magic, the supernatural, and events that are novel. They should able to relate to rejoicing over unexpected recovery from illness or physical disability. Attempts to purchase influence or prominence appear far too frequently in the news. This passage corrects multiple attitudes, including the idea that all religions are equal, the suggestion that it is possible to combine the gospel with other forms of spirituality, fascination with the occult, and attempts to hide a sinful heart attitude from God. It commends faithful proclamation of the truth of God's Word, the response of faith to the gospel, acceptance of other people groups as part of the church, and the willingness to examine our heart attitudes and change them to align with God's way of thinking.

PHILIP'S WITNESS IN SAMARIA (8:4–25)

LITERARY STRUCTURE AND THEMES (8:4–25)

The passage is the first of two that recount Philip's ministry in Samaria (8:4–25) and Judea (8:26–40). The link-word εὐαγγελίζομαι occurs five times in the two passages (8:4, 12, 25, 35, 40) including three summary verses that form *inclusios* around the two narratives.

8:4	διερχομαι . . . εὐαγγελίζομαι . . . λογος
8:25	λογος . . . εὐαγγελιζομαι
8:40	διερχομαι . . . εὐαγγελιζομαι

In Acts 8:4–25, the verbal echo of οἱ μὲν οὖν διεσπαρέντες in verse 4 and οἱ μὲν οὖν διαμαρτυράμενοι in verse 25 reinforces the framing. The passage itself divides into two sections, each with two paragraphs. The first section (8:5–13) focuses on Philip and Simon, with πόλις framing the first paragraph that describes Philip's ministry (8:5–8), and ἐξίστημι framing the second paragraph that describes Simon's magic (8:9–13). Occurrences of λόγος and Ἱεροσόλυμα frame the second section (8:14–24), which focuses on Peter and Simon, with the first paragraph describing the apostles' visit and the coming of the Holy Spirit (8:14–17), and the second paragraph describing Simon's attempt to purchase the authority to bestow the Spirit (8:18–24).

- ***The Gospel Comes to Samaria (8:4–13)***
- ***The Spirit Comes to the Samaritans (8:14–25)***

EXPOSITION (8:4–25)

Acts 8:4–25 opens the second major division of the book. Beginning at Pentecost, the focus of the new movement had been in Jerusalem and the surrounding villages (1:1–8:3). Stephen's ministry crossed the cultural threshold from Hebraic Jews to Hellenistic Jews (6:8–15), but it also prompted persecution that dispersed the church into the regions of Judea and Samaria (8:1–3). Philip, one of seven men chosen to care for the needs of the Hellenistic widows (6:1–7), was among the disciples who left Jerusalem to escape the persecution. By choosing to travel to Samaria, Philip carried the gospel outward both geographically and culturally.

His ministry also led to an encounter between Christianity and Samaritan syncretism in the person of Simon the magician. As Dunn notes, Simon represents the gospel's first confrontation with non-Jewish theology (1996, 107). It is also the first of several encounters with magic (13:6–11; 16:16–18; 19:11–20). Luke organizes the passage into two sections that highlight the contrast between Philip and Peter as true ministers of the one true God and Simon, the supposed "Great Power" of "god." In 8:5–13, he sets the ministry of Philip and the magic of Simon in parallel.

When the Samaritans responded to Philip's ministry by believing and being baptized (8:12), their actions made it clear that the gospel was the superior message. Even Simon believed and was baptized (8:13). Soon thereafter, Peter and John visited, and God granted the Samaritans the gift of the Holy Spirit (8:14–17). When Simon responded to the apostles' ministry by trying to purchase their authority, Peter's rebuke made it clear that the Spirit was the superior power (8:18–24). As Larkin writes, "the power of the gospel is not magic and cannot be bought" (1995, 125). In Christianity's first confrontation with another religious system, Luke shows the clear superiority of the gospel's message and power.

	Philip	**Simon**
Message	Preaching the Messiah (8:5) ἐκήρυσσεν τὸν Χριστόν	Claiming to be someone great (8:9) λέγων εἶναί τινα ἑαυτὸν μέγαν
Attestation	Miraculous signs (8:6–7) τὰ σημεῖα ἃ ἐποίει	Feats of magic (8:9, 11) μαγεύων . . . ταῖς μαγείαις
Audience	Crowds (8:6) οἱ ὄχλοι	All (8:10) πάντες
Response	Close attention (8:6) προσεῖχον	Close attention (8:10, 11) προσεῖχον
Reaction	Great joy (8:8) πολλὴ χαρά	Amazement (8:9) ἐξιστάνων
Result	Faith in Philip's message (8:12) ἐπίστευσαν τῷ Φιλίππῳ	Assent to Simon's claim (8:10) λέγοντες οὗτός ἐστιν ἡ δύναμις τοῦ θεοῦ ἡ καλουμένη Μεγάλη

The Gospel Comes to Samaria (8:4–13)

Philip travels to Samaria, preaches the Messiah in a context of religious syncretism, and baptizes the Samaritans who respond in faith.

8:4. This summary verse is the first of three that structure Luke's account of Philip's ministry. He introduces a new text section with μὲν οὖν (1:6; 13:4; 15:30; 23:31; 26:4), resumes the narrative of 8:2 by referring to "those who had been scattered" (LEB, οἱ διασπαρέντες), and describes their activity as "going from place to place telling the good news of the word" (cf. CEV). Peterson notes correctly that translating εὐαγγελιζόμενοι τὸν λόγον as "preaching the word" (e.g., ESV) might be too narrow if it is understood only as "giving a sermon," because the activity can take many forms (2009, 279). The verb εὐαγγελίζομαι first occurred in 5:42, but it now becomes a key term for the disciples' witness (10:36; 11:20; 13:32; 14:7, 15, 21; 15:35; 16:10; 17:18) and is the link-word in the two connected accounts of Philip's ministry (8:4, 12, 25, 35, 40). See 6:2 on Luke's use of "the word" (τὸν λόγον) as shorthand for the gospel. The term occurs three times in this passage and highlights the fact that the gospel was the central message those who had been scattered (8:4), Philip (8:14), and the apostles (8:25) shared wherever they went.

8:5. Among those who had been scattered was Philip, one of the seven men who had been tasked with caring for the Hellenistic widows in the Jerusalem church (6:5). Like his colleague Stephen, Philip's ministry went beyond the initial role for which he had been set apart, to the extent that he eventually became known as "the evangelist" (21:8). Leaving Jerusalem, he "went down" (κατελθών) to Samaria—since that phrase always described movement from Jerusalem to other places (Barrett 1994, 401)—and "began proclaiming the Messiah to them" (ἐκήρυσσεν αὐτοῖς τὸν Χριστόν, inceptive imperfect). The Samaritans considered their theology distinct from and superior to Jewish theology, but their Samaritan Pentateuch also taught them to expect the prophetic figure Moses had promised (Deut. 18:15–19). His coming would introduce "a day of final judgment, of vengeance and reward, when the temple of Gerizim would be restored, the sacrifices reinstated and the heathen converted" (Larkin 1995, 125).

Samaria and the Samaritans

Samaria was the central district of first-century Palestine, bordered by Judea on the south, the Mediterranean Sea on the west, the Jordan River on the east, and Galilee on the north (Josephus, *B.J.* 3.3.4–5). It became part of the northern kingdom of Israel when Jeroboam led ten tribes in rebellion against Rehoboam ca. 930 B.C. and built Shechem as his capital city (1 Kings 12). When the Assyrians conquered the northern kingdom ca. 722 B.C., they resettled foreigners there (2 Kings 17). When Zerubbabel and Ezra led the remnant back to Palestine after the Babylonian exile ca. 585 B.C., the Samaritans opposed the work of rebuilding the temple in Jerusalem (Ezra 4–5; Josephus, *A.J.* 11.4.3–9) and soon built their own temple on Mount Gerizim ca. 450 B.C. (Josephus, *A.J.* 11.8.2–4). They also opposed Nehemiah's work of rebuilding the wall around Jerusalem ca. 445 B.C. (Nehemiah 4, 6; Josephus, *A.J.* 11.5.6–8). They distanced themselves from the Jews during the Seleucid occupation ca. 167–64 B.C. (Josephus, *A.J.* 12:5.5), and John Hyrcanus destroyed both the city and the Gerizim temple ca. 127 B.C. (Josephus, *A.J.* 13.9.1; 13.10.1). In return, Samaritans defiled the Jerusalem temple ca. A.D. 6–9 by scattering bones in the outer court (Josephus, *A.J.* 18.2.2). During Jesus's time, the Samaritans continued to worship on Mount Gerizim (John 4:20) and were looking for the messiah (John 4:25), most likely the prophetic figure Moses had promised (Deut. 18:15–19). The Jews and Samaritans had

no dealings with one another (John 4:9), a situation reflected in the Samaritans' unwillingness to receive Jesus on his journey to Jerusalem and the disciples' intense reaction to that rejection (Luke 9:51–56). When Luke refers to "the city of Samaria" (Acts 8:5; P[74], ℵ, A, B), he might have been thinking of the major political city of Sebaste or the major religious city of Samaria (Bock 2007, 337). The specific city is less important than Philip's willingness to cross the long-standing cultural and religious gulf between the Jews and the Samaritans.

8:6–8. Crowds of Samaritans were paying attention (προσεῖχον οἱ ὄχλοι) "with one accord" (ὁμοθυμαδόν) to Philip, not only because of what he was saying (τοῖς λεγομένοις ὑπὸ τοῦ Φιλίππου), but also because of the signs he was doing (τὰ σημεῖα ἃ ἐποίει). The signs included casting out unclean spirits (πνεύματα ἀκάθαρτα . . . ἐξήρχοντο) and healing many who were paralyzed and lame (πολλοὶ παραλελυμένοι καὶ χωλοὶ ἐθεραπεύθησαν). Those attesting signs filled the city with great joy (πολλὴ χαρά). The combined activities of sharing good news (εὐαγγελίζομαι) and healing (θεραπεύω) recall the ministries of Jesus (Luke 4:38–44) and the apostles—both during Jesus's ministry (Luke 9:6) and after his ascension (Acts 3:2; 5:16). For Luke, rejoicing is a characteristic response of those who find the lost (Luke 15:5, 6, 7, 9, 10, 32), hear the good news of salvation (Acts 8:39; 13:48), and are filled with the Spirit (13:52).

8:9–11. Among those who were paying close attention to Philip's words and signs was a certain man named Simon. He had been in the city before Philip arrived (προϋπῆρχεν ἐν τῇ πόλει; cf. Barrett 1994, 406), performing feats of magic (μαγεύων) that amazed the people of Samaria (ἐξιστάνων τὸ ἔθνος τῆς Σαμαρείας) and supported his claim that he was someone great (λέγων εἶναί τινα ἑαυτὸν μέγαν). Because he had for a long time (διὰ τὸ ἱκανῷ χρόνῳ) amazed them (ἐξεστακέναι αὐτούς) by his feats of magic (ταῖς μαγείαις), everyone "from the least to the greatest" (ἀπὸ μικροῦ ἕως μεγάλου) were paying attention to him (προσεῖχον αὐτῷ) and were calling him "the power of god that is called 'Great'" (ἡ δύναμις τοῦ θεοῦ ἡ καλουμένη Μεγάλη).

Simon Magus

The Simon whom Luke introduces in Acts 8 was a magician (μάγος) who astonished everyone by his feats of magic (μαγεύων . . . ταῖς μαγείαις). Justin Martyr writes that Simon was a Samaritan from the city of Gitta, who did mighty acts of magic and whom almost all the Samaritans considered to be a god (*1 Apol.* 26). The Samaritans' assessment, however, that "this man is the power of God that is called 'Great'" (LEB, οὗτός ἐστιν ἡ δύναμις τοῦ θεοῦ ἡ καλουμένη Μεγάλη) suggests that they did not view him as the supreme God but, rather, "that of all the Powers of God, he was the great one" (Barrett 1994, 407). He later moved to Rome, and Irenaeus names him as the originator of Gnosticism (*Haer.* 1.23). The term "simony," the practice of buying or selling a church office or ecclesial preferment, has its thirteenth-century origin in Simon's attempt to purchase the ability to bestow the Holy Spirit by laying on hands (8:18–19). Bruce notes that in apocryphal works such as the Acts of Peter, Simon was "the untiring adversary of Peter, not only in Samaria . . . but also at Caesarea. Antioch, and Rome (1990, 218).

8:12. When the Samaritans heard Philip sharing the good news about the kingdom of God and the name of Jesus the Messiah, however, they believed his message (ἐπίστευσαν τῷ Φιλίππῳ) instead of Simon's and were baptized (ἐβαπτίζοντο). The parallel descriptions of Simon's magic and Philip's ministry highlight the change that took place in the lives of the Samaritans. Previously, they had paid attention to Simon and had been amazed because of his magic acts (8:9, 11). Now, they paid attention to Philip and

rejoiced because of his miraculous healings (8:6, 8). Previously, they had given credence to Simon's claims (8:10). Now, they committed themselves to Philip's Christ (8:12). The message of "the kingdom of God" (τῆς βασιλείας τοῦ θεοῦ), of course, was congruent with Jesus's message (Luke 4:43; 8:1; 9:2, 11; 11:20), and "the name of Jesus" (τοῦ ὀνόματος Ἰησοῦ) was congruent with the apostles' message (Acts 2:21, 38; 3:6, 16; 4:10, 12; 5:41). Χριστοῦ echoes the content of Philip's preaching (8:5).

8:13. Even Simon himself (ὁ Σίμων καὶ αὐτός, anaphoric article) responded to Philip's message by believing (ἐπίστευσεν) and being baptized (βαπτισθείς). He then "began following Philip wherever he went" (NLT, ἦν προσκαρτερῶν τῷ Φιλίππῳ), because he continued to be amazed (γινομένας ἐξίστατο) as he saw the miraculous signs and powerful works (θεωρῶν τε σημεῖα καὶ δυνάμεις μεγάλας) Philip was doing. Luke uses the verb προσκαρτερέω elsewhere to describe "devotion" to prayer (1:14; 6:4), to the apostle's teaching (2:42), to worship in the temple (2:46), and to the ministry of the word (6:4). Bock notes that its use to describe Philip as an object of devotion is unusual (2007, 329), but the periphrastic participle serves to highlight Simon's strong fascination with the miraculous aspects of Philip's ministry. Subsequent events would make it clear that his fascination would lead him into error, but there is nothing in Luke's account to suggest that Simon's faith was anything other than genuine or that Philip had baptized him prematurely (Schnabel 2012, 409).

The Spirit Comes to the Samaritans (8:14–25)

Peter and John visit from Jerusalem, pray for the Samaritans to receive the Holy Spirit, and correct Simon's false ideas about God's giving of the Spirit.

8:14–16. When the Jerusalem apostles (οἱ ἐν Ἱεροσολύμοις ἀπόστολοι) heard that the people of Samaria had received the word of God (δέδεκται τὸν λόγον τοῦ θεοῦ; cf. 11:1; 17:11), they sent Peter and John to investigate the report. When Peter and John arrived, they prayed for the Samaritans in order that they might receive the Holy Spirit (ὅπως λάβωσιν πνεῦμα ἅγιον). Ἡ Σαμάρεια is a metonymy for the residents of the region (Culy and Parsons 2003, 155). See 8:4 on ὁ λόγος τοῦ θεοῦ. Later, the Jerusalem church would send Barnabas to Antioch on a similar mission (11:22), but Marshall's characterization of that congregation as a conservative body that never initiated any new ventures is overly critical (1980, 156).

Luke does not explain how the apostles knew that the Spirit had not yet fallen on any of the Samaritans (οὐδέπω ἦν ἐπ' οὐδενὶ αὐτῶν ἐπιπεπτωκός), although they had already been baptized (pluperfect periphrastic participle). Bruce suggests that the Samaritans "having being baptized in the name of the Lord Jesus" (βεβαπτισμένοι ὑπῆρχον εἰς τὸ ὄνομα τοῦ κυρίου Ἰησοῦ) "bears public witness to having passed into the ownership of Jesus, now acknowledged as Lord" (1988, 159). The apostles acknowledged the Samaritans' response to the gospel as genuine, but evidence of the Spirit's presence was missing. Schnabel notes that elsewhere "realities such as rejoicing (8:39; 16:34) or missionary ministry (9:20–22) are taken as adequate ongoing evidence of the presence of the Holy Spirit" (2012, 411). Apparently, such evidence was not yet present among the Samaritans.

8:17. The apostles began laying hands on the Samaritans (ἐπετίθουν τὰς χεῖρας ἐπ' αὐτούς), who began receiving the Holy Spirit (ἐλάμβανον πνεῦμα ἅγιον). Luke does not elaborate on the Spirit's coming, although it is possible to infer from verse 18 that there was some sort of outward manifestation that Simon observed (Bruce 1990, 222). See 6:6 for the practice of laying on hands. Peterson suggests that it is an act of identification with and concern for the individual (2009, 286), which seems to be the more likely significance here than Schnabel's view that it was a transfer of authority (2012, 412). Prayer appears to have been part of the process (8:15; cf. 6:6; 13:3; 28:8).

Receiving the Holy Spirit was Jesus's parting promise (1:8), and the phrase occurs on four subsequent occasions: Peter's sermon at Pentecost (2:38), Peter and John's ministry in Samaria (8:15, 17, 19), Peter's ministry in Caesarea (10:47), and Paul's ministry in Ephesus (19:2). Each of those occasions represented the incorporation of a new group into the movement—the Jews, the Samaritans, the Gentiles, and the disciples of John. Interestingly, they also echoed the four geographical regions Jesus included in his command/promise: Jerusalem, Samaria, Judea, and the Roman Empire at large.

Is the Samaritans' Experience of the Spirit Normative?

Stott asks, "Does Luke intend his readers to understand the Samaritans' divided experience . . . as typical or atypical, normal or abnormal? Is it set before us as the usual pattern for Christian experience today, or as an exception which we should expect to be repeated?" (1990, 152). When seeking to derive normative elements from narrative passages, the best approach is to look for consistent repeated patterns (Harvey 2015, 93–96). As the following table makes clear, there is no consistent pattern in Acts related to receiving the Spirit (Bock 2007, 331; Larkin 1995, 128).

	Time of Baptism	Laying on Hands	Outward Manifestation	Members of the Twelve Present
Pentecost (2:37–42)	Coincident (inferred, 2:38)	Not mentioned	Not mentioned	All
Samaria (8:5–17)	Prior (8:12)	Yes (8:17)	Inferred (8:18–19)	Peter and John
Paul (9:1–19)	Subsequent (9:18)	Yes (9:17)	Not mentioned	No
Cornelius (10:34–48)	Subsequent (10:48)	Not mentioned	Yes (10:46)	Peter
Ephesus (19:1–7)	Coincident (19:5)	Yes (19:6)	Yes (19:6)	No

Sometimes, the coming of the Spirit happens at the time of baptism (2:38; 19:5); sometimes, it precedes baptism (9:18; 10:48); sometimes, it follows baptism (8:12). On some occasions, the laying on of hands is mentioned (8:17; 9:17; 19:6); on other occasions, it is not. In some instances, there is an outward manifestation of the Spirit's coming (8:18–19; 10:46; 19:6); in other instances, there is not. Sometimes members of the Twelve are present; other times they are not. In still other instances, Luke does not even mention the coming of the Spirit when a person responds to the gospel in faith (8:36–39; 16:14–15, 30–34). Elsewhere in the NT, however, didactic passages indicate that the Spirit indwells all those who belong to Jesus (Rom. 8:9; 1 Cor. 12:3, 13; Eph. 1:13). When Luke highlights one or more individuals receiving the Spirit in his narrative, therefore, the best understanding is that he is calling attention to God's special working as the gospel moves across cultural and religious thresholds.

8:18–19. Simon was already fascinated by the miraculous signs and powerful works Philip had been doing (8:13). When he saw (ἰδών) that the apostles' act of laying on hands (διὰ τῆς ἐπιθέσεως τῶν χειρῶν τῶν ἀποστόλων) resulted in receiving the Spirit (δίδοται τὸ πνεῦμα), his interest deepened. He offered them money (προσήνεγκεν αὐτοῖς χρήματα) and asked to purchase the same ability (τὴν ἐξουσίαν ταύτην), which he obviously viewed as an even greater exercise of power.

Larkin writes that Simon's approach "reflects the typically idolatrous and pagan understanding of the way to acquire supernatural power that one would then control" (1994, 129).

Simon had carried his previous understanding of how spiritual power worked into his new relationship with Christ. Marshall notes that Luke's concern was not with whether Simon was a true believer but, rather, with "his sinful desire to have spiritual power for the wrong reasons and to gain that power by the wrong means" (1980, 158). In that regard, his attitude and actions echo Ananias and Sapphira's attempt to enhance their reputations by the wrong means (5:1–11). Two Lukan themes connect the incidents: the desire for prestige and the misuse of money (Bock 2007, 333; cf. Luke 12:13–21; 16:14–15). As Peter's response will make clear, the combination is potentially disastrous.

8:20–21. Peter's response to Simon's request was immediate and piercing: "May your silver be destroyed along with you, because you thought you could acquire the gift of God by means of money" (LEB). Barrett argues that Peter's rebuke was not a curse (1994, 414), a conclusion Bock supports for three reasons: (1) Simon did not die immediately as Ananias and Sapphira had, (2) the verb εἴη expressed a wish (voluntative optative), and (3) Peter called Simon to repent (2007, 34). Regardless, Simon's problem was that he misunderstood an important truth: "money cannot buy the gift of God" (Peterson 2009, 288). Further, Simon's request reflected a heart that "was not right with God" (οὐκ ἔστιν εὐθεῖα ἔναντι τοῦ θεοῦ). For that reason, Simon had "absolutely no share" (οὐκ . . . μερὶς οὐδὲ κλῆρος; cf. Culy and Parsons 2003, 158) in "this matter" (ἐν τῷ λόγῳ τούτῳ)—that is, the matter of bestowing the Spirit (so Schnabel 2012, 414; contra Larkin 1994, 129).

8:22–24. Peter continued by admonishing Simon to repent from his wickedness (μετανόησον ἀπὸ τῆς κακίας σου ταύτης) and "implore the Lord" (δεήθητι τοῦ κυρίου; cf. NET note) "in the hope that perhaps" (εἰ ἄρα; cf. Moule 1953, 158) the intent of his heart would be forgiven (ἀφεθήσεταί σοι ἡ ἐπίνοια τῆς καρδίας σου). Simon's spiritual condition was serious; he was "full of bitter jealousy and . . . held captive by sin" (NLT, εἰς χολὴν πικρίας καὶ σύνδεσμον ἀδικίας). He needed to change direction immediately. His response, however, has generated considerable discussion, since—rather than praying for himself—he asked Peter to pray for him (δεήθητε ὑμεῖς ὑπὲρ ἐμοῦ πρὸς τὸν κύριον). Witherington offers six reasons to view Simon's response negatively (1998, 288), but Schnabel views it as clear indication that Simon has repented (2012, 415). It might be that Luke intentionally left the ultimate resolution of the encounter open in order to challenge his readers to examine their own hearts in light of the condition of Simon's heart (Bock 2007, 336).

8:25. A second summary verse closes the Samaritan episode with a repetition of μὲν οὖν (cf. 8:4), the third occurrence of λόγος (cf. 8:4, 14), a repetition of Ἱεροσόλυμα (cf. 8:14), and the third occurrence of εὐαγγελίζομαι (cf. 8:4, 12). Peter and John concluded their ministry in the city by solemnly charging the Samaritans (διαμαρτυράμενοι) and speaking the Word of the Lord (λαλήσαντες τὸν λόγον τοῦ κυρίου) to them. They then began their return trip to Jerusalem (ὑπέστρεφον εἰς Ἱεροσόλυμα, inceptive imperfect) and were "bringing the good news to many Samaritan villages on the way" (NEB, πολλάς κώμας τῶν Σαμαριτῶν εὐηγγελίζοντο, iterative imperfect). The participles διαμαρτυράμενοι and λαλήσαντες are adverbial of time (e.g., LEB). In this context, διαμαρτύρομαι has the sense of "solemnly charge" (1 Tim. 5:21; 2 Tim. 2:14; 4:1). See 8:4 on λόγος and εὐαγγελίζομαι. See 9:31; 16:5; 23:31 for Luke's use of μὲν οὖν to close a section (Longenecker 2005, 198).

THEOLOGICAL FOCUS

Acts 8:4–25 introduces a new section of Luke's narrative, as the persecution following Stephen's martyrdom dispersed the disciples from Jerusalem. Philip's bold act of leaving Jerusalem and sharing the good news of the Messiah with the Samaritans moved the church's mission to the next phase in Jesus's command/promise. He crossed a new geographical and cultural threshold, saw his listeners forsake the power of magic they had previously admired, and provided the opportunity for the apostles to validate the Samaritans' incorporation into the church. His ministry in Samaria sets the trajectory for the events of the second major section of Acts (8:4–12:25) in which the church rapidly extends its witness throughout Judea, Samaria, and the Roman province of Syria.

Theologically, Acts 8:4–25 demonstrates that the gospel is superior to competing religious systems, excludes other forms of spirituality, and accepts on an equal basis all who respond in faith. Although it is easy to be distracted by questions that the passage leaves unanswered (Which city in Samaria? Was Simon regenerate? Did he really repent?), Luke structures the passage to highlight the power encounter that takes place between the gospel, in the persons of Philip, Peter, and John; and magic, in the person of Simon. First, he sets Philip's ministry parallel to Simon's magic and demonstrates that the gospel is superior to competing religious systems (8:5–13). Then, he sets the giving of the Spirit through Peter and John parallel to Simon's misguided attempt to purchase the Spirit's power and demonstrates that the gospel cannot be mixed with other forms of spirituality (8:14–24). In so doing, he demonstrates the exclusivity of the gospel. The delayed coming of the Spirit poses another puzzle, but when properly understood, it demonstrates the inclusivity of the gospel. The centuries of hostility between the Jews and the Gentiles had created a prejudice that required special persuasion to overcome. When the apostles laid their hands on the Samaritans who received the Holy Spirit, their experience made it clear that God had accepted this previously despised people group as full participants in the salvation blessings Jesus had promised.

PREACHING AND TEACHING STRATEGIES

Exegetical/Theological Synthesis

As Jesus's witnesses moved outward from Jerusalem, Luke's first-century readers would have wanted to know what would happen when the gospel encountered non-Jewish cultures and religious systems. Would the disciples or the apostles compromise the truth of the gospel or the power of the Spirit? Would the Jewish disciples view non-Jewish believers as having equal status in the church? Given the centuries-long hostility between the Jews and the Samaritans, the latter people group provided a perfect test case for what would happen as the gospel encountered a new ethnic-cultural-religious threshold. Luke's account of, first, the gospel coming to Samaria and then, the Holy Spirit coming to the Samaritans makes it clear that the gospel overcomes all obstacles, whether those obstacles involve geography, history, culture, religion, spiritual opposition, or the syncretistic human tendency to add previous spiritual attitudes and practices to the truth of the gospel. With the original audience, the twenty-first-century audience shares the need to understand that the gospel overcomes all obstacles and incorporates into the church on an equal basis all who respond in faith, so that they will be faithful in sharing the truth of the gospel regardless of ethnic, cultural, and religious differences.

Preaching/Teaching Idea

The gospel is both exclusive and inclusive.

Contemporary Connections

What does it mean?
The gospel of Jesus is indeed good news that is inclusive for all who would repent and believe. It is also exclusive in that Jesus is superior to all other gods and beliefs and will not share his throne with them. The inclusivity of Jesus is on full display in this chapter. Because of the heated history between Jews and Samaritans outlined above, Jesus's commission to "Samaria" might have been harder to swallow than the final frontier to "the ends of the earth." If the early church was reluctant to initiate this next phase on her own, though, God initiated it for her by persecution that set her fleeing in the direction of Samaria. The results in Samaria are as shocking as Jonah's results in Nineveh. The despised Samaritans heard the good news, welcomed Jesus, were baptized, and received the Holy Spirit. The exclusivity of Jesus is also on full display. Men and women cannot serve both God and Mammon, or God and magicians. By receiving the gospel, the people let go of Simon. For his part, Simon sought a way to do both. Simon jumped at the

gospel with feet of faith and baptism but tried to keep his stature of power among the people by offering to buy the authority to dispense the Holy Spirit. Peter soundly rebuked him, because Jesus will not share.

Is it true?

The stakes could not have been higher as the gospel reached its first frontier outside Jewish orthodoxy and culture. This passage reminds us that rather than waiting expectantly for the revealing of the Christ, the world is organizing its own gospels of authority, power, and truth. The parallels between Philip and Simon's ministries underscore this reality. Long before Philip brought a message attested by signs to Samaritan crowds seeking their response, Simon brought a message attested by signs to Samaritan crowds seeking their response. Philip preached Jesus; Simon preached Simon. Both claimed to speak for God. The lesson John the Baptist readily cherished would have been hard on Simon: Jesus must increase, we must decrease. This town was not big enough for two gospels. Simon's disciples, like John's, flocked to Jesus. Even Simon was impressed. The one who had a career in amazing others (8:11) was himself amazed (8:13). Yet, the story remains open-ended. Amazement itself cannot save. Only genuine faith and submission to Jesus—at the exclusion of all other faiths—is God's means of salvation.

Now what?

Christians today must be clear on the inclusivity and exclusivity of the gospel. The gospel is inclusive, available to all. Well did Peter preach from Joel in Acts 2:21, "everyone who calls upon the name of the Lord shall be saved." There is not a person in our perverse culture today to whom this warm invitation is not offered—immoral, idolater, rich, poor, those who struggle with same-sex attraction, the adulterer, even the self-righteous celibate. The gospel, however, is also exclusive and shared by none. Well did

Peter preach in Acts 3:19, "repent therefore and turn" from every other claim.

Christians must also be clear that we are never only the messenger. We are always recipients of the same message we share. We must beware of the allure of power, money, and prestige. We must be on guard against mixing faith in Christ with anything else. Jesus will not share his preeminence with our lust for self. Like Simon, we fancy calling ourselves Christians, but then we jostle for bigger status over other Christians. For Simon, it was using money to buy power to gain prestige. His aim was similar to the aim of Ananias and Sapphira. For us, it might be trying to use spiritual gifts, natural talents, or our own righteousness to take the limelight off Jesus and put it on ourselves within God's people. Peter's message for this insidious tendency is a stinging rebuke: "Repent, therefore, of this wickedness of yours" (8:22).

Creativity in Presentation

Barbara Robinson's 1972 book *The Best Christmas Pageant Ever* cleverly tells the story of six naughty non-Christian kids from the Herdman family, who land roles in the neighborhood church's annual Christmas pageant. The kids cuss, smoke, drink, shoplift, and make life difficult for public school teacher and Sunday school teacher alike. Needless to say, the town is not excited to have this family taint their pageant, but something remarkable happens. As the Herdmans hear the Christmas story for the first time in rehearsal and finally on stage, they experience the story in ways the tired Christians of the town did not. In the end, it is the unlikeliest of all, the Herdmans, who deliver the truest understanding of the gospel.

We can all think of the persons in our lives who seem least likely to be saved. We all know Herdmans. They might be wild, flagrant sinners or cold, callous moralists. They might be staunch atheists, or they might have tried every religion out there. They might have rejected Christianity many times and might even have dabbled in deep, dark anti-Christian things. For whatever reason, we have written them off as impossible. Then we run smack into this story of the gospel crossing the impossible barrier of the Samaritans. These people had married pagans, resisted the rebuilding of the Jerusalem temple, built their own temple, defiled the true temple, and even blocked Jesus himself on his journey through the territory (Luke 9). They make the Herdmans look like saints. Yet even the Samaritans were not outside God's love or God's reach. They were radically converted. Even the conversion of their town's chief deceiver, Simon himself, appears to be genuine.

A natural way to divide a sermon into three parts from the "Theological Focus" above, would be to begin with the inclusivity of the gospel for all (8:4–8), move to its exclusivity against competing religions and ideas (8:9–13), and end with its refusal to be mixed with anything else for the believer (8:14–24). When all is said and done, the gospel is both inclusive and exclusive.

- The gospel is inclusive for all who believe (8:4–8).

- The gospel is exclusive against competing beliefs (8:9–13).

- The gospel cannot be mixed with anything else (8:14–24).

DISCUSSION QUESTIONS

1. In what ways does Philip's ministry in Samaria provide a good model for crossing ethnic, cultural, and/or religious boundaries?

2. Why was Simon "devoting himself to Philip" (ἦν προσκαρτερῶν τῷ Φιλίππῳ) after he was baptized? What do his actions reveal about his attitudes?

3. Why did the Jerusalem church think it was necessary to send Peter and John to investigate the report of the Samaritans receiving the Word of God? What mindset do you think it reflects?

4. Is the Spirit's delayed reception by the Samaritans normative for all Christians? Why or why not? What theological truth(s) does it teach about God's working and his church?

5. What does Simon's offer to purchase the ability to lay on hands so that others might receive the Holy Spirit suggest about his understanding of the nature of the gospel and the power related to it?

Acts 8:26–40

EXEGETICAL IDEA

Following divine directions, Philip preached the gospel to an Ethiopian official whom he baptized, and then continued evangelizing coastal Judea.

THEOLOGICAL FOCUS

God guides his witnesses to individuals who are prepared to hear and respond to the gospel.

PREACHING IDEA

Divine appointments create gospel opportunities.

PREACHING POINTERS

Are there such things as "chance encounters"? When we find ourselves seated next to someone new on a train or in an airplane, how should we view the situation? When our travel plans suddenly change, does it bother us or excite us? Our answers to those questions probably depend on our understanding of God's providence. Philip's experience on the road to Gaza suggests that we should hold our plans loosely, be open to what God might be doing, and be ready to make the most of the evangelistic opportunities that might present themselves. With Luke's original readers, we need to understand that God is at work in the hearts of "seekers" and will take whatever actions might be necessary to get the gospel to them, including arranging divine appointments that create opportunities for his witnesses to share the good news.

People today should be able to relate to the ideas of surprise encounters, meeting new people while they are traveling, sudden changes in travel plans, meeting prominent individuals, and needing assistance in understanding unclear information. This passage corrects several ideas: that men or women of high social status have no interest in spiritual matters, that individuals have little value in God's eyes, that people can find their own way to Jesus, or that there is such a thing as a "chance encounter." It commends openness to spiritual truth, obedience to divine guidance, sensitivity to the spiritual condition of others, the ability to contextualize passages from any portion of Scripture to listeners' needs, and the ability to adapt evangelistic methods to the need of the moment. Philip's encounter with the Ethiopian embodies Peter's injunction always to be "ready to make a defense to everyone who asks you to give an account for the hope that is in you" (1 Peter 3:15).

PHILIP'S WITNESS TO AN ETHIOPIAN (8:26–40)

LITERARY STRUCTURE AND THEMES (8:26–40)

The passage consists of three sections: a narrative opening (8:26–29), a "conversion report" (8:30–38; cf. Schnabel 2012, 421), and a narrative closing (8:39–40). It is worth noting that verse 37 was most likely not part of the original account. Divine instructions to Philip (8:26, 29) frame the opening narrative that introduces the characters in the episode. The conversion report includes three parts: the Ethiopian's request for guidance in understanding the passage of Isaiah he was reading (8:30–31), Philip's proclamation about Jesus based on that passage (8:32–35), and the Ethiopian's request for baptism (8:36, 38). The closing narrative recounts subsequent events as the Ethiopian went on his way rejoicing (8:39) and the Spirit carried Philip away to Azotus for further evangelistic ministry (8:40). References to Philip frame the narrative (8:26, 40), and verse 40 serves as the third summary statement that structures the account of Philip's ministry (cf. 8:5, 26). Occurrences of διερχομαι and εὐαγγελιζομαι form an *inclusio* around the paired narratives (8:5, 40).

- *God Directs Philip to Meet an Ethiopian Official (8:26–29)*
- *Philip Preaches Jesus to the Ethiopian (8:30–38)*
- *The Ethiopian and Philip Resume Their Travels (8:39–40)*

EXPOSITION
(8:26–40)

Acts 8:26–40 continues Luke's account of Philip's ministry as an angel instructed him to travel the road from Jerusalem to Gaza, where the Holy Spirit directed him to approach an important Ethiopian official who had been worshipping in Jerusalem. Like the Samaritans, the Ethiopian identified with Judaism but was on its margins. As was true in Samaria, Philip became the messenger God used to bring the Ethiopian into the church as it continued its geographical and cultural expansion outward from Jerusalem. Although the two narratives have their connections to Judaism in common, however, there are significant differences between the accounts.

	Samaritans (8:4–25)	Ethiopian (8:26–40)
Circumstances	Scattering because of persecution	Direction by angel and the Spirit
Audience	People group	Individual
Miraculous Signs	Prominent	Absent
Message	Messiah (Deut. 18:15–19)	Suffering Servant (Isa. 53:7–8)

Luke lays special emphasis on the divine direction that Philip received (8:26, 29, 39), which Ananias (9:10–16) and Peter (10:9–22) would also soon experience. The Ethiopian is the first of three individual converts, soon to be followed by Paul (9:1–19a) and Cornelius (10:1–48). Bock notes that Luke takes particular interest in individuals of higher social status who show an interest in spiritual matters, most likely because Theophilus could relate to them (2007, 347). The account makes it clear that the christological explanation of Scripture rather than miraculous signs is the key factor when someone responds in faith to the gospel.

God Directs Philip to Meet an Ethiopian Official (8:26–29)

An angel instructs Philip to travel the road from Jerusalem to Gaza, where the Holy Spirit directs him to approach an important Ethiopian official.

8:26. Luke's narrative returns to Philip and his evangelistic ministry, as an angel of the Lord spoke to him and gave him instructions that were both urgent and specific. He was to "go at once" (ἀνάστηθι καὶ πορεύου; Culy and Parsons 2003, 161) south (κατὰ μεσημβρίαν) on the uninhabited road that ran from Jerusalem to Gaza. See 5:19 on ἄγγελος κυρίου, who was the messenger God also used to give instructions to the apostles (5:20), Cornelius (10:1–8; 11:13), and Paul (27:23). Bock notes that Gaza was "the last water stop in southwestern Israel before entering the desert on the way to Egypt" (2007, 341).

A number of interpretive issues cluster around the angel's instructions to Philip. The first issue is the phrase κατὰ μεσημβρίαν, which can designate time ("at noon") or direction ("to the south"), with the latter sense referring to the position of the sun at midday (cf. Barrett 1994, 423). The phrase refers to time in Acts 22:6, and Marshall suggests that a temporal understanding makes the instruction more

unusual, since "at noon the road would be deserted of travelers because of the heat" (1980, 161). Other commentators and most English versions, though, conclude that direction makes better sense (Schnabel 2012, 424).

The second issue is the parenthetical clause αὕτη ἐστὶν ἔρημος ("this is desert"), which can be understood as referring either to the road or to the city of Gaza. There was both an old Gaza that Alexander Jannaeus razed in 96 B.C. (Josephus, *A.J* 13.13.3) and a new Gaza that Gabinius rebuilt in 57 B.C. (Josephus, *A.J.* 14.5.3). Since Strabo refers to the former as "remaining desolate" (Strabo, *Geogr.* 16.2.30), it is possible that the clause refers to the "desert" city. As Peterson notes, however, the city plays no role in the episode, and it is more natural to understand the description as applying to the road (2009, 293). Bock's suggestion that the clause refers to a portion of the road that was close to old Gaza might be on target (2007, 341), and the fact that ἔρημος can carry the sense of "an uninhabited region or locality" (BDAG s.v. "ἔρημος" 2, 392) supports that possibility. Although Barrett writes that it is not clear whether Philip and the Ethiopian met on the coast road from Caesarea or on the direct road from Jerusalem (1994, 423), Luke explicitly refers to it as "the road that is going down from Jerusalem to Gaza" (τὴν ὁδὸν τὴν καταβαίνουσαν ἀπὸ Ἰερουσαλὴμ εἰς Γάζαν), which would have reflected the fact that Gaza was 2,400 feet lower than Jerusalem. Larkin notes that the Jerusalem road was paved, suitable for a carriage, and more direct (1995, 131).

8:27–29. Luke highlights Philip's immediate and complete obedience by repeating the verbs in the angel's command to describe his next actions (ἀναστὰς ἐπορεύθη). Surprisingly (καὶ ἰδού), there was another traveler on the road. He was the "minister of finance" (Longenecker 1981, 364) for the queen mother of Ethiopia (δυνάστης Κανδάκης βασιλίσσης Αἰθιόπων, ὃς ἦν ἐπὶ πάσης τῆς γάζης αὐτῆς), who had been in Jerusalem to worship (ὃς ἐληλύθει προσκυνήσων εἰς Ἰερουσαλήμ). He had begun his one thousand-mile return journey home (ἦν ὑποστρέφων), was traveling in a carriage (καθήμενος ἐπὶ τοῦ ἅρματος αὐτοῦ), and was reading from the prophet Isaiah (ἀνεγίνωσκεν τὸν προφήτην Ἠσαΐαν). The "carriage" (ἅρμα) was a traveling vehicle that apparently was large enough to accommodate three people (cf. 8:38), although it is difficult to know how elaborate it was (Barrett 1994, 426). When the carriage came into view, Philip received additional instructions—this time from the Holy Spirit—who told him to "approach and join this carriage" (πρόσελθε καὶ κολλήθητι τῷ ἅρματι τούτῳ).

Ethiopia and the Ethiopian

Ethiopia (Αἰθίοψ) was another name for the area the OT calls Cush (Gen. 2:13; Ezek. 29:10). It was the kingdom south of Aswan in Egypt in the area that is now part of the Sudan. It was considered the southern edge of the earth (Homer, *Od.* 1:23) and the last inhabited land to the south (Herodotus, *Hist.* 3.25.114). Its inhabitants had "black skin and wooly hair" (Strabo, *Geogr.* 15.21). They believed that their king was the divine child of the sun god (Bruce 1990, 226). The effective head of the government was Candace (Κανδάκη), a hereditary dynastic title given to the queen mother (Pliny, *Nat.* 6.186.25). Luke describes the individual Philip encountered as an Ethiopian male (ἀνὴρ Αἰθίοψ), who was a minister of Candace (δυνάστης Κανδάκης) with authority over all her treasury (ὃς ἦν ἐπὶ πάσης τῆς γάζης αὐτῆς), and who had traveled to Jerusalem to worship (ὃς ἐληλύθει προσκυνήσων). He was, therefore, exotic, upper class, influential, and devout. He was also a eunuch (εὐνοῦχος), a term that can be understood in several ways, including a castrated male (Lev. 21:20), an impotent or celibate male (Matt. 19:12), or a high government official (Jer. 34:19; 38:7). If he was a eunuch physically, he would have

been barred from the assembly of Israel (Deut. 23:1), yet he had been to Jerusalem to worship, and he possessed a scroll of Isaiah (8:28), an item that would have been difficult to acquire if he were not Jewish (Larkin 1995, 133). The options are that he was a Diaspora Jew who was physically unfit to worship in the temple (Reeves 2004, 120), that he was proselyte to Judaism who was described as a eunuch because of his governmental office (Schnabel 2012, 425), or that he was a castrated Gentile "would-be proselyte," similar to the Godfearer Cornelius (Peterson 2009, 292). Regardless, Luke logically pairs the Ethiopian in Luke's narrative with the Samaritans not only because both he and they benefited from Philip's ministry but also because both he and they represented "a half-way house between a movement still completely within Judaism . . . and the later mission of Paul to the Gentiles" (Dunn 1996, 113). They were still "under the broad umbrella of Judaism" (Witherington 1998, 280) but on its margins.

Philip Preaches Jesus to the Ethiopian (8:30–38)

Beginning with a passage from Isaiah, Philip preaches Jesus to the Ethiopian, who responds with a request to for baptism.

8:30–31. Following the Spirit's instructions, Philip ran toward (προσδραμών) the carriage, where he heard the Ethiopian reading from the scroll of Isaiah the prophet and asked whether he understood what he was reading. The official acknowledged his need for spiritual guidance (πῶς ἂν δυναίμην ἐὰν μή τις ὁδηγήσει με;) and invited Philip to join him in the carriage (παρεκάλεσέν τὸν Φίλιππον ἀναβάντα καθίσαι σὺν αὐτῷ). In the largely oral culture of the first century, dictating aloud was the normal method of composition, and reading aloud was the predominant practice (Harvey 1998, 52). "Isaiah the prophet" (Ἠσαΐαν τὸν προφήτην) is a metonymy for his writings. Bock notes the wordplay in Philip's question (γινώσκεις ἃ ἀναγινώσκεις;) that contrasts understanding and reading (2007, 342). Marshall notes that the official's request for an interpreter reflects the incomplete character of OT revelation (1980, 163). Philip's actions demonstrated his obedience and spiritual sensitivity, while the Ethiopian's response demonstrated his humility and spiritual sincerity, as the Spirit put them together for a divine appointment.

8:32–35. The portion (ἡ περιοχή) of the scroll that Philip heard the Ethiopian reading was Isaiah 53:7–8, in a form that follows the LXX "with small variations" (Barrett 1994, 429). The verses are part of Isaiah's fourth Servant Song (Isa. 52:13–53:12). Jesus specifically applied that song to himself as numbered with transgressors (Luke 22:37; cf. 53:12), and "it was from him that the early church learned to read Isaiah 53 in this way" (Stott 1990, 161). From the passage, they also subsequently drew the themes of Jesus's healing (Matt. 8:14–17; cf. Isa. 53:4), his glorification (Acts 3:12–13; cf. Isa. 52:13), and his uncomplaining response to unjust treatment (1 Peter 2:21–25; cf. Isa 53:9) as part of their own teaching. In Isaiah 53:7–8 the emphasis is on the injustice that the servant experienced. When the Ethiopian asked Philip to whom Isaiah was referring (περὶ τίνος ὁ προφήτης λέγει τοῦτο;), therefore, it was understandable that Philip could begin with that Scripture (ἀρξάμενος ἀπὸ τῆς γραφῆς ταύτης) and share the good news about Jesus with him (εὐηγγελίσατο αὐτῷ τὸν Ἰησοῦν).

8:36, 38. Luke provides no details about Philip's gospel presentation, but the Ethiopian's response of faith was evident from his request for baptism. As they continued their journey (ὡς ἐπορεύοντο κατὰ τὴν ὁδόν), they came to some water (ἦλθον ἐπί τι ὕδωρ), and the Ethiopian asked whether there was anything that would stand in the way of his being baptized (τί κωλύει

με βαπτισθῆναι;). He commanded the carriage to stop (ἐκέλευσεν στῆναι τὸ ἅρμα), they both stepped down into the water (κατέβησαν ἀμφότεροι εἰς τὸ ὕδωρ), and Philip baptized him (ἐβάπτισεν αὐτόν). Luke gives no indication of where they came across the water, how much water was present, or what mode of baptism Philip used. Any attempt to be specific goes beyond the evidence of the text. Nor does Luke explain how the Ethiopian knew about baptism or its connection with salvation. Perhaps Philip followed Peter's example (2:38). Regardless, the point is that the Ethiopian responded positively to the good news about Jesus and, as a result, "a eunuch, a black, God-fearing Gentile" (Polhill 1992, 226) became part of the church.

TEXTUAL ANALYSIS: Variant Readings in Acts 8:36–40
There are two variant readings in 8:36–40, neither of which is likely original, but both of which are theologically interesting. The first is in 8:37, where the Western text adds a conversation between Philip and the Ethiopian. The latter asks, "What prevents me from being baptized?" Philip answers, "If you believe with all your heart, you may." The Ethiopian then replies, "I believe that Jesus Christ is the Son of God." Metzger notes that there is no reason for scribes to have omitted the verse (*TCGNT*, 315), and Marshall writes, "the content of the addition is perfectly sound theology, but the style is not that of Luke and the [manuscript] evidence is weak" (1980, 165). The second is an addition to 8:39, where the Western text reads "the *Holy* Spirit *fell upon the eunuch, and an angel* of the Lord carried Philip away." Since the wording of the Greek variant is πνεῦμα ἅγιον ἐπέπεσεν ἐπὶ τὸν εὐνοῦχον ἄγγελος δὲ κυρίου ἥρπασεν τὸν Φίλιππον, Marshall concedes that scribes might have omitted the additional words between πνεῦμα and κυρίου accidentally (1980, 165). The shorter reading, however, has stronger manuscript support, and it seems more likely that scribes added the words to make it clear that the Ethiopian also received the Spirit after his baptism.

The Baptism of the Eunuch by Pieter Lastman. Public domain.

The Ethiopian and Philip Resume Their Travels (8:39–40)

The Ethiopian continues his journey, and the Spirit transports Philip to Azotus, where he continues his evangelistic ministry.

8:39–40. After they came up out of the water (ἀνέβησαν ἐκ τοῦ ὕδατος), the Ethiopian joyfully resumed his travels (ἐπορεύετο τὴν ὁδὸν αὐτοῦ χαίρων). He no longer saw his spiritual guide, however, because the Spirit of the Lord carried Philip away (πνεῦμα κυρίου ἥρπασεν τὸν Φίλιππον). As a result, Philip found himself in Azotus, approximately twenty-five miles north of Gaza. From there, he kept on sharing the good news (εὐηγγελίζετο) as he was passing through (διερχόμενος) the cities on his way to Caesarea, approximately fifty-five miles farther north (21:8). See 8:8 on rejoicing as the response to the good news of salvation. The verb ἁρπάζω can denote "to take away to a different place" (23:10) or "to catch up into heaven" (1 Thess. 4:15–17). Peterson writes that the latter sense "is obviously not the meaning in this context," and argues that Luke simply describes "a forceful direction of Philip" (2009, 297). There is no *a priori* reason, however, to rule out an instantaneous supernatural relocation by the Spirit (cf. Bock 2007, 346; Schnabel 2012, 429).

THEOLOGICAL FOCUS

Acts 8:26–40 continues the account of Philip's evangelistic ministry, as first an angel then the Holy Spirit guided him to a divine appointment with an individual who, like the Samaritans, was on the margins of Judaism. The man he met on the road to Gaza was a powerful, highly placed government official from a kingdom that was considered to be at "the end of the earth." When the Ethiopian responded to the good news about Jesus, Philip baptized him into the movement as a member on equal footing with the Jews and the Samaritans before him. This segment of Luke's narrative develops his account of the progress of Jesus's command/promise in several ways. Historically, it continues the account of the Hellenistic Jewish witness that would resume in Antioch (11:19–30). Geographically, it foreshadows the spread of the gospel to the ends of the earth. Culturally, it expands the church's witness to those on the margins of Judaism and moves another step closer to the gospel reaching the Gentiles (10:1–48).

Theologically, Acts 8:26–40 provides a fresh perspective on Luke's theology of conversion with an individual at the center of the action. To this point in Acts, all the conversion stories involved groups: the crowds at Pentecost (2:1–40), the crowds in the temple (3:1–26), the crowds from the towns surrounding Jerusalem (5:12–16), and the crowds in Samaria (8:4–25). In this second excerpt from Philip's evangelistic ministry, the focus is on the conversion of an individual. Acts 2:1–42 establishes the basic sixfold pattern of witness: God acts (2:1–4), the listeners respond with interest (2:5–13), the witness explains from Scripture (2:14–36), the listeners respond with understanding (2:37), the witness calls for a decision (2:38–40), and the listeners respond with commitment (2:41–42). In his account of the Ethiopian's conversion, Luke highlights four of those six elements.

At Pentecost, God acted by using the miraculous to capture the attention of the listeners; on the road to Gaza, God acted by using an angel to capture the attention of the witness, and the Holy Spirit subsequently acted to provide additional divine guidance. Philip's obedience to that divine guidance was key to keeping his appointment with the Ethiopian. The Ethiopian's initial interested response reflected a prepared heart that demonstrated four qualities: It seeks God (8:27–28), it studies Scripture (8:30–33), it receives spiritual instruction (8:34–35), and it responds to truth (8:36–39). Philip focused his explanation from Scripture on Christ and contextualized it to his audience. Stott points out that in his preaching to the Samaritans, Philip focused on the coming of the Messiah (Deut. 18:15–19), because the Samaritans revered the writings of Moses but rejected the OT prophets. In his conversation with the Ethiopian, though, he focused on Isaiah's suffering servant (Isa. 53:7–8), because the Ethiopian was studying that portion of the OT (1990, 163). Finally, there was nothing half-hearted or ambivalent about his committed response, as he took the initiative in suggesting baptism and, afterward, went on his way rejoicing. If we are to believe early church tradition, the Ethiopian went on to become the first missionary to Central Africa (Irenaeus, *Haer.* 4.23.2; Eusebius, *Hist. eccl.* 2.1.13).

PREACHING AND TEACHING STRATEGIES

Exegetical/Theological Synthesis

Philip's ministry in Samaria had continued the pattern of evangelism among the crowds—in Jerusalem, in villages surrounding Jerusalem, and in the cities of Samaria. Yet, members of the Jewish ruling class had consistently opposed the gospel. Luke's first-century readers would have wanted to know whether the gospel was only for "the masses." Would someone in a position of power from another culture respond in the same way the Jewish rulers had? That question would have been of particular interest to "most excellent" Theophilus (Luke 1:3), who was most likely a highly placed Roman official. Were such individuals likely to be open to the gospel? How would they respond to the good news about Jesus? Would God welcome them into the new movement? As a quintessential "seeker" on the fringes of Judaism, the Ethiopian was exotic, upper class, influential, and devout. His divine appointment with Philip answers these questions and more. With the original audience, the twenty-first-century audience shares the need to understand that God welcomes "seekers" regardless of ethnicity, culture, or social status and will take whatever steps might be necessary to get the gospel to them. In response, they need to be obedient to the Spirit's guidance and take advantage of the divine appointments he arranges to share the good news about Jesus with the individuals he brings across their paths.

Preaching/Teaching Idea

Divine appointments create gospel opportunities.

Contemporary Connections

What does it mean?
The Holy Spirit beautifully orchestrates each movement of the gospel's advance. Divine appointments are everywhere. Waiting for the city to surge in population at Pentecost to reach the Diaspora, healing a man born lame to reach the temple crowd, mercy ministry at the divide of Hellenistic Jews, and persecution that drives the church outward and onward are just a few highlights of such marvelous light. Were there no Spirit-work in Acts, there would be no gospel fruit. Philip with the Ethiopian official is a prime example. Not one for subtly, the Holy Spirit tells Philip exactly where and when to go, exactly to whom he should speak, and presumably what to say. Just imagine the million little details that went into arranging for two men from very different backgrounds, who lived a thousand miles from each other, to cross paths on a lonely desert road, bent over Isaiah of all prophets and the Servant Song of all passages, ready to talk about Jesus. It's a miraculous encounter in a scene otherwise without miracles. And it underscores just how providential the work of witness and conversion really is.

Is it true?
Having pressed into the very heart of the Jewish nation in Jerusalem with the gospel, the Holy Spirit now brings opportunities to Judaism's margins. The Great Commission gathers right to the border of her Gentile reach, but tarries just a little longer. There is more work to do here. First, Philip witnesses to Samaritans. Now, he witnesses to an Ethiopian seeker. Just like that, the gospel leaps the gap. It leaps the eternal gap of a sinner now joined to God. It leaps the continental gap from Asia to Africa. It leaps the socioeconomic gap into a new region of political power and influence. It is ready to leap the frontier gap to pagan nations.

The simplicity of evangelism and conversion stands out perhaps more in this one-on-one encounter than in previous mass preaching and conversions. This unnamed Ethiopian has a heart for the one true God of Israel. He worshipped in Jerusalem and studied his Bible. He sounds like Cornelius. By the Spirit's help, Philip is able to contextualize the unchangeable good news into a way he could understand. Whereas the Samaritans heard about the coming Messiah they were looking for, the Ethiopian heard about the Suffering Servant he was curious about. All this talk of Jesus made this searching soul ready to receive baptism as the sign of his union with God.

Now what?
The Holy Spirit's providence is on full display in bringing Philip and the Ethiopian together for a divine appointment. Philip could not have created this scene if he tried. He would never have thought to put it in his weekly schedule. He would hardly even know how to pray for an opening like it. It makes no difference—the "wind blows where it wishes" (John 3:8). The Spirit surprises beyond human expectation. So it is with us. God can upend, invert, or turn inside out even our best plans to be faithful in his work. We might beat our heads against a closed door, only to find a nearby door swing wide open. Whether in evangelism, or an act of mercy, or speaking truth in love to a believer, or any good work, God creates divine appointments through his Spirit. His work, however, does not mitigate

human responsibility. Philip was preaching before this call (8:2), and he preached after it (8:40), but God swung this door wide in a memorable way. So also, we proclaim, warn, teach with all wisdom, but readily acknowledge his energy working in us (Col. 1:28–29). We are "zealous for good works" (Titus 2:14) while knowing that God has "prepared [them] beforehand that we should walk in them" (Eph. 2:10).

Creativity in Presentation

It would be fascinating to lay out many of the links of the chain that brought Philip the Jew and the Ethiopian eunuch together in this glorious, providential encounter. Think about the upbringing of this Ethiopian, who lived a thousand miles from Jerusalem and yet came to know the God of Israel. Think about the "chance" international trip he made just as the gospel was spilling outside Jerusalem city limits and into new cultures. Think about how rare it was to own a Scripture scroll, how remarkable his place in the text was that very day, and how perfectly his question became a soft pitch to Philip to hit with evangelistic fervor. In an informal setting, one could use actual chain links, metal or paper, to show sovereign details stretch out one after another.

What is the probability of all these possibilities coming together at once? The chance of flipping a coin five times and getting five heads, for example, is 3 percent. The chance of these remarkably different links joining is surely less. Essentially, apart from the Spirit's working, there is no chance. Apart from the Spirit's working, this episode would have been a very short story: an unnamed Ethiopian travels home. With the Spirit at work, though, gospel faith in Africa advances supernaturally. As believers, we must see the world differently. The world is pulsing with the Spirit, who is present, active, moving, and orchestrating. We are not a series of random collisions, chance events, or haphazard interactions. We Christians are under the direction of the Spirit, moved by him into the work he has for us. What are the chances?

Divine appointments create gospel opportunities.

- A divine appointment (8:26–30)
- A gospel opportunity (8:31–40)

DISCUSSION QUESTIONS

1. What do we learn about divine guidance from Philip's experience on the road to Gaza?

2. What makes the Ethiopian a good case study for how to recognize someone whose heart God has been preparing?

3. What do we learn from Philip's approach about how to share the gospel with a seeker?

4. How might Philip have gone about "preaching Jesus" from Isaiah 53:7–8?

5. What does the Ethiopian's request for baptism say about his understanding of the gospel?

Acts 9:1–19a

EXEGETICAL IDEA

Jesus appears to Saul on the road to Damascus and sends Ananias to confirm Saul's incorporation into "the Way."

THEOLOGICAL FOCUS

God's sovereign intervention results in the total transformation of every life he touches.

PREACHING IDEA

Only Jesus can transform an adversary into an advocate.

PREACHING POINTERS

Have you ever known anyone who thought he or she was doing what was right when it was totally wrong? Perhaps you know someone whose behavior was self-destructive, although he or she was unable or unwilling to acknowledge it. One way to address such a situation is to hold an "intervention," a carefully planned course of action designed to confront that person and put him or her on the right track. In Acts 9:1–19a, we find what might be the ultimate divine intervention as Jesus appeared to Saul on the road to Damascus in all his heavenly glory and confronted him with the shocking truth that what he thought was helping God's cause was actually opposing God's purposes. In so doing, he transformed Saul from a vessel destined for destruction into a vessel destined for glory.

People today should be able to relate to individuals making radical changes of direction in their lives. They might know about the circumstances or experiences that led to such changes. They might even be aware of the practice of holding an "intervention" to confront a loved one about the consequences of his or her self-destructive behavior. This passage corrects the ideas that there might be people who are beyond God's reach, or that God never intervenes in the lives of individuals. It also corrects the ideas that God has no interest in the sufferings of his followers, or that following Jesus makes a person immune from suffering. It commends an attitude of openness to what God is doing; the expectation that God will work in the lives of those around us; obedience to his instructions or commands; and the willingness to welcome, care for, and support every person God brings to himself. It is a testimony to the truth that God can and will intervene in the lives of even his most dedicated opponents, if it suits his purposes to do so.

JESUS'S APPEARANCE TO AND CONFIRMATION OF SAUL (9:1–19a)

LITERARY STRUCTURE AND THEMES (9:1–19a)

The passage consists of two sections recounting Saul's vision on the road to Damascus (9:1–9) and Ananias's vision that led him to the street called Straight (9:10–19a). The first section begins with a summary of Saul's activities as he persecuted the church (9:1–2), records Jesus's appearance to Saul in which he identified himself and gave Saul instructions (9:3–7), and concludes with Saul's companions leading him into the city of Damascus where he remained for three days (9:8–9). The second section records Jesus's appearance to Ananias in which he gave him instructions and explained Saul's new role (9:10–16), and concludes with Ananias's visit to a house on the street called Straight where Saul regained his sight and was baptized into the movement (9:17–19a).

- ***Appearance on the Road to Damascus (9:1–9)***
- ***Confirmation on the Street Called Straight (9:10–19a)***

EXPOSITION (9:1–19a)

God continued to push his witnesses outside their comfort zones. First, he used persecution to move Philip out of Jerusalem and into Samaria (8:4–25). Then, he used divine guidance to make it possible for Philip to meet the Ethiopian (8:26–40). Both the Samaritans and the Ethiopian had been on the margins of Judaism. Now, they were members of the new movement on an equal basis with the Jews. Next, he would appear to Saul and would use Ananias to bring him into the fellowship of the church (9:1–19a).

Saul had been the disciples' most feared adversary. Now, he was Jesus's chosen instrument to extend the mission to the Gentiles. Soon, God would overcome Peter's prejudice against the Gentiles and use him to share the good news with Cornelius (10:1–48) and persuade the Jerusalem church that the repentance leading to life had come to the Gentiles as well (11:1–18). In Acts 8–10, God uses three different witnesses—Philip, Ananias, and Peter—to intervene in the lives of three different individuals—the Ethiopian, Saul, and Cornelius. Luke "stresses the similarity of the mission that central characters share" (Tannehill 1994, 115). At the same time, the mission Jesus had given his disciples was continuing to expand. At the center of those three accounts is Jesus's appearance to and confirmation of Saul.

Scholars differ on how to characterize Luke's account of Paul's experience in Acts 9:1–19a. Bock highlights the similarities to the OT calling accounts of Samuel, Isaiah, and Jeremiah (2007, 353). Peterson emphasizes Saul's changed relationship to God that would be central to a conversion account (2009, 299). Barrett concludes that the account records both Saul's conversion and his call (1994, 442), and Schnabel views the passage as including both a conversion narrative and a commissioning narrative (2012, 438). There might be a better place to focus, however, than on the question of conversion and/or calling. Throughout the passage, the key actor is Jesus, who reveals himself to Saul, tells Saul to enter the city and await further instructions, appears to Ananias in a vision and tells him to seek out Saul, explains to Ananias Saul's new role as a chosen instrument, and ultimately heals Saul's blindness and fills him with the Holy Spirit. Although Saul's life and ministry changed dramatically, it was Jesus who had transformed him.

Acts 9:1–19a is one of three passages in Luke's narrative that includes an account of Saul's encounters with Jesus and Ananias. As the following table makes clear, there are differences between the accounts; but as Barrett notes, "the agreements are much more important than the disagreements" (1994, 441). The two most important agreements are that Jesus appeared to Saul and that Jesus communicated his plan to use Saul as a witness to the Gentiles. It is worth noting that the latter information is communicated in three different ways. In Acts 9, Jesus communicates Saul's new role to Ananias; in Acts 22, Ananias communicates that new role to Saul; in Acts 26, Jesus communicates it directly to Saul.

Sequence of Events	Acts 9:3–18	Acts 22:6–16	Acts 26:12–18
Saul approaches Damascus	9:3a	22:6a	26:12
A light shines around Saul	9:3b	22:6b	26:13
Saul falls to the ground	9:4a	22:7a	26:14a
A heavenly voice addresses Saul	9:4b	22:7b	26:14b
Saul asks who is speaking	9:5a	22:8a	26:15a
Jesus identifies himself	9:5b	22:8b	26:15b
Jesus appoints Saul as a witness	--	--	26:16–18
Saul asks what to do	--	22:10a	--
Jesus tells Saul to enter Damascus and wait	9:6	22:10b	--
Saul's companions are confused	9:7	22:9	--
Saul discovers that he is blind	9:8a	22:11a	--
Saul's companions lead him to Damascus	9:8b	22:11b	--
Saul does not eat or drink for three days	9:9	--	--
Jesus instructs Ananias to assist Saul	9:10–12	--	--
Jesus explains Saul's new role to Ananias	9:13–16	--	--
Ananias arrives to assist Saul	9:17	22:12–13a	--
Saul regains his sight	9:18a	22:13b	--
Ananias explains Saul's new role to him	--	22:14–15	--
Ananias baptizes Saul	9:18b	22:16	--

In this first account, distinct elements include Saul's period of waiting (9:9), Jesus's instructions to Ananias to seek out and assist Saul (9:10–12), and Jesus's explanation of Saul's new role to Ananias (9:13–16). By including those elements, it appears that Luke's emphasis in 9:1–19a is more on Ananias's need to understand Saul's new relationship to the church than on Saul's need to understand his own conversion and/or calling. Ananias and the other disciples in Damascus no longer needed to fear Saul (9:13–14), because he was Jesus's chosen instrument to bear his name before the Gentiles and to suffer for his name's sake (9:15–16). Saul was now a member of "the Way" and a key participant in its mission.

Appearance on the Road to Damascus (9:1–9)

Jesus appears to Saul on the road to Damascus, strikes him blind, and instructs him to enter the city and await further instructions.

9:1–2. While Philip was on his way to Caesarea, Saul was on his way to Damascus. Luke reintroduces Saul (ὁ Σαῦλος, anaphoric article), who was last present in Jerusalem "dragging off women and children and putting them in prison" (8:3). In the interim, he had still (ἔτι) continued (iterative present) "making threats to murder" (L&N §33.293, ἐμπνέων ἀπειλῆς καὶ φόνου) toward Jesus's followers. Not content to limit his activity to Judea, Saul approached the high priest and asked him for letters that would allow him to travel to Damascus and visit the synagogues there. If he found any who were "of the Way" (τῆς ὁδοῦ ὄντας)—whether men or women (ἄνδρας τε καὶ γυναῖκας)—he was authorized to return them bound (δεδεμένους) to Jerusalem, presumably for a trial like Stephen's before the Sanhedrin.

Culy and Parsons understand ἀπειλῆς καὶ φόνου as a hendiadys that they translate "murderous threats" (2003, 169; cf. NIV), while Longenecker sees the phrase as reflecting the two stages of Jewish legal proceedings (1981,

368). Regardless, Larkin notes that "Luke builds up the picture of Saul as a rampaging wild beast in his hateful opposition to the disciples of the Lord" (1995, 137). Damascus was a major city in the Roman province of Syria, approximately 140 miles north-northwest of Jerusalem, with a Jewish population large enough to have multiple synagogues (Josephus, *B.J.* 2.20.2; 7.8.7). See Bruce on the background of letters of extradition (1988, 180). "The Way" (19:9, 23; 24:14, 22) is a shortened form of "the way of salvation" (16:17), "the way of the Lord" (18:25), or "the way of God" (18:26) that refers to the Christian movement.

9:3–4. While he was drawing near to Damascus (αὐτὸν ἐγγίζειν τῇ Δαμασκῷ) and without any previous warning, a brilliant light flashed around Saul and caused him to fall to the ground. Saul then heard an audible voice asking him why he was persecuting the speaker. The details of the account highlight its special character. The unexpected nature of the occurrence (ἐξαίφνης; cf. BDAG s.v. "ἐξαίφνης" 344) suggests supernatural intervention (Luke 2:13). The "light from heaven" (φῶς ἐκ τοῦ οὐρανοῦ) that came at midday (22:16; 26:13) was brighter than the sun (26:13). It "flashed brightly all around" (περιήστραψεν; cf. BDAG s.v. "περιαστράπτω" 799) Saul in a manner reminiscent of the lightning (ἀστραπή) that accompanied God's presence in the OT (Exod. 19:16; Ezek. 1:14), that will accompany Jesus's return (Luke 17:24), and that emanates from God's heavenly throne (Rev 4:5; 11:19; 16:18). In response, Saul fell to the ground (πεσὼν ἐπὶ τὴν γῆν), which was the normal response to a divine visitation (Ezek. 1:28; Dan. 8:17; 10:9; Rev. 1:17).

As the lightning from God's throne is accompanied by voices, so the light on the Damascus road was accompanied by an audible voice (φωνήν) such as the one that Jesus heard at his baptism (Luke 3:20) and the three disciples heard at his transfiguration (Luke 9:35). By repeating Saul's name (Σαοὺλ Σαούλ) in the same way that God addressed Abraham (Gen. 22:11), Jacob (Gen. 46:2), Moses (Exod. 3:4), and Samuel (1 Sam. 3:4, 6), the voice highlighted the importance of the message. When the speaker asked, "Why are you persecuting me?" (τί με διώκεις;), he made clear his identification with Saul's victims (Luke 10:16). The event, therefore, was more than a bodily postresurrection appearance (Luke 24:15–31; Acts 1:3–8). When Saul later wrote that Jesus appeared to him (1 Cor. 9:1; 15:5–8) and when Barnabas reported that Saul had seen the Lord (Acts 9:27), they were describing a christophany in which Jesus revealed himself to Saul in all his heavenly glory.

9:5–7. Clearly, Saul was not certain of the speaker's identity, because he asked, "Who are you, Lord?" (τίς εἶ, κύριε;). When he heard,

"I am Jesus whom you are persecuting" (ἐγώ εἰμι Ἰησοῦς ὃν σὺ διώκεις), the answer must have shocked him. Jesus followed that answer with specific instructions for Saul to enter the city, where someone would tell him what to do. "Lord" (κύριε) in Saul's question was the appropriate way to address a heavenly figure (cf. 10:4). Bock notes that it was more than "sir" but less than a christological title (2007, 358). Jesus's answer used the "I am" (ἐγώ εἰμι) form that echoed God's self-identification (Exod. 3:6, 14). By adding "whom you are persecuting," he again identified himself with the very people Saul had thought were opposed to God and, so, required Saul to make a total change in his attitude and action.

Jesus's instructions to "enter the city at once" (ἀνάστηθι καὶ εἴσελθε εἰς τὴν πόλιν; cf. 8:26) emphasized his authority, expected immediate obedience by Saul, and echoed his instructions to the Eleven immediately before he ascended (1:4–5). The fact that Saul spent his time in the city praying (9:11) is also reminiscent of the way in which the Jerusalem disciples spent their time while they waited (1:14). Luke highlights the fact that this experience was for Saul alone (Peterson 2009, 305) by including the note that his traveling companions (οἱ δὲ ἄνδρες οἱ συνοδεύοντες αὐτῷ) stood speechless (εἱστήκεισαν ἐνεοί). They had heard the voice (ἀκούοντες τῆς φωνῆς), but they had seen no one (μηδένα θεωροῦντες). Nevertheless, they served as objective witnesses that Saul had experienced something unusual (Larkin 1994, 140; Marshall 1980, 171).

9:8–9. Jesus had instructed Saul to enter the city at once (9:6). His response was to get up from the ground (ἠγέρθη Σαῦλος ἀπὸ τῆς γῆς) and enter the city. His companions had to lead him by hand (χειραγωγοῦντες), though, because the light had blinded him. When he opened his eyes (ἀνεῳγμένων τῶν ὀφθαλμῶν αὐτοῦ), he was unable to see (οὐδὲν ἔβλεπεν).

His blindness was more than momentary (progressive imperfect); he remained blind for the next three days (ἦν ἡμέρας τρεῖς μὴ βλέπων), while he also refrained from eating and drinking (καὶ οὐκ ἔφαγεν οὐδὲ ἔπιεν). Larkin's suggestion that Saul's blindness was an acted parable "showing the bankruptcy of his pre-Christian condition" (1995, 141) aligns well with what the converted Pharisee would later write to the Corinthians (2 Cor. 4:4; cf. 3:15). Saul's fasting might have been an act of penitence (Marshall 1980, 170), preparation for his restoration (Larkin 1995, 142), and/or a way of preparing to receive additional revelation (Peterson 2009, 305).

Confirmation on the Street Called Straight (9:10–19a)

After Jesus appears to Ananias and gives him instructions regarding Saul, Ananias seeks out Saul, lays hands on him, and baptizes him.

9:10. Next, Luke's account shifts away from Saul, as Jesus appeared to Ananias, "a certain disciple in Damascus" (τις μαθητὴς ἐν Δαμασκῷ) and the witness who would incorporate Saul into the movement he had previously persecuted. Saul would subsequently describe Ananias as "a godly man, deeply devoted to the law, and well regarded by all the Jews of Damascus" (22:12, NLT). When the Lord spoke to him by name in a vision (ἐν ὁράματι), Ananias's response was immediate and unequivocal: "Here I am, Lord!" (NET, ἰδοὺ ἐγώ, κύριε). The paired visions of Saul and Ananias parallel the paired visions Cornelius and Peter will experience (10:1–23). Ananias's response to Jesus echoed Samuel's (1 Sam. 3:4) and "indicates both his presence and his readiness to carry out the Lord's will" (Barrett 1994, 453). Jesus's call and Ananias's response demonstrated that he was "a duly authorized prophet" (Bruce 1988, 188), who would speak on behalf of the one who would send him to Saul.

9:11–12. Jesus had specific instructions for Ananias. He was to go at once to the street in Damascus that was called "Straight," find the house owned by Judas, and ask for "a man from Tarsus named Saul" (NASB, Σαῦλον ὀνόματι Ταρσέα). He would know that he had met the right individual when he found someone who had been praying and had seen Ananias in a vision. When he found him, Ananias was to lay hands on Saul so that he would regain his sight. Clearly, Jesus was directing events as he called Ananias; commissioned Ananias by telling him where to go, whom to find, and what to do; as well as preparing Saul for Ananias's arrival. See 8:26 as a parallel to ἀναστὰς πορεύθητι ("go at once"). "The street called Straight" (τὴν ῥύμην τὴν καλουμένην Εὐθεῖαν) was the major east-west avenue in Damascus (Longenecker 1981, 373). Saul's act of continued prayer (προσεύχεται, iterative present) followed the pattern of the disciples in the upper room prior to Pentecost (1:14) and would have been a natural activity during his time of fasting. See 6:6 for the practice of laying on hands. The blind recovering sight was both a sign of the presence of the kingdom of God (Luke 7:18–23) and a metaphor for salvation (Luke 18:35–43).

9:13–14. Ananias, though, reacted strongly to the task Jesus gave him because of reports from many people (ἀπὸ πολλῶν) concerning Saul (περὶ τοῦ ἀνδρὸς τούτου), specifically reports about what he had been doing in Jerusalem and what he was planning on doing in Damascus. In Jerusalem, he had done many evil things (κακὰ . . . ἐποίησεν) to Jesus's followers (τοῖς ἁγίοις σου). In Damascus, he intended to use authority from the high priest (ἔχει ἐξουσίαν παρὰ τῶν ἀρχιερέων) to arrest all those who were calling on Jesus's name (δῆσαι πάντας τοὺς ἐπικαλουμένους τὸ ὄνομά σου).

Luke Timothy Johnson notes that in raising these issues Ananias serves as "the community's (and reader's) spokesperson in voicing reluctance and fear at so rapidly accepting into fellowship this murderous fellow" (1992, 169). His reluctance and fear were understandable. Saul was more than a "seeker"; he was an active persecutor. Was it reasonable to expect that those he had been persecuting would accept him into "the Way" on an equal status with his former victims? Jesus's answer to Ananias's concerns would confirm that Saul should be accepted into the church along with the other saints (9:13) who were calling on Jesus's name (9:14). Just as the Spirit's coming had overcome Jewish prejudice against the Samaritans, and just as the Ethiopian's unsolicited request for baptism had overcome any potential prejudice against him because of his background or physical imperfection, so Jesus's appearance to Ananias would help overcome his understandable antipathy toward the movement's most active adversary.

9:15–16. Rather than addressing Ananias's concerns directly, Jesus repeated the command to "Go" (πορεύου) and in explaining why (ὅτι) set out four aspects of his new role for Saul. First, Saul was Jesus's chosen instrument (σκεῦος ἐκλογῆς ἐστίν μοι οὗτος). Elsewhere, the verb ἐκλέγομαι denotes God's gracious choice, whether to salvation (Luke 18:7; Acts 13:17) or to a special role (Luke 6:13; 9:35; Acts 1:2). The latter applies here. The noun σκεῦος can denote someone with a role to perform (BDAG s.v. "σκεῦος" 3, 927). The combination σκεῦος ἐκλογῆς, therefore, describes Saul as someone God has graciously chosen to perform a special role for him. Paul's later comment that "we have this treasure in earthen vessels [ὀστρακίνοις σκεύεσιν]" is a possible echo of the idea (2 Cor. 4:7). Second, Saul's ministry would be to bear Jesus's name (τοῦ βαστάσαι τὸ ὄνομά μου). The verb βαστάζω can denote bearing something that is burdensome (BDAG s.v. "βαστάζω" 2, 171), whether a cross (Luke 14:27; John 19:17) or the cares of others (Gal. 6:2). "Name" (ὄνομα) encompasses both Jesus himself as an object of faith resulting in salvation (2:38; 3:16; 4:12) and

his power and authority (3:6; 4:7, 10, 30). Saul would assume the burden of presenting the salvation and power that was available through Jesus. He would soon do so both in Damascus (9:20) and in Jerusalem (9:28–29).

Third, the scope of Saul's ministry would extend to the Gentiles, kings, and the sons of Israel (ἐνώπιον ἐθνῶν τε καὶ βασιλέων υἱῶν τε Ἰσραήλ). Although much of his ministry would focus on the Gentiles (13:45–49; 14:8–20; 16:14–34; 17:16–34), it would not be limited to them. In fact, his mission practice would be to begin his work in a city by interacting with Jews in the local synagogue (13:15–41; 14:1–4; 17:1–4, 10–12; 18:1–7). He would also stand before Agrippa (25:13–26:29) and Caesar (25:10–12). His ministry, therefore, would be broad both in ethnic scope and in social scale. Fourth, it would be necessary (δεῖ) for Saul to suffer many things on behalf of Jesus's name (αὐτὸν ὑπὲρ τοῦ ὀνόματός μου παθεῖν). Both in this verse and in verse 6, δεῖ points to "the divine necessity inherent in [Saul's] calling" (Bock 2007, 358). Part of that necessity would be following the example of Jesus's sufferings (Phil. 1:29; Col. 1:24; 1 Peter 2:21), and Paul later writes that he bore "in the body the brand marks of Jesus" (Gal. 1:17). He would soon begin to experience rejection both in Damascus (9:23–25) and in Jerusalem (9:29–30).

9:17–19a. With his own assignment reaffirmed and Saul's new role explained, Ananias left (ἀπῆλθεν) the venue where Jesus had appeared to him and entered the house (εἰσῆλθεν εἰς τὴν οἰκίαν) to which Jesus had sent him. There, he laid hands on Saul, explained that Jesus had sent him, and described the purpose of his visit. Saul regained his sight (ἀνέβλεψεν), was baptized (ἐβαπτίσθη), broke his fast (λαβὼν τροφήν), and regained his strength (ἐνίσχυσεν). When he met Saul, Ananias addressed him as "brother" (Σαοὺλ ἀδελφέ), which acknowledged his new status as a fellow disciple. Ananias also made it clear that the Lord had sent him (ὁ κύριος ἀπέσταλκέν με) and that he was aware of Saul's encounter with Jesus on the road ('Ἰησοῦς ὁ ὀφθείς σοι ἐν τῇ ὁδῷ ᾗ ἤρχου). Saul would both regain his sight (ἀναβλέψῃς) and be filled with the Spirit (πλησθῇς πνεύματος ἁγίου). Those results would confirm his incorporation into the movement. See 6:6 for laying on hands, 9:12 for regaining sight, and 2:4 for filling with the Spirit. The "something like scales" (ὡς λεπίδες) that fell from Saul's eyes might have been a scar tissue (Larkin 1995, 143), but the important factor was the immediacy (εὐθέως) with which the healing occurred (cf. Luke 5:13). The fact that Saul was baptized at once (ἀναστὰς ἐβαπτίσθη; cf. 9:6, 11) echoes the Ethiopian's response and serves as further confirmation of his incorporation into "the Way."

THEOLOGICAL FOCUS

Acts 9:1–19a is the first of two accounts (along with 9:19b–31) describing "the sovereign, merciful intervention of God in Saul's life" (Peterson 2009, 298). Together, the paired accounts advance Luke's narrative in two ways. They continue the pattern of unexpected conversions that resulted from the scattering that followed Stephen's martyrdom—moving from the Samaritans to the Ethiopian to Saul, the church's most active adversary—and they set the stage for the prominent role Saul will have in the mission to the Gentiles. On its own, Acts 9:1–19a continues to highlight the way in which Jesus directs the progress of the mission he has given his witnesses. On the one hand, he appeared to Saul on the road to Damascus to intervene in the life of his chosen instrument. On the other hand, he appeared to Ananias to direct his witness to the street called Straight, so that Saul could regain his sight, be filled with the Holy Spirit, and be baptized into the church. The mission continued to advance exactly as Jesus had promised/commanded.

Theologically, Acts 9:1–19a reinforces the truths of God's sovereign intervention in the lives of individuals he brings into a relationship with himself and the total transformation that results from his intervention. When Jesus intervened in Saul's life, it was entirely at his initiative. He revealed himself to Saul and instructed him on what he should do. He appeared to Ananias and told him to seek out Saul. When Ananias expressed concerns, he explained Saul's new role as a chosen instrument. He healed Saul's blindness and filled him with the Holy Spirit. As Saul would later write to the Galatians, God set him apart from his mother's womb, called him through his grace, and was pleased to reveal his Son in him (Gal. 1:15–16). Further, when Jesus intervened in Saul's life, the transformation was total. Saul's role changed from persecutor of Jesus's followers to Jesus's chosen instrument. His passion changed from making a name for himself to bearing the name of Jesus. His focus changed from the purity of Israel to the obedience of the Gentiles. His experience changed from inflicting suffering on Jesus's followers to sharing Jesus's own sufferings. As Saul would later write to the Philippians, everything he had previously valued, he now counted as rubbish for the surpassing value of knowing Christ (Phil. 3:7–8). Taken together, the truths of God's sovereign intervention and the total transformation that results from his intervention demonstrate that only Jesus can transform an adversary into an advocate.

PREACHING AND TEACHING STRATEGIES

Exegetical/Theological Synthesis

The gospel was moving outward from Jerusalem. Through Philip's ministry, it had moved north into the cities of Samaria and south on the road to Gaza. As the gospel moved outward, however, persecution followed it. Reports of the gospel reaching Damascus in Syria apparently reached Jerusalem and prompted Saul to travel to that city to search out and arrest any disciples he might find in the synagogues of that city. Anyone who knew "the rest of the story," however, would know that somehow Jesus transformed Saul from one of the gospel's most aggressive opponents to one of its most effective witnesses. Luke's first-century readers would have wanted to understand how Saul became a member of the very movement he had persecuted. How had Jesus done it? Had he used supernatural means or the faithful witness of his disciples? Why had Jesus done it? Did he have special plans for Saul? If so, what were they? How had the church responded? Did they reject Saul, or did they accept him? Luke's narrative in Acts 9:1–19a answers those questions and more. With the original audience, the twenty-first-century audience shares the need to realize that God can intervene in the lives of even his most dedicated opponents and will do so, if it suits his purposes. In response, they need to welcome, care for, and support every person God transforms by his grace and for his purposes.

Preaching/Teaching Idea

Only Jesus can transform an adversary into an advocate.

Contemporary Connections

What does it mean?
It is certainly rare and striking to see such a definitive conversion from such a dark place. We last left Saul collecting coats at Stephen's brutal execution (7:58). It gets worse. That was Saul's springboard to rip into the church body, bursting into homes and dragging Christians to prison (8:3). It gets worse still. When he ran out of believers to hurt in Jerusalem, he received special permission to seek them out in Damascus. His intention was to arrest men and women there and bring them back to Jerusalem. On the now famous road to Damascus, however, Jesus intervened in a spectacular way. He appeared in transfigured flashing light. Saul was thunderstruck, confused, and cowed.

What Jesus said next is not a gospel presentation per se but assumes all kingdom authority and expects immediate, full obedience. Jesus told Saul exactly what to do. Saul jumped to obey. Later as the dust settled, through prayer and Ananias, Saul understood his salvation and his calling. The word *Lord* that probably meant respect back on the Damascus road now resonated as *Lord of all*, and certainly *Lord of Saul*. He gained physical sight as he regained spiritual sight, was baptized, and was strengthened for a road ahead that was much longer than the Damascus road had been.

Is it true?
Ananias's hesitation to have anything to do with Saul makes complete sense to any reader. "Lord, I have heard from many about this man, how much evil he has done" (9:13) is an understatement. Saul was a real, ghastly, violent sinner, and he left a wake of destruction in his path. There would have been actual flesh-and-blood saints nearby who had lost loved ones to death or prison at his hands. We are touched by Saul/Paul's later admission of himself as *chief of sinners* (1 Tim. 1:15). That self-designation was no quaint, glossy false humility. It was gross. It was costly. His real sin hurt real people in despicable ways.

Paul's experience puts flesh on the good news of the gospel. It always lands on shameful sinners—not well-heeled slip-up-once-in-a-while sinners, but vile rebels, bent away from God and his kingdom. To understand Jesus in the gospel in that way is to love him even more. His grace is sufficient even for Saul; it is sufficient even for all. At the same time, this gospel brings those who are *wounding* into its reach, and it cares for the *wounded* who are already there. When Jesus confronted Saul, he did not ask, "Why are you hurting those Christians in Jerusalem?" He demanded, "Why are you hurting *me*?" (9:4–5). Jesus identifies and cares for the wounded, as he would for himself. When the church suffers, Jesus feels the hurt. What a marvelous Jesus, who comforts the wounded, converts the wounding, and draws us both to himself.

Now what?

The good news that Jesus transforms adversaries into advocates is not just for the most publicly heinous of sinners—the Manassehs, the Pauls, the John Newtons. That good news is for *all*. *All* sin, resist, rebel, and pit ourselves against God. Some of us were flagrant, public sinners with punchy testimonies of drugs, alcohol, and adultery. Others of us were hidden, private sinners with "boring" testimonies of legalism, self-righteousness, rote obedience with no love. Some of us were unwashed tombs and some of us were whitewashed tombs, but a tomb is a tomb. Adversaries of God come in as many shapes and sizes as there are people, which makes Jesus's firm mercy here all the more delightful. In a world of unkindness, he is willing to absorb the worst we throw at him and his people, and still offer terms of peace with God through his death and resurrection. *Enemy* Saul becomes *Brother* Saul through God's adoption into his family of faith. More than saving us—although salvation alone is marvelous—he engages us in his kingdom work, to be his advocates in our needy neighborhoods. Our pasts never render us unusable. Jesus entrusts the most adversarial among us with real work to do for his glory.

Creativity in Presentation

There is more than one way to skin a cat, and there is more than one way to save a soul. Talk of testimonies opens the door wide to many creative ways to illustrate and present Saul's conversion here that fit within the myriad of ways God saves. One approach would be to trace some of the more radical testimonies from Scripture. For example, Manasseh was one of Judah's worst kings. He dabbled in every idol, medium, or omen available and even sacrificed his sons as pagan offerings. Like Saul, he had blood on his hands. Yet God transformed this hardened adversary into an advocate who became zealous for God's work (2 Chron. 33). An equally striking testimony in Scripture is Nebuchadnezzar. Like Saul, this king used power to persecute God's people, and like Saul, at the height of his power, God struck him down but did not destroy him. He returned to his throne praising God (Dan. 4).

Postbiblical history is replete with stories of Jesus transforming men and women. John Newton stands at the fore as one of the starkest turns. Newton was a godless, wicked man who worked his way up on slave ships to become a captain and make several slave-trading journeys. Christ grabbed his life and transformed him into a pastor who went on to write hymns like "Amazing Grace" and "Glorious Things of Thee Are Spoken." Both the OT Scriptures and history illustrate that God has been churning out miraculous testimonies for a long time.

Of course, living, breathing testimonies bring their own power to draw an audience into the text. Having friends share the stories of their conversion is a beautiful way to illuminate this Scripture. It is always wise to share several different kinds of stories of conversion so that they do not pigeonhole the way God saves or elevate certain kinds of testimonies as more important than others. In the end, what should shine in testimonies is what shines in the text, literally—Jesus. Attended by bright flashing light, armed with all resurrection authority, and able to take sight and give sight in a moment, Jesus stands at the center of Saul's story. In his kindness, he spares Saul's earthly life (a kindness Saul did not show Stephen) and gives him eternal life. Newton's right: "Amazing grace, how sweet the sound, that saved a wretch like me." Truly, only Jesus can transform an adversary into an advocate.

- Saul the adversary persecutes Christ (9:1–9).

- Saul the advocate is transformed by Christ (9:10–19a).

DISCUSSION QUESTIONS

1. Which aspects of Saul's experience are normative for people today? Which were unique to his individual encounter with Jesus?

2. Why are Jesus's initial statement to Saul and his answer to Saul's subsequent question significant? What do they reveal about Jesus's identification with his followers?

3. Why did Jesus delay three days before sending Ananias to assist Saul? What do Saul's actions during that period suggest about him?

4. Did Ananias act properly in raising his concerns after Jesus instructed him to find and assist Saul? Why or why not?

5. What steps did Jesus take to persuade Ananias that Saul should be accepted into the church? What did each contribute to his understanding?

Acts 9:19b–31

EXEGETICAL IDEA

Saul's early ministry in Damascus and Jerusalem included acceptance by the church, preaching in the synagogues, opposition from the Jews, and escape from opponents.

THEOLOGICAL FOCUS

A new disciple's willingness to connect to the body of Christ, witness in the name of Christ, and endure suffering for the cause of Christ attests to the depth of his or her relationship with Christ.

PREACHING IDEA

Genuine faith in Christ yields genuine fruit for Christ.

PREACHING POINTERS

How can we know that a person's profession of faith is genuine? Are there indicators that can help us as we work to integrate a new believer into a local church? Should we insist on a probationary period to evaluate the depth of his or her commitment? If ever there was situation that would seem to require caution, it was Saul's. He was a notorious persecutor of the church who had come to Damascus to continue his activities. He had no doubt arrested, imprisoned, and interrogated many members of the Jerusalem church. Yet there he was in both cities professing to follow the very name he had persecuted. What did he do to demonstrate that his commitment to Christ was genuine? He immediately sought to connect to the body of Christ both in Damascus and in Jerusalem. Once he was connected, he engaged actively in the life and the witness of the congregation, and he demonstrated significant growth in areas of his giftedness and calling. When opposition arose, he was willing to suffer for the cause of Christ. His example demonstrates the truth that genuine faith yields genuine fruit.

People today should be able to relate to skepticism that might arise about a person who makes a sudden and radical change in his or her attitude, action, or lifestyle. They can probably also relate to someone serving as a sponsor to introduce someone new to a group. Dramatic escapes or rescues from danger occur frequently, whether in the news, in books, or in movies. The passage corrects several possible wrong attitudes, including any suggestion that someone who comes to Christ can continue living "life as usual," that new disciples have no need of connecting with the body of Christ, or that it is necessary to make certain new disciples are "ready" before permitting them to engage in ministry. It commends the importance of helping new believers connect with a local congregation, allowing new believers to engage early and often in the active life and ministry of a congregation, and providing mutual support and assistance to members of the congregation who might be facing difficulties or be in trouble.

SAUL'S WITNESS IN DAMASCUS AND JERUSALEM (9:19b–31)

LITERARY STRUCTURE AND THEMES (9:19b–31)

The passage consists of two paragraphs that document Saul's early ministry activities in Damascus (9:19b–25) and Jerusalem (9:26–30). Both paragraphs follow a pattern of acceptance, preaching, opposition, and escape, and they foreshadow a similar pattern of synagogue preaching and Jewish opposition during his later ministries in Pisidian Antioch (13:13–52), Iconium (14:1–6), Thessalonica (17:1–9), Berea (17:10–15), Corinth (18:1–18), and Ephesus (19:8–10). The passage concludes with a summary statement (9:31) that highlights the church's growth (cf. 6:7), concludes the period of persecution in which Saul played a major role (8:1–9:31), and closes Luke's account of the events that began with Stephen's ministry to Hellenistic Jews in Jerusalem (6:8–9:31).

	Damascus	Jerusalem
Acceptance by Disciples	9:19b	9:26–27
Preaching in Synagogues	9:20–22	9:28
Jewish Opposition	9:23–24	9:29
Escape from the City	9:25	9:30

- *Witness in Damascus (9:19b–25)*
- *Witness in Jerusalem (9:26–31)*

EXPOSITION (9:19b–31)

After Jesus appeared to him on the road to Damascus (9:1–9) and Ananias visited him on the street called Straight (9:10–19a), Saul immediately began preaching in the synagogues of the city (9:19b–22) and encountered opposition from the Jews that led to his escape from the city (9:23–25). He then traveled to Jerusalem where he met with the apostles (9:26–27), preached in the Hellenistic synagogues as Stephen had (9:28), and encountered opposition from the Jews that led to his escape from the city (9:29–30).

The street called "Straight" in Damascus by Félix Bonfils. Public domain.

The apostle later recounts the same events in Galatians 1 and mentions his escape from Damascus in 2 Corinthians 11. The authors' different purposes shape their accounts and explain the variations between them (Longenecker 1981, 375). The Acts account focuses on the fulfillment of Saul's calling as a witness who would suffer and his continuity with the Jerusalem church, while the Galatians account focuses on the distinctiveness of Saul's gospel and his independence from the Jerusalem apostles.

	Acts Account	Galatians Account
Encounter with Jesus	Acts 9:1–9	Galatians 1:15–16
Confirmation by Ananias	Acts 9:10–19a	--
Ministry in Damascus	Acts 9:19b–22	--
Time in Arabia (Nabatean kingdom)	--	Galatians 1:17a
Return to Damascus	--	Galatians 1:17b
Escape from Damascus	Acts 9:23–25	(2 Corinthians 11:32–33)
Meeting with Jerusalem Apostles	Acts 9:26–27	Galatians 1:18–19
Ministry in Jerusalem	Acts 9:28–29	--
Travel to Tarsus/Syria and Cilicia	Acts 9:30	Galatians 1:21

The primary differences are that Acts omits any mention of Saul's three years in Arabia while Galatians omits any mention of Saul's initial ministry in Damascus. The best resolution is to place Saul's three years in Arabia (Gal. 1:17) between his initial ministry in Damascus (Acts 9:19b–22) and his subsequent escape from that city (Acts 9:23–25). "After many days" in Acts 9:23, therefore, corresponds to "three years later" in Galatians 1:18.

Witness in Damascus (9:19b–25)

Saul's preaching in the synagogues of Damascus results in a plot against his life and leads to his escape from the city.

9:19b–22. Luke moves directly to Saul's activities in Damascus after Ananias's visit. Those activities began immediately (εὐθέως) and took place over an indefinite period (ἡμέρας τινάς), during which Saul spent time with the disciples in the city (ἐγένετο μετὰ τῶν ἐν Δαμασκῷ μαθητῶν) and preached repeatedly in the synagogues (ἐν ταῖς συναγωγαῖς ἐκήρυσσεν). His preaching focused on the truth that Jesus was the Son of God (ὅτι οὗτός ἐστιν ὁ υἱὸς τοῦ θεοῦ). His preaching also generated constant amazement in everyone who heard it (ἐξίσταντο πάντες οἱ ἀκούοντες), because they knew that Saul had previously tried to destroy the disciples in Jerusalem (ὁ πορθήσας ἐν Ἰερουσαλήμ) and had come to Damascus with the same purpose in mind (ὧδε εἰς τοῦτο ἐληλύθει). Saul's preaching "became more and more powerful" (NLT, μᾶλλον ἐνεδυναμοῦτο), to the point that he was consistently astonishing (συνέχυννεν) his opponents as he was able to show for certain (συμβιβάζων) that Jesus was the Messiah (ὅτι οὗτός ἐστιν ὁ Χριστός). The use of imperfect tense verbs (ἐκήρυσσεν . . . ἐξίσταντο . . . ἔλεγον . . . ἐνεδυναμοῦτο . . . συνέχυννεν) and present tense participles (ἀκούοντες . . . συμβιβάζων) emphasizes the fact that Saul's preaching ministry in Damascus was both vigorous and protracted. In contrast, the aorist participle πορθήσας and the pluperfect verb ἐληλύθει both point to activities that were in his past.

"Son of God" (ὁ υἱὸς τοῦ θεοῦ) occurs only here in Acts, although "my Son" occurs in a quotation of Psalm 2:7 in Acts 13:33. The latter term was understood during intertestamental times as messianic (4 Ezra 7:28–29), and the Father used it to refer to Jesus at his baptism (Luke 3:22) and transfiguration (Luke 9:35). Larry Hurtado suggests that it refers to "Jesus's unique standing and intimate favor with God" (2003, 104). The title "Son of God" became a key concept in Paul's Christology (Rom 1:4; 2 Cor. 1:19; Gal. 2:20). "Messiah" (ὁ Χριστός) was central to the preaching of both Peter (Acts 2:31, 36; 3:18) and Philip (8:5). It would become central to Saul's preaching as well (9:22; 17:3; 26:23) and encompassed Jesus's suffering, resurrection, and exaltation. Saul's preaching, therefore, aligned fully with both the OT Scriptures and the NT church's message.

Πορθέω carries the sense of "to attack and cause complete destruction" (BDAG s.v. "πορθέω" 853). Paul himself describes his persecuting activities using the same verb (cf. Gal. 1:13, 23). Συγχύννω is a Hellenistic form of συγχέω (BDAG s.v. "συγχέω" 953) and denotes an action that "causes such astonishment as to bewilder" (L&N §25.22). Συμβιβάζω describes a process that "causes something to be known as certain and therefore dependable" (L&N §28.46). Bruce suggests that Saul set out OT promises about the Messiah and then explained their fulfillment (1988, 191). The extent and effectiveness of Saul's witness in Damascus sets the pattern for his future activities. As Larkin writes, "Just as

instantaneous as [Saul's] healing is his fulfillment of his calling" (1995, 144).

9:23–25. One part of Saul's calling was to bear Jesus's name before Gentiles, kings, and Israel (9:15). His witness began in Damascus. The other part of his calling was to suffer many things on behalf of Jesus's name (9:16). His suffering also began in Damascus. Whether that suffering had its origin with the Jews in the city (Acts 9:23), with the ethnarch representing Aretas in the city (1 Cor. 11:32), or a combination of both, Saul found it necessary to leave Damascus in a hurry after "many days had passed" (ESV, ἐπληροῦντο ἡμέραι ἱκαναί). The Jews Saul had been confounding (9:22) plotted together (συνεβουλεύσαντο) to kill him and were guarding the city's gates (παρετηροῦντο . . . τὰς πύλας) around the clock (ἡμέρας τε καὶ νυκτός). Their plan (ἡ ἐπιβουλὴ αὐτῶν), however, became known to Saul (ἐγνώσθη τῷ Σαύλῳ), and his friends helped him escape during the night (νυκτός). They let him down through the city wall (διὰ τοῦ τείχους καθῆκαν αὐτόν) by lowering him in a large basket (χαλάσαντες ἐν σπυρίδι). Wallace's category of "pluperfective" imperfect might apply to ἐπληροῦντο, since it describes time antecedent to that of the main verb (*GGBB*, 549); most English versions translate it as a past perfect. Culy and Parsons suggest, "as time went on the situation was becoming increasingly intolerable" (2003, 181). "His disciples" (οἱ μαθηταὶ αὐτοῦ) might refer to new friends and sympathizers (Bruce 1988, 192), or more naturally, to converts under Saul's ministry (Larkin 1995, 145).

> **Who Was Guarding the City Gates?**
> In Acts 9:24, Luke writes that the Jews plotted to kill Saul and watched the city gates. In 2 Corinthians 11:32, however, Paul writes that the ethnarch under Aretas the king was guarding the city. Aretas IV (9 B.C.–A.D. 39) ruled the Nabatean kingdom, which included Arabia where Saul spent three years (Gal. 1:17). If Saul's time in

Arabia included missionary preaching as Bruce suggests (1988, 191), Aretas was most likely aware of his activity, particularly if he had stirred up trouble among Jewish communities there (Marshall 1980, 174). An ethnarch (ὁ ἐθνάρχης) was an official appointed to rule over a particular area or constituency on behalf of a king (BDAG s.v. "ἐθνάρχης" 276). Perhaps in this case, the ethnarch was the king's representative among the Arabian community in Damascus. If so, "certain Jews and an Arab [ethnarch] might have seen fit to join in common cause against Saul" (Longenecker 1981, 377).

Witness in Jerusalem (9:26–31)

After Barnabas introduces him to the apostles, Saul preaches boldly in Jerusalem and leaves the city when the church learns of a plot against his life.

9:26–27. After he arrived in Jerusalem (παραγενόμενος εἰς Ἰερουσαλήμ), Saul did his best to associate with the disciples there (ἐπείραζεν κολλᾶσθαι τοῖς μαθηταῖς), but all of them were afraid of him (πάντες ἐφοβοῦντο αὐτόν) because they did not believe that he was a disciple (μὴ πιστεύοντες ὅτι ἐστὶν μαθητής). Barnabas, however, took the bold step of introducing Saul to the apostles (ἤγαγεν πρὸς τοὺς ἀποστόλους), and explaining in detail (διηγήσατο) that Saul had seen and heard the Lord, and that he had spoken out boldly (ἐπαρρησιάσατο) in the name of Jesus (ἐν τῷ ὀνόματι Ἰησοῦ) in Damascus.

Πειράζω suggests a context of futility (BDAG s.v. "πειράζω" 1, 792), and κολλάω refers to associating with someone on intimate terms (BDAG s.v. "κολλάω" 2b, 556; cf. 5:13; 10:28). A comparison with Galatians 1:18–20 makes it clear that the apostles (οἱ ἀπόστολοι) with whom Saul met were Peter and John (Bruce 1988, 193). Διηγέομαι describes the process of providing detailed information in a systematic manner (L&N §33.201); the cognate noun διήγησις occurs in Luke 1:1 to describe "an orderly account." "Speaking boldly" (παρρησιάζομαι) becomes a characteristic Lukan description of Saul's public proclamation (9:28; 13:46; 14:3; 18:26; 19:8; 26:26).

Some scholars question how the disciples in Jerusalem could have been unaware of Saul's conversion (Haenchen 1971, 336). Larkin, however, notes that it is "plausible when we consider that Paul has been away in Arabia a good portion of that time and that a persecuted community is naturally suspicious of any good news about its most violent adversary" (1995, 146; cf. Bock 2007, 368; Longenecker 1981, 378). As Schnabel suggests, "many in Jerusalem had been arrested, imprisoned, and interrogated by Saul" (2012, 456). Barnabas's report to the apostles includes the facts that Saul had seen the risen Jesus, had received a commission from Jesus, and had preached boldly in Jesus's name. He had each of those experiences in common with the Twelve (Larkin 1995, 146).

Verbal Aspect in 9:26–30

Although there might be a tendency to focus on Barnabas as the "sponsor" who introduced Saul to the Jerusalem apostles, Luke's use of verbal aspect in this episode suggests that his focus is on Saul and the reactions to him by the disciples and the Hellenists. The aorist adverbial participle of time (παραγενόμενος) that introduces the narrative carries events forward into the new episode. A shift to the imperfect and present tenses in the remainder of verse 26 (ἐπειραζεν κολλᾶσθαι) brings Saul and his activities to the foreground, along with the reaction of the disciples (ἐφοβοῦντο . . . μη πιστεύοντες), and gives those activities prominence. In verse 27, Barnabas's actions (ἐπιλαβόμενος . . . ἤγαγεν . . . διηγήσατο) and his account of Saul's Damascus experiences (εἶδεν . . . ἐλάλησεν . . . ἐπαρρησιάσατο) recede into the background with the use of the aorist tense. A shift back to the imperfect and present tenses in verses 28–29 (ἦν . . . εἰσπορευόμενος . . . ἐκπορευόμενος . . . παρρησιαζόμενος . . . ἐλάλει . . . συνεζήτει) again brings Saul and his activites to the foreground, along with the Hellenists' reaction (ἐπεχείρουν). A return to the aorist tense in verse 30 (ἐπιγνόντες . . . κατήγαγον . . . ἐξαπέστειλαν) carries the narrative to its conclusion by describing the actions of the Jerusalem disciples.

9:28–30. After Barnabas introduced him to the apostles, Saul immediately became active in the life and witness of the Jerusalem church—"moving about freely . . . [and] speaking out boldly in the name of the Lord" (NASB, εἰσπορευόμενος καὶ ἐκπορευόμενος . . . παρρησιαζόμενος ἐν τῷ ὀνόματι τοῦ κυρίου). In particular, he engaged the Hellenistic segment of the Jewish community (ἐλάλει τε καὶ συνεζήτει πρὸς τοὺς Ἑλληνιστάς). The result was another plot against his life (οἱ δὲ ἐπεχείρουν ἀνελεῖν αὐτόν). When the other disciples learned of the plot (ἐπιγνόντες οἱ ἀδελφοὶ), they took him to Caesarea (κατήγαγον αὐτὸν εἰς Καισάρειαν) and sent him off to Tarsus (ἐξαπέστειλαν αὐτὸν εἰς Ταρσόν).

Saul's witness to the Hellenists in Jerusalem resumed the ministry Stephen had begun, was equally effective, and resulted in similar—potentially deadly—opposition (6:8–14). Although Saul was active in the life and witness of the Jerusalem church, he later wrote that he "was unknown in person to the churches in Judea" (LEB; Gal. 1:22), which suggests that his ministry was limited to the city. Since Caesarea Maritima was the principal port of Palestine, it is most likely that Saul traveled to Tarsus by sea (Bock 2007, 370). Saul's experience in Damascus of acceptance, preaching, opposition, and escape repeated itself in Jerusalem. Summarizing Saul's early ministry in Damascus and Jerusalem, Stott

highlights four characteristics: it was Christ-centered, Spirit-empowered, courageous, and costly (1990, 178).

9:31. Luke concludes the passage with a summary statement that highlights the church's growth (cf. 6:7), ends the period of persecution in which Saul played a major role (8:1–9:31), and closes the account of the events that began with Stephen's ministry to Hellenistic Jews in Jerusalem (6:8–9:31). "The church throughout all Judea and Galilee and Samaria" (ESV, ἡ ἐκκλησία καθ᾽ ὅλης τῆς Ἰουδαίας καὶ Γαλιλαίας καὶ Σαμαρείᾳ) encompasses the entire Jewish homeland of Palestine (Longenecker 1981, 379).

Peterson notes that, although it is a single Greek sentence, most English versions divide the verse into two sentences (2009, 318). The grammatical issue is the relationship between the finite verbs that begin and end the sentence and the two participles that stand between them (εἶχεν . . . οἰκοδομουμένη καὶ πορευομένη . . . ἐπληθύνετο). English versions tend to take οἰκοδομουμένη with εἶχεν and πορευομένη with ἐπληθύνετο (e.g., CSB, ESV, NIV). Schnabel, on the other hand, divides the verse into three statements (2012, 466–67) and echoes Dunn's description of "a period of relative peace, consolidation, and steady growth" (1996, 128).

Since the feminine singular participles (οἰκοδομουμένη καὶ πορευομένη) both agree with the feminine singular noun that immediately precedes them (εἰρήνην), it seems most natural grammatically to divide the verse between the two dative phrases: τῷ φόβῳ τοῦ κυρίου and τῇ παρακλήσει τοῦ ἁγίου πνεύματος. If so, Luke highlights two results: peace and growth. Continuing peace (εἶχεν εἰρήνην), characterized by continuing progress in piety (οἰκοδομουμένη καὶ πορευομένη), was the product of reverence for the Lord (τῷ φόβῳ τοῦ κυρίου), while continuing numerical growth (ἐπληθύνετο) was the product of encouragement by the Holy Spirit (τῇ παρακλήσει τοῦ ἁγίου πνεύματος).

THEOLOGICAL FOCUS

In Acts 8:4–11:18, Luke presents three paired accounts focusing on three different witnesses. First, he traces Philip's ministry as he shares the good news of the gospel with the Samaritans (8:4–25) and with the Ethiopian (8:26–40). Next, he records Saul's encounter with Jesus (9:1–19a) and his initial ministry activities (9:19b–31). Finally, he will recount Peter's ministry in coastal Judea (9:32–43) and his witness to Cornelius's household (10:1–11:18). The narratival function of Acts 9:19b–31, therefore, is to conclude Luke's introduction of Saul and set the stage for Peter's ministry during the period of peace that began with Saul's departure for Tarsus (9:30–31) and would end with the persecution initiated by Herod Agrippa I (12:1–24). The persecution that began after Stephen's martyrdom ended when Jesus transformed his chief adversary into his faithful advocate. Luke's account of Saul's witness in Damascus and Jerusalem demonstrates four facts beyond the shadow of a doubt. Saul's purpose had changed (9:21). His preaching was aligned with both the OT Scriptures and the message of the NT church (9:21, 23, 28). He was accepted by the Twelve (9:26–27). He was willing to suffer for the sake of the name of the one he had previously opposed (9:25–25, 29–30).

Theologically, Acts 9:19b–31 provides a graphic illustration of the difference an encounter with Jesus makes in the life of a person who responds to him in faith. Others could testify to a noticeable change in Saul's life. He sought to connect immediately with the body of Christ, both in Damascus where Ananias could vouch for him and in Jerusalem where the church initially rebuffed him. Once he was connected, he engaged actively in the life and the witness of the congregation, both in Damascus and in Jerusalem. Saul understood the truth of the gospel accurately, communicated it effectively, and demonstrated significant growth in areas of his giftedness and calling. When opposition arose, he was willing to suffer for the cause of Christ. How can we know whether an individual's profession of faith is genuine? One way is to look at the sort of evidence Saul's life provides. The passage also highlights the role the church should play in the lives of new believers. In both Damascus and Jerusalem, a member of the congregation stepped forward to facilitate Saul's entry into the body. Both congregations provided opportunities for him to be engaged in the life and ministry of the body. Members of both congregations took active steps to protect Saul when he was in danger. How can we support men and women as they begin their walk with Christ? One way is to care for them actively, in the way the disciples in Damascus and Jerusalem cared for Saul.

PREACHING AND TEACHING STRATEGIES

Exegetical/Theological Synthesis

Jesus had totally transformed the life of one of the gospel's most feared opponents, so that he had become one of its most fearless witnesses. He had called Saul to bear his name before Gentiles, rulers, and Israel and to suffer for his name's sake. How would the church view him? Would they accept him? How would he fit into the life and work of the congregations with which he associated? How would his initial ministry activities relate to his calling? How would his message relate to that of the OT Scriptures and that of the apostles? Luke's first-century readers would have wanted to know how Saul connected to and became active in the movement he had previously persecuted. With the original audience, the twenty-first-century audience shares the need to know whether there are indicators that can help them as they seek to integrate new believers into local congregations. Luke's account of Saul's early witness in Damascus and Jerusalem in Acts 9:19b–31 provides a dramatic example of how a new follower of Christ can and should relate to the body of Christ. It also suggests that a new disciple's willingness to connect to the body of Christ, witness in the name of Christ, and endure suffering for the cause of Christ attests to the depth of his or her relationship with Christ. Was Saul an imposter, a wolf who came in sheep's clothing to infiltrate the new movement? Jesus himself said, "You will know them by their fruits" (Matt. 7:15–20; cf. Luke 6:43–45). Both in Damascus and in Jerusalem, Saul demonstrated that he was a good tree by the good fruit he yielded.

Preaching/Teaching Idea

Genuine faith in Christ yields genuine fruit for Christ.

Contemporary Connections

What does it mean?

At his conversion, Jesus used Ananias to explain to Saul two aspects of his new life of faith. First, he would be an evangelist in Jesus's name, and second, he would suffer much for that name (9:15–16). These statements were not Jesus's best guesses as to how Saul's Christian life would unfold. They were the fruits Jesus planned to yield through Saul's genuine faith. As Saul/Paul would later articulate the relationship between faith and fruit: "For we are his workmanship, created in Christ Jesus for good works, which God prepared beforehand, that we should walk in them" (Eph. 2:10).

True to his word, Jesus began bearing these good fruits in Saul's life. "Immediately," as though God had shot him out of an evangelistic cannon, Saul began preaching in local synagogues. We can safely assume that "the letters to the synagogues at Damascus" (9:2),

condemning Christians he brought to the city, never made it to those leaders. Instead, he brought a different message: "[Jesus] is the Son of God" (9:20). Before long, the Jews made the first of many attempts on Saul's life. The second attempt came shortly afterward in Jerusalem. It appears that genuine faith in Christ yields genuine fruit for Christ. Jesus called this unlikeliest of converts to witness and suffer, and then empowered Saul to fulfill his calling both in Damascus and in Jerusalem.

Is it true?

In the previous chapter of Acts, we read a conversion story that seemed too good to be true. Simon the magician believed, was baptized, and was amazed at God's power, but we left him with a stern rebuke from Peter that if he did not repent and turn, his so-called conversion was too good to be true (8:9–24). Those events put the reader on notice that there is more to conversion than a decision, a baptism, and a marveling at God's power. If Jesus grabs hold of someone's life, he will bear fruit in that individual. A converted life will look and feel different from an unconverted life. Jesus told his disciples, "If anyone would come after me, let him deny himself, and take up his cross daily and follow me" (Luke 9:23). Saul bears the cross Jesus gives him and produces the fruit Jesus prepares for him. Saul's first visit to Jerusalem demonstrates this truth dramatically. In the city where Stephen died in Saul's presence for his witness to Hellenists, Saul picks it up and carries it forward in witness to that same group (9:29). All the while, the church is there to bear this fruit with him. They help him escape Damascus and then help him to escape Jerusalem. The very one who afforded the church no refuge was delivered by her kind refuge. In the final summary in verse 31, it is Jesus's church, not Saul, who is Christ's shining fruit, built up and multiplying.

Now what?

We saw in the previous section that no conversion story is normative. There is no single way God chooses to save sinners. All of us can point to different ways and places he pointed, prodded, confronted, intervened, and snapped us into his kingdom. Although the details might differ, the core elements never do. We have already witnessed the staple elements of the gospel: repentance from sin and faith in the death and resurrection of Jesus, God's Messiah. Now we see repeated insistence on ongoing fruit. Where Jesus brings genuine faith, he will also bring genuine fruit.

That truth should challenge all of us. Genuine conversion is not "easy believism." It is not contained in a sinner's prayer, a walk down the aisle, the affirmation of a creed, or even baptism. It is not a nod to Jesus's words without producing Jesus's works. Jesus himself stressed, "Everyone who comes to me and hears my words *and does them*" is like the man whose house is built upon the rock (Luke 6:47). Genuine faith means being a hearer *and* doer of the word. We do not earn our salvation in the doing; we prove Jesus is really at work by bearing the good fruit he promised. Our lives should look like cross-carrying, Jesus-adoring, Spirit-empowered, costly discipleship. That victory is the one Jesus wins in us for his glory.

Creativity in Presentation

A creative presentation of this section could start with stories of narrow escapes. There have been many memorable ones in history and more recently—from prison, from kidnappers, from unsafe nations. A notorious story from history was Frank Morris and the Anglin brothers, who escaped from Alcatraz in 1962. Saul's early Christian life has its own flare for the dramatic. He narrowly escaped twice with his life, once from Damascus and once from Jerusalem.

The real action of the text and the sermon, however, centers on Jesus and the fruit he bears. Genuine faith in Christ yields genuine fruit for Christ. To see that truth most vividly in Saul and the church, it might be helpful to remind the audience about the myriad of responses to Jesus so far in Acts. The earliest Pentecost crowd was a mix of amazed, perplexed, and mocking (2:12–13). Ananias and Sapphira appeared to have faith but struggled with fruit (5:1–11). Other crowds esteemed Jesus, but they would not join him (5:13). Simon the magician seemed to convert but then let greed for power run ahead of him (8:9–24).

All these examples remind us that not every decision, sinner's prayer, walk down an aisle, raising a hand, signing a card, confirmation, dedication, or baptism is genuine faith for Jesus. The proof is in the fruit. Jesus said so: "I am the true vine, and my Father is the vinedresser. Every branch in me that does not bear fruit he takes away, and every branch that does bear fruit he prunes, that it may bear more fruit" (John 15:1–2). A message based on this passage gets to highlight the precious, salvation-confirming fruit that is all over Saul and the church, to the glory of Jesus.

True faith in Christ yields good fruit for Christ.

- Saul grows in genuine faith in Christ (9:19b–22).

- Christ bears genuine fruit in Saul (9:23–31).

DISCUSSION QUESTIONS

1. What are some indicators to draw from Saul's experience about how to assess the genuineness of an individual's commitment to Christ?

2. Should new believers be required to undergo a probationary period before they begin to engage in public witness for Jesus? If so, why? If not, why not?

3. What does the title "Son of God" reveal about who Jesus is?

4. How might a witness use the OT Scriptures to demonstrate that Jesus is the promised Messiah?

5. Did the disciples in Damascus and Jerusalem act wisely, or was their faith weak when they helped Saul escape from plots against his life? How do their actions relate to Jesus's teaching (Matt. 10:16–23) and practice (Matt. 12:15; 14:13; 15:21)?

Acts 9:32–43

EXEGETICAL IDEA

Miraculous works that resulted in widespread conversions characterized Peter's witness in Lydda and Joppa.

THEOLOGICAL FOCUS

Jesus exercises his power through his witnesses to advance his mission according to his sovereign will.

PREACHING IDEA

Jesus uses his power to build his church.

PREACHING POINTERS

What determines when God chooses to transcend the laws of nature? Why does he choose to act miraculously in some circumstances but not in others? How do miraculous works relate to the proclamation of the gospel message and the advance of the Christian mission? Peter's witness in coastal Judea raises these questions and more. His healing of paralyzed Aeneas and his raising of lifeless Dorcas demonstrated Jesus's power, sent shock waves throughout the region, and resulted in widespread conversions as Jesus worked through his witness to heal and to save. As the gospel spread outward geographically and ethnically from Jerusalem, Jesus continued to use his apostolic witnesses according to his sovereign will to accomplish his kingdom purposes as they depended on him to exercise his power, authenticate their witness, and advance his mission.

People today should be able to relate to individuals who suffer from prolonged illness or paralysis, grief over the loss of a loved one, and the sense of helplessness that can arise from such situations. They should also be able to relate to the rapid spread of reports about dramatic news such as the events in Lydda and Joppa. The passage corrects suggestions that there are no such things as miracles, that God does not intervene in human affairs, or that any situation is beyond hope of God's help. It commends trusting in and depending on God, turning to him for help in desperate circumstances, and responding in faith when he does the unexpected. As his people, we need to understand that Jesus uses whomever he wishes in whatever circumstances he wishes to accomplish whatever he wishes, in order to advance mission in whatever way he wishes.

PETER'S WITNESS IN COASTAL JUDEA (9:32–43)

LITERARY STRUCTURE AND THEMES (9:32–43)

The passage consists of two healing narratives—the healing of paralyzed Aeneas in Lydda (9:32–35) and the raising of lifeless Dorcas in Joppa (9:36–43). Both narratives include the same four elements of arrival, report, healing, and conversion, although the second narrative reverses the order of the first two elements. The close of the second narrative also notes that Peter remained in Joppa for many days (9:43), which sets the stage for the Cornelius episode that follows (cf. 10:5–6, 23).

	Aeneas in Lydda	**Dorcas in Joppa**
Travel and Arrival	9:32	9:38–39
Report of Illness/Death	9:33	9:36–37
Healing/Raising	9:34	9:40–41
Resulting Conversions	9:35	9:42–43

- *Healing Aeneas in Lydda (9:32–35)*
- *Raising Dorcas in Joppa (9:36–43)*

EXPOSITION (9:32–43)

Since he and John had returned to Jerusalem after visiting Philip's work in Samaria (8:14–25), Peter had been "off stage" in Luke's narrative. With the church in Judea, Galilee, and Samaria enjoying a period of peace (9:31), he engaged in travel throughout Palestine that brought him to the Judean coastal cities of Lydda (cf. Josephus, *B.J.* 3.3.5) and Joppa (cf. Josephus, *B.J.* 3.9.3). His ministry in those cities was characterized by the sort of miraculous works that God had used to accredit OT messengers such as Elijah (1 Kings 17:17–24) and Elisha (2 Kings 4:32–37) and that he would soon use to accredit Paul during his missionary travels (Acts 14:8–12; 20:7–12). In particular, the two miracle stories in Acts 9:32–43 show "how Peter acted as Jesus's agent in doing works similar to those in the Gospels" (Marshall 1980, 178; cf. Luke 5:17–26; 7:11–17; 8:41–56). Stott notes that Peter's ministry "followed the example of Jesus," as he performed miracles "by the power of Jesus," that were "signs of the salvation of Jesus," and "redounded to the glory of Jesus" (1990, 183). Peter might have been off stage temporarily, but his work in advancing Jesus's mission was not over.

Healing Aeneas in Lydda (9:32–35)

In Lydda, Peter heals paralyzed Aeneas, and many turn to Jesus.

9:32–35. As Peter was traveling (διερχόμενον) throughout Palestine, he came to Lydda in western Judea, about a day's journey from Jerusalem. There, he encountered (εὗρεν) Aeneas, who was one of the disciples living in that city (τοὺς ἁγίους τοὺς κατοικοῦντας Λύδδα), and who had been paralyzed for eight years. Peter declared, "Jesus Christ heals you" (ἰᾶταί σε Ἰησοῦς Χριστός), and commanded him to "get up and roll up your mat" (NIV, ἀνάστηθι καὶ στρῶσον σεαυτῷ). The healing was immediate (εὐθέως ἀνέστη) and led to widespread conversions among the population of Lydda and the surrounding Sharon coastal plain (πάντες οἱ κατοικοῦντες Λύδδα καὶ τὸν Σαρῶνα).

The verb διέρχομαι suggests that Peter was engaged in missionary activity (8:4, 40; 10:38; 11:19; 13:6; 14:24; 15:41; 18:23; 19:1). Schnabel suggests translating the phrase διὰ πάντων as "throughout the country" and concludes that it refers to the regions of Judea, Galilee, and Samaria just mentioned in 9:31 (2012, 467). Although ἐξ ἐτῶν ὀκτὼ could possibly be translated as "from the age of eight," the phrase more likely denotes "for eight years" (Barrett 1994, 480). The pluperfect periphrastic participle ἦν παραλελυμένος ("had been paralyzed") emphasizes the long-term nature of Aeneas's condition. The command to "roll up your mat" (NIV, στρῶσον σεαυτῷ) is best understood as the act of making up a bed after using it (L&N §40.10) and would demonstrate the reality of the cure (Marshall 1980, 179). The description of many "turning to the Lord" (ἐπέστρεψαν ἐπὶ τὸν κύριον) echoes Peter's call to repentance after the temple healing (3:19) and becomes a common way of describing conversion (11:21; 14:15; 15:19, 26; 18:20). Bock suggests that it is synonymous with "believing in the Lord" (ἐπίστευσαν ἐπὶ τὸν κύριον) in verse 42 (2007, 379).

Raising Dorcas in Joppa (9:36–43)

In Joppa, Peter raises lifeless Dorcas, and many believe in Jesus.

9:36–37. Meanwhile, there was a certain female disciple (τις μαθήτρια) living in Joppa whose Hebrew name was Tabitha and whose Greek name was Dorcas. She was well-known for doing good works and for giving alms to the poor (πλήρης ἔργων ἀγαθῶν καὶ ἐλεημοσυνῶν). During the period Luke describes (ἐν ταῖς ἡμέραις ἐκείναις), she became sick and died (ἀσθενήσασαν αὐτὴν ἀποθανεῖν). After the disciples washed her body (λούσαντες), they placed her in an upper room (ἔθηκαν ἐν ὑπερῴῳ). The addition of ἐποίει (customary imperfect) to describe her charitable activities highlights them as her regular and repeated practice. Dorcas's generosity is reminiscent of Barnabas's (4:32–37), and in Larkin's view, she "gives us a model of Christian charity to the

marginalized in society" (1995, 152). Bock suggests that the unusual act of washing her body and placing it in an upper room for viewing reflects a Hellenistic Jewish approach to burial (2007, 378).

9:38–39. When the disciples in Joppa heard (ἀκούσαντες) that Peter was in nearby Lydda, they sent two men to him to ask for help (ἀπέστειλαν δύο ἄνδρας πρὸς αὐτόν). Peter promptly went with the men (ἀναστὰς Πέτρος συνῆλθεν αὐτοῖς), and when he arrived (παραγενόμενον), they led him to the upper room (ἀνήγαγον εἰς τὸ ὑπερῷον) where Dorcas was lying. There, all the widows (πᾶσαι αἱ χῆραι) whom Dorcas had helped were present, weeping (κλαίουσαι) and showing Peter the inner and outer garments (ἐπιδεικνύμεναι χιτῶνας καὶ ἱμάτια) she had made. Joppa was located approximately ten miles west of Lydda on the Mediterranean coast. The NLT translates the disciples' request (μὴ ὀκνήσῃς διελθεῖν ἕως ἡμῶν) as "Please come as soon as possible," which captures the sense of urgency and loss they felt. The participle ἀναστάς suggests that Peter responded at once (8:26, 27; 9:6, 11, 18). The presence of the widows (αἱ χῆραι) suggests that Dorcas's charity extended beyond the local community of disciples (Bruce 1988, 199). A χιτών was an inner garment worn next to the skin under an outer garment (ἱμάτιον).

9:40–41. Peter put everyone else outside the room (ἐκβαλὼν ἔξω πάντας), knelt (θεὶς τὰ γόνατα), prayed (προσηύξατο), turned to Dorcas's body (ἐπιστρέψας πρὸς τὸ σῶμα), and commanded her to rise (εἶπεν, Ταβιθά, ἀνάστηθι). In response, Dorcas opened her eyes (ἤνοιξεν τοὺς ὀφθαλμοὺς αὐτῆς), looked at Peter (ἰδοῦσα τὸν Πέτρον), and sat up (ἀνεκάθισεν). He, in turn, gave her his hand (δοὺς αὐτῇ χεῖρα), helped her up (ἀνέστησεν αὐτήν), called in the disciples and widows (φωνήσας δὲ τοὺς ἁγίους καὶ τὰς χήρας), and presented her to them alive (παρέστησεν αὐτὴν ζῶσαν). Asking others to leave the room followed Jesus's example when he raised Jairus's daughter (Mark 5:40), and his words to Dorcas echoed Jesus's command to the younger girl (Mark 5:41; Luke 8:54). Kneeling and praying demonstrated Peter's submission to and dependence on God. Her return to life was immediate, as was the confirmation of the miracle by others.

9:42–43. When the miracle became known throughout Joppa (γνωστὸν . . . καθ' ὅλης τῆς Ἰόππης), many responded with faith in Jesus (ἐπίστευσαν πολλοὶ ἐπὶ τὸν κύριον). Peter then remained in Joppa many days (ἐγένετο ἡμέρας ἱκανὰς μεῖναι ἐν Ἰόππῃ) with another Simon, who was a leather worker (παρά τινι Σίμωνι βυρσεῖ). Although Dunn sees significance in Peter's choosing to stay with someone whose work would make him ceremonially unclean (1996, 130), Bock concludes that it would be better not to press the issue too far (2007, 379; cf. Schnabel 2012, 471). Larkin suggests that the detail simply serves to distinguish Simon Peter from his host (1995, 152).

THEOLOGICAL FOCUS

Acts 9:32–43 serves several narrative functions. It illustrates the growth of the church throughout Judea, Galilee, and Samaria that Luke summarized in 9:31. It continues the expansion of the church's mission geographically and ethnically to the "semi-Gentile population" of the Judean coastal plain (Bruce 1988, 198; cf. Barrett 1994, 483; Larkin 1995, 149). It returns Peter to the forefront of the action, authenticates him as an itinerant witness following the model Jesus set, and sets the stage for his encounter with Cornelius by noting his extended stay in Joppa.

Theologically, Acts 9:32–43 raises the question of the relationship between the miraculous, the proclamation of the gospel message, and the advance of the church's mission, because it is one of eight passages in which signs and wonders are prominent.

Text	Sign/Wonder	Response	Preaching/Teaching
Acts 3:1–26 (Jerusalem)	Paralytic healed (3:7–9)	Amazement (3:10)	Sermon (3:12–26)
Acts 5:12–16 (Jerusalem)	Sick and demonized healed (5:15–16)	Respect (5:13)	None noted
Acts 8:4–13 (Samaria)	Sick and demonized healed (8:7)	Attention and rejoicing (8:6, 8)	Preaching (8:5, 12)
Acts 9:32–43 (Judea)	Paralytic healed and dead raised (9:39, 41)	None noted	None noted
Acts 13:4–12 (Cyprus)	Magician blinded (13:10–11)	Amazement (13:12)	Teaching (13:12)
Acts 14:8–18 (Lystra)	Paralytic healed (14:10)	Syncretism (14:12–13, 18)	Sermon (14:14–17)
Acts 16:16–21 (Philippi)	Demonized girl healed (16:18)	Opposition (16:19–21)	Proclaiming (16:17, 21)
Acts 19:8–20 (Ephesus)	Sick and demonized healed (19:12)	Syncretism (19:13–16)	Speaking boldly (19:8–10)

It is possible to make several observations related to these passages. First, seven of the eight passages involved immediate, complete, and indisputable deliverance from serious physical conditions. Second, onlookers responded in various ways, both positively and negatively. Third, the signs served to attract attention (3:11; 5:16; 14:11), silence opposition (13:10), and/or authenticate the witness (8:9–13). Fourth, in six of the eight passages, gospel preaching or teaching accompanied the signs. Fifth, in six of the eight passages, the result was an advance of the church's mission (4:4; 5:14; 8:12; 9:35, 42; 13:12; 19:20).

There are some incidents in Acts when miracles did not result in a response of faith (6:8–15), and other incidents when people responded in faith apart from miracles (8:26–40). It is best to conclude, therefore, that miraculous signs do not automatically lead to conversions or church growth and that a lack of miracles does not hinder or prevent conversions or church growth (Schnabel 2012, 471). Marshall notes that God can display his power both in act and in word (1980, 178). Larkin suggests that the best perspective is to recognize that miraculous works give credence to the witness and his message (1995, 151). In fact, authentication of the witness appears to be the role those works play during Peter's missionary activity in Lydda and Joppa. They demonstrated that Jesus was still at work to exercise his power to heal and to save through his faithful witness as he advanced his mission to new geographical and ethnic frontiers.

PREACHING AND TEACHING STRATEGIES

Exegetical/Theological Synthesis
The mission was expanding geographically and ethnically beyond an exclusively Jewish movement centered in Jerusalem, and other individuals were assuming prominent roles in that expansion. Stephen had crossed the cultural threshold to the Hellenistic Jews. Philip had extended the mission to the margins of Judaism by sharing the gospel with the Samaritans and the Ethiopian. In Damascus, Jesus had used Ananias to help Saul understand that he would be instrumental in taking the gospel to the Gentiles. In the meantime, Peter and John had functioned as validators of Philip's ministry in Samaria, but they had not served as front-line itinerant missionaries beyond, possibly, the towns surrounding Jerusalem. Jesus had commissioned the original twelve apostles to be his witnesses "to the ends of the earth," but when the persecution following Stephen's death scattered the disciples, the Twelve had remained in Jerusalem. Luke's first-century readers would have wanted to know what role the original apostles played in crossing geographical and cultural thresholds as Jesus continued to advance his mission. The account of Peter's witness in Lydda and Joppa provides a snapshot of the way in which Jesus continued to authenticate his apostolic witnesses as they faithfully carried the gospel outward from Jerusalem in obedience to his command. With the original audience, the twenty-first-century audience shares the need to understand how Jesus works to advance his mission through his witnesses as they follow his example and rely on his power, and they need to learn to depend on him to use them as he sees fit to accomplish his purposes.

Preaching/Teaching Idea
Jesus uses his power to build his church.

Contemporary Connections

What does it mean?
Peter had faded into the background for a while as Luke shifted the focus to Philip and Saul. Now they fade, and Peter returns. The characters are interchangeable, but the Christ and his commission is not. Peter leaves his perch in Jerusalem in obedience to this Christ and sets about missionary work outside of Jerusalem

among the coastal cities of Judea. Like a rock thrown into a still pool of water that creates a series of ripples radiating outward, so Jesus's servants move in waves from Jerusalem to the surrounding regions. The power and witness promised in Jesus's commission are here. Jesus attends to Peter's ministry with incredible miraculous power, a power to heal a paralyzed man and even greater power to raise a woman from the dead. There is also power in Dorcas. Jesus gives her power for good works and gracious charity. In this text, both displays of power draw people in and build Jesus's church.

Is it true?
There is a sweetness in watching Peter watching Jesus. What he saw and heard from his Savior in the Gospels, he does and says in Acts. He becomes a little less like Peter and a little more like Jesus. When Peter heals Aeneas, he speaks in Jesus's name, and even sounds like Jesus telling a paralytic to get up and pick up their mat (John 5). When Peter heals Dorcas, he more or less re-enacts Jesus's healing of Jairus's daughter (Mark 5). They are Peter's words and deeds, but he comes by them honestly. He saw Jesus do them first, which means Jesus's power here is not just in the miraculous healings but also in the miraculous change in this Galilean fisherman.

There is power in Dorcas too. Her faith was "full of good works and acts of charity" (9:36). A host of mourners proved it. Jesus's power is at work again, turning inward-facing sinners to outward-facing sons and daughters of radical property-selling, dinner-table-sharing, tunic-making generosity. It is significant, of course, that Peter raised Dorcas from the dead. Resurrection power occurs sparingly and pointedly in the Bible. Jesus raised three people from the dead besides himself. Peter did it once. Paul did it once. Elijah and Elisha each did it once (not counting Elisha's bones). Resurrections are rare. We sit up and take notice of the brazen display of death-defeating power. Many people in the Bible die and stay dead, including the apostles

themselves, but not Dorcas. Jesus has yet more good work to do through her.

Now what?
We are the recipients of Jesus's power too. For a few of us, it might be the biblically rare miraculous act of healing. For many of us, we pray, it will be the biblically everyday miraculous acts of good works and generosity. Both are remarkable, countercultural fruits of life in Jesus and both raise the eyebrows of a watching world. Do we see that power at work in our lives and in our churches? If so, we can say with Paul, "The kingdom of God does not consist in talk but in power" (1 Cor. 4:20).

Jesus's power in us is never an end in itself, though. It comforts us, but its aim is never to make us comfortable. Jesus's power is an outward display to glorify himself before a watching world. In both scenes, new friends came running into the kingdom. Might they come running today, too? Might they see Jesus so beautifully and powerfully displayed in us and in our church body that they turn from themselves and toward him? May there be friends and neighbors around us who feel the loving care of Jesus through us and believe in him. May his power indeed build his church today as it did in Peter's day.

Creativity in Presentation
A creative presentation could start by grabbing people's attention. In an informal teaching setting, a loud noise, a cheesy magic trick, someone noisily arriving late to the talk could do the trick. In a formal setting, it might be examples of times and places of infamous publicity stunts. Memorable advertising by companies comes to mind; so do scandalous quotes by famous people. They say that there is no such thing as bad publicity. Of course, none of those creative illustrations parallel what is going on in the text. There are a million ways to grasp for attention, ranging from questionable or silly to disgraceful. But here in this passage, miracles and charity

are the best of signposts because they lead to the glory of Jesus and the good of people.

There are no magic tricks here seeking cheap thrills. A man receives the gift of walking. A woman receives the gift of life. There is no fawning for the attention of so-called important people. Dorcas's charity is providing clothing for marginalized widows on the razor's edge of poverty. Jesus's power in this place is for good, for health, for binding up what is broken. All miracles and acts of generosity read that way in Acts. The fruit of Jesus's power here is building up Jesus's church. Gimmicks and stunts chase self-glory. Jesus's power in and through us seeks Jesus's glory. At the end of both stories, people are turning to and trusting in Jesus. Peter and Dorcas fade. We fade. Jesus stands forever as he uses his power to build his church.

- Jesus's power restores what is lost (9:32–34, 36–41).

- Jesus's power strengthens the church (9:35, 42–43).

DISCUSSION QUESTIONS

1. How does the account of Peter's witness in Lydda and Joppa relate to the events that preceded and followed it?

2. Why was Peter traveling throughout Palestine at this time, when the apostles had previously remained in Jerusalem?

3. How did the miracles that Peter performed echo similar miracles from the OT and from Jesus's ministry? What are some specific examples?

4. What role did miraculous works play in this snapshot of Peter's ministry? Why does Luke choose to highlight those works in this particular passage?

5. Were the specific actions Peter took in the upper room with Dorcas significant? Why or why not? What did they suggest about his approach to seemingly hopeless circumstances?

Acts 10:1–48

EXEGETICAL IDEA
God uses divine guidance, christocentric proclamation, and Holy Spirit confirmation to overcome Peter's prejudice and bring forgiveness to Cornelius and his household.

THEOLOGICAL FOCUS
The impartial God uses the "more light" principle to bring the truth about Jesus, the Lord and judge of all, to responsive seekers from every people group.

PREACHING IDEA
God gives us the light we need to save us and sanctify us.

PREACHING POINTERS
How does God help us overcome our ethnic/religious/social prejudices? How does he orchestrate events to get the gospel to genuine seekers from people groups who have never heard the good news about Jesus? Luke's account of Peter's divinely orchestrated appointment with Cornelius illustrates the answers to both questions and highlights two complementary themes: the impartiality of God and the universality of the gospel. As God leads Peter step by step to acknowledge that he welcomes individuals from every people group, he also leads Cornelius step by step to accept Jesus as the Lord of all and the judge of the living and dead. What ties together the experiences of Peter and Cornelius is the principle that God gives more light to men and women who respond to the light they have. Luke's narrative recounts the parallel journeys of two men who are obedient to the light God gives them and, as a result, reach the different but important goals he has for each of them.

There are elements of the passage that people today might find strange, such as seeing angels, hearing heavenly voices, and concern about strict dietary rules. Nevertheless, they should be able to relate to ethnic/religious/social differences as well as to the idea of religious piety expressed by prayer and good works. The passage corrects the idea that God makes distinctions between people because of ethnicity, religious heritage, or social status. Instead, as the old hymn says, "at the foot of the cross, everyone stands the same." The passage also corrects any suggestion that good works alone are all that God requires of a person. Otherwise, Cornelius would have had no need to summon Peter to hear the words that God had commanded him to speak. Positively, the passage commends the attitudes of being open to the truth, being responsive to the light God provides, and being willing to obey divine guidance immediately. If we adopt those attitudes, we can be confident that God will bring us to the place where he wants us to be, whether it is to an acknowledgement of God's impartial stance toward humankind or to an acceptance of Jesus's universal lordship.

PETER'S WITNESS TO A GODFEARER (10:1–48)

LITERARY STRUCTURE AND THEMES (10:1–48)

The passage consists of six scenes grouped into three pairs consisting of two visions and two journeys, followed by a message and a response. After Cornelius experiences the first vision in Caesarea (10:1–8), Peter experiences a second vision in Joppa (10:9–16). While Cornelius's messengers are traveling to Joppa, the Holy Spirit speaks to Peter (10:17–23a); Peter then travels to Caesarea and meets Cornelius (10:23b–33). While Peter is still preaching a message to the group Cornelius had called together (10:34–43), the Holy Spirit falls upon everyone who is listening (10:44–48).

Peter's message divides into four parts: an introduction (10:34b–35), a thesis (10:36), proofs (10:37–42), and a conclusion (10:43). Declarations in verses 36 and 42 that Jesus is Lord of all (οὗτός ἐστιν πάντων κύριος) and judge of the living and the dead (οὗτός ἐστιν ... κριτὴς ζώντων καὶ νεκρῶν) frame the body of the message.

10:34b–35	Introduction (*exordium*)	*In every people group*, God finds acceptable the person who fears him and practices righteousness. (cf. Deut. 10:12–13)
10:36	Thesis (*propositio*)	God sent a message of peace to the Jewish people through Jesus Christ, *who is Lord of all*. (cf. Ps. 107:20; Isa. 52:7)
10:37–42	Proofs (*confirmatio*)	Following his ministry, death, resurrection, and appearances God appointed Jesus *judge of the living and the dead*. (cf. Deut. 21:22–23; Isa. 61:1)
10:43	Conclusion (*peroratio*)	The prophets witnessed to the forgiveness of sins through Jesus's name *to all who believe in him*. (Jer. 31:34; 33:8)

- *An Angel Appears to Cornelius (10:1–8)*
- *Peter Sees a Heavenly Vision (10:9–16)*
- *Messengers Arrive in Joppa (10:17–23a)*
- *Peter Arrives in Caesarea (10:23b–33)*
- *Peter Preaches Jesus (10:34–43)*
- *The Spirit Confirms Salvation (10:44–48)*

EXPOSITION (10:1–48)

The mission had moved steadily outward, crossing cultural boundaries from Hebraic Jews to Hellenistic Jews, to Samaritans, to the Ethiopian, to the ethnically mixed area of the Judean coastal plain. Crossing the cultural boundary to the Gentiles, however, would be a major step for the new movement. In his sovereignty, God chose Peter, perhaps the most prominent apostle, to share the good news about Jesus with

Cornelius, an exemplary Gentile, who had responded to the light of the Jewish religion by adopting key practices of that religion. Now, God provided more light to Cornelius by sending an angel to instruct him to summon Peter, who would speak the message God had commanded. At the same time, God was also dealing with Peter to overcome his ethnic prejudice against non-Jews. A heavenly vision, as well as specific guidance by the Holy Spirit, persuaded Peter to respond to Cornelius's summons and share the truth that the good news of peace through Jesus extended to members of all people groups who respond in repentance and faith. To confirm the inclusion of the Gentile listeners, the Holy Spirit interrupted Peter's message by falling upon all those who were present.

Although the Spirit's intervention cut it short, Peter's message included seven truths about Jesus. He is Lord of all (10:36b). God anointed him with the Holy Spirit and power (10:38a). He went about doing good and healing (10:38b). He died by crucifixion (10:39b). God raised him on the third day (10:40). God appointed him judge of the living and the dead (10:42b). Forgiveness of sins is available through his name (10:43). The central theme of the message, however, is the universal scope of the gospel message about Jesus that Peter highlights in six declarations: God welcomes individuals from every people group (10:35). Jesus is Lord of all (10:36). His ministry encompassed all of Judea, beginning in Galilee (10:37). He healed all whom demons oppressed (10:38). He is judge of the living and the dead (10:41). Forgiveness of sins is available to all who believe in him (10:43).

In keeping with other sermons in Acts, Peter's message included four of the six essentials of the gospel message: according to Scripture (10:43a), Christ must suffer (10:39b), Christ must rise (10:40a), and promise of forgiveness (10:43b). Both the call to repentance and the promise of blessing are missing because God intervened when he caused the Holy Spirit to fall on the listeners. The coming of the Spirit (10:44),

however, fulfilled the promise of blessing and supplies a fifth essential: Peter also affirmed the apostles' role as Jesus's witnesses (10:39a, 41).

An Angel Appears to Cornelius (10:1–8)

An angel appears to Cornelius and instructs him to send for Peter in Joppa.

10:1–3. Luke introduces Cornelius by highlighting his professional credentials and his spiritual condition. Professionally, he was a centurion (ἑκατοντάρχης), which made him the equivalent of a platoon sergeant who assists a commissioned junior officer. Spiritually, he was devout (εὐσεβής), feared God in such a way that his piety influenced his entire household (φοβούμενος τὸν θεὸν σὺν παντὶ τῷ οἴκῳ αὐτοῦ), gave alms generously to those in need (ποιῶν ἐλεημοσύνας πολλὰς τῷ λαῷ), and prayed to God regularly (δεόμενος τοῦ θεοῦ διὰ παντός). "In broad daylight" (Longenecker 1981, 386; φανερῶς), around 3:00 in the afternoon, he saw an angel who entered and addressed him by name (εἰσελθόντα πρὸς αὐτὸν καὶ εἰπόντα αὐτῷ, Κορνήλιε).

A "cohort" (σπεῖρα) was a military unit of six hundred men (L&N §55.9), divided into six groups of one hundred with a centurion (ἑκατοντάρχης) over each group of one hundred. Dunn suggests that Cornelius might have been retired and notes that he was "one of Luke's good centurions" (1996, 135; cf. Luke 7:5; Acts 27:43). Polybius's famous description of a centurion's character is that they "are desired not to be bold and adventurous so much as good leaders, of steady and prudent mind, not prone to take the offensive or start fighting wantonly, but able when overwhelmed and hard pressed to stand fast and die at their post" (Polybius, *Hist.* 6.24.9). The cohort "called Italian" (τῆς καλουμένης Ἰταλικῆς) was most likely an auxiliary unit stationed in Caesarea under the command of the Roman governor (Schnabel 2012, 485).

Commentators debate whether "Godfearer" (φοβούμενος τὸν θεόν; cf. 13:16, 26; 16:14;

18:7) was an established first-century category, although most conclude that it was a general rather than technical term that describes Cornelius as "a pious and intensely religious man" (Longenecker 1981, 385; cf. Bruce 1990, 252; Schnabel 2012, 494). Alms and prayer were key elements of Jewish piety (3:1–6). Larkin notes the importance of visions (ὀράματα) for the advance of the Christian mission (1995, 154; cf. 9:10–12; 16:9–10; 18:9). The ninth hour (ὡσεὶ περὶ ὥραν ἐνάτην τῆς ἡμέρας) was the time of the evening sacrifice and evening prayer (3:1–3). See 5:19 on "an angel of God" (ἄγγελος τοῦ θεοῦ) and the frequent appearance of angels in Luke-Acts.

Caesarea Maritima

Herod the Great completed his construction of Caesarea in 13 B.C., named it in honor of Augustus Caesar, and improved its harbor. Located sixty-five miles northwest of Jerusalem and thirty miles south of Joppa, it served as Herod's capital as well as the principal port for his kingdom. Beginning in A.D. 6, Caesarea served as the administrative center for the Roman governors of Judea as well as the military headquarters for the Roman forces in the province. The city was the home of Philip the evangelist (Acts 8:40; 21:8–9); the base for the Italian cohort of which Cornelius was a centurion (Acts 10:1); and the scene of Paul's trials before Felix (Acts 24:1–21), Festus (25:1–12), and Agrippa (Acts 26:1–29).

10:4–6. Cornelius "stared at [the angel] in terror" (NLT; ἀτενίσας αὐτῷ ἔμφοβος γενόμενος) and asked him, "What is it, lord?" (τί ἐστιν, κύριε;). The angel's answer included a word of encouragement and a word of command. The encouragement was that God was aware of and pleased with Cornelius's spiritual receptivity. His prayers and his acts of charity (αἱ προσευχαί σου καὶ αἱ ἐλεημοσύναι σου) had ascended as a memorial before God (ἀνέβησαν εἰς μνημόσυνον ἔμπροσθεν τοῦ θεοῦ). The

command required immediate attention (νῦν). He was to send messengers to Joppa (πέμψον ἄνδρας εἰς Ἰόππην) and summon (μετάπεμψαι) Peter.

The verb ἀτενίζω carries the sense of "to fix the eyes on an object continually and intensely" (L&N §24.49; cf. 1:10; 3:4, 12; 6:15; 7:55). Bock suggests that ἔμφοβος carries the idea of "startled and caught by surprise" (2007, 387). Schnabel prefers "fear" and notes that this episode is the first time "Luke explicitly ascribes fear to the recipient of a vision, explained by the fact that Cornelius is the first Gentile to see a vision" (2012, 486). "Lord" (κύριε) in Cornelius's question was the appropriate way to address a heavenly figure (cf. 9:4); it does not necessarily imply deity. The angel's report regarding Cornelius's prayers and alms echoes the language of a sacrifice that God accepts as pleasing (Exod. 17:14; Lev. 2:2; Ps. 141:2; Rom. 12:102; Phil. 4:8; Heb. 13:15–16). In order to make certain that the messengers found the correct Simon, the angel included three details: his other name was Peter (ὃς ἐπικαλεῖται Πέτρος), he was staying with another Simon who was a leatherworker (οὗτος ξενίζεται παρά τινι Σίμωνι βυρσεῖ), and the latter's house was beside the sea (ᾧ ἐστιν οἰκία παρὰ θάλασσαν).

10:7–8. As the angel departed (ὡς ἀπῆλθεν ὁ ἄγγελος), Cornelius immediately responded by calling two of his household servants (φωνήσας δύο τῶν οἰκετῶν) and one of his devout military attendants (στρατιώτην εὐσεβῆ τῶν προσκαρτερούντων αὐτῷ), explaining everything to them (ἐξηγησάμενος ἅπαντα αὐτοῖς), and sending them to Joppa (ἀπέστειλεν αὐτοὺς εἰς τὴν Ἰόππην).

Peter Sees a Heavenly Vision (10:9–16)

Peter sees a vision and hears a voice that challenges his understanding of what God considers clean and unclean.

10:9–10. Around noon (περὶ ὥραν ἕκτην) the next day (τῇ ἐπαύριον), while Cornelius's messengers were on the way (ὁδοιπορούντων) and were drawing near (ἐγγιζόντων) to Joppa, Peter went up on the roof (ἀνέβη Πέτρος ἐπὶ τὸ δῶμα) of the house to pray (προσεύξασθαι). Peter was hungry (ἐγένετο πρόσπεινος) and wanted to eat (ἤθελεν γεύσασθαι), but while the members of the household were preparing a meal (παρασκευαζόντων αὐτῶν), "a trance came over him" (NET; ἐγένετο ἐπ᾽ αὐτὸν ἔκστασις). Peter will experience another trance in 12:17, and Paul reports on his own trance in 22:17. Because the distance from Caesarea to Joppa was approximately thirty miles, the messengers either traveled through the night (Haenchen 1977, 334) or on horseback (Bruce 1990, 254) in order to arrive on the next day. Marshall notes, "Luke often emphasizes how God speaks to people when they are at prayer" (1980, 185; cf. 13:2; Luke 3:21; 9:29).

10:11–13. In his trance, Peter saw heaven opened (τὸν οὐρανὸν ἀνεῳγμένον) and "something like a big sheet being let down to earth by its four corners" (NJB, σκεῦός τι ὡς ὀθόνην μεγάλην τέσσαρσιν ἀρχαῖς καθιέμενον ἐπὶ τῆς γῆς). In the sheet were all sorts of four-footed animals (πάντα τὰ τετράποδα), reptiles (ἑρπετὰ τῆς γῆς), and birds (πετεινὰ τοῦ οὐρανοῦ). A voice accompanied the vision, telling Peter to "Get up . . . kill, and eat" (NIV, ἀναστάς . . . θῦσον καὶ φάγε). A shift to the historical present tense (θεωρεῖ . . . καταβαῖνον . . . καθιέμενον) heightens the vividness of Peter's vision. The list of animals, reptiles, and birds in the sheet echoes the lists in Genesis 7:14, 8:19, and Romans 1:23. Larkin, following Derrett, sees in the list a

possible "reestablishing [of] the eating practices available to Noah" in Genesis 9:3 (1995, 157). As it has elsewhere, ἀναστάς suggests a call to immediate action (8:26; 9:6, 11, 18). The heavenly origin of the sheet and its contents as well as the heavenly voice reinforce the divine nature of the combined visual-verbal communication.

10:14–16. Peter's response was immediate and emphatic—"Not a chance!" (L&N §69.6, μηδαμῶς)—and included a reason: he had never eaten anything common and unclean (οὐδέποτε ἔφαγον πᾶν κοινὸν καὶ ἀκάθαρτον). So, the voice spoke a second time (ἐκ δευτέρου), telling Peter that he should not call common (σὺ μὴ κοίνου) anything that God has made clean (ἃ ὁ θεὸς ἐκαθάρισεν). The voice spoke a third time (τοῦτο ἐγένετο ἐπὶ τρίς), and the sheet was immediately taken up into heaven (εὐθὺς ἀνελήμφθη τὸ σκεῦος εἰς τὸν οὐρανόν). Peter's rationale echoes Ezekiel's answer in similar circumstances (Ezek. 4:14).

The phrase κοινὸν καὶ ἀκάθαρτον occurs only here in the NT, although κοινὸν ἢ ἀκάθαρτον occurs in 10:28 and 11:8. Culy and Parsons suggest that the doublet "emphasizes Peter's abhorrence of the idea" of obeying the command (2003, 198). The pronoun σύ in the second heavenly declaration is emphatic. Schnabel notes that the threefold repetition "underscores both the novelty of the practice and the importance of the divine revelation" (2012, 491). The explicit significance of the vision is that it sets aside the OT food laws (Marshall 1980, 186), although the wider implications will become clear to Peter as the episode progresses (cf. 10:19–20, 28, 34).

Holy, Clean, and Unclean

Leviticus 11 set out laws for animals the Israelites were permitted to eat and those they were not (cf. 20:24–26). In addition, Leviticus 22:17–33 set out laws for animals that the Israelites were permitted to use for various sacrifices. Together, these passages suggest three categories of animals: holy (sacrificial), clean (edible), and unclean (detestable). Following Jacob Milgrom, Schnabel suggests that Israel also applied the categories of holy, clean, and unclean to people and to spaces (2012, 488–90).

	Holy	Clean	Unclean
Spaces	Tabernacle/Temple	The Land	The World
People	Priests	Israel	Gentiles
Animals	Sacrificial	Edible	Detestable

The voice in Peter's vision removed the distinction between clean and unclean animals. As the episode progressed, however, Peter came to understand that God had also removed the distinction between clean and unclean human beings. Whereas Israel's food laws had reinforced Israel's separation from the nations (Bock 2007, 390), the removal of those laws also removed the need for Jesus's followers to avoid contact with people previously considered unclean.

Messengers Arrive in Joppa (10:17–23a)

When Cornelius's messengers arrive at the house where he is staying, the Holy Spirit instructs Peter to accompany them without making any distinction regarding their ethnicity.

10:17–18. "By providential circumstance" (Larkin 1995, 159), while Peter continued to be perplexed inwardly (ὡς ἐν ἑαυτῷ διηπόρει ὁ Πέτρος) about what the vision he saw might mean (τί ἂν εἴη τὸ ὅραμα ὃ εἶδεν), Cornelius's messengers arrived. They had found their way to the house by asking questions (διερωτήσαντες τὴν οἰκίαν), stood at the front gate (ἐπέστησαν ἐπὶ τὸν πυλῶνα), and repeatedly inquired (ἐπυνθάνοντο, iterative imperfect) whether Simon, called Peter, was staying there (εἰ Σίμων ὁ ἐπικαλούμενος Πέτρος ἐνθάδε ξενίζεται). The verb διαπορέω carries the sense of being perplexed (Culy and Parsons 2003, 199; cf. Luke 9:7; Acts 2:12; 5:24); the progressive imperfect highlights the continuing state of Peter's bewilderment. The optative of εἴη reinforces Peter's uncertainty over how to understand the vision. The participle διερωτήσαντες describes the act of acquiring information by asking questions (L&N §27.11).

10:19–20. The messengers' arrival "was the situation for which the dream was meant to prepare

Peter" (Marshall 1980, 187). While Peter was still "puzzling over" (NLT, διενθυμουμένου, progressive present) the vision, the Holy Spirit spoke to him with information, instruction, and interpretation. The information was that three men were seeking him (ἄνδρες τρεῖς ζητοῦσίν σε). The instruction was to descend from the roof immediately (ἀναστὰς κατάβηθι) and go with them (πορεύου σὺν αὐτοῖς). The interpretation of the circumstances was that the Spirit had sent the men (ἐγὼ ἀπέσταλκα αὐτούς), and therefore, Peter should not make any distinction (μηδὲν διακρινόμενος) regarding their ethnicity.

The verb διενθυμέομαι has the sense of "to ponder" something (BDAG s.v. "διενθυμέομαι" 244) or "to think seriously" about something (L&N §30.2). Ἀναστάς again suggests a call to immediate action (cf. 10:13). The Spirit's explanation was the second step in Peter's education. The first step was to understand that God had removed the distinction between clean and unclean animals (10:15). This second step applied the same principle to human beings (10:20). The third step would follow Cornelius's explanation of his experience (10:34). As Larkin writes, "obedience to the Spirit will lead to understanding; understanding demands further obedience" (1995, 160).

There are three variant readings regarding the number of messengers in verse 19—ἄνδρες τρεῖς ("three men"), ἄνδρες δύο ("two men"), and ἄνδρες ("men"). The first reading has the strongest and most widely distributed manuscript support; it also agrees with 11:11. The second reading is more difficult and supported by a single manuscript (B); it might reflect the two household servants in 10:7. The third reading is shorter, and it could have led scribes to add a number to agree with 10:7 or 11:11. Metzger concludes that the first reading is "the least unsatisfactory solution" (*TCGNT*, 328).

TEXTUAL ANALYSIS: "making no distinction"
The primary sense of διακρίνω is "to make a distinction by separating" (BDAG s.v. "διακρίνω" 2, 231) or "to judge that there is a distinction" (L&N §30.113), although when the verb occurs in the middle voice it can have the secondary sense of "to doubt" (L&N §31.37). When the Holy Spirit instructs Peter to go with Cornelius's messengers μηδὲν διακρινόμενος, therefore, does he tell him to go "without hesitation" (most English versions) or "without distinction" (many commentators)? Although Peterson argues for a double meaning (2009, 332). The sense of "making no distinction" seems more likely for two reasons. First, as Bock notes, the similar phrase μηδὲν ἀνακρίνοντες occurs in 1 Corinthians 10:25 and 10:27 with the sense of "not raising questions of conscience" (2007, 391). Second, in the summary discussion of clean and unclean animals in Leviticus 20:25, Moses tells Israel, "You shall make a distinction [ἀφοριεῖτε] between the clean . . . and the unclean." Stott's suggestion, therefore, is "making no gratuitous distinction between Jew and Gentile" (1990, 187).

10:21–23a. In obedience to the Spirit's instruction, Peter descended from the roof (καταβάς), identified himself to the men (ἐγώ εἰμι ὃν ζητεῖτε), and asked the reason for their presence (τίς ἡ αἰτία δι' ἣν πάρεστε;). The messengers explained who Cornelius was, that he had received divine direction to summon Peter, and that he hoped to hear what Peter had to say. In response, Peter invited them in (εἰσκαλεσάμενος) and entertained them as guests (ἐξένισεν). The messengers' description of Cornelius—a centurion, righteous, and fearing God—echoes the description in 10:1–2 and adds the commendation that he was "respected by all the Jewish people" (NIV, μαρτυρούμενός τε ὑπὸ ὅλου τοῦ ἔθνους τῶν Ἰουδαίων).

The phrase ἐχρηματίσθη ὑπὸ ἀγγέλου ἁγίου identifies the information Cornelius received as a divine disclosure (Bock 2007, 392; cf. Matt. 2:12, 22; Luke 2:26). The infinitival purpose phrase ἀκοῦσαι ῥήματα παρὰ σοῦ adds the new information that Cornelius wanted to listen to what Peter had to say (Marshall 1980, 187). Peter's willingness to entertain the men "does not go beyond what a law-abiding Jew might do," although it is "a sign that he agrees to their request [to visit a Gentile], which was not permitted for a Jew" (Larkin 1995, 160).

Peter Arrives in Caesarea (10:23b–33)
Peter travels to Caesarea, where he finds that Cornelius has gathered his relatives and friends to hear the message God has commanded Peter to speak.

10:23b–26. On the next day (τῇ ἐπαύριον), Peter immediately departed (ἀναστὰς ἐξῆλθεν), accompanied by Cornelius's messengers (σὺν αὐτοῖς) and a group of brothers from Joppa (τινες τῶν ἀδελφῶν τῶν ἀπὸ Ἰόππης). A day later (τῇ ἐπαύριον), they arrived in Caesarea (εἰσῆλθεν εἰς τὴν Καισάρειαν), where Cornelius was expecting them (ὁ Κορνήλιος ἦν προσδοκῶν αὐτούς) and had called together (συγκαλεσάμενος) a group of relatives (τοὺς συγγενεῖς αὐτοῦ) and close friends (τοὺς ἀναγκαίους φίλους). Acts 11:12 specifies the number of brothers from Joppa at six (οἱ ἓξ ἀδελφοὶ οὗτοι) for a total traveling party of ten. The larger group probably increased the travel time, so that they arrived on the fourth day (10:30).

When Peter arrived (τοῦ εἰσελθεῖν τὸν Πέτρον), Cornelius met him (συναντήσας αὐτῷ ὁ Κορνήλιος) and fell at his feet in worship (πεσὼν ἐπὶ τοὺς πόδας προσεκύνησεν). Peter "pulled him up" (NLT, ἤγειρεν αὐτόν) while telling him to get up (ἀνάστηθι), explaining that he was also a human being. Although the verb προσκυνέω can denote "to prostrate oneself before someone as an act of reverence, fear, or supplication" (L&N §17.21), the more likely sense here is "to worship" (L&N §53.56), which is the common reaction to the appearance of an angelic messenger (Rev. 19:10; 22:8). Peter's response (καὶ ἐγὼ αὐτὸς ἄνθρωπός εἰμι) is "a highly emphatic statement" (Culy and Parsons 2003, 205), combining the adjunctive καί, the personal pronoun ἐγώ, and the intensive pronoun αὐτός—"I myself am also" (LEB). Ἄνθρωπος denotes Peter's humanity rather than his maleness. "Contrary to what Cornelius thought, Peter was not a god or an angelic being, but a mere mortal" (NET).

10:27–29a. Peter continued talking with Cornelius (συνομιλῶν αὐτῷ), entered (εἰσῆλθεν), and found many who had come together (εὑρίσκει συνεληλυθότας πολλούς). Peter had a three-part preliminary announcement for the assembled group. First, his listeners were aware (ὑμεῖς ἐπίστασθε) that it was "indecent" (ἀθέμιτον; cf. Bock 2007, 393) for a Jew to associate with (κολλᾶσθαι ἢ προσέρχεσθαι) a non-Jew (ἀλλοφύλῳ). Second, God had shown (ἔδειξεν) him that no one (μηδένα) should call another person common or unclean (κοινὸν ἢ ἀκάθαρτον λέγειν ἄνθρωπον). Third, he had come "without raising any objection" (BDAG s.v. "ἀναντιρρήτως" 69) when he was summoned (μεταπεμφθείς).

The adjective ἀθέμιτος describes something that was contrary to ancient custom rather than forbidden by the Mosaic law (i.e., ἄνομος); Bruce suggests the idea of "taboo" (1988, 209). The custom is reflected in Jubilees 22:16, which enjoins, "Keep yourself separate from the nations, and do not eat with them; and do not imitate their rites, nor associate yourself with them." The reason not to associate on intimate terms (κολλᾶσθαι) with non-Jews was that it could lead to ritual defilement. A Jew could become unclean by entering a Gentile building (John 18:28), and table fellowship with Gentiles was "intolerable" because of the potential for eating food that was prohibited, had been sacrificed to idols, or contained blood (Bruce 1998, 210). Ἀλλόφυλος describes someone or something that is "foreign" (i.e., not Jewish). Μηδένα is best understood as the subject of the infinitive λέγειν (Culy and Parsons 2003, 206). Κοινὸν ἢ ἀκάθαρτον echoes Peter's initial objection to the heavenly command to "kill and eat" (10:14). His statement to the group, however, made it clear that he now understood the implications of the vision: God no longer applied distinctions either to food (10:15) or to people (10:20).

10:29b–33. The natural question for Cornelius, therefore, was why he had summoned Peter (πυνθάνομαι τίνι λόγῳ μετεπέμψασθέ με;). Cornelius began by rehearsing the events that had taken place four days previously (ἀπὸ τετάρτης ἡμέρας). He recounted the circumstances, the vision of a man "in dazzling apparel" (ἐν ἐσθῆτι λαμπρᾷ; cf. Bock 2007, 394), the good news that God had looked favorably on his prayers and acts of charity, the command to summon Peter from Joppa, and his immediate (ἐξαυτῆς) obedience to the command. He then acknowledged Peter's kindness in coming (σύ καλῶς ἐποίησας παραγενόμενος) and explained that everyone who had gathered (πάντες ἡμεῖς … πάρεσμεν) considered themselves to be in God's presence (ἐνώπιον τοῦ θεοῦ) and were ready to hear everything God had commanded Peter to say (ἀκοῦσαι πάντα τὰ προστεταγμένα σοι ὑπὸ τοῦ κυρίου).

Although Barrett considers Cornelius's opening words in verse 30 to be unclear (1994, 516), NLT captures the meaning well: "Four days ago I was praying in my house about this same time, three o'clock in the afternoon." The mention of four days involves inclusive counting (Bruce 1988, 209): on the first day Cornelius sent the messengers (10:8), on the second day the messengers arrived in Joppa (10:9), on the third day Peter set out for Caesarea (10:23), on the fourth day Peter arrived at Cornelius's house (10:24). The description of the man's bright clothing is consistent with other angelic appearances (Luke 24:4; Acts 1:10). The combination of "before God" and "has been commanded by the Lord" reflects Cornelius's realization that "God is responsible for their being together . . . [and] is a witness to what is taking place" (Bock 2007, 395). As Larkin notes, "the Gentile mission was God's will and would not have happened apart from divine intervention" (1995, 162).

Peter Preaches Jesus (10:34–43)

Peter shares the good news of peace through Jesus, who is the universal Lord and judge and is sent by the impartial God to seekers from every people group.

10:34–35. What the Lord had commanded Peter to say was a proclamation of the universal scope of the message about Jesus. Specifically, God is not one who shows favoritism (οὐκ ἔστιν προσωπολήμπτης). Instead (ἀλλ᾿), he welcomes those individuals in every people group who fear him and practice righteousness. Following David Daube, Barrett suggests that the phrase ἀνοίξας τὸ στόμα reflects a rabbinic formula denoting "to open a lecture on Scripture" (1994, 431; cf. Daube 1956, 434), which fits well with other NT occurrences (Matt. 5:2; Acts 8:35). "In truth I understand" (LEB, ἐπ᾿ ἀληθείας καταλαμβάνομαι) reinforces the genuineness of Peter's new conviction. "In every nation" (ἐν παντὶ ἔθνει) introduces the universal scope of the gospel that is central to Peter's message. Προσωπολήμπτης ("one who shows favoritism") reflects the OT concept of showing favor by "raising up the face of one who has

prostrated himself" (Barrett 1994, 519). Other NT occurrences are Romans 2:11, Ephesians 6:9, and Colossians 3:25 (cf. ἀπροσωπολήμπτης in 1 Peter 1:17).

"Fearing [God] and practicing righteousness" (φοβούμενος αὐτὸν καὶ ἐργαζόμενος δικαιοσύνην) echoes both Deuteronomy 10:12–13 and Cornelius's reputation for prayer and almsgiving (Schnabel 2012, 499). The adjective δεκτός pertains "to that which is pleasing in view of its being acceptable" (L&N §25.85). "Acceptable," however, does not mean "accepted." God was pleased with Cornelius's progress to this point, but he still needed to hear the gospel and respond to it in repentance and faith. As Marshall notes, "a good life is acceptable in God's sight only when it leads to recognition of its own inadequacy and to acceptance of the gospel" (1980, 190).

10:36. This God, who does not show favoritism but welcomes individuals from every people group, sent a message (τὸν λόγον ὃν ἀπέστειλεν) to the people of Israel (τοῖς υἱοῖς Ἰσραήλ) proclaiming the good news of peace through Jesus Christ (εὐαγγελιζόμενος εἰρήνην διὰ Ἰησοῦ Χριστοῦ). The content of that message was that Jesus is Lord of all (οὗτός ἐστιν πάντων κύριος). Although it is difficult, this verse provides the thesis statement for Peter's message. Larkin suggests that "it contains the gospel message on the pattern of its first announcement to the shepherds" (1995, 165; cf. Luke 2:10–14), and Peterson notes that "peace in Luke-Acts is a synonym for salvation" (2009, 336; cf. Isa. 52:7).

Although many commentators take οὗτός ἐστιν πάντων κύριος as grammatically parenthetical (Culy and Parsons 2003, 210), it provides the conceptual theme of the message (Bock 2007, 397). The clause, however, does not necessarily need to be understood as parenthetical. If the initial noun phrase (τὸν λόγον) is taken as an accusative of respect, it is possible to read the concluding clause as the subject of the sentence: "As for the word that he sent . . . [it is that] this one (i.e., Jesus Christ) is Lord of all." This God, who welcomes all people, sent the message about salvation through Jesus, who is Lord of all people—including the group of Gentiles gathered in Cornelius's house.

TEXTUAL ANALYSIS: "as for the word that he sent . . ."
Barrett views the language of verses 36–38 as "so difficult as to be untranslatable" and "a piece of careless and uncorrected writing" (1994, 521, 524). A textual variant regarding the presence or absence of the relative pronoun ὅν *in verse 36 complicates the situation. English versions have translated the syntax in four ways. The NEB and CSB omit the relative pronoun from verse 36 and treat it as a separate sentence ("He sent the message"). The RSV, NIV, and NET supply a verb at the beginning of verse 36 ("You know the message which he sent"). The NKJV and NASB understand verse 36 as a sentence that Peter began but did not complete ("The word which he sent"). The ESV and LEB understand* τὸν λόγον *as an accusative of respect ("As for the word which he sent") introducing a phrase that qualifies either "this one is Lord of all," or verse 37. The more difficult reading includes the relative pronoun, and adding a verb is unnecessary. Longenecker follows the third solution and suggests that "the awkwardness . . . probably stems from Peter himself as he spoke before his Gentile audience in somewhat 'broken' Greek" (1981, 392). Larkin prefers the fourth solution and argues that the verse "should be allowed to maintain its independent status with a minimum of emendation" (1995, 164).*

10:37–39a. Peter's first proof that Jesus is Lord of all was his public ministry. That ministry began in Galilee (ἀρξάμενος ἀπὸ τῆς Γαλιλαίας) after the baptism that John preached (μετὰ τὸ βάπτισμα ὃ ἐκήρυξεν Ἰωάννης) and extended throughout Judea (καθ' ὅλης τῆς Ἰουδαίας). The account (τὸ γενόμενον ῥῆμα) was so public that Cornelius and his household already knew about it (ὑμεῖς οἴδατε). Peter underscored three elements of Jesus's public ministry. First, God had set Jesus apart for the task and empowered him by the Holy Spirit (ἔχρισεν αὐτὸν ὁ θεὸς πνεύματι ἁγίῳ καὶ δυνάμει). Second, Jesus went about (διῆλθεν) doing good (εὐεργετῶν) and healing all who were oppressed by the devil (ἰώμενος πάντας τοὺς καταδυναστευομένους ὑπὸ τοῦ διαβόλου). Third, God was with Jesus (ὁ θεὸς ἦν μετ' αὐτοῦ). Peter concluded the proof by stressing the fact that he and the other apostles were witnesses (μάρτυρες) of everything that Jesus did both in Judea and in Jerusalem (πάντων ὧν ἐποίησεν ἔν τε τῇ χώρᾳ τῶν Ἰουδαίων καὶ Ἰερουσαλήμ).

The phrase τὸ γενόμενον ῥῆμα resumes τὸν λόγον of verse 36 (Bruce 1990, 262). The accusative phrase Ἰησοῦν τὸν ἀπὸ Ναζαρέθ moves to the front of the construction to announce the topic; the pronoun αὐτόν resumes the topic within the clause (Culy and Parsons 2003, 36). Jesus from Nazareth, therefore, was clearly the focus of Peter's message. The verb χρίω carries the sense of "setting apart for special service under divine direction" (BDAG s.v. "χρίω" 1091). Jesus himself called attention to the special nature of his task (Luke 4:18; cf. Acts 4:27; Heb. 1:9). Peterson notes that Peter's use of the verb "testified to [Jesus's] messianic status and role" (2009, 337; cf. Isa. 11:1–3; 42:1; 61:1). Barrett suggests that the phrase πνεύματι ἁγίῳ καὶ δυνάμει is a hendiadys that communicates the sense that "the bestowal of the Spirit resulted in power" (1994, 524). Elsewhere in Acts, the verb διέρχομαι denotes missionary activity (8:4, 40; 9:32). The verb εὐεργετέω describes the act of rendering exceptional service, especially to a community (BDAG s.v. "εὐεργετέω" 405; cf. Acts 4:9), and καταδυναστεύω carries the sense of "to oppress, exploit, dominate" (BDAG s.v. "καταδυναστεύω" 516).

10:39b–42. Peter's second proof included four elements of Jesus's passion and postresurrection ministry. First, the Jews in Jerusalem (NCV; cf. Barrett 1994, 526) executed Jesus by crucifixion (ὃν καὶ ἀνεῖλαν κρεμάσαντες ἐπὶ ξύλου). Second, God raised Jesus on the third day (τοῦτον ὁ θεὸς ἤγειρεν τῇ τρίτῃ ἡμέρᾳ). Third, God also granted that Jesus should become visible (ἔδωκεν αὐτὸν ἐμφανῆ γενέσθαι; cf. LEB). Fourth, Jesus commanded his followers to preach and bear witness (παρήγγειλεν ἡμῖν κηρύξαι . . . καὶ διαμαρτύρασθαι) to the truth God that has designated Jesus the judge of both the living and the dead (ὅτι οὗτός ἐστιν ὁ ὡρισμένος ὑπὸ τοῦ θεοῦ κριτὴς ζώντων καὶ νεκρῶν). Peter's listeners could trust the veracity of these facts, because Jesus had appeared to Peter and the other apostles (ἡμῖν), whom God had chosen in advance (προκεχειροτονημένοις ὑπὸ τοῦ θεοῦ). They were witnesses (μάρτυσιν) who had eaten and drunk (συνεφάγομεν καὶ συνεπίομεν) with Jesus after he rose from the dead (μετὰ τὸ ἀναστῆναι αὐτὸν ἐκ νεκρῶν).

Both the relative pronoun ὃν and the demonstrative pronoun τοῦτον resume the topic—Jesus from Nazareth—after Peter had mentioned the apostles' role as witnesses (10:39a). Ἀνεῖλαν is the aorist indicative of ἀναιρέω and refers to the act of "getting rid of by execution . . . mostly killing by violence" (BDAG s.v. "ἀναιρέω" 2, 64). The participial phrase κρεμάσαντες ἐπὶ ξύλου ("by hanging on a tree") specifies the means of execution. Outside the Gospels, references to Jesus rising "on the third day" (τῇ τρίτῃ ἡμέρᾳ) occur only here and in 1 Corinthians 15:4 (Barrett 1994, 526). The adjective ἐμφανῆ refers to a person being or becoming visible (BDAG s.v. "ἐμφανής" 1, 325), and in extrabiblical literature describes someone who is present and manifest, as in open court (Barrett 1994, 526). "To all the people" (παντὶ τῷ λαῷ) refers to all the Jews in Jerusalem, Judea, and/or Galilee rather than to the people of all nations (Schnabel 2012, 503; contra Bock 2007, 399).

The fact that the preappointed witnesses ate and drank with Jesus testifies to the physical reality of his resurrection and appearances. The verb ὁρίζω denotes the act of appointing or designating a person to be something (BDAG s.v. "ὁρίζω" 2b, 723). Here, Peter declares that Jesus has been appointed to be the judge of the living and the dead (cf. Acts 17:31; 2 Tim. 4:1; 1 Peter 4:5); in Romans 1:4, Paul describes Jesus as designated the Son of God with power.

10:43. Having demonstrated that Jesus is the universal Lord (10:36) and the universal judge (10:42), Peter moved from proof to persuasion by pointing to the OT prophets, who had borne witness that everyone who believed in Jesus (πάντα τὸν πιστεύοντα εἰς αὐτόν) would receive forgiveness of sins (ἄφεσιν ἁμαρτιῶν λαβεῖν) through his name (διὰ τοῦ ὀνόματος αὐτοῦ). Barrett (1994, 528) and Bock (2007, 399) argue that the demonstrative pronoun τούτῳ is neuter and refers to the facts about Jesus that Peter had just presented. Both Peter's practice of emphasizing his topic by fronting a reference to Jesus (10:38, 39a, 40) and the fact that the antecedent of the pronouns that follow all refer to Jesus, however, suggest that the initial pronoun is best understood as masculine ("To this man—that is, to Jesus from Nazareth—all the prophets bear witness"). Each of the components in Peter's statement corresponds to the early apostolic preaching—the testimony of the OT (Luke 24:44; Acts 2:16, 30; 3:18, 21, 24; 5:30), the forgiveness of sins (Luke 24:47; Acts 2:38; 3:19; 5:31), the authority of Jesus's name (Luke 24:47; Acts 2:21, 38; 3:6, 16; 4:30; 5:28; 8:12; 9:28), and the response of faith (Acts 2:44; 4:4; 5:14; 8:12; 9:42).

The Spirit Confirms Salvation (10:44–48)

When the Holy Spirit interrupts his message by falling upon the members of Cornelius's household, Peter directs them to be baptized and incorporated into the church.

10:44–46a. While Peter was still speaking (ἔτι λαλοῦντος τοῦ Πέτρου), the Holy Spirit interrupted him by falling upon (ἐπέπεσεν; cf. 11:15) everyone who was hearing his message (πάντας τοὺς ἀκούοντας τὸν λόγον). The disciples who had traveled from Joppa with Peter were "astonished" (ἐξέστησαν) because the Holy Spirit had been poured out (ἐκκέχυται) on the Gentiles (ἐπὶ τὰ ἔθνη). As evidence of the Spirit's coming, they were hearing (ἤκουον) the members of Cornelius's household speaking in tongues (λαλούντων γλώσσαις) and praising God's greatness (μεγαλυνόντων τὸν θεόν). When he describes the Holy Spirit as "falling upon" (ἐπιπίπτω) Cornelius's household, Luke uses the same language that he used for the Samaritans' experience (8:16) and that he will use for the experience of John's disciples in Ephesus (19:17). See the discussion on 8:16–17. The Holy Spirit's coming, therefore, confirmed the Gentiles' acceptance into the community of Christ-followers.

The description of the men who traveled with Peter from Joppa as "the faithful ones from the circumcision" (οἱ ἐκ περιτομῆς πιστοί) identifies them as Jewish-background believers (Barrett 1994, 529; cf. 11:2; Col. 4:12). The verb ἐξίστημι denotes "a state in which things seem to make little or no sense" (BDAG s.v. "ἐξίστημι" 1, 350), which graphically captures the observers' total bewilderment in the face of what they were experiencing (2:12; 8:13; 9:21; 12:16). Peter had previously described the coming of the Holy Spirit as a "gift" (δωρεά) at Pentecost (2:38) and in Samaria (8:20). He would do so again in his report to the Jerusalem church (cf. 11:17). It is not possible to reach a conclusion on the nature of the Gentiles' speaking in tongues from Luke's brief comment (Larkin 1995, 168). Whether the tongues were known languages or ecstatic utterances, however, the phenomenon praised God for his greatness (μεγαλυνόντων τὸν θεόν; cf. L&N §33.358).

10:46b–48. Peter's response to the Holy Spirit's coming (τότε ἀπεκρίθη Πέτρος) was not astonishment but acknowledgment. He had reached the final step on his journey to full understanding (10:15, 20, 34). The conclusion was inescapable: God had granted salvation to the Gentiles (cf. 11:18). If the Gentiles had received the Holy Spirit as the Jews also had (οἵτινες τὸ πνεῦμα τὸ ἅγιον ἔλαβον ὡς καὶ ἡμεῖς), could anyone object to them being incorporated into the church through baptism (NLT, μήτι τὸ ὕδωρ δύναται κωλῦσαί τις τοῦ μὴ βαπτισθῆναι τούτους;)? So, Peter ordered them to be baptized in Jesus's name (προσέταξεν αὐτοὺς ἐν τῷ ὀνόματι Ἰησοῦ Χριστοῦ βαπτισθῆναι), and the new disciples asked Peter to remain in Caesarea for several days (ἠρώτησαν αὐτὸν ἐπιμεῖναι ἡμέρας τινάς). Peter's willingness to spend additional time with Cornelius and his household signaled his full acceptance of the new disciples and allowed time for a report of the conversions to reach Jerusalem (Barrett 1994, 531).

THEOLOGICAL FOCUS

Narratively, Acts 10:1–48 concludes the series of unexpected conversions that followed Stephen's martyrdom—the Samaritans, the Ethiopian, Saul, and Cornelius—as the gospel continued moving outward from Jerusalem both geographically and culturally. Saul was Jesus's chosen instrument to bear his name to the Gentiles (9:1–31), but how would he help his Jewish-background disciples overcome their centuries-long prejudice against the unclean Gentiles? While Saul's post-Damascus-road travels had taken him to Jerusalem, Caesarea, and Tarsus, Peter's missionary travels had brought him to the Judean coastal plain (9:32–43). Now, God would sovereignly superintend the process that brought Peter, one of the original Jerusalem apostles, to Caesarea and helped the church cross the final cultural threshold to the Gentiles. At the same time that Peter's encounter with Cornelius concludes the gospel's expansion in Judea, Galilee, and Samaria (9:31), it also sets the stage for the mission to the Gentiles that would soon expand from its center in Syrian Antioch (11:19–30) to reach Cyprus, Asia Minor, and Greece (13:1–20:38).

Theologically, Acts 10:1–48 weaves together two important themes: the impartiality of God and the universality of the gospel. As Peter gradually understands the truth that God is not one who shows favoritism but instead welcomes men and women from every people group, his experience teaches us four principles to apply in overcoming ethnic and cultural prejudice. First, we must understand that God welcomes all ethnic groups impartially. Second, we must associate with members of other ethnic groups freely. Third, we must engage them with the truth about Jesus effectively. Fourth, we must accept them into Christian fellowship unconditionally.

As Cornelius gradually moves to the point of responding in faith to the good news of peace that is available through Jesus, his experience teaches us four truths about the universal scope of the gospel. First, Jesus is the Lord of every person from every people group. Second, Jesus is the judge of every person who lives or dies. Third, Jesus offers forgiveness of sins to every person who believes in him. Fourth, Jesus gives the gift of the Holy Spirit to every person who responds to the gospel in repentance and faith. Further, their combined story teaches us about the process God uses to bring the good news about Jesus to people who have never heard it. He begins by making his light available to those who live in darkness. He then leads his witnesses to those individuals who respond to the light they have. When his witnesses share the truth about Jesus, the Holy Spirit confirms a genuine response of faith.

PREACHING AND TEACHING STRATEGIES

Exegetical/Theological Synthesis

Cornelius and Peter shared a connection to the Jewish religion. Cornelius feared God and adopted the Jewish practices of prayer and almsgiving. Peter had followed the customs of Judaism from his birth. They were, however, men from different cultural backgrounds. One was a Gentile; the other was a Jew. In the first century, that difference established a seemingly insurmountable barrier between the two groups. Observant Jews were diligent in avoiding any contact with Gentiles that might make them ritually unclean. Yet Jesus had commanded his disciples to be his witnesses to the ends of the earth. As Luke's first-century readers followed his narrative of how that mission continued to expand, they would have wanted to know how God would deal with the barrier that existed between Jew and Gentile. Luke's account of the events that led Peter, the observant Jew, to the home of Cornelius, the unclean Gentile, illustrates the principle that God gives more light to men and women who respond obediently to the light they have (Larkin 1995, 154). Cornelius and Peter both heard from God through visions. They both promptly obeyed the revelation they received. As they obeyed, they both moved closer to the goals God had for each of them. For Peter, the goal was an acknowledgement of God's impartial stance toward humankind. For Cornelius, the goal was an acceptance of Jesus's universal lordship. The result was a double breakthrough for Jesus's mission. With Luke's original audience, twenty-first-century readers share the need to understand and apply the truth that as they respond promptly and obediently to God's instructions, he will lead them to the place where he wants them to be in their relationship with him.

Preaching/Teaching Idea

God gives us the light we need to save us and sanctify us.

Contemporary Connections

What does it mean?

There are two "conversions" in Acts 10, not one. God converts both Cornelius's soul and Peter's imagination by his guiding light. These two movements parallel each other and point to God's work to save and to sanctify. God gave Cornelius a searching soul. We meet a deeply devout, religious man, bringing his whole household along into the key pious practices of prayer and generosity. Then, God revealed more of himself, announcing through an angel about how to find Peter. Cornelius obeyed at once. Next, God revealed more, bringing Peter to preach Jesus. Cornelius and household listen eagerly. Finally, God revealed his utmost, as his Spirit fell upon the group, opening hearts and minds fully to salvation. It is a beautiful divine dance of increasing revelation met with increasing faith.

God gave Peter a humble soul. Peter experienced his own increased revelation and increased obedience toward his further sanctification. God revealed his heart to Peter in a threefold cryptic vision. Still perplexed, Peter answered the call to go with his visitors to Caesarea. God revealed more of himself in Peter's exchange with Cornelius. Peter obeyed, making the connection between the vision and the present opportunity, and preaches Jesus. Finally, God revealed his utmost, as Peter was ready to baptize new Gentile believers and stayed with them in fellowship and teaching.

Is it true?

God uses a myriad of ways to save and sanctify. He can save dramatically, in a moment, as he did at Pentecost and with Saul, or he can guide slowly, warming movement toward himself as he did with the Ethiopian eunuch. This passage provides an instance of the latter. In God's perfect providence, he gave Cornelius what seemed to be a long season of responding to little light. He feared God, he prayed to God, and he gave generously in God's name. Although it might not have looked like much, in God's economy, those prayers and alms were a precious memorial before God and preparation for the new things God has in store for him (10:4). Had God not given Cornelius this searching soul and these little acts of obedience, we would have never heard of him. God gave him light, gave him obedience to respond to light, and finally lavished more light.

Peter's conversion of imagination is powerful for believers longing to grow up into their salvation. Peter had already spent three years with Jesus, which was surely the greatest seminary education the world has ever known. The Holy Spirit had filled him since Pentecost. He had spent his days devoting himself to prayer and Scripture (6:4). If any Christian could be fully formed this side of heaven, it would have been Peter. Yet, God was not finished with him. There was so much more for Peter to learn, to love, and to experience. Was the threefold vision a subtle reminder for Peter that his tests come in threes? Just like Cornelius, Peter had his own divine dance of God's revelation matched by God's indwelling power to obey. By the end of the chapter, Peter was an even more radically transformed believer, nearer to the image of God.

Now what?

There is something deeply encouraging for us today as we watch the slow but sure dual movements of salvation and sanctification. As we witness to friends and family, we would love to see Pentecost moments. We want to say just the right thing in the Spirit and hear our loved one ask, "What must I do to be saved?" This story of slow-building revelation to Cornelius is often how God works today. There are little ways in thousands of moments that God's light shines into a person's heart. He uses our simple faithfulness to pray, to speak kind words, to be open with others about our faith, and to live our lives honoring to him. God might use any and all of these things to reveal himself slowly but surely to another in the long road of conversion. He did it with Cornelius; he can do it with our friends.

This same, often slow, revealing work is as true of our sanctification as it was for Peter. We are not the only ones too dense to grasp the fullness of God's abundant life the first time around. Watching Peter struggle through God's multiple visions, his visit to Cornelius's house, his backpedaling later on (Gal. 2:11–14), everything seems familiar. God is doing this work in us, little by little revealing himself and changing us. He breaks down prejudices, builds up new community, and shows us more of the kingdom we inhabit.

Creativity in Presentation

It is hard to get inside Peter's devout Jewish mind on matters of food and fellowship. God is asking him to do things he has never done before. He responds to the vision of eating unclean animals, "I have never eaten anything that is common or unclean" (10:14). He admits to Cornelius's household, "You yourselves know how unlawful it is for a Jew to associate with or to visit anyone of another nation" (10:28). To what could we compare his hesitation?

God telling Peter to eat unclean animals would be kind of like God telling us never to wash our hands before we eat. We have always done it (hopefully). Our parents have always told us that it is for our good. It would bother us every time we reached for food with filthy hands. It is a little bit like that for Peter. Only God's command to Peter runs deeper. It is not just a matter of hygiene, but a matter of right and wrong too. Food, however, is just the warm-up. God breaks down unclean food for Peter to free him from his prejudice against unclean people (10:28).

A brilliant illustration of letting one area of prejudice or resistance inform another is Harper Lee's novel *To Kill a Mockingbird*. Lee throws her readers into the racially charged climate of Alabama in the 1930s as she describes a trial of a black man accused of abusing a white woman. While that prejudice consumes the reader, others slip in. There is prejudice against the accuser Mayella Ewell and her poor white family and prejudice against the recluse Boo Radley. As each prejudice is slowly exposed, the reader must look within, at his or her own prejudices.

In Acts 10, God was doing that good work with Peter. In scandalizing fashion, he reveals more and more to Peter until he was ready for sanctifying change deep within and a new kingdom life without prejudice ahead. God gives us the light we need to save us and sanctify us.

- God gives Cornelius and household increasing light to save them (10:1–8, 44–48).

- God gives Peter increasing light to sanctify him (10:9–43).

DISCUSSION QUESTIONS

1. How frequently should we expect God to use visions and audible voices as part of the process of drawing people to himself? Why?

2. Why is the concept of God's impartiality important? What implications does it have for addressing ethnic, cultural, and social tensions?

3. If God viewed Cornelius as acceptable because of his prayers and alms, why was it necessary for him to summon Peter from Joppa to hear the message God had given him?

4. What are other examples of the "more light" principle in the Bible? How do they compare with Cornelius's and Peter's experiences?

5. Why was the Holy Spirit's interruption of Peter's message noteworthy? What did his coming upon the members of Cornelius's household signify?

Acts 11:1–18

EXEGETICAL IDEA
In response to concerns from some of the disciples, Peter reports on what God accomplished in Caesarea, resulting in praise from the church.

THEOLOGICAL FOCUS
God expects us to praise him when he works in unexpected ways, not criticize the means he uses to accomplish his purposes.

PREACHING IDEA
Focus on what God does, not on how he does it.

PREACHING POINTERS
Are you guilty of putting God in a box? In his classic book *Your God Is Too Small*, J. B. Phillips writes that we are crippled by limited concepts of God. One of those limited concepts is "God-in-a-Box"—a God whom we have "captured and tamed and trained to [our] own liking" and have "forced into little man-made boxes with neat labels upon them" (1961, 37). That is exactly what we do when we expect God to act according to our expectations, prejudices, or traditions. When he dares to act counter to those expectations, prejudices, or traditions, we become confused, uncomfortable, and even angry. Yet, we cannot put the God of the Bible in a box. He does what he does in the way he chooses for the reasons he knows are best. Never was that truth more evident than in the events that led Peter to share the gospel with Cornelius and his household. Because Peter's actions ran counter to centuries of Jewish tradition, a segment of the disciples took exception to what he had done. In response, Peter reported that God had directed every step along his way. Instead of looking in the rearview mirror at the way Judaism had always done things, the church needed to look forward to what Jesus was doing to make it possible for repentance to be preached in his name to all the nations (Luke 24:47).

People today should be able to relate to being criticized for their actions. Members of churches or individuals engaged in Christian leadership can also relate to disputes over ministry-related decisions or activities. The passage corrects the practices of criticizing others for their ministry activities, resisting what God might be doing when it runs contrary to our expectations, or perpetuating divisions within the body of Christ. It commends openness to God's leading, willingness to confront our prejudices, acceptance of others who are different from us, and praise for God's work in saving others. As his followers, we must understand that God expects us to praise him when he works in unexpected ways, not criticize the people or the means he uses to accomplish his purposes. Instead, we should focus on him and the results he produces.

DEFENSE OF PETER'S WITNESS TO THE GENTILES (11:1–18)

LITERARY STRUCTURE AND THEMES (11:1–18)

The passage consists of two brief narrative sections that frame the central panel of Peter's report to the Jerusalem church. The opening narrative (11:1–3) sets the report in the context of concerns raised by a segment of the church. The report itself (11:4–17) recounts Peter's experiences in Joppa and Caesarea and divides into four sections (Stott 1990, 194–95): divine revelation (11:4–10), divine instruction (11:1–12a), divine preparation (11:12b–14), and divine confirmation (11:15–17). The closing narrative (11:18) records the church's response to Peter's report.

- ***Criticism by the Circumcised (11:1–3)***
- ***Report by Peter (11:4–17)***
- ***Acceptance by the Church (11:18)***

EXPOSITION (11:1–18)

The amount of his narrative that Luke devotes to Peter's ministry in western Judea (9:32–43), his experiences in Joppa and Caesarea (10:1–48), and his report to the Jerusalem church (11:1–18) signals the importance of those events for the early Christian movement. Longenecker captures well their significance when he writes, "the conversion of Cornelius was a landmark in the history of the gospel's advance from its strictly Jewish beginnings to its penetration of the Roman Empire" (1981, 396). How would members of the movement that had its origins in Judaism, which historically drew a sharp line between Jews and Gentiles, respond to news that one of the twelve original apostles had arranged the baptism of a household of Gentiles?

Acts 11:1–18 answers that question. Reports of other unexpected conversions had already raised questions (8:14–15; 9:21), and it was inevitable that word of the events in Caesarea would spread throughout the church.

When he returns to Jerusalem, therefore, Peter encounters a segment of the community that takes exception to his actions. In response, he offers a summary of his experiences that is "considerably abbreviated and told in the first person from [his] point of view" (Marshall 1980, 196). The emphasis throughout his report is on God's sovereign working to ensure that "the Gentiles' salvation is divinely worked, complete, and authentic" (Larkin 1995, 168). When his listeners respond with praise that God has granted repentance and life to the Gentiles, both the leadership and the membership of the church confirm the legitimacy of Peter's actions, the authenticity of the Gentiles' commitment to the gospel, and their equal status as members of the movement.

Criticism by the Circumcised (11:1–3)

When he returns to Jerusalem, Peter encounters criticism for his actions in Caesarea.

11:1–3. The report that the Gentiles received the Word of God (τὰ ἔθνη ἐδέξαντο τὸν λόγον τοῦ θεοῦ) spread to the disciples throughout Judea (οἱ ὄντες κατὰ τὴν Ἰουδαίαν) so that it reached both the church's leaders (οἱ ἀπόστολοι) and its members (οἱ ἀδελφοί). After an unspecified period (10:48), Peter returned to Jerusalem (ἀνέβη Πέτρος εἰς Ἰερουσαλήμ), where certain members of the church kept on taking exception to his actions (διεκρίνοντο πρὸς αὐτόν, iterative imperfect). Their criticism was that he entered the home of uncircumcised men (εἰσῆλθες πρὸς ἄνδρας ἀκροβυστίαν ἔχοντας) and ate with them (συνέφαγες αὐτοῖς). Barrett notes that δέχομαι denotes receiving and accepting God's Word so as to become believers (1994, 536; cf. 8:14; 17:11; 1 Thess. 1:6; 2:13).

"Those of the circumcision" (οἱ ἐκ περιτομῆς) denotes a group that is narrower than Jewish-background believers in general (10:45) but broader than the advocates of circumcision who later disrupted the church in Antioch (15:1; Gal. 2:11–12). Bock describes them as "the more conscientious of the Hebrew Christians" (2007, 406). Bruce regards them as "those Jewish believers who were specially zealous for the law and insisted that there should be no social intercourse between circumcised and uncircumcised" (1988, 220; cf. Larkin 1995, 170). Their religious scruples led them to express their disapproval (διεκρίνοντο; cf. L&N §33.412) toward Peter and his actions. Dunn calls their criticism "the logic of religious purity," in that good Jews would avoid becoming unclean by avoiding Gentile households and meal tables (1996, 149). Although there was no specific evidence that Cornelius had served food that was unclean, as Barrett writes, "with Gentiles, you never know" (1994, 538). Longenecker suggests that the critics were concerned that Peter's actions could endanger the church's relations with the Jewish nation (1981, 397).

TEXTUAL ANALYSIS: Peter's Return to Jerusalem It is interesting to note that the Western text expands verse 2 considerably. The variant reads, "Therefore, after a considerable time, Peter wished to go to Jerusalem; and after he had gathered the brothers and had strengthened them, [he went out] doing much preaching and teaching throughout the country; who also went to meet them [i.e., the apostles and brothers in verse 1] and announced to them the grace of God. But those of the circumcision disputed with him." As Metzger notes, the intent of the addition appears to be to counter any impression that Peter was compelled to stop his missionary activity immediately and report to Jerusalem to justify his actions in Caesarea (*TCGNT*, 338).

Report by Peter (11:4–17)

In response to the criticism, Peter recounts his experiences in Joppa and Caesarea.

11:4–10. Peter began (ἀρξάμενος) by explaining (ἐξετίθετο, inceptive imperfect) his experience "point by point" (BDAG s.v. "καθεξῆς" 490). His explanation followed the four steps in God's progressive revelation to him, beginning with his initial vision in Joppa. The account in verses 5–10 parallels the events previously described in 10:9–16.

Peter prays in Joppa	11:5a	10:9
Peter becomes hungry	--	10:10a
Peter falls into a trance	11:5b	10:10b
Peter sees a vision of a sheet	11:5c–6	10:11–12
A voice commands Peter to kill and eat	11:7	10:13
Peter reacts negatively	11:8	10:14
The voice speaks a second time	11:9	10:15
The interchange occurs three times	11:10a	10:16a
The sheet is taken back up into heaven	11:10b	10:16b

The differences in the two accounts are minimal. Peter omitted the fact that he had gone up on the roof to pray, omitted the details about becoming hungry, and added wild animals (τὰ θηρία) to the contents of the sheet. The point for the listeners was the same as it was for Peter: what God made clean, he should not consider defiled (ἃ ὁ θεὸς ἐκαθάρισεν σὺ μὴ κοίνου).

11:11–12a. Next, Peter described the Spirit's command to accompany the messengers without making a distinction. The account parallels the events previously described in 10:17–23a, although it is considerably less detailed.

Cornelius's messengers arrive	11:11	10:17–18
The Spirit speaks to Peter	11:12a	10:19–20
Peter welcomes the messengers	--	10:21–23a

Peter reported the arrival of the messengers from Caesarea without mentioning either how they found Simon's house or their repeated inquiries about whether Peter was there (10:18). Nor did he mention his conversation with the messengers or his invitation for them to stay overnight (10:21–23a). The important element was the Spirit's instruction to Peter, which applied the vision about removing the distinction between clean and unclean animals to human beings. He was to go with the men without making any distinction (συνελθεῖν αὐτοῖς μηδὲν διακρίναντα).

11:12b–14. Peter continued by recounting how he and those who accompanied him to Caesarea learned about another man's vision. The account parallels the events previously described in 10:23b–33, although it is again condensed.

Peter enters Cornelius's house in Caesarea	11:12b	10:23b–29
Cornelius recounts his experience	11:13–14	10:30–33

Peter noted the number of brothers who accompanied him (οἱ ἓξ ἀδελφοὶ οὗτοι), acknowledged that they all entered the house (εἰσήλθομεν εἰς τὸν οἶκον τοῦ ἀνδρός), but omitted his initial interaction with Cornelius (10:25–29). The abbreviated report of Cornelius's experience includes the appearance of the angel and the angel's instruction to send for Peter in Joppa. Peter added the reason for summoning Peter: That he would speak words by which Cornelius and all his house would be saved (ὃς λαλήσει ῥήματα πρὸς σὲ ἐν οἷς σωθήσῃ σὺ καὶ πᾶς ὁ οἶκός σου). Peter did not name Cornelius, but simply referred to him as "the man" (τοῦ ἀνδρός), which shifted the focus from an individual Godfearer to a representative Gentile (Bock 2007, 408). The theme of salvation runs throughout the book (2:21, 40; 4:9, 12; 14:9; 16:30), and household conversions later occur in Philippi (16:15, 31) and Corinth (18:8). Although Peter left unspoken his conclusion from hearing about God's work of preparing Cornelius and his household, at the time it led him to declare that God is not one who shows favoritism (10:34).

11:15–17. Peter ended his report by explaining the conclusion he reached when the Spirit interrupted him by coming upon the listeners. The account parallels the events previously described in 10:34–48, although it omits the content of Peter's message (10:34–43), the amazement of the brothers from Joppa (10:45–46a), Peter's order to baptize the members of Cornelius's household (10:48a), and the invitation for Peter to remain in Caesarea (10:48b).

Peter preaches Jesus	--	10:34–43
The Spirit falls on Cornelius's household	11:15	10:44
The brothers from Joppa are amazed	--	10:45–46a

Peter acknowledges God's gift of the Spirit	11:16–17	10:46b–47
Peter orders baptism of the new believers	--	10:48a
Cornelius invites Peter to stay in Caesarea	--	10:48b

It is best to understand Peter's statement that the Spirit fell upon his listeners "as [he] began to speak" (ἐν τῷ ἄρξασθαί με λαλεῖν) as describing an interruption before he concluded what he had intended to say. In fact, he had not yet mentioned the promise of God's blessing—the gift of the Holy Spirit—which was one of the essentials of the apostolic proclamation (e.g., 5:30–32). Peter specifically noted the parallel of the Spirit's coming in Caesarea to the Jerusalem disciples' experience at Pentecost (ὥσπερ καὶ ἐφ᾽ ἡμᾶς ἐν ἀρχῇ). The event also reminded him of Jesus's postresurrection teaching that he would baptize his disciples with the Holy Spirit (1:5). The only logical conclusion to draw (οὖν) was that if God granted to the Gentiles of Cornelius's household the same gift (τὴν ἴσην δωρεάν) he had granted to the Jerusalem disciples who had believed in Jesus (πιστεύσασιν ἐπὶ τὸν κύριον Ἰησοῦν Χριστόν), he would not stand in God's way (ἐγὼ τίς ἤμην δυνατὸς κωλῦσαι τὸν θεόν;). As Stott writes, "Water-baptism could not be forbidden to these Gentile converts, because God could not be forbidden to do what he had done, namely give them Spirit baptism" (1990, 196). As was the case in Samaria, the Spirit's coming validated the Gentiles' acceptance into the church.

Acceptance by the Church (11:18)

Peter's explanation silences his critics and leads the rest of the disciples to praise God.

11:18. After Peter's audience heard his report (ἀκούσαντες ταῦτα), they responded in two ways: they became silent (ἡσύχασαν), and they glorified God (ἐδόξασαν τὸν θεόν). The verb ἡσυχάζω describes the act of "maintain[ing] a state of silence with a possible focus on the attitude involved" (L&N §33.119). It describes the hostile silence of the Pharisees in Luke 14:1–6 and suggests that Peter's critics held their peace publicly but continued to hold their opposing position privately. The more important assessment, however, was that God had granted to the Gentiles "the repentance that leads to life" (NASB, τὴν μετάνοιαν εἰς ζωήν). As the events preceding the Jerusalem Council would make clear (15:1–5), details related to Gentile participation in the church remained unaddressed. The principle, however, was established. As Bruce writes, "their objections ceased; their praise began; the practical problems . . . did not arise" (1988, 223).

THEOLOGICAL FOCUS

Narratively, Acts 11:1–18 concludes the three accounts of Peter's ministry in western Judea by returning him to Jerusalem in preparation for the events Luke will describe in Acts 12. His report to the Jerusalem church reinforces the importance of the conversion of Cornelius's household by repeating the way in which God orchestrated the events and confirmed the outcome. The church's response establishes the validity of the Gentiles' incorporation into the movement on an equal footing with other people groups who respond to the gospel with faith. The passage also prepares the way for the Gentile mission that will soon find itself based in Syrian Antioch (11:19–30).

Theologically, Acts 11:1–18 takes direct aim at the way we respond to the way God works. The center panel of the passage repeated the events of Acts 10 and made it clear that God was at work. He used divine revelation and instruction to bring Peter and Cornelius together. He used divine preparation to lay the groundwork for Cornelius and his household to hear the gospel. He used divine confirmation to validate their response of faith. God had brought the gospel to the Gentiles. He had granted them the repentance that leads to life. He had given them the gift of the Holy Spirit. The response within the church should have been praise and rejoicing. Instead, when he returned to Jerusalem, Peter encountered condemnation, not commendation.

The narrative frame around Peter's report highlights two possible responses to the way God works: criticism or praise. The criticism focused on Peter and his actions. He had violated Jewish taboos by associating with unclean Gentiles. The praise focused on God and his actions. He had abolished the barrier between Jew and Gentile by incorporating Cornelius and his household into the church on equal footing with Hebraic Jews, Hellenistic Jews, Samaritans, and the Ethiopian. Peter's report silenced his critics and led the rest of the disciples to praise God. The bottom line is: God expects us to praise him when he works in unexpected ways, not criticize the means he uses to accomplish his purposes.

PREACHING AND TEACHING STRATEGIES

Exegetical/Theological Synthesis

Luke's first-century readers would have wanted to know how a movement that had its roots in Judaism and, so far, had focused on people groups that were at least on the margins of Judaism would respond to Peter's ministry to Cornelius and his Gentile household. For centuries, the Jews had considered Gentiles unclean and had done their best to avoid unnecessary contact with them. Yet, Peter had intentionally entered a Gentile home and had eaten with the members of the household. His actions ran counter to Jewish expectations, prejudices, and traditions. How could he have done such a thing? Peter had an explanation: the central issue was not the possibility of defilement; it was the salvation of people (Schnabel 2012, 511). The latter took absolute precedence over the former. His report to the Jerusalem church should have made it doubly clear for Luke's readers that God had

orchestrated both Peter's meeting with Cornelius and the outcome of that meeting.

Repetition adds emphasis, and by repeating Peter's experience in his own words Luke signals the importance of the gospel crossing the cultural threshold to the Gentiles. As Stott writes, the events "demonstrated conclusively that God had now welcomed believing Gentiles into his family on equal terms with believing Jews" (1990, 196). Yet, when God works in ways that run counter to our expectations, prejudices, or traditions, it is easy to fall into the trap of saying "we have never done it that way" or "God would not do such a thing." A segment of the Jerusalem church fell into that trap and took objection to what Peter had done. Their perspective needed adjustment, and Peter's report sought to shift their focus from their tradition to God's salvation. With the original audience, the twenty-first-century audience shares the need to know how to respond when God leads in ways that run counter to their expectations, prejudices, or traditions. The proper response is to focus on God and the results he produces rather than on the people and the means he uses to produce those results.

Preaching/Teaching Idea

Focus on what God does, not on how he does it.

Contemporary Connections

What does it mean?

Luke clearly does not want his readers to miss the significance of what has happened in this passage. After a careful, detailed, forty-eight-verse telling of the grand story of Cornelius's conversion and Peter's reimagining of the kingdom, he adds an eighteen-verse retelling of those events. That is sixty-four verses! By comparison, Luke recounts Saul's monumental conversion in nineteen verses, or less than a third of this story. The reader is compelled to pay attention again to God's salvific work to an unlikely convert through controversial means.

The incredible news of Gentile conversions—glorious news fitting with Jesus's Great Commission—is met with icy criticism from suspicious Hebrew Christians. All they could muster in response to God's growing kingdom was criticism: "You went to the uncircumcised men and ate with them." They focused on the speck of misunderstanding rather than celebrating the log of miraculous conversions. They missed God's commendation by their finger-wagging condemnation. On the other hand, God was gracious. Just as he did with Peter, whose initial response was off, he gave another chance. In the end, they joined in joyous praise.

Is it true?

These are the early rumblings of an issue that will dog the NT—what Gentiles must do to be saved. It will get far more intense than this criticism. In fact, the Jerusalem church must soon make a ruling in Acts 15. The knee-jerk response of the circumcision party, however, shows ready suspicion. Rather than focusing on God, they went after Peter ("you," 11:3). Rather than considering the call to souls at the ends of the earth, they zeroed in on covenant membership ("uncircumcised men"). Rather than celebrating salvation, they could not get past table fellowship ("ate with them"). They reduced God's glorious movement in Acts 10 to a purely human exchange. In doing so, they sound a lot like Jesus's critics, harping on handwashing and Sabbath observance when something much grander was before them. They missed the forest for a single tree. Once Peter explained, their response is hard to read. They fall silent. Then "they" (just some of them?) praise God. Since there is more trouble to come from within the circumcision party, it is hard to know what is really going on in their hearts. Some might have genuinely realized their rash criticism and repented. Others might have nursed their frustrations for a later time. At least in this moment, however, celebration replaced criticism.

Now what?

Why is it so hard to see and celebrate the good God is doing? Why is it especially hard to celebrate the good things God does *through others*? Watching Hebrew Christians pounce on Peter is unsettling because it hits so close to home. We are more like they were than we care to admit. We have a fleshly knack for knocking over perceived pedestals to make sure no one stands higher in God's kingdom than we do. That attitude starts us looking for what is wrong in each other rather than what is right. In doing so, we miss the good God is doing right in front of our proud faces.

Today's term for this phenomenon is "cancel culture." We withdraw support or ostracize those with whom we do not agree. In a social media age, it happens as quick as lightning. The world is training us to spot, disagree, and expose as quickly as possible. It is scary to realize how good we can get at something so bad. There is certainly a place to engage true wrong, but this is something else. It is looking for a fight, and the joy we could have had in mutual celebration with a brother or sister is lost in that first moment of knee-jerk criticism. Praise God, he does not treat us the same way.

Creativity in Presentation

Personal examples abound of being quick to criticize or of being quickly criticized. In an informal setting, the group could share stories of what it felt like to be attacked over a false accusation, or what it felt like to confront someone without all the facts only to learn we were in the wrong. In a formal setting, we could share personally.

A creative presentation could explore the dynamics that probably lay just below the surface of the Hebrew Christians' hasty criticism. We can imagine the scene all too well. Peter is starting to look too big for his britches. He has had more than his fair share of celebrity. He is one of the Twelve and one of the inner three. He is the outspoken leader of the movement.

He keeps showing up in the right place at the right time and doing things nobody has done before. Folks are starting to whisper that Peter needs to be brought down a notch. This latest stunt of sharing a meal with uncircumcised Gentiles is the last straw.

There is symmetry to this passage and presentation. The Hebrew Christians' realization that God gives repentance to Gentiles is its own kind of reversal for them. Their praise is their repentance. They are turning from criticism to celebration to acknowledge what God has done and restore the relationship with Peter. Just as God through Christ gives lavish forgiveness to foreign, uncircumcised Gentiles, so he gives it repeatedly to those he has already adopted into his home. That forgiveness is cause for celebration. It is the story of the prodigal and self-righteous sons, only with a happy ending. In this telling, the self-righteous older brother joins the party.

In the end, this passages remind us to focus on what God does, not on how he does it.

- Man's criticism (11:1–3)

- God's kindness (11:4–17)

- Man's repentance and rejoicing (11:18)

DISCUSSION QUESTIONS

1. What are some of the expectations, prejudices, and/or traditions Christians might have that can get in the way of a proper perspective on how God works? How can they hinder the progress of the gospel?

2. Should the church engage in public discussion of theological positions, ministry directions, and/or missiological methods? Why or why not?

3. What examples have you seen of God's direction, preparation, and/or confirmation as he has worked to bring others to faith in Christ?

4. How does Peter's report provide a helpful model for responding to criticism by others? What principles can you draw from his approach?

5. What are some of the ways in which you tend to put God in a box? Where do you need to adjust your perspective on him and the way(s) in which he works?

Acts 11:19–30

EXEGETICAL IDEA
The church in Antioch was planted by bold witnesses, nurtured by gifted leaders, characterized by explosive growth, and committed to the welfare of God's people.

THEOLOGICAL FOCUS
God is at work to build his church in every geographical location and in every cultural context.

PREACHING IDEA
When you see God moving, get on board.

PREACHING POINTERS
"Watch to see where God is working and join him in his work." That axiom is one of Henry Blackaby's best-known quotations. Acts 11 suggests a similar principle guided Barnabas's life. It is a reasonable inference that he observed God at work among the first disciples and joined them in their commitment to Jesus. As a member of the Jerusalem church, he saw God moving to meet the needs of others and became an example of Christian generosity. As a member of the Jerusalem church, he also heard reports of Saul's conversion and evangelistic effectiveness and took the initiative in introducing him to the apostles. When the Jerusalem church heard reports of what God was doing in Antioch and sent him to that city as its representative, he saw the grace of God at work, rejoiced, encouraged the new disciples, and recruited Saul to provide additional leadership for the new congregation. Later, he would respond to the Holy Spirit's direction by becoming one of the first missionaries commissioned by the church in Antioch. God was moving in Antioch, Barnabas saw it, and he got on board. Are we willing to do the same?

People today can relate to large crowds and popular movements. The Billy Graham crusades of the twentieth century drew huge crowds; public demonstrations of the twenty-first century provide more recent examples. They should also be able to relate to reports of widespread food shortages and solicitation for funds to feed the hungry. The passage corrects any suggestion that evangelistic efforts should be limited by ethnicity, that a single leader can "do it all," or that individual congregations stand alone with no connection to other groups of believers. It commends faithful witness to all people and groups, the importance of gifted leadership for congregational nurture, the importance of balancing edification and evangelization in ministry, generosity toward others who are in need, and promoting unity and connectedness between local congregations. As Jesus's disciples, we need to understand that God is at work to build his church, and we must be willing to join him in what he is doing.

BOLD WITNESS IN SYRIAN ANTIOCH (11:19–30)

LITERARY STRUCTURE AND THEMES (11:19–30)

The passage records three narrative snapshots of the early days of the church in Antioch. The first snapshot describes how disciples who had been scattered by the persecution that followed Stephen's martyrdom planted the church in Antioch (11:19–21). The second snapshot describes how Barnabas and Saul established the church in Antioch after the church in Jerusalem sent Barnabas to that city (11:22–26). The third snapshot describes how the Antioch church repaid the Jerusalem church's spiritual investment by sending Barnabas and Saul back to Jerusalem to deliver a financial gift for famine relief (11:27–30).

- ***Planting the Church in Antioch (11:19–21)***
- ***Establishing the Church in Antioch (11:22–26)***
- ***Benevolent Action by the Church in Antioch (11:27–30)***

EXPOSITION (11:19–30)

As the church expanded geographically and culturally, Luke's account has focused more on individuals than on people groups. The exception, of course, was Philip's ministry in Samaria. In that episode, however, Luke chose to highlight the superiority of the gospel message over magic and the confirmation provided by the Spirit's coming upon the Samaritans. He tells his readers little about the church that must have been planted among that ethnic group. The situation is different with the Gentiles. Acts 10:1–11:18 had already provided the details of God's leading, the content of Peter's message, the unexpectedness of the Spirit's coming upon the Gentile audience, and a theological defense of Peter's actions. In Acts 11:19–30, Luke turns his attention to the first major people movement among the Gentiles—God's working in the city of Syrian Antioch. The three snapshots in that passage describe the new church's origin, its growth, and its charity. They also include striking parallels to the early days of the church in Jerusalem.

Bold witness led to explosive growth. Spirit-filled leaders edified those inside the church and evangelized those outside the church. Commitment to caring for fellow disciples led to benevolent giving that met financial needs. The gospel might spread to other geographical locations and to other ethnic groups, but the essentials of early church life remained constant. The Gentile church in Antioch looked a lot like the Jewish church in Jerusalem. Further, there was a dynamic relationship between the two churches. The church in Jerusalem sent leadership assistance to the new disciples in Antioch; the church in Antioch sent financial assistance to the needy disciples in Jerusalem. The new work among the Gentiles in Antioch was not a splinter movement; it was an integral part of what God was doing to build Christ's church and to see the gospel go beyond Jerusalem, Judea, and Samaria to the ends of the earth.

Planting the Church in Antioch (11:19–21)

Disciples who had been scattered by the persecution following Stephen's death move northward through Phoenicia and Syria and share the good news about Jesus with Gentiles in Antioch.

11:19. As Philip had left Jerusalem in the aftermath of Stephen's death and had ministered in

Samaria and Judea (8:4–40), other disciples left the city and traveled northward to Phoenicia, Cyprus, and into Syria. Most of them limited their witness to other Jews (μηδενὶ λαλοῦντες τὸν λόγον εἰ μὴ μόνον Ἰουδαίοις). The substantival participle οἱ διασπαρέντες ("the ones who were scattered") appears to be a deliberate echo of 8:4, as does the verb διῆλθον that elsewhere denotes missionary activity (8:4, 40; 9:32; 10:38), and their act of speaking "the Word" (λαλοῦντες τὸν λόγον). The phrase "during the persecution after Stephen's death" (NLT, ἀπὸ τῆς θλίψεως τῆς γενομένης ἐπὶ Στεφάνῳ) sets the disciples' activity parallel to 8:4–9:30, since the persecution ended with the conversion of Saul (9:31).

Phoenicia was a narrow region that began just north of Caesarea and stretched northward approximately one hundred miles along the Mediterranean coast. Luke later notes the existence of churches in the Phoenician cities of Tyre (21:3–4), Ptolemais (21:7), and Sidon (27:3). Cyprus was the third largest island in the Mediterranean—after Sicily and Sardinia—and was located just south of Asia Minor. It was easy to reach by boat from Caesearea. Antioch was the administrative center of the Roman province of Syria, located three hundred miles north of Jerusalem. The preposition "as far as" (ἕως) suggests that the missionary activity Luke describes expanded northward from Jerusalem and Damascus throughout Syria until it reached the provincial capital.

11:20–21. Not all the travelers, however, limited their evangelistic activities. When certain men from the island of Cyprus and from Cyrene in North Africa (τινες . . . ἄνδρες Κύπριοι καὶ Κυρηναῖοι; cf. 2:10; 6:9) came to Antioch (ἐλθόντες εἰς Ἀντιόχειαν), they also began speaking (ἐλάλουν, inceptive imperfect) to the non-Jewish population of the city (πρὸς τοὺς Ἑλληνιστάς). The content of their message of good news (εὐαγγελιζόμενοι) was "the Lord Jesus" (τὸν κύριον Ἰησοῦν). God blessed their efforts, and a great number who believed (πολύς ἀριθμὸς ὁ πιστεύσας) turned to the Lord (ἐπέστρεψεν ἐπὶ τὸν κύριον).

Bruce notes that the preaching of "the Lord Jesus" made good sense among the Greek population of Antioch. He writes, "To present him as Messiah to people who knew nothing of the hope of Israel would have been a meaningless exercise, but the Greek terms 'Lord' and 'Savior' were widely current in the religious world of the eastern Mediterranean" (1988, 225). "The hand of the Lord" (χεὶρ κυρίου) is an anthropomorphism for God's power and favor (Ezra 7:5, 9; Isa. 66:14; Luke 1:66) and might also suggest the presence of signs and wonders (4:30; cf. 2:43; 5:12; 6:8). "A great number" (πολύς ἀριθμός) echoes other accounts of significant church growth (2:47; 4:4; 5:36; 6:7; 9:35). To "turn to the Lord" (ἐπέστρεψεν ἐπὶ τὸν κύριον) is one of Luke's ways of describing salvation (3:19; 9:35; 14:15; 15:19; 26:18, 20). Bock notes that the combination of ἐπιστρέφω and πιστεύω occurs only here and indicates that "faith entails turning to the Lord Jesus" (2007, 414).

TEXTUAL ANALYSIS: "speaking also to the Greeks"
The fact that Ἑλληνιστάς occurs only three times in the NT (Acts 6:1; 9:29; 11:20) has generated considerable discussion over the identity of those with whom the men from Cyprus and Cyrene shared the good news about the Lord Jesus (11:20). Barrett's suggestion seems most likely: in 6:1 the word refers to Greek-speaking Jewish Christians, in 9:29 the word refers to Greek-speaking Jews, in 11:20 the word refers to Greek-speaking Gentiles (1994, 550). Larkin (1995, 176) and Peterson (2009, 535) concur, with Larkin describing them as "Greek-speaking persons who practice Greek ways—that is, the mixed non-Jewish population of Antioch." That understanding most likely explains the less difficult variant reading of Ἕλληνας in P⁷⁴, ℵ², A, and D*.

Establishing the Church in Antioch (11:22–26)

The Jerusalem church sends Barnabas to Antioch, where he rejoices at what he observes, encourages the new disciples, and recruits Saul to assist in ministry.

11:22–24. The church in Jerusalem heard the report (ὁ λόγος) about the events in Antioch and sent (ἐξαπέστειλαν) Barnabas to travel to Antioch. See 4:36 for further details on Barnabas. When he arrived (παραγενόμενος) and saw (ἰδών) that the grace of God (τὴν χάριν τοῦ θεοῦ) was at work, Barnabas rejoiced (ἐχάρη) and engaged in ongoing encouragement

(παρεκάλει) of the new believers. As a result of Barnabas's ministry, "a great crowd" (ὄχλος ἱκανός) "was added to the Lord" (προσετέθη … τῷ κυρίῳ). Culy and Parsons explain the phrase ἠκούσθη εἰς τὰ ὦτα ("was heard in the ears") as an idiom referring to information coming to someone's attention (2003, 226). "The grace of God" (τὴν χάριν τοῦ θεοῦ) includes the content of the gospel (20:24), the experience of God's care (13:43; 15:40), and God's enabling for ministry (14:26; cf. Eph. 3:2, 7). Barrett notes the wordplay of χάριν … ἐχάρη (1994, 552). The content of Barnabas's encouragement (παρεκάλει) was to remain faithful to the Lord (προσμένειν τῷ κυρίῳ) by resolving in advance to set their hearts on that pursuit (τῇ προθέσει τῆς καρδίας). The verb προστίθημι occurs elsewhere to describe extensive church growth (2:41, 47; 5:14). Here, it is a divine passive (προσετέθη) that highlights God's involvement in the process.

Luke describes Barnabas as "a good man and full of the Holy Spirit and faith" (11:24). That combination highlights his exemplary character (ἀγαθός) as one who was kind, generous, and an asset to the community, his genuine spirituality (πλήρης πνεύματος ἁγίου) as one who lived and ministered by the power of the Spirit, and his total devotion (πίστεως) as one who trusted God and his working. His ongoing ministry of encouragement in Antioch (παρεκάλει, iterative imperfect) was in accordance with the name the Jerusalem apostles had given him as "son of encouragement" (11:23; cf. 4:36). It seems clear that his previous observation of Saul's effectiveness in ministry prompted him to bring Saul to Antioch from Tarsus (11:25; cf. 9:26–29). It is worth considering the extent to which Barnabas's previous commitment to generosity might have influenced the members of the church in Antioch to arrange the famine relief collection for Jerusalem (11:29).

11:25–26. As the ministry in Antioch exploded, Barnabas recognized the need for additional leadership. Accordingly, he left Antioch to travel to Tarsus and locate (ἀναζητῆσαι) Saul. When he found him (εὑρών), Barnabas brought Saul back to Antioch (ἤγαγεν εἰς Ἀντιόχειαν), where for an entire year (ἐνιαυτὸν ὅλον), they met with the church (συναχθῆναι ἐν τῇ ἐκκλησίᾳ) and taught even more people (διδάξαι ὄχλον ἱκανόν). Because the verb ἀναζητέω carries the sense of "try[ing] to locate by searching" (BDAG s.v. "ἀναζητέω" 62), Schnabel suggests that Saul was not in Tarsus but instead "was engaged in missionary outreach in cities and towns in Cilicia" (2012, 523). The distance by land from Antioch to Tarsus was 130 miles, and Barnabas would have needed at least a week to make the one-way trip. It is possible that the two infinitives describe different activities with συναχθῆναι ἐν τῇ ἐκκλησίᾳ ("to meet with the church," NASB) referring to instructing those who were part of the church and διδάξαι ὄχλον ἱκανόν ("to teach considerable numbers," NASB) referring to evangelizing those who were outside the church (Schnabel 2012, 524). Luke notes that the disciples were first given the name (χρηματίσαι) "Christians" (Χριστιανούς) in Antioch.

> **"The disciples were first given the name Christians in Antioch."**
>
> To this point in his narrative, Luke has described Jesus's followers as believers (οἱ πιστεύοντες, 2:44), disciples (οἱ μαθηταί, 6:1), and brothers (οἱ ἀδελφοί, 6:3). In Antioch, a new name arose—Christians (Χριστιανοί; cf. 26:28; 1 Peter 4:16). The verb χρηματίζω can mean "to go under the name of" (BDAG s.v. "χρηματίζω" 2, 1089) or "to give a name to" (L&N §33.127). Larkin notes that the residents of Antioch had a reputation for "coining jesting nicknames" (1995, 175), and it seems more likely that the residents gave the name to the disciples rather than adopting it themselves. The ending -ιανος carries the sense of "followers" or perhaps "servants" (Stott 1990, 205). Bock writes, "the name was significant because it shows that it

was the identification with Jesus . . . as the Messiah that people noticed" (2007, 416). That explanation is possible, although Bruce suggests that the Greeks would have understood Χριστός as an additional name of Jesus (1990, 272). Schnabel suggests that the Roman authorities adopted the name to refer to a new religious group that was distinct from Judaism (2012, 525). In the second century, Clement of Alexandria would use the name as a badge of honor and write, "we who worship God in a new way, as the third race, are Christians" (*Strom.* 6.5.41.6).

Benevolent Action by the Church in Antioch (11:27–30)

When a prophet predicts a widespread famine, members of the church in Antioch send a financial gift for famine relief to the disciples in Judea.

11:27–28. Luke's next snapshot of the church began when itinerant prophets from Jerusalem visited Antioch. While they were there, the Holy Spirit (διὰ τοῦ πνεύματος) prompted one of them to predict a major famine (λιμὸν μεγάλην) that would be widespread (ἐφ᾽ ὅλην τὴν οἰκουμένην) and would occur during the reign of Claudius (ἥτις ἐγένετο ἐπὶ Κλαυδίου). Although the phrase "in those days" (ἐν ταύταις ταῖς ἡμέραις) is indefinite, it most likely refers to an event that occurred during the year Luke mentions in 11:26. New Testament prophets (προφῆται) could be either resident (13:1) or itinerant (11:27; cf. Did. 11:7–12). In Acts, they sometimes encouraged and strengthened the church (15:32–33) and other times foretold the future (21:10–11). Agabus (Ἄγαβος), the prophet, reappears in Caesarea on Paul's final trip to Jerusalem (cf. 21:7–14). The verb σημαίνω denotes the act of making something specific and clear (L&N §33.153); Bock suggests that it refers to the giving of oracles (2007, 417). "The whole world" (ὅλην τὴν οἰκουμένην) could refer to the earth as an inhabited area or to the world as an administrative unit (BDAG s.v. "οἰκουμένη" 2, 699). It is best understood as referring to the Roman Empire and its inhabitants (L&N §1.83). In 11:28, the phrase indicates that the famine extended beyond an isolated region.

> **The Famine in Judea**
>
> The great famine (λιμὸν μεγάλην) that would be over the whole world (ἐφ᾽ ὅλην τὴν οἰκουμένην) in the days of Claudius (ἐπὶ Κλαυδίου) most likely dates to A.D. 46–47. Claudius ruled from A.D. 41 until A.D. 53 (Barrett 1994, 563). Peterson notes that a poor harvest in Egypt in A.D. 45 led to a grain shortage and high prices that would have affected Judea in A.D. 46–48 (2009, 357). Josephus mentions such a famine during Claudius's reign (A.J. 3.15.3) and records a trip by Helena, queen of Adiabene, in A.D. 45–47, during which she took food to Jerusalem because of the famine (A.J. 20.2.5; 20.5.2). Agabus most likely gave his prophecy during the year that Luke mentions in 11:26 (ca. A.D. 42). Barnabas and Saul's visit (12:25) followed the death of Herod Agrippa I that Luke describes in 12:20–24 (ca. A.D. 44).

11:29–30. In response to Agabus's prophecy, the disciples organized a collection to send (πέμψαι) to their brothers and sisters in Judea (τοῖς κατοικοῦσιν ἐν τῇ Ἰουδαίᾳ ἀδελφοῖς). They collected funds from those who had the resources (καθὼς εὐπορεῖτό τις), and Barnabas and Saul delivered the funds to the elders (πρὸς τοὺς πρεσβυτέρους) in Jerusalem. Luke fronts the genitive phrase τῶν μαθητῶν to make it clear that the idea for the famine relief collection came from the disciples in Antioch rather than the prophets from Jerusalem. He resumes the subject later in the sentence with the phrase ἕκαστος αὐτῶν.

The verb εὐπορέω carries the sense of "be[ing] well off financially" (BDAG s.v. "εὐπορέω" 410); the conjunction καθὼς denotes measure (Culy and Parsons 2003, 229).

Louw and Nida suggest the translation "in proportion to the amount of possessions he owned" (L&N §57.27). The process the disciples in Antioch used was parallel to the practice of the Jerusalem church (4:34–35). Διακονία echoes the description of the care of the widows in the Jerusalem church (6:1). The phrase διὰ χειρὸς Βαρναβᾶ καὶ Σαύλου ("through the hand of Barnabas and Saul") identifies Barnabas and Saul as the agents who delivered the money the disciples had collected. See the introduction for a discussion of the number and timing of Paul's visits to Jerusalem.

> **The Jerusalem Elders**
>
> Acts 11:30 is the first mention of elders in the Jerusalem church although it was Paul's later practice to appoint elders in the churches he planted (14:23; 16:4; 20:17). The account of the Jerusalem Council mentions "the apostles and the elders" (οἱ ἀπόστολοι καὶ οἱ πρεσβύτεροι) multiple times (15:2, 4, 6, 22, 23), which suggests that the elders ministered alongside the apostles. In the account of the famine relief visit, the elders appeared to be responsible for administering financial aid, a ministry (διακονία) that was parallel to the role of the Seven prior to Stephen's martyrdom (6:1–6). If the other members of the Seven left Jerusalem at the same time Philip did (8:4–5), it seems likely that the elders mentioned in 11:30 took their places (Larkin 1995, 181).

THEOLOGICAL FOCUS

Acts 11:19–30 draws together a number of threads from Luke's narrative of the early church's expansion. It resumes the account of the scattering that followed Stephen's death. It follows naturally on the account of the events surrounding the incorporation into the church of Cornelius's household as the first Gentile converts. It continues the outward geographical movement of Jesus's witnesses beyond Judea and

Samaria to Phoenicia, Cyprus, and Syrian Antioch. It introduces a major people movement among members of a new cultural group—the Gentiles. It echoes aspects of early church life that were present in Jerusalem. It highlights the unity that characterized the movement. The passage also lays the foundation for the second half of Luke's narrative by providing an account of the early days of the church in Antioch, the church that would become the base for the Gentile mission described in chapters 13–20.

Acts 11:19–30 also reinforces a number of theological truths about local church life and ministry. Those truths include God's active involvement in the life of his church, the normativity of certain aspects of church life, and the interdependence that exists among congregations and crosses local boundaries. Luke repeatedly highlights God's involvement in the events in Antioch. The hand of the Lord was upon the witnesses (11:21). The grace of God was clearly apparent to Barnabas when he arrived (11:23). Barnabas himself was full of the Holy Spirit (11:24). The result of his ministry was that many were added to the Lord (11:24, divine passive). The church in Antioch organized the famine relief visit to Jerusalem in response to prophetic revelation through the Holy Spirit (11:28).

The similarities between the experiences of the church in Jerusalem and the church in Antioch are notable. In both cities, bold witness led to explosive growth, Spirit-filled leaders edified those inside the church and evangelized those outside the church, and commitment to caring for fellow disciples led to benevolent giving that met financial needs. The famine relief collection—organized in response to Agabus's prophetic utterance—highlights the unity and interdependence that exists within the body of Christ. It also reflects the principle Paul articulated for the Romans regarding his later collection for the Jerusalem church: "If the Gentiles have shared in [the Jerusalem saints'] spiritual things, they are indebted to minister to them also in material things" (Rom. 15:27).

PREACHING AND TEACHING STRATEGIES

Exegetical/Theological Synthesis

Following Luke's extended account of the events surrounding Peter's witness to Cornelius and his household, it is likely that his first-century readers would have had multiple questions come to mind. Were those events the exception or the rule? How would other Gentiles—particularly those who did not have the same interest in Judaism that Cornelius had—respond to the gospel? Would the movement catch on among Gentiles in regions outside Judea? If it did, how would those disciples relate to the Jerusalem church, and vice versa? The account of the gospel's arrival in Syrian Antioch answers those questions and more, because Luke's snapshots of the early days of the Gentile church in Antioch highlight the similarities to the early days of the Jewish church in Jerusalem. In both cities, God used the bold preaching of faithful witnesses to plant the church. In both cities, Spirit-filled leaders nurtured the church through a balance of edification and evangelization. In both cities, the unity of the church was evident in its active care for those in need. God was moving among the Gentiles in Antioch in the same way he had moved among the Jews in Jerusalem. With the original audience, the twenty-first-century audience shares the need to understand that God is at work to build his church in every geographical location and in every cultural context and that he wants his people to join him in what he is doing. In other words, when you see God moving, get on board!

Preaching/Teaching Idea

When you see God moving, get on board.

Contemporary Connections

What does it mean?
God was clearly moving. The spread of believers fleeing persecution looks random and chaotic

until the dust settles and we see the gospel preached and churches planted in their wake. The evangelistic visit to Syrian Antioch was no detour from God's commission, but rather his guiding hand into new regions and peoples. Lest there be any mistake, Luke spells it out clearly: "the hand of the Lord was with them" (11:21). God also moved in Antioch, just as dramatically as he did in Jerusalem. God drew many new believers to himself through nameless evangelists from Cyprus and Cyrene. God established this fledgling church through his servants Barnabas and Saul. God then mobilized the new church that had received so much to give of herself back to Jerusalem. All this divine movement opened doors for believers to get on board. Those once persecuted have a hand in evangelizing Jews over the three-hundred-mile stretch from Jerusalem. Those coming from North Africa and the Mediterranean get to share with Gentiles. The Jerusalem church selects Barnabas and sends him to help. Barnabas travels to Tarsus to recruit Saul to aid him. That is an inspiring scene. In God's remarkable grace, he lets his saints tag along to take part in his kingdom work.

Is it true?

There is both a contrast and a parallel in this passage. The contrast is between Barnabas now and the Hebrew Christians earlier; the parallel is between the Antioch church now and the Jerusalem church earlier. By way of contrast, when the Hebrew Christians heard the report of Gentile conversions, they criticized Peter for eating with the uncircumcised (11:2–3). It took considerable explaining to prompt praise instead. When Barnabas showed up in Antioch and witnessed Gentile conversions, however, "he was glad" (11:23). He was able to get right to work exhorting and teaching toward faithfulness in the Lord because he had received the Lord's evident work with praise. The fruit of God's work through the Hellenistic Jewish evangelists, Barnabas, and Saul displays a striking parallel between Antioch and Jerusalem. Both churches

were born by God's power through evangelism. Both churches grew up under faithful teaching. Both churches demonstrate true gospel grace by seeking to meet the physical needs of others. The picture that emerges is one of interdependent believers, churches, and cities serving each other for the sake of God's growing kingdom.

Now what?

Our culture is quick to criticize, to find what is wrong, and to cancel one another. We hunt for drama. We feed on gossip. Stories of dramatic failure draw us more than stories of slow and steady success. We have been discipled into a way of the world that hunts for the glass half empty and throws it on social media for all to see. Our culture can make us poorly equipped in the flesh to spot God's grace at work and join in. Enter Barnabas, son of encouragement (see 4:36), full of the Holy Spirit (11:24), and looking with expectation for God's grace to appear where his people are doing his work. The Spirit in Barnabas is showing us another way that contrasts sharply with the worldly one to which we have grown accustomed. The Spirit's way does not pick petty squabbles, split hairs, or try to expose what is missing. Instead, as a preacher once said, the Spirit in us loves the Spirit in another and is eager to encourage and celebrate. This expectation of grace wherever God is makes us all the quicker to join in what he is doing.

Creativity in Presentation

A creative presentation highlights *seeing* the grace of God and *joining* the grace of God. Seeing God's grace is not easy. Think of the ways people in our lives spot what is not rather than what is. There will always be the coach who runs up the score on another team, only to nitpick their players in the locker room for petty issues. There will always be the boss who sees a job well done and assigns another task without remark. There will always be the parent whose child brings home a nearly perfect report card but harps on the single B grade. Finding what is wrong comes easily. Celebrating what is right is learned behavior. Seeing God's grace in the first place is the fruit of Spirit-filled practice.

It is one thing to spot God's grace moving; it is another thing to step in and join it. So many hands join God's movement in our passage—scattered believers from Jerusalem, men of Cyprus and Cyrene, Barnabas, Saul, Jerusalem prophets like Agabus, and new disciples in Antioch. It all looks like an Amish barn raising. Barn raisings in early America, and among the Amish today, entail whole communities working together to build a barn that would be cost- and labor-prohibitive for a single family to do alone. It is remarkable to watch. You can find time-lapse videos on YouTube. That is what is happening in our passage. This entire community is joining in God's grace. Where God is moving, they get on board, to the mutual benefit of one another and to the beautiful glory of God.

- God's grace moves mightily (11:19–21)

- Many hands join in God's movement (11:22–30)

DISCUSSION QUESTIONS

1. What similarities do you see between the life of the early church in Jerusalem and the life of the early church in Antioch? Which of those qualities and/or practices are normative for local churches today?

2. How can you nurture exemplary character, genuine spirituality, and total devotion like Barnabas's in other believers? In which of those areas do you need to grow? Why?

3. Why was Barnabas's initiative in recruiting Saul an important step in the life of the church in Antioch? What principles does it suggest about congregational leadership and ministry?

4. Why is it that so many local congregations tend to minister in isolation? What can they do to foster cooperation at the local and regional levels?

5. Where do you see God moving and calling you to join him in his work?

Acts 12:1–25

EXEGETICAL IDEA
God responded to Herod Agrippa's persecution of the Jerusalem church by miraculously delivering Peter from prison and striking down Herod in judgment.

THEOLOGICAL FOCUS
Although Christ's disciples will encounter persecution, God will protect his people, punish their persecutors, and prevail over opposition.

PREACHING IDEA
Kings might persecute, but God always prevails.

PREACHING POINTERS
No one can oppose God and win. Previous kings had tried. Previous kings had failed. Pharaoh thought he could keep the Israelites in Egypt; he lost his army in the Red Sea (Exodus 14). Saul did his best to kill David; he lost his kingdom, his sons, and his life (1 Samuel 31). Nebuchadnezzar claimed the sovereignty that belonged to God alone; he lost his mind and ended up eating grass like a cow (Daniel 4). It makes you wonder what Herod Agrippa I was thinking when he executed the apostle James and arrested the apostle Peter. As much as we might tend to focus on Peter and his miraculous escape from prison, the main characters in Acts 12 are the king of Judea and the King of the universe, and Herod's futile attempt to oppose what God was doing through the Jerusalem church is the focus of the chapter. Herod let his arrogance, pride, and political ambition get in the way of a proper perspective on the God of heaven who removes and establishes kings (Dan. 2:21). He thought he could oppose God, and he ended up eaten by worms. In the most drastic way possible, he learned the lesson we all need to remember: kings might persecute, but God always prevails.

People today should be familiar with individuals being arrested and held in jail as well as with the frantic search that follows when someone escapes from jail or prison. They might also be aware of religious persecution from civil authorities in other countries and the need for missionaries to leave a country to avoid trouble. The passage corrects an attitude of pride or self-glorification. It also corrects any idea that it might be possible to oppose God and be successful. It commends trust in God's care, the importance of prayer, humility in recognizing God's rule, and the wisdom of withdrawing from danger when necessary. As Jesus's disciples, we need to understand that God continues to care for his people so that we will remain steadfast in the face of opposition, will continue in prayer, and will trust God to work in the face of seemingly impossible circumstances.

OPPOSITION FROM HEROD AGRIPPA I (12:1–25)

LITERARY STRUCTURE AND THEMES (12:1–25)

Barrett notes that 12:1–23 forms a continuous narrative (1994, 572), while 12:24–25 serves as a combined summary/transition statement. Although Walter Schmithals has suggested a "chiastic" construction for 11:27–12:25 (1982, 115), it is better to understand 12:1–23 as forming an ABA' pattern, with two narratives focused on Herod framing the description of Peter's miraculous release from prison:

A	Persecution by Herod	12:1–4
B	Release of Peter	12:5–17
A'	Death of Herod	12:18–23

The center panel follows the common pattern for biblical narrative passages, with Peter's statement in verse 11 as the main point of the passage:

12:5	Context	Peter is under guard in prison
12:6–10	Rising Action	An angel leads Peter out of prison
12:11	Climax	Peter declares that God has rescued him
12:12–16	Falling Action	Peter goes to Mary's house
12:17	Conclusion	Peter explains his release and departs

Schnabel identifies 12:6–11 as a miracle story (2012, 530). An adjusted and simplified analysis is: the person in distress (12:5–6), the miracle (12:7–8), the confirmation of the miracle (12:9–10), and response to the miracle (12:11; cf. 12:16). The final verses of the chapter summarize the continuing growth of the church (12:24) and shift the attention of the narrative from the church in Jerusalem to the church in Antioch by noting Barnabas and Saul's return after delivering the famine relief collection (12:25; cf. 11:30)

- ***The King Executes James and Arrests Peter (12:1–4)***
- ***God Sets Peter Free (12:5–17)***
- ***God Judges the King (12:18–23)***
- ***God's Word Continues to Advance (12:24–25)***

EXPOSITION (12:1–25)

After Stephen's death, Luke's account of the early church's witness moved away from Jerusalem to Samaria (8:4–25), southern Judea (8:26–40), Damascus (9:1–25), western Judea (9:32–43), Caesarea (10:1–48), and Antioch (11:19–30). Jerusalem, however, continued to be the center of the movement. Peter and John traveled from Jerusalem to Samaria in the aftermath of Philip's ministry (8:14–24). Saul traveled to Jerusalem to meet the apostles after his conversion (9:26–30). Paul defended his witness to the Gentiles before the Jerusalem church (11:1–18). Barnabas traveled from Jerusalem to Antioch after hearing reports of God at work in that city (11:22–26). Now, in Acts 12:1–25, Luke brings his readers back to Jerusalem in order to close the first major section of the book that focused on the early church's witness based in Jerusalem (1:1–12:25).

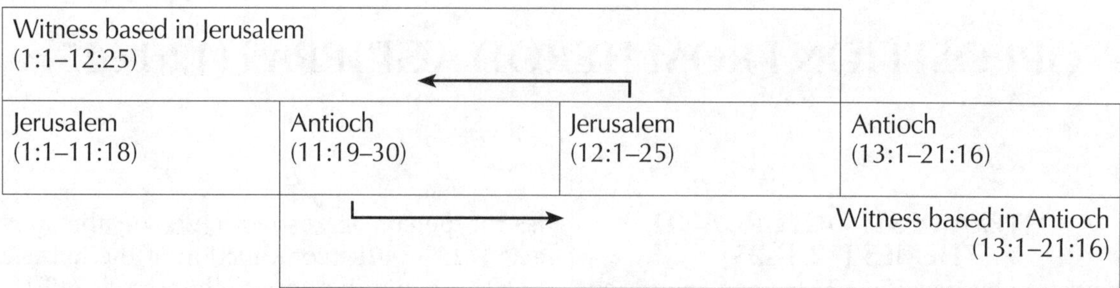

As 11:19–30 pointed forward to the second half of Luke's narrative by providing an account of the early days of the church in Antioch, so 12:1–25 points backward to the first half of his narrative by highlighting themes from earlier accounts of the church in Jerusalem. Barrett notes four: the cost of witness, God's care of his people, the prayers of the church, and victory over opponents (1994, 572). The church in Jerusalem had experienced persecution before, but a period of peace followed Saul's conversion (9:31). Now, persecution arose from a different source. Yet, "as the persecution intensifies . . . God's protection is still at work" (Bock 2007, 421). King Herod Agrippa I might execute James and arrest Peter, but God set Peter free and judged the king, with the result that his word continued to advance.

The King Executes James and Arrests Peter (12:1–4)
King Herod Agrippa I launches a persecution in which he executes the apostle James and arrests the apostle Peter.

12:1–2. Although the church in Jerusalem had experienced peace since Saul's conversion (9:31), the recently arrived king, Herod Agrippa I, launched a new period of persecution by laying hands on (ἐπέβαλεν . . . τὰς χεῖρας) some from the church (τινας τῶν ἀπὸ τῆς ἐκκλησίας) for the purpose of causing them harm (κακῶσαι, infinitive of purpose). One of his actions was to execute James the brother of John. Since Herod

Agrippa I ruled in Judea from A.D. 41 until A.D. 44, "about that time" (κατ᾽ ἐκεῖνον τὸν καιρόν) sets the events generally parallel to Agabus's prophecy in 11:27–28 (ca. A.D. 41–42) and prior to Barnabas and Saul's delivery of the collection in 11:29–30 (ca. A.D. 46–47). See 10:39 for ἀνεῖλεν (aorist of ἀναιρέω); μαχαίρῃ most likely refers to beheading, possibly reflecting a political charge (Schnabel 2012, 535).

Martyrdom of St. James by Giovanni Battista Piazzetta. Public domain.

Herod Agrippa I

Herod Agrippa I was the son of Aristobulus, the nephew of Herod Antipas, and the grandson of Herod the Great. He grew up in Rome, where he had both enemies and friends. Among the latter was Gaius Caligula, who granted him the title of "king," gave him control over the tetrarchies of Philip and Lysanias in A.D. 37 (Josephus, *A.J.* 18.6.10), and added the regions of Galilee and Perea in A.D. 39 (Josephus, *A.J.* 18.7.2). Subsequently, Claudius added the regions of Judea and Samaria in A.D. 41 (Josephus, *A.J.* 19.5.1), which gave him control of territory that was essentially the same as that of his grandfather. He returned to Judea in that same year. Like his grandfather, he was a builder, both in Judea (Josephus, *A.J.* 19.7.2) and in Phoenicia (Josephus, *A.J.* 19.7.5). He took active steps to win favor with the Jews (Josephus, *A.J.* 19.7.3) and "was especially pious, at least when he was in Jerusalem" (Bock, 2007, 424; cf. Josephus, *A.J.* 19.6.2). When he died unexpectedly in A.D. 44 (Josephus, *A.J.* 19.8.2), Claudius appointed Fadus to serve as procurator of Judea (Josephus, *A.J.* 19.9.2).

12:3–4. Luke does not record Herod's motives for launching the persecution, but when the king saw that his actions pleased the Jews (ἀρεστόν ἐστιν τοῖς Ἰουδαίοις), he also arrested Peter (προσέθετο συλλαβεῖν καὶ Πέτρον) during the days of unleavened bread. He put Peter into prison (ἔθετο εἰς φυλακήν) and entrusted him to four squads of soldiers to stand continuous guard over him (φυλάσσειν αὐτόν). His plan (βουλόμενος) was to present Peter for public execution after the Passover. The parenthetical note that the arrest took place during the days of unleavened bread (ἦσαν ἡμέραι τῶν ἀζύμων) explains the delay between Peter's arrest and the king's intended action. Along with the mention of the Passover (μετὰ τὸ πάσχα), it also echoes the timing of Jesus's passion (Bock 2007, 425). The "four groups of four soldiers each" (GNB, τέσσαρσιν τετραδίοις στρατιωτῶν) rotated

their duty every three hours. Herod's plan "to lead him out to the people" (ἀναγαγεῖν αὐτὸν τῷ λαῷ) suggests the intent of public execution (Barrett 1994, 577).

God Sets Peter Free (12:5–17)

In response to the prayers of the church, God sends an angel to free Peter from prison so that he can continue his ministry elsewhere.

12:5. While Peter was in prison, the church was praying for him. The imperfect tenses indicate that both the imprisonment (ἐτηρεῖτο ἐν τῇ φυλακῇ) and the prayer (προσευχὴ ἦν γινομένη) lasted multiple days (Marshall 1980, 208); the adverb ἐκτενῶς denotes the high degree of intensity and/or persevance the church devoted to Peter's situation (L&N §68.12; cf. Luke 22:44; Acts 26:7). Longenecker notes that "prayer is the natural atmosphere of God's people and the normal context for divine activity" and lists a dozen cross-references from previous chapters (1981, 409; cf. 1:14, 24; 2:42; 4:24–31; 6:4, 6; 9:40; 10:2, 4, 9, 31; 11:5).

12:6–8. At the last minute, on the night before Herod was about to carry out his plan (ὅτε δὲ ἤμελλεν προαγαγεῖν αὐτὸν ὁ Ἡρῴδης), God acted instead. Peter was asleep (κοιμώμενος) in his cell, bound by two chains (δεδεμένος ἁλύσεσιν δυσίν) to soldiers on either side of him (μεταξὺ δύο στρατιωτῶν), with two more standing guard at the door (πρὸ τῆς θύρας ἐτήρουν τὴν φυλακήν). Suddenly an angel of the Lord stood over him (ἐπέστη), and a bright light shone in the cell (ἐν τῷ οἰκήματι). The angel struck Peter's side (πατάξας τὴν πλευρὰν τοῦ Πέτρου), woke him (ἤγειρεν αὐτόν), and told him to get up quickly (ἀνάστα ἐν τάχει). When Peter did, the chains fell off his hands (ἐξέπεσαν αὐτοῦ αἱ ἁλύσεις ἐκ τῶν χειρῶν). Then, the angel told Peter to fasten his belt (ζῶσαι), put on his sandals (ὑπόδησαι τὰ σανδάλιά σου), put on his outer garment (περιβαλοῦ τὸ ἱμάτιόν σου), and follow him (ἀκολούθει). See 5:19 for "an angel of the Lord" (ἄγγελος κυρίου). A bright light (φῶς ἔλαμψεν) often accompanies heavenly visits or visions (cf. Luke 2:9; Acts 9:3; 22:11). Ζῶσαι is the aorist middle infinitive of ζώννυμι, "to gird oneself" (BDAG s.v. "ζώννυμι" 431); ἱμάτιον refers to an outer garment such as a cloak or robe (BDAG s.v. "ἱμάτιον" 2, 475).

12:9–10. Peter obeyed immediately, even though he was not entirely certain that what the angel was doing (τὸ γινόμενον διὰ τοῦ ἀγγέλου) was real (οὐκ ᾔδει ὅτι ἀληθές ἐστιν). Instead, he thought he was seeing a vision (ἐδόκει δὲ ὅραμα βλέπειν). The next events, however, confirmed the reality of the miracle. The angel led Peter through two chambers of the prison or past two sets of guards (διελθόντες πρώτην φυλακὴν καὶ δευτέραν) until they came to the main gate that led to the city (ἐπὶ τὴν πύλην τὴν σιδηρᾶν τὴν φέρουσαν εἰς τὴν πόλιν). That gate opened of its own accord (αὐτομάτη ἠνοίγη). After they had gone one block (προῆλθον ῥύμην μίαν), the angel suddenly departed (εὐθέως ἀπέστη ὁ ἄγγελος) and left Peter on his own. Since Peter was no stranger to angelic releases (5:17–20) or to visions (10:9–16) his confusion is a bit curious. Larkin suggests that his recent vision in Joppa colored his judgment (1995, 184). Others ascribe it to sleepiness (Longenecker 1981, 409). Regardless, Dunn notes the contrast in detail between this experience and the briefer account in 5:17–20 and observes that "Luke glories unreservedly in the supernatural character of the event" (1996, 160). Clearly, there was a divine hand in Peter's release.

12:11. When the angel departed, Peter "finally came to his senses" (NLT, ἑαυτῷ γενόμενος; cf. Barrett 1994, 582) and understood that what he had not been certain was real (ἀληθές; cf. 11:9) was, in fact, a certainty (ἀληθῶς). His statement of understanding—which Bock correctly identifies as the main point of the passage (2007,

The Liberation of St. Peter
by Gerard van Honthorst. Public domain.

427)—highlights the Lord (ὁ κύριος) as the source of the miracle, the angel (τὸν ἄγγελον αὐτοῦ) as the agent God sent (ἐξαπέστειλεν) to execute the miracle, and deliverance (ἐξείλατο) as the result of the miracle. The verb "rescued" (ἐξείλατο, aorist of ἐξαιρέω) describes "God's protecting hand on his witnesses to make certain they fulfill their responsibilities" (Larkin 1995, 184). Later in Acts, it applies to Paul (26:17). In the OT it applied to Moses whom God rescued from Pharaoh (Exod. 18:4–10) and to the three Hebrew youths whom God rescued from the fiery furnace (Dan. 3:28). "The hand of Herod" (χειρὸς Ἡρῴδου) is a metonymy for Herod's power. The noun προσδοκία carries the sense of "expect[ing] something to happen, whether good or bad" (L&N §30.55). In this instance, it was the expectation the Jews of Jerusalem would have had that the king would carry out his intention of executing Peter (12:4). In this early conflict between the church and the state, it was clear to Peter that the saving power of God was superior to the destructive power of the king (Stott 1990, 207).

12:12–14. When this realization "dawned on him" (NIV, συνιδών), Peter went directly to a house owned by Mary, the mother of John Mark, where many of the disciples had gathered (οὗ ἦσαν ἱκανοὶ συνηθροισμένοι) and were continuing to pray (προσευχόμενοι) for him. When Peter knocked (κρούσαντος αὐτοῦ), a female slave (παιδίσκη) who answered to the name of Rhoda (ὑπακοῦσαι ὀνόματι Ῥόδη) came to the gate. Although she recognized Peter's voice (ἐπιγνοῦσα τὴν φωνὴν τοῦ Πέτρου), she was so overcome by joy (ἀπὸ τῆς χαρᾶς) that she did not open the gate right away (οὐκ ἤνοιξεν τὸν πυλῶνα). Instead, she ran into the house (εἰσδραμοῦσα) and announced (ἀπήγγειλεν) to the praying group that Peter was standing at the gate (ἑστάναι τὸν Πέτρον πρὸ τοῦ πυλῶνος). Mary's house was, most likely, one of numerous private homes where groups of disciples met on a regular basis for fellowship and prayer (2:46–47). It was large enough to have a courtyard and an outer gate. Barrett suggests that "the door of the gate" (τὴν θύραν τοῦ πυλῶνος) describes a large gateway that had a smaller access door set into it (1994, 584). In early Christian literature, παιδίσκη always refers to the slave class (BDAG s.v. "παιδίσκη" 749), but it is likely that Rhoda was also a member of the house church that had met to pray for Peter. See 15:37 for Mary's son, John Mark.

12:15–16. The group's first response was to declare that Rhoda was out of her mind (μαίνη). When she kept on insisting that it was so (διϊσχυρίζετο οὕτως ἔχειν), they next suggested that she had heard Peter's angel. Meanwhile, Peter kept on knocking (ἐπέμενεν κρούων). When they finally opened the door and saw him, they were amazed (ἐξέστησαν). The verb διϊσχυρίζομαι describes being emphatic or resolute about something (BDAG s.v. "διϊσχυρίζομαι" 246). The iterative imperfect emphasizes Rhoda's repeated insistence that Peter actually was standing at the gate. The reference to Peter's angel (ὁ ἄγγελός ἐστιν αὐτοῦ) might reflect Jewish belief in "protecting and guiding angels . . . thought to resemble the human beings they protected" (Barrett 1994, 585), although that belief first appears in later rabbinic literature (Schnabel 2012, 540). It is

difficult to know for certain what the disciples were thinking, although they do not appear to have been expecting the miraculous release that God delivered, since they were completely astonished when they saw Peter. See 10:45 for ἐξίστημι.

12:17. Silencing the commotion by motioning with his hand (κατασείσας αὐτοῖς τῇ χειρί; cf. 13:16; 21:40), Peter explained in detail (διηγήσατο) how the Lord had used the angel to lead him out of the prison (πῶς ὁ κύριος αὐτὸν ἐξήγαγεν ἐκ τῆς φυλακῆς). He then gave the group instructions to communicate everything to James and the other brothers, left (ἐξελθών), and went to an unspecified location (ἐπορεύθη εἰς ἕτερον τόπον). The verb διηγέομαι denotes giving a detailed account of something (Luke 8:39; 9:10; Acts 9:27). See 15:13 for James and his role in the Jerusalem church. "The brothers" (τοῖς ἀδελφοῖς) were either other disciples in general or the elders mentioned in 11:30 (Schnabel 2012, 540; cf. 21:18). Larkin notes five locations that others have suggested for the phrase "to another place" (1995, 186); Bock adds a sixth (2007, 429). Paul's comments in Galatians are at least suggestive that the phrase points to Syrian Antioch (Gal. 2:11–21). Clement of Alexandria writes that the apostles remained in Jerusalem for twelve years and then engaged in missionary activity among Jews of the Diaspora (*Strom.* 6.5.43). Schnabel suggests that the large number of pilgrims who left the city after Passover would have made it easy for Peter also to leave unnoticed (2012, 541).

God Judges the King (12:18–23)

God strikes King Herod Agrippa I with a sudden fatal illness when he accepts public acclaim as a god.

12:18–19. With Peter now out of prison and off stage, Luke returns to the king who had put him there. At daybreak (NET, γενομένης δὲ ἡμέρας; cf. BDAG s.v. "ἡμέρα" 1, 436), there was a major uproar (τάραχος οὐκ ὀλίγος) among the soldiers (ἐν τοῖς στρατιώταις) over what had happened to Peter (τί ἄρα ὁ Πέτρος ἐγένετο). Herod launched an unsuccessful search for Peter (ἐπιζητήσας αὐτὸν καὶ μὴ εὑρών), interrogated the guards (ἀνακρίνας τοὺς φύλακας), commanded that they be executed (ἐκέλευσεν ἀπαχθῆναι), and left Jerusalem for Caesarea (κατελθὼν ἀπὸ τῆς Ἰουδαίας εἰς Καισάρειαν), where he spent some time (διέτριβεν). "Not a little commotion" (τάραχος οὐκ ὀλίγος) is one of Luke's frequent uses of litotes, in which he makes a statement by negating the opposite idea (4:20; 5:26). According to Roman law (Justinian, *Cod.* 9.4.4), the guards who allowed Peter to escape would suffer the same penalty he would have (Larkin 1995, 186). Herod's departure "from Judea" (ἀπὸ τῆς Ἰουδαίας) refers to the immediate vicinity of Jerusalem, since Caesarea was the administrative capital of the province (Marshall 1980, 211).

12:20. In Caesarea, the king faced another issue posed by his relations with the neighboring free cities of Tyre and Sidon. Luke does not explain why the king was "very angry" (θυμομαχῶν) with the cities, although Haenchen suggests a trade war of some sort (1971, 386). Regardless, the cities sent a joint delegation to the king (ὁμοθυμαδὸν παρῆσαν πρὸς αὐτόν) and persuaded (πείσαντες) Blastus, one of his administrators, to intercede for them (ἠτοῦντο εἰρήνην). Their concern was that they relied on Judea to provide them with food (διὰ τὸ τρέφεσθαι αὐτῶν τὴν χώραν). Louw and Nida describe Blastus, who was "over the bed-chamber of the king" (ἐπὶ τοῦ κοιτῶνος τοῦ βασιλέως), as "a highly respected person with considerable responsibility for the king's living quarters and personal affairs" (L&N §7.29). The fact that Tyre and Sidon relied on Judea for food places this episode before the famine in A.D. 46–48 (11:27–28).

12:21–23. On the day appointed (τακτῇ ἡμέρᾳ) for meeting with the Phoenician delegation, the king appeared, sat on his judicial bench (ἐπὶ τοῦ βήματος; cf. BDAG s.v. "βῆμα" 3, 175), and began delivering a public address (ἐδημηγόρει, inceptive imperfect). While he was speaking, the assembled crowd kept on calling out loudly (ἐπεφώνει, iterative imperfect) that they were hearing the voice of a god not of a man (θεοῦ φωνὴ καὶ οὐκ ἀνθρώπου). Immediately (παραχρῆμα), an angel of the Lord afflicted the king with a fatal disease (ἐπάταξεν αὐτὸν ἄγγελος κυρίου), because he accepted the glory that belonged to God alone (ἀνθ' ὧν οὐκ ἔδωκεν τὴν δόξαν τῷ θεῷ). His gruesome end was that he "was eaten by worms" (σκωληκόβρωτος) and "breathed his last" (ἐξέψυξεν).

According to Josephus, the king's royal clothing (ἐσθῆτα βασιλικήν) was woven silver that reflected the sun's brightness, and the delegation's time in Caesarea coincided with a festival held to honor Caesar (Josephus, *A.J.* 19.8.2). The latter detail explains the popular assembly (ὁ δῆμος; cf. BDAG s.v. "δῆμος" 1, 223) that was present. Πατάσσω means "to slay by means of a mortal blow or disease" (L&N §20.73); Luke previously used ἐκψύχω to describe Ananias and Sapphira's deaths (cf. 5:5, 10). The two verbs highlight the divine source of the disease (BDAG s.v. "πατάσσω" 2, 786) and the divine judgment resulting from it. Larkin notes seven medical options for Herod's being "eaten by worms" (σκωληκόβρωτος) and concludes that a combination of perintonitis and intestinal roundworms seems to be the best explanation (1995, 188). The phrase has parallels in the deaths of two other kings who opposed God's purposes: Antiochus Epiphanes (2 Macc. 9:5–12) and Herod the Great (Josephus, *A.J.* 17.6.5). Josephus writes that the king died five days after the angel struck him (*A.J.* 19.8.2).

God's Word Continues to Advance (12:24–25)

Despite the king's failed persecution, God's word continues to advance, as the focus of the mission shifts from Jerusalem to Antioch.

12:24–25. Verse 24 is Luke's third summary statement (6:7; 9:31) and demonstrates that, despite the king's persecution, the mission continues to expand. Verse 25 reintroduces Barnabas and Saul, resumes the narrative that Luke paused in 11:30, and adds John Mark to the disciples who are present in Antioch. It is possible to understand the combination ηὔξανεν καὶ ἐπληθύνετο as "a doublet used to emphasize the degree to which God's message spread" (Culy and Parsons 2003, 242). In the parallel statement of 6:7, the Word of God grows, and the number of disciples increases, which suggests ongoing growth (progressive imperfects) that is both qualitative and quantitative. Chronologically, verse 25 takes place two or three years after verse 23, as Luke writes thematically rather than sequentially.

TEXTUAL ANALYSIS: "to Jerusalem" or "from Jerusalem" (12:25)?
The UBS[5] reading of 12:25 (ὑπέστρεψαν εἰς Ἰερουσαλήμ) has good manuscript support (‫א‬, B), is the more difficult reading, and according to Metzger is "the least unsatisfactory" option (TCGNT, 352). If, however, the church in Antioch sent Barnabas and Saul to Jerusalem with the famine relief collection in 11:30, it seems more natural to the narrative for them to return from Jerusalem in 12:25. Other variants substitute the prepositions ἀπό (D) and ἐξ (P[74], A), both of which would be easier readings. In the NT, ὑποστρέφω ἐκ occurs only once (2 Peter 2:21) and ὑποστρέφω ἀπό occurs only three times (Luke 4:1; 24:9; Heb. 7:1), while ὑποστρέφω εἰς occurs seventeen times (Culy and Parsons 2003, 242), making it the more congruent reading (fifteen times elsewhere in Luke-Acts) that best explains the others. Longenecker suggests that εἰς was "a slip of copyist's pen or a marginal gloss" (1981, 417), and Stott writes, "the textual evidence needs to be overridden by the demands of context" (1990, 215). Barrett, however, notes that "Luke did not always adopt the 'correct' order of words" (1994, 596), and other commentators choose to take the prepositional phrase with what follows: "Barnabas and Saul returned when they had fulfilled their mission to Jerusalem" (NASB; cf. Bock 2007, 435; Bruce 1990, 290; Larkin 1995, 189; Peterson 2009, 371).

THEOLOGICAL FOCUS

The narratival function of Acts 12:1–25 is to conclude the first half of Luke's narrative by giving readers a final look at the "mother church" in Jerusalem. Since persecution scattered many of the Jerusalem disciples in 8:4, the major blocks of the narrative have moved from the Hellenistic witness of Philip and Saul (8:4–9:31) to the Hebraic witness of Peter (9:32–11:18) and back to the Hellenistic witness of Barnabas and Saul (11:19–30). In 12:1–24, Luke brings his readers back to the Hebraic Jewish witness in Jerusalem for a final visit before the action shifts to the Hellenistic witness in Antioch and the missionary work that would soon be based in that city (13:1–20:16). A brief note about Barnabas and Saul in 12:25 connects back to Acts 11:19–30 and facilitates the transition.

Theologically, Acts 12:1–25 resumes Luke's picture of the church's experience of persecution. The Jerusalem church had faced persecution before. It began with the arrest of Peter and John and led to a warning by the religious leaders (4:1–22). It escalated to the arrest of the apostles followed by a beating (5:17–42). It reached a zenith with the death of Stephen and the widespread attack on the church led by Saul, the Pharisee (8:1–3), who pursued the disciples to Damascus (9:1–2). With Saul's conversion, religious persecution ended and the church in Judea enjoyed approximately ten years of peace (9:31). Luke's account of Herod Agrippa's new phase of persecution against the church reinforces several truths found in earlier chapters. First, prayer should be the church's first response to persecution (12:5, 12; cf. 4:23–30). Second, God might choose to deliver miraculously (12:6–10; cf. 5:17–20). Third, God does not promise deliverance; persecution might result in death (12:1–2; cf. 7:54–60). Fourth, God's Word advances despite persecution (12:24; cf. 4:31; 6:1).

The passage also introduces two new elements. The first is that civil authority can be the source of the persecution. Previous persecutions had their origins with Jewish religious authorities. Although Herod's actions pleased the Jews, his actions were self-serving in that they helped consolidate his political popularity. Paul's experiences later in Acts will develop further the theme of the church's interaction with governmental authorities (16:22–40; 18:1–17; 24:24–27; 25:1–22; 26:30–32). The second new element is that God will deal with the persecutor(s). Although Gamaliel had warned the Sanhedrin that they might find themselves to be fighting against God (5:35–39), Herod learned the consequences of actually doing it. The bottom line is that God will ultimately judge those who oppose him. Herod Agrippa's judgment came quickly. Not every opponent will necessarily experience immediate judgment, but judgment is inevitable, as Paul wrote to the Thessalonians, "judgment will finally overtake them" (TNT, 1 Thess. 2:16).

PREACHING AND TEACHING STRATEGIES

Exegetical/Theological Synthesis
After only mentioning Jerusalem periodically in his recent narrative, and with the early church's witness increasingly moving away from that city, Luke's first-century readers would have wanted to know whether God might be finished with his work there. So, Luke returns to Jerusalem for one final look at the life of the church, and his answer is an emphatic "No!" The Jerusalem church was still persevering in the face of persecution, was still trusting God through intense prayer, was still experiencing God's miraculous deliverance, and was still seeing God's word grow qualitatively and quantitatively. With the original audience, the twenty-first-century audience shares the need to know that God does not abandon the work he has begun. In fact, he continues to protect his people and pursue his purposes, even in the face of persecution by civil authorities. If they understand that truth, they will remain steadfast in the face of opposition, will continue in prayer, and will trust God in the face of seemingly impossible circumstances, because God always prevails.

Preaching/Teaching Idea
Kings might persecute, but God always prevails.

Contemporary Connections

What does it mean?
The passage might begin with a reference to Herod's "violent hands," but it makes much of God's sovereign hand throughout. Kings persecute. Jerusalem is still a dangerous place to be a Christian. Luke had just reminded his readers of the scattering from Stephen's martyrdom (cf. 11:19). Now Herod beheads the apostle James to the thrill of the Jews and throws the apostle Peter into prison. Two-thirds of Jesus's innermost circle are out of action. The authority and military presence of Herod Agrippa's power certainly feels supreme. In response, the church earnestly prayed—again. She had prayed with devotion in the upper room awaiting the Spirit (1:14) and had prayed when Peter and John were threatened early on (4:24). The church believed what Herod would learn in short order: God always prevails. The God who was able to bring about the resurrection of his martyred son around Passover is easily able to bring about the liberation of his disciple around Passover so many years later. The God who thwarted Herod's grandfather is

able to frustrate the grandson's plans. God is sovereign; his will be done.

Is it true?

God's sovereign display harkens back to Jesus's conversation with Peter by the sea. When Jesus told Peter he would die a martyr's death, Peter asked him about John, who followed them. Jesus told Peter that if he willed, John would live out his natural life. Sure enough, although Peter and John spent a couple times in prison together, it was James whom Herod grabbed and put to death. Peter's time had not come. John's would not. God holds all timing in his hands.

There are comical scenes of God's work in this passage. One is the sovereignty of God and its relationship with prayer. When hardship comes, the church does not wait around for God's inevitable prevailing power to show up. She prays, earnestly. She prays late into the night while others sleep. As the church prays, God answers. In fact, God answers so fast, the church cannot recognize his answer when it comes in Peter's knock at the door. The church nearly ignores answered prayer so that she can get back to praying.

The other comical scene is Peter in his cell. Jerusalem is ablaze with persecution—James is dead, Herod plots, sentries guard, the church prays, and Peter is fast asleep. He is sleeping so deeply that the angel needs to strike him to get him up and moving. In God's hands, Peter is safe wherever he is—in an upper room or a prison cell. Maybe a good night's sleep is a radical act of faith. He looks like Jesus sleeping on the boat through a storm. If God is at work, there is certainly a place to pray hard. Then there is also a place to sleep deeply.

Now what?

What is our own knee-jerk reaction to trials and hardships? How we respond tells us a lot about what we believe. As always, orthopraxy (right living) reveals orthodoxy (right believing). Praying people display a prevailing God. If we pray in the face of hardship, a growing part of us must believe God hears, God cares, and God has all power to answer how he wills. Praying when we suffer is a beautiful act of faith because it ascribes all those things to God. Once we have prayed earnestly for things outside *our* control but firmly in *God's* control, sleeping can be a great act of faith too. It is important to remember that even though God always prevails, our prevailing in him does not always look the same. James and Peter are both arrested. James and Peter are both on death row. We can assume the church prayed for both James and Peter. Yet, James was beheaded, and Peter was released. God's prevailing sovereignty did not guarantee our particular safety. If the Lord wills, we suffer. If the Lord wills, we experience dramatic release from suffering. Whatever he wills and however he prevails, blessed be the name of the Lord.

Creativity in Presentation

The story in Acts 12 has such dramatic twists and turns that the action is in the telling. An informal teaching space lends itself to acting out the story, including the comical scenes of Peter's deep sleep and Rhoda's leaving Peter knocking at the door. A formal teaching space might simply retell the story. Peter has been in and out of prison so often in Acts, he is starting to feel like the proverbial cat of many lives. Herod might well say to Peter in exasperation what Romeo's friend Mercutio demands of Juliet's murderous cousin Tybalt: "Good king of cats, nothing but one of your nine lives!" Still, Peter joins the ranks of Samson, Jeremiah, Daniel, Shadrach and friends, and others sprung by God's sovereign hand from certain death.

John Paton was a missionary to the violent, cannibal islanders of the New Hebrides and knew this sovereign hand's power to prevail. Before Paton went, a certain Mr. Dickson challenged Paton as to the danger, shouting, "The cannibals! You will be eaten by cannibals!" Paton's famous response was,

> Mr. Dickson, you are advanced in years now, and your own prospect is soon to be laid in the grave, there to be eaten by worms. I confess to you, that if I can but live and die serving and honoring the Lord Jesus, it will make no difference to me whether I am eaten by Cannibals or by worms. In the Great Day my Resurrection body will rise as fair as yours in the likeness of our risen Redeemer.

Indeed. Should the Lord will that we die by sword soon (James), by crucifixion later (Peter), or by old age last (John), may his will be done. Should our part be to sit in prison (Peter) or to sit all night in the prayer meeting (Rhoda), may his will be done. Whatever our assignment, although kings might persecute, God always prevails.

- King Herod persecutes God's people (12:1–5).

- God prevails by freeing Peter (12:6–19).

- God prevails by striking down Herod (12:20–25).

DISCUSSION QUESTIONS

1. What principle(s) can you draw from the fact that Herod executed James but God delivered Peter?

2. How does the Jerusalem church's response to persecution serve as a model for Christians who experience persecution today?

3. Why is it significant that the angel had to awaken Peter before he led him out of prison? What does that detail suggest about Peter's mental and emotional states?

4. In what ways does the passage contrast Herod's power with God's power? What does that contrast teach about each?

5. What principle(s) does the passage suggest about the relationship between persecution and the progress of the gospel?

CYPRUS, GALATIA, AND THE JERUSALEM COUNCIL (ACTS 13:1–15:35)

The events of Acts 12 closed Luke's account of the mission based in Jerusalem. The gospel moved outward geographically from Jerusalem through Judea, Samaria, and Syria, and it moved outward culturally from Hebrew-speaking Jews to Greek-speaking Jews to Samaritans to an Ethiopian official to the Gentiles. Acts 13 opens the account of a new mission based in Syrian Antioch. That mission extends through Acts 20 as Paul—first in partnership with Barnabas and then in partnership with Silas—carries the gospel to Cyprus, Galatia, Greece, and Asia. The mission encompasses the evangelistic activities of what are usually described as Paul's three "missionary journeys." The first major section comprises the third division of the book and recounts Barnabas and Saul's ministries in Cyprus and Galatia (13:1–14:28) as well as the events of the Jerusalem Council (15:1–35).

	Region	Text Section	People Group	Missionaries
Acts 3–7	Jerusalem	Acts 3:1–5:42	Hebrew-speaking Jews	Peter and John
		Acts 6:1–7:60	Greek-speaking Jews	Stephen
Acts 8–12	Judea Samaria Syria	Acts 8:4–25	Samaritans	Philip
		Acts 8:26–40	Ethiopian (adherent)	Philip
		Acts 10:1–48	Cornelius (Godfearer)	Peter
		Acts 11:19–30	Gentiles	Barnabas
Acts 13–20	Cyprus Galatia Greece Asia	Acts 13:1–14:28	Gentiles	Barnabas and Paul
		Acts 15:36–18:17	Greeks	Paul and Silas
		Acts 19:1–20:28	Greeks	Paul

As the division progresses, a pattern emerges that will characterize Paul's mission strategy: The missionaries focus on major population centers. Whenever possible, they begin their witness in Jewish synagogues. When opposition arises from the Jews in the city, they shift their attention to receptive Gentiles. If opposition in a city becomes dangerous, they move on to the next city. The events surrounding the start of the church in Antioch and the subsequent mission to Cyprus and Galatia also suggest a paradigm for how mission work should proceed. The sending church in Jerusalem commissioned a missionary team to support the witness in Antioch (11:19–22).

The missionary team planted a mission church (11:23–26). The mission church in Antioch became a sending church by commissioning a missionary team (13:1–3). The missionary team planted mission churches in Galatia (13:13–14:24). The missionary team reported to the church in Antioch that commissioned them (14:25–28). Subsequently, the mission churches in Lystra and Derbe would continue the pattern by commissioning Timothy to join the missionary team of Paul and Silas (16:1–5). The events recounted most likely cover the period of A.D. 46–48.

46	Winter	Syrian Antioch (13:1–3)	Missionary call (13:2)
	Spring	Cyprus (13:4–12)	John Mark departs (13:13)
	Summer		
	Fall	Pisidian Antioch (13:13–52)	
47	Winter	Iconium (14:1–7)	
	Spring	Lystra (14:8–19)	
	Summer		
	Fall	Derbe (14:20)	
48	Winter	Derbe to Antioch (14:21–26)	
	Spring		
	Summer	Syrian Antioch (14:27–28)	Galatians
	Fall	Jerusalem (15:1–35)	Jerusalem Council (15:6–29)

Homiletically, the third division consists of four preaching sections. The first describes Barnabas and Saul's commissioning and their witness on the island of Cyprus (13:1–12). The second records their witness in Pisidian Antioch (13:13–52). The third recounts their witness to Jews in Iconium and Gentiles in Lystra and their return to Syrian Antioch (14:1–28). The fourth traces the origins, deliberations, and decisions of the Jerusalem Council (15:1–35).

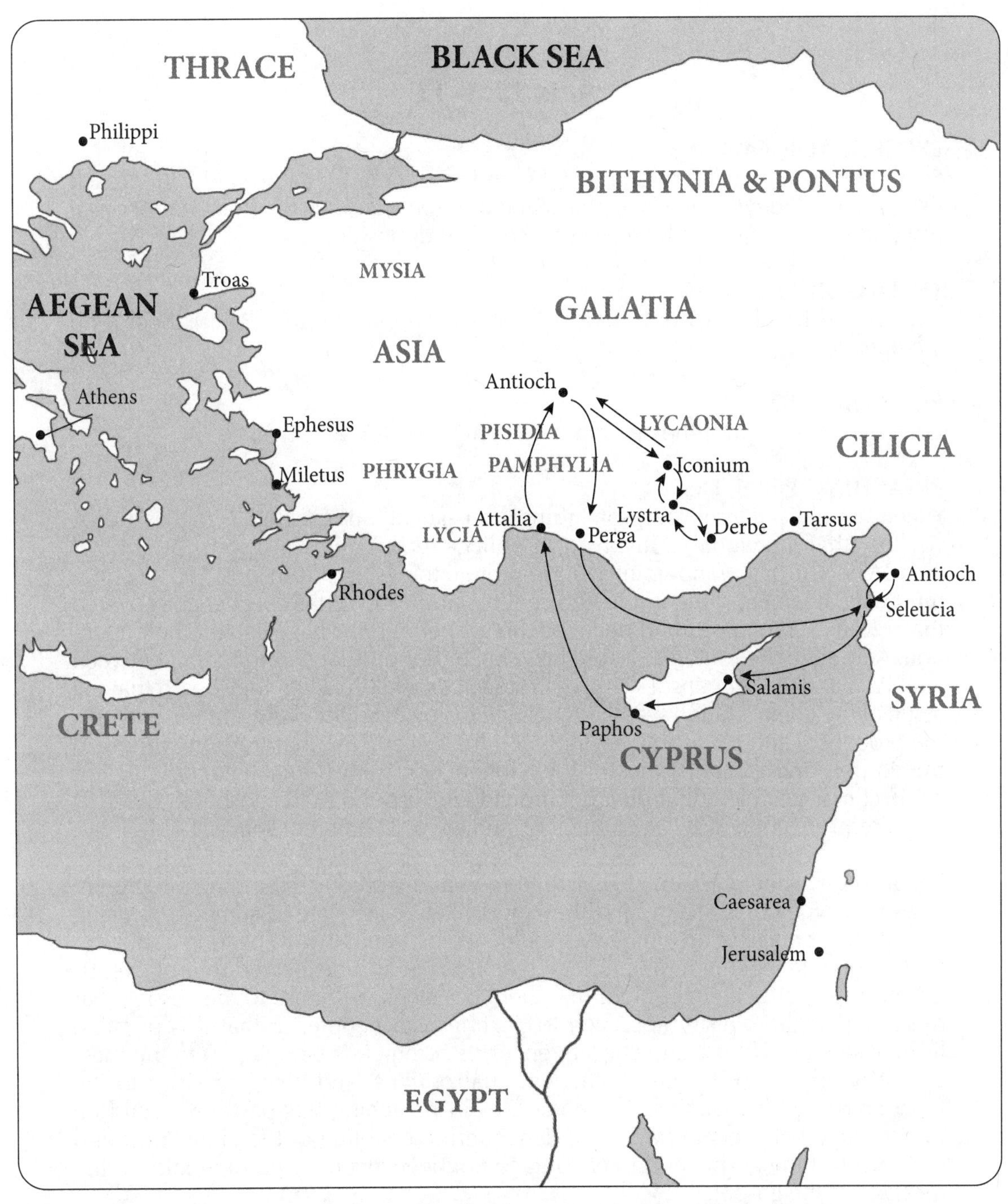

Paul's First Journey

Acts 13:1–12

EXEGETICAL IDEA
Sent out by the Holy Spirit and the church in Antioch, Barnabas and Saul preach the gospel in the synagogues on the island of Cyprus and see the Roman proconsul respond in faith to God's word despite spiritual opposition.

THEOLOGICAL FOCUS
God's word has the power to defeat those who oppose it and deliver those who are open to it.

PREACHING IDEA
God's word confounds the resistant and convinces the receptive.

PREACHING POINTERS
When a public figure does something unusual or unexpected it makes news, whether that individual is involved in politics, entertainment, sports, or another area. When he or she shows interest in spiritual things, it turns heads. The response must have been the same in the first century, and when Luke's readers discovered that a Roman proconsul had believed the gospel, it must have caught their attention. Adding to their interest would have been the spiritual confrontation between Saul/Paul and the proconsul's court astrologer, especially when they heard that the result of the confrontation was the magician losing his sight. The contrasts between the proconsul and his astrologer included their character, their responsiveness to the gospel, and the outcomes of their interaction with Barnabas and Saul. The contrast makes it clear that different individuals respond to the gospel in different ways, require different styles of ministry, and arrive at different spiritual outcomes.

People today should be able to relate to men and women responding in different ways to an idea or concept, and they most likely can relate to someone seeking to oppose a course of action. They should also be familiar with hearing about important people making news and being amazed at an unexpected turn of events. The passage corrects suggestions that there is a single response to the gospel, that there is a single ministry approach to dealing with people, or that it is possible to oppose God without any consequences. It commends being open to the message of God's word, rejecting other spiritual options, and being sensitive to the Holy Spirit and his leading. The objectives in preaching this passage should be to challenge believers to have confidence in the enabling of the Holy Spirit and the power of the gospel and to encourage nonbelievers to respond in faith to the message of the gospel.

WITNESS ON CYPRUS (13:1–12)

LITERARY STRUCTURE AND THEMES (13:1–12)

Acts 13:1–12 brings together three brief narratives that lead to the conversion of the Roman proconsul Sergius Paulus. A commissioning narrative introduces the main characters and explains the impetus behind their activities (13:1–3). A brief travel narrative shifts the location of events from Antioch to Cyprus and sets the context for the main action of the passage (13:4–5). A longer conversion narrative describes a high-level Roman official's positive response to the gospel (13:6–12) and includes an embedded "confrontation miracle" (13:9–11; cf. Bock 2007, 441) that demonstrates the gospel's superiority over spiritual opposition and authenticates Saul/Paul as God's messenger.

- *The Church in Antioch Commissions Barnabas and Saul (13:1–3)*
- *Barnabas and Saul Preach in the Synagogues of Cyprus (13:4–5)*
- *A Roman Official Believes the Word of God (13:6–12)*

EXPOSITION (13:1–12)

This brief passage begins the third major division of the book. Herod's persecution, Peter's release, and Herod's death in chapter 12 closed Luke's focus on the mission based in Jerusalem on a positive note. Action would return to that city for the deliberations of the Jerusalem Council and for Paul's arrest and trials, but chapter 13 shifts Luke's focus to the mission based in Syrian Antioch. The opening account of Barnabas and Saul's commissioning and ministry on the island of Cyprus highlights a number of similarities with the mission based in Jerusalem. The work is characterized by the Holy Spirit's direction (cf. 8:29; 10:19) and filling (cf. 4:8; 6:3; 11:24). It encounters and overcomes hostile spiritual forces when it enters new territory (cf. 8:4–24). It results in judgment for those who oppose it (cf. 5:1–11; 12:18–23). A new element, which will become a recurring theme as the mission expands into other areas of the Roman Empire, is the sympathetic response of an important government official. In addition, the sharp contrast between the receptive proconsul, Sergius Paulus, and the resistant magician, Bar-Jesus, highlights the truth that different individuals respond to the gospel in different ways, require different styles of ministry, and arrive at different outcomes.

The Church in Antioch Commissions Barnabas and Saul (13:1–3)

The Holy Spirit directs the church in Antioch to set apart Barnabas and Saul for the work to which he has called them.

13:1. Luke already began the transition to the church in Antioch in 12:25. Now, he introduces the church's leadership team, consisting of five prophets and teachers (προφῆται καὶ διδάσκαλοι). Although the five men Luke introduces were most likely all Hellenistic Jews, they came from diverse backgrounds. Barnabas was a Diaspora Jew from Cyprus and was a landowner and a Levite. Simeon's name makes it likely that he was Jewish, although his Roman name (ὁ καλούμενος Νίγερ) suggests that he was possibly a "black" proselyte from Africa. Lucius had a Roman name and came from Cyrene in Northern Africa. Tradition records that he returned to his homeland and became its first bishop. Manaen was a Palestinian Jew, who had aristocratic connections to the former tetrarch

Herod Antipas. Saul was a Diaspora Jew from Cilicia in eastern Asia Minor and was a free-born Roman citizen. Together, they comprised an ethnically and culturally diverse group, representing a cosmopolitan urban congregation.

The phrase κατὰ τὴν οὖσαν ἐκκλησίαν is best understood as indicating that the prophets and teachers ministered throughout the various house churches in the city (Culy and Parsons 2003, 243). See 11:27 for prophets (προφῆται). Teachers (διδάσκαλοι) occurs only in Acts 13:1, although διδαχή occurs four times, and διδάσκω occurs sixteen times. Throughout Acts, teaching occurred in both public and private venues (2:42; 5:42; 20:20), and included both instruction of those inside the church (2:42; 11:26; 15:1) and evangelism of those outside the church (4:2; 5:21; 15:25; 18:25). Although Barnabas and Saul both engaged in teaching in Antioch (11:26), Luke provides no details about the gifting and/or roles of the five members of the leadership team. The Latin adjective *niger* that others applied to Simeon refers to being dark-complexioned (BDAG s.v. "Νίγερ" 672). The adjective σύντροφος that describes Manaen refers to an intimate childhood companion (L&N §34.515), who was raised with an individual either as a foster brother or as a close friend (BDAG s.v. "σύντροφος" 976).

13:2–3. While the leaders were worshipping the Lord (NLT, λειτουργούντων τῷ κυρίῳ) and fasting (νηστευόντων), the Holy Spirit instructed them to set apart (ἀφορίσατε) Barnabas and Saul to engage in the task (εἰς τὸ ἔργον) for which he had called them (ὃ προσκέκλημαι αὐτούς). In response, they fasted (νηστεύσαντες), prayed (προσευξάμενοι), laid on hands (ἐπιθέντες τὰς χεῖρας), and "sent off" (NRSV, ἀπέλυσαν) Barnabas and Saul. Λειτουργέω describes the act of performing religious rites out of devotion to God (BDAG s.v. "λειτουργέω" 1, 591) and sometimes refers to priestly service (Luke 1:23; Heb. 10:11). Bock believes that in this context, it refers to prayer (2007, 440), although it seems more naturally to refer to worship in general. Fasting (νηστεύω/νηστεία) was one of the major practices of Jewish piety (Matt. 6:16–18) and along with regular worship and prayer characterized the prophetess Anna in Luke 2:37 (νηστείαις καὶ δεήσεσιν λατρεύουσα νύκτα καὶ ἡμέραν). The NT mentions the practice only occasionally as part of the life of the church, although Paul practiced it as part of the process of appointing elders (Acts 14:23).

Although some commentators suggest that the Spirit's instructions came to the entire congregation (Marshall 1980, 215), the more natural antecedent of the subject of the genitive absolute (λειτουργούντων αὐτῶν . . . καὶ νηστευόντων) is the group of five prophets and teachers just identified. Luke gives no indication of how the Spirit spoke. Bruce suggests that it was through an inspired utterance by one of the prophets (1988, 245); Peterson thinks that it was a conviction given to each one present (2009, 376). Regardless, this incident is one of several in which the Spirit speaks directly to the early disciples (8:29; 10:19; 11:12; 19:1 [textual variant in D]; 21:11). The verb ἀφορίζω denotes the act of selecting someone out of group for a purpose (BDAG s.v. "ἀφορίζω" 2, 158). In his letters, Paul uses the same verb to describe his call (Rom. 1:1; Gal. 1:15). The "work" (τὸ ἔργον) was the special task to which the Spirit had already called (προσκέκλημαι) Barnabas and Saul (BDAG s.v. "προσκαλέω" 1a, 881). The perfect tense makes it clear that the Spirit was speaking of a past calling that was still in effect (9:15–16). The laying on of hands, therefore, describes the church identifying itself with Barnabas and Saul's work (Marshall 1980, 216).

Barnabas and Saul Preach in the Synagogues of Cyprus (13:4–5)

Barnabas and Saul sail to Cyprus, where they begin proclaiming the Word of God in the Jewish synagogues on the island.

13:4–5. Sent out by the Holy Spirit (ἐκπεμφθέντες ὑπὸ τοῦ ἁγίου πνεύματος), Barnabas and Saul—accompanied by John Mark—traveled sixteen miles to the seaport of Seleucia and set sail for Cyprus (ἀπέπλευσαν εἰς Κύπρον). When they arrived in Salamis (γενόμενοι ἐν Σαλαμῖνι), they began proclaiming (κατήγγελλον, inceptive imperfect) the Word of the Lord (τὸν λόγον τοῦ θεοῦ) in the Jewish synagogues (ἐν ταῖς συναγωγαῖς τῶν Ἰουδαίων). Schnabel suggests two reasons that Barnabas and Saul chose Cyprus as their initial destination (2012, 555): Barnabas was a native of Cyprus (4:36), and believers from Cyprus and Cyrene had carried the gospel northward from Jerusalem, to Phoenicia, Cyprus, and Antioch (11:19–20).

Synagogues were natural venues in which to find potentially receptive audiences, and it became standard practice for the missionaries to begin their preaching there whenever possible (13:14; 14:1; 17:1, 10, 17; 18:4, 19; 19:8). See 15:37 for John Mark. A ὑπηρέτης refers to someone who functions as a helper, frequently in a subordinate capacity (BDAG s.v. "ὑπηρέτης" 1035). The basic idea is an individual who renders service to another. Luke does not specify the nature of the service John Mark rendered, but Timothy would fill a similar role on Paul and Silas's next round of missionary activity (16:1–5). Stott captures the dynamic involved in the sending of Barnabas and Saul nicely: "The Spirit sent them out, by instructing the church to do so, and the church sent them out, having been directed by the Spirit to do so" (1990, 218).

A Roman Official Believes the Word of God (13:6–12)

In Paphos, Barnabas and Saul encounter a magician who opposes the gospel and a proconsul who responds to it in faith.

13:6–8. The missionary team left Salamis on the eastern end of the island and traveled (διελθόντες) westward across "the whole island" (ὅλην τὴν νῆσον) until they reached Paphos on the western end. The adverbial participle διελθόντες suggests missionary activity (8:4, 40; 9:32; 10:38; 11:19). Schnabel suggests that the distance involved would have taken about seven days on foot plus the time they spent in cities along the way (2012, 557). In Paphos, they encountered two men: Bar-Jesus and Sergius Paulus.

Luke describes Bar-Jesus as a magician (μάγος) and a false prophet (ψευδοπροφήτης). The first term identifies him as "a person skilled in the use of incantations with the goal of influencing or controlling transcendent powers to overcome public or private problems" (Schnabel 2012, 557). See 8:9 on Simon Magus, who was also a magician. The second term identifies him as someone who "claimed falsely to be a medium of divine revelation" (Bruce 1988, 249). The fact that he was Jewish places him among the Jews who practiced sorcery and magic (Luke 11:19;

Acts 19:13–16), even though it was officially forbidden (Exod. 22:18; Lev. 19:26, 31; 20:6; Deut. 18:10). He most likely served as the proconsul's court astrologer (Barrett 1994, 614; Dunn 1996, 175; Larkin 1995, 194). Bock suggests that his role "would involve healing and looking for signs using formulas, incantations, amulets, and other forms of inducing discernment" (2007, 445).

Sergius Paulus was the proconsul (ἀνθύπατος) in charge of the Roman province. Luke describes him as "intelligent" (συνέτος), which describes someone who is "able to understand with discernment" (BDAG s.v. "συνέτος" 970). He also was receptive to the gospel, because he summoned (προσκαλεσάμενος) Barnabas and Saul and wanted to hear the Word of the Lord (ἐπεζήτησεν ἀκοῦσαι τὸν λόγον τοῦ θεοῦ). In contrast, Bar-Jesus "resisted" (ἀνθίστατο) Barnabas and Saul and kept on seeking (ζητῶν) to lead the proconsul away from the faith (διαστρέψαι τὸν ἀνθύπατον ἀπὸ τῆς πίστεως). Luke places the two men in stark contrast. Sergius Paulus was discerning, receptive to the truth, and ultimately believed (13:12); Bar-Jesus was deceitful (cf. 13:9), resistant to the truth, and ultimately was blinded (13:11). Bock summarizes the contrast: "they are two kinds of people who are outside the faith: one strenuously objected to it, and one is . . . open and needs to learn the first things about the faith" (2007, 447).

13:9–11a. Under the control of the Holy Spirit (πλησθεὶς πνεύματος ἁγίου), Saul confronted the magician by looking straight at him (ἀτενίσας εἰς αὐτόν), denouncing his character, attitude, and activity (Larkin 1995, 195), and pronouncing judgment on him. Regarding his character, Bar-Jesus was "full of all kinds of deceit and trickery" (CSB, πλήρης παντὸς δόλου καὶ πάσης ῥᾳδιουργίας). Regarding his attitude, he was "an enemy of all righteousness" (ESV, ἐχθρὲ πάσης δικαιοσύνης). Regarding his activity, he was continually "perverting the true ways of the Lord" (NLT, διαστρέφων τὰς ὁδοὺς τοῦ

κυρίου τὰς εὐθείας). As a result, the hand of the Lord (χεὶρ κυρίου) would cause him to be blind (τυφλός) and temporarily unable to see the sun (μὴ βλέπων τὸν ἥλιον ἄχρι καιροῦ).

The shift of name from Saul to Paul (Σαῦλος ὁ καὶ Παῦλος) most likely reflects the shift from Jewish synagogue audiences to the Roman proconsul. The fact that Luke describes Paul as "filled with the Holy Spirit" highlights the importance of the event (Barrett 1994, 616) and echoes the descriptions of Peter (4:8), Stephen (6:3), and Barnabas (11:24). The CEV renders the phrase πλήρης παντὸς δόλου καὶ πάσης ῥᾳδιουργίας colorfully as "You are a liar and a crook"; the 1961 edition of NEB translates the phrase as "an utter imposter and charlatan." The noun ῥᾳδιουργία describes someone who seeks to gain a personal end by trickery as a "con man" might (BDAG s.v. "ῥᾳδιουργία" 902–3). Righteousness (δικαιοσύνης) most likely refers to ethical behavior rather than to forensic status (Barrett 1994, 617). The verb διαστρέφω occurs with two nuances in this passage. In verse 8 it carries the sense of "mislead" or "cause to be uncertain about a belief"; in verse 10 it carries the sense of "pervert" or "cause to depart from an accepted standard" (BDAG s.v. "διαστρέφω" 237). See 11:21 on "the hand of the Lord."

13:11b–12. God acted immediately (παραχρῆμα), and "mist and darkness" (ἀχλὺς καὶ σκότος) fell upon Bar-Jesus, so that he began going around (περιάγων) looking for people to lead him by the hand (ἐζήτει χειραγωγούς). When Sergius Paulus saw what had happened (ἰδὼν . . . τὸ γεγονός), he believed (ἐπίστευσεν), because he was amazed (ἐκπλησσόμενος) at the teaching about the Lord (ἐπὶ τῇ διδαχῇ τοῦ κυρίου). In classical literature, ἀχλύς ("mist") is used "of one whom a god deprives of the power of seeing and knowing others" (LSJ, s.v. "ἀχλύς" 1, 297). The verb ἐκπλήσσω denotes being filled with amazement to the point of being overwhelmed (BDAG s.v. "ἐκπλήσσω" 308; cf. Luke 2:48; 4:32; 9:43). The participle ἐκπλησσόμενος is adverbial of cause. The genitive of τοῦ κυρίου is objective (Barrett 1994, 619).

Peterson notes that the act of blinding Bar-Jesus both removed an obstacle to faith and authenticated Paul as God's messenger (2009, 382). Although some commentators have questioned whether the proconsul was converted (Witherington 1998, 402), the explicit contrast between the two responses argues that he was (Bock 2007, 447). The focus of the episode is on the power of the gospel to overcome spiritual opposition in the context of witness to a pagan Gentile who is also a highly placed official in the Roman government. Larkin writes, "by juxtaposing the [magician's] judgment to Sergius Paulus's faith response, Luke clearly shows how the gospel's power is greater than the power of the occult" (Larkin 1995, 195).

THEOLOGICAL FOCUS

The narratival function of Acts 13:1–12 is to open the next major movement of the gospel outward from Jerusalem, Judea, and Samaria as it continues its progress toward the ends of the earth. The passage resumes Luke's account of the church in Syrian Antioch, which began as a mission church (11:19–21), became a growing church (11:22–26), and embraced the opportunity to be a cooperating church (11:27–30). In those early stages, it engages in the important ministries of edification, evangelism, cooperation, and assistance. In 13:1–12 the church reaches maturity as it becomes a sending church that engages in the ministries of mission and church planting. Under the leading of the Holy Spirit, the church in Syrian Antioch was the first church to pursue intentional mission activity. The account of Barnabas and Saul's commissioning and their initial ministry on the island of Cyprus explains how that work began and sets the stage for the work that would eventually reach "from Jerusalem and all the way around to Illyricum" (Rom. 15:19, ESV).

Theologically, Acts 13:1–12 reinforces several truths that were present in previous passages. God takes the initiative in moving his people outward in witness, as the Holy Spirit provides direction (13:2, 4; cf. 8:29; 10:19). The Holy Spirit's filling empowers Saul/Paul as he engages in ministry (13:9: cf. 4:8; 6:3; 11:24). The preaching of the gospel encounters spiritual opposition when it enters new territory (13:8–11; cf. 8:4–24). God's messenger denounces false spirituality (13:9–11a; cf. 5:3–4, 9; 8:20–24). An opponent of the gospel experiences judgment for his actions (13:11b; cf. 12:20–23). The gospel overcomes opposition (13:12; cf. 4:31; 5:41–42; 8:4; 12:24).

The focus of the passage, however, is on the power of the gospel to overcome spiritual opposition in the context of witness to a pagan Gentile who is also a highly placed official in the Roman government. Luke makes his point by contrasting the experiences of two individuals, the resistant magician, Bar-Jesus, and the receptive proconsul, Sergius Paulus. Bar-Jesus was deceitful (13:9) and resistant to the truth (13:8). Saul/Paul condemned his character, attitude, and activity. As a result, the magician experienced short-term physical blindness, ironically reflecting his longer-term spiritual blindness (13:11). Sergius Paulus was discerning (13:7) and receptive to the truth (13:7). Based on previous evidence (9:19b–21), Saul/Paul explained to him the truth about Jesus. As a result, the proconsul responded in belief (13:12). The outcome was defeat for one and deliverance for the other. From a practical perspective, their contrasting experiences also make it clear that different individuals respond to the gospel in different ways, require different styles of ministry, and arrive at different spiritual outcomes.

PREACHING AND TEACHING STRATEGIES

Exegetical/Theological Synthesis

Acts 12 ended with Herod Agrippa I dead, God's word growing and multiplying throughout Palestine, and Barnabas and

Saul back in Syrian Antioch. At this point in Luke's narrative his first-century readers would have wanted to know: What happened next? Herod had opposed the gospel. Would other civil officials respond in the same way? What did God have in mind next for the church in Antioch as well as for Barnabas and Saul? Would the gospel continue to cross geographical borders and cultural boundaries? Acts 13:1–12 begins to answer those questions by introducing the mission based in Syrian Antioch. Barnabas and Saul's initial witness in Cyprus would have been of particular interest to Theophilus and others in his circle because it featured the proconsul for the province. As an official of the Roman government, Sergius Paulus was intelligent, from the middle-class, and well connected politically. He was interested enough in spiritual things to summon Barnabas and Saul to his court because he wanted to hear the Word of God. He was, however, also under the influence of his court astrologer. His response of faith to the teaching of the Lord, despite the opposition of Bar-Jesus, represented another breakthrough for the gospel in new territory and involving a new segment of Roman society. With the original audience, twenty-first-century readers share the need to understand that God's word has the power to persuade receptive listeners of any background in any context, even in the face of spiritual opposition.

Preaching/Teaching Idea

God's word confounds the resistant and convinces the receptive.

Contemporary Connections

What does it mean?

This entire missionary journey across Cyprus is God-initiated and God-empowered. The multicultural leadership team in Antioch was not content with the past fruit they had experienced previously. They continued to worship, fast, and seek the Spirit's will. God's Spirit impressed upon them to commission Barnabas and Saul to go. These men were "sent off" by the church and "sent out by the Holy Spirit" (13:3–4), proclaiming God's word as they went from east to west across the island. Sergius Paulus was receptive to the word, but Bar-Jesus was resistant. The message intrigued Sergius, and he summoned the missionaries to hear more (13:7). The blinding of his advisor must have shocked him, but he was even more "astonished" by the message of Jesus (13:12). His receptivity results in a happy conversion, but the result with Bar-Jesus was drastically different. He immediately set to work trying to keep his boss away from faith. Saul rebuked him and struck him blind. At least for now, his resistance kept him from the kingdom.

Is it true?

The contrast between Sergius Paulus and Bar-Jesus is striking. As noted above, Sergius is distinguished for his discernment; Bar-Jesus is known for his deceit. Bar-Jesus sought to bar Sergius from Jesus, fancying himself as the one who saw rightly. For that villainy, Saul struck him blind for a time to be led around by the hand, which is ironic because Saul himself was struck blind for a time to be led around by the hand. So, the resistant false prophet became as blind physically as he was spiritually. The receptive proconsul *sees* it all (13:12) and responds in faith. It is not just Sergius who is receptive to God's word, but Antioch's leadership is, too. By humbly submitting themselves to God in worship and fasting, these men were in tune to hear God call them to action. They readily responded, sending off their best and brightest leaders for the sake of Cyprus and beyond.

Now what?

Am I receptive to the Word of God? Receptivity looks different for unbelievers and believers, but there is evidence in both. Like Sergius, an unbeliever who is sympathetic and curious about God's Word seeks out answers. She will reach out to learn more, ask good questions, listen well, and respond to the evidence staring back at her. A resistant unbeliever will do no such thing. He does not want to learn more, listens only to argue, asks questions to set traps, and ignores evidence.

For a believer, receptivity is even more effusive in its welcome. For Antioch's leadership and for us, it means seeking the Lord in worship, prayer, fasting, and discernment. It means surrounding ourselves with like-minded believers doing the same. It also means responding when the Lord calls us to hard and sacrificial things. These are the fruits of a heart of stone that's been made into a heart of flesh to receive God and his Word.

Creativity in Presentation

Bar-Jesus's evil hold on the proconsul Sergius Paulus reminds us of Grima Wormtongue in *The Lord of the Rings: The Two Towers*. Grima was the chief advisor to King Theoden of Rohan. Tolkien described him with a pale face and a pale tongue. The movie depicts him as a deathly white greasy figure with his eyebrows shaved off. Gandalf thinks him a snake. It soon becomes apparent that Grima works for evil Saruman and has darkly influenced the king for evil. Ultimately, the spell breaks, Theoden shakes off the dulling of deceit, and he joins the forces of good in the fight.

A creative presentation might show that film clip or describe the scene. Of course, the movie's depiction works hard to help the audience identify Grima as evil right away. It is essential that we see him as he is, even before the king does. In our text, however, we have no indication that Bar-Jesus's appearance held any sinister clues. He probably did not shave his eyebrows. Clearly, Sergius Paulus, who was "a man of intelligence," trusted him (13:7). Sergius Paulus could not see Bar-Jesus for what he was, but Paul could. Paul is able to "look intently" (13:9) and see right through his evil counsel. Such a presentation could go on to contrast two audiences: one that is resistant to God's will and word and one that is receptive. Find the differences in the text and then expound on how we today exhibit those differences. Strikingly, the receptive see even more keenly while the resistant lose what little sight they had.

God's word confounds the resistant and convinces the receptive.

- God's word goes forth (13:1–6).

- God's word confounds those who resist him (13:7–11).

- God's word convinces those who are receptive to him (13:12).

DISCUSSION QUESTIONS

1. What principles can you draw from this passage about who sends missionaries? What roles do the local church and the Holy Spirit play?

2. Why did Barnabas and Saul decide to begin their travels by sailing to Cyprus? What principle can you draw from their decision?

3. Why did Barnabas and Saul begin their preaching in Jewish synagogues? What principle can you draw from their practice?

4. Is Saul/Paul's action of denouncing Bar-Jesus normative for Christians today? Why or why not? If so, what guidelines apply?

5. Why was Sergius Paulus's interest in and openness to the gospel significant for the progress of the church?

Acts 13:13–52

EXEGETICAL IDEA

Paul and Barnabas's ministry in Pisidian Antioch began with preaching in the synagogue, resulted in conversions followed by Jewish opposition, and led them to shift their focus to the Gentiles.

THEOLOGICAL FOCUS

The gospel message and mandate do not change, even if the mission strategy must.

PREACHING IDEA

Mission must be adaptable in its approach but consistent in its message.

PREACHING POINTERS

Have you ever faced the need to change direction—whether in your own life or in ministry? How did you decide which direction to take? What was negotiable? What was nonnegotiable? What did you continue? What did you discontinue? Why? That was the challenge Paul and Barnabas faced during their ministry in Pisidian Antioch. They were following their usual strategy, and everything seemed to be going well, with conversions among both Jews and Gentiles. Then, things went off the rails when Jews in the city stirred up prominent civic leaders to begin a persecution against the missionaries. How did they respond? What aspects of their ministry changed? What aspects remained constant? What lessons can we learn from their approach? A look at Acts 13:13–52 helps us with the answers to those questions.

People today should be able to relate to individuals who are invited to speak in public settings, opportunities provided by receptive audiences, and divisions over religious differences. They should also be able to relate to people becoming jealous over the success of others and to people seeking the support of prominent members of society. The passage corrects any suggestion that the Jews are somehow irrelevant to God's plan, or that a witness to the Gentiles is somehow a change in direction to that plan. It also corrects the idea that it is wrong to change ministry strategy or that it is necessary to pursue a particular strategy indefinitely if it is not productive. The passage commends the ability to contextualize the gospel message to different audiences, the ability to apply Scripture to the circumstances of ministry, and the ability to discern when changes in ministry strategy might be needed because of complications and/or challenges. Overall, the passage commends the need to understand that the gospel message and mandate do not change even if the mission strategy must and to adopt an approach to ministry that is adaptable but consistent with a mission God has launched.

WITNESS IN PISIDIAN ANTIOCH (13:13–52)

LITERARY STRUCTURE AND THEMES (ACTS 13:13–52)

The passage begins with a brief travel narrative that moves the missionary team from the island of Cyprus to the highlands of South Galatia (13:13–15). The centerpiece of the passage is a synagogue homily that Paul delivers in response to an invitation by the synagogue leaders (13:16–41). After Paul's message, a longer narrative section describes the events that followed on that Sabbath and the next (13:42–52).

- ***Traveling Inland from Perga to Pisidian Antioch (13:13–15)***
- ***Preaching in the Synagogue (13:16–41)***
- ***Turning to the Gentiles (13:42–52)***

EXPOSITION

Paul and Barnabas's ministry in Cyprus had included preaching in Jewish synagogues, although Luke passed over that activity briefly in order to focus on their encounter with Sergius Paulus and Bar-Jesus (13:1–12). During their time in Pisidian Antioch, Luke provides a closer look at Paul's synagogue preaching, as he delivered a message in response to an invitation by the synagogue leaders. Barrett notes the correspondence between his message and a recognized form of a synagogue homily (1994, 624). His homily began with a survey of Israel's history as background to his thesis that Jesus was the promised Savior from the offspring of David. Two proofs, centered on Jesus's death and resurrection, supported Paul's thesis and led to the conclusion that forgiveness and justification are available in Jesus to everyone who believes.

13:16–22	Background (*narratio*)	God led Israel out of Egypt, brought them into Canaan, and raised up David to be their king.
13:23–25	Thesis (*propositio*)	Jesus is the offspring of David and the promised Savior, whom John the Baptist proclaimed.
13:26–37	Proofs (*confirmatio*)	Proof #1: Jesus was crucified and buried.
		Proof #2: God raised Jesus from the dead.
13:38–41	Conclusion (*peroratio*)	Forgiveness of sins and justification are available to everyone who believes.

Paul's message also included the six essentials of the gospel, with a particularly Pauline nuance. Scripture runs throughout the message, including a review of Israel's history from the patriarchs to David (13:17–22, 27, 29, 33, 34, 35). The truths that Christ must suffer (13:27–29) and rise (13:30, 33, 37) form the two proofs that support his thesis. The mention of John the Baptist's preaching introduces the call for repentance (13:24). Forgiveness of sins constitutes one of the blessings of salvation (13:38). The characteristic Pauline mention of justification constitutes the other (13:38–39), replacing the promise of the Holy Spirit.

The events following Paul's homily included an initial positive response by many of the Jews and Godfearing proselytes. When the Jews saw the crowds that gathered on the next Sabbath and became hostile, Paul and Barnabas turned to the Gentiles. Increased opposition led them to move on to Iconium, in a pattern that would recur frequently in Paul's missionary travels.

Traveling Inland from Perga to Pisidian Antioch (13:13–15)

After landing in Perga, Paul and Barnabas travel inland to Pisidian Antioch, where they enter the synagogue and share a word of encouragement.

13:13–14a. From Cyprus, the team sailed (ἀναχθέντες) north to Perga in Pamphylia on the southern coast of Asia Minor, a trip of approximately 150 miles. At that point, John Mark left the team (ἀποχωρήσας ἀπ' αὐτῶν) and returned (ὑπέστρεψεν) to Jerusalem. From Perga, Paul and Barnabas traveled (διελθόντες) inland and arrived (παρεγένοντο) at the Roman colony of Pisidian Antioch. "Paul and his companions" (ESV, οἱ περὶ Παῦλον) marks Paul as the team's leader. Luke does not explain John Mark's departure, but after dismissing six possible explanations for his departure, Erbey Galvan Valdez argues for theological differences between John Mark and Paul (2020, 50–56).

In other contexts, διελθόντες suggests a preaching tour, although Barrett rejects that nuance in this passage without explanation (1994, 627). The direct route from Perga to Pisidian Antioch ran northward for approximately 115 miles, although Mark Wilson suggests that a more westerly route of 155 miles would have been "by far the easiest and probably the safest" (2009, 482). Antioch was actually in the ancient region of Phrygia, near the border of Pisidia. Some documents refer to it as "Antioch toward Pisidia" (Ἀντιόχεια πρὸς Πισιδίαν; cf. Barrett 1994, 627) to distinguish

it from the other Antioch in Phrygia. It was the main garrison city for South Galatia and the center of civil administration for the region, with a Jewish population of approximately two thousand families (Josephus, *A.J.* 12.3.4).

Scholars have often raised the question of why Paul and Barnabas left Perga so quickly and traveled inland to Pisidian Antioch. The most common suggestion, tracing back to Sir William Ramsay, is that Paul had fallen sick with malaria or another illness, and the team wanted to reach the healthier highlands farther inland (Stott 1990, 221). There is, however, little evidence to support that explanation. Another suggestion is that Paul saw South Galatia as the next logical region to evangelize, since it lay immediately to the west of his home province of Cilicia (Allen 1977, 12). It would have been easier, however, to travel westward from Syrian Antioch through Cilicia to reach the region from the east as Paul and Silas did, when they revisited the churches in South Galatia (15:41–16:6). Wilson offers the intriguing idea, based on ancient inscriptions noted by Stephen Mitchell, that Sergius Paulus was originally from Pisidian Antioch. After his conversion, the proconsul suggested that the team visit his home city and provided letters of introduction for them (Wilson 2016, 230–32). Thomas Davis and Wilson suggest elsewhere that Paphos was a more natural point of departure for North Africa and Egypt and that Barnabas and Saul might have originally intended to follow a circuit from Cyprus to Cyrene to Alexandria and back to Palestine and Syria. At the proconsul's urging, however, they changed their plans and headed for the Roman colony and governmental center of Pisidian Antioch (Davis 2016, 1–10). Such an approach would align well with Paul and Silas's later strategy in Macedonia and Achaia.

13:14b–15. On the next Sabbath day (τῇ ἡμέρᾳ τῶν σαββάτων), Paul and Barnabas entered the synagogue (εἰσελθόντες εἰς τὴν συναγωγήν) and took seats (ἐκάθισαν). Following the readings from the Law and the Prophets (μετὰ δὲ τὴν ἀνάγνωσιν τοῦ νόμου καὶ τῶν προφητῶν) that were part of the regular synagogue order of service, the leaders of the synagogue (οἱ ἀρχισυνάγωγοι) invited the visitors to share a word of encouragement (λόγος παρακλήσεως) they might have for those who were assembled (πρὸς τὸν λαόν). Schnabel suggests that Paul and Barnabas would have introduced themselves earlier in the week and that the synagogue officials would have known that Paul had trained as a rabbi under Gamaliel (2012, 574). Others have suggested that the reading from the Law was Deuteronomy 4:25–46 and the reading from the Prophets was 2 Samuel 7:6–16 (Bruce 1988, 254).

Preaching in the Synagogue (13:16–41)

Paul explains that Jesus fulfills the OT promise of salvation and offers forgiveness of sins and justification to everyone who believes in him.

13:16–25. Paul rose (ἀναστάς), motioned with his hand (κατασείσας τῇ χειρί), addressed the gathering, and asked them to listen to what he had to say (ἀκούσατε). By addressing both Jews (ἄνδρες Ἰσραηλῖται) and Gentiles (οἱ φοβούμενοι τὸν θεόν) in his opening, Paul signaled his understanding that the gospel was intended for an inclusive audience (13:26, 43). As background for his intended thesis, he began with a brief survey of Israel's history, covering one thousand years from the patriarchs to King David. In rapid succession, Paul described ten of God's powerful acts on behalf of Israel. He chose the fathers (13:17a; cf. Deut. 7:6–7), made the people great in Egypt (13:17b; cf. Exod. 1:7), brought them out with a demonstration of his power (13:17c; cf. Exod. 12:51), and put up with them in the wilderness (13:18; cf. Num. 14:34). He destroyed seven nations in Canaan (13:19a;

cf. Deut. 7:1), distributed the land as an inheritance (13:19b; cf. Josh. 14:1), and gave the people both judges (13:20a; cf. Judg. 2:16) and Samuel the prophet (13:20b; cf. 1 Sam 3:20). He gave them Saul in response to their request for a king (13:21; cf. 1 Sam. 10:20–21) and raised up David as the king who would do all of God's will (13:22; cf. 1 Sam. 13:14).

Longenecker suggests that the Paul's survey is "a confessional summary that for Jews epitomized the essence of their faith" (1980, 425). Ἐξελέξατο ("he chose our fathers") in verse 17 is an indirect middle and highlights God's personal interest in his choice of Israel. Frederick Danker defines ὑψόω as "to cause enhancement in honor, fame, position, power, of fortune" and suggests "made them great in numbers and in power" for ὕψωσεν in verse 17 (BDAG s.v. "ὑψόω" 2, 1046). Later in the same verse, μετὰ βραχίονος ὑψηλοῦ ("with an uplifted arm") describes manner (i.e., powerfully) rather than means (Culy and Parsons 2003, 253). Ἐτροποφόρησεν ("he put up with them") in verse 18 describes bearing with someone's manner or moods (BDAG s.v. "τροποφορέω" 1017). LXX uses the same verb in Deuteronomy 1:31 to describe Israel's wilderness experience, and NASB translates the verse as "the Lord your God carried you, just as a man carries his son." Bock suggests that the expression highlights God's faithfulness despite Israel's faithlessness (2007, 452).

Καθελών (from καθαιρέω) in verse 19 carries the sense of "to conquer or destroy." In Luke 1:52, it describes God's act of bringing rulers down from their thrones. Also in verse 19, κατεκληρονόμησεν ("he distributed their land as an inheritance") describes the act of giving someone something as a rightful possession (BDAG s.v. "κατακληροδοτέω" 518) or causing someone to receive something of value as a gift (L&N §57.135). The 450 years Paul mentions in verse 20 (ἔτεσιν τετρακοσίοις καὶ πεντήκοντα) encompasses the sojourn in Egypt (four hundred years), the wilderness wandering (forty years), and the conquest of the land (ten years). The detail that Saul was "a man from the tribe of Benjamin" (ἄνδρα ἐκ φυλῆς Βενιαμείν) in verse 21 echoes Paul's own heritage (Rom. 11:1; Phil. 3:5). Paul's statement that God "raised David" (ἤγειρεν τὸν Δαυίδ) in verse 22 refers to his act of bringing David on the scene of history. Bock points out that ἐγείρω (cf. 13:30, 37) is an important link word for the passage (2007, 452).

13:23–25. Paul then jumped forward in history one thousand years and introduced his thesis that Jesus was the offspring of David, the promised Savior, whom John the Baptist proclaimed. It was from David's seed (τούτου . . . ἀπὸ τοῦ σπέρματος) and according to his promise to David (κατ' ἐπαγγελίαν) that God brought to Israel (ἤγαγεν τῷ Ἰσραήλ) a Savior, who was Jesus (σωτῆρα Ἰησοῦν). Jesus and his resurrection were, therefore, the "climax of salvation-history" (Hansen 1967, 300), because all of Israel's history led to him and his work on the cross. John the Baptist, however, preceded Jesus, and Paul summarized John's ministry succinctly. First, John's public ministry preceded that of Jesus (πρὸ προσώπου τῆς εἰσόδου αὐτοῦ; cf. Mark 1:2). Second, John proclaimed in advance a baptism of repentance (προκηρύξαντος . . . βάπτισμα μετανοίας; cf. Luke 3:3) to all the people of Israel (παντὶ τῷ λαῷ Ἰσραήλ; cf. Luke 3:7–14). Finally, while John was finishing his work (ὡς ἐπλήρου Ἰωάννης τὸν δρόμον), he repeatedly (ἔλεγεν) pointed forward to Jesus, whose sandal he was not worthy to untie (ἰδοὺ ἔρχεται μετ' ἐμὲ οὗ οὐκ εἰμὶ ἄξιος τὸ ὑπόδημα τῶν ποδῶν λῦσαι; cf. Luke 3:16).

In verse 23, τούτου is fronted to make explicit the connection to David, and σωτῆρα Ἰησοῦν is delayed to the end of the clause for emphasis. The verse also includes a textual variant that replaces ἤγαγεν ("brought") with ἤγειρεν ("raised"). The latter reading is most likely a scribal alteration (*TCGNT*, 359), influenced by verse 22 and possibly added to form an *inclusio* with verse 37. It is interesting that,

in a synagogue context, Paul chose to emphasize Jesus as Savior (σωτήρ) rather than as Messiah (χριστός). Larkin suggests, "[Paul] avoids the use of Messiah, with its connotations of a purely political deliverer. He indicates that the liberation is much greater, for God is its source, bringing the final salvation according to the Old Testament" (1995, 199). Most commentators conclude that the promise (κατ' ἐπαγγελίαν) in verse 23 is God's promise to David in 2 Samuel 7:12–16 (Marshall 1980, 224), although Longenecker suggests that the underlying OT allusion is to Isaiah 11:1–11 (1981, 425). By including John the Baptist at this point in his homily, Paul marks John's ministry as beginning a new era in what God was doing (Marshall 1980, 224), clarifies John's role in preparing the way for Jesus, and echoes Peter's mention of John in 10:37.

13:26–29. Paul began the second major section of his homily with an address (ἄνδρες ἀδελφοί, υἱοὶ γένους Ἀβραὰμ καὶ οἱ ἐν ὑμῖν φοβούμενοι τὸν θεόν) that reaffirmed the inclusive scope of the gospel (13:16). In support of his thesis, Paul then offered two proofs that Jesus was the Savior God had promised to send to Israel (13:23). The first proof was that Jesus died as the OT had promised in "the message about this salvation" (ὁ λόγος τῆς σωτηρίας ταύτης, objective genitive) that was sent out (ἐξαπεστάλη) to his listeners. "This salvation" connects back to Jesus's designation as Savior in 13:23. The voices of the prophets (τὰς φωνὰς τῶν προφητῶν) that were read every Sabbath (τὰς κατὰ πᾶν σάββατον ἀναγινωσκομένας) predicted his death, and the actions of his executioners both fulfilled (ἐπλήρωσαν) what the prophets had said and completed (ἐτέλεσαν) everything that had been written about him (πάντα τὰ περὶ αὐτοῦ γεγραμμένα).

Those executioners included both the inhabitants of Jerusalem (οἱ κατοικοῦντες ἐν Ἰερουσαλήμ) and their rulers (οἱ ἄρχοντες αὐτῶν). Both groups acted out of ignorance (ἀγνοήσαντες), condemned him (κρίναντες) despite finding no grounds for it (μηδεμίαν αἰτίαν θανάτου εὑρόντες), and asked Pilate to execute him (ἠτήσαντο Πιλᾶτον ἀναιρεθῆναι αὐτόν). As confirmation of his death, Jesus's executioners took him down from the cross (καθελόντες ἀπὸ τοῦ ξύλου), and his followers placed him in a tomb (ἔθηκαν εἰς μνημεῖον). The OT passages that lay behind Paul's exposition were most likely Deuteronomy 21:22–23, Isaiah 53:3–9, and Psalm 118:22 (Marshall, 1980, 225; Schnabel, 2012, 579). See 3:17 for the idea of "acted out of ignorance" and 10:39 for ἀναιρέω.

13:30–37. Paul's second proof was that God raised Jesus from the dead (ὁ θεὸς ἤγειρεν αὐτὸν ἐκ νεκρῶν). As confirmation of his resurrection, Jesus appeared for many days (ὤφθη ἐπὶ ἡμέρας πλείους) to those who had traveled with him (τοῖς συναναβᾶσιν αὐτῷ) from Galilee to Jerusalem (ἀπὸ τῆς Γαλιλαίας εἰς Ἰερουσαλήμ). Those to whom he appeared were now his witnesses to the people (οἵτινες νῦν εἰσιν μάρτυρες αὐτοῦ πρὸς τὸν λαόν), who shared with them the good news (ὑμᾶς εὐαγγελιζόμεθα) about the promise made to the fathers (τὴν πρὸς τοὺς πατέρας ἐπαγγελίαν γενομένην). By raising Jesus (ἀναστήσας Ἰησοῦν), God had made this promise come to fruition (ταύτην ὁ θεὸς ἐκπεπλήρωκεν) in three ways. First, Psalm 2:7 confirmed that God appointed Jesus as the divine Son who would carry out salvation (υἱός μου εἶ σύ, ἐγὼ σήμερον γεγέννηκά σε; cf. Bock 2007, 456). Second, Isaiah 55:3 confirmed that, through Jesus, God renewed the covenantal promise of salvation (δώσω ὑμῖν τὰ ὅσια Δαυὶδ τὰ πιστά; cf. Beale and Carson 2007, 586). Third, Psalm 16:10 confirmed that God made certain Jesus would not see decay (οὐ δώσεις τὸν ὅσιόν σου ἰδεῖν διαφθοράν), and the indestructible life (cf. Heb. 7:16) that was his would enable him to be the source of eternal life/salvation (13:46, 48; cf. Heb. 5:9). The third

prophecy must apply to Jesus, because David served his own generation (Δαυὶδ ἰδίᾳ γενεᾷ ὑπηρετήσας), fell asleep (ἐκοιμήθη), was laid among his fathers (προσετέθη πρὸς τοὺς πατέρας αὐτοῦ), and saw corruption (εἶδεν διαφθοράν). Jesus, however, did not see corruption (οὐκ εἶδεν διαφθοράν), because God raised him (ὃν ὁ θεὸς ἤγειρεν).

The promise might have been made to the fathers (πρὸς τοὺς πατέρας), but it was immediately applicable to Paul's audience. The message of salvation was sent "to you" (ἡμῖν; 13:26). Paul and Barnabas shared the good news with "you" (ὑμᾶς; 13:32). God brought the promise to fruition "for us, their children" (τοῖς τέκνοις αὐτῶν ἡμῖν; 13:33). The holy and sure blessings of David are "for you" (ὑμῖν; 13:35). In his conclusion, Paul would make it clear that forgiveness of sins was being announced "to you" (ὑμῖν; 13:38). In verse 31, "from Galilee to Jerusalem" echoes 10:37, and "witnesses" echoes 1:8; 2:32; 5:32; and 10:39. In verse 33, ταύτην is fronted to focus attention on the promise, and the verb ἐκπληρόω denotes the act of causing something to come to fruition (BDAG s.v. "ἐκπληρόω" 308). The phrase "for us, their children" (τοῖς τέκνοις αὐτῶν ἡμῖν) in verse 33 is complicated by the text critical question of whether the original reading included αὐτῶν (C³, E, 33) or ἡμῶν (P⁷⁴, א, A, B, C*, D). See Metzger for a discussion (*TCGNT*, 362). Paul's quotation of Psalm 16:10 in verse 35 echoes Peter's use in 2:27. Longenecker notes the correspondence between Paul's presentation in 13:28–31 and his confessional statement in 1 Corinthians 15:3–8 (1980, 425): Jesus died (13:28; cf. 1 Cor. 15:3), was buried (13:29; cf. 1 Cor. 15:4a), was raised (13:30; cf. 1 Cor. 15:4b), and appeared to witnesses (13:31; cf. 1 Cor. 15:5–8).

13:38–41. With a third instance of direct address (ἄνδρες ἀδελφοί), Paul moved to his conclusion (οὖν) that forgiveness of sins and justification are available to everyone who believes. What he has said is something that is imperative for his listeners to know (γνωστὸν ἔστω ὑμῖν) and included two key elements. The first is forgiveness of sins (ἄφεσις ἁμαρτιῶν), which is being announced (καταγγέλλεται, progressive present) to them (ὑμῖν) through Jesus (διὰ τούτου). The second element is that by Jesus (ἐν τούτῳ) everyone who is believing (πᾶς ὁ πιστεύων) is being justified (δικαιοῦται) from everything (ἀπὸ πάντων) the law of Moses (ἐν νόμῳ Μωϋσέως) was unable to address (οὐκ ἠδυνήθητε . . . δικαιωθῆναι). Paul then stressed the seriousness of the decision before his listeners by warning them (βλέπετε) not to let come upon them (μὴ ἐπέλθῃ) the circumstances about which the prophets had spoken (τὸ εἰρημένον ἐν τοῖς προφήταις). God was doing a work in their days (ἔργον ἐργάζομαι ἐγὼ ἐν ταῖς ἡμέραις ὑμῶν) that they would never believe (ὃ οὐ μὴ πιστεύσητε) unless someone explained it to them in detail (ἐάν τις ἐκδιηγῆται ὑμῖν). If they treated it with contempt (οἱ καταφρονηταί; cf. BDAG s.v. "καταφρονέω" 1, 529), they would be destroyed (ἀφανίσθητε).

Forgiveness of sins (ἄφεσις ἁμαρτιῶν) has been one of the essentials of the gospel witness throughout Acts (2:38; 3:19; 5:31; 10:43); being justified (δικαιόω) in the sense of conferring forensic status has not. Rather, "righteous" (δίκαιος) and "righteousness" (δικαιοσύνη) have denoted ethical behavior (3:14; 4:19; 10:22, 35; 13:10). In 13:38–39, however, the verbs carry the Pauline sense of God's act of declaring a person righteous (BDAG s.v. "δικαιόω" 2bβ, 249), and Paul declares that what the Mosaic Law could not do, Jesus could. Jesus is, in fact, the intermediate agent through whom both forgiveness and justification are available. Both διὰ τούτου (13:38) and ἐν τούτῳ (13:39) are fronted in their respective clauses and have Jesus as their antecedent (Hansen 1967, 305). "Everyone who is believing" (πᾶς ὁ πιστεύων) would include both the Jews and the Gentiles in the audience (Larkin 1995, 204). The final

OT quotation in Paul's homily was Habakkuk 1:5 (LXX). In the prophet's time, the "work" (ἔργον) God was doing was judgment through the agency of the Chaldeans (Hab. 1:5). In the time of Paul's first-century audience, it denoted either the apostolic mission (Beale and Carson 2007, 587) or, more likely, Jesus's resurrection and the salvation that came from it (Hansen 1967, 306). The verb ἐκδιηγέομαι describes the process of giving a detailed account (BDAG s.v. "ἐκδιηγέομαι" 245), which is what Paul had been doing in his homily. His point in quoting Habakkuk was that the listeners ignored the account at their peril.

Turning to the Gentiles (13:42–52)

On the next Sabbath, when the Jews stir up opposition against them, Paul and Barnabas turn to the Gentiles, leave the city, and move on to Iconium.

13:42–43. While Paul and Barnabas were leaving (ἐξιόντων αὐτῶν, genitive absolute), the synagogue attenders kept on asking them (παρεκάλουν, iterative imperfect) to return on the next Sabbath (εἰς τὸ μεταξὺ σάββατον) to tell them more (λαληθῆναι αὐτοῖς τὰ ῥήματα ταῦτα). After the synagogue meeting was over (λυθείσης τῆς συναγωγῆς, genitive absolute), many of those present followed (ἠκολούθησαν) Paul and Barnabas, who kept on persuading them (ἔπειθον, iterative imperfect) to continue in the grace of God (προσμένειν τῇ χάριτι τοῦ θεοῦ). When used as an adverb, μεταξύ marks an interval that separates, either of space or time, and carries the sense of "afterward, next" (BDAG s.v. "μεταξύ" 1, 641). The phrase εἰς τὸ μεταξὺ σάββατον, therefore, is best translated "on the next Sabbath." The groups that followed Paul and Barnabas included "many of the Jews and the devout proselytes" (πολλοὶ τῶν Ἰουδαίων καὶ τῶν σεβομένων προσηλύτων). The latter group most likely refers to Gentiles who regularly attended the synagogue and whom Paul had addressed in 13:16 (οἱ φοβούμενοι τὸν θεόν) and 13:26 (οἱ ἐν ὑμῖν φοβούμενοι τὸν θεόν). The verb προσμένω describes the act of continuing in something without wavering (BDAG s.v. "προσμένω" 1b, 883; cf. 11:23). Barrett's conclusion seems correct that the phrase "implies arrival at a point at which the hearers are encourged to continue; they have become Christians and must not give up their new faith" (1994, 654).

> TEXTUAL ANALYSIS: "While they were leaving, they were asking . . ."
> The ambiguity of the subjects in verse 42 led to a variety of textual variants. One Byzantine reading has the Jews leaving the synagogue (ἐξιόντων ἐκ τῆς συναγθφῆς τῶν Ἰουδαίων). Another has the Gentiles asking Paul and Barnabas to return on the next Sabbath (παρεκάλουν τὰ ἔθνη εἰς τὸ μεταξὺ σάββατον). If the UBS[5] reading is preferred (ἐξιόντων αὐτῶν παρεκάλουν εἰς τὸ μεταξὺ σάββατον), the best understanding is to take Paul and Barnabas as the subject of the genitive absolute and the synagogue attenders as the subject of the finite verb (e.g., NET).

13:44–45. On the following Sabbath (τῷ ἐρχομένῳ σαββάτῳ), nearly the entire city (σχεδὸν πᾶσα ἡ πόλις) assembled (συνήχθη) to hear Paul and Barnabas speak the Word of the Lord (ἀκοῦσαι τὸν λόγον τοῦ κυρίου). When the Jews saw the crowds (ἰδόντες οἱ Ἰουδαῖοι τοὺς ὄχλους), however, they were filled with jealousy (ἐπλήσθησαν ζήλου) and began contradicting (ἀντέλεγον, inceptive imperfect) and slandering (βλασφημοῦντες) Paul. It is not necessary to understand "almost the whole city" (σχεδὸν πᾶσα ἡ πόλις) as exaggeration (Marshall 1980, 229). Schnabel suggests that the crowd might have included several thousand people, especially if Paul and Barnabas had arrived with letters of introduction from Sergius Paulus on Cyprus and had met the leading families in the city (2012, 586). See 5:17 for ζῆλος. Βλασφημοῦντες is an adverbial participle of manner. When applied to a human

being the verb carries the sense of speaking in a disrespectful way that demeans, denigrates, or maligns (BDAG s.v. "βλασφημέω" b, 178).

13:46–47. In response, Paul and Barnabas spoke out boldly (παρρησιασάμενοι) and declared four truths. First, it was necessary (ἀναγκαῖον) for the Word of God to be spoken (λαληθῆναι τὸν λόγον τοῦ θεοῦ) to them first (ὑμῖν . . . πρῶτον). Second, in rejecting (ἀπωθεῖσθε) the message, the listeners had passed judgment on themselves (κρίνετε ἑαυτούς) as unworthy of eternal life (οὐκ ἀξίους . . . τῆς αἰωνίου ζωῆς). Third, the good news of salvation was not limited to Jews alone (ἰδοὺ στρεφόμεθα εἰς τὰ ἔθνη). Fourth, their action in turning to the Gentiles was in accordance with the Lord's command (οὕτως ἐντέταλται ἡμῖν ὁ κύριος) in Isaiah 49:6. See 9:27–28 for παρρησιάζομαι (cf. 2:29; 4:13, 29, 31 for the cognate noun παρρησία).

The idea of "to the Jews first" was an important Pauline concept (Rom. 1:16; 2:9) that would guide his missionary strategy. The verb ἀπωθέω describes the action of pushing aside, rejecting, or repudiating (BDAG s.v. "ἀπωθέω" 126–27). Although the idea of eternal life (τῆς αἰωνίου ζωῆς) occurs only twice in Acts (13:46, 48), it is clearly a Pauline concept (Rom. 2:7; 5:21; 6:22, 23; Gal. 6:8; 1 Tim. 1:16; 6:12; Titus 1:2; 3:7). The perfect tense of ἐντέταλται highlights the continuing validity of the Lord's command. Peterson notes that by turning to the Gentiles, Paul and Barnabas fulfilled the OT servant's role (2009, 396). First Israel, then Jesus, and now the church were responsible to carry the light of God's salvation to the ends of the earth (Isa. 42:6; 49:6; 51:4; 60:1–3; cf. Luke 2:32).

13:48–50. When the Gentiles in the crowd heard Paul and Barnabas's declaration (ἀκούοντα τὰ ἔθνη), they responded in three ways. They began rejoicing and glorifying (ἔχαιρον καὶ ἐδόξαζον) the Word of the Lord (τὸν λόγον τοῦ κυρίου), they placed their faith in Jesus (ἐπίστευσαν), and they began carrying (διεφέρετο) the message about Jesus (ὁ λόγος τοῦ κυρίου) throughout the entire region (δι᾽ ὅλης τῆς χώρας). In contrast, the Jews also responded in three diametrically opposite ways. They aroused the emotions (παρώτρυναν) of the devout women of high standing (τὰς σεβομένας γυναῖκας τὰς εὐσχήμονας) and the leaders of the city (τοὺς πρώτους τῆς πόλεως), they stirred up persecution (ἐπήγειραν διωγμόν) against Paul and Barnabas, and they drove them out of the region (ἐξέβαλον αὐτοὺς ἀπὸ τῶν ὁρίων αὐτῶν).

The three inceptive imperfects (ἔχαιρον . . . ἐδόξαζον . . . διεφέρετο) highlight both the beginning and the continuing expression of the Gentiles' response. The description of the Gentiles who believed as "as many as had been appointed to eternal life" (ὅσοι ἦσαν τεταγμένοι εἰς ζωὴν αἰώνιον) combines the perfect tense with a divine passive to highlight God's sovereign work over salvation (Bock 2007, 464). Barrett writes, "The present verse is as unqualified a statement of absolute predestination . . . as is found anywhere in the NT. Those believed who were appointed . . . to do so. The rest, one infers, did not believe, did not receive eternal life, and thus were appointed to death" (1994, 658). The verb παροτρύνω describes the act of stirring up strong emotion against someone or something (BDAG s.v. "παροτρύνω" 780). The outward spread of the gospel from a major population center is a recurring pattern in Acts (5:16; 13:49; 19:10).

13:51–52. Following both Jesus's instructions to his disciples (Luke 9:5; 10:11) and his practice of withdrawing in the face of opposition (Matt. 12:15; 14:13; 15:21), Paul and Barnabas shook off the dust of their feet (ἐκτιναξάμενοι τὸν κονιορτὸν τῶν ποδῶν) against the Jews (ἐπ᾽ αὐτούς), and traveled approximately ninety miles east-southeast along the Via Sebaste to Iconium (ἦλθον εἰς Ἰκόνιον). Luke closes the account with the note that, despite the opposition raised by the Jews, the disciples (οἱ μαθηταί) were consistently being filled (ἐπληροῦντο, progressive imperfect) with joy (χαρᾶς) and the Holy Spirit (πνεύματος ἁγίου). Bruce notes that the gesture of shaking off the dust of the feet showed that "the community against which it was directed was doomed (possibly self-doomed) to destruction" (1988, 268). Marshall writes that it was "tantamount to regarding [the residents] as pagan Gentiles" (1980, 231).

Joy (χαρά) was one of the results of Philip's ministry in Samaria (cf. 8:8), and being filled with the Holy Spirit regularly characterized the early disciples (2:4; 4:31; 6:3, 5; 7:55; 9:17; 11:24; 13:9). Although Larkin, Longenecker, and some English versions understand "the disciples" to refer to the believers in Antioch (Larkin 1995, 208; Longenecker 1980, 430; GNB; CEV), the conjunction τε appears to connect the disciples to Paul and Barnabas, who shook off the dust of their feet against the Jews in Antioch (Marshall 1981, 231; Peterson 2009, 400; Schnabel 2012, 591).

THEOLOGICAL FOCUS

Acts 13:13–52 continues Luke's narrative of Paul and Barnabas's evangelistic activity by relating their ministry in the South Galatian city of Pisidian Antioch. The account provides an example of Paul's preaching in Jewish synagogues, the mixed responses of the listeners, and the theological rationale for the strategy Paul articulated in Romans as "to the Jew first and also to the Greek" (Rom. 1:16; 2:9). The account also continues the series of parallels between Paul's ministry and Peter's ministry. In 13:1–13, Paul's rebuke of spiritual opposition on Cyprus corresponded to Peter's rebuke of Simon Magus in Samaria (8:14–24). Now in 13:13–52, Paul's preaching in Pisidian Antioch corresponds to Peter's preaching at Pentecost (2:14–40).

The series will continue in 14:8–18, when Paul will heal a man who is lame from his mother's womb and follow the healing with a message as Peter did (3:1–26). Together, Acts 13–14 serve as a paradigm for the witness of the mission based in Antioch in the same way that Acts 2–5 served as a paradigm for the witness of the mission based in Jerusalem (Peterson 2009, 383, who limits the parallel to Acts 13 and Acts 2).

Theologically, Acts 13:13–52 demonstrates the continuity of Paul's message and mission strategy with that of Peter and the original disciples. Dunn provides a good summary of the parallels between Paul's message in the synagogue in Pisidian Antioch and Peter's message at Pentecost (1996, 177). Both messages begin with a contextualized introduction (13:16–25; cf. 2:14–21), the core of each message focuses on Jesus's death and resurrection (13:26–31; cf. 2:22–24), both messages highlight the fulfillment of OT prophecy (13:32–37; cf. 2:25–36), and both messages conclude with offers of forgiveness (13:38–41; cf. 2:38–39). In addition, Paul's brief survey of Israel's history is reminiscent of Stephen's much longer survey (13:17–22; cf. 7:2–50). The message also includes essentials of the gospel that have been part of earlier messages in Acts—the scriptural basis, Jesus's suffering and resurrection, the importance of repentance, the forgiveness of sins, and the blessings that accompany salvation.

The theme of continuity relates to mission objective as well. The mission Jesus gave his original followers was to be witnesses in Jerusalem, in Judea and Samaria, and to the ends of the earth (1:8). That mission was not new, because God had already commissioned Israel to be his witnesses (Isa. 43:10, 12; 44:8) and a light to the nations (Isa. 49:6; 51:4; 60:3), with the result that God's salvation would extend to the ends of the earth (Isa. 45:22; 52:10; cf. Ps. 65:5; 98:3). Although the opposition of the Jews in Pisidian Antioch was regrettable, it aligned with what the prophets had written (Hab. 1:5), and it allowed Paul and Barnabas to be obedient to God's command that his people would be a light to the nations to the ends of the earth (Isa. 49:6). The change in the focus of their witness, therefore, was not a departure from the mission Jesus had given his followers. Rather, it was fully congruent with that mission, in that it was necessary for the good news to go to the Jews first. When they rejected the message, it was both right and necessary that God's witnesses share that good news with the Gentiles as well.

PREACHING AND TEACHING STRATEGIES

Exegetical/Theological Synthesis

The focus of Luke's narrative has shifted from the witness based in Jerusalem to the witness based in Antioch, and Paul has supplanted Peter as the major character in that narrative. The account of Paul's ministry on Cyprus demonstrated one aspect of the continuity of his ministry with Peter's in rebuking spiritual opposition, but it passed over his synagogue preaching. Luke had already characterized Paul's preaching as "speaking boldly" (παρρησιάξομαι; cf. 9:27–28) and would continue to do so (13:46; 14:3; 19:8; 26:26; 28:31), but he had provided no details. Luke's first-century readers would have wanted to know the content of Paul's preaching, how it aligned with Peter's, and how his approach to mission aligned with the original mission Jesus had given his followers. The account of the witness in Pisidian Antioch includes an example of Paul's preaching that is congruent with both Peter's preaching at Pentecost and Stephen's preaching before the Sanhedrin. In addition, by quoting Isaiah 49:6 to support their decision to shift the focus of their ministry in the city from the Jews to the Gentiles, Paul made it clear that their change in strategy was consistent with God's original plan for his people to be witnesses to the ends of the earth (Acts 1:8). With the original audience, twenty-first-century readers share the need to understand that the gospel message and mandate do not change even if the mission strategy must, so that they will be adaptable in their approach but consistent in the content of their message and their commitment to the mission.

Preaching/Teaching Idea

Mission must be adaptable in its approach but consistent in its message.

Contemporary Connections

What does it mean?

Gospel presentations in the book of Acts are like snowflakes—no two are alike. All the key elements are there, but their structure and emphases are as varied as their audiences are. These presentations demonstrate faithful adaptability at its finest. The message never changes but the mouthpiece and the hearers do. As the good news moves from the messenger Peter to the messenger Paul and from audiences in Jerusalem to a far-flung audience in Pisidian Antioch, the key pronouncements of forgiveness and justification in Jesus stay the same. There is joy and the Holy Spirit too (2:41, 46–47; 13:52). Pisidian Antioch looks like Pentecost Jerusalem. Saul sounds like Stephen. The same Jesus presides over all.

Is it true?

The theological consistency from the OT to this newest revelation brings great apologetic comfort. Like Peter and Stephen, Paul relies on the Scriptures. In this abridged telling, he refers to Exodus, Joshua, and Samuel. He directly quotes Psalms, Samuel, Isaiah, and Habakkuk. The Bible is Paul's touchstone. He does not speculate or innovate. Instead, he exegetes God's continued work of tremendous grace to gather a sinful people to himself. The missional consistency through the earliest church under the Twelve's leadership and into a new team launched from a different place is a great relief. Paul and Barnabas carry the mantle of a message for the nations. They saw it in the Jerusalem church, they anticipated it in Habakkuk's prophecy, and they obeyed it in Isaiah's call. Including the Gentiles as an audience is what God had planned all along. Both the same message and the new audience are the fruits of his eternal plan.

Now what?

It is striking to watch other groups first receive the gospel message to which we might have grown so accustomed that it has lost its freshness. When Paul and Barnabas preached this message of forgiveness and justification in Jesus, the synagogue listeners' first response was to beg them to return to share more (13:42). Those same listeners followed Paul and Barnabas throughout the following week (13:43). They must have grabbed friends and neighbors, because by the following Sabbath nearly the whole city turned out (13:44). The Gentiles' response was even wilder. They rejoiced, glorified God, spread the word, and endured collateral persecution. This response to the consistent message and mission of Jesus is an invitation to reinvigorate our own daily response. We must once again absorb the awe of God's redemption plan in Jesus and allow it to lead us to happy worship. This good news makes us hungry to hear more. It overflows in us to tell friends and neighbors. It readies us to endure anything for Jesus's sake.

Creativity in Presentation

Everybody knows Steve Wozniak and Steve Jobs. Few people have heard of Ronald Wayne. Back in 1976, they cofounded a little start-up company called Apple Computer. Twelve days later, Ronald sold his 10 percent share of the company for $800. He clearly did not know what he had. Today Apple's market capitalization is north of $2 trillion. Only a handful of entire countries in the world have a gross domestic product value higher. To add insult to injury, he sold the original contract of that deal in the 1990s for $500. Sotheby's later auctioned the three typed and signed pages for $1.6 million. Looking back, Wayne must have found that passing on what turned out to be million and billion dollar deals to be excruciating.

His loss is nothing, however, compared with the bitter loss in the text. The Jews of Pisidian Antioch initially met this grand news of forgiveness and justification in Jesus with enthusiasm. They pressed to hear more, listened to Paul and Barnabas all week, and invited friends. Soon after, though, everything changed. In a fit of jealousy and hot persecution, these souls passed on the free gift of eternal life. A priceless gift exchanged hands for nothing. What was theirs for the receiving passed to the Gentiles. The synagogue's loss was the Gentiles' gain. They saw immediately the eternal wealth that was available to them, and they responded with heartfelt worship. They could not help but pass it around the surrounding region. It was too valuable not to keep and too valuable not to share. When they have been there ten thousand years, bright shining as the sun, they will not regret for a moment receiving God's glorious gift.

Mission must be adaptable in its approach but consistent in its message.

- The missionaries adapt their approach in new places with new audiences (13:13–15, 44–52).

- The message never changes (13:16–43).

DISCUSSION QUESTIONS

1. Why did Paul and his companions choose to bypass Pamphylia and focus their attention on Pisidian Antioch? What principle of mission strategy does their action suggest?

2. How is Paul's partial survey of Israel's history similar to Stephen's? How is it different? Why did Paul choose to focus on the events he did?

3. How is the content of Paul's message similar to that of Peter's messages? How is it different? What elements reflect his own theology and emphases?

4. How does Paul's homily reflect both continuity with Israel and openness to the Gentiles?

5. What principles can you draw from Paul and Barnabas's actions in the aftermath of their synagogue ministry?

Acts 14:1–28

EXEGETICAL IDEA
Paul and Barnabas's witness in the cities of South Galatia resulted in numerous conversions, encountered active opposition, strengthened the new churches, and concluded with a return to Syrian Antioch.

THEOLOGICAL FOCUS
God's grace opens doors for his witnesses to fulfill the work he has given them despite the tribulations they might experience.

PREACHING IDEA
God's work triumphs over tribulations.

PREACHING POINTERS
Are you an optimist or a pessimist? Do you see the proverbial glass as half-full or half-empty? Paul and Barnabas must have been God-oriented optimists, because they were able to focus on the good news of what God was doing despite the difficulties they faced. A superficial look at Acts 14 might lead some to see all the problems the missionaries faced, including opposition from Jews, Gentiles, and civil authorities; divided public opinion; misunderstanding of their message; mob violence; and—in Paul's case—stoning. Yet, when they reported to the church in Syrian Antioch about their ministry in Cyprus and South Galatia, where did they focus? They gathered the church together and described everything God had accomplished with them and how he had opened a door of faith for the Gentiles. They clearly understood that God's work triumphs over (and through) tribulations.

People today should be able to relate to multiple aspects of the Acts 14:1–28, including people with serious physical or health issues, quick shifts in public opinion, and a mob mentality. Paul and Barnabas's experiences epitomize the saying "trouble follows him" as the Jews followed them from Pisidian Antioch to Iconium to Lystra. They can probably also relate to the idea of reporting on progress at the end of an assigned task or project. The passage corrects any inclination to ascribe supernatural powers to human beings as well as the tendency to adopt incorrect views of God. It also corrects the idea that violence can stop the progress of the gospel or an approach to ministry that suggests evangelism alone is the mission of the church. It commends persevering in the face of opposition, depending on God and his working, being able to address wrong ideas about God, knowing how to care for new believers, and being accountable in ministry. The objective in communicating the passage is to help listeners understand that tribulations might arise but God's triumph is certain, so that they will learn to see the doors he opens instead of the difficulties they face.

FURTHER WITNESS IN SOUTH GALATIA (14:1–28)

LITERARY STRUCTURE AND THEMES (14:1–28)

Acts 14:1–28 consists of three narrative sections of varying length. The first section describes Paul and Barnabas's ministry in Iconium (14:1–7), repeating the "reception-opposition" pattern that was present in the preceding account of events in Pisidian Antioch (Bock 2007, 468). The longer second section describes their ministry in Lystra (14:8–20), beginning with a healing miracle and the listeners' misguided reaction to it (14:8–13), continuing with Paul and Barnabas's call to turn from idols to the one true God (14:14–18), and concluding with the events that led the missionaries to move on to Derbe (14:19–20). The third section describes the return trip from Derbe to Syrian Antioch (14:21–28), including a summary narrative of the missionaries' work in strengthening the new churches throughout South Galatia (14:21–23) and a travel narrative that describes their travel by land through Pamphylia and by sea to Syria (14:24–28).

- *Witness in Iconium (14:1–7)*
- *Witness in Lystra (14:8–20)*
- *Return to Syrian Antioch (14:21–28)*

EXPOSITION (14:1–28)

Paul and Barnabas's ministry on Cyprus (13:1–12) and in Pisidian Antioch (13:13–52) set the pattern for the remainder of their missionary travels together. If there was a synagogue in the city, they began by sharing the gospel with potentially receptive attenders there. If they encountered opposition from local Jews, they focused their attention on seeking Gentiles. If the opposition became intense, they moved on to the next city. After leaving Pisidian Antioch, they continued their church planting activities across the southern plateau of the Roman province of Galatia. Luke's narrative includes a concise account of their ministry in Iconium, a fuller account of their ministry in Lystra, and a summary account of their return travel to Syrian Antioch.

The narrative of the witness in Iconium (14:1–7) repeats the basic pattern in Pisidian Antioch—witness, conversions, opposition, and withdrawal—although with fewer details. The difference is that opposition arises from both Jews and Gentiles. The narrative of the ministry in Lystra (14:8–20) is the first instance of missionary witness to a purely Gentile audience and involves an encounter with the "old gods of classical Greece" (Dunn 1996, 189). It includes an example of the missionaries' preevangelistic response to an incorrect understanding of deity. From Derbe, they retraced their travels through South Galatia, preached in Pamphylia, and returned by sea to their sending church in Syrian Antioch (14:21–28). An important element of their return trip was their ministry of appointing elders in the churches they had planted.

Witness in Iconium (14:1–7)

Although many Jews and Greeks respond positively to their ministry in Iconium, potentially deadly opposition ultimately leads Paul and Barnabas to withdraw to Lystra and Derbe.

14:1–2. In Iconium, the team followed their established practice of entering the local synagogue (εἰσελθεῖν αὐτοὺς εἰς τὴν συναγωγήν), where "they spoke so effectively that" (NIV, λαλῆσαι οὕτως ὥστε) a large number of both Jews and Greeks believed (πιστεῦσαι Ἰουδαίων τε καὶ Ἑλλήνων πολὺ πλῆθος). Unbelieving

Jews (οἱ ἀπειθήσαντες Ἰουδαῖοι), however, again stirred up trouble (ἐπήγειραν) and "poisoned the minds of the Gentiles" (NLT, ἐκάκωσαν τὰς ψυχὰς τῶν ἐθνῶν) against the new believers. Iconium was located on the Via Sebaste approximately ninety miles east-south-east of Pisidian Antioch, still in the ancient region of Phrygia. Although the city had been designated a Roman colony, it had resisted Roman influence and had retained the ethos of a Greek city-state (Longenecker 1981, 431).

The phrase κατὰ τὸ αὐτό ("as they did in Antioch," ERV) indicates that Paul and Barnabas used the same approach that they had in the previous episode. The combination ἐπήγειραν καὶ ἐκάκωσαν is difficult. Culy and Parsons suggest that it is a periphrastic construction that "means something like 'to begin to mistreat'" (2003, 272). The phrase ἐκάκωσαν τὰς ψυχάς is idiomatic for "to cause to have hostile feeling toward someone" (L&N §88.200). Bock notes the strong emotional component (2007, 469). "Against the brothers" (κατὰ τῶν ἀδελφῶν) could refer either to Paul and Barnabas (e.g., NLT) or the new believers in the city (e.g., CEV). The latter seems more likely (Schnabel 2012, 603).

TEXTUAL ANALYSIS: The Connection Between Verses 2 and 3
Some commentators see the connection between verses 2 and 3 as so difficult they suggest that the order should be reversed (Williams 1989, 161). The Western text resolves the difficulty by inserting "but the Lord soon gave peace" at the end of verse 2 (TCGNT, 371). It is simpler, however, to see Paul and Barnabas's decision to remain in Iconium as motivated by the new believers' need for support in the face of opposition (Barrett 1994, 669). Bock characterizes their action as "resolve in the face of opposition" (2007, 470). Only when the opposition became potentially deadly (14:6), did the missionaries leave the city.

14:3–4. Despite the opposition, Paul and Barnabas remained (διέτριψαν) in the city for an extended period of time (ἱκανὸν χρόνον) while they continued their bold witness (παρρησιαζόμενοι). They drew their boldness from the Lord (ἐπὶ τῷ κυρίῳ), who repeatedly testified to the word of his grace (τῷ μαρτυροῦντι τῷ λόγῳ τῆς χάριτος αὐτοῦ) by granting them the ability to perform signs and wonders. The result was a divided city (ἐσχίσθη τὸ πλῆθος τῆς πόλεως). Some citizens sided with the Jews (οἱ μὲν ἦσαν σὺν τοῖς Ἰουδαίοις); others sided with Paul and Barnabas (οἱ δὲ σὺν τοῖς ἀποστόλοις). Bold witness (παρρησιάζομαι) consistently characterized the early church's ministry (2:29; 4:13, 29, 31; 9:27–28; 13:46).

The phrase ἐπὶ τῷ κυρίῳ is best understood as pointing to the Lord as the reason for their boldness (Barrett 1994, 670). Signs and wonders (σημεῖα καὶ τέρατα) regularly authenticated Jesus's witnesses (2:22, 43; 4:30; 5:12; 6:8; 8:6), and Paul mentioned them when he wrote to the churches in Galatia (Gal. 3:4–5). Although the signs and wonders occurred through the intermediate agency of the apostles (διὰ τῶν χειρῶν αὐτῶν), the ultimate agent was the Lord, who kept on granting (διδόντι) both the necessary authority and ability. The "population of the city" (LEB, τὸ πλῆθος τῆς πόλεως) might refer to the assembly that conducted the business of a Greek city-state (Longenecker 1981, 433) or, more likely to the general populace (Schnabel 2012, 604).

Were Paul and Barnabas "Apostles"?
Luke uses the word "apostles" (ἀπόστολοι) to describe individuals other than the original Twelve only in Acts 14, where he applies it to Barnabas and Paul (14:4, 14). Barrett offers four possible explanations: (1) Luke was careless; (2) Luke's admiration for Paul was so great that he used the word although he knew he should not; (3) the word applies to the message Barnabas and Paul proclaimed; (4) Barnabas and Paul

were apostles, although in a different sense than the Twelve (1994, 671). Marshall suggests that Luke knew there was a group of apostles—wider than the Twelve—whom Jesus had commissioned, and Barnabas and Paul belonged to that wider group (1980, 234). Schnabel (2012, 604) concludes that Barnabas and Saul were "apostles" in the sense that Paul was sent out by the risen Lord (9:15), Barnabas was sent out by the church in Jerusalem (11:22), and they were both sent out by the Holy Spirit from the church in Antioch (13:4). Larkin adopts Barrett's fourth explanation that Luke uses the word with the broader sense of "missionary" (1995, 210; cf. 1 Cor. 9:4–6; 2 Cor. 8:23; Phil. 2:25). Based on the use of Isaiah 49:6 in 13:47, Peterson suggests that Barnabas and Paul were fulfilling Jesus's commission in Acts 1:8 as apostles to the nations (2009, 405). One of the latter two explanations seems most likely.

14:5–7. Acting on impulse, the Gentiles (τῶν ἐθνῶν), the Jews (Ἰουδαίων), and their rulers (σὺν τοῖς ἄρχουσιν αὐτῶν) decided to mistreat (ὑβρίσαι) and stone (λιθοβολῆσαι) Paul and Barnabas. When the missionaries became aware (συνιδόντες) of the plan, they "fled for refuge" (κατέφυγον; cf. Bruce 1990, 319) to the Lycaonian cites of Lystra and Derbe, where they continued sharing the good news. Louw and Nida categorize ὁρμὴ γίνομαι as an idiom that refers to "making a decision to carry out some action, with emphasis on the impulse involved" (L&N §30.78). The verb ὑβρίζω denotes the act of treating a person in an insolent or spiteful manner (BDAG s.v. "ὑβρίζω" 1022). "Their rulers" (τοῖς ἄρχουσιν αὐτῶν) were most likely the civic leaders. If so, "the opposition spans the whole society" (Bock 2007, 471). Since Iconium was the easternmost city in the region of Phrygia, Paul and Barnabas's travel onward from that city involved

their crossing into the neighboring region of Lycaonia. "The surrounding region" (τὴν περίχωρον) suggests that their evangelistic activity was not limited to the two Lycaonian cities Luke mentions. The periphrastic construction εὐαγγελιζόμενοι ἦσαν highlights the sustained nature of the missionaries' activities.

Witness in Lystra (14:8–20)

When Paul heals a lame man in Lystra, the crowds want to offer sacrifices to him and Barnabas as gods, but Jews from Pisidian Antioch and Iconium persuade the crowds to stone him instead.

14:8–10. In Lystra, Paul and Barnabas encountered a lame man who listened attentively to what Paul was saying (οὗτος ἤκουσεν τοῦ Παύλου λαλοῦντος). When he looked closely at the man (ἀτενίσας αὐτῷ), Paul perceived that he had the faith to be healed (ἰδὼν ὅτι ἔχει πίστιν τοῦ σωθῆναι). So, in a loud voice (μεγάλη φωνῇ), he commanded the man to stand upright on his feet (ἀνάστηθι ἐπὶ τοὺς πόδας σου ὀρθός). The man immediately jumped up (ἥλατο) and began walking (περιεπάτει, inceptive imperfect). Lystra lay approximately twenty miles south-southwest of Iconium in the ancient region of Lycaonia. Since the city had also been designated a Roman colony, it had a Roman ruling class. Greeks controlled the commerce in the city, and the Jewish influence was minimal (Longenecker 1981, 434). Schnabel argues that the city might been less "rustic" than sometimes has been suggested (2012, 605).

Luke describes the lame man in three ways: he was unable to use his feet (ἀδύνατος τοῖς ποσὶν; cf. BDAG s.v. "ἀδύνατος" 1a, 22), he was born that way (χωλὸς ἐκ κοιλίας μητρὸς αὐτοῦ), and he had never walked (ὃς οὐδέποτε περιεπάτησεν). Together, those details highlight the complete hopelessness of his condition. The parallel to the lame man whom Peter healed is obvious (3:2), and the healing is the third in Luke's series of parallels between Peter and Paul. See 10:4 for ἀτενίζω. In this context, the verb σῴζω refers to deliverance from physical disability, although as Barrett comments, "in a Christian writer the word is seldom without an overtone" of spiritual deliverance (1994, 675; cf. Bock 2007, 475).

14:11–13. When the crowds saw what Paul had done (οἳ ὄχλοι ἰδόντες ὃ ἐποίησεν Παῦλος), they misinterpreted the source of the healing and concluded that Barnabas and Paul were the gods Zeus and Hermes, who had taken human likeness and come down from heaven to visit them (οἱ θεοὶ ὁμοιωθέντες ἀνθρώποις κατέβησαν πρὸς ἡμᾶς). Then, the priest of Zeus (ὁ ἱερεὺς τοῦ Διός), whose temple was located "just outside the city" (NET, πρὸ τῆς πόλεως), brought bulls and garlands to the city gates (ταύρους καὶ στέμματα ἐπὶ τοὺς πυλῶνας ἐνέγκας) and persisted in wanting to offer sacrifices (ἤθελεν θύειν, iterative imperfect) with the crowds (σὺν τοῖς ὄχλοις).

The Lystrans called Barnabas Zeus (Δία), perhaps because he was more dignified (Longenecker 1981, 435) or older (Bock 2007, 476). Luke notes that they called Paul Hermes (Ἑρμῆν) because he was "the chief speaker" (αὐτὸς ἦν ὁ ἡγούμενος τοῦ λόγου). The "garlands" (στέμματα) were "wreath[s] of wool to which leaves and flowers might be added and either wound around a staff or woven into a garland to be worn on the head" and "were an important part of the ritual involved in the worship of pagan gods in the ancient world" (L&N §6.193). Some commentators suggest that, because the crowds shouted in the dialect of their region (ἐπῆραν τὴν φωνὴν αὐτῶν Λυκαονιστί), the missionaries were not initially aware of what was happening (Marshall 1980, 236; Peterson 2009, 408). As Schnabel notes, however, such

an inference goes beyond what the text says (2012, 607).

Possible Background for the "Zeus and Hermes" Incident

Most commentators point to a legend from Ovid (*Metam.* 8.626–724) as possible background for the citizens in Lystra identifying Barnabas and Paul as Zeus and Hermes (Longenecker 1981, 435). The legend says that Zeus and Hermes visited the Phrygian hill country disguised as men. After they asked for lodging at a thousand houses, an elderly couple finally took them into their cottage and provided a banquet for them. In appreciation, the gods transformed the couple's cottage into a temple with a golden roof and marble columns, flooded the surrounding valley, and destroyed those who had refused them lodging.

14:14–18. When they heard about what was happening (ἀκούσαντες), Paul and Barnabas tore their outer garments (διαρρήξαντες τὰ ἱμάτια αὐτῶν), rushed into the crowd (ἐξεπήδησαν εἰς τὸν ὄχλον), and urged them to stop. It is better to classify their message as an apologetic response to an incorrect understanding of deity rather than a missionary speech. It followed a four-part structure: address (14:15a), point of contact (14:15b), call to turn from their traditional gods to the living God (14:15c), and explanation of God's true character (14:15d–17). With their words, they were able—although with difficulty (μόλις; cf. BDAG s.v. "μόλις" 1, 657)—to quiet (κατέπαυσαν) the crowds enough that they did not sacrifice to them (τοῦ μὴ θύειν αὐτοῖς). Tearing their garments (διαρήσσω) was a symbol of horror associated with sacrilege (L&N §19.32). That act and their headlong rush into the crowd (ἐκπηδάω) reflected the depth of their emotional reaction to what they heard.

The missionaries' apologetic response began with direct address (ἄνδρες) followed immediately by a question (τί ταῦτα ποιεῖτε;).

Bock notes that the question ("Why are you doing these things?") was actually a request that the listeners stop what they had been doing (2007, 477). The crowd's response was improper because Paul and Barnabas were not gods; they were men who were similar in feelings and circumstances (ὁμοιοπαθεῖς; cf. BDAG s.v. "ὁμοιοπαθεῖς" 706) to the Lystrans. That statement established common ground with the listeners and led directly to the heart of their message. The missionaries were bringing good news (εὐαγγελιζόμενοι) that consisted of the opportunity to turn (ἐπιστρέφειν) from the powerless gods (ἀπὸ τούτων τῶν ματαίων) of ancient Greece to the living God (ἐπὶ θεὸν ζῶντα) of the OT.

It was important that the crowd understood three truths about the one true God. First, he is the sovereign God, who made the heaven, the earth, the sea, and all the things in them (ὃς ἐποίησεν τὸν οὐρανὸν καὶ τὴν γῆν καὶ τὴν θάλασσαν καὶ πάντα τὰ ἐν αὐτοῖς). Second, he is the merciful God, who did not execute judgment on the nations despite their long-term waywardness (ὃς ἐν ταῖς παρῳχημέναις γενεαῖς εἴασεν πάντα τὰ ἔθνη πορεύεσθαι ταῖς ὁδοῖς αὐτῶν). Third, he is the good God, who uses common grace to bear witness to himself (οὐκ ἀμάρτυρον αὐτὸν ἀφῆκεν ἀγαθουργῶν, οὐρανόθεν ὑμῖν ὑετοὺς διδοὺς καὶ καιροὺς καρποφόρους, ἐμπιπλῶν τροφῆς καὶ εὐφροσύνης τὰς καρδίας ὑμῶν).

The content of the message incorporates OT concepts as well as concepts from Paul's letters. The language of turning from idols to serve the living God echoes 1 Thessalonians 1:9. The truth of God as creator occurs in multiple OT passages (Exod. 20:11; Neh. 9:6; Ps. 146:6). The language of God withholding judgment for previously committed sins echoes Romans 3:25. The truth of God's goodness in the fruitfulness of creation also occurs in multiple OT passages (Lev. 26:4; Ps. 147:8; Jer. 5:24). Paul's longer message on Mars Hill (17:22–31) uses a similar apologetic approach.

14:19–20. The pattern of opposition Paul and Barnabas had encountered in Pisidian Antioch and Iconium continued in Lystra, when Jews from those cities arrived (ἐπῆλθαν), won over the crowds (LEB, πείσαντες τοὺς ὄχλους), stoned Paul (λιθάσαντες τὸν Παῦλον), dragged him outside the city (ἔσυρον ἔξω τῆς πόλεως), and left him for dead (νομίζοντες αὐτὸν τεθνηκέναι). When the disciples gathered around him (κυκλωσάντων τῶν μαθητῶν αὐτόν), however, he got up (ἀναστάς) and went back into the city (εἰσῆλθεν εἰς τὴν πόλιν). The next day (τῇ ἐπαύριον), he and Barnabas departed for Derbe (ἐξῆλθεν . . . εἰς Δέρβην).

The Jews from Pisidian Antioch had traveled more than one hundred miles to reach Lystra, while those from Iconium had traveled approximately twenty miles. Schnabel describes the radical reversal of public opinion about Paul and Barnabas as "the raw side of popular piety" (2012, 612). Paul seems to refer to this incident in 2 Corinthians 11:25, 2 Timothy 3:11, and possibly Galatians 6:17. The disciples who gathered around Paul were new converts from Lystra (Peterson 2009, 412). Derbe lay approximately sixty miles farther eastward along the Via Sebaste. It was a Lycaonian town close to the South Galatian border with Cilicia. See 16:1 on the question of whether Timothy was from Derbe or Lystra.

Return to Syrian Antioch (14:21–28)

After sharing the gospel in Derbe, Paul and Barnabas retrace their route through South Galatia to strengthen the churches they had planted and return to their sending church in Syrian Antioch.

14:21–22. After they has shared the good news (εὐαγγελισάμενοι) and made many disciples (μαθητεύσαντες ἱκανούς) in Derbe, Paul and Barnabas returned (ὑπέστρεψαν) to the cities they had previously visited—Lystra, Iconium, and Pisidian Antioch. In those cities, they strengthened (ἐπιστηρίζοντες) the new disciples, by encouraging (παρακαλοῦντες) them to continue in the faith (ἐμμένειν τῇ πίστει) and to remind them that they must encounter many tribulations (διὰ πολλῶν θλίψεων) before they would enter the kingdom of God (ἡμᾶς εἰσελθεῖν εἰς τὴν βασιλείαν τοῦ θεοῦ).

The verb μαθητεύω occurs elsewhere only in Matthew 13:5, 27:57, and 28:19. Στηρίζω carries the sense of "causing someone to become more firm and unchanging in an attitude or belief" (L&N §74.19). The phrase "the souls of the disciples" (τὰς ψυχὰς τῶν μαθητῶν) is a synecdoche for the disciples themselves (Culy and Parsons 2003, 282). The challenge to continue in the faith (ἐμμένειν τῇ πίστει) echoes similar encouragements to continue in the Lord in 11:23 (προσμένειν τῷ κυρίῳ) and to continue in the grace of God in 13:43 (προσμένειν τῇ χάριτι τοῦ θεοῦ). As in previous instances, δεῖ ("it is necessary") indicates conformity to the divine plan (1:16, 21; 3:21; 4:12; 9:6, 16); in this instance, the necessity is suffering. See 1:3 for the kingdom of God.

14:23. Instruction was one of three ways in which Paul and Barnabas cared for the new disciples. The second was to appoint elders (χειροτονήσαντες . . . πρεσβυτέρους) for them (αὐτοῖς) in each of the new churches (κατ᾽ ἐκκλησίαν). The third was to entrust them to the Lord's protection (παρέθεντο αὐτοὺς τῷ κυρίῳ) with prayer and fasting (προσευξάμενοι μετὰ νηστειῶν). The verb χειροτονέω denotes the act of electing or choosing someone for a specific office or task (BDAG s.v. "χειροτονέω" 1083). Larkin notes that although the occurrence of the verb in this context might allow for the congregation playing a part in the process (1:23; 6:1–6; 13:1–3), the basic sense points to the missionaries doing the appointing (1995, 217).

Although some commentators believe the reference to elders is anachronistic (Marshall 1980, 241), Luke has previously mentioned the Jerusalem elders in 11:30 (cf. 15:2, 4, 6, 22, 23; 16:4; 21:18). He later notes the presence of elders in Ephesus (20:17–38). Further, Paul speaks of recognized leaders in other local churches (1 Cor. 16:15–18; Gal. 6:6; Phil. 1:1; 2:29; 1 Thess. 5:12–13). "Prayer with fasting" (προσευξάμενοι μετὰ νηστειῶν) echoes the same activities that accompanied Paul and Barnabas's appointment for missionary service (13:3). The verb παρατίθημι describes the act of entrusting someone or something to another for safekeeping (BDAG s.v. "παρατίθημι" 3b, 772).

Although at least some English translations understand the individuals (αὐτούς) whom Paul and Barnabas commended to the Lord to be the newly appointed elders (e.g., NLT), the parallel to αὐτοῖς in the preceding clause suggests that the antecedent of both pronouns is the disciples in each church (Schnabel 2012, 614). The relative clause εἰς ὃν πεπιστεύκεισαν ("in whom they had believed," intensive pluperfect) highlights both the disciples' initial response to the gospel and "the ongoing nature of [their] faith" (Bock 2007, 483). The missionaries' three actions on their return trip through South Galatia—instruction, leadership identification, and spiritual care—demonstrate well-rounded support for the new churches they had planted.

14:24–26. From Pisidian Antioch, Paul and Barnabas traveled (διελθόντες) southward through Pisidia and Pamphylia to Perga, the main city of the latter province. After they spoke the Word (λαλήσαντες τὸν λόγον) in that city, their next stop was the port city of Attalia. From there (κἀκεῖθεν), they set sail (ἀπέπλευσαν) for Syrian Antioch. Although Marshall notes that the Pisidia was "wild country where there was probably little opportunity for evangelism" (1980, 242), the participle διελθόντες suggests that their travel included at least some evangelistic activity (13:14). Paul and Barnabas had passed through Perga quickly on their outward travels, but they now took the opportunity to preach there.

The second half of verse 26 brings the narrative of chapters 13–14 full circle by describing Syrian Antioch as the place "from which they had been entrusted to the grace of God for the work they had fulfilled" (ὅθεν ἦσαν παραδεδομένοι τῇ χάριτι τοῦ θεοῦ εἰς τὸ ἔργον ὃ ἐπλήρωσαν). The periphrastic construction ἦσαν παραδεδομένοι highlights the continuing nature of their commission. The verb παραδίδωμι denotes the act of entrusting someone for care or preservation (BDAG s.v. "παραδίδωμι" 2, 762). It was God and his grace who had cared for them, preserved them, and enabled them to fulfill the work (τὸ ἔργον) for which the Holy Spirit has set them apart (13:2).

14:27–28. After they arrived (παραγενόμενοι) in Syrian Antioch, Paul and Barnabas gathered (συναγαγόντες) the church and reported (ἀνήγγελλον) on two topics: everything God had done with them (ὅσα ἐποίησεν ὁ θεὸς μετ' αὐτῶν) and the way in which he had opened a door of faith for the Gentiles (ἤνοιξεν τοῖς ἔθνεσιν θύραν πίστεως). They then spent (διέτριβον) "a long time" (GNB) with the disciples. The imperfect tense of ἀνήγγελλον in verse 27 highlights the extended nature of their report, and the imperfect tense of διέτριβον in verse 28 indicates their stay in Syria was extended. The phrase χρόνον οὐκ ὀλίγον ("not a little time") is another instance of Luke's use of litotes (1:5; 4:20; 12:18). The phrase μετ' αὐτῶν highlights the divine cooperation that characterized the missionaries' work.

The statement that God "opened a door" (ἤνοιξεν θύραν) echoes Paul's own language (1 Cor. 16:9; 2 Cor. 2:12; Col. 4:3) and refers to opportunities for witness. Schnabel characterizes the result as a "breakthrough" (2012, 616). The sweeping conversions provided further confirmation that the way of faith was open to the Gentiles, as the Jerusalem church had concluded after Cornelius's conversion (11:18). The combination of "the grace of God" in verse 26 along with "everything that God did with them" and "God opened a door of faith" in verse 27 makes it clear that "God is truly the hero of the first missionary journey" (Larkin 1995, 217).

THEOLOGICAL FOCUS

Acts 14:1–28 serves a threefold narrative function. First, it continues the account of Paul and Barnabas's ministry activity and establishes the strategy Paul would use throughout his ministry. The team focused on cities to reach a region, made initial contacts in settings where people were interested in spiritual things, invested in segments of the population that were receptive to the gospel, withdrew when opposition became potentially deadly, revisited and nurtured the churches that resulted, and remained accountable to the church that had sent them. Second, it demonstrates that God had opened a door of faith for the Gentiles. Although Peter had made the initial breakthrough with Gentiles in Caesarea, and although the church in Syrian Antioch was a predominantly Gentile church, Paul and Barnabas were the first witnesses to engage in intentional ministry among the Gentiles and to see widespread Gentile responses to the gospel. Third, it set the stage for the Jerusalem Council. With a large-scale ingathering of Gentile disciples, the church would need to deal with the place of those Gentiles in the movement. Paul and Barnabas's report on their experiences in Cyprus and South Galatia would play a crucial role in that debate (15:4, 12).

Theologically, Acts 14:1–28 highlights the nature and work of the one true God. As Larkin notes, God is truly the hero of the narrative. He is the source of confidence for boldness in the face of severe opposition and the one who gives the authority to do signs and wonders that attest to the word of his grace (14:3). He is the sovereign, merciful, good God, who is the only true object of worship (14:15–17). It is his plan that requires his followers to enter his kingdom through many tribulations (14:22). It is to him that the missionaries present the new disciples after they place their faith in him (14:23). It is to his grace that the sending church originally entrusted the missionaries for protection (14:26). He is the one who works with his witnesses and opens a door of faith for the Gentiles (14:27).

The passage also sets the intense but temporary nature of tribulations in the context of the ultimate triumph of the gospel. The missionaries faced opposition that arose from multiple sources, took many forms, and was potentially deadly. They encountered opposition from Jews, Gentiles, and civil authorities. They endured divided public opinion, plots against them, and misunderstanding of their message. In Lystra, a crowd stoned Paul and left him for dead. In nearly every respect, their experience paralleled that of the apostles in the Jerusalem church. Yet, God's mission was unstoppable. In every city, the missionaries spoke out boldly, made many disciples, and left a church to continue the work they had begun. On their return travels, they encouraged the disciples in those churches by reminding them that "through many tribulations we must enter the kingdom of God" (14:22). Paul would later echo that truth when he wrote to the Corinthians, "Our momentary, light suffering is producing for us an eternal weight of glory far beyond all comparison because we are not looking at what can be seen but at what cannot be seen. For what can be seen is temporary, but what cannot be seen is eternal" (2 Cor. 4:17–18, NET). Because God is the one who opens doors for his witnesses, they can be certain that the tribulations they face are temporary, and he will ultimately triumph as he grows his church.

PREACHING AND TEACHING STRATEGIES

Exegetical/Theological Synthesis
Paul and Barnabas's missionary work had begun well. They had seen Sergius Paulus, the proconsul of Cyprus, respond in faith despite spiritual opposition. In turn, he had suggested that the cities of South Galatia might well be receptive to the gospel. In the important garrison city of Pisidian Antioch, many Jews and Godfearing proselytes had responded positively to their initial witness in the synagogue. Then the situation had changed dramatically as jealous Jews stirred up persecution against them and drove them out of the region. As a result, they traveled farther into the interior. As Luke's account continued, his first-century readers would have wanted to know whether the pattern of response followed by opposition that Paul and Barnabas had experienced in Pisidian Antioch would reoccur in other cities. If it did, would that continuing opposition deter the missionaries from fulfilling the mission for which the Holy Spirit and the church in Syrian Antioch had commissioned them?

In fact, the opposition continued. In Iconium, unbelieving Jews poisoned the minds of the Gentiles, divided the city against the missionaries, and intended to stone them. In Lystra, popular acclaim turned to mob violence when Jews from Pisidian Antioch and Iconium incited the crowds against the missionaries, stoned Paul, and left him for dead. It would have been easy for Luke's readers to see all the difficulties, especially when the missionaries reminded the new disciples that they would encounter many tribulations before they entered God's kingdom. Paul and Barnabas, however, saw the open doors, not the difficulties. God was at work among the Gentiles of South Galatia, and their role was to fulfill the work for which the Holy Spirit had set them apart. So, they drew their confidence from God, spoke out boldly in the face of opposition, and encouraged their new Gentile converts to continue in the faith. With the original audience, twenty-first-century readers share the need to learn to see the open doors instead of the difficulties. They need to remember that tribulations might arise, but God's triumph is certain. As David wrote, "Weeping might last through the night, but joy comes with the morning" (Ps. 30:5, NLT).

Preaching/Teaching Idea
God's work triumphs over tribulations.

Contemporary Connections

What does it mean?
We get a rare glimpse at the growth of churches at every stage from gospel seeds to fully formed, fruit-bearing trees. Derbe was the most distant stop for Paul and Barnabas on this missionary journey. In the first stage of their travels, they sowed gospel seeds and saw abundant fruit in fledgling disciples. Next, the apostles retraced their steps to Lystra and Iconium and moved these church plants into the second stage. They encouraged the disciples, appointed elders, and committed them to the Lord through prayer and fasting. Finally, upon their return to Antioch, they reported to a fully formed church that sent its own missionaries and received them back, bearing gospel fruit near and far. What the Jerusalem church had already experienced at great cost, however, the Antioch church was quickly learning: God's triumphs of local church growth come in the face of tribulations. The missionary team was threatened and forced to flee, and ultimately Paul was stoned and presumed dead. Below the surface, there may well have also been a struggle over deep bitterness for the unfair treatment by Jewish hearers bent on their demise. The church truly suffered.

Is it true?
The power of this passage is God's sovereignty in the triumphs *and* the tribulations. As noted above, God—not Paul, Barnabas, or the sending church in Antioch—stands squarely at the center of every stage of the action. The Lord bore witness to his grace through signs. He sustained his people through suffering. He helped new Christians endure. All triumphs are God's triumphs, but he also holds the tribulations in this passage. God told Paul at his conversion that he would suffer much (9:16). God was not guessing. He sovereignly holds all things, and nothing happens outside of his control. Paul's fate was in God's hands, not in the hands of the angry crowd. That truth is the reason Paul earnestly committed the churches they planted in South Galatia into those same sovereign hands (14:23).

Now what?
Anyone who follows Jesus will encounter tribulation. Jesus promised, "In the world you will have tribulation" (John 16:33). Paul affirmed, "All who desire to live a godly life in Christ Jesus will be persecuted" (2 Tim. 3:12). As Christians, we must not seek ways to avoid pain, hardship, suffering, or persecution, because suffering will come our way. We must follow Jesus's example in suffering (1 Peter 2:21–25). That is, we must embrace the suffering God allows, in order to see the glories God will bring in us, in our churches, and in our neighbors.

One product of godly endurance in suffering is seeing God grow our churches to the point of maturity. Paul describes the objective of the proper functioning of the body of Christ in this way: "That we might grow up in every way into him who is the head, even Christ" (Eph. 4:15). We start as new disciples receiving good news. We grow into adolescent congregations, appointing elders, receiving Christ's encouragement, and holding fast through fasting and prayer. Then, Lord willing, our congregations start to look like those in Antioch and Jerusalem—giving more than receiving for the sake of the nations. Our journey will not end there, of course, but it will experience greater and greater depths of the reality that God triumphs in the face of tribulations as he grows his church.

Creativity in Presentation
There is something soothing about cooking channels. The soft banter of a dressed-down chef in a clean space making good food is homey. That soothing tone is probably why cooking channels play in unlikely spaces, like courthouses or hospital waiting rooms. What is

so mesmerizing is that the action keeps moving. No sooner does a dish go in the oven than the chef pulls out an already baked one from another oven. There is no waiting involved; fully prepared dishes roll out at every stage. Seeing a whole chapter of churches at different stages has the same effect. As soon as Iconium and Lystra go in the mixing bowl in the first half of the chapter, they are ready to go into the oven in the second half of the chapter. By the end of the passage, Antioch appears fully baked.

These stages represent God's triumph over tribulations. They are his grains of wheat, buried and breaking, to produce much fruit. Each stage is a beautiful triumph. John the Baptist once sent messengers from his prison cell to ask whether Jesus was the Messiah. Jesus told them to tell John that the blind see and the lame walk (Matt. 11:2–5). In a word, *yes,* he is—as his triumphs clearly showed. Imagine if some imprisoned Christians sent messengers to Paul and company to inquire whether the church was really growing. Was God really triumphing in the face of tribulations? The leadership could gladly report that the gospel is preached, friends are converted, disciples are encouraged and trained, believers fast and pray, and sending churches grow stronger and more generous. In the face of tribulations, God triumphs.

- Man delivers tribulations at every turn of ministry (14:1–20).

- God provides triumphs at every turn of ministry (14:21–28).

DISCUSSION QUESTIONS

1. What parallels do you see between Paul's ministry and Peter's? What parallels do you see between Paul and Barnabas's experiences and the experiences of the Jerusalem church?

2. Why did Paul and Barnabas initially decide to remain in Iconium despite opposition but later decide to leave the city because of it? What factor(s) guided their decision-making?

3. How does Paul's response to the Lystrans' attempt to sacrifice to them provide a model for relating to non-Christian religions? How does it compare with his message in the synagogue in Pisidian Antioch?

4. Why do you think Paul and Barnabas chose to retrace their route westward rather than continuing farther eastward from Derbe to Tarsus and Syrian Antioch?

5. What principles for mission and church planting can you draw from Paul and Barnabas's ministry in South Galatia?

Acts 15:1–35

EXEGETICAL IDEA

The Jerusalem Council resolved a dispute over whether it was necessary to circumcise Gentile disciples by reviewing the history of the mission to the Gentiles, applying OT prophecy to the situation, and establishing guidelines that would facilitate table fellowship between Jews and Gentiles.

THEOLOGICAL FOCUS

A balanced approach to mission maintains a commitment to essential doctrines, recognizes cultural differences, and respects personal convictions in secondary matters of faith and practice.

PREACHING IDEA

Wise counsel guards the truth without binding the conscience.

PREACHING POINTERS

"In essentials unity, in nonessentials liberty, and in all things charity." This saying seems particularly applicable to the decision of the Jerusalem Council in Acts 15. How should the church balance commitment to essential doctrines, recognition of cultural differences, and respect for personal convictions in secondary matters of faith and practice? That was the challenge the early church faced when certain law-observant Jewish members advocated requiring circumcision of the large number of Gentile disciples who were entering the church through the missionary work of Paul and Barnabas. The decision they reached and the way in which they reached it reminds us that we must interpret what God is doing in light of Scripture, so that we are careful to guard the truth without binding the conscience.

People today can relate to church conferences, debates over religious practices, or reaching a compromise to preserve unity. They should also be able to relate to taking an issue to a higher court, appealing to precedent, documenting a decision in writing, and rejoicing over a favorable decision. The passage corrects imposing cultural values or practices on others, being dogmatic on nonessentials, putting God to the test by questioning what he is doing, or suggesting that religious practices must supplement faith in order for a person or a group to gain salvation. It commends recognizing and respecting God's working, respecting cultural differences, turning to Scripture for guidance in decision-making, seeking resolutions that maintain unity, and being willing to limit personal liberty out of respect for the convictions of others. The objective in communicating the passage should be to help listeners understand that their identity in Christ supersedes their cultural identity so that they will learn to balance a commitment to truth with respect for their brothers and sisters in Christ.

THE JERUSALEM COUNCIL (15:1–35)

LITERARY STRUCTURE AND THEMES (15:1–35)

The passage consists of five sections. An opening narrative describes the origin of the dispute that led to the consultation in Jerusalem (15:1–5). A speech by Peter reviews how the Gentiles first heard the gospel (15:6–11). A speech by James proposes a solution to the dispute (15:12–21). A letter records the church's decision (15:22–29). A closing narrative describes the delivery of the council's letter to Antioch (15:30–35). The resulting concentric structure places James's speech at the center of the passage as the key element.

A Paul and Barnabas travel from Antioch to Jerusalem (15:1–5)

B The apostles and elders gather to look into the matter (15:6–11)

C James proposes a solution (15:12–21)

B′ The apostles, elders, and church adopt the proposal (15:22–29)

A′ Paul and Barnabas travel from Jerusalem to Antioch (15:30–35)

The correspondence between the two travel narratives of A and A′ is clear. Four verbal links support the correspondence between B and B′. References to the apostles and elders appear in the opening clauses of each paragraph (15:6, 22). Three of the book's seven occurrences of the verb ἐκλέγομαι appear in the two paragraphs (15:7, 22, 25). The only references in the chapter to the Holy Spirit occur in verses 11 and 28, and the only references to "the Lord Jesus" occur in verses 11 and 26.

- *Paul and Barnabas Deliver the Report to Jerusalem (15:1–5)*
- *Peter Reviews the Beginning of the Gentile Mission (15:6–11)*
- *James Proposes a Solution (15:12–21)*
- *The Council Adopts the Proposal (15:22–29)*
- *Judas and Silas Deliver the Letter to Antioch (15:30–35)*

EXPOSITION (15:1–35)

Dunn calls Acts 15:1–35 "a watershed of Luke's whole narrative" (1996, 194). Haenchen writes, "the episode . . . rounds off and justifies the past developments, and makes those to come intrinsically possible" (1971, 461). The gospel has steadily crossed cultural boundaries from devout Jews to pagan Gentiles. First, God used Peter to share the gospel with the Godfearing Gentile Cornelius. Then, Hellenistic Jewish missionaries shared the gospel with Gentiles in Syrian Antioch. Now, God had opened a door for the Gentiles as Paul and Barnabas had engaged in intentional mission among them in Cyprus and South Galatia. Peter's report after the conversion of Cornelius and his household approximately ten years previously had persuaded the Jerusalem church that God had accepted the Gentiles into the new movement on an equal basis.

Yet, with the large-scale ingathering of Gentile disciples, the question of how to integrate them into the church arose. One group of disciples advocated a proselyte model in which the Gentiles must become observant Jews. Paul and Barnabas, however, took exception to that approach. In order to seek a resolution to the dispute, the church in Antioch sent representatives to Jerusalem. The resulting consultation brought together all the major leaders of the movement—Paul and Barnabas, the Jerusalem apostles and elders, Peter, and James, the brother of Jesus. The final solution was an eschatological model that recognized the fulfillment of the OT promise that the Gentiles would seek the Lord. The church, therefore, would not require Gentiles to adopt the practices of Jewish piety. Instead, they should be sensitive to Jewish concerns when they found themselves in situations involving table fellowship. The Gentile mission could move forward unhindered and enjoying the full support of a unified church.

Paul and Barnabas Deliver the Report to Jerusalem (15:1–5)

When a dispute over the necessity of circumcision arises in Antioch, the church sends Paul and Barnabas to Jerusalem to report on their missionary work.

15:1–2. While Paul and Barnabas were still in Syrian Antioch (14:28), an unspecified group of visitors (τινες) arrived from Jerusalem and began teaching (ἐδίδασκον, inceptive imperfect) the disciples that no one was able to be saved (οὐ δύνασθε σωθῆναι) unless they were circumcised (ἐὰν μὴ περιτμηθῆτε) according to the Mosaic practice (τῷ ἔθει τῷ Μωϋσέως). When "not a little" (οὐκ ὀλίγης) dispute and discussion (στάσεως καὶ ζητήσεως) arose between Paul and Barnabas and the itinerant teachers, the church appointed Paul, Barnabas, and certain others from the congregation (τινας ἄλλους ἐξ αὐτῶν) to travel to Jerusalem and meet with the apostles and elders concerning the particular point of disagreement (περὶ τοῦ ζητήματος τούτου).

Verse 5 suggests that the "some" of verse 1 were individuals from the religious party of the Pharisees, and a Western insertion brings the wording of verse 5 forward to clarify that understanding (τινες τῶν πεπιστευκότων ἀπὸ τῆς αἱρέσεως τῶν Φαρισαίων). Wallace classifies ἔθει as a dative of rule (*GGBB*, 155);

Schnabel notes that the idea is one of long-established practice (2012, 628). Στάσις denotes a lack of agreement regarding policy (BDAG s.v. "στάσις" 3, 940), and ζήτησις denotes the process of "searching for truth through public inquiry and debate" (Barrett 1998, 713). Culy and Parsons note that the doublet and Luke's use of litotes "strongly emphasize the serious nature of the dispute" (2003, 286). Ζήτημα describes a controversial issue (BDAG s.v. "ζήτημα" 428). Verse 3 subsequently suggests that the whole church appointed (ἔταξαν) the representatives and sent them to Jerusalem. Metzger provides a helpful discussion of the Western alterations to the text of verses 1–5 (*TCGNT*, 376–78).

15:3–4. While the representatives who were sent on their way by the church (οἱ προπεμφθέντες ὑπὸ τῆς ἐκκλησίας) were traveling (διήρχοντο) southward through Phoenicia and Samaria, they kept on reporting in detail (ἐκδιηγούμενοι, iterative present) about the conversion of the Gentiles (τὴν ἐπιστροφὴν τῶν ἐθνῶν). In so doing, they brought great joy (ἐποίουν χαρὰν μεγάλην) to all the brothers (πᾶσιν τοῖς ἀδελφοῖς). When they arrived in Jerusalem (παραγενόμενοι εἰς Ἰερουσαλήμ), the church, the apostles, and the elders all welcomed (παρεδέχθησαν) them, and they reported on everything God had done with them. The verb προπέμπω describes assisting in making a journey (BDAG s.v. "προπέμπω" 2, 873), and the verb ἐκδιηγέομαι refers to providing detailed information when telling something (BDAG s.v. "ἐκδιηγέομαι" 300). The fact that the churches in Samaria and Phoenicia were the product of the Hellenistic Jewish witness (8:4–25; 11:19) and were comprised predominantly of non-Jews would have made Paul and Barnabas's report particularly welcome in those congregations. The clause ἀνήγγειλάν ὅσα ὁ θεὸς ἐποίησεν μετ' αὐτῶν echoes Paul and Barnabas's previous report to the church in Syrian Antioch (14:27).

15:5. The debate that had initially arisen in Antioch, however, soon resurfaced in Jerusalem. Some individuals from the religious party of the Pharisees who had believed the gospel (τινες τῶν ἀπὸ τῆς αἱρέσεως τῶν Φαρισαίων πεπιστευκότες) argued that it was necessary (δεῖ) to circumcise the Gentiles (περιτέμνειν αὐτούς) and command (παραγγέλλειν) them to keep the Mosaic Law (τηρεῖν τὸν νόμον Μωϋσέως). It should not be surprising that some Jews from that group had believed, since many priests had been converted (6:7), and since Paul himself later used his background as a Pharisee in his defense before the Sanhedrin (cf. Acts 23:6; Phil. 3:5). They were particularly zealous for the law (cf. 21:20), they based their argument on what they considered to be divine necessity (δεῖ; cf. 1:16, 21; 3:21; 4:12; 5:29; 9:6, 16; 14:22), and their position extended beyond submitting to circumcision to obeying the entire Mosaic Law. Essentially, their position was that the Gentiles must become Jews in order to enjoy the blessings of God's covenant with his people. They were advocating a proselyte model of conversion (Longenecker 1981, 446). In Stott's words, the Gentiles "must let Moses complete what Jesus had begun, and let the law supplement the gospel" (1990, 243).

Peter Reviews the Beginning of the Gentile Mission (15:6–11)

Peter reminds the church in Jerusalem about God's initiative in making it possible for the Gentiles to hear and believe the message of the gospel.

15:6–7. The apostles and elders assembled (συνήχθησαν) to look into the matter (ἰδεῖν περὶ τοῦ λόγου τούτου). After considerable debate (πολλῆς ζητήσεως γενομένης), Peter addressed the gathering. His speech proceeded in three steps. First, he affirmed divine initiative by reminding them that approximately ten years previously God chose (ἐξελέξατο) him as the agent through whom the Gentiles

heard (ἀκοῦσαι) and believed (πιστεῦσαι) the message of the gospel (τὸν λόγον τοῦ εὐαγγελίου). Schnabel suggests that verse 6 introduces a different meeting from the one mentioned in verse 4 (2012, 632). The first was a meeting of the entire assembly; the second was an "executive session" of the apostles and elders that extended through verse 21. In verse 22, the leaders presented the proposed solution to the entire assembly. According to Culy and Parsons, the phrase ἀφ' ἡμερῶν ἀρχαίων ("from ancient days") is an idiom describing events that took place "some time ago" (2003, 289). In this case, the conversion of Cornelius and his household had occurred approximately ten years previously. The fact that God chose Peter highlights his divine initiative. "Through my mouth" (διὰ τοῦ στόματός μου) is a synecdoche for Peter himself as the agent through whom God chose to act.

15:8–9. Next, Peter affirmed divine acceptance by reminding his listeners that God bore witness to the Gentiles' response (ἐμαρτύρησεν αὐτοῖς) by giving them the Holy Spirit (δοὺς τὸ πνεῦμα τὸ ἅγιον) just as he had done with the Jews at Pentecost (καθὼς καὶ ἡμῖν). In so doing, he removed the distinction (οὐθὲν διέκρινεν) between Jews and Gentiles (μεταξὺ ἡμῶν τε καὶ αὐτῶν). The external evidence provided by God's giving the Holy Spirit reflected the inner work that he had done in the hearts of Cornelius and his household. He both knew their hearts (ὁ καρδιογνώστης θεός) and cleansed their hearts (καθαρίσας τὰς καρδίας αὐτῶν) in response to their faith (τῇ πίστει).

15:10–11. In the third step in his speech, Peter affirmed divine grace by reminding his listeners that they accepted as axiomatic (πιστεύομεν, gnomic present) the truth that both they and the Gentiles (κἀκεῖνοι) are saved in the same way (καθ' ὃν τρόπον)—by the grace of the Lord Jesus. If salvation is by grace, the logical question (οὖν) is why anyone would want to add to it a burden that is too heavy to bear. To do so would be to put God to the test (πειράζετε τὸν θεόν). As Schnabel notes, the adversative conjunction that connects these verses (ἀλλά) places the emphasis on verse 11 and the conviction that God's salvation is by grace (2012, 635). The prepositional phrase διὰ τῆς χάριτος τοῦ κυρίου Ἰησοῦ is fronted to emphasize grace as the means by which God grants salvation (Culy and Parsons 2003, 290). The genitive of τοῦ κυρίου is subjective. Σωθῆναι is a divine passive that marks God as the ultimate agent. The idea of testing God has OT roots (Exod. 17:2; Num. 14:22; Deut. 6:16; Ps. 95:9) and invites his judgment, as the deaths of Ananias and Sapphira demonstrated (5:9). Rabbinic literature tended to view the "yoke" (ζυγόν) of the law—that is, the obligation to obey it—as a blessing (Barrett 1998, 718). Peter's point, however, was that requiring the Gentiles to keep the law as a means of salvation (15:5) was a requirement that neither he and his listeners (ἡμεῖς) nor their ancestors (οἱ πατέρες ἡμῶν) had been able to meet.

James Proposes a Solution (15:12–21)

James uses a passage from the OT prophet Amos to propose a solution that removes the burden of circumcision from the Gentiles and provides guidelines for table fellowship between Jews and Gentiles.

15:12–14. Following Peter's speech, the entire group became silent (ἐσίγησεν πᾶν τὸ πλῆθος) and began listening (ἤκουον) to Barnabas and Paul while they were explaining (ἐξηγουμένων) all the signs and wonders (σημεῖα καὶ τέρατα) God did among the Gentiles (ἐν τοῖς ἔθνεσιν) through them (δι' αὐτῶν). After Barnabas and Paul stopped speaking (μετὰ τὸ σιγῆσαι αὐτούς), James called for attention (ἄνδρες ἀδελφοί, ἀκούσατέ μου). He began his speech with a summary of Peter's argument (15:14), which should have reminded them of the precedent (πρῶτον) God set when he visited (ἐπεσκέψατο) with the purpose of taking from among the Gentiles (λαβεῖν ἐξ ἐθνῶν) a people for his name (λαὸν τῷ ὀνόματι αὐτοῦ).

The mention of signs and wonders echoes 14:4 and affirms God's divine validation of Paul and Barnabas's ministry. As Bock notes, James's summary of Peter's speech includes several important theological ideas (2007, 503). Both the OT and Luke use ἐπισκέπτομαι to denote divine oversight (Exod. 3:16; 4:31; Jer. 39:41; Luke 1:68, 78; 7:16). The verb carries the sense of making an appearance to help (BDAG s.v. "ἐπισκέπτομαι" 3, 378) and has messianic overtones (Bock 2007, 502). The idea of God "taking a people for his name" echoes God's choice of Israel (Exod. 19:5; Deut. 7:6; 14:2). Marshall, however, notes an interesting difference: "whereas Deuteronomy refers to God selecting Israel to be his special people *separate from the nations*, James here appears to mean that God is now taking a group of people *out of the Gentile nations* to be a people for himself" (2007, 589; emphasis original). Larkin notes that Luke elsewhere uses λαός to refer to the Jews as God's people (1995, 223; cf. 4:10; 10:42; 13:17; 26:17, 23; 28:17). James, however, applies the term to the Gentiles and includes them among God's "people."

James the Just

James, the brother of Jesus (Matt. 13:55; Mark 6:3; Gal. 1:19), was one of the individuals to whom Jesus appeared after his resurrection (1 Cor. 15:7) and one of the "pillars" of the Jerusalem church (Gal. 2:9). He was known as James the Just because of "the excellence of his virtue" (Eusebius, *Hist. eccl.* 2.1.2). In describing his exceptional piety, Hegesippus wrote that "his knees became horny like that of a camel's by reason of his constantly bending the knee in adoration of God and begging forgiveness for the people" (Eusebius, *Hist. eccl.* 2.23.6). He played a key role in the Jerusalem consultation (Acts 15:13–21) and was appointed the first bishop of Jerusalem (Eusebius, *Hist. eccl.* 2.1.2).

He was the author of the canonical letter that bears his name, most likely written during the period of A.D. 40–48 (Davids 1982, 22). He met his death by stoning in A.D. 61 (Josephus, *A.J.* 20.9.1).

15:15–18. James next appeals to the OT, first by noting that the words of the prophets (οἱ λόγοι τῶν προφητῶν) agree with (συμφωνοῦσιν) Peter's summary, then by quoting Amos 9:11–12. James's reference to "the prophets" might point to the book of the twelve Minor Prophets of which Amos is a part (Marshall 1980, 252) or, more likely, to the OT prophets as a whole. By noting that the prophets "agree with" Peter's summary, James affirmed that the events were a direct fulfillment of what the prophets had predicted (Bock 2007, 503). The introductory formula (καθὼς γέγραπται) highlights the continuing validity of Amos's prophecy.

The quotation itself consists of four parts. The first line of verse 16 (μετὰ ταῦτα ἀναστρέψω)—perhaps an echo of Hosea 3:5 and/or Jeremiah 12:15—connects the prophecy to the days when God will return and act on behalf of Israel. The remaining three lines of verse 16 promise that he will restore Israel through the work of the Davidic messiah. The first two lines of verse 17 establish that God's ultimate purpose (ὅπως ἄν) is to incorporate the Gentiles into his people. The final line of verse 17 (λέγει κύριος ποιῶν ταῦτα)—with the addition of what might be an echo of Isaiah 45:21 (γνωστὰ ἀπ' αἰῶνος)—confirms that what God is doing has been his intention from eternity.

"The tent of David that has fallen" (τὴν σκηνὴν Δαυὶδ τὴν πεπτωκυῖαν) refers to "the dynasty of David that had come to an end when Jehoiachin and Zedekiah were forced into exile in Babylon" (Schnabel 2012, 638). The "rest of humankind" (οἱ κατάλοιποι τῶν ἀνθρώπων) who will seek the Lord are, in fact (καί), "all the Gentiles" (πάντα τὰ ἔθνη). The participle ἐπικέκληται is an intensive perfect and a divine passive, which highlights the fact that

God had already claimed the Gentiles as his own. The Lord's declaration that the Gentiles had "my name" (τὸ ὄνομά μου) called upon them echoes James's statement in verse 14. Larkin captures the essence of the quotation well when he writes, "Rightly interpreted, the rebuilt Davidic tent refers to a restored Israel, which in the person of Jewish Christians God chooses to inaugurate the Gentile mission. That was, after all, the purpose of Israel's restoration: that the remainder of men may seek the Lord" (Larkin 1995, 224).

TEXTUAL ANALYSIS: James's Quotation of Amos 9:11–12
Longenecker notes that James's quotation of Amos 9:11–12 "differs from the MT in meaning and the LXX in form" and itemizes both sets of differences (1981, 447). Marshall provides a detailed discussion of the differences (2007, 589–92). Gleason Archer and Gregory Chirichigno suggest that there was a Hebrew text that stood behind the LXX and Acts and of which the MT was a corruption (1983, 155), but Bock evaluates that possibility as "less than clear" (2007, 504). Although he was a Jewish Christian, there is no reason to conclude that James could not have quoted the Greek LXX (contra Haenchen 1971, 448), especially if he was being sensitive to the Hellenistic context of the issue under discussion (Bock 2007, 504). Schnabel argues that the formal variations from the LXX are the result of James interpreting Amos in light of related texts with which it shared words (i.e., *gezerah shawah*), namely Hosea 3:4–5, Jeremiah 12:15–16, Zechariah 8:22, and Isaiah 45:20–23 (2012, 636–41). Regardless, James's use of Amos 9:11–12 provides the OT support for the argument he makes.

15:19–21. Following logically (διό) on Peter's speech, Paul and Barnabas's report, and Amos's prophecy, James proposed (ἐγὼ κρίνω) a solution that addressed two aspects of the issue under discussion. On the one hand, the church should stop creating unnecessary difficulties (μὴ παρενοχλεῖν) for those from among the Gentiles who were turning to God (τοῖς ἀπὸ τῶν ἐθνῶν ἐπιστρέφουσιν ἐπὶ τὸν θεόν) by circumcising them or commanding them to keep the Mosaic Law (contra 15:5). On the other hand (ἀλλά), the church should inform by letter (ἐπιστεῖλαι) those same Gentiles to abstain (τοῦ ἀπέχεσθαι) from four practices that their Jewish brothers found objectionable. The first was eating food polluted by idols (τῶν ἀλισγημάτων τῶν εἰδώλων). The second was engaging in sexual immorality (τῆς πορνείας). The third was eating meat of animals killed by strangling (τοῦ πνικτοῦ). The fourth was consuming blood (τοῦ αἵματος). The rationale (γάρ) for these particular guidelines was that from ancient times (NET, ἐκ γενεῶν ἀρχαίων) Jews in the synagogues (ἐν ταῖς συναγωγαῖς) in every city (κατὰ πόλιν) on every Sabbath (κατὰ πᾶν σάββατον) both read (ἀναγινωσκόμενος) and preached (κηρύσσοντας) Moses. The first part of James's proposal invoked the principle of Christian liberty by rejecting limits on Gentile freedom. The second part of his proposal invoked the principle of Christian love by providing guidelines for respecting Jewish cultural sensitivity. The rationale invoked the principle of Christian unity by extending the scope of his proposal to table fellowship between Gentiles and Jews "in every city."

Κρίνω describes the act of coming to a conclusion after a cognitive process (BDAG s.v. "κρίνω" 4, 568). Stott notes that the verb has a range of meaning that includes "expressing an opinion" at one end of the spectrum and "issuing a decree" at the other end. He then advocates for the mediating sense of "stating a conviction" (1990, 248). Peterson suggests that μὴ παρενοχλεῖν should be understood as "'stop annoying,' since the Gentiles have already been troubled with the regard to the necessity of circumcision" (2009, 433). The middle voice of ἀπέχω carries the sense of avoiding contact with something or someone and takes a genitive object to mark separation (BDAG s.v. "ἀπέχω"

5, 103). The noun ἀλίσγημα denotes pollution or defilement; the cognate verb ἀλισγέω describes the act of making someone or something ceremonially impure (BDAG s.vv. "ἀλίσγημα"; "ἀλισγέω" 44). Εἰδώλων is a subjective genitive. Verse 29 clarifies the phrase as referring to "meat offered to idols" (εἰδωλοθύτων). Πορνεία describes "various kinds of unsanctioned sexual intercourse" (BDAG s.v. "πορνεία" 1, 854). In this context, the noun might refer to sexual activity that accompanied pagan rites and feasts in pagan temples (Witherington 1998, 463), but more likely, it has the broader sense (Peterson 2009, 433). Πνικτός denotes something that has been choked to death (BDAG s.v. "πνικτός" 838) and, therefore, had not been subjected to the ritually prescribed slaughtering process, which included draining blood from the animal (Barrett 1998, 733). At least some English versions translate the word as "the meat of strangled animals" (e.g., NIV). Αἷμα "most naturally refers to the consumption of blood in any form" (Peterson 2009, 434) and reflects the Jewish association of blood and life (Gen. 9:4; Lev. 17:11, 14; Deut. 12:23). Metzger provides a detailed discussion of the textual variants related to verses 20 and 29 and to the subsequent reference in 21:25 (*TCGNT*, 379–83).

Provisions of the Jerusalem Decree

James's proposal to the apostles and the elders, in addition to removing the burden of circumcision from the Gentiles who turned to God (15:19), included four practices from which Gentile disciples should abstain (15:20). Schnabel lists six suggestions for including these specific practices: (1) they were a practical measure to facilitate table fellowship, (2) they reflected the commandments of the Noahic covenant, (3) they were cardinal sins Jews should never commit, (4) they were part of a list of vices and virtues used in teaching proselytes, (5) they were practices related to pagan worship, and (6) they were regulations drawn from Leviticus 17–18

(2012, 644–45). The connection to Leviticus 17–18 seems closest (Larkin 1995, 225; Marshall 1980, 246; Stott 1990, 250). Abstaining from food offered to idols corresponds to Leviticus 17:8–9; abstaining from blood corresponds to Leviticus 17:10–13; abstaining from the meat of strangled animals corresponds to Leviticus 17:14–16; and abstaining from sexual immorality corresponds to Leviticus 18:6–23. In addition, Gentiles living as aliens in Israel were included under these particular injunctions (Lev. 17:8, 10, 13; 18:26). These provisions served three functions. Theologically, they integrated the Gentiles into the people of God (Schnabel 2012, 644). Culturally, they highlighted areas of Jewish sensitivity (Bock 2007, 507; Dunn 1996, 205). Ethically, they facilitated table fellowship between Jews and Gentiles (Longenecker 1981, 448).

The Council Adopts the Proposal (15:22–29)

The assembled church in Jerusalem adopts James's proposal and drafts a letter to send to the churches in Antioch, Syria, and Cilicia.

15:22–23. James's proposal was met with approval from the apostles, the elders, and the whole church (σὺν ὅλῃ τῇ ἐκκλησίᾳ). In response, it seemed good (ἔδοξε) to them to write a letter (γράψαντες διὰ χειρὸς αὐτῶν) and choose (ἐκλεξαμένους) two leaders from the Jerusalem church (ἄνδρας ἡγουμένους ἐν τοῖς ἀδελφοῖς)—Judas Barsabbas and Silas—to send to Syrian Antioch with Paul and Barnabas. The letter's salutation followed the standard first-century form: sender (nominative) to recipients (dative) followed by a greeting (χαίρειν). The senders were the apostles (οἱ ἀπόστολοι) and the elders (οἱ πρεσβύτεροι), who further identified themselves as "brothers" (ἀδελφοί). The recipients were also "the brothers" (τοῖς ἀδελφοῖς). Ethnically, they were from among the Gentiles (τοῖς ἐξ ἐθνῶν); geographically,

they were located in Antioch, Syria, and Cilicia (κατὰ τὴν Ἀντιόχειαν καὶ Συρίαν καὶ Κιλικίαν). The use of ἀδελφοί to describe both the Jewish leaders in Jerusalem and the Gentile disciples in Syria and Cilicia placed the two groups on equal footing and emphasized the unity that crossed ethnic and geographical boundaries.

15:24–27. The body of the letter addressed the two issues James had identified in his proposal. The first issue had brought Paul and Barnabas to Jerusalem—the dispute caused by some who had gone out from the Jerusalem church (τινὲς ἐξ ἡμῶν ἐξελθόντες), but to whom the church had not given orders (οἷς οὐ διεστειλάμεθα) to require circumcision. Those individuals had "troubled and upset [the Gentile believers] by what they said" (L&N §25.231, ἐτάραξαν ὑμᾶς λόγοις ἀνασκευάζοντες τὰς ψυχὰς ὑμῶν). The consultation in Jerusalem agreed unanimously (ἔδοξεν ἡμῖν γενομένοις ὁμοθυμαδόν) to disown those itinerant teachers and offer a threefold endorsement of Barnabas and Paul. They were "our beloved ones" (τοῖς ἀγαπητοῖς ἡμῶν), who had "handed over their souls" (παραδεδωκόσι τὰς ψυχὰς αὐτῶν) on behalf of the name of the Lord Jesus Christ, and whose teaching Judas and Silas would confirm (αὐτοὺς διὰ λόγου ἀπαγγέλλοντας τὰ αὐτά) when they delivered the letter.

Barrett notes that ἔδοξεν ("it seemed best") frequently introduced decrees (1998, 742). Luke has used the adverb ὁμοθυμαδόν ("with one mind") to describe the unity of the church (1:14; 2:46; 4:24; 5:12). Now he uses it to describe the unity of the assembly in making its decision. Although English versions translate the participial phrase παραδεδωκόσι τὰς ψυχὰς αὐτῶν as "who have risked their lives" (e.g., NIV, ESV), Schnabel's argument that the verb more naturally describes "the constant dedication of the two missionaries to Jesus and to the proclamation of the good news about Jesus as Israel's Messiah and Lord" (2012, 649) seems preferable. As the chosen (ἐκλεξαμένους) messengers officially sent out (ἀπεστάλκαμεν) by the church, Judas and Silas would not only deliver the letter but would also be able to provide an authoritative explanation of its contents (Harvey 1998, 54–55).

15:28–29. Then, the letter addressed the issue of table fellowship. It seemed good (ἔδοξεν) to both the consultation and the Holy Spirit to place no greater burden (μηδὲν πλέον ἐπιτίθεσθαι βάρος) on the new Gentile disciples beyond certain "essentials" (πλὴν τούτων τῶν ἐπάναγκες).

The adverb ἐπάναγκες describes something that is necessary or compulsory (BDAG s.v. "ἐπάναγκες" 358). Those essentials—although in a slightly different order—were the four practices set out in verse 20: abstaining (ἀπέχεσθαι) from food offered to idols (εἰδωλοθύτων), from blood (αἵματος), from the meat of strangled animals (πνικτῶν), and from sexual immorality (πορνείας). If Gentile disciples kept themselves (διατηροῦντες ἑαυτούς) from these practices, they would do well (εὖ πράξετε). As Bock notes, by observing these essentials they would avoid causing offense both to Jews and to God (2007, 513). The letter closes with the standard farewell wish to "be healthy" (ἔρρωσθε; cf. 2 Macc. 9:27; 11:21; 3 Macc. 3:12; 7:1, 9).

Judas and Silas Deliver the Letter to Antioch (15:30–35)

Judas and Silas accompany Paul and Barnabas on their return trip and deliver the letter to the church in Antioch.

15:30–35. With the issues resolved and the letter written, Luke moves the narrative quickly to a conclusion (Barrett 1998, 748). Paul, Barnabas, Judas, and Silas were sent on their way (ἀπολυθέντες) and traveled (κατῆλθον) to Syrian Antioch, where they called together (συναγαγόντες) the congregation and delivered (ἐπέδωκαν) the letter. When Judas and

Silas read (ἀναγνόντες) the letter, the church rejoiced (ἐχάρησαν) because of the encouragement (ἐπὶ τῇ παρακλήσει) it gave them. Both Judas and Silas—who were also prophets (αὐτοὶ προφῆται ὄντες)—encouraged (παρεκάλεσαν) and strengthened (ἐπεστήριξαν) the disciples through an extended message (διὰ λόγου πολλοῦ). They spent an unspecified period of time (ποιήσαντες χρόνον) with the church, before being sent on their way with peace (ἀπελύθησαν μετ᾽ εἰρήνης) to the Jerusalem church that had dispatched them (πρὸς τοὺς ἀποστείλαντας αὐτούς). Meanwhile, Paul and Barnabas remained (διέτριβον) in Antioch, where they—along with many others (μετὰ καὶ ἑτέρων πολλῶν)—resumed their ministry of teaching (διδάσκοντες) and sharing the good news (εὐαγγελιζόμενοι) about the Word of the Lord (τὸν λόγον τοῦ κυρίου). The Western text includes verse 34, which scribes most likely inserted to explain why Silas was present in Antioch in verse 40. The variant reads, "But it seemed good to Silas that they remain, and Judas journeyed alone." Strong manuscript evidence (P[74], א, A, B, E, Ψ), however, supports the omission.

THEOLOGICAL FOCUS

The narratival function of Acts 15:1–35 is to bring together the previously separate Jewish and Gentile missions as the united means by which Jesus would use his witnesses to reach beyond Jerusalem, Judea, and Samaria to the ends of the earth. The entire episode revolves around questions that arose from the church's missionary enterprise: How do men and women become Christ-followers and, having begun following him, how do they relate to one another? Luke highlights the chapter's pivotal role by bringing together the major leaders of the movement: Peter, Paul, Barnabas, and James. Most commentators note that Peter makes his final appearance in Acts 15, but as Longenecker observes, he appears as a missionary rather than as an administrator (1981, 445). His account of the conversion of Cornelius's household emphasized two factors that were central in bringing the first Gentile believers into the church: divine initiative in choosing Peter to be the messenger and divine acceptance in bestowing the Holy Spirit. Although Luke includes no speech by either Paul or Barnabas, he specifically notes that their report included divine validation of the Gentile mission by the signs and wonders God worked through them. James made the proposal that replaced the former proselyte model of entry into the people of God with a new eschatological model and established clear guidelines for table fellowship between Gentiles and Jews. The council's letter put a stamp of approval on Paul, Barnabas, and the Gentile mission and set the direction for the remainder of the narrative. Through the actions of the Jerusalem Council, the church authorized both missions to carry out the overarching task Jesus had given his followers.

Theologically, Acts 15:1–35 clarifies the relationship between truth and conscience, between unity and diversity, and between liberty and love. Doctrinally, the decision of the council established that entry into the people of God is through "faith alone rooted in the grace of God through Christ alone" (Bock 2007, 493). On the one hand, there is no need to add anything to the essential truth of the gospel, including culture-bound religious practices. On the other hand, holding to that essential truth does not allow any believer to overrule the conscience of another believer on nonessential practices. Missiologically, the decision of the council established that believers' identity in Christ "both supersedes and allows for their cultural identity" (Larkin 1995, 224). On the one hand, when God brings an individual to faith, he or she becomes a member of the body of Christ with a new identity. On the other hand, there is no need to require any new believer to discard his or her cultural identity in order to become part of the people of God. Ethically, the decision of the council established that followers of Christ must "exercise their liberty with wisdom, restraint, and love" (Peterson 2009, 440). On the one hand, in secondary matters of faith and practice, believers have liberty to follow their convictions. On the other hand, they must be willing to limit their liberty if doing so edifies other believers and advances the progress of the gospel.

PREACHING AND TEACHING STRATEGIES

Exegetical/Theological Synthesis

During their itinerant ministry in Cyprus and South Galatia, Paul and Barnabas had found an open door through which the Gentiles were turning to God. The rapid growth of the Gentile portion of the church raised concerns among the more law-observant Jews in the movement. Bruce observes, "Many Jewish Christians no doubt feared that the influx of so many converts from paganism would bring about a weakening of the church's moral standards" (1988, 286). The solution suggested by some of the Pharisees who had believed was to require the Gentiles to become Jews. Paul and Barnabas strenuously opposed that approach and advocated allowing the Gentiles to retain their cultural identity. Which approach would the church embrace? How would the church respect the convictions of its Jewish members? How would it protect the freedom of its Gentile members? How would it decide what to do? Luke's first-century readers would have wanted to know how a movement that had its origins in Judaism and had many members who practiced Jewish piety would respond to what God was doing among the Gentiles through Paul and Barnabas's ministry. His account of the events surrounding the Jerusalem Council provides the answers, as the church reached a solution that balanced truth and conscience, unity and diversity, liberty and love. With the original audience, twenty-first-century readers share the need to maintain a commitment to essential doctrines, recognize cultural differences, and respect personal convictions in secondary matters of faith and practice.

Preaching/Teaching Idea

Wise counsel guards the truth without binding the conscience.

Contemporary Connections

What does it mean?
Christian liberty is the precious, miraculous, joyful, blood-bought, cosmos-culminating victory of God in Christ, "that we will be saved through the grace of the Lord Jesus" (15:11). God's salvation is all grace. God's grace is all the Lord Jesus. Throughout Acts, the gospel message never changed. From Pentecost onward, Jesus's disciples proclaimed the forgiveness of sins in Jesus to all who would respond with repentance and faith (2:38–39). When the Pharisaical push to add circumcision and law obedience to that gracious gift arose, the Jerusalem Council soundly denounced it. At the risk of appearing to compromise gospel grace, but in pursuit of Christian love, the council proposed key observances to foster unity. Abstaining from food offered to idols, sexual immorality, things strangled, and blood are not additions to the gospel that will allow God's people to gain his grace. Instead, these Levitical observances made it possible for God's grace-receiving family to get along together and enjoy one another. Peter required repeated visions and the voice of God's Spirit to challenge his lifelong commitment to food laws (Acts 10). It will take time for the rest of the church to come along.

Is it true?
Although there is considerable debate over how exactly first-century Jews understood the Mosaic Law's role in salvation, this chapter makes clear how Jews from the circumcision party thought. They put it bluntly: "Unless you are circumcised according to the custom of Moses, you cannot be saved" (15:1). To that requirement, some of the Pharisees who had believed added another: "observe the law of Moses" (15:5). As Stott notes, some were seriously suggesting that Moses must complete what Jesus started. This issue arises repeatedly in the NT, perhaps most dramatically in Galatians, where Paul asks, "Are you so foolish? Having begun by the Spirit, are you now being perfected by the flesh?" (Gal. 3:3) and declares, "We have been justified by faith in Christ and not by works of the law" (Gal. 2:15). Jesus's death is all-sufficient, and we receive it by faith alone. The council's emphatic stand makes their guidelines for the Gentiles even more striking. Would listing all the things Gentiles should avoid add works of the law to Jesus? Might the list get miscommunicated and misused abroad? The risk was real, but the value of unity was so great that the church took the risk to guard Christian fellowship. If certain practices would doom any hope of mutual hospitality between Jewish and Gentile believers, it was worth sacrificing rights in the gospel in order to encourage love for one another.

Now what?
As a largely Gentile church today, we do not struggle with adding the same things to Jesus's all-sufficiency that the first-century church did. We are not tempted to make circumcision or food laws essential to salvation. The impulse toward *work* over *grace*, though, is alive and well. The gospel sounds too good to be true, and so, we add a little here and a little there. Salvation becomes Jesus *plus* church attendance, or Jesus *plus* a resolve to do better morally, or Jesus *plus* promises to do more ministry. We want a gospel we can control, can quantify, and can earn. We will not find that gospel in Scripture. The Bible's gospel is all Jesus and all grace.

Ironically, although we are more than willing to add duties to grace for God's acceptance, we resist strongly the idea of limiting our own liberty for the sake of Christian unity. If we think we can earn credit with God, we will add the heaviest yoke available. If the issue is the welfare of another brother or sister, though, we are reluctant to pick up the lightest straw. Scripture teaches clearly that practices, observances, or indulgences can hinder another believer's faith. Even if they are permissible, it is better to go without so that we can "pursue what makes for peace and for mutual upbuilding" (Rom. 14:19). Seeing God's kingdom advance is more important than insisting on my own happiness (1 Cor. 9:19–23).

Creativity in Presentation

It is an amusing but awkward experience to watch a mother or father with little ones in tow trying to navigate the grocery store. For every item on the list the parent places into the grocery cart, the children add two treats for good measure. When the kids are not looking, the treats return to the shelves. When the parents are not looking, more treats appear. Ultimately, the cashier will decide who wins the battle. Our passage describes a similar putting-in/taking-out struggle for what is essential to the gospel. In some congregations, it is grace alone, through faith alone, in Christ alone. In others, circumcision, law-keeping, and other elements keep going into the cart. A creative presentation might play up this tussle.

To illustrate giving up freedom for fellowship, think about what we would sacrifice for mere physical health or civility. I hope I would not serve friends a dish they did not like, even if it was my favorite food. I hope I would not grow a plant to which my neighbor was allergic, even if it would look great along the fence line. If we are willing to limit our rights for the tastes and health of others, how much more should we make them subservient to the spiritual well-being of others? There are concerns that are far more important than getting my way.

The reformer Martin Luther made this point winsomely in his treatise *On the Freedom of a Christian* (1520): "A Christian is a perfectly free lord of all, subject to none. A Christian is a perfectly dutiful servant of all, subject to all." With respect to salvation, we are justified by faith in Christ alone, and subject to nothing else. With respect to my neighbor, however, I am bound by love to perfect subjection in Jesus's name. We are absolutely free and simultaneously, absolutely bound. It will take our entire Christian lives to learn and live out our freedom and subjection. Wise counsel guards the truth without binding the conscience.

- The problem (15:1–11)

- The wise solution (15:12–35)

    - A solution that guards the truth.

    - A solution that does not bind the conscience.

DISCUSSION QUESTIONS

1. Why did Paul and Barnabas object so strenuously to what the visitors from Judea were teaching about circumcision?

2. How did Peter's speech affirm God's action in opening a door for the Gentiles?

3. How did James's proposal change the paradigm for incorporating Gentiles into the church?

4. How did the council's letter balance doctrine and duty?

5. What principles can you draw from this passage about balancing Christian unity with cultural diversity?

MACEDONIA AND ACHAIA (ACTS 15:36–18:17)

The decision of the Jerusalem Council cleared the way for Paul to set out on a new stage of the Gentile mission. The popular label often applied to this period of travel and ministry is Paul's "second missionary journey." Five missiological principles run throughout this section. First, church planting should target key cities from which new believers can reach surrounding areas. Second, initial evangelistic activity should focus on potentially receptive audiences. Third, clear proclamation of God's Word must be central to evangelistic activity. Fourth, evangelistic activity will result in opposition as well as in conversions. Fifth, there is a time when it is wiser to move to another location than to continue evangelistic efforts in the face of widespread opposition. The section also includes three instances of the gospel's interaction with civil authorities. The events recounted most likely cover the period from early A.D. 49 through early A.D. 52.

49	Winter	Syrian Antioch (15:36–40)	Split over John Mark (15:37–40)
	Spring	Antioch to Troas (15:41–16:10)	Timothy circumcised (16:3)
	Summer		Macedonian vision (16:9)
	Fall	Philippi (16:11–40)	
50	Winter	Thessalonica (17:1–9)	
	Spring	Berea (17:10–15)	Silas and Timothy remain (17:14)
	Summer	Athens (17:16–34)	
	Fall		Silas and Timothy arrive (18:5)
51	Winter		1–2 Thessalonians
	Spring	Corinth (18:1–17)	Corinthian vision (18:9–10)
	Summer		Before Gallio (18:12–17)
	Fall		
52	Winter		
	Spring	Cenchrea to Jerusalem (18:18–21)	Visit to Ephesus (18:19–21)
	Summer	Syrian Antioch (18:22)	
	Spring	Syrian Antioch to Ephesus (18:23)	

This fourth division consists of five preaching sections. The first records how the Holy Spirit led Paul and Silas to cross into Europe (15:36–16:10). The second describes the missionary team's witness in Philippi as well as their arrest and release from prison (16:11–40). The third details their witness in Thessalonica and Berea as they moved westward along the Via Egnatia (17:1–15). The fourth records Paul's solo witness in Athens, including his speech before the Areopagus Council (17:16–34). The fifth describes the team's witness in Corinth (18:1–17).

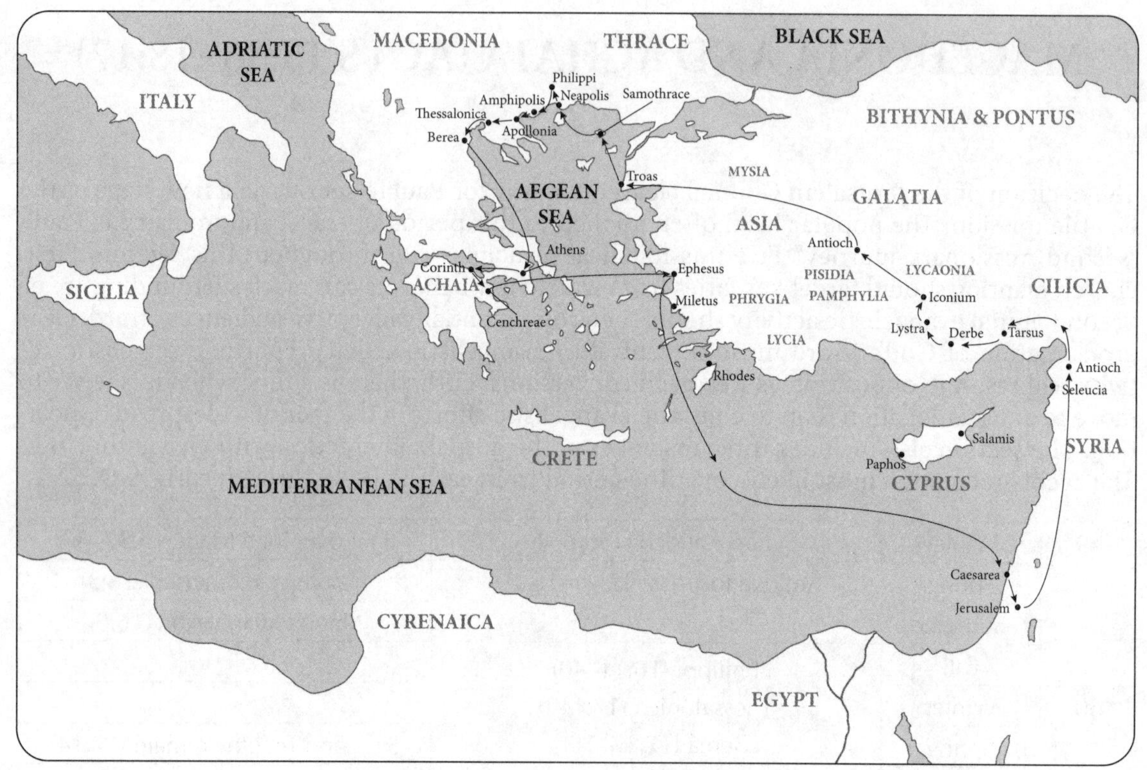

Paul's Second Journey

Acts 15:36–16:10

EXEGETICAL IDEA

The process that led Paul to minister in Europe involved resolving interpersonal differences, addressing cultural considerations, and following the Holy Spirit's guidance.

THEOLOGICAL IDEA

Taking the gospel to new frontiers requires discernment in order to maintain team unity, to be culturally sensitive, and to follow the Spirit's guidance.

PREACHING IDEA

The progress of God's gospel demands discernment by God's people.

PREACHING POINTERS

Christian ministry is not easy; it can be a minefield with multiple opportunities to step in the wrong place. Paul and Barnabas discovered that interpersonal issues could threaten team unity. Paul had to make a tough decision about how to be culturally sensitive. As Paul and Silas traveled together, they repeatedly encountered closed doors. In each instance, God's witnesses needed discernment and the Holy Spirit's guidance to navigate the process of taking the gospel to new frontiers. With the original readers of Acts, we need to understand how God works to take the gospel to new frontiers, and we need to know how to make the right choices along the way.

People today should be able to identify with the potential pitfalls of ministry, because those issues echo everyday life in general—disagreements with coworkers and unexpected changes in plans are just two examples. In that regard, the account of how God expanded the scope of the church's outreach to Gentile Europe corrects any notion that ministry is simple or easy. At the same time, this passage commends the virtues of discernment, perseverance, and obedience, as Paul and his missionary team follow the Holy Spirit's leading to new avenues of outreach. It reminds us that the progress of God's gospel demands discernment by God's people.

THE ROAD TO EUROPE (15:36–16:10)

LITERARY STRUCTURE AND THEMES (15:36–16:10)

The passage consists of three paragraphs. The first describes a dispute between Paul and Barnabas over whether to include John Mark on a return visit to the churches they had planted (15:36–40). The second describes Paul and Silas's visit to the churches in southern Asia Minor as well as Timothy's addition to the missionary team (16:1–5). The third describes the way in which the Holy Spirit guided the team northward to Troas, where Paul received a vision that led them to cross over into Macedonia (16:6–10).

- ***Split over John Mark (15:36–40)***
- ***Visiting the Churches (16:1–5)***
- ***Macedonian Call (16:6–10)***

EXPOSITION (15:36–16:10)

This passage begins the fourth major division of the book. Previously, the gospel had moved outward geographically from Jerusalem (1:1–8:3) to Judea/Samaria/Syria (8:4–12:25) to Cyprus/Galatia (13:1–14:28). Now, in the aftermath of the Jerusalem Council and their report to the congregation in Syrian Antioch (15:1–35), Paul and Barnabas were eager to inform the churches they had recently planted of the good news about the decisions the council reached. Since the inland road from Antioch through Syria and Cilicia ultimately led to Ephesus, the fourth largest city in the empire, it seems likely that Paul had in mind further missionary work in western Asia Minor after visiting the churches in southern Galatia. The Holy Spirit, however, had other plans for the team as he led them northward in preparation for the next stage of gospel expansion—into Macedonia and Achaia (16:11–18:22). This passage traces Paul's steps on the road to Europe and covers the period from winter through summer of A.D. 49. Larkin suggests that one contribution of this passage is to set out the means by which the church can identify the right purpose, the right people, and the right place for its missionary efforts (1995, 229–34). The virtues of discernment, perseverance, and obedience are crucial in exercising these means in pursuit of the progress of the gospel.

Split over John Mark (15:36–40)

After Paul and Barnabas disagree over whether to take John Mark with them on a second trip, two missionary teams leave Syrian Antioch with different destinations.

15:36. "After some days" (μετὰ τινας ἡμέρας) most likely denotes the winter months (Marshall 1980, 257), since there was no sea travel on the Mediterranean from mid-November through mid-March (Larkin 1995, 369). With the coming of spring, Paul proposed a visit to the churches he and Barnabas had planted on their first cycle of travels. "The brothers in every city" (τοὺς ἀδελφοὺς κατὰ πόλιν πᾶσαν) highlights the comprehensive nature of the plan. "Let us visit" (ἐπισκεψώμεθα) highlights special care and concern for God's people (Luke 1:68; 7:16; Acts 7:43; 15:14). Paul's proposal reflects his normal practice as seen at the end of his first cycle of travels (14:21–28) and during the winter of his third cycle of travels (20:1–5). It also reminds the reader of the continuing connection between the missionary and mission churches.

15:37–39a. Barnabas had already "determined to take along" (ἐβούλετο συμπαραλαβεῖν) his cousin John Mark (Col. 4:10). John Mark was originally from the Jerusalem church (12:12), but he had traveled north when Paul and Barnabas returned to Syrian Antioch after the famine relief visit (12:25). He accompanied the team when they evangelized Cyprus (13:5) but returned to Jerusalem when they crossed over to Pamphylia (13:13). Apparently, he was back in Syrian Antioch more than three years later. Paul "thought it best not to take along" (ἠξίου . . . μὴ συμπαραλαμβάνειν) John Mark, "who had deserted them" (τὸν ἀποστάντα ἀπ' αὐτῶν) on their first cycle of travels.

Luke gives no reason either for Barnabas's desire to include John Mark (although Larkin suggests possible motives; 1995, 230–31) or for John Mark's previous departure (although Longenecker argues that John Mark disagreed with Paul's willingness to approach Gentiles directly; 1981, 421). Regardless, Paul had decided that John Mark was not to be trusted (Barrett 1998, 755) and should not accompany them. The result was a "sharp disagreement" (παροξυσμός) and the formation of two missionary teams. Dunn suggests that the disagreement over table fellowship in Antioch (Gal. 2:11–14) might have strained the relationship between Barnabas and Paul, if that incident took place during this general time period (1996, 209), but Schnabel rejects this notion (2012, 662).

TEXTUAL ANALYSIS: "A Sharp Disagreement"
Although most English versions translate the verb ἐβούλετο in 15:37 as "wanted" (NASB, ESV, NIV, NRSV, CSB), a better choice might be "planned" or "intended" (BDAG s.v. "βούλομαι" 2, 182). KJV translates the verb as "determined," which captures the idea that Barnabas had already made up his mind to include John Mark. Paul's response in 15:38 (ἠξίου) is variously translated as "decided" (NRSV), "kept insisting" (NASB, CSB), and "did not think it right" (KJV, GNB, ESV, NIV). Culy and Parsons note that when the verb occurs in the imperfect indicative, the sense is "to think something

best," and that it is wise not to overemphasize the function of the imperfect (2003, 304). It is better to understand the description of John Mark in 15:38 (τὸν ἀποστάντα ἀπ' αὐτῶν) as substantival ("one who had deserted them," NRSV, NASB, CSB, ESV, KJV) than as causal ("because he had deserted them," NLT, GNB, NIV). The verb itself (ἀφίστημι) can mean "withdraw" (ESV) or "depart" (KJV), but the cognate noun (ὁ ἀποστάτης) carries the nuance of "deserter" and explains the more frequent choice of "deserted" (NIV, NLT, CSB, NASB, NRSV). Luke 8:13 and 1 Timothy 4:1 suggest the severity of the failure. The result of Paul's and Barnabas's differences of opinion in 15:39a (παροξυσμός) is "a state of irritation expressed in argument" (BDAG s.v. "παροξυσμός" 2, 780). The cognate verb (παροχύνω) describes the action of causing someone to become inwardly angry.

15:39b–41. Barnabas and John Mark "sailed away for Cyprus" (ἐκπλεῦσαι εἰς Κύπρον) to revisit the predominantly Jewish churches there (13:5), and subsequent comments by both Paul (2 Tim. 4:11; Philem. 24) and Peter (1 Peter 5:13) validate Barnabas's confidence in his younger cousin. Paul, in turn, chose Silas as his teammate. Silas was a highly respected member of the Jerusalem church (15:22), perhaps an elder (Barrett 1998, 739), definitely a prophet (15:32), and a Roman citizen (16:21, 37). He was also an able amanuensis (1 Thess. 1:1; 2 Thess. 1:1; 1 Peter 5:12). The Jerusalem church had sent him as an envoy to Syrian Antioch (15:22), where he had remained for a while and then returned to Jerusalem (15:33), perhaps the previous autumn. Now, he was back in Syrian Antioch. Adding him to the missionary team affirms Paul's solidarity with the Jerusalem church (Peterson 2009, 448).

The leaders of the church "commended [them] to the grace of the Lord" (παραδοθεὶς τῇ χάριτι τοῦ κυρίου), which gave Paul and Silas the same stamp of approval they had previously given Paul and Barnabas (14:26). Paul and Silas took the land route westward that would lead them from Antioch in Syria through Cilicia. Paul, of course, was born in the Cilician city of Tarsus (21:39; 22:3) and had spent time ministering in that province after his conversion (9:30; Gal. 1:21). He was in Tarsus when Barnabas originally recruited him to be help with the work in Syrian Antioch (11:25–26). As they traveled, they "strengthened the churches" (ἐπιστηρίζων τὰς ἐκκλησίας). A variant reading in the Western text adds that they did so by "delivering the commands of the elders" (παραδιδοὺς τὰς ἐντολὰς τῶν πρεσβυτέρων).

Visiting the Churches (16:1–5)

While reporting the decision of the Jerusalem Council to the churches in southern Asia Minor, Paul and Silas add Timothy to their team.

16:1–3. The road from Syria through Cilicia led to the territory of Lycaonia at the southern end of the Roman province of Galatia, where Paul and Silas, traveling from east to west, "arrived [first] in Derbe and [then] in Lystra" (κατήντησεν εἰς Δέρβην καὶ εἰς Λύστραν). Although Origen notes that Timothy was from Derbe (*Comm. Rom.* 10.39), commentators lean toward Lystra (Marshall 1980, 259). Timothy was a "disciple" (μαθητής), most likely one of Paul's own converts (2 Cor. 4:17) from his first visit (14:4–20). "His mother was a Jewish believer" (γυναικὸς Ἰουδαίας πιστῆς, NLT) as was his grandmother (2 Tim. 1:5), and he was "respected by the brothers in Lystra and Iconium" (ἐμαρτυρεῖτο ὑπὸ τῶν ἐν Λύστροις καὶ Ἰκονίῳ ἀδελφῶν; cf. 6:3; 10:12; 22:12 for μαρτυρέω; Culy and Parsons 2003, 306, suggest the translation "respected").

Paul wanted to add Timothy to the team "but his father was a Greek" (πατρὸς δὲ Ἕλληνος), probably not a believer, and possibly deceased (Larkin 1995, 232). Under Jewish law, a child took the religion of the mother, but under Greek law, the father dominated the household (Longenecker 1981, 455). The Jews in Lystra and Iconium "all knew that [Timothy's] father

was a Greek" (ᾔδεισαν ἅπαντες τὸν πατέρα αὐτοῦ ὅτι Ἕλλην ὑπῆρχεν). They would have viewed Timothy, therefore, as ethnically Jewish but "technically apostate" (Bruce 1990, 352) because his parents had not circumcised him, and they would have denied him access to their synagogues.

For Paul, circumcision was unimportant (Gal. 5:6; 6:15) unless others demanded it as essential for salvation, in which case he argued forcefully against imposing it (Acts 15:1–2; Gal. 5:2–4). In support of his position, the Jerusalem Council had ruled that circumcision was not required for Gentile believers (15:19–22). Practically, though, Paul was willing to become "all things to all men that I might save some of them" (1 Cor. 9:22). Because part of his evangelistic strategy in cities was to begin by preaching in local synagogues and because Timothy was ethnically Jewish, Paul "took and circumcised" (λαβὼν περιέτεμεν) Timothy to remove any possibility of offending Jews to whom they might preach. Peterson notes that this incident accomplishes three functions. First, it shows that the Jerusalem Council did not abolish Jewish-Christian tradition. Second, it shows that Paul had not abandoned his commitment to Judaism Third, it shows that Paul did not insist that Jews forsake the Mosaic law (2009, 451).

16:4–5. With Timothy on board, the team continued their travels. "They delivered the decisions" points to the faithful passing on (παρεδίδοσαν; cf. Rom. 6:17; 1 Cor. 11:2, 23; 15:3) of decrees that must be observed (τὰ δόγματα; cf. Luke 2:1). The Jerusalem Council had passed enduring judgment (τὰ κεκριμένα) on those decrees, and they were binding (φυλάσσειν). The result of this ministry was both qualitative, in that the churches "were strengthened in the faith" (ἐστερεοῦντο τῇ πίστει; cf. Col. 2:5), and quantitative, in that the churches "grew daily in numbers" (ἐπερίσσευον τῷ ἀριθμῷ καθ' ἡμέραν; cf. 2:47; 5:14; 6:7; 9:31; 12:24).

Verbal Aspect in 16:1–5

Culy and Parsons discuss the significance of verbal aspect in this paragraph (2003, 305–6). The aorist tense verb in 16:1 (κατήντησεν) provides the background for the events, and the aorist tense verbs in 16:3 (ἠθέλησεν . . . ἐξελθεῖν . . . λαβὼν . . . περιέτεμεν) advance the narrative. The imperfect tense verbs in 16:2 (ἐμαρτυρεῖτο), 16:4 (διεπορεύοντο . . . παρεδίδοσαν), and 16:5 (ἐστερεοῦντο . . . ἐπερίσσευον) highlight significant actions. The perfect tense of τὰ κεκριμένα in 16:4 emphasizes the established nature of the Jerusalem Council's decision.

Macedonian Call (16:6–10)

Providentially hindered from entering the territory of Asia and the province of Bithynia, Paul and Silas travel to Troas where God calls them to preach the gospel in Macedonia.

16:6–8. Divine guidance takes two forms in this section. First, the Holy Spirit provided negative guidance at two points in the team's travels. When they approached the border of the territory of Asia, they were "prevented by the Holy Spirit" (κωλυθέντες ὑπὸ τοῦ ἁγίου πνεύματος) from preaching there. Then, when they came to the border of Mysia (ἐλθόντες κατὰ τὴν Μυσίαν) and were attempting to enter the province of Bithynia (ἐπείραζον εἰς τὴν Βιθυνίαν πορευθῆναι), "the Spirit of Jesus did not permit them" (οὐκ εἴασεν αὐτοὺς τὸ πνεῦμα Ἰησοῦ) to do so. Luke does not say what means the Spirit used or how he communicated his guidance in either instance, but it is clear that "Jesus himself through the Spirit was guiding the progress of the gospel" (Marshall 1980, 263). Blocked from going eastward into Bithynia, they "went down to Troas" (κατέβησαν εἰς Τρῳάδα) "passing by" (παρελθόντες) the opportunity to preach the gospel in Mysia (Bruce 1990, 355).

16:9–10. A second, positive form of divine guidance occurred when "a vision appeared to Paul in the night" (ὅραμα διὰ τῆς νυκτὸς τῷ Παύλῳ ὤφθη; cf. NASB). This vision was not Paul's first (9:1–9; 22:6–21; 26:12–18), nor would it be his last (18:9–10; 27:23–24; cf. 2 Cor. 12:1–6). The vision specifically directed the team to cross over to the province of Macedonia (διαβὰς εἰς Μακεδονίαν). The team "immediately" (εὐθέως) "put together" (συμβιβάζοντες) the negative and positive guidance and sought to depart for northern Greece (ἐζητήσαμεν ἐξελθεῖν εἰς Μακεδονίαν). In so doing, they "showed unhesitating obedience to a divine command" (Barrett 1998, 772), which is precisely the response Jesus expects from his disciples. The change to the first-person plural ("we sought to go on into Macedonia, concluding that God had called us") in 16:10 introduces the first of five "we" passages in the later chapters of Acts (16:10–17; 20:5–15; 21:1–18; 27:1–29; 28:1–16).

THEOLOGICAL FOCUS

The narratival function of Acts 15:36–16:10 is to recount the process of how God expanded the church's outreach to Gentile Europe. The passage introduces the fourth major section of the book and traces Paul's steps from Syrian Antioch to Troas, where he experienced the vision that led him to conclude that his next stop should be Macedonia. Along the way, he needed to make critical choices about how to proceed in light of the decision reached by the Jerusalem Council. The council had validated the mission to the Gentiles. What implications did that verdict have regarding who was best suited for the mission, how to negotiate the differences between Jewish and Gentile culture, and where to pursue the mission next?

At the core, each of these issues is a theological issue. Was John Mark truly on board with the theology of the Gentile mission? Was Silas the better coworker because he was fully committed to the council's decision? Would the fact that Timothy's father was a Greek offend Jewish audiences? Would circumcising Timothy be sacrificing doctrinal truth to pragmatic concerns? Should the next target city be Ephesus? Should it be somewhere else? How would the team discern the Holy Spirit's guidance? Taking the gospel to new frontiers requires discernment in order to maintain team unity, to be culturally sensitive, and to follow the Spirit's guidance. Luke's account of the road Paul and Silas took to Europe provides concrete examples of how the team addressed each of these issues.

PREACHING AND TEACHING STRATEGIES

Exegetical/Theological Synthesis

Luke's first-century readers would have wanted to know the factors that led Paul and Silas to take the gospel to the new frontier of Europe. With his original readers, the twenty-first-century audience shares the need to understand how God works to take the gospel to new frontiers, and they need to know how to navigate the choices they must make along the way. The logical follow-up to his ministry in Cyprus and Asia Minor would have been to go back on the road with Barnabas, first to revisit the churches they had planted then to press westward toward Ephesus. No sooner did Paul suggest the idea, however, than issues arose that required choices. Would John Mark or Silas be the better choice for the team? Would Timothy's background become an issue? If not Ephesus, where? Paul ultimately made decisions that were theologically sound, mission driven, and Spirit led. Left to our own resources, we will inevitably go astray. Fortunately, we can draw on the truth of God's Word, the counsel of God's people, and the leading of God's Spirit as we seek to exercise discernment in following the guidance he provides.

Preaching/Teaching Idea

The progress of God's gospel demands discernment by God's people.

Contemporary Connections

What does it mean?

In Christian life and ministry, discernment is the ability to evaluate several courses of action and choose the one that most closely aligns with Scripture's teaching and the Holy Spirit's leading. Discernment is essential to the progress of the gospel because, although the mission is clear, the strategy might not be. We know our marching orders: to be Spirit-empowered witnesses to the ends of the earth (Acts 1:8). That commission is nonnegotiable, but we might not readily know how, where, or with whom to take the next step. Finding the right purpose, the right people, and the right place takes discernment.

In his classic work *Decision-Making and the Will of God*, Garry Friesen (1980) identifies eight "road signs" that point to making wise decisions: the Bible, circumstances, inner impressions, mature counsel, personal desire, common sense, special guidance, and results. In Acts 15:36–16:10, we see four of those road signs at work as Paul made ministry-related decisions: mature counsel (15:40; 16:2), Scripture (16:4), inner impressions (16:6–7), and special guidance (16:9). Exercising discernment, therefore, means examining all the pertinent road signs and balancing them wisely.

Is it true?

We need discernment for ministry today just as Paul did on the road to Europe. At each leg of the Great Commission journey, the church must always seek to discern God's leading. All four of the road signs of discernment in our passage are present and active in such directing today. First, God used *mature counsel* to commend Paul and Silas on their journey (15:40) and to recommend Timothy's addition to the team (16:2). Godly counsel is the way of wisdom; Proverbs implores "in an abundance of counselors there is safety" (Prov. 11:14), "a wise man listens to advice" (Prov. 12:15), and "whoever walks with the wise becomes wise" (Prov. 13:20). Today, we are watching the rise and fall of celebrity pastors, heavy on power and light on counsel. We are enamored with hard-nosed, forward-thinking, quick-acting, lone-ranger leaders, but God loves to use the godly, together, to discern his leading.

Second, God used *his inspired Word* to guide the young congregations (16:4). The churches Paul and his team visited grew in strength and in conversions (16:5). Will we trust his Scripture to lead us to the same? Our generation flirts with leadership literature to fill this role. We can be quicker to reach for podcasts than for the prophets, to reach for TED Talks than for Torah. We want to know what works for corporations and try it on our churches. To be sure, we learn from all kinds of avenues, but Scripture always holds a more prominent place in God's direction. Finally, God's Spirit was highly active in *impressing and guiding* (16:6–7, 9). He took keen interest in where his gospel went. Does he not also do so today? His Spirit opens and shuts doors, prompts and redirects. The question is not whether he will speak but whether we will slow down enough to listen.

Now what?
We share the enormous challenge Paul and his team did: to strengthen the reached and evangelize the unreached. The cities, towns, and neighborhoods where we live, work, and play are full of people who have never heard the good news clearly explained, may think they are Christians but are not truly born again, or have been burned by the church and want nothing to do with it. They will not come to us. The church must go to them. If Acts is any indication, we will not reach them with lone-ranger leaders, the best leadership books, or well-intentioned busyness. We will not reach them idly, cheaply, without real strain on our membership, or without Spirit-infused prayer. The task is too great, the need is too profound, and the obstacles are too insidious for the church to wing it or to do what she has always done. Real gospel progress demands real discernment by God's people. The church today must seek God to guide through mature counsel, Scripture, inner impressions, and special guidance. We do that longing to see what the early church saw: "churches were strengthened in the faith, and they increased in number daily" (16:5).

Creativity in Presentation
Have you ever entered an address into your phone's GPS, followed every turn without thinking, and ended up in the entirely wrong place? Sometimes it can be comical. We can so trust our device that we turn down gravel roads or into industrial areas, all the while believing that the soft, calm voice on our phones speaking *lefts* and *rights* surely knows best. Truly, directions are like discernment—it matters who is telling us where to go.

Our passage lends itself to a sermon that starts with a destination, ends with an arrival, and gives us several *left and right turns* throughout the story to get us there.

- God's Destination (15:36)

- God's Directions

  - God Leads Through His People (15:36–16:3)

  - God Leads Through His Word (16:4–5)

  - God Leads Through His Spirit (16:6–10)

- God's Arrival (16:5, 10)

Paul shares the destination at the outset: to strengthen and grow the church (15:36). Of all the things that the church, the Jerusalem

Council, and Paul and Barnabas themselves would disagree about, the destination is not one of them. The early church took its commission seriously to strengthen and grow believers. Do we share that same clarity? Are we all plugging the same address into our GPS devices?

God gives his directions (our discernment) in several ways: (1) God leads through his people, (2) God leads through his Word, and (3) God leads through his Spirit. Of course, the story here and in our lives is not a series of tight, clearly marked *lefts* and *rights*. Paul and Barnabas sharply disagreed over whom to take. Paul made a cultural sensitivity judgment call about Timothy's circumcision. The team meandered a bit before setting out toward Macedonia. God proved faithfully, however, in every turn to lead and guide.

The validation of discerning God's directions is the church's arrival. God used his people and Word to strengthen churches in the faith and increase conversions (16:5). God used his Spirit to direct the missionary team to new fields in Macedonia (16:10). Acts is truly the story of what Jesus continues to do and teach (1:1). After setting the church off in the right direction, Jesus does not leave us to get lost. He gives us directions to discern what is theologically sound, mission driven, and Spirit led. Our job is to trust that he will accomplish his aims and bring his church to his arrival. The progress of God's gospel demands discernment by God's people.

DISCUSSION QUESTIONS

1. In light of the Jerusalem Council's decision, what questions might have arisen in Paul's mind while he was on "home ministry assignment" in Syrian Antioch (15:30–35)?

2. Was Barnabas wrong to insist on including John Mark on their visit to the churches they had previously planted? Was Paul wrong to insist John Mark not accompany them?

3. Did Paul's decision to circumcise Timothy contradict his previous insistence that Titus should not be circumcised (cf. Gal. 2:1–10)?

4. How can we discern the Holy Spirit's guidance as we seek to make ministry-related decisions?

5. What roles do God's Word and God's people play in making ministry-related decisions?

Acts 16:11–40

EXEGETICAL IDEA
God uses Paul and Silas's witness in Philippi to open the hearts of a Godfearing woman and a jailer to the gospel, to cast a demon out of a slave girl, and to establish the legitimacy of the newly planted church.

THEOLOGICAL IDEA
The preaching of the gospel disrupts the religious, spiritual, economic, personal, and civic lives of the individuals who encounter it.

PREACHING IDEA
The gospel changes everything.

PREACHING POINTERS
Whether through firsthand experience or through secondhand news reports, everyone understands the disruption a major earthquake can create. Earthquakes were common in the Eastern Mediterranean, and the ancient Greeks considered them to be the expression of "the earth-shaker" Poseidon's anger (Homer, *Il.* 20.57–58). When Paul arrived in Philippi, the gospel hit the city like a 9.0 magnitude earthquake—both literally and in every other way. The gospel touched—and disrupted—the lives of everyone in the city. With the original readers of Acts, we need to understand that God's working through the gospel touches every aspect of life and culture.

People today can easily relate to the disruptions of life, whether religious, spiritual, economic, personal, or civic. It is rare for an installment of the evening news to end without at least some mention of one or more such events. The account of Paul and Silas's ministry in Philippi corrects any idea that the gospel leaves other aspects of life and culture untouched. It commends the responses of saving faith and shared life in response to God's working. It reminds us that we should expect the gospel to "shake up" our own lives and the lives of those around us, because wherever it is preached, the gospel changes everything.

WITNESS IN PHILIPPI (16:11–40)

LITERARY STRUCTURE AND THEMES (16:11–40)

The passage consists of four paragraphs that follow the basic pattern of biblical narrative. Luke sets the stage with Paul and Silas's arrival in Philippi and Lydia's conversion (16:11–15). The action builds when they encounter the slave girl, cast out the spirit that possesses her, and find themselves in prison as a result (16:16–24). The action reaches its high point with the earthquake that frees Paul and Silas and leads to the jailer's dramatic request for salvation (16:25–34). The action winds down with their public release, encouragement of the church, and departure from the city (16:35–40).

- ***Conversion of a God-worshipping Woman (16:11–15)***
- ***Exorcism of a Slave Girl (16:16–24)***
- ***Conversion of a Jailer (16:25–34)***
- ***Protection of the New Church (16:35–40)***

EXPOSITION (16:11–40)

Following both providential and extraordinary guidance to cross into Europe (16:6–10), Paul and Silas left Troas by boat. After stopping at the island of Samothrace, they landed in the port city of Neapolis (16:11). They then traveled inland about eight miles to Philippi, where they stayed "for several days" (16:12, GNB and NLT), most likely during the fall of A.D. 49. This passage details their ministry in that city. The fact that first-person narrative ends at 16:17 and resumes in 20:5 has led some scholars to suggest that Luke remained in Philippi to assist the new church when Paul and Silas departed for Thessalonica, and then rejoined Paul when he passed through Macedonia on his final trip to Jerusalem five or six years later (Longenecker 1981, 467).

Throughout the narrative, God uses his witnesses to open hearts to the gospel, overcome spiritual oppression, correct unjust treatment by civil authorities, and establish the legitimacy of the new church. Williams suggests that including the gospel's impact on a woman (16:11–15), a slave (16:16–24), and a jailer (16:25–34) highlights the crossing of gender, social, and ethnic barriers (1989, 280). Larkin notes that the exorcism in Philippi (16:18) parallels similar activities by Peter in Judea (5:16) and Philip in Samaria (8:7) and epitomizes the gospel's liberating advance into Europe (1995, 238). Indeed, wherever it is preached, the gospel changes everything.

Conversion of a God-worshipping Woman (16:11–15)

After Paul and Silas arrive in Philippi, the Lord opens Lydia's heart to the gospel.

16:11–12. Obediently following the divine guidance they had received (16:9–10), Paul and Silas set sail from Troas (ἀναχθέντες ἀπὸ Τρῳάδος). They sailed first to the island of Samothrace, where they spent the night. On the next day (τῇ ἐπιούσῃ) they completed their 156-mile voyage and arrived in the port city of Neapolis. Philippi lay ten miles inland along the Via Egnatia, the major Roman road through the region, and was "a major city of that part of Macedonia" (πρώτη τῆς μερίδος τῆς Μακεδονίας πόλις). The team made Philippi their first Macedonian destination and stayed there "several days" (ἡμέρας τινάς). In addition to being a major city, Philippi was also a Roman colony (κολωνία). A Roman colony was "a piece of Rome transplanted abroad" (Bruce 1990, 357). Its citizens enjoyed the right to self-government, freedom from taxation, and the same legal system as Rome (Barrett 1998, 780). Paul's subsequent letter to the Philippian church suggests that the residents of that city were particularly conscious of their Roman citizenship (Phil. 1:27; 3:20).

TEXTUAL ANALYSIS: "The first city of Macedonia".
The province of Macedonia was divided into four districts, and Thessalonica was the "first" (i.e., greatest) city in the province as a whole. Amphipolis was the capital of the district in which Philippi was located. For these reasons, scholars debate the original reading of the city's description in 16:12. Marshall (1980, 266) and Bruce (1990, 357) choose to follow the UBS[5] majority reading "a city of the first district of Macedonia" (GNB). Others follow the better-attested reading "a major city of that district of Macedonia" (NLT; cf. Culy and Parsons 2003, 311).

Philippi

Philip of Macedon founded Philippi ca. 360 B.C., ten miles from the north end of the Aegean Sea, and named it after himself. Wars subsequently destroyed the city, but Octavius rebuilt it after he consolidated his control of the empire ca. 40 B.C. He settled the new city with veterans from his army and designated it a Roman colony. It was a major stop on the Via Egnatia, ten miles inland from its port city of Neapolis. The population was predominantly Roman with a significant number of Macedonian Greeks. Luke's comment about Paul visiting "a place of prayer" outside the city gates (16:13) suggests that the Jewish community in Philippi was not large enough to support a synagogue. Philippi was famous for its medical school, and if Luke was a doctor as tradition records, it is interesting to consider his possible connection to Philippi. The fact that the "we" passages begin with Paul's vision of the man from Macedonia (16:9–11) has led some to suggest that Luke himself was the man in the vision (Ramsay 1895, 204). Bruce (1988, 308) hints that Luke might have been practicing as a doctor in Troas when Paul, Silas, and Timothy arrived there. If Luke was from Philippi or had studied in the medical school in Philippi, that fact might explain the prominence he gives to the city. Richard Ascough (1998, 101–3) ascribes the "first city" description in 16:12 to the civic pride of someone who was from Philippi, whether a source or Luke himself.

16:13–15. When the Sabbath arrived, Paul, Silas, and Timothy went outside the city gate (ἐξήλθομεν ἔξω τῆς πύλης) beside the Gangites River, where they "supposed there was a place of prayer" (ἐνομίζομεν προσευχὴν εἶναι). Upon finding the place, Paul and his companions began speaking to the women who had assembled (ἐλαλοῦμεν ταῖς συνελθούσαις γυναιξίν). Among the group they encountered was a certain woman by the name of Lydia (τις γυνὴ ὀνόματι Λυδία), who is described in three ways. She was a "dealer in purple cloth" (πορφυρόπωλις), "from the city of Thyatira" (πόλεως Θυατίρων), and a "worshipper of [the one true] God" (σεβομένη τὸν θεόν). As the result of her continued listening (ἤκουεν), the Lord "opened her heart" (διήνοιξεν τὴν καρδίαν) so that she "was paying close attention" (προσέχειν) to what Paul was saying. She and her house were baptized (ἐβαπτίσθη καὶ ὁ οἶκος αὐτῆς), and she invited Paul and Silas into her home (εἰσελθόντες εἰς τὸν οἶκόν μου μένετε).

The descriptions of Lydia, along with her Latinized name and the fact that she had a house large enough for hospitality (16:15), suggest that she was Roman, either freeborn or a freed slave, a devout adherent to Judaism, and at least moderately wealthy. As such, she was the first of four such women Paul would encounter in Macedonia and Achaia. The others were Priscilla in Corinth (18:2–3; Rom. 16:3–5), Phoebe in Cenchrea (Rom. 16:1–2), and Chloe in Corinth (1 Cor. 1:11). Her experience is a reminder that God's act of opening hearts is key to a person understanding and believing the truth of Scripture (Luke 24:45; Acts 13:48). Her subsequent baptism and offer of hospitality provide clear evidence that she is faithful to the Lord (πιστὴν τῷ κυριῳ εἶναι) and reaffirm the truth that saving faith makes a difference in the way people live. The baptism of her household (16:15) is the second of four "household conversions" in Acts (10:48; 16:33; 18:8; cf. 1 Cor. 1:16).

TEXTUAL ANALYSIS: "A place of prayer"
The existence of multiple textual variants complicates the process of determining the exact wording of 16:13 (Barrett 1998, 780–81). The reading adopted by UBS[5] (ἐνομίζομεν προσευχήν) is most likely the original, although Bruce disagrees (1990, 358). In the NT, προσευχή most frequently refers to the act of prayer (Acts 1:14; 2:42; 3:1; 6:4). It can, however, designate a time of prayer (Acts 3:1) or a place of prayer (Acts 16:16; cf. Luke 19:46). The latter is the sense in Acts 16:13. Bock concludes that the word refers to a synagogue (2007, 533), but it seems more likely that it designates an informal place of prayer—perhaps in the open air (Larkin 1995, 235) or possibly in a building (Schnabel 2012, 679).

Lydia of Thyatira

Although it is possible that Lydia was an itinerant trader, it is more likely that she had migrated from the Roman province of Asia and had established herself in Philippi as a retail merchant. Thyatira was located in the ancient kingdom of Lydia in the Lycus Valley of western Asia Minor. Its original settlers were from Macedonia, and the city was famous for its purple dye as early as Homer's time (Bruce 1990, 358). Luke 16:19 suggests that "purple" denoted luxury goods that only the wealthy could afford, and 1 Maccabees 10:62 connects those goods with royalty, although Schnabel disagrees (2012, 680). There was a Jewish community in Thyatira, and it is likely that Lydia was attracted to Judaism there (Dunn 1996, 219). See 10:2 for a discussion of "Godfearers."

Exorcism of a Slave Girl (16:16–24)

The exorcism of a demon-possessed slave girl results in imprisonment for Paul and Silas.

16:16–17. Subsequently (ἐγένετο δέ), as the team was returning to the place of prayer where they had encountered Lydia, a slave girl (παιδίσκη) met (ὑπαντῆσαι) them. Larkin notes that she was "twice bound, spiritually and economically" (1995, 237). She was possessed by "a spirit of divination" (ἔχουσαν πνεῦμα πύθωνα), and she was exploited by her masters, to whom she kept on bringing great profit (ἐργασίαν πολλὴν παρεῖχεν τοῖς κυρίοις αὐτῆς) by forecasting the future (μαντευομένη). As she followed Paul and his companions, she kept on crying out (ἔκραζεν, iterative imperfect) that they were "servants of the Most High God" (δοῦλοι τοῦ θεοῦ τοῦ ὑψίστου) and were proclaiming "a way of salvation" (ὁδὸν σωτηρίας). Both the title and the message provided potential points of contact but could have been misunderstood and would have needed correction. "Most High God" was "a divine title current among both Jews and Greeks" (Bruce 1990, 360). For Jews, it would point to the one true God, but for Gentiles, it could designate whatever deity the hearer might consider supreme (e.g., Ζεὺς ὕψιστος). Similarly, for Jews, "a way of salvation" would denote a way to acquire divine deliverance from sin, but for Gentiles, it would refer to "release from the powers governing the fate of man and of the material world" (Longenecker 1981, 462).

TEXTUAL ANALYSIS: "A spirit of divination" Luke describes the slave girl as having "a spirit of divination" (ESV). The Greek phrase πνεῦμα πύθωνα could be translated either as "a spirit [named] Python" (taking πύθωνα as a noun in apposition) or as "a Pythonian spirit" (taking πύθωνα as a noun used adjectivally). The spirit expressed itself by "giving oracles" (μαντεύομαι), and its name reflected common terminology in the ancient world. Python was the name of the serpent/dragon Apollo killed at Delphi and from which he acquired the power to forecast the future (Larkin 1995, 237). The priestesses at the Delphi shrine were "Pythiai," and supposedly, a spirit dwelling in their bellies spoke through them. By extension, the term came to designate someone (usually a woman) through whom a god or a spirit spoke. For Luke, it clearly had evil connotations (Schnabel 2012, 682). See Bock on magic and oracles in the ancient world (2007, 535).

16:18. When the slave girl persisted in her public statements for many days (τοῦτο ἐποίει ἐπὶ πολλὰς ἡμέρας), Paul "reached the end of [his] patience" (διαπονηθείς; cf. Barrett 1998, 787). Scholars debate why Paul decided to address the issue when he did after he had tolerated it previously, but possibly he grew tired of the spirit's proclamation "getting more of a hearing than the proclamation of the gospel" (Longenecker 1981, 462). His response paralleled Jesus's actions in similar situations (Luke 4:35, 41; 8:28)—he turned (ἐπιστρέψας), spoke to the spirit (τῷ πνεύματι εἶπεν), and commanded it to come out of the slave girl (παραγγέλλω σοι . . . ἐξελθεῖν ἀπ' αὐτης). The result was immediate (ἐξῆλθεν αὐτη τῇ ὥρᾳ), and Paul's use of Jesus's name (ἐν ὀνόματι Ἰησοῦ Χριστοῦ) was consistent with the early church's understanding of its source of authority (3:6, 16; 4:10; cf. 19:13, 17). Larkin adds the practical note that "exorcism must be approached today . . . with much care,

humility and prayer. But there must also be bold confidence that Jesus is still bringing release to the captives" (1995, 239).

16:19–21. When the spirit "went out from her" (ἐξελθεῖν ἀπ' αὐτῆς), the slave girl's masters saw that their "hope of profit went out" (ἐχῆλθεν ἡ ἐλπὶς τῆς ἐργασίας) as well. In response, they laid hold of Paul and Silas and dragged them "into the marketplace before the rulers" (εἰς τὴν ἀγορὰν ἐπὶ τοὺς ἄρχοντας). Although the actual impact of the exorcism was economic—as would also be the case later in Ephesus (19:23–27)—the slave girl's masters brought charges against Paul and Silas that were designed to be far more damaging. Their charges involved three areas, which Larkin characterizes as "appeals to law-and-order nationalism, anti-Semitic prejudice and ethnic traditionalism" (1995, 239).

First, the accusers charged Paul and Silas with "throwing the city into confusion" (NASB, ἐκταράσσουσιν . . . τὴν πόλιν). That is, they were disturbing the public order, which would have been a direct challenge to the magistrates' primary responsibility (Schnabel 2012, 685). Second, the accusers charged them with "being Jews" (Ἰουδαῖοι ὑπάρχοντες). That is, they were associated with the troublemakers whom Claudius had recently expelled from Rome (cf. 18:2; Suetonius, *Claud.* 25.3–4). Third, the accusers charged them with "proclaiming customs that it is not permitted to receive or do" (καταγγέλλουσιν ἔθη ἃ οὐκ ἔξεστιν . . . παρδέξεσθαι οὐδὲ ποιεῖν), since the residents of Philippi were Romans (Ῥωμαίοις οὖσιν). That is, they threatened the stability of the city by advocating practices that could turn residents away from their "faithful citizenship to Rome" (Bock 2007, 538). None of these charges addressed the real issue: loss of financial profit. Instead, as Dunn notes, the accusers "adopted a tactic repeated countless times in the history of communities the world over: the appeal to prejudice against small ethnic minorities commonly known for their peculiar customs" (1996, 222).

TEXTUAL ANALYSIS: "Into the marketplace before the rulers"
The ἀγορά ("marketplace") was the center of a Greek city's public life (17:17), a place for children to play (Luke 7:32), and a venue for public events, including announcing lawsuits (Demosthenes, *Macart.* 57). GNB translates the word as "public square." It would have had "a raised judgment seat, the βῆμα, where the magistrates sit to render judgment" (Bock 2007, 537). In 16:20, Luke calls the officials before whom Paul and Silas appeared ἄρχοντες ("rulers"), which was a general title for Gentile officials. He subsequently refers to them as στρατηγοί ("chief magistrates"), which was the courtesy designation for the highest official in a Greco-Roman city (BDAG s.v. "στρατηγός" 1, 947; cf. 16:22, 35, 36, 38). Josephus attests to that title for officials in Pergamum (*A.J.* 14.247) and Sardis (*A.J.* 14.259). The official Roman title was *duoviri* (Barrett 1998, 789), which appears nowhere in the NT. Each magistrate was attended by two ῥαβδοῦχοι ("officers," literally "rod-bearers"; cf. 16:35, 38), who carried bundles of rods about five feet long, served as the magistrate's household guard, cleared his way in crowds, and punished offenders as he directed. Their title was *lictor* (Bruce 1990, 366).

16:22–24. The accusers' inflammatory charges had the desired effect. The crowd that had gathered "joined in and showed its hostility" (NJB, συνεπέστη) toward Paul and Silas. The magistrates ordered them stripped (περιρήξαντες αὐτῶν τὰ ἱμάτια), beaten severely with rods (ῥαβδίζειν πολλάς . . . πληγάς), and imprisoned (ἔβαλον εἰς φυλακήν). Ordered to keep them securely (ἀσφαλῶς τηρεῖν αὐτούς), the jailer put Paul and Silas in the inner prison (εἰς τὴν ἐσωτέρον φυλακήν) and secured their feet in stocks (τοὺς πόδας ἠσφαλίσατο αὐτῶν εἰς τὸ ξύλον). The intent of the beating was most likely to discourage Paul and Silas's followers from further preaching (Bock 2007, 538). The intent of the stocks was most likely to ensure security rather than to inflict torture (Barrett 1998, 793; contra Bruce 1990, 363).

Conversion of a Jailer (16:25–34)
When an earthquake frees Paul and Silas, their jailer responds with saving faith.

16:25–26. At midnight (κατὰ τὸ μεσονύκτιον), Paul and Silas were in the process of praying (προσευχόμενοι) and singing praises to God (ὕμνουν), while the other prisoners were listening (ἐπηκροῶντο). Suddenly (ἄφνω), an earthquake shook the foundations of the prison, all the doors opened immediately, and "the chains of all (the prisoners) came loose" (Culy and Parsons 2003, 318, πάντων τὰ δεσμὰ ἀνέφη). In their praying and their "joy amid suffering" (Marshall 1980, 271), they were following the practice (2:42; 3:23–30; 6:4; 11:5; 12:12; 13:3) and example (5:41) of the early church as well as Paul's own practice (9:11) and teaching (cf. Phil. 1:19; 4:11–13). Tertullian alludes to this episode when he writes, "the leg suffers nothing in the stocks while the mind is in heaven" (*Mart.* 2). Longenecker notes and refutes suggestions that verses 25–34 comprise an "independent legend" or a conventional story describing a miraculous escape (1981, 464).

16:27–28. The same earthquake that shook the foundations of the prison also shook the foundations of the jailer's life (Larkin 1995, 242). He awoke to find the prison doors open (ἀνεῳγμένας τάς θύρας τῆς φυλακῆς) and, he supposed, the prisoners gone (νομίζων ἐκπεφευγέται τοὺς δεσμίους). Because under Roman law, a guard who allowed a prisoner to escape was liable to the same penalty as the escaped prisoner (Justinian, *Cod.* 9.4.4), the jailer drew his sword (σπασάμενος τὴν μάχαιραν) and prepared to kill himself (ἤμελλεν ἑαυτὸν ἀναιρεῖν). Compare 12:19 and 27:42 for similar circumstances and responses. Luke does not explain how Paul knew of the jailer's intention—which raises questions for some commentators (Conzelmann 1987, 132; Haenchen 1971, 501)—but it is reasonable to suggest that Paul heard what was going on (Marshall 1980, 272). Regardless, Paul called out loudly (ἐφώνησεν μεγάλη σωνῆ) to the jailer, urged him not to harm himself (μηδὲν πράξῃς σεαυτῷ κακόν), and assured him that all the prisoners were still in custody (ἅπαντες ἐσμεν ἐνθάδε).

16:29–30. In response to Paul's call, the jailer asked for lights (αἰτήσας φῶτα), rushed into (εἰδεπήδησεν) the inner cell (cf. 16:24), and "threw himself trembling at the feet of Paul and Silas" (NJB). Elsewhere, trembling (ἔντρομος) is connected with fear (Heb. 12:21), and falling at someone's feet (προσπίπτω) is the act of a supplicant (Mark 5:33; 7:25; Luke 8:47). The jailer's response was one of alarmed appeal rather than of worship (Bock 2007, 541). After leading them outside (προαγαγὼν αὐτοὺς ἔξω)—perhaps into the prison's courtyard (Schnabel 2012, 691)—the jailer asked the question to which the action has been building, "Sirs, what must I do to be saved?" (NLT).

16:31–32. The jailer's question might well reflect the slave girl's repeated declarations that Paul and Silas were proclaiming "the way of salvation" (16:17). Their initial answer included three key elements of the gospel proclamation in Acts. First, faith (πίστευσον) is the appropriate response to God's working (8:12–13; 13:12). Second, the Lord Jesus (ἐπὶ τὸν κύριον' Ἰησοῦν) is the appropriate

object of faith (9:42; 11:17). Third, salvation (σωθήσῃ) is the certain result of saving faith (2:21; 11:14). The title "Lord Jesus" echoes similar statements in Paul's letters (Rom. 10:9; 1 Cor. 12:3; Phil. 2:11), and Larkin notes that "Paul knows no separation between receiving Jesus as Savior and following him as Lord" (1995, 242). The addition of "you and your household" (σύ καὶ ὁ οἶκός σου) extends the offer of salvation to the jailer's extended family. Paul and Silas elaborated on this succinct exhortation by speaking the Word of the Lord (τὸν λόγον τοῦ κυρίου) to both the jailer (αὐτῷ) and to all those in his house (πᾶσιν τοῖς ἐν τῇ οἰκίᾳ αὐτοῦ).

Saving Faith in Luke-Acts

The jailer's question and Paul's response bring together two significant themes from Luke-Acts: believing and salvation. The verb πιστεύω occurs forty-six times in Luke-Acts, while the verb σῴζω and the noun σωτηρία occur forty times. The latter number comprises more than one quarter of the occurrences of both words in the New Testament as a whole.

Πιστεύω can describe the act of entrusting something to someone (Luke 16:11) or the act of giving credence or intellectual ascent to someone or something (Luke 1:20, 45; 20:5; 22:67; 24:25; Acts 9:26; 13:41; 24:14; 26:27 [twice]; 24:25). The largest group of occurrences (thirty-four times), however, refers to the act of committing the whole person to someone or something in trust and obedience. Σῴζω and σωτηρία can describe deliverance from a range of circumstances including enemies (Luke 1:71; Acts 7:25), hostile spirits (Luke 8:36), sickness/disease (Luke 8:48, 50; 17:19; 18:42; Acts 4:9; 14:19), or physical death (Luke 23:35 [twice], 37, 39; Acts 27:20, 31, 34). The largest group of occurrences (twenty-four times), however, refers to deliverance from "transcendent danger or destruction" (BDAG s.v. "σῴζω" 2, 982). In Acts 16:31, Paul urges the jailer to commit his whole person to Jesus (πίστευσον ἐπὶ τὸν κύριον Ἰησοῦν) in order to experience deliverance from his sin-cursed life and destiny (ἵνα σωθήσῃ).

In Luke-Acts, a person is saved by believing (Luke 8:12), which is an act of God's grace (Acts 15:11) that is extended to all those whom God has appointed (Acts 13:48). Most importantly, a person believes in the Lord Jesus Christ (Acts 5:14; 9:42; 11:17, 21; 14:23; 22:19). Alternately, a person believes in God (Acts 16:34) or the message of the gospel (Acts 4:4; 15:7). The benefits of salvation include eternal life (Acts 13:48), forgiveness of sins (Luke 1:77; Acts 10:43; cf. Luke 24:47), redemption (Luke 1:69), justification (Acts 13:39), and the gift of the Holy Spirit (Acts 11:17). It is entirely possible that Paul explained these aspects of saving faith when he "spoke the Word of the Lord to [the jailer] together with all who were in his house" (Acts 16:32).

16:33–34. Luke highlights the jailer's unhesitating response to the gospel by noting that he acted "in that hour of the night" (ἐν ἐκείνῃ τῇ ὥρᾳ τῆς νυκτός) and "immediately" (παραχρῆμα). His actions provide vivid evidence of the dramatic change that had taken place in his life. He extended physical care to the missionaries by washing their wounds (ἔλουσεν ἀπὸ τῶν πληγῶν). He identified with Christ and submitted to his authority by being baptized (ἐβαπτίσθη). He extended hospitality to Paul and Silas by taking them into his home (ἀναγαγών αὐτοὺς εἰς τὸν οἶκον) and feeding them (παρέθηκεν τράπεζαν). He expressed the heartfelt joy (ἠγαλλιάσατο) that accompanies salvation (cf. 8:39; 13:48).

Schnabel provides helpful background on "the impropriety or even illegality" of the jailer's actions in light of first-century prison culture (2012, 692). The meal is more naturally understood as an outworking of the common life of the early church (2:46) rather than as a celebration of the Eucharist as some have suggested. The perfect tense that describes the jailer's faith (πεπιστευκὼς τῷ θεῷ) "suggests its enduring quality" (Bock 2007, 543). The notes that "all his family" (GNB, οἱ αὐτοῦ πάντες) were baptized and that the jailer believed "with his entire household" (ESV, πανοικεί) are the third and fourth references to the jailer's extended family (16:31–32). They reinforce the fact that "the New Testament takes the unity of the family seriously, and when salvation is offered to the head of the household, it is as a matter of course made available to the rest of the family group (including dependents and servants) as well" (Marshall 1980, 273).

Protection of the New Church (16:35–40)

By demanding a public release from prison, Paul and Silas establish that the new church is not a threat to Roman law.

16:35–36. In the morning (ἡμέρας γενομένης), the magistrates (οἱ στρατηγοί) instructed their attending officers (τοὺς ῥαβδούχους)—who had most likely beaten Paul and Silas (cf. ῥαβδίζειν in 16:22) the previous day (Bock 2007, 543)—to release the prisoners. Luke provides no motive for the magistrates' decision, although a textual variant in the Western text ascribes it to fear resulting from the nocturnal earthquake (ἀναμνησθέντες τὸν σεισμὸν τὸν γεγονότα ἐφοβήθησαν). Another suggestion is that they "regarded the beating and night's imprisonment as sufficient exercise of their authority . . . for so trivial an offence" (Marshall, 1980, 274). The officers apparently communicated the order to the jailer (ὁ δεσμοφύλαξ), because he informed Paul and Silas of their release (ἀπέσταλκαν οἱ στρατηγοὶ ἵνα ἀπολυθῆτε) and encouraged them to "Come out and go in peace" (ἐξελθόντες πορεύεσθε ἐν εἰρήνῃ).

Shared Life as Evidence of Saving Faith

Larkin describes the jailer and his family as "quintessential converts" (1995, 243), which highlights a recurring pattern in Acts. Luke includes the same elements when he describes both the conversion of Lydia and the conversion of the jailer. After they hear the word, they respond in faith. After they receive baptism, they share their lives with other disciples. The same pattern appears in the account of Pentecost (2:40–44), in the account of Cornelius's conversion in Caesarea (10:44–48), and in subsequent events surrounding Crispus's conversion in Corinth (18:5–8).

	Pentecost (2:40–42)	Cornelius (10:44–48)	Lydia (16:14–15)	Jailer (16:31–34)	Crispus (18:5–8)
Hear the Word	2:40	10:44a	16:14b	16:32	18:5
Respond in Faith	2:41a "received his word"	10:44b cf. 11:17 "after believing in the Lord Jesus Christ"	16:14b "opened her heart to respond"	16:34b "having believed in God"	18:8a "believed in the Lord"
Receive Baptism	2:41b	10:48a	16:15b	16:33	18:8b
Share Life with Others	2:42	10:48b	16:15b	16:34a	18:7

Shared life among disciples was a key characteristic of the early church (2:43–47; 4:32–37), and these passages make it clear that willingness to participate in that shared life serves as evidence of saving faith. What was true for the early church is equally true for the contemporary church.

16:37. Because he and Silas were Roman citizens (ἀνθρώπους Ῥωμαίους ὑπάρχοντας), however, Paul emphatically rejected the offer of release (οὐ γάρ; cf. Barrett 1998, 802). The magistrates had previously acted in public (δημοσίᾳ) and without due process (ἀκατακρίτους). Now, they tried to act in secret (λάθρᾳ). They had beaten Paul and Silas (δείραντες) and had "thrown [them] into prison" (ἔβαλεν εἰς φυλακήν). Now, they were trying to "throw [them] out" (ἐκβάλλουσιν) of prison without acknowledging their abuse of authority. Instead, Paul demanded that the magistrates come personally (ἐλθόντες αὐτοί) and escort them out of prison (ἡμᾶς ἐξαγαγέτωσαν).

TEXTUAL ANALYSIS: "Men who are Romans"
By asserting their status as Romans, Paul invoked the legal rights associated with citizenship. Authorities could not inflict humiliating public punishment on citizens, and citizens were entitled to a trial before being punished (Larkin 1995, 243). The magistrates had clearly violated both rights, and citizens had the right to seek legal redress

for such violations (Barrett 1997, 801). There is considerable discussion about how Paul and Silas might have proven their citizenship (Barrett 1997, 802) and why they did not invoke their rights earlier in the process (Bruce 1990, 336). There is no evidence available to answer the first question, and the most likely answer to the second question is that Paul thought raising the issue at the time of their release was in the best interests of the new Philippian congregation (Peterson 2009, 473).

16:38–39. The officers reported Paul's response (ἀπήγγειλαν ... τὰ ῥήματα ταῦτα) to the magistrates. When they heard that Paul and Silas were Romans (ἀκούσαντες ὅτι Ῥωμαῖοι εἰσιν), the magistrates were justifiably "alarmed" (NLT, NIV, ἐφοβήθησαν) because they were open to punishment or even dismissal for violating the rights of Roman citizens (Peterson 2009, 474). They went to the prison, "appealed" (παρεκάλεσαν) to Paul and Silas, escorted them out (ἐξαγαγόντες), and "repeatedly asked" (ἠρώτων; cf. Bock 2007, 545) them to leave the city (ἀπελθεῖν ἀπὸ τῆς πόλεως). The Western text again adds supposed details—this time, that the magistrates brought many friends with them, declared that they did not realize Paul and Silas were righteous men, and were concerned that the slave girl's masters would again cause trouble (Longenecker 1981, 467).

16:40. After leaving the prison (ἐξελθόντες ἀπὸ τῆς φυλακῆς), Paul and Silas returned to Lydia's house (εἰσῆλθον πρὸς τὴν Λυδίαν) where they "encouraged the brothers" (παρεκάλεσαν τοὺς ἀδελφούς) and, then, departed (καὶ ἐξῆλθαν). The third-person narrative leads several commentators to conclude that Luke remained in Philippi when Paul, Silas, and Timothy departed (Longenecker 1981, 467; Marshall 1980, 275; Schnabel 2012, 695). At that point, the congregation consisted of the members of Lydia's household, the members of the jailer's household, and, most likely, the slave girl (Peterson 2009, 475). Paul's demands and the magistrates'

response confirmed the legitimacy of the new church and established a peaceful context in which it could continue to grow. Larkin (1995, 244) draws three practical principles from this episode. First, when Christians suffer at the hands of the civil authorities, it should be as innocent victims rather than as guilty troublemakers (cf. 1 Peter 4:15–16). Second, when their rights are violated, Christians should appeal unjust treatment to the civil authorities. Third, Christians should expect those authorities to correct their errors.

THEOLOGICAL FOCUS

The narratival function of Acts 16:11–40 is to recount the impact of the gospel as it crosses a new cultural threshold into Europe. The gospel has moved outward geographically from Jerusalem (2:42–8:1), to Judea/Galilee/Samaria (8:2–9:31), to Syria (9:32–12:25), and to Cyprus/Asia Minor (13:1–16:5). It has also moved outward culturally from Hebrew-speaking Jews (2:42–6:7), to Greek-speaking Jews (6:8–8:1), to Samaritans (8:2–25), to a proselyte (8:25–40), to a Godfearer (10:1–48), and to Gentiles (11:19–30). To this point, God's witnesses have preached the gospel primarily in cities with Jewish communities, and their strategy has been to begin in the local synagogues. Now, God has led his witnesses into Macedonia and eventually Achaia, the birthplace of Greek religion and culture. What impact would the gospel have in this new religious and cultural context? Would God's witnesses need to adjust their message and/or their method? Would the gospel continue to spread as it had to this point in the narrative (6:7; 9:31; 12:24; 16:5)?

Theologically, Acts 16:11–40 highlights the continuity of the gospel's advance into this new context. Faith continues to be the means of salvation (16:31; cf. 5:14; 9:42; 11:17) and continues to include households (16:31; cf. 2:39; 10:44–48). The name of Jesus continues to exercise authority over evil spirits (16:18; cf. 5:16; 8:7). The gospel continues to be a perceived threat to the existing order (16:19–21; cf. 4:1–22; 5:17–42; 6:8–12; 13:50; 14:2–6, 19–20) and continues to lead to imprisonment (16:22–24; cf. 5:17–18; 12:1–4). Previously, the opposition had come primarily from Jews; now, it also comes from Gentiles. Previously, the concerns had been primarily religious and social; now, they also include political and economic elements. Deliverance from imprisonment, however, continues to be in response to the prayers of God's people (16:25; cf. 5:19–20; 12:5–12). Luke's account of Paul and Silas's ministry in Philippi demonstrates that the gospel crosses cultural thresholds as effectively as it crosses geographical boundaries and that when it does, it changes everything.

PREACHING AND TEACHING STRATEGIES

Exegetical/Theological Synthesis
Luke's first-century readers would want to know the impact the gospel would have as it crossed the geographical and cultural border from Asia to Europe. With his original readers, the twenty-first-century audience shares the need to understand that the gospel makes a difference in the lives of the individuals it touches. It causes a major upheaval in every aspect of life and culture—whether religious, spiritual, economic, personal, or civic—regardless of the context in which it is proclaimed. As they proclaim that gospel in whatever context they might find themselves, God's witnesses can draw encouragement from the resources he provides. Those resources include his sovereign working to open hearts (16:14), the truth of his word (16:14, 32), his authority over hostile spiritual powers (16:18), his response to prayers for deliverance (16:25), the shared life of those who come to him in faith (16:15, 34), and the integrity of the civil authorities to correct injustice (16:37–39). They can be confident in both the power of the gospel and the Lord who is the source of the gospel that changes everything.

Preaching/Teaching Idea
The gospel changes everything.

Contemporary Connections

What does it mean?
The gospel changes everything. Wherever God draws people to himself in conversion or confronts principalities and powers in gospel proclamation, real change happens in individuals, families, workplaces, and communities. The Philippian slave owners had it right: "they are disturbing our city" (16:20). The Thessalonians will say as much and more (17:6). Ephesian idol-makers would agree (19:27). The gospel does not play nice with principalities. Lydia receives new life. A slave girl receives her freedom. A jailor receives a new direction. Philippi is duly disturbed. Lord willing, that disruption is coming to a city near you.

As the gospel fans out from Jerusalem to the ends of the earth, spanning millennia, it effects real change. Lydia's conversion alone crosses racial, social, gender, and socioeconomic barriers, and her life is transformed immediately. This successful international businesswoman influences her whole household toward faith and makes her home the hub of the mission team's work in that city. The Philippian jailer's conversion is just as dramatic. Whole lives and households headed in one direction make about-faces and head in another.

In between those stories is a far more sinister one. Lydia dealt in purple goods. Others dealt in slavery and sorcery. Nameless owners exploited a young, demon-possessed slave girl. They cared about their wallets, not her welfare, happily making money off her misery. Gospel expansion and demonic oppression, however, do not mix well. At great risk to himself Paul cast out the spirit in Jesus's name, and broke the bonds of her suffering and her marketability in a moment of divine power. Lydia, little girl, jailer, households, and markets are irreparably changed.

Is it true?

This section resonates deeply with younger generations of believers and unbelievers alike. Our culture is stuck in a paradox: we subscribe to individualized, relativized, what's-true-for-me spirituality—except in certain situations. It is a cardinal cultural sin to tell another person what to believe—except when it comes to justice. Scroll through any millennial social media feed and a clarion call for absolute justice abounds: Black Lives Matter; Blue Lives Matter; racial reconciliation; #woke; sexual abuse scandals; welfare reform; immigration policy; and the plight of the poor, oppressed, unborn, and refugee. These movements are God-given impulses for real, abiding, spiritual and societal change, but they are olive branches of peace cut off from the trunk of the very gospel that feeds and sustains them. It is only God in Christ in his gospel that can effect the lasting change the world longs for.

While our culture, just like Philippi's culture, presses us to keep our beliefs to ourselves where they cannot hurt or offend anyone else, the gospel spills over neatly drawn lines of political correctness and upends the present order. The gospel is good news for body and soul, civic community, and church community. Throughout history, where the gospel goes, it brings with it justice, reconciles races, uplifts the poor, and practices hospitality in the unlikeliest of places. Converted communities get their hands dirty. The Amy Carmichaels, William Wilberforces, and Martin Luther King Jrs. come by their callings honestly. The gospel is explosive.

Now what?

A wise pastor once asked his church, "If Jesus answered *yes* to all of the prayers you prayed last week, what would happen today?" His question exposes thin expectations. Do we actually expect the gospel to shake things up in our lives, our churches, our cities? Have we resigned ourselves to a domestic, house-cat Christianity content to dwell quietly and privately inside the doors of our hearts? Watching God work as the gospel spreads in Philippi reawakens our imagination as to what is possible.

The nineteenth-century British missionary to India William Carey once said, "Expect great things from God. Attempt great things for God." We can quibble about the wording, but expecting and attempting go hand in hand. The more we expect the power of God for salvation and transformation in our communities, the more we will attempt those very things by his power. We will preach the gospel to the wealthy, looking for Lydias. We will labor for the gospel's implicit value of all people, even the poor and oppressed, looking for the slave girls. We will heartily rejoice in God, even in suffering. The faithful witness is not in prison, but the worldly jailor is.

Creativity in Presentation

Few things inspire our faith in a God whose gospel changes everything more than stories. Stories told firsthand are even more inspiring. Accounts of people converted or freed from addiction or possession prove God is alive and active. Luke was so sure of this truth, that he aimed his two-book project chockful of eyewitnesses at bringing "*certainty* concerning the things you have been taught" (Luke 1:4). As Joel Green says, "For Luke . . . narration is proclamation" (1995, 19). The sermon here is in the story.

This preaching section is special because *Luke was there.* His narration-as-proclamation switches from "they" (16:8) to "we" (16:10) through 16:17. That change means Luke himself was either present or close by for all three dramatic scenes. A first-person narrative sermon, where the preacher assumes Luke's view and voice, can be effective here. For example, the abridged version of the beginning of Lydia's story might go something like this:

Philippi was different from the places we had seen God work before. This wasn't Asia anymore. This was Europe. Our strategy had been to find synagogues first and witness to the Jews there. Philippi didn't have a synagogue. What could we do? It finally dawned on us that even if there wasn't a synagogue, Jews and those interested in God would still meet and pray where they could on the Sabbath. The next Saturday, we found a place outside the city near the river. Here's what happened.

Tell all three scenes. (Note: Luke is not present in the final jail scene but reports what Paul and Silas presumably told him shortly afterward.) Since Luke is great with details, there is no need to embellish. Be sure to keep the main preaching point in view in every scene: The gospel changes everything. Highlight the changes. Lydia was a wealthy, Roman, Godfearing woman. When God opens her heart, she wins her household to Christ, receives baptism, and uses her wealth for the kingdom by opening her home to the team. The gospel changes everything. Next, when Paul cast a demon out of a slave girl, it sets her free and totally disrupts the wicked business of her owners. The gospel changes everything. Finally, a jailer on the verge of suicide finds life and eternal life, invites his prisoners into his home, cares for their wounds, and receives baptism with his household. Indeed, the gospel changes everything.

- The gospel changes hearts (16:11–15).

- The gospel changes cities (16:16–24).

- The gospel changes households (16:25–40).

DISCUSSION QUESTIONS

1. Why was the team's travel from Troas in Asia Minor to Philippi in Macedonia significant, both geographically and culturally?

2. What implications can you draw from the "household baptisms" that followed both Lydia's and the jailer's conversions?

3. Why is it significant that both Lydia and the jailer extended hospitality to Paul and Silas after their conversions?

4. What lessons can you draw from the way in which Paul and Silas responded to their imprisonment?

5. Why was Paul's appeal to his Roman citizenship important? What lessons can you draw from his appeal and the magistrates' response?

Acts 17:1–15

EXEGETICAL IDEA
The gospel's advance in Macedonia continued in the synagogues of Thessalonica and Berea, involving careful argument from and study of the Old Testament, resulting in positive responses among Jews and Gentiles, and leading to persistent opposition from zealous Jews.

THEOLOGICAL FOCUS
Effective preaching of the gospel includes engagement, explanation, and exposition, while appropriate receptivity to the gospel manifests itself in openness, eagerness, and thoroughness.

PREACHING IDEA
Proper presentation of the gospel encourages careful consideration of its claims.

PREACHING POINTERS
Although we live in an increasingly post-Christian society, many men and women retain a degree of biblical preunderstanding. The teachings of the OT were foreign to the Greco-Roman citizens of Macedonia, but God had planted Jewish synagogues throughout the empire in accordance with his plan to use Israel as a light to the nations (Isa. 42:6; 49:6). The men and women who worshipped in those synagogues possessed a high degree of biblical preunderstanding and represented potentially receptive audiences for the gospel. With Luke's original readers, we need to understand how to present the gospel effectively to listeners with a biblical preunderstanding, and we need to be able to recognize open-minded receptivity to the gospel when we encounter it.

People today should be able to relate to the suggestion that they be open to ideas that run counter to their preconceptions. The call for "tolerance" is widespread in contemporary society. The accounts of Paul and Silas's ministry in Thessalonica and Berea correct any notions that the gospel will always produce a positive response, all Jews are hostile to the gospel, or civil authorities will always respond benevolently when acting in response to charges against God's witnesses. The accounts commend both a commitment to presenting the gospel carefully and an attitude of open-minded receptivity to truth. It reminds us that proper presentation of the gospel encourages careful consideration of its claims.

WITNESS IN THESSALONICA AND BEREA (17:1–15)

LITERARY STRUCTURE AND THEMES (17:1–15)

The passage consists of two paragraphs. The first paragraph recounts Paul and Silas's travel to and ministry in Thessalonica (17:1–9). The second documents their travel to and ministry in Berea (17:10–15). Both accounts follow the same basic pattern, which is parallel to Paul and Barnabas's previous experiences in Pisidian Antioch (13:13–52) and Iconium (14:1–6).

	Thessalonica	**Berea**
Travel	17:1	17:10a
Synagogue preaching	17:2–3	17:10b
Positive response	17:4	17:11–12
Jewish opposition	17:5–9	17:13–15

- *Opposition in Thessalonica (17:1–9)*
- *Openness in Berea (17:10–15)*

EXPOSITION (17:1–15)

Leaving Philippi, the team followed the Via Egnatia farther into Macedonia until they reached the provincial capital of Thessalonica (17:1). Resuming their customary strategy of preaching in Jewish synagogues (13:5, 14; 14:1), they spent three consecutive Sabbaths reasoning from the OT Scriptures (17:2–3). The result was that some Jews, a large group of Godfearing Greeks, and a number of leading women were persuaded that Jesus is the Christ (17:4). As was true in Philippi, the gospel again aroused opposition, this time from zealous Jews (17:5–9). Moving on in the face of persecution (cf. Matt. 10:23), the team traveled to Berea where there was another synagogue (17:10). The Jews in Berea were eager to check the validity of the message of the gospel, and the result was that many Jews as well as a large number of prominent Greek women and men believed (17:11–12). Renewed Jewish opposition prompted Paul to leave the city and travel to Athens (17:13–15).

The narrative highlights the centrality of God's Word, the proper response of careful consideration and faith, and the reality of the opposition that accompanies the preaching of the gospel. Schnabel dates the ministry in Thessalonica and Berea to October A.D. 49 through January A.D. 50 (2012, 699). Paul's letter to the church in Thessalonica attests to this portion of his ministry, mentioning his mistreatment in Philippi (1 Thess. 2:1), his preaching in the face of opposition (2:2) that came from Jews who drove him out of the city (2:14–16), and his subsequent time in Athens (3:1–2). When he later revisited the congregations he planted in Macedonia (Acts 20:1–2), Aristarchus and Secundus from Thessalonica as well as Sopater from Berea accompanied Paul on his collection visit to Jerusalem (Acts 20:4). His letter to the Romans attests to the churches' generous contribution to that collection (Rom. 15:26–28).

Opposition in Thessalonica (17:1–9)

When Paul and Silas reason from the OT in the synagogue, their ministry leads to committed responses from some Jews and strong opposition from others.

17:1. When they left Philippi, Paul and Silas "took the road through" (διοδεύσαντες; cf.

Bruce 1990, 368) Amphipolis and Apollonia to Thessalonica, the provincial capital of Macedonia. Luke's brief account of their travel suggests that they did not linger in either place, most likely because neither city had a synagogue (Barrett 1998, 809). Hemer's suggestion that they made the trip in three days is simply a conjecture (1989, 115). A trip of that length (one hundred miles) in so short a time would have been possible, however, if they were traveling by horseback. When they arrived in Thessalonica, they found what they were seeking: a synagogue of the Jews (ὅπου ἦν συναγωγὴ τῶν Ἰουδαίων).

From Philippi to Athens via Thessalonica and Berea

Leaving Philippi after their release from prison, Paul and Silas traveled southwest along the Via Egnatia for thirty-three miles until they reached Amphipolis, which was the capital of the district that also included Philippi. From Amphipolis, they continued west for another twenty-eight miles to Apollonia and, from that city, thirty-eight additional miles to Thessalonica. Located at the head of the Thermaic Gulf, Thessalonica was the capital and chief port of the Roman province of Macedonia. It had a significant Roman population as well as a Jewish community large enough to support a synagogue. Granted status as a free city in 42 B.C., it had the right to follow the Greek pattern of government with a public assembly (δῆμος) and non-Roman magistrates (πολιτάρχαι). After at least three weeks of ministry in Thessalonica, strong Jewish opposition prompted Paul and Silas to leave the Via Egnatia and travel west-southwest for forty-five miles to Berea, where there was another Jewish synagogue. Berea was in a different district and had a large population, although it was of little historical importance. It had the advantage for Paul and Silas of "being off the beaten track" (Cicero, *Pis.* 36.89). Pursued by Jewish opponents from Thessalonica, Paul left Silas and Timothy in Berea and traveled "as far as the sea," perhaps

to Pydna on the Aegean Sea (Barrett 1998, 820). From that port, he traveled two hundred miles south to Athens—most likely by boat (Hemer 1989, 116; contra Longenecker 1981, 471).

17:2–3. In Thessalonica, Paul resumed his customary strategy (κατὰ τὸ εἰωθὸς τῷ Παύλῳ) of entering the synagogue (εἰσῆλθεν πρὸς αὐτούς) where he expected to encounter a potentially receptive audience (13:5, 14; 14:1). For three Sabbaths in a row (ἐπὶ σάββατα τρία), Paul pursued a three-part method of proclamation. He began by engaging his listeners in conversation centered on the Scriptures (διελέξατο ἀπὸ τῶν γραφῶν). He then explained Scripture in a way that enabled his listeners to understand it (διανοίγων). Finally, he expounded the truth of Scripture by setting out the evidence in a systematic way (παρατιθέμενος; cf. Culy and Parsons 2003, 325) to prove that Jesus is the Jewish Messiah (οὗτός ἐστίν ὁ Χριστὸς ὁ Ἰησοῦς), who must suffer and rise from the dead (τὸν Χριστὸν ἔδει παθεῖν καὶ ἀναστῆναι ἐκ νεκρῶν). Larkin notes the syllogistic logic of Paul's argument (1995, 245).

TEXTUAL ANALYSIS: "for three Sabbaths in a row"

Since τό σάββατον can refer either to the seventh day of the week or a period of seven days ending on the Sabbath (BDAG s.v. "σάββατον" 909–10), the phrase ἐπὶ σάββατα τρία has been variously interpreted as "for three weeks" (RSV), "on three Sabbath days" (NET), or "for three Sabbaths in a row" (NLT). It has also raised the question of the duration of Paul and Silas's ministry in Thessalonica, because Paul's letters to the Thessalonians (1 Thess. 2:9; 2 Thess. 3:7–10) and the Philippians (4:16) suggest a period longer than three weeks. The pattern of Paul's ministries in Corinth and Ephesus also supports a longer time. In both of the latter cities, Paul began his work in the synagogue but subsequently moved to another location—to the house of Titius Justus for eighteen months in Corinth (Acts 18:7–11) and to the hall of Tyrannus for two years in Ephesus (Acts 19:9–10). The fact that the mob in Thessalonica went to Jason's house when they were looking for Paul and Silas suggests that his house might have served a similar function in Thessalonica. Most likely, Paul and Silas spent their first three Sabbaths in Thessalonica engaging the Jews and God-worshipping Greeks in the synagogue and subsequently moved to Jason's house for an unspecified period. The fact that Paul describes the members of the congregation in Thessalonica as "turn[ing] to God from idols, to serve the living and true God" (1 Thess. 1:9) suggests that the team's ministry had a significant impact among Gentiles from outside the synagogue during the latter period.

17:4. Luke describes the response of some of Paul's Jewish listeners (τινες ἐξ αὐτῶν) in two ways: they "were persuaded" (ἐπείθησαν), and they "were joined" (προσεκληρώθησαν) with Paul and Silas. The first indicates that the listeners accepted the truth of the message, and the second indicates that they committed themselves to what Luke elsewhere calls "the Way" (9:2; 19:9, 23; 24:22). The passive voice of the verbs highlights God's initiative in both actions (13:14; 16:14)—"the conversion of the new believers [and] the foundation of the new community" (Schnabel 2012, 705). Along with some of the Jews, "a great multitude of the devout Greeks" (ESV, τῶν σεβομένων Ἑλλήνων πλῆθος πολύ) and "not a few of the leading women" (ESV, γυναικῶν τῶν πρώτων οὐκ ὀλίγαι) also responded. Once again, the appeal of the gospel extended beyond its initial Jewish audience.

17:5–6a. Driven by misguided zeal for their traditions (ζηλώσαντες; cf. Rom. 10:2–3)—as well, perhaps, by jealousy over Paul's ability to persuade large numbers of synagogue attenders to join him and Silas (cf. Acts 13:45)—other Jews resorted to the same strategy the slave girl's masters in Philippi used: public accusation

before the civil authorities. On this occasion, the Jewish opponents gathered "some wicked men from those in the marketplace" (τῶν ἀγοραίων ἄνδρας τινὰς πονηρούς), "formed a mob" (οχλοποιήσαντες), and "began to set the city in an ongoing uproar" (ἐθορύβουν τὴν πόλιν). They "attacked Jason's house" (NET, ἐπιστάντες τῇ οἰκίᾳ Ἰάσονος) and "were seeking to bring out" (ἐζήτουν . . . προαγαγεῖν) Paul and Silas to the public assembly (εἰς τὸν δῆμον). Failing to find the new congregation's leaders (μὴ εὑρόντες αὐτούς), the mob dragged (ἔσυρον) Jason and "some of the other believers" (NLT, τινας ἀδελφούς) before the magistrates (ἐπὶ τοὺς πολιτάρχας), where they repeatedly shouted (βοῶντες) their accusations. Once again, the opposition was organized, determined, and violent. This episode is the second of four such incidents that Luke records (16:19–21; 18:12–13; 19:23–27). See 19:23–41 for a discussion of the response of civil officials to the gospel.

17:6b–7. The mob's accusations echoed those brought against Jesus (Luke 23:2–4) and included three specific charges. The first charge—against Paul and Silas—was that they were threatening the stability of the empire (οἱ τὴν οἰκουμένην ἀναστατώσαντες οὗτοι). Later in Acts, the verb ἀναστατόω describes "the Egyptian . . . who . . . stirred up a revolt" (21:38). In Luke 2:1, Caesar Augustus's decree encompassed "all the world" (πᾶσαν τὴν οἰκουμένην)—that is, the entire portion of the inhabited world governed by Rome.

The second charge—against Jason—was that he had given and continued to give refuge to the troublemakers (οὓς ὑποδέδεκται Ἰάσων). By welcoming Paul and Silas and extending hospitality to them and their followers, Jason was also guilty of threatening the stability of the empire. Jason's act of hospitality reflects the same evidence of saving faith that Lydia and the Philippian jailer exhibited (16:15, 34). In Thessalonica, however, it also carried significant consequences.

The third charge—against all the members of the group (οὗτοι πάντες)—was that they were practicing sedition against the emperor (ἀπέναντι τῶν δογμάτων Καίσαρος πράσσουσιν) by proclaiming another king (βασιλέα ἕτερον λέγοντες εἶναι Ἰησοῦν). Schnabel discusses the possible options for understanding precisely which "decrees of Caesar" the missionaries were accused of violating (2012, 708). The kernel of truth in the third charge most likely lies in Paul's teaching about God's kingdom (1 Thess. 2:12), the coming of Christ (1 Thess. 1:10; 2:19; 3:13; 4:15), and the ultimate destruction of the man of lawlessness (2 Thess. 2:3–12). The charge, however, radicalizes that teaching in a way that Paul never did (Rom. 13:1–7; 1 Tim. 2:1–2). As in Philippi, the accusers designed the charges to alarm; they did not reflect the actual issue, which in this instance was that people were deserting the synagogue in order to follow the Jesus whom Paul and Silas preached.

17:8–9. Not surprisingly, the charges "disturbed" (ἐτάραξαν) both the crowd and the magistrates. Before they released Jason and the others, therefore, the magistrates demanded and received bail money (λαβόντες τὸ ἱκανόν) as a pledge that they would cause no further trouble in the city. See Bock for the legal practice involved, which he considers a "moderate" solution on the part of the magistrates (2007, 553).

Openness in Berea (17:10–15)

Paul's and Silas's ministry in the synagogue receives an attentive hearing from open-minded Jews and launches a new multiethnic congregation.

17:10. Perhaps as part of the bail arrangement they had just made (Barrett 1998, 816), the disciples in Thessalonica (οἱ ἀδελφοί) immediately (εὐθέως) sent Paul and Silas to Berea by night (διὰ νυκτός). Following their customary strategy when they arrived (παραγενόμενοι), the team entered the Jewish synagogue (εἰς τὴν συναγωγὴν τῶν Ἰουδαίων ἀπῄεσαν). It is logical to suppose that Paul and Silas used the same sort of tactics in presenting the gospel as they had in Thessalonica (17:2–3). Luke provides no details of their presentation but focuses instead on the response of the Jews in Berea, which stands in sharp contrast to that of the Jews in Thessalonica.

17:11. The Jews in Berea were different in three ways: their openness, their eagerness, and their thoroughness. Luke describes the Bereans as "more noble-minded" (NASB, εὐγενέστεροι) than the Jews in Thessalonica. Noble-mindedness was an attitude associated with well-bred persons (BDAG s.v. "εὐγενής" 2, 404) and in this context carries the sense of "a willingness to learn and evaluate something fairly" (L&N §27.48). Because of their openness, they "received the word with all eagerness" (ἐδέξαντο τὸν λόγον μετὰ πάσης προθυμίας). The noun προθυμία describes exceptional interest in engaging in an activity or event (BDAG s.v. "προθυμία" 870; L&N §25.68) and falls in the same semantic range as ζηλόω (L&N §25.76). Luke's choice of προθυμία in this context heightens the contrast between the commitment of the Berean Jews to the OT and the commitment of the Thessalonian Jews to their traditions (17:5). Their eagerness led them to "[search] the Scriptures day after day to see if Paul and Silas were teaching the truth" (NLT, καθ᾽ ἡμέραν ἀνακρίνοντεςτὰς γραφὰς εἰ ἔξοι ταῦτα οὕτως). The verb ἀνακρίνω denotes the practice of engaging in the careful study of a question (BDAG s.v. "ἀνακρίνω" 1, 66). Elsewhere in Acts, it describes the legal examination of a witness (4:9; 12:19; 24:8; 28:18). Peterson suggests that the Jews in Berean "cross examined" Scripture and characterizes them as "rational and reflective," while the Jews in Thessalonica were "jealous and emotive" (2009, 484).

17:12. The results of Paul and Silas's ministry in Berea were also different, at least in the distribution of those who responded positively to the gospel (cf. 17:4). In Berea, "many" of the Jews believed (πολλοὶ . . . ἐξ αὐτῶν ἐπίστευσαν); in Thessalonica, only "some" were persuaded (τινες ἐξ αὐτῶν ἐπείσθησαν). In Berea, Luke mentions no large group of "devout Greeks" as he did in Thessalonica (τῶν σεβομένων Ἑλλήνων πλῆθος πολύ), although Bruce suggests that "Greeks" in the next phrase includes both God-fearers and pagans (1990, 374). In Berea, not only did prominent women (γυναικῶν τῶν πρώτων) believe as in Thessalonica, but prominent Greek men (τῶν Ἑλλινίδων γυναικῶν τῶν εὐσχομόνων καὶ ἀνδρῶν) also responded to the gospel. Although Luke's account is brief, it seems fair to conclude from these results that, as was true in other cities, Paul and Silas did not limit their ministry to the synagogue but most likely engaged individuals in other venues as well (Schnabel 2012, 710). The resulting Christian community included Jews and Greeks, men and women, and individuals of different socioeconomic levels.

17:13–15. As Jews from Pisidian Antioch and Iconium had pursued Paul to Lystra (14:19), so Jews from Thessalonica (οἱ ἀπὸ τῆς Θεσσαλονίκη Ἰουδαῖοι) now came to Berea when they knew (ὡς ἔγνωσαν) that Paul was proclaiming the Word of God (ὁ λόγος τοῦ θεοῦ) there also. The Jews appear to have followed the same tactics they used in Thessalonica. They "incited" (NET) the crowds with their accusations (cf. 17:6–7) and so "disturbed" (NET) them (cf. 17:8), no doubt hoping for punitive action by the city magistrates. The present tense of both participles (σαλεύοντες καὶ ταράσσοντες) suggests a sustained effort, and doubling the terms emphasizes the energy behind that effort (Culy and Parsons 2003, 330). The NEB suggests that the Jews "came . . . to stir up trouble and rouse the rabble." In response, the disciples immediately (εὐθέως) sent

Paul out of the city (ἐξαπέστειλαν), while Silas and Timothy remained in Berea (ὑπέμειναν . . . ἐκεῖ). The disciples who accompanied Paul (οἱ καθιστάνοντεχ τὸν Παῦλον) escorted him as far as Athens (ἕως Ἀθηνῶν), and then returned to Berea with instructions for Silas and Timothy to join Paul as soon as possible (ἵνα ὡς τάχιστα ἔλθωσιν πρὸς αὐτόν).

TEXTUAL ANALYSIS: "to go as far as the sea"
The phrase πορεύεσθαι ἕως ἐπὶ τὴν θάλασσαν has generated several suggested understandings. One is that the Berean believers sent Paul "as if to go to the sea" as misdirection and then conducted him by land to Athens (Longenecker 1981, 471). Another is that they sent him "to the coast," but—since there is no mention of Paul taking a boat to Athens—he traveled to Athens over land (Bruce 1990, 374). A third is that they sent him "as far as the sea" where he took a boat to Athens (Barrett 1998, 820). Regardless, Paul arrived in Athens, ministered there on his own (17:16–34; cf. 1 Thess. 3:1), and then, moved on to Corinth, where Silas and Timothy joined him (18:1–5; cf. 1 Thess. 3:6).

THEOLOGICAL FOCUS

The narratival function of these two brief vignettes is to move Paul from Philippi, "the first city of Macedonia," to "learned Athens" (Ovid, *Her.* 2.83), the cradle of Greek philosophy, architecture, and art in Achaia. Along the way, he and Silas resume their primary strategy of focusing on the major cities in a region and beginning their presentation of the gospel in the Jewish synagogues of those cities, where they had reason to anticipate that they would encounter receptive listeners who had a biblical preunderstanding. How effective would that strategy be in Macedonia? How would Paul and Silas present the gospel to the hellenized Jews they encountered? How would those Jews respond? Would Jewish opposition arise in Europe as it had in Asia Minor? If it did, would the opposition follow the same pattern it had elsewhere during Paul's travels? Luke's account of the gospel witness in Thessalonica and Berea answers each of these questions.

Theologically, Acts 17:1–15 presents two paradigms—one for the proper presentation of the gospel in contexts where the listeners possess a biblical preunderstanding; the other for the careful consideration those listeners should give to the gospel when they encounter it. The team's ministry in Thessalonica illustrates the former paradigm, which begins by engaging others in conversation about Scripture, follows that engagement by explaining the details of Scripture, and backs the explanation by an exposition of the supporting evidence from Scripture. Their ministry in Berea illustrates the latter paradigm, which moves from openness to new ideas, to eagerness to hear those ideas, to thoroughness in examining the evidence for those ideas. The presentation paradigm of Scripture-suffering-resurrection (17:2–3) aligns exactly with Jesus's statement of the gospel message in Luke 24:44–48 (Larkin 1995, 23–29) and summarizes both Peter's preaching (2:14–40) and Paul's preaching (13:16–41) in Jewish contexts, with Messiah's suffering and resurrection at the heart of their messages.

	According to Scripture	Messiah Suffers	Messiah Rises	Call to Repentance	Promise of Forgiveness
Luke 24:44–48	24:46a	24:46b	24:46c	24:47a	24:47b
Acts 2:14–40	2:25–28	2:23	2:24–32	2:38–40	2:38
Acts 13:16–41	13:27, 29	13:27–29	13:30–37	13:40–41	13:38–39

PREACHING AND TEACHING STRATEGIES

Exegetical/Theological Synthesis

Luke's first-century readers would want to know the strategy Paul and Silas used to penetrate new territory in Europe and the results that strategy produced. Their strategy focused on Jewish synagogues in major cities. Because of their familiarity with the OT, the Jews who worshipped in those synagogues represented a segment of Greco-Roman society to whom Paul and Silas could appeal using Scripture as a starting point. With the original readers, the twenty-first-century audience shares the need to understand both how to communicate the gospel effectively to men and women with a biblical preunderstanding and how to recognize receptivity to the gospel when they meet it. Effective communication of the gospel to such an audience includes careful explanation of the facts of Messiah's suffering and resurrection, systematic exposition of support from the Scriptures, and logical reasoning that leads listeners to a conclusion about Jesus. Receptivity to the gospel message shows itself in willingness to learn, active engagement with the facts, and careful study of the evidence presented. Proper presentation of truth encourages receptive hearers to consider that truth carefully and respond to it positively.

Preaching/Teaching Idea

Proper presentation of the gospel encourages careful consideration of its claims.

Contemporary Connections

What does it mean?

Proper presentation and careful consideration are the two sides of sharing the good news. The giver presents. The hearer considers. Both roles have big responsibilities according to our passage. Paul and Silas exemplify the presentation role in Thessalonica. Carefully, over the course of weeks in the synagogue and presumably time outside the synagogue, these men reasoned, explained, proved from Scripture Jesus's suffering, death, and resurrection as God's Christ. Where there is even the most remote exposure to the Bible—be it first-century Jews and sympathetic Gentiles or a twenty-first-century post-Christian society—clear explanation of Scripture spurs a response, positive or negative. Sadly, in Thessalonica it was mostly negative.

The Bereans exemplified the considering role. Foreign visitors and new teachings did not impress them. Scripture was their filter. They did not receive Paul per se. Instead, they "received *the Word* with all eagerness, examining the Scriptures daily" (17:11, emphasis added). Paul did not mind. He had always been anxious to let his ministry fade so that Christ crucified could shine (1 Cor. 2:1–5). To see a synagogue digging into their Bibles must have been beautiful to behold. The result was that "many" were converted and a diverse Christian community was born.

Is it true?
Critics of Christianity love to dub conversion as a "leap of faith." The phrase conjures images of mindless lemmings cliff-diving, or at least brittle-minded evangelicals about to have their worldview upended in a freshman biology class. The tired secular refrain is that the gospel asks us to check our brains at the door and join Jesus's prescientific world where people were willing to believe just about anything. To be sure, some of those critiques are well deserved. Many Christians have unthinkingly subscribed to the religion of their family or community. It helps to remember, though, that God expects and celebrates thoughtful, deliberate examination of his claims. For thousands of years, Berean-like hearers have checked and double-checked what is true. Jesus himself likened the process to a man carefully counting the cost of building a tower or a king deliberating his ability to go to war (Luke 14:28–32). He invited hard questions and found it worth giving complicated answers.

Sadly, space for such careful consideration has fallen on hard times in the public square today. Ideologies are deeply entrenched. We reduce our competing agendas into sarcastic sound bites and fire them at each other from behind the safety of our mobile screens. The thick skins and long attention spans so essential to the exchange of ideas are in short supply. It is hard to imagine a Berean-like scene on *any* issue today, much less the ultimate issue of eternal life. All these considerations make Acts 17 timely. It rejects the strawman fallacy that evangelism depends on thoughtless decisions. It commends space for careful explanation and thorough engagement.

Now what?
Any pastor will tell you that a highlight of preaching is watching people in pews, chairs, couch cushions, bent over paper Bibles or the ambient glow of digital ones, weighing *the pastor's* words against *the* Word. The grass withers, the flower fades, the pastor retires, but the Word of God stands forever. Any teaching of eternal value invites the believer or unbeliever to see for *herself* what God says about *himself.*

The rise of the digital, mobile, frenetic age has some teachers second-guessing the place of sustained exposition. We fear a Netflix-nursed culture might be reticent to engage a book-bound faith. Instead of creating environments of proper presentation and careful consideration, we dabble in events and gimmicks in search of ever-elusive relevance. Contextualization is a good thing, but not at the expense of the time-tested, Acts-endorsed space to present and consider God's claims from God's Word.

You have to love Paul and Silas's approach in consecutive cities. After poor results in Thessalonica, the approach did not change in Berea. You would think inciting an angry mob might take the wind out of a Word-based approach to evangelism and discipleship. It does not. Gather hearers. Preach the Word. Invite people to respond. What might get you killed in one city turns out to be a revival in another.

Creativity in Presentation

Preaching Thessalonica and Berea side by side, comparing and contrasting, is startling. The book of Proverbs often uses this teaching strategy to compare wise and foolish audiences. Jesus used it in his parable of the house built on the rock versus the house built on the sand (Matt. 7:24–27). The Thessalonians and the Bereans were a living parable of how we present and respond to God's Word.

In 1859, Charles Dickens published his historic novel *A Tale of Two Cities*. His memorable opening lines sound as much like Thessalonica and Berea as his intended Paris and London.

> It was the best of times; it was the worst of times. It was the age of wisdom; it was the age of foolishness. It was the epoch of belief; it was the epoch of incredulity. It was the season of Light; it was the season of Darkness. It was the spring of hope; it was the winter of despair. We had everything before us; we had nothing before us. We were all going direct to Heaven; we were all going direct the other way.

You might consider structuring the sermon in two parts: compare and contrast. The comparison section would highlight Paul and Silas's careful explanation from Scripture in both places. They traveled to a new location (17:1 and 17:10a) and found a synagogue where there would be a receptive audience (17:2–3 and 17:10b). They preached from the Word (17:2 and 17:11) and navigated the peoples' response (17:4–9 and 17:11–15). We have seen this approach repeatedly in Acts. The centerpiece of the comparison section should be on the preaching. Paul reasoned, explained, proved week after week (17:2–3), day after day (17:11) from Scripture about Jesus. He trusted the power of God behind his Word to make his Christ shine. He let the Word do the talking. This would be a great place to illustrate with ways you have seen the Word have power in evangelism and discipleship. It also invites rich application for how we might use our Bibles in winsome ways to share with others.

The contrast section highlights the open, eager, thorough response of Berea over Thessalonica. The centerpiece would be the different responses that Luke clearly wants to highlight. Although there was fruit in Thessalonica, the dominant response was jealousy, resistance, and anger. Led by "wicked men," the city erupted into riotous uproar—attacking, dragging, and falsely accusing. The scene resembles an amped-up version of college campus debates in the media today. The response in Thessalonica could not be further from the response in Berea. The Bereans were eager and interested to engage, but they were not pushovers. They checked their Bibles for themselves. The result was that many believed.

Proper presentation of the gospel encourages careful consideration of its claims.

- Comparison: Same Approach (17:1–15)

- Contrast: Different Responses (17:4–9, 11–12)

DISCUSSION QUESTIONS

1. What principles about mission strategy can you draw from Paul and Silas's movements and ministries in Acts 17:1–15?

2. Can you identify other examples of the Scripture-suffering-resurrection presentation paradigm (17:3) elsewhere in Acts?

3. What similarities and differences are there between the opposition in Philippi and the opposition in Thessalonica?

4. What connections can you find between Acts 17:1–15 and Paul's two letters to the Thessalonians?

5. What OT passages might Paul have used in demonstrating that it was necessary for Messiah to suffer and rise from the dead?

Acts 17:16–34

EXEGETICAL IDEA
Paul's ministry in Athens began with teaching in the synagogue and marketplace, culminated with a speech before the council of the city, and produced mixed results.

THEOLOGICAL FOCUS
Scripture's truth about God's acts of creation and providence offers a foundation to contextualize the gospel for those who lack a biblical preunderstanding.

PREACHING IDEA
The truth of Scripture challenges the dogmas of human philosophies.

PREACHING POINTERS
Because we live in an increasingly post-Christian society, it becomes increasingly important for us to know how to contextualize the message of God's love and forgiveness for men and women who lack a biblical preunderstanding. Ancient Athens provided the perfect setting for Paul to engage the prominent philosophical thinking of his day. His speech before the Areopagus Council offers one example of how to present the gospel to such an audience. With Luke's original readers, we need to understand that Scripture challenges the dogmas of human philosophies, but it is still possible to interact with postmodern thinkers in a manner that is both scriptural and respectful.

People today should be able to relate to having an interest in "something new." The prospect of Apple releasing a new iPhone or the opening of a new episode in a popular movie franchise is enough to send users/followers into a frenzy. The account of Paul's ministry in Athens corrects multiple ideas—that the world simply "happened," that pantheism and deism are plausible explanations for God's relationship to his creation, that there is no purpose to life, and that there is no possibility of knowing God. The same account commends a proper understanding of God's works of creation, providence, and judgment as well as the need for men and women to repent of their wrong concepts of who God is and how he acts.

WITNESS IN ATHENS (17:16–34)

LITERARY STRUCTURE AND THEMES (17:16–34)

The passage consists of two narrative sections framing a speech addressed to Greek philosophers. The first narrative section describes Paul's ministry in the synagogue and the marketplace and sets the stage for his speech before the council of the Areopagus (17:16–21). The speech consists of an introduction asserting that it is possible to know the "unknown God" whom the Athenians worship in ignorance (17:22–23), two proofs demonstrating that God is both the transcendent Creator (17:24–25) and the providential Sustainer (17:26–29), and a conclusion calling all people everywhere to repent (17:30–31). The closing narrative section records the aftermath of Paul's speech and the results of his ministry in the city (17:32–34). In style and content, if not in form and length, the speech is closest to Paul's earlier speech in Lystra (14:15–17; cf. Peterson 2009, 493).

- *Engagement in the Synagogue and the Marketplace (17:16–21)*
- *Speech Before the Areopagus Council (17:22–31)*
- *Mixed Responses (17:32–34)*

EXPOSITION (17:16–34)

The disciples from Berea who had escorted Paul to Athens had returned to Macedonia (17:15), leaving Paul on his own in "learned Athens." The city was the birthplace of Socrates and Plato, as well as the adopted city of Aristotle, Epicurus, and Zeno (Bruce 1990, 375). As the cradle of Greek philosophy, Athens was the ideal setting for Paul to interact with the ideas of non-Jewish thinkers and, so, allows Luke to highlight "the diverse character of preaching necessary for the Christian mission" (Dunn 1996, 231). As his second evangelistic speech (cf. 13:13–43), "Paul's speech on the Areopagus is . . . a model of how the gospel may be proclaimed in a cross-cultural situation where the traditions of Judaism . . . are foreign" (Losie 2004, 233). As such, it provides the perfect counterpart to Paul's preaching in the Jewish contexts of Thessalonica and Berea. Schnabel suggests that Paul makes nine points of contact with his philosopher listeners and identifies ten points of contradiction (2012, 746–48). The primary emphases (proofs) in the speech are God's works of creation and providence as Paul uses the truth of Scripture to challenge the dogmas of human philosophies.

Introduction (*exordium* and *propositio*)	17:22–23
Thesis: The "unknown God" can be known (17:23)	
Proofs (*probatio*)	17:24–29

Proof #1:	The transcendent, self-sufficient Creator made the world and gives life to everything in it (17:24–25).	
God's creative power (17:24a)	He made the world and all things in it.	Exod. 20:11 Ps. 146:6
God's transcendence (17:24b)	He does not dwell in temples made with hands.	1 Kings 8:27 Isa. 66:1–2
God's self-sufficiency (17:25a)	He is not served by human hands, as though he needed anything.	Job 22:2 Ps. 50:9–12
God's life-giving power (17:25b)	He gives to all life, breath, and all things.	Job 33:4 Isa. 42:5
Proof #2:	The providential Sustainer orders humankind's origin, history, purpose, and piety (17:26–29).	
Humankind's origin (17:26a)	God made from one every nation of humankind to live on the earth.	Gen. 1:27–28 Gen. 10:32
Humankind's history (17:26b)	God determined the times and boundaries of their habitation.	Deut. 32:8 Ps. 74:17
Humankind's purpose (17:27)	They are to seek and find God, who is not far from each one.	Deut 4:29 Ps. 145:18
Humankind's dependence (17:28)	In God all live, move, and exist.	Job 12:10 Dan. 5:23
Humankind's piety (17:29)	God is not an image formed by the art and thought of humanity.	Isa. 44:9–20 Jer. 10:2–6
Conclusion (*peroratio*) 17:30–31		
Application: The God who can be known calls all to repent (17:30).		

The most likely timing for Paul's ministry in Athens was spring of A.D. 50 before he moved on to Corinth (Schnabel 2012, 715). There is no additional biblical or extrabiblical information about the length of time Paul spent in Athens or his ministry in the city.

Engagement in the Synagogue and the Marketplace (17:16–21)

Paul's teaching in the synagogue and marketplace opens the door for him to speak before the Areopagus Council.

17:16–17. While he was waiting for Silas and Timothy, Paul observed that Athens was a city "submerged in idols" (κατείδωλον; cf. Stott 1990, 278), and "his spirit became greatly upset within him" (Culy and Parsons 2003, 333). The verb παροξύνομαι can include grief, anger, or both; in the OT, it describes God's anger at idolatry (Isa. 65:3; Hos. 8:5). See 15:39 for the cognate noun παροξυσμός. In response, Paul spent "every single day" (Culy and Parsons 2003, 333; κατὰ πᾶσαν ἡμέραν) "dialoguing" with Jews and God-worshippers in the synagogue (ἐν τῇ συναγωγῇ τοῖς Ἰουδαίοις καὶ τοῖς σεβομένοις) and with those who happened to be present in the marketplace (ἐν τῇ ἀγορᾷ . . . πρὸς τοὺς παρατυγχάνοντας). The verb διαλέγομαι denotes "a dialogical style of teaching . . . that allowed the audience to ask questions and make comments," and the imperfect tense highlights extended activity (Schnabel 2012, 724).

Athens

Tradition records the founding of Athens around 1500 B.C. Named for the goddess Athena, it became a center of Greek art, science, and philosophy, reaching the height of its power and influence in the fifth century B.C. with a peak population of at least 250,000. The Romans conquered Athens in 146 B.C., but out of respect for its history, they designated it a free city with the right to follow the Greek pattern of government. It lay five miles inland from the port of Piraeus on the Aegean Sea. When Paul arrived, its population had dwindled in size to ten thousand, but it was still the home of a notable university. Its citizens worshipped the Greek pantheon, and the culture was pagan Greek. Marshall describes Athens as a "blend of superstitious idolatry and enlightened philosophy" (1981, 281). The Areopagus Council was "the effective government of Roman Athens and its chief court" (Barnes 1969, 413). As such, it was the main administrative body of the city and "the supervisor and judge of public instruction" (Fitzmyer 1998, 606).

17:18. Among the individuals Paul engaged in the marketplace were a number of Epicurean and Stoic philosophers (τινὲς τῶν Ἐπικουρείων καὶ Στοικῶν φιλοσόφων) who "kept on contributing their opinions to the discussion" (συνέβαλλον; cf. Schnabel 2012, 724). The two groups of philosophers evaluated Paul's teaching differently. One group, most likely the Epicureans, described him by using the derogatory term σπερμολόγος, which was "originally used of birds picking up grain, then of scrap collectors searching for junk, then extended to those who snapped up the ideas of others and peddled them as their own without understanding them" (Longenecker 1981, 474). The

other group, most likely the Stoics, described Paul as a proclaimer of "strange deities" (ξένων δαιμονίων . . . καταγγελεύς), which echoes the long-ago charges against Socrates (Dunn 1996, 233). Bock concludes that the two groups "had no clue about what Paul [was] saying" (2007, 562), when in fact, he was preaching Jesus and the resurrection (τὸν Ἰησοῦν καὶ τὴν ἀνάστασιν εὐηγγελίζετο).

Epicurean and Stoic Philosophers

Epicurus founded the school of Greek philosophy that bore his name in the fourth century B.C. He taught that the cosmos is the accidental result of the random collision of suitable atoms. Gods exist and enjoy lives of pleasure, but they take no part in the affairs of the world. For an Epicurean, the goal of living was to be free of disturbance and fear through the exercise of free will. Zeno founded Stoicism in the third century B.C. He taught that the world consists solely of material objects and their interaction. God is present in all matter as the impersonal force that controls the universe, and everything happens according to deterministic laws that allow for no exceptions. For a Stoic, the goal of living was to achieve harmony with the universe by mastering reactions to the events it dictates.

17:19–21. The philosophers brought Paul to the Areopagus Council, which licensed traveling lecturers (Larkin 1995, 253), so that he could explain "this new teaching" (ἡ καινὴ αὕτη . . . διδαχή) and either receive permission to continue preaching or be barred from further preaching in the city (Longenecker 1981, 474). Paul's message included "some rather strange things" (NLT, ξενίζοντα τινα), and the philosophers wanted to know what they meant. Their curiosity was characteristic of the Athenians and visitors to the city who "used to spend their time in nothing other than telling or listening to something new" (NET, εἰς οὐδὲν ἕτερον ηὐκαίρουν ἢ λέγειν τι ἢ ἀκούειν τι καινότερον).

TEXTUAL ANALYSIS: "they brought [Paul] to the Areopagus Council"
The clause ἐπὶ τὸν Ἄρειον Πάγον ἤγαγον (17:19) can be understood to mean either that the philosophers brought Paul "to" a location on the height called Mars Hill, or that they brought him "before" the Mars Hill Council. In 17:22, Luke writes that Paul stood "in the middle of the Areopagus" (ἐν μέσῳ τοῦ Ἀερίου πάγου), which could, theoretically, refer to a place on Mars Hill but, more likely, refers to a meeting of the council (cf. 2:22; 27:21). English versions consistently choose the latter option (e.g., NIV, NASB, NET, CSB, ESV), with NLT making the idea explicit: "took him to the high council of the city . . . standing before the council." It is possible that the council met on Mars Hill, although Hemer suggests that Paul delivered his speech before the court in the agora (1989, 117). Whether the purpose of bringing Paul before the council was to hold a formal judicial proceeding or to give him an opportunity for a more formal presentation of his teaching is unclear, but Lynn Allan Losie notes that "Luke is thus setting the scene for a discourse by Paul that can engage the philosophical thinkers of the Greco-Roman world" (2004, 225).

Speech Before the Areopagus Council (17:22–31)

Paul explains that the one true God makes himself known through his works of creation and providence and directs all to repent of their ignorant worship.

17:22–23. Standing among the members of the Areopagus Council (σταθεὶς ἐν μέσῳ τοῦ Ἀρείου πάγου), Paul began his speech by addressing those present (Ἄνδρες Ἀθηναῖοι) and underscoring their interest in spiritual things (κατὰ πάντα ὡς δεισιδαιμονεστέρους ὑμᾶς). He had seen their interest while he was passing through (διερχόμενος) the city and observing (ἀναθεωρῶν) their objects of worship (τὰ σεβάσματα). Among those objects, he had "come across" (εὗρον; cf. Barrett 1998, 837) an

altar with the inscription "to an unknown god" (ἀγνώστῳ θεῷ). Paul was not, therefore, "a proclaimer of strange deities" as the philosophers had suggested (17:18). He was proclaiming (καταγγέλλω) the one true God about whom the Athenians lacked accurate information (ἀγνοοῦντες). He would now provide them with the information they needed.

TEXTUAL ANALYSIS: "very religious in all respects"
The comparative adjective δεισιδαιμονεστέρους can be understood negatively as "too superstitious" (KJV), positively as "extremely religious" (NRSV), or neutrally as simply "religious" (Barrett 1998, 835). A. T. Robertson suggests "more religious . . . than ordinary or than I had supposed" (1934, 665), which seeks to account for the comparative form. Most commentators and English versions understand the term positively. The NJB translates as "extremely scrupulous . . . in all religious matters." Larkin suggests, "Paul puts the ambiguity to good use" and concludes, "Here we have a respectful recognition of religious endeavors but not an acknowledgment that they lead to saving faith" (1995, 255).

St. Paul Preaching in Athens by Raphael. Public domain.

17:24–25. First, in order to correct their ignorance, the Athenians needed to understand that this one true God whom Paul proclaimed was the transcendent Creator. He "made the world and all things in it" (ὁ ποιήσας τὸν κόσμον καὶ πάντα τὰ ἐν αὐτῷ). Not only has he created the physical universe, he also "gives to all [who live in that universe] life and breath and all things" (διδοὺς πᾶσι ζωὴν καὶ πνοὴν καὶ τὰ πάντα). Further, he is the "Lord of heaven and earth" (οὐρανοῦ καὶ γῆς . . . κύριος), who exists entirely apart from his creation. He neither lives in temples made by human hands (οὐκ ἐν χειροποιήτοις ναοῖς κατοικεῖ) nor is he served by human hands (ὑπὸ χειρῶν ἀνθρωπίνων θεραπεύεται). He has given all things to his creation, but there is nothing his creation can give to him in return (Rom. 11:35). The Epicureans believed that the world was the result of a fortunate accident; the Stoics believed that the gods were present in the preexistent matter of the universe. Both of the prominent Greek philosophies of Paul's day were ignorant of the truth about God; he is the transcendent Creator, who created all things and exists apart from his creation.

17:26–29. Second, in order to correct their ignorance, the Athenians needed to understand that the one true God whom Paul proclaimed was the providential Sustainer. "Every race of humankind" (πᾶν ἔθνος ἀνθρώπων) dwells on the face of the earth (κατοικεῖν ἐπὶ παντὸς προσώπου τῆς γῆς) according to the times God has appointed (προστεταγμένους καιρούς) and within the boundaries he has set (τὰς ὁροθεσίας τῆς κατοικίας αὐτῶν). He has given them a true purpose for life: "to seek God" (ζητεῖν τὸν θεόν), even if their best efforts are like groping in the darkness (ψηλαφήσειαν). In him they "live and move and exist" (ζῶμεν καὶ κινούμεθα καὶ ἐσμέν), a triadic construction that "brings out all sides of man's absolute dependence on God" (Gärtner 1955, 155). Yet humankind continues to demonstrate its ignorance by supposing (νομίζειν) that it can capture God in gold, silver, or stone images formed

by their own art and thought. The Epicureans believed that the gods took no part in the affairs of the world; the Stoics believed that "god" was an impersonal force that worked according to deterministic laws. Both prominent Greek philosophies of Paul's day were ignorant of the truth about God; he is the providential Sustainer, who actively governs his creation with the good of his creatures in mind.

TEXTUAL ANALYSIS: "the epochs of their history and the limits of their territory"
Bock notes that προστεταγμένους καιρούς ("appointed times") can refer to (1) seasons of national dominance or (2) seasons of divine provision, while τὰς ὁροθεσίας τῆς κατοικίας αὐτῶν ("boundaries of their habitation") can refer to (3) national boundaries or (4) natural boundaries (2007, 566). Culy and Parsons choose (2) and (3): "orderly seasons and boundaries within which to live" (2003, 232). Schnabel chooses (1) and (3): "epochs in history . . . political boundaries" (2012, 735). Witherington points to Deuteronomy 32:8 and Genesis 10–11 as support for national dominance and boundaries (1998, 527), and most English versions adopt the same understanding (e.g., NEB: "the epochs of their history and the limits of their territory").

17:30–31. The combination μὲν οὖν ("therefore") marks a shift in content (17:17). In this instance, the shift is to Paul's concluding application. The phrase "times of ignorance" (τοὺς χρόνους τῆς ἀγνοίας) summarizes humankind's misunderstanding of God and forms an *inclusio* with the "unknown God" (ἀγνώστῳ θεῷ) whom the Athenians "worship in ignorance" (ὃ ἀγνοοῦντες εὐσεβεῖτε; cf. 17:23). Although God has previously overlooked those times of ignorance, circumstances have changed—he "now" (νῦν) commands "everyone everywhere" (πάντας πανταχοῦ) to repent (μετανοεῖν; cf. 2:38; 3:19; 8:22; Luke 24:47). The reason (καθότι) they should repent is that God's activities as Creator and Sustainer give him the right to judge the world (κρίνειν τὴν οἰκουμένην). In that third role, he has established a day (ἔστησεν ἡμέραν) for judgment, he has designated a man (ἐν ἀνδρί ᾧ ὥρισεν) to act as judge, and he has provided proof (πίστιν παρασχών) of that man's right to judge (Schnabel 2012, 741). The Western text specifies "the man" as Jesus (ἀνδρὶ Ἰησοῦ). God delivered the proof by "raising him from the dead" (ἀναστήσας αὐτὸν ἐκ νεκρῶν). With this mention of the resurrection, Paul returns to one of the "new teachings" that had led his listeners in the marketplace to bring him before the council (17:18–19).

Mixed Responses (17:32–34)
Paul's speech results in ridicule, procrastination, and belief.

17:32–33. When his listeners heard Paul mention the resurrection (17:31), some (οἱ μέν) began to ridicule him (ἐχλεύαζον); others (οἱ δέ) asked to hear more from him again (ἀκούσόμεθά σου περὶ τούτου καὶ πάλιν). Most likely, the first group included the Epicureans, who believed only in a mortal existence, and the second group included the Stoics, who allowed for a limited immortality of the soul (Bock 2007, 571). Bruce notes, "there was no place in Greek thinking for the resurrection of the body" (1990, 387), and Bock writes succinctly, "Greeks believed dead people remained dead" (2007, 570). The effect of the council's failure to reach a decision was to delay Paul's licensing to continue preaching. Schnabel interprets the nondecision positively and concludes that since no Athenian laws were involved, those who chose to follow Paul could be left alone (2012, 743). It seems more likely, however, that the delayed decision was a factor in Paul moving on to Corinth, the capital of the province of Achaia.

17:34. Luke summarizes the results of Paul's ministry in Athens by noting that "some people" (NET, τινὲς ἄνδρες) joined Paul (κολληθέντες αὐτῷ) and believed (ἐπίστευσαν). Among others (ἕτεροι) were Dionysius, a member of the council (Διονύσιος ὁ Ἀρεοπαγίτης), and a woman named Damaris (γυνὴ ὀνόματι Δάμαρις). Scripture records nothing further about either of them, although tradition names Dionysius as the first bishop of Athens (Eusebius, *Hist. eccl.* 3.4.10; 4.23.3). It is likely that Dionysius heard Paul's speech before the council, but the others might well have been the product of his teaching in the synagogue and the marketplace. Longenecker concludes, "in overall terms the Christian mission in the city must be judged a failure" (1981, 478), but the responses of ridicule, procrastination, and belief are not that different from those Paul experienced elsewhere. Losie concludes, "the response, in fact, is much the same as the response to Paul's speech to the Jewish and Jewish-sympathizing audience in Antioch in Pisidia" (2004, 233), the venue in which Luke records Paul's other evangelistic speech (13:42–52). Although Luke nowhere mentions a church in Athens, it is reasonable to conclude with Peterson, "Paul left behind a small group of believers" (2009, 504).

THEOLOGICAL FOCUS

The narratival function of Acts 17:16–34 is to recount the major events of Paul's ministry in Athens as he waited for Silas and Timothy to arrive from Macedonia. In Philippi, he had encountered a variety of audiences—a God-worshipping businesswoman from Asia Minor, a demon-possessed slave girl, and a Roman jailer. In Thessalonica and Berea, he had interacted with Jewish-background audiences who responded with opposition and openness respectively. What sort of response would he encounter in "learned Athens," the cradle of Greek philosophy, architecture, and art? How would he present the gospel in that context? What role would Scripture play in his presentation? How effective would his ministry be? What could Luke's readers learn from Paul's experience?

Theologically, Acts 17:16–34 provides insight into how to share truth with men and women who lack a biblical preunderstanding. Since the Athenians were not familiar with the teachings of the OT and ridiculed the very idea of the resurrection, Paul did not quote or argue from Scripture as he had with the Jews in Thessalonica and the Berea. That fact, however, does not mean that his speech ignored Scripture. In fact, he grounded his entire speech in OT teaching. Paul knew the prominent philosophies of his time well enough to find points of commonality with those philosophies, identify key beliefs, and address those beliefs in a respectful manner. In particular, Paul used the biblical truths of God's acts of creation and providence to challenge the dogmas of the Epicurean and Stoic philosophers. He also challenged their understandings of the purpose of life.

	Paul	Epicureans	Stoics
Creation	God is the transcendent Creator who made the world and gives life to all who are in it.	The world is the accidental result of the random collision of suitable atoms.	The world consists of preexistent material objects and their interactions.
Providence	God is the providential Sustainer who cares for humankind and orders its history.	The gods have material bodies, live apart from the world, and take no part in its affairs.	God is the impersonal force present in all matter that controls the universe according to deterministic laws.
Purpose of Life	The goal of living is to seek and find God, who is near to all and in whom humankind exists.	The goal of living is to be free of disturbance and fear through the exercise of free will.	The goal of living is to live in harmony with the universe by accepting the events it dictates.

In so doing, Paul highlighted nine important truths about the one true God:

- God is Creator (17:24–25).
- God is Sustainer (17:26–29).
- God is Judge (17:30–31).
- God cannot be confined in our temples (17:24).
- God cannot be controlled by our service (17:25).
- God cannot be conformed to our image (17:29).
- We depend on God; he does not depend on us (17:25).
- We live in God; he does not live in us (17:28).
- We seek blindly for God, yet he is not far from us (17:27).

The focus of the gospel witness should always be on God and his grace, and we can be confident that the truth about him as revealed in Scripture will challenge the dogmas of human philosophies as we call for a response to that truth.

PREACHING AND TEACHING STRATEGIES

Exegetical/Theological Synthesis

Luke's first-century readers would want to know how the Greek intelligentsia of Athens would respond to the gospel as Paul continued his mission in Europe. His audience would have no biblical preunderstanding and would most likely think that Paul's message was novel at best and totally foreign at worst. With his original readers, the twenty-first-century audience shares the need to understand how to contextualize Scripture without compromising its truth. Paul's strategy in his speech before the Areopagus Council suggests seven principles for presenting God's truth to men and women who lack a biblical preunderstanding:

1. Understand key beliefs the audience holds.
2. Find one or more points of commonality.
3. Stay focused on a few key ideas.
4. Present a logical argument.
5. Contextualize the teaching of Scripture to correct misunderstanding.
6. Call for a decision based on the truth of Scripture.
7. Expect a variety of responses.

Preaching/Teaching Idea

The truth of Scripture challenges the dogmas of human philosophies.

Contemporary Connections

What does it mean?

The God of Scripture trumps the unknown gods of culture. We must test every human hypothesis of who god might be against God as he is. Since the force of Paul's challenge to the people of Athens hangs on the hinges of creation and providence, it is worth understanding these weighty theological concepts further. The Westminster Shorter Catechism affirms that God executes his eternal decrees in his works of creation and providence (Question 8). It continues by describing God's work of creation as "making all things of nothing, by the word of his power, in the space of six days, and all very good" (Question 9). His works of providence are "his most holy, wise, and powerful preserving and governing all his creatures and all their actions" (Question 11). Numerous Scripture references support these two truths. This teaching is the core of Paul's challenge. The unknown god

of Athens is the knowable God of creation and providence. He is the transcendent Creator of the universe (17:24–25) and the providential Sustainer of its inhabitants (17:26–29). He is not dependent on creation (17:24–25) but humanity is dependent on him for life (17:25–28) and eternal life (17:30–31). As such, he is the supreme Judge who calls all men and women to repentance (17:30–31).

Is it true?

Much of the West is more Athens than Thessalonica, more Epicurean than Berean. *Post-Christian* is a polite euphemism for *non-Christian* and in many places *anti-Christian*. There are pockets of people who still respect what the Bible has to say and are willing to listen to it. There are also groups who find it archaic, out of touch, mythical, or bigoted. Statistics show a steady rise in those with no religious affiliation—the "nones," as some have dubbed them. Our culture's opinions on creation and providence do not fall too far from the trees of Epicurean and Stoic thought. Many perceive creation largely as a cosmic accident. Given enough time, enough speed, enough temperature, enough ingredients, the universe simply burst into being. You are welcome to overlay the material world with spiritual opinions as long as you keep them to yourself. The material world is the dry, factual cake. Spiritual musings are the icing that make existence edible. Scripture flips this perspective on its head. God precedes the material world. Everything we see and cannot see, every breath we take, and every move we make— God's creating and sustaining hand makes them all possible. The grass withers, the flowers fade, philosophers are buried, and hypotheses are overturned, but the Word's witness to God's creating and sustaining power stands forever.

Now what?

Paul's "Men of Athens, I perceive that in every way you are very religious" (17:22) is today's "I perceive that in every way you are very informed/spiritually sensitive/self-aware." Paul saw their attitude as an open door, not an obstacle. He identified their places of worship (17:22), quoted their poets (17:28), and met them where they gathered (17:17, 19). Using their own perceptions of god, he pivoted toward the knowable God of creation, his justice, his rescue plan of the resurrection, and his call for repentance.

We can hardly improve on that approach in our context today. Surely, the idolatry of our generation provokes our spirits (17:6). It also has much to teach us. Where our culture goes for meaning, pleasure, and security is today's version of an altar to the unknown god. It is a roadmap of her felt needs. Take our sex-saturated landscape. Novelist Bruce Marshall (often attributed to G. K. Chesterton) wrote, "I still prefer to believe that sex is a substitute for religion and that the young man who rings the bell at the brothel is unconsciously looking for God." He is right. God made us for worship, pleasure, and fulfillment. God made the Athenians to know him, the very one they feared might be unknowable. Our felt needs have a lot to teach us.

Creativity in Presentation

Once again, we are essentially preaching a sermon on a sermon. The passage gives the preacher the choice of either talking *about* Paul and his approach or talking *as* Paul in his approach. In the latter, we preach to our people as Paul preached to Athens, trusting for unbelievers to repent and believers to be inspired in their own evangelism of this great, creating, sustaining God. In Athens, Paul's preaching unfolds in three parts: appeal (17:22–23), attributes (17:24–29), and application (17:30–31).

The advertising industry knows how to make an appeal. It knows you get one shot to capture an audience's interest—one billboard picture, one radio line, one opening television commercial scene. If you fail to connect to what your listeners actually need (or think

they need), you have lost them. Illustrations abound here. Consider funny and memorable ads that have hooked your interest. Even though Paul knows God does the ultimate heart-hooking, he still works hard to engage his hearers thoughtfully and creatively. He has spent time with them (17:22). He has toured their altars (17:23). He has read their writers (17:28). He is not presuming he knows these people already. He humbles himself to learn, and the payoff is huge. Paul finds a crack in the cradle of Western philosophy, an agnostic doubt that perhaps for all the talk of god and gods, he might be unknown. Some call it the "felt need." What is the felt need of our audience today? Where do the fault lines of doubt, guilt, or shame lie? Perhaps it is feelings of discontent, boredom, or restlessness. Paul, like us, proclaims that the unknown God is knowable; that there are answers to our greatest felt needs and fears. Our appeal meets our hearers where they are.

Next, Paul highlights the attributes of God that meet the felt needs of his hearers. God creates (17:24–25) and God sustains (17:26–29). Paul quotes the philosophers and poets popular in Athens positively—they are saying more than they know. What does our pop culture get right today? How does it reflect partial truth about God? In the 1990s Joan Osborne sang, "What if God was one of us?" In 2004, Kanye West sang, "We are at war with terrorism, racism, but most of all we are at war with ourselves. God show me the way because the devil's trying to break me down. Jesus walks with me." What are our influencers saying today? Paul's application is abridged, but our application is the place in preaching and teaching to be clear about the gospel. God is Creator and Sustainer, he made the world and placed us here that we might seek him, he has sent his Son Jesus who died and rose again for our sins (17:18, 31), and he commands us to repent.

The truth of Scripture challenges the dogmas of human philosophies.

- The appeal to hearts (17:22–23)

- The attributes of God that speak to our hearts (17:24–29)

- The application of how our hearts might respond (17:30–31)

DISCUSSION QUESTIONS

1. What are some of today's prevalent philosophies, fears, or felt needs?

2. What are the major beliefs of each of these?

3. How does Scripture address and/or correct those beliefs?

4. What truths about God are particularly pertinent for interacting with each set of beliefs?

5. What are some potential points of connection for Christian witness?

Acts 18:1–17

EXEGETICAL IDEA
During Paul's bivocational and full-time ministry in Corinth, fellow believers helped him, God reassured him, and the Roman proconsul vindicated him.

THEOLOGICAL IDEA
God uses ordinary and extraordinary means to assure and guide his obedient witness in the face of financial need, religious opposition, and legal challenge.

PREACHING IDEA
God gives us what we need, to do what he asks us to do.

PREACHING POINTERS
At some point, every individual, family, congregation, or ministry experiences need. The need might be financial, physical, spiritual, or legal. Sometimes the needs occur sequentially; other times they occur simultaneously. Whatever the nature or timing of the needs, they are opportunities for God to act to meet them. He might meet them in ways we expect, or his provision might be totally unexpected. During his ministry in Corinth, Paul experienced a variety of needs. In each instance, God provided the resources Paul needed to witness faithfully for the Lord Jesus. His experience reminds us that God gives us what we need, so that we can do what he asks us to do.

People today should be able to relate to experiencing financial need and/or uncertainty, working for a living, being encouraged by friends or colleagues, and being involved in legal proceedings. The account of Paul's ministry in Corinth corrects suggestions that religion—including missionary activity—is illicit or illegal, or that the state has authority over church affairs. The same account commends trust in God's promises and guidance as well as faithfulness in witness despite difficult circumstances. It reinforces the theological truth that God uses both ordinary and extraordinary means to advance his kingdom purposes.

WITNESS IN CORINTH (18:1–17)

LITERARY STRUCTURE AND THEMES (18:1–17)

The passage consists of three paragraphs describing the eighteen months Paul spent in Corinth. The first paragraph describes Paul's initial period of bivocational witness in the Jewish synagogue (18:1–4). In the second paragraph, Paul resumes full-time witness, shifts his base of ministry to the house of Titius Justus, and turns his attention to Gentiles in the city (18:5–11). The paragraph includes an account of a divine vision that assures Paul of God's protection (18:9–10). The third paragraph recounts a hearing before Gallio, the proconsul, who summarily dismisses the charge brought against Paul by the Jews (18:12–17).

- ***Bivocational Witness (18:1–4)***
- ***Full-time Witness (18:5–11)***
- ***Hearing Before Gallio (18:12–17)***

EXPOSITION (18:1–17)

From Athens, Paul moved westward to Corinth, a major commercial center and the capital of the Roman province of Achaia. During eighteen months in that city, Paul experienced support from ministry colleagues, opposition from the Jews, receptivity from the Gentiles, reassurance from a divine vision, and vindication from the Roman proconsul. The selectivity of Luke's account highlights divine guidance (18:9–11) and the gospel's relationship to civil authorities (18:12–17). The passage incorporates multiple Lukan themes, including witness in major cities, involvement of Paul's colleagues, references to secular history, evaluation of Christian witness by civil authorities, and the gospel's encounter with Judaism (Barrett 1998, 858). Once again, that encounter with Judaism moved from engagement to opposition to separation to advance (Larkin 1995, 264).

There are also multiple points of connection between this passage and Paul's first letter to the Corinthians. They include the Corinthians' familiarity with Aquila and Priscilla (1 Cor. 16:19), Paul's secular employment (1 Cor. 9:12, 15–18), Timothy's involvement in the Corinthian mission (1 Cor. 4:17; 16:10–11), Paul's preaching to both Jews and Gentiles (1 Cor. 1:22–25; 9:19–23), and the conversion and baptism of Crispus (1 Cor. 1:14). See also Bock (2007, 576), and Schnabel (2012, 749); both include Sosthenes (18:17) as the same individual named in 1 Corinthians 1:1.

The reference to Claudius's edict expelling the Jews from Rome and an inscription in Delphi allow comparatively precise dating of Paul's ministry in Corinth. Claudius issued his edict in A.D. 49 (Seutonius, *Claud.* 25.4; cf. Bruce 1990, 390–91), and Aquila and Priscilla had relocated to Corinth following that edict (18:2). The inscription dates from A.D. 52 and follows Gallio's proconsulship in Achaia (Barrett 1998, 871). It is probable that Gallio served from July of A.D. 51 through June of A.D. 52 (Schnabel 2012, 761), and that Paul appeared before him early in his term but after Paul had been in Corinth for some time—perhaps the summer of A.D. 51 (Longenecker 1981, 485). Most likely, therefore, Paul's time in Corinth began in the fall of A.D. 50 and extended through the summer of A.D. 52.

Bivocational Witness (18:1–4)

When Paul meets Aquila and Priscilla in Corinth, he combines secular employment as a leatherworker with religious engagement in the synagogue.

18:1. Sometime after the events surrounding his ministry in Athens (μετὰ ταῦτα), Paul left that city (χωρισθεὶς ἐκ τῶν Ἀθηνῶν) and traveled to Corinth (ἦλθεν εἰς Κόρινθον), a three-day journey westward along the coast of the Saronic Gulf.

> ### Corinth
> Lying forty miles west of Athens, Corinth was located on a ten-mile-wide isthmus between the port of Cenchrea on the east and the port of Lechaem on the west. It was also astride the main road between the mainland to the north and the Peloponnesus to the south, making it a major commercial center. The Romans destroyed the original city in 146 B.C., but Julius Caesar rebuilt it in 46 B.C. as a Roman colony. It became the capital of the province of Achaia in 27 B.C. and was the site of the Isthmian Games every two years. It had a population of at least two hundred thousand and was home to Greeks, Romans, Jews, freedmen, lower classes, and slaves. The Corinthians enjoyed wealth, luxury, and immorality. "To live like a Corinthian" became a common description for someone who lived a particularly immoral life. The temple of Aphrodite attracted worshippers from across the ancient world.

18:2–3. On his own in that major commercial center, Paul sought out an opportunity to support himself and met (εὑρών) Aquila, who was from the province of Pontus in Asia Minor (Ἀκύλα, Ποντικὸν τῷ γένει), and his wife Priscilla (Πρίσκιλλαν γυναῖκα αὐτοῦ).

This Jewish couple had recently arrived from Italy (προσφάτως ἐληλυθότα ἀπὸ τῆς Ἰταλίας) because Claudius had ordered all Jews to depart from Rome. They were leatherworkers by trade (σκηνοποιοὶ τῇ τέχνῃ), and since he was also (διὰ τὸ ὁμότεχνον), Paul approached them (προσῆλθεν), stayed with them (ἔμενεν), and began working with them (ἠργάζετο) for an unspecified period of time.

18:4. While he was working his secular job, however, Paul also followed his customary strategy of regular religious engagement in the Jewish synagogue (διελέγετο ἐν τῇ συναγωγῇ; cf. 13:5, 14; 14:1; 17:1–2, 10, 16). He was present "every Sabbath without fail" (κατὰ πᾶν σάββατον; cf. Culy and Parsons 2003, 345), repeatedly persuading both Jews and Greeks (ἔπειθέν τε Ἰουδαίους καὶ Ἕλληνας) that the Messiah was Jesus (cf. 17:3; 18:5). The Western text adds the phrase "inserting the name of the Lord Jesus" (ἐντιθεὶς τὸ ὄνομα τοῦ κυρίου Ἰησοῦ), which Bruce suggests Paul did "where appropriate . . . as the scriptures were read" (1990, 392).

Full-time Witness (18:5–11)

When Silas and Timothy arrive from Macedonia with financial support, Paul resumes full-time ministry that is effective despite Jewish opposition and sustained by divine reassurance.

18:5. Silas and Timothy had remained in Berea when Paul left that city (17:14), but he had also given directions for them to join him in Achaia as soon as possible (17:15). First Thessalonians indicates that Timothy had subsequently joined Paul in Athens (1 Thess. 3:1) but that Paul had sent him back to Thessalonica to check on the status of the disciples there (1 Thess. 3:2). Now, however, both Silas and Timothy joined Paul in Corinth (κατῆλθον ἀπὸ τῆς Μακεδονίας ὅ τε Σιλᾶς καὶ ὁ Τιμόθεος), most likely bringing financial support from the churches in Macedonia (2 Cor. 11:8–9; Phil. 4:15). That financial support made it possible for Paul to "[begin] to devote himself exclusively to the ministry of the word and to continue to do so throughout his stay in Corinth" (συνείχετο τῷ λόγῳ; cf. Longenecker 1981, 482). Their arrival marked the shift from Paul's bivocational witness to his full-time witness in Corinth. Central to that witness among the Jews was the truth that "the Messiah was Jesus" (διαμαρτυρόμενος τοῖς Ἰουδαίοις εἶναι τὸν Χριστὸν Ἰησοῦν; cf. 17:3).

18:6. Not surprisingly, the Jews opposed (ἀντιτασσομένων) and slandered (βλασφημούντων) Paul. In response, he "shook out his garments" (ἐκτιναξάμενος τὰ ἱμάτια) in a symbolic gesture that demonstrated the seriousness of their rejection of the gospel (13:51; Neh. 5:13; Luke 10:11). Marshall notes that Jews typically performed this action against Gentiles (1980, 294), which highlights the irony of Paul's subsequent turning to the Gentiles. Paul accompanied that symbolic action with a denunciation, a declaration, and an announcement. The denunciation parallels the Jews' rejection of Jesus: "Your blood be upon your head" (τὸ αἷμα ὑμῶν ἐπὶ τὴν κεφαλὴν ὑμῶν; cf. Matt. 27:25; Acts 5:28). The declaration parallels Pilate's declaration of innocence: "I am clean" (καθαρὸς ἐγώ; cf. Matt 27:24). The announcement states his intention to redirect his witness in Corinth to focus on the Gentiles: "From now on, I will go to the Gentiles" (ἀπὸ τοῦ νῦν εἰς τὰ ἔθνη πορεύσομαι; cf. 13:46; 28:28).

18:7–8. What might have been inferred to be Paul's practice elsewhere (17:2) became explicit in Corinth. After leaving the synagogue (μεταβὰς ἐκεῖθεν), he relocated to the house of Titius Justus (εἰσῆλθεν εἰς οἰκίαν ... Τιτίου Ἰούστου), one of the God-worshipping Gentiles (σεβομένου τὸν θεόν), whose house was next door to the synagogue (συνομοροῦσα τῇ συναγωγῇ) and became Paul's base of operations for the remainder of his stay (cf. 19:8–10). Bruce, among others, suggests that the full name of Paul's Roman host was Gaius Titius Justus and, therefore, that he was the same Gaius named in Romans 16:23 and 1 Corinthians 1:14 (1990, 393), but Schnabel cautions that such an identification is hypothetical (2012, 739). Titius Justus is the last "Godfearer" mentioned in Acts (Bock 2007, 579).

The other notable convert in Corinth was Crispus, who was the leader of the synagogue (ὁ ἀρχισυνάγωγος), who "believed in the Lord with his whole household" (ἐπίστευσεν τῷ κυρίῳ σὺν ὅλῳ τῷ οἴκῳ αὐτοῦ), and who is mentioned—along with Gaius—in 1 Corinthians 1:14. His household is the last of four "household conversions" in Acts (10:48; 16:15, 33). They were not, however, the only converts. Luke notes, "Many of the Corinthians" (πολλοὶ τῶν Κορινθίων) "were hearing, believing, and being baptized" (ἀκούοντες ἐπίστευον καὶ ἐβαπτίζοντο). Peterson notes that the three verb tenses highlight iterative action and point to "an ongoing pattern of response to the preaching of the gospel" that highlights the effectiveness of Paul's ministry in Corinth (2009, 512).

18:9–11. Although Marshall correctly notes that Luke provides no specific reason for God to give Paul the vision he next experienced (1980, 295), that fact has not stopped commentators from suggesting reasons for God's action. Longenecker writes at some length about Paul's dejected mood after leaving Athens (1981, 479). Peterson suggests that the Jewish opposition he expected to encounter troubled Paul (2009, 513). Regardless, this vision was the fourth of six God gave Paul to guide him in his ministry. In the first vision, Jesus told him to enter Damascus where he would receive further instructions (9:3–9). In his second vision, Jesus sent him to the Gentiles (22:17–21). His third vision had directed him to Macedonia (16:9–10). This fourth vision encouraged Paul to minister in Corinth for a period of eighteen months (ἐνιαυτὸν καὶ μῆνας ἕξ), "teaching the Word of God among them" (διδάσκων ἐν αὐτοῖς τὸν λόγον τοῦ θεοῦ). Peterson considers this vision a recommissioning and compares it to other NT commissioning passages (2009, 513–15). Larkin notes that three promises undergird three commands (1995, 265):

Commands	Promises
"Stop being afraid" (μὴ φοβοῦ)	"I am with you" (ἐγώ εἰμι μετὰ σοῦ)
"Keep on speaking" (λάλει)	"No one will attack you to harm you" (οὐδεὶς ἐπιθήσεταί σοι τοῦ κακῶσαί σε)
"Do not be silent" (μὴ σιωπήσῃς)	"I have many people in this city" (λαός ἐστί μοι πολύς ἐν τῇ πόλει ταύτῃ)

Hearing Before Gallio (18:12–17)

When the Jews bring charges against Paul, Gallio dismisses the case, ruling that missionary activity is legal and the state is not competent to judge religious questions.

18:12–13. As was true on the road to Europe (16:6–10), divine guidance took two forms to reassure Paul that he should remain in Corinth. First, God used the extraordinary means of a divine vision (18:9–11). Then, he used the ordinary means of human events to confirm that guidance as well as his promise that "no one will attack you to harm you." Although Luke connects the next set of events to the period when Gallio was proconsul of Achaia (Γαλλίωνος ἀνθυπάτου ὄντος τῆς Ἀχαΐας), there is no indication of when during Paul's eighteen-month stay in Corinth those events occurred. It was far enough into his stay, however, that the effectiveness of his ministry aroused unified Jewish opposition.

"With one accord" (ὁμοθυμαδόν), the Jews attacked (κατεπέστησαν) Paul and led him before the place of judgment (ἤγαγον αὐτὸν ἐπὶ τὸ βῆμα). Longenecker describes the βῆμα as "a large, raised platform that stood in the Agora . . . in front of the residence of the proconsul and served as the forum where he tried cases" (1981, 486). Barrett cautions, however, that since the place where the judge held court was determined by where the judge was, the specific

venue cannot be confirmed (1998, 871). The charge the Jews brought against Paul was that he was "inciting people to worship God contrary to the law" (παρὰ τὸν νομόν ἀναπείει . . . τοὺς ἀνθρώπους σέβεσθαι τὸν θεόν). See Longenecker (1981, 485) for background information on Gallio.

TEXTUAL ANALYSIS: "inciting people to worship God contrary to the law"
Commentators observe that the Jews' charge against Paul was potentially ambiguous. As Larkin notes, the wording raises questions about the identity of the "people" and the nature of the "law" involved (1995, 266). Were the people (τοὺς ἀνθρώπους) Jews, Gentiles, or Roman citizens? Was the law (τὸν νόμον) the Jewish Torah (Bock 2007, 581), the Roman prohibition against proselytizing (Bruce 1990, 396), or the Roman law that Jewish customs and practices were to be respected (Peterson 2009, 516)? Or were they accusing Paul of preaching rebellion against Caesar as had been the case in Thessalonica (Schnabel 2012, 762; cf. 17:7)? Because Gallio was responsible for administering Roman law, it would make the most sense for the charge to imply a breach of that law. Given previous instances of accusers falsifying charges against Paul (16:20–21; 17:6–7), however, it might be that "there was a deliberate and conscious ambiguity in the accusation which demonstrates a certain cunning, but also the weakness of the plaintiffs' case against Paul" (Tajra 1989, 56). Regardless, Gallio saw through their ploy as raising questions "about a word and names and your own law" and summarily dismissed the charge (18:15–16).

18:14–16. Although Paul was prepared to defend himself (μέλλοντος τοῦ Παύλου ἀνοίγειν τὸ στόμα), the proconsul preempted him. Using a contrary-to-fact conditional construction (εἰ . . . ἄν), Gallio declared that he would have been prepared to be patient with the Jews (ἀνεσχόμην ὑμῶν), if they had brought a charge related to a "wrongdoing or vicious crime" (ESV, ἀδίκημα ἢ ῥᾳδιούργημα πονηρόν). Instead, they had brought him points of disagreement (ζητήματα) "about a word and names and law" (περὶ λόγου καὶ ὀνομάτων καὶ νόμου), which Longenecker understands as Paul's message, messianic titles, and a particular interpretation of the Jewish law (1981, 486). Gallio was, therefore, unwilling to be a judge of such matters (κτιτὴς ἐγὼ τούτων οὐ βούλομαι εἶναι) and drove them away (ἀπήλασεν αὐτούς). In so doing, Gallio ruled that followers of this new message were not breaking Roman law, and that disputes over that message were internal to the Jewish community (Dunn 1996, 244–45). The broader principles that may be drawn are that missionary activity is legal and the state is not competent to judge religious questions (Larkin 1995, 267).

18:17. Gallio's commitment to nonintervention included a total lack of concern about the events that followed his ruling (οὐδὲν τούτων τῷ Γαλλίωνι ἔμελεν). It is unclear who subsequently attacked Sosthenes. "All" (πάντες) might refer to the Jews (Schnabel 2012, 765), the Greek bystanders (as the Western text specifies), or both groups—the Jews for his ineffectiveness in dealing with Paul and the Greeks for being Jewish (Barrett 1998, 875). Regardless, they took hold of him (ἐπιλαβόμενοι) and beat him repeatedly (ἔτυπτον) on the spot (ἔμπροσθεν τοῦ βήματος). The Sosthenes mentioned here might be the same individual included in the salutation of Paul's first letter to Corinth (1 Cor. 1:1), although Sosthenes was a fairly common name (Schnabel 2012, 765).

THEOLOGICAL FOCUS

The narratival function of Acts 18:1–17 is to recount key events from Paul's extended ministry in cosmopolitan Corinth, the largest city and commercial hub of Greece. As Bock notes, the account is selective with special attention given to the hearing before Gallio, the Roman proconsul (2007, 576). In addition to providing insight into Paul's church-planting strategy—particularly his practice of working to support himself—therefore, the passage has an apologetic function. Corinth was the third Greek city where Paul appeared before civil authorities. In Philippi (16:19–24, 35–40) and Thessalonica (17:5–9), before both Roman and Greek magistrates, the results had been negative. In Athens (17:22–33), before the Areopagus Council, the question had been left unresolved. As a well-regarded Roman proconsul, however, Gallio's ruling set a precedent for provincial governors across the empire. Longenecker describes his decision as "tantamount to the recognition of Christianity as a *religio licita*" (1981, 486). If Theophilus and other well-placed Roman readers like him had any doubt about the legitimacy of the gospel Paul preached, Gallio's verdict should have removed them. The town clerk in Ephesus subsequently confirmed that verdict.

Theologically, the high point of the passage is Paul's vision in 18:9–11. In that vision, the Lord Jesus (cf. 23:11) issues three commands undergirded by three promises. Together, those elements underscore an important theological principle: God's provisions enable us to fulfill our obligations. The promises of the vision suggest:

- His presence calms our fears.
- His protection fuels our witness.
- His predestination nurtures our boldness.

In the passage as a whole, God provides gainful employment through Aquila and Priscilla (18:1–4), missionary support through the churches in Macedonia (8:5–8), reassurance through a vision (8:9–11), and a legal validation through Gallio (8:12–17). Those provisions made it possible for Paul to sustain his obedient witness in the face of financial need, religious opposition, and legal challenge. His experience in Corinth teaches us that God gives us what we need, so that we can do what he asks us to do.

Accusers	Issue	Charge(s)	Official(s)	Verdict
Gentiles in Philippi (16:19–24, 35–40)	Economic	Disturbing the public order and advocating customs contrary to Roman practice	Roman magistrates	Beaten with rods, jailed, and released
Jews in Thessalonica (17:5–9)	Religious	Threatening the stability of the empire and advocating sedition against the emperor	Greek magistrates	Posted bond and released
Greeks in Athens (17:22–33)	Philosophical	Proclaiming strange deities	Greek city council members	No decision
Jews in Corinth (18:12–17)	Religious	Advocating worship that is contrary to the law	Roman proconsul	Charges dismissed as without merit
Gentiles in Ephesus (19:23–41)	Economic	Advocating rejection of Artemis and gods made with hands	Greek town clerk	Charges dismissed as without merit

PREACHING AND TEACHING STRATEGIES

Exegetical/Theological Synthesis

Luke's first-century readers would want to know what happened when Paul brought the gospel to Corinth, the largest city in Greece, a cosmopolitan commercial center, and the capital of the Roman province of Achaia. So far, he had been forced to leave Philippi, Thessalonica, and Berea, and he had encountered skepticism and ridicule in Athens. How would Paul respond when financial need joined religious opposition and legal challenge? Would his time in Corinth be equally brief and tumultuous, or would God order events differently? With Luke's original readers, the twenty-first-century audience shares the need to understand that they can expect God to use both ordinary and extraordinary means to assure and guide the witness who trusts his promises and obeys his commands. Characteristics of such a witness include flexibility, steadfastness, and faith. In turn, he or she can depend on the support of God's people, the faithfulness of God himself, and the neutrality of civil authorities.

Preaching/Teaching Idea

God gives us what we need, to do what he asks us to do.

Contemporary Connections

What does it mean?
God called his church to be Spirit-empowered witnesses to the ends of the earth (1:8). God called Paul to be "a chosen instrument of mine to carry my name before the Gentiles and

kings and the children of Israel" (9:15). That is God's "ask." It is the clarion, costly call to be his mouthpiece in a world infatuated with its own voice. Everything God asks of us, however, he provides for us. Just like he gives his Spirit so that we might bear spiritual fruit (Galatians 5), and provides a way of escape so that we might resist temptation (1 Corinthians 10), so also he provides all that is needed to fulfill his Great Commission. Paul, whom we could caricature as a self-made missionary, was dependent on God's provision every step of the way. From friends, to work, to a place to live, to coworkers carrying financial support, to a place to preach, to receptive hearers, God's providing hand was everywhere. Still, Paul was afraid, but again God provided—this time in a vision to encourage him with more provision to come. Truly, God gives us all we need to do what he asks us to do, but often, he gives us above and beyond what we need, to help us every step of the way, to do what he asks us to do.

Is it true?
Asking about God's provision today is essentially asking if Jesus is still true to his Great Commission promise two millennia ago. He told us, "All authority in heaven and on earth has been given to me. Go, therefore and make disciples" (Matt. 28:18–19). He backed that command with a promise: "And behold, I am with you always, to the end of the age" (Matt. 28:20). The book of Acts is like one big testament to believers today that God's Word is still good.

As Acts shows, however, *what* God's presence and provision involves might look different in every situation. In Philippi, Paul was beaten and jailed. In Corinth, his case was dismissed. God still provided. In Corinth, Paul escaped but Sosthenes was attacked. God was still present. It seems like there was much less evangelistic fruit in Athens than in Corinth. God still predestines. This lesson is important. We cannot put parameters on exactly what God's presence and protection will look like in our lives today. We

might wish we could. We might wish we could dictate how God ought to act on our behalf. We would not even mind picking the timetable. Of course, we are going to do things God's way and not our way. He picks the provision we need for the work he gives us to do, and he is always right.

Now what?
Where are we stepping out in faith in such a way that we even *need* God's provision? That is the heart of our application question for today. We would like God's provisions to pile up in our lives so that we can spend them in the future. In our passage, however, they come like manna—one day's supply, one day at a time. God meets the needs that arise out of the commands he gives. Jesus taught us to pray, "Your kingdom come, your will be done," before we pray, "Give us this day our daily bread" (Matt. 6:9–13). God's mission precedes God's supply, which is a good thing. Following him means taking risks to obey him and trusting that he will supply the need. These needs and provisions come in all shapes and sizes. When we face loneliness, joblessness, homelessness, threats from without and threats from within, uncertainty about the future, or personal attacks, we run to God for his help. Paul learned that if God has given us his Son Jesus in our salvation, "how will he not also with him graciously give us all things?" (Rom 8:32).

A secondary theme that has been building in Acts is that the state vindicates Christianity. Luke has been eager to show us how responsibly this new faith can grow up under Rome without threatening her stability. The parallels are important in our world that is growing hostile to Christianity. The Roman Empire was a far more threatening place, and we can learn from the early church when to obey the state and when to resist.

Creativity in Presentation
There is a big difference between starting a puzzle and finishing a puzzle. Putting together the first ten pieces and the last ten pieces could

not feel more different. The first ten are a challenge. You know that they are there (if it is a freshly opened puzzle), but it takes a lot of patience to find them and place them. The last ten are a breeze, and you can hardly slap them in place quickly enough. The changing seasons of God's provision can feel that way. There are seasons where it feels like God meets every need that comes into our lives with his clear, specific, perfectly placed help. There are other seasons where we might know his promises to care for and equip us with everything we need for life and godliness (2 Peter 1:3), but it is hard to see at the time.

A creative way to present this overarching principle is to compare the different ways God has provided for his church in Acts so far. Both seasons are present. There are times when street preaching leads to conversions, and there are times when street preaching leads to martyrdom. There are times when arrest leads to a miraculous deliverance, and there are times when it leads to execution. There are harder seasons of ministry like Thessalonica and Athens, and there are sweet seasons like Corinth and Ephesus. In every season, God is present and providing, but it might not look like we expect. This principle opens the way to celebrate the season Paul enjoys, which God underscores with a vision in 18:9–11. God meets Paul's fear with his presence, Paul's vulnerability with his protection, and Paul's temptation to stay silent with his promise that there are many predestined in Corinth to believe. These examples of real help meet real needs. Paul will not reach the Corinthians in his own strength. He is dependent on God to provide.

God gives us what we need, to do what he asks us to do.

- God gives us what we need (18:1–3, 5, 9–11)

- To do what he calls us to do (18:4, 6–8, 12–17)

DISCUSSION QUESTIONS

1. How can bivocational ministry be a helpful approach to church planting for both the church planter and the church plant?

2. Should full-time ministry be considered superior to bivocational ministry? Why or why not?

3. Does a time come when continuing to witness to an individual or a group becomes counterproductive? If so, how do you determine when that time has arrived?

4. Is it realistic to expect civil authorities to be neutral with regard to religious matters? Why or why not?

5. What are some examples you have experienced when God provided what you needed so that you could do what he asked you to do?

ASIA (ACTS 18:18–20:38)

Gallio's dismissal of the charges against Paul allowed the apostle to continue his ministry in Corinth before departing for Syrian Antioch by way of Ephesus and Jerusalem. He then returned to Ephesus for an extended time of ministry in Asia. The popular label often given to this period of travel and ministry is Paul's "third missionary journey," although Dunn views the events of chapters 16–20 as a sustained "Aegean mission" with two main phases (1996, 212): the first centered in Corinth for at least eighteen months (18:11); the second centered in Ephesus for three years (20:31).

This division continues motifs from the preceding division, including witness in major metropolitan centers, synagogue preaching emphasizing Jesus as the Messiah, Jewish opposition leading to a turning to the Gentiles, the victory of the gospel over competing spiritual powers, vindication of the gospel by civil authorities, and the importance of continuing contact with mission churches. It closes with Paul recalling his ministry in Asia. The events Luke reports most likely cover the period from early A.D. 52 through the middle of A.D. 57.

52	Spring	Cenchrea to Jerusalem (18:18–21)	Visit to Ephesus (18:19–21)
	Summer	Syrian Antioch (18:22)	
	Fall	Antioch to Ephesus (18:23)	
53	Winter		Apollos in Ephesus (18:24–26)
	Spring		Apollos in Achaia (18:27–28)
	Summer		
	Fall		
54	Winter		
	Spring		
	Summer		"Previous letter" to Corinthians
	Fall	Ephesus (19:1–40)	
55	Winter		
	Spring		1 Corinthians
	Summer		Riot over Artemis (19:23–40)
	Fall		"Severe letter" to Corinthians
56	Winter		
	Spring		
	Summer	Macedonia (20:1–2)	2 Corinthians
	Fall		
57	Winter	Corinth (20:3)	Romans
	Spring	Troas to Miletus (20:7–20:38)	Farewell in Miletus (20:17–38)

This fifth division consists of five preaching sections. The first records the beginning of the Christian witness in Ephesus—first, Paul's visit; then, Apollos's visit (18:18–28). The second describes Paul's extended ministry in Ephesus (19:1–22). The third records the riot that took place during the second half of Paul's time in the city (19:23–40). The fourth recounts Paul's return visit to Macedonia and Achaia and the beginning of his travel to Jerusalem (20:1–16). The fifth describes his farewell to the Ephesian elders in Miletus (20:17–28).

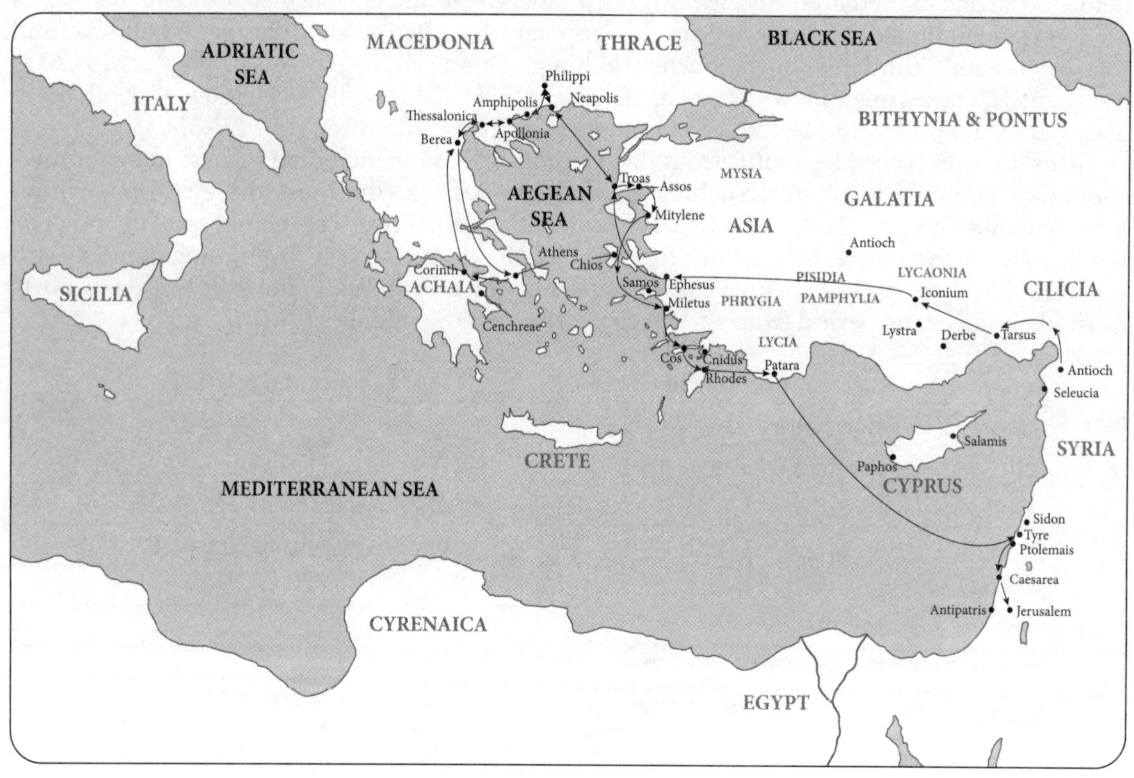

Paul's Third Journey

Acts 18:18–28

EXEGETICAL IDEA

Paul's initial witness, Apollos's apologetic ministry, and Priscilla and Aquila's continuing care laid the foundation for Ephesus to become the center of gospel outreach in Asia.

THEOLOGICAL IDEA

God uses a variety of people, each with different giftings, to advance his purposes.

PREACHING IDEA

It takes a team to do God's tasks.

PREACHING POINTERS

Hillary Clinton's 1996 book *It Takes a Village* brought to prominence the African proverb that says, "It takes a village to raise a child." The proverb captures the idea that an entire community of people must participate if children are to grow up in a healthy environment. The same principle applies to the growth of works that God begins. In his sovereign working he used Paul, Apollos, Priscilla, and Aquila to begin a work in Ephesus that would ultimately make an impact throughout western Asia Minor. With Luke's original readers, we need to understand that God uses different people in different ways to accomplish his kingdom purposes. If we do, we will be intentional about looking for our roles in what God is doing and will fill those roles as he empowers us to do so.

People today should be able to relate to multiple elements from this passage, including overseas travel, eloquent speakers, and working with coaches. Men and women who are familiar with mission work can most likely relate to the ideas of a "vision trip" to explore a possible future area for ministry and of a "home ministry assignment" after a term on the mission field. The accounts of Paul's and Apollos's ministries in Ephesus correct the ideas that "lone ranger" ministry is a valid option and that there is no need to learn from others. The accounts commend the values of trust in God's will and teachability as well as the practice of private correction when a fellow believer is in error. They remind us that—because God uses different people in different ways—it takes a team to do God's tasks.

EARLY EVENTS IN EPHESUS (18:18–28)

LITERARY STRUCTURE AND THEMES (18:18–28)

The passage consists of two paragraphs describing early events related to the Christian witness in Ephesus. The first paragraph documents Paul's travels, beginning in Corinth and extending through the start of his return trip to Ephesus (18:18–23). It divides into two itineraries: Corinth to Cenchrea to Ephesus (18:18–21) and Caesarea to Jerusalem to Syrian Antioch (18:22–23). The second paragraph introduces Apollos and his ministry (18:24–28). It also divides into two parts: his visit to Ephesus (18:24–26) and his visit to Achaia (18:27–28). Together, they cover the founding of the church that was destined to become the center of gospel outreach for the province of Asia.

- ***Paul's Initial Witness in Ephesus (18:18–23)***
- ***Apollos's Witness in Ephesus and Achaia (18:24–28)***

EXPOSITION (18:18–28)

Having completed his ministry in Corinth, Paul embarked on a return trip to Syrian Antioch so that he could report to the church there as was his established practice (14:21–28). Leaving Corinth from the eastern port of Cenchrea, he stopped in Ephesus, the most important city in western Asia Minor, where he followed his normal strategy of engaging the Jews in the synagogue (18:18–21). Leaving Priscilla and Aquila there and promising to return, he continued his voyage, first by sea to Caesarea, then by land to Jerusalem and Syrian Antioch (18:22–23). At some time after Paul left Ephesus, Apollos arrived there (18:24). When he began engaging the Jews in the synagogue, Priscilla and Aquila recognized that Apollos needed additional instruction and took him aside to provide it (18:25–26). Equipped with a more accurate understanding of the gospel and carrying a letter of recommendation from the Christians in Ephesus, Apollos traveled to Achaia where he watered the seeds that Paul had planted (18:26–27; cf. 1 Cor. 3:6).

The passage summarizes events over the course of approximately one year—from spring A.D. 52 through spring A.D. 53—and serves as a narrative transition from Paul's extended ministry in Corinth, the major commercial center of Greece, to his extended ministry in Ephesus, the major commercial center of Asia Minor. Peterson notes that Paul's patterns of ministry in the two cities were similar (2009, 523). The cities were, in effect, the twin headquarters of what Dunn calls Paul's "Aegean mission" (1996, 212), and the events recounted in 18:18–28 prepare the reader for the second half of that mission in Ephesus.

Paul's Initial Witness in Ephesus (18:18–23)

Paul stops in Ephesus before visiting the church in Jerusalem, reporting on his activity to the church in Syrian Antioch, and strengthening the churches in South Galatia.

18:18. Luke notes that after the hearing before Gallio (18:12–17), Paul stayed on (προσμείνας) in Corinth for "many days" (ἡμέρας ἱκανάς). Schnabel thinks Paul stayed for a comparatively short time and left before sea travel ended in November of A.D. 51 (2012, 766), while Bruce thinks Paul stayed for a longer time and left after the Aegean reopened for travel in March of A.D. 52 (1990, 397). The latter explanation seems more natural, and underscores the fact that Paul left Corinth voluntarily, unlike his departures from Philippi, Thessalonica, and Berea. Accompanied by Priscilla and Aquila, he set sail from Cenchrea with Syria as his ultimate destination (ἐξέπλει εἰς τὴν Συρίαν). Since Luke does not mention Silas or Timothy, Peterson offers the possibility that Paul might have left them in Achaia to continue the work there as he had previously done when he left Macedonia (2009, 519). Luke also notes that while Paul was in Cenchrea he cut his hair, because he was under a vow (κειράμενος … τὴν κεφαλήν, εἶχεν γάρ εὐχήν).

TEXTUAL ANALYSIS: "he had his hair cut, because he was under a vow"
Luke's comment about Paul's action in Cenchrea is cryptic at best and—setting aside the suggestion that is an unhistorical Lukan insertion (Weiser 1985, 497–98)—has led to four proposed explanations. Following *NewDocs* 1.24, Barrett suggests that it reflects "a standard Greek cultural reaction to some dream through which came divine guidance" (1998, 877). This option is possible, although a Jewish background seems more natural. Dunn believes that a Nazirite vow is in view (Num. 6:1–21) and proposes that Cenchrea was the place where Paul last cut his hair before he began the vow. He would not cut his hair until God granted him safety during his impending travel to Jerusalem (Dunn 1996, 246). Connecting Paul's action to a Nazirite vow seems more natural, although Dunn's suggestion of a final haircut preceding the vow seems forced. Bruce rejects the possibility of a Nazirite vow, because fulfilling such a vow would be difficult outside Israel given the possibility of defilement through contact with Gentiles (1990, 398; cf. Bock 2007, 586). He suggests that Paul's action marks the end of a private vow of thanksgiving that he took following the vision in Corinth (18:9–10). Although it is impossible to know for certain (Schnabel 2012, 768), the suggestion that it was the conclusion of a Nazirite vow for protection after Paul's Macedonian vision (Larkin

1995, 268) or his Corinthian vision (Longenecker 1981, 488) seems most natural. Marshall notes that the individual could cut his hair outside Israel (1981, 300; cf. m. Naz. 3:6; 5:4). Paul could subsequently have offered the hair in Jerusalem after the required thirty days of purification. Such an explanation would establish the length of time Paul spent in Jerusalem prior to "going down" to Syrian Antioch (18:22).

18:19–21. En route to Syria, Paul reached Ephesus (κατήντησαν εἰς Ἔφεσον), where—as was his custom (17:2, 17; 18:2)—he entered the synagogue (αὐτὸς εἰσελθὼν εἰς τὴν συναγωθήν) and engaged the members of the Jewish community (διελέξατο τοῖς Ἰουδαίους). They responded positively and asked Paul to spend more time with them (ἐρωτώντων αὐτῶν ἐπὶ πλείονα χρόνον μεῖναι). Paul, however, was eager to get to Jerusalem, and the Western text inserts his reason in verse 21: "I must by all means keep this coming feast in Jerusalem" (NKJV). Since the sea lanes had just opened in mid-March and Passover was in early April that year, it might be that the textual variant captures Paul's intent. Alternately, the addition might be an assimilation to 20:16. Regardless, he left Priscilla and Aquila in Ephesus to carry on the work he had begun (κἀκείνους κατέλιπον; the clause is placed unexpectedly early in verse 19), took his leave (ἀποταξάμενος), promised to return (πάλιν ἀνακάμψω πρὸς ὑμᾶς) if God was willing (τοῦ θεοῦ θέλοντος), and set sail again (ἀνήχθη).

> **Ephesus**
> The early history of Ephesus is undocumented, although mythology alludes to its founding by the race of female warriors known as the Amazons. The site "was probably inhabited by a combination of Carians, Leleges, and indigenous peoples" (*DPL*, 249). Ionian colonists founded the original Greek city of Ephesus around 1100 B.C. and constructed the temple

of Artemis in the seventh century B.C. The Persians controlled the city from the sixth century B.C. until Alexander the Great conquered Asia Minor. The temple was rebuilt in the first half of the third century, and Lysimachus redesigned the city to relocate it close to the harbor. Control of the city passed to the Romans in 133 B.C. By the first century, Ephesus was the fourth largest city in the empire with an estimated population of 250,000 and was the capital of the Roman province of Asia. The city had a theater that seated twenty-four thousand, a market that measured 110 meters square, baths, gymnasiums, and a medical school. It was also the home of the common games of Asia. The population was predominantly Gentile but also included a Jewish population large enough to support a synagogue (Harvey 2012, 128–29). It was a free city with its own Greek assembly.

Colonnade in Ephesus. Public domain.

18:22. Although his ultimate destination was Syria (18:18), Paul booked passage on a ship that sailed for Caesarea (κατελθὼν εἰς Καισάρειαν). The trip from Ephesus would have covered 650 miles and would have taken five to ten days (Schnabel 2012, 769), most likely with stops for supplies along the way (Barrett 1998, 880). From Caesarea, Paul "went up and greeted the church" (ἀναβὰς καὶ ἀσπασάμενος τὴν ἐκκλησίαν). Since the verb ἀναβαίνω often refers to "going up" to Jerusalem (Luke 18:31; 19:28; Acts 11:2; 13:31; 15:2; 21:12, 15; 25:1), the reference is more naturally to the church in Jerusalem than to the church in Caesarea. Jerusalem also makes good sense if Paul was completing his Nazirite vow (18:18) and/or seeking to celebrate the Passover as the Western text suggests (18:21). See the introduction on Paul's visits to Jerusalem. Peterson is most likely correct when he suggests that the visit was "part of [Paul's] strategy to maintain good links between the Gentile churches and the centre from which the gospel first came" (2009, 522). From Jerusalem, Paul "went down" to Syrian Antioch (κατέβη εἰς Ἀντιόχειαν), a trip of more than three hundred miles that would have taken about three weeks on foot (Schnabel 2012, 769).

18:23. By highlighting the continuity between verse 22 and verse 23, Culy and Parsons refute the suggestion that verse 23 begins a new section (2003, 354; contra Fitzmyer 1998, 633, 636). In contrast to Jerusalem, where Paul merely "greeted the church," he "spent some time" (ποιήσας χρόνον τινά) in Syrian Antioch (compare "not a little time" in 14:28). Since the church in that city had committed him and Silas to the work in which they had been engaged (15:40), he most likely spent the time reporting on what God had been doing through them as he and Barnabas had done after their first extended time in the field (14:27). Then, following his practice from three years previously (15:41; 16:4–5), he visited the churches in South Galatia once again (διερχόμενος καθεξῆς τὴν Γαλατικὴν χώραν καὶ Φρυγίαν) with the express purpose of "strengthening all the disciples" (ἐπιστηρίζων πάντας τοὺς μαθήτας).

Apollos's Witness in Ephesus and Achaia (18:24–28)

Apollos arrives in Ephesus and begins preaching in the synagogue, before traveling to Achaia for further witness.

18:24–25. In Paul's absence, another itinerant Jewish teacher arrived in Ephesus—Apollos from Alexandria in Egypt (Ἀλεξανδρεύς τῷ γένει). Luke characterizes Apollos in five ways. First, he was an "eloquent" or "learned" man (λόγιος ἀνήρ). The adjective Luke uses can carry either meaning (BDAG s.v. "λόγιος" 598). Most English translations choose "eloquent" (e.g., CSB, ESV, NASB, NRSV), although NIV chooses "learned." Barrett suggests that it is "fruitless to inquire which is intended," since Hellenistic education included extensive training in rhetoric (1998, 887). Second, he was "capable" in the Scriptures (δυνατὸς ἐν ταῖς γραφαῖς). English translations variously choose "mighty/powerful" (e.g., NASB) or "well-versed" (e.g., NSRV). Third, he had been "catechized" (κατηχημένος) with regard to "the way of the Lord" (τὴν ὁδὸν τοῦ κυρίου). Fourth, he was "fervent in the Spirit" (ζέων τῷ πνεύματι). Fifth, he taught "accurately" (ἀκριβῶς) concerning Jesus (τὰ περὶ τοῦ Ἰησοῦ). The picture, therefore, is of an individual who had received both a thorough secular education and a thorough scriptural grounding, who was empowered by the Holy Spirit, and who could communicate the truth he knew eloquently and accurately. His understanding of the truth, however, was imperfect in that he "knew only John's baptism" (ἐπιστάμενος μόνον τὸ βάπτισμα Ἰωάννου).

18:26. Following a strategy that mirrored Paul's, Apollos centered his ministry in the Jewish synagogue (ἐν τῇ συναγωγῇ), where he began to speak out boldly (ἤρξατο παρρησιάζεσθαι). When Priscilla and Aquila heard him speak, they realized that they could help him. Luke gives no details as to what aspect(s) of his teaching might have needed correction, although the previous comment about Apollos knowing only John's baptism is suggestive. Rather than confronting him publicly, Priscilla and Aquila "took him aside" (προσελάβοντο αὐτόν) and coached him privately. They "filled him in more accurately" (ἀκριβέστερον αὐτῷ διελθεῖν) regarding "the

way of God" (τὴν ὁδὸν τοῦ θεοῦ). Bock suggests that Priscilla and Aquila "update[d] Apollos on baptism, moving him beyond John's baptism, probably to the gift of the Spirit, telling Apollos that the Spirit has come and acquainting him with the importance of the arrival of this eschatological promise" (2007, 593).

Apollos and the Twelve Disciples in Ephesus

The way in which Luke places in close proximity the accounts of Apollos's visit in Ephesus (18:24–26) and Paul's encounter with the twelve disciples in Ephesus (19:1–7) invites comparison, since Luke describes both Apollos and the twelve disciples as knowing only John's baptism. The differences are that Apollos "had been instructed in the way of the Lord" and was "fervent in Spirit" (18:25), but the twelve required instruction that Jesus was the one who was coming after John (19:4) and had not yet received the Holy Spirit (19:6). Larkin notes that the twelve were "living without either the truth or the power of the Christian gospel" (1995, 273). Apollos exhibited both: not only did he understand the truth, he was able to "[teach] accurately the things concerning Jesus" (18:25). The presence of the definite article in the phrase "being fervent in the Spirit" (ζέων τῷ πνεύματι) and the parallel to Romans 12:11, where the same phrase applies to Christians, support the conclusion that the reference is to the Holy Spirit rather than to Apollos's human spirit. Marshall suggests that the "more accurate" (ἀκριβέστερον) instruction Apollos received from Priscilla and Aquila (18:26) brought his "garbled understanding" of the gospel into alignment with "distinctive Pauline doctrines" (1980, 303–4). The fact that there is no mention of Priscilla and Aquila baptizing Apollos suggests that "[his] earlier 'baptism of repentance' was considered Christian baptism when viewed as pointing to Jesus and was therefore not to be redone every time there was a growth in understanding" (Longenecker 1981, 491; cf. Bruce 1990, 403).

18:27a. After Priscilla and Aquila instructed him, Apollos expressed a desire to cross over to Achaia (βουλομένου αὐτοῦ διελθεῖν εἰς τὴν Ἀχαΐαν). Luke provides no motivation for the proposed change of venue. Perhaps Priscilla and Aquila told Apollos about their recent experiences in Achaia. Peterson suggests that it was apparent how effective Apollos could be in refuting the Jewish opposition they had encountered there (2009, 527). As is often the case, the Western text supplies an explanation: "And some Corinthians who were on a visit to Ephesus and had heard him invited him to cross over with them to their native place." Barrett discusses the variant reading and the related issues at some length (1998, 890–91). Regardless, the brothers (οἱ ἀδελφοί) in Ephesus encouraged (προτρεψάμενοι) Apollos to make the trip and wrote a letter of recommendation, asking the disciples in Achaia to welcome him (ἔγραψαν τοῖς μαθηταῖς ἀποδέξασθαι αὐτόν). Dunn's identification of "the brothers" as "a group within the synagogue, who probably met during the week in the home of Priscilla and Aquila" (1997, 251) seems to be supported by Paul's comment in 1 Corinthians 16:19 about the church that met in that couple's house.

18:27b–28. When he arrived (παραγενόμενος) in Achaia, Apollos "proved to be of great benefit to those who, by God's grace, had believed" (NLT, συνεβάλετο πολὺ τοῖς πεπιστευκόσιν διὰ τῆν χάριτος). His ministry was both public (δημοσίᾳ) and vigorous (εὐτόνως). He "overwhelmed" (διακατηλέγχετο; cf. Bock 2007, 593) the Jews by showing through the Scriptures that the Messiah was Jesus (ἐπιδεικνὺς διὰ τῶν γραφῶν εἶναι τὸν Χριστὸν Ἰησοῦν; cf. 17:3; 18:5). Luke does not say whether Apollos ministered elsewhere in Achaia, but Paul's first letter to the Corinthians attests to his effectiveness in that city—to the extent that some Corinthian believers identified strongly with him (1 Cor. 1:12). It is clear, however, that Paul did not view Apollos as a competitor or a threat. Instead, he

acknowledged that, as a fellow worker, Apollos built on the foundation he had laid (1 Cor. 3:6–9). Later, when they were again in Ephesus at the same time, Paul urged Apollos to revisit Corinth (1 Cor. 16:12).

THEOLOGICAL FOCUS

The narratival function of Acts is to document the events during the transition in Paul's ministry from his time in Corinth until his time in Ephesus. Having experienced God's assurance and Gallio's validation, both of which enabled him to remain in Corinth for an extended period of ministry, what would his next steps be? Would he move directly to a new field of ministry, or would he return to Syrian Antioch as he had done at the end of his first period of itinerant ministry? If the former, how would he determine where that new field would be? Would he follow the same strategy that he had used in Europe? If the latter, would he also visit Jerusalem to provide an update on the Gentile mission? Luke's account of Paul's travels answers those questions by telling readers that Paul did both—he combined a "vision trip" to Ephesus with a visit to Jerusalem and an extended time in Syrian Antioch. In so doing, Luke provided background on the initial gospel witness in Ephesus, introduced Apollos, and explained the Alexandrian Jewish apologist's connection with the church in Corinth.

Theologically, Acts 18:18–28 illustrates a truth about the body of Christ that Paul teaches explicitly in his letters, particularly in his letter to the Ephesians: God uses the whole body to produce the growth of the body (Eph. 4:11–16). Paul, Apollos, and the husband-wife team of Priscilla and Aquila each played a role in the founding of the church in Ephesus. To borrow (and adapt) the metaphor Paul uses in 1 Corinthians 3:6–9: Paul planted the seeds through his initial engagement with the Jews in the city, Apollos watered the seeds through his preaching, and Priscilla and Aquila tended the garden through their ministry of pastoral care as seen in their coaching of Apollos. The group of believers in Ephesus was then able to recommend Apollos to the church in Corinth.

It is also worth noting that one way to determine normativity in biblical narrative is through identifying repeated patterns. Luke's account of the initial events in Ephesus repeats the pattern he had set out earlier with the church in Syrian Antioch. Evangelism (18:19–21; cf. 11:19–21) precedes edification (18:24–26; cf. 11:22–26), which results in extension of mission to other areas (18:27–28; cf. 13:1–4).

PREACHING AND TEACHING STRATEGIES

Exegetical/Theological Synthesis

Luke's first-century readers would want to know how Ephesus became the center for gospel outreach for the province of Asia. By combining the account of Paul's travels after he left Corinth with the introduction of Apollos, Luke is able to recount the early events in Ephesus that laid the foundation for Paul's subsequent three-year ministry in that city. He is also able to make his readers aware of the key figures who played a part in laying that foundation. With the original readers, the twenty-first-century audience shares the need to understand the way in which God uses different people with different gifts to advance his kingdom purposes. Luke's narrative incorporates individuals with the gifts of apostleship/evangelism (Paul), prophecy/teaching (Apollos), and discernment/pastoring (Priscilla and Aquila). Together, these individuals illustrate the way in which diversity of gifting and unity of purpose within the body of Christ can combine to establish a group of believers whose commitment to the progress of the gospel extended beyond the limits of their own city. The effectiveness of this multifaceted ministry makes it clear that it takes a team to do God's tasks.

Preaching/Teaching Idea

It takes a team to do God's tasks.

Contemporary Connections

What does it mean?

This preaching unit is a celebration of God's design to bring the church body together to do his work. The text shows each participant playing his or her role in turn. First, Paul marched ahead into the synagogue to plant the seed of witness among the Jews (18:19). Next, Apollos appeared in Paul's absence and watered these seeds with eloquent, competent, fervent, accurate doctrine about Jesus (18:24–25). Finally, Priscilla and Aquila reappeared, tending the garden by sharpening Apollos's understanding (18:26). Each person had the right gift for the right role at the right time. That kind of providence leaves us standing in awe of God. Fittingly, a passage that displays a team to do God's work begins, ends, and has at its center God's church. Paul lingered with the brothers in Corinth (18:18). Paul traveled on to greet the church at Caesarea and Antioch (18:22) and onward to churches in Galatia and Phrygia (18:23). The believers in Ephesus encouraged Apollos, and the church in Achaia received him (18:27). Even though the passage highlights the unique contributions of Paul, Priscilla and Aquila, and Apollos, they stand on the shoulders of nameless Christians in all corners, each fulfilling God's role for them.

Is it true?

God gains supreme glory when he entrusts his people with different gifts to use together for his kingdom. This Paul-Apollos-Priscilla-Aquila combination is a shining example of that truth. Paul will write later to this church plant in Ephesus that God makes one church body, baptized into the one triune God, and gives each a different "measure of Christ's gift" (Eph. 4:7). "When each part is working properly," Paul exhorts, Christ "makes the body grow so that it builds itself up in love" (Eph. 4:16). Paul would know. The Ephesians would know. It had happened in their city. God did not need to do it this way, of course. He could have given Paul extra gifts, like the humility and pastoral care of Priscilla and Aquila, making their role redundant. He could have made Priscilla and Aquila a little louder like Apollos so that the church would not need his extra help. It certainly would have simplified things. It certainly would have removed any hint of a division that haunts capable leaders (1 Cor. 1:10–17). Then, however, we would have a different book. This passage would read more like the Acts of Paul than the Acts of the Spirit. Lone ministries need little Spirit. God has a different story to tell. His story is one of a God-dependent team with God-given gifts working together toward God's mission.

Now what?

This glimpse of a multigifted team at work from the earliest days of the Ephesian church planting movement is a microcosm of how God has always acted in Scripture and in history. Think of the diverse people, talents, nationalities, and personalities that populate both testaments. What was Moses without Aaron, Nehemiah without Ezra, or Esther without Mordecai? Jesus doubled down on this principle by choosing a colorful cast of disciples. Matthew the tax collector and Simon the zealot were different people with different backgrounds. Loud-mouthed Peter and affectionate John were different personalities. God loves to make us dependent *on* him by making us dependent on each other *in* him.

If anything, the church today has grown more diverse, colorful, and interdependent since the events recorded in Acts, as it has expanded to the nations. These heady days of watching God at work show us his glory through these brothers and sisters in our midst and around the globe. He assigns some to plant and some to water so that he can give the growth (1 Cor. 3:6–8). He makes some to be eyes to see and some to be hands to touch so that he can empower (1 Corinthians 12). He is really calling the *whole* church into his mission today.

Creativity in Presentation

It is easy to think of different personalities and gifts, especially those the most different from ours, as more of a liability than an asset. We know better than to say so aloud, but surely most of us have thought, "If only everybody would do this *my way* then we would see some real change." Then, God goes ahead and humbles us by making us dependent on each other to do what he is calling us to do. No single believer can carry all the gifts and roles. We need each other.

Think about a mousetrap. It is a simple system. It has four parts: a platform, a spring, a hammer, and a latch. No individual part looks impressive. What happens, though, when one simple, unimpressive piece is missing? There is no mousetrap. All the parts must be in place if the system is to function properly. Using this illustration or a similar one, a sermon could creatively walk through the text, "attempting" to remove each person and role.

What if Paul were not the point of the spear to start witnessing to Jews in the synagogue? How would the work have turned out if Apollos had not followed up with sound teaching? Where would Ephesus have been if Priscilla and Aquila had never gently guided Apollos more accurately in the way? Would there even have been a Paul, an Apollos, a Priscilla, or an Aquila without a faithful church body standing behind them to send them, receive them, encourage them, support them, and pray for them? Missing church members are like missing mousetrap parts.

The whole thing fails to function without each member doing his or her part.

It is critical to make this passage practical within the church today. Pioneer church planting work in Ephesus can feel disconnected from the day-to-day lives of the people in the pews. Spiritual gift lists in places like 1 Corinthians 12 and Romans 12 should help. Just as the absence of any member of the Ephesian team would change the work, so the absence of these gifts within a local church body would change the way in which God is calling us to live out his mission today. It takes a team to do God's tasks.

- God uses Paul to plant the seeds (18:18–23).

- God uses Apollos to water the seeds (18:24–25).

- God uses Priscilla and Aquila to tend the garden (18:26–28).

DISCUSSION QUESTIONS

1. What strategies for mission/church planting can you draw from Luke's account of the early events in Ephesus described in Acts 18:18–28?

2. What do Paul's movements in Acts 18:22–23 teach you about the relationships among the missionary, the sending church, and the mission churches planted by the missionary?

3. What does Luke's description of Apollos teach you about the qualities that should be present in an effective witness for Christ (18:24–26)?

4. What lessons can you learn from the way in which Priscilla and Aquila interacted with Apollos after they heard him speak in the synagogue (18:26)?

5. What principles can you draw from the way in which the believers in Ephesus responded to Apollos's desire to travel to Achaia (18:27–28)?

Acts 19:1–22

EXEGETICAL IDEA

During Paul's extended ministry in Ephesus, the gospel spread to Jews and Greeks throughout the province of Asia as he proclaimed the kingdom of God and performed works of power.

THEOLOGICAL FOCUS

Opening new frontiers for the gospel requires God's witness to address other theological systems, proclaim the good news about Jesus, rely on divine empowerment, and be sensitive to the Spirit's leading.

PREACHING IDEA

The church advances when God's power accompanies gospel proclamation.

PREACHING POINTERS

What does it take to open new areas for the gospel? Should we expect to see God perform signs and wonders? What is the relationship between supernatural demonstrations of God's working and the preaching of the gospel? How should we go about evangelizing the cities where we live? As we seek to obey Jesus's commission to be his witnesses, what strategies might we need to use, and how can we keep them in proper balance? Luke's account of Paul's ministry in Ephesus points the way to answers by presenting the key elements of his missionary activity. He was working not only in an area where Jesus's name had not been named but also in one of the major metropolitan centers of the empire. As the result of his extended work in the city, all the inhabitants of the province of Asia had the opportunity to hear the good news about Jesus. The objective in communicating the passage should be to help listeners understand the strategic ingredients of gospel ministry so that they will be bold in proclaiming Jesus and faithful in relying on God for his enabling and leading.

People today should be able to relate to encountering people who misunderstand what God expects of them, combine different religious systems, or attempt to appropriate supernatural power for their own purposes. They can certainly relate to making travel plans, and they might have heard about instances of book burning. This passage corrects any suggestion that a partial understanding of the gospel is adequate, that it is possible to mix other religious systems with biblical truth, that Jesus's name is simply a magical formula, or that involvement with the occult is appropriate for Jesus's followers. It commends a commitment to upholding orthodox doctrine, to teaching biblical truth faithfully and consistently, to relying on divine enabling and leading, and to being willing to acknowledge and confess sin. It reinforces the theological truth that the church advances when God's power accompanies gospel proclamation.

WITNESS IN EPHESUS (19:1–22)

LITERARY STRUCTURE AND THEMES (19:1–22)

The passage consists of four narrative vignettes. In the first, Luke recounts Paul's arrival in the city and his encounter with twelve men who knew only John's baptism of repentance (19:1–7). In the second, he provides a concise summary of Paul's teaching ministry in the city (19:8–10). In the third, Luke records the impact of the works of power God performed through Paul (19:11–20). In the fourth, he notes Paul's plans to leave Ephesus and travel to Macedonia, Achaia, Jerusalem, and Rome (19:21–22).

- ***Correcting Incorrect Theology (19:1–7)***
- ***Proclaiming the Kingdom of God (19:8–10)***
- ***Prevailing over Religious Syncretism (19:11–20)***
- ***Following the Spirit's Leading (19:21–22)***

EXPOSITION (19:1–22)

Together, the four segments of Acts 19:1–22 provide a comprehensive picture of Paul's ministry in Ephesus. They also represent "the culmination and resolution of Paul's calling and mission" (Towner 1998, 419), in that they present all the key elements of his missionary ministry and strategy in a single account.

In Ephesus, Paul ministered in a major urban center for an extended period (19:10) as he had in Corinth (18:11), and his ministry affected an entire region (19:10) as it had in South Galatia (13:49). He encountered and corrected incomplete theology (19:1–7) as he had in Lystra (14:15–17) and Athens (17:22–31). He proclaimed the kingdom of God (19:8–10; cf. 20:25) as he previously had in South Galatia (14:22) and

later would in Rome (28:23, 31). He exercised divine power (19:11–12) as he had in Iconium (14:3), Lystra (14:8–10), and Philippi (16:16–18), and he prevailed over religious syncretism (19:13–20) as he had on Cyprus (13:8–11). At the end of his time in Ephesus, he followed the Holy Spirit's leading (19:21–22) as he had been sensitive to similar guidance in Syrian Antioch (13:1–4) and on the road to Europe (16:6–10).

In Ephesus, Paul began his witness in the synagogue (19:8) as he had in Pisidian Antioch (13:14), Iconium (14:1), Thessalonica (17:2), Berea (7:10), and Corinth (18:4). He engaged in persuasive dialogue (19:8) as he had in Pisidian Antioch (13:46), Iconium (14:3), and Corinth (18:26). He saw positive responses from both Jews and Gentiles (19:10) as he had in Pisidian Antioch (13:43), Iconium (14:1), Thessalonica (17:4), and Corinth (18:7). When he faced Jewish disobedience (19:9) as he had in Pisidian Antioch (13:45), Iconium (14:2), Thessalonica (17:5), Berea (7:13), and Corinth (18:6), he withdrew to a base outside the synagogue (19:9) as he had in Thessalonica (17:5) and Corinth (18:7).

Correcting Incorrect Theology (19:1–7)

When he arrives in Ephesus, Paul encounters twelve men who know only John's baptism of repentance and corrects their incorrect theology.

19:1–2. While Paul followed an inland route westward from Syrian Antioch to Ephesus (18:23), Apollos concluded his ministry in the city and crossed the Aegean to Corinth (18:24–28). Luke describes Paul's movement with the participle διελθόντα, which often denotes missionary travel (8:4, 40; 9:32; 13:6, 14; 14:24; 16:6; 17:23). The phrase τὰ ἀνωτερικὰ μέρη ("the upper regions") describes "an inland or higher area, presumably away from the shoreline" (L&N §1.65). In 18:23, Luke specifies the route as passing "through the region of Galatia and Phrygia" (ESV). See 18:19 for the city of Ephesus.

When he arrived in Ephesus (ἐλθεῖν εἰς Ἔφεσον), Paul "found some disciples" (εὑρεῖν τινας μαθητάς), whom he engaged by asking whether they received the Holy Spirit when they believed (εἰ πνεῦμα ἅγιον ἐλάβετε πιστεύσαντες;). They responded that they had not even heard that there is a Holy Spirit (οὐδ᾽ εἰ πνεῦμα ἅγιον ἔστιν ἠκούσαμεν). Luke does not explain what led Paul to ask these men about their experience of the Holy Spirit, but clearly, something was missing. Since they had been baptized into John's baptism (19:3), and since John had publicly connected the baptism of the Spirit with Jesus and his appearing (Luke 3:15–17), their response most likely reflects ignorance of the events at Pentecost (Stott 1990, 304). The adverbial aorist participle πιστεύσαντες denotes action that is coincident with the aorist main verb ἐλάβετε (Barrett 1998, 894; cf. *GGBB*, 624). It does not provide support for a "second experience" of the Spirit subsequent to responding to the gospel in repentance and faith. See 18:26 for similarities and differences between these twelve "disciples" and Apollos.

19:3–7. The men's admission of their ignorance about the Holy Spirit led Paul to ask a further question about the nature of their baptism (εἰς τί οὖν ἐβαπτίσθητε;). When they responded that they had received John's baptism (εἰς τὸ Ἰωάννου βάπτισμα), Paul was able to explain the true focus of the forerunner's message. That message called John's listeners (τῷ λαῷ λέγων) to go beyond repentance to faith (ἵνα πιστεύσωσιν) in the one who was coming after John (εἰς τὸν ἐρχόμενον μετ᾽ αὐτόν)—namely, Jesus (τοῦτ᾽ ἔστιν εἰς τὸν Ἰησοῦν). Baptism into Jesus's name (ἐβαπτίσθησαν εἰς τὸ ὄνομα τοῦ κυρίου Ἰησοῦ) and the Spirit's subsequent coming upon them (ἦλθε τὸ πνεῦμα τὸ ἅγιον ἐπ᾽ αὐτούς) confirmed the genuineness of their response to Paul's message.

As Stott writes, "The norm of Christian experience, then, is a cluster of four things: repentance, faith in Jesus, water baptism, and the gift of the Spirit . . . the four belong together and are universal in Christian initiation" (1990, 305). In this fourth example of the church incorporating a new group of disciples—as was true at Pentecost (2:4), in Samaria (8:17), and in Caesarea (10:45–46)—the twelve men began speaking in tongues and prophesying (ἐλάλουν γλώσσαις καὶ ἐπροφήτευον, inceptive imperfects). Paul's act of laying hands on the men (ἐπιθέντος αὐτοῖς τοῦ Παύλου χεῖρας) parallels Peter and John's action in Samaria (8:17) and legitimatizes his ministry (Gaventa 2003, 266). Luke adds a note that there were "about twelve men" in the group (ἦσαν οἱ πάντες ἄνδρες ὡσεὶ δώδεκα), but the number is an estimate not symbolic (Bock 2007, 600).

Proclaiming the Kingdom of God (19:8–10)

Paul proclaims the kingdom of God for more than two years, first in the Jewish synagogue then in the hall of Tyrannus.

19:8. As was his custom (13:5, 14; 14:1; 17:2, 17; 18:2, 19), Paul entered the synagogue (εἰσελθὼν εἰς τὴν συναγωγήν) and began engaging the Jewish community in the city for a period of three months (ἐπὶ μῆνας τρεῖς). Paul engaged the synagogue attenders in three ways—by speaking boldly (ἐπαρρησιάζετο; cf. 9:27–28; 13:46; 14:3; 18:26), debating (διαλεγόμενος; cf. 17:2, 17; 18:4, 19), and persuading (πείθων; cf. 13:43; 14:19; 17:4; 18:4)—which echo his methods earlier in Acts. Barrett suggests that ἐπαρρησιάζετο refers to inspired speech and διαλεγόμενος refers to reasoned discourse (1998, 903). Paul's intent was to persuade his listeners regarding matters related to the kingdom of God (περὶ τῆς βασιλείας τοῦ θεοῦ; cf. 14:22). See 1:3 for the kingdom of God. Larkin notes that in his farewell address to the Ephesian elders Paul characterized his witness in Ephesus as emphasizing repentance, faith, and grace (Acts 20:21, 24), which "all speak of the reign of God in the lives of those for whom Jesus is Lord" (1995, 274). The imperfect tense verb and the two present tense participles highlight the ongoing nature of Paul's ministry in the synagogue.

19:9. After three months, "some" (τινες) of Paul's Jewish listeners began resisting his teaching. They greeted it with three responses—hardening (ἐσκληρύνοντο; cf. Heb. 3:8, 13, 15; 4:7), disobeying (ἠπείθουν; cf. 14:2; Rom. 2:8; 11:30–31; 1 Peter 3:1; 4:17), and speaking evil (κακολογοῦντες; cf. Matt. 15:4; Mark 7:10; 9:39) of "the Way" (τὴν ὁδόν). Together, the three verbs emphasize the Jews' complete rejection of Paul's message (Bock 2007, 601). The two

imperfect tense verbs and the present tense participle highlight their sustained opposition. See 9:2 for "the Way" (cf. 16:17; 18:25–26).

Paul then withdrew to the hall of Tyrannus, where he continued teaching on a daily basis (καθ' ἡμέραν διαλεγόμενος). Dunn notes that Paul's act of withdrawing from his opponents (ἀποστὰς ἀπ' αὐτῶν) and taking the disciples away (ἀφώρισεν τοὺς μαθητάς) describes voluntary separation from his Jewish opponents rather than forced expulsion from the synagogue (1996, 258). The "hall" (σχολῇ) where Paul continued teaching might have been a formal lecture hall or a large space he rented in a building owned by Tyrannus (Schnabel 2012, 792). The Western text adds the detail that Paul lectured from the fifth hour (11:00 a.m.) until the tenth hour (4:00 p.m.), which corresponded to the Asian midday rest period (Longenecker 1981, 495). Bruce suggests that the timing would have allowed Paul to work at his trade during the morning (cf. 20:33–35) and teach in the afternoon (1988, 366).

19:10. Paul's teaching ministry in Ephesus continued for two more years (ἐπὶ ἔτη δύο). The result (ὥστε) was that "all those who were dwelling in Asia" (πάντας τοὺς κατοικοῦντας τὴν Ἀσίαν)—both Jews and Greeks (Ἰουδαίους τε καὶ Ἕλληνας)—heard the gospel. "Asia" refers to the Roman province of Asia, which encompassed most of western Asia Minor. Most likely, disciples who came to faith through Paul's ministry in Ephesus extended the evangelistic work outward from that city. Acts 20:4 mentions Tychicus and Trophimus "of Asia" (cf. Col. 4:7), and in his letter to the church in Colossae, Paul reminds his readers that they learned the gospel from Epaphras, his "beloved fellow bond-servant" (Col. 1:7; cf. Col. 4:12–13). Again, Luke refers to the gospel as "the Word of the Lord" (8:25; 13:44, 48, 49; 15:35, 36; 16:32), which anticipates the summary statement of 19:20 and Paul's farewell to the Ephesian elders in 20:35.

Prevailing over Religious Syncretism (19:11–20)

God's miraculous working through Paul results in a demon acknowledging Jesus's name and disciples repudiating their involvement in the practice of magic.

19:11–12. In addition to bold proclamation, works of extraordinary power (δυνάμεις οὐ τὰς τυχούσας) characterized Paul's ministry in Ephesus. Luke is careful to identify God as the one who was doing the works (ὁ θεὸς ἐποίει) and Paul as the agent through whom he was working (διὰ τῶν χειρῶν Παύλου). The results (ὥστε) were healings (ἀπαλλάσσεσθαι ἀπ' αὐτῶν τὰς νόσους) and exorcisms (τά πνεύματα τὰ πονηρὰ ἐκπορεύεσθαι). Δυνάμεις denotes deeds that demonstrate power (BDAG s.v. "δύναμις" 3, 263). The verb τυγχάνω describes the act of meeting someone or something (BDAG s.v. "τυγχάνω" 1, 1019). The phrase οὐ τὰς τυχούσας ("not those commonly met"), therefore, is an instance of litotes that most English versions translate as "extraordinary" (e.g., ESV). Διὰ τῶν χειρῶν Παύλου ('through Paul's hands') is a synecdoche for Paul himself (Culy and Parsons 2003, 364). See 9:32–43 for the relationship between works of power and proclamation of the gospel.

The works of power involved a practice that might seem unusual to contemporary readers. Individuals would secure objects that had touched Paul's skin (ἀπὸ τοῦ χρωτὸς αὐτοῦ) and would carry (ἀποφέρεσθαι) those objects to others who were incapacitated (ἐπὶ τοὺς ἀσθενοῦντας) in order to release them (ἀπαλλάσσεσθαι) from their suffering. The practice was similar to that of the woman who was healed after she touched Jesus's garment (Luke 8:43–48; cf. 6:19) and that of the residents of Jerusalem who laid out in the street those who were ill so that Peter's shadow could fall on them (5:15). Schnabel suggests that it represented an understanding among the citizens of Ephesus that miraculous power could

be stored in material items for later use (2012, 795; cf. Klauck 2000, 98). Peterson concludes that "God healed people in this way, graciously accommodating to human beliefs and expectations, to encourage them to draw near and discover what his messenger was proclaiming to them" (2009, 537).

Ἀσθένεια denotes a debilitating condition that renders a person incapacitated (L&N §23.143), while νόσος denotes a physical malady or disease (L&N §23.155). Χρωτός ("skin") is most likely a synecdoche for Paul's body (Culy and Parsons 2003, 364). Danker defines σουδάριον as a "face cloth for wiping perspiration" (BDAG s.v. "σουδάριον" 934), and Louw and Nida define σιμικίνθιον as a "workman's cloth to protect clothing" (L&N §6.179). Most English versions translate the combination as "handkerchiefs or aprons" (e.g., NRSV). Barrett suggests that σουδάριον refers to a rag worn on the head to prevent sweat from running into the eyes, while σιμικίνθιον refers to a rag carried in hands for general mopping up (1998, 907).

19:13. Apparently hearing about Paul's miracle ministry, some itinerant Jewish exorcists (τινες καὶ τῶν περιερχομένων Ἰουδαίων ἐξορκιστῶν) attempted (ἐπεχείρησαν) to imitate it by speaking Jesus's name (ὀνομάζειν . . . τὸ ὄνομα τοῦ κυρίου Ἰησοῦ) over those who had evil spirits (ἐπὶ τοὺς ἔχοντας τὰ πνεύματα τὰ πονηρά). The verb ἐπεχειρέω ("to set one's hand") is a wordplay on διὰ τῶν χειρῶν Παύλου in verse 11. The adjectival participle περιερχομένων describes the practice of going from place to place (BDAG s.v. "περιέρχομαι" 1, 800). The verb ὁρκίζω ("command/charge") denotes the act of binding someone by an oath to keep a command (BDAG s.v. "ὁρκίζω" 723). Although the name of Jesus is an important theme in Acts (2:21, 38; 3:6, 16; 4:10, 12, 30; 8:12; 9:15, 16, 21, 27, 28; 10:48; 15:26; 16:18), the Jewish exorcists misappropriated it in a syncretistic way. Their attempted misuse of Jesus's name as a source of power in this episode stands in contrast to Paul's proper use earlier in the passage (19:5). Paul performed a similar exorcism in Philippi (16:18). For other Jewish exorcists, see Luke 9:49 and 11:19.

19:14–16. Seven sons of a certain Jewish priest named Sceva (τινος Σκευᾶ Ἰουδαίου ἀρχιερέως ἑπτὰ υἱοὶ τοῦτο) tried using the practice (ἦσαν . . . τοῦτο ποιοῦντες, tendential imperfect)—with unexpected results. When they commanded a spirit to come out of a certain man, the spirit answered that he knew Jesus (τὸν Ἰησοῦν γινώσκω) and was acquainted with Paul (τὸν Παῦλον ἐπίσταμαι), but he did not know them (ὑμεῖς δὲ τίνες ἐστέ;). The demon-possessed man (ἐν ᾧ ἦν τὸ πνεῦμα τὸ πονηρόν) first leapt upon them (ἐφαλόμενος ὁ ἄνθρωπος ἐπ' αὐτούς) then "mastered and overpowered them" (ESV, κατακυριεύσας . . . ἴσχυσεν κατ' αὐτῶν), so that (ὥστε) they fled from the house (ἐκφυγεῖν ἐκ τοῦ οἴκου ἐκείνου) naked and seriously wounded (γυμνοὺς καὶ τετραυματισμένους).

Sceva might have been "a member of one of the families in Jerusalem from whom high priests were appointed" or, more likely, was "a member of the Jewish priestly aristocracy in Asia Minor" (Schnabel 2012, 797). The verb τραυματίζω ("wounded") denotes physical trauma that results in a mark or permanent scar (L&N §20.28). Luke uses ἰσχύω to characterize the advance of the gospel in 19:20. Peterson (2009, 540) notes the contrast with the Gerasene demoniac (Luke 8:26–39). Ironically, the evil spirit makes Luke's point: Jesus's name is superior, but it is not a magical formula. Larkin notes, "Only those with a personal relationship with Christ and who invoke his name in humble faith are in the correct position to see God act to drive out demons" (1995, 277).

19:17–19. When all the Jews and Greeks living in Ephesus (πᾶσιν Ἰουδαίοις καὶ Ἕλλησιν τοῖς κατοικοῦσιν τὴν Ἔφεσον) heard about the incident, it provoked respectful reverence among them (ἐπέπεσεν φόβος ἐπὶ πάντας αὐτούς) and caused them to hold the name of Jesus in greater esteem (ἐμεγαλύνετο τὸ ὄνομα τοῦ κυρίου Ἰησοῦ; cf. BDAG s.v. "μεγαλύνω" 2, 623). The incident had an even greater impact on many of the new disciples in the city (πολλοί τῶν πεπιστευκότων). They began confessing and disclosing (ἐξομολογούμενοι καὶ ἀναγγέλλοντες) their practices (τὰς πράξεις αὐτῶν), and a number who had been practicing witchcraft (ἱκανοὶ δὲ τῶν τὰ περίεργα πραξάντων) collected their books (συνενέγκαντες τὰς βίβλους) and burned them in public (κατέκαιον ἐνώπιον πάντων).

Φόβος ("fear") denotes respectful reverence (2:43; 3:10; 5:11). As the result of the exorcists' attempt to appropriate "the name of the Lord Jesus" (τὸ ὄνομα τοῦ κυρίου Ἰησοῦ), it received the esteem it deserved. Bruce notes that the perfect tense of πεπιστευκότων highlights the enduring nature of the disciples' faith (1990, 412). The imperfect tenses of ἐμεγαλύνετο, ἤρχοντο, and κατέκαιον suggest that the actions took place over an extended period of time. Ἐξομολογέω describes the admission of wrongdoing (BDAG s.v. "ἐξομολογέω" 351), and ἀναγγέλλω suggests considerable detail in the process of disclosure (L&N §3.197). Culy and Parsons suggest that ἐξομολογέω describes general confession and ἀναγγέλλω describes specific disclosures (2003, 368). Περίεργος ("witchcraft") describes the practice of magic based on superstition (L&N §53.99), often prompted by misdirected curiosity (BDAG s.v. "περίεργος" 2, 800). The "books" (τὰς βίβλους) were scrolls containing magic spells, and the disciples' action in burning them demonstrated the depth of their commitment to Jesus. With silver selling at $14 per ounce in September 2009, Schnabel calculated the value of the 50,000 silver coins at $98,000 (2012, 799). With silver selling at $22 per ounce in May 2022, the total is nearly $155,000.

19:20. The new disciples' willingness to discard their former magical practices reflected the way in which (οὕτως) the gospel message (τοῦ κυρίου ὁ λόγος) spread throughout Asia (19:10). The standard was a demonstration of power (κατὰ κράτος)—what Larkin calls "power advance" (1995, 276). The results were numerical growth (ηὔξανεν) and the defeat (ἴσχυεν) of competing religious beliefs and practices. Although the order is unusual, it is best to understand the genitive τοῦ κυρίου as modifying ὁ λόγος rather than κράτος on the grammatical principle that both a noun and its genitive modifier normally either have or lack the definite article (*GGBB*, 239; contra Schnabel 2012, 800). Paul echoes the combination of κράτος ("might, power") and ἰσχύς ("strength") when he later writes to the Ephesians (Eph. 1:19; 6:10). The verb αὐξάνω occurs in the summary statements of 6:7 and 12:24. This summary statement is the fourth in Luke's narrative that highlights the gospel's growth among different ethnic, cultural, and religious groups (6:7; 9:31; 12:24).

Following the Spirit's Leading (19:21–22)
Prompted by the Holy Spirit, Paul declares his intent to travel to Rome after visiting Macedonia, Achaia, and Jerusalem.

19:21–22. As the preceding events drew to a close (ἐπληρώθη ταῦτα), the Holy Spirit prompted Paul to begin making travel plans. After traveling through Macedonia and Achaia (διελθὼν τὴν Μακεδονίαν καὶ Ἀχαΐαν), he planned to visit Jerusalem (πορεύεσθαι εἰς Ἱεροσόλυμα), with the long-range goal of also seeing Rome (δεῖ με καὶ Ῥώμην ἰδεῖν). In preparation for the first stage of his itinerary, he sent (ἀποστείλας) Timothy and Erastus ahead of him (εἰς τὴν Μακεδονίαν), while he remained a little longer in Asia (αὐτὸς ἐπέσχεν χρόνον εἰς τὴν Ἀσίαν).

The verb ἐπληρώθη points to divine timing (1:16; 7:30). The impersonal verb δεῖ points to "divine compulsion" (Dunn 1996, 262; cf. 1:16, 21; 3:21; 4:12; 5:29; 9:6; 14:22; 16:30; 17:3; 20:35; 23:11; 27:24, 26). The phrase ἐν τῷ πνεύματι ("by the Spirit") points to divine prompting. The middle voice of ἔθετο ("purposed") highlights Paul's personal resolve (Bock 2007, 605). Although in many places διέρχομαι indicates missionary travel (8:4, 40; 9:32; 13:6, 14; 14:24; 16:6; 17:23; 19:1), the use in 15:41 specifically links the verb to the purpose of strengthening the churches Paul had previously planted (cf. 18:23; 20:2). The latter sense is more likely the intent here.

Of the two representatives Paul sent into Macedonia, Timothy (Τιμόθεος) had joined Paul on his return visit to South Galatia (16:1–3) and had worked with him in Berea (17:14–15) and Corinth (18:5). Paul also mentions individuals by the name of Erastus (Ἔραστος) in Romans 16:23 and 2 Timothy 4:20. It is unclear whether the reference in all three passages is to the same person, although on balance it seems likely that the Erastus of Acts 19 is the same as Paul's co-worker in 2 Timothy 4 but different from the city official in Romans 16 (Larkin 1995, 279). Luke describes them as "two of his helpers" (NIV, δύο τῶν διακονούντων αὐτῷ). The verb διακονέω is multifaceted and can denote rendering assistance (Luke 4:39), fulfilling administrative responsibilities (cf. Acts 6:2), or carrying out ministerial duties (1 Tim. 3:10). Paul's letters confirm his plans for visiting Macedonia and Achaia (1 Cor. 16:5; 2 Cor. 2:13; 7:5), Jerusalem (Rom. 15:25; 1 Cor. 16:3), and Rome (Rom. 15:24).

THEOLOGICAL FOCUS
The narrative function of Luke's account of Paul's extended ministry in Ephesus (Acts 19:1–22) is to begin the transition from Paul's missionary activity in the east to the

events that would ultimately bring him to Rome in the west. It is at least possible that Paul intended to visit the fourth largest city in the empire when the Holy Spirit redirected him and Silas northward and westward to Europe (16:6–10). It is certain that he hoped to return to Ephesus after his brief stop in the city en route from Corinth to Jerusalem (18:18–21). After ministering in Cilicia, Syria, Cyprus, South Galatia, Pamphylia, Macedonia, and Achaia, it was logical that Paul would view the province of Asia as the climax of his work in the eastern empire, and it was natural that he would turn his eyes westward toward Rome and beyond. By describing Paul's activities in Ephesus in Acts 19:1–20, Luke reviews Paul's missionary ministry and strategy in Acts 13–19, and by noting Paul's anticipated itinerary in Acts 19:21–22, he previews Paul's upcoming travels in Acts 20–28.

Theologically, Acts 19:1–22 brings together Paul's teaching ministry (19:8–10) and his miracle ministry (19:11–20) and raises the issue of what Wimber labels "power evangelism," which he defines as evangelism that is "preceded and undergirded by supernatural demonstrations of God's presence" (1985, 46). In 19:11, Luke describes the signs and wonders that accompanied Paul's ministry as "works of extraordinary power" (δυνάμεις οὐ τὰς τυχούσας). He also notes that it was "according to power" (κατὰ κράτος) that the gospel reached the entire province of Asia (19:20). Luke also mentions "signs and wonders" (σημεῖα καὶ τέρατα) or "signs and miracles" (σημεῖα καὶ δυνάμεις) in four previous passages where power accompanied proclamation: the apostles' early ministry to Hebraic Jews in Jerusalem (2:41–47; 4:30; 5:12), Stephen's ministry to Hellenistic Jews in Jerusalem (6:8–15), Philip's ministry to the Samaritans (8:4–12), and Saul and Barnabas's ministry to Greeks in Iconium (14:1–7; cf. 15:12).

	Power	Proclamation
Acts 2:41–47	σημεῖα καὶ τέρατα (2:43)	τῇ διδαχῇ τῶν ἀποστόλων (2:42)
Acts 6:8–15	σημεῖα καὶ τέρατα (6:8)	τῇ σοφίᾳ καὶ τῷ πνεύματι ᾧ ἐλάλει (6:10)
Acts 8:4–13	σημεῖα καὶ δυνάμεις (8:13)	εὐαγγελιζομένῳ περὶ τῆς βασιλείας τοῦ θεοῦ (8:12)
Acts 14:1–7	σημεῖα καὶ τέρατα (14:3)	παρρησιαζόμενοι ἐπὶ τῷ κυρίῳ (14:3)

The common factor in those episodes was that each involved the gospel penetrating new territory—culturally, geographically, or both. The signs and wonders opened the door for the gospel and authenticated its messengers. The same dynamic was at work in Ephesus. Paul's teaching ministry included "speaking boldy" (ἐπαρρησιάζετο), "debating" (διαλεγόμενος), and "persuading" (πείθων), and Luke is careful to note that it was "the Lord's Word" (τοῦ κυρίου ὁ λόγος) that "was growing" (ηὔξανεν) and "prevailing" (ἴσχυεν). As was true of Peter's ministry in Lydda and Joppa (9:32–43), miraculous signs did not automatically lead to conversions or church growth, but they opened the door for witness. In fact, in Ephesus, the miracles followed Paul's preaching rather than preceding it. God's powerful working through Paul furthered the spread of the gospel and inspired the new disciples in the city to deepen their commitment to the Lord. Power and proclamation, therefore, are complementary, but miraculous works are no substitute for faithful witness.

PREACHING AND TEACHING STRATEGIES

Exegetical/Theological Synthesis

Since his experience on the Damascus road, Paul had borne Jesus's name before both Jews and Greeks in Cilicia, Syria, Cyprus, South Galatia, Pamphylia, Macedonia, and Achaia. There remained one unreached region that would allow Paul to complete his Aegean mission: the province of Asia with its capital of Ephesus, the fourth-largest city in the empire. As Paul headed westward from Syrian Antioch toward Ephesus, Luke's first-century readers would have wanted to know how Paul approached ministry in one of the major cities of the empire. Luke's account of Paul's witness in Ephesus provides the answer by capturing the key elements of his extended ministry in that city. Those elements included correcting incorrect theology, systematically proclaiming gospel truth, relying on divine enabling, and being sensitive to the Spirit's leading. As result, all the inhabitants of the province had the opportunity to hear about Jesus. With Luke's original readers, the twenty-first-century audience shares the need to understand the strategic ingredients of pioneer gospel ministry. Paul's ministry in Ephesus suggests that those ingredients include focusing on urban centers, proclaiming the Lord Jesus, relying on the Father's enabling, and following the Spirit's leading. Particularly prominent in Luke's narrative are the complementary aspects of proclamation and power. Although God might not choose to grant his witnesses the ability to perform miraculous works in every ministry situation, the gospel itself is the "power of God for salvation to everyone who believes" (Rom. 1:16), and it is the power of God's Spirit at work through God's people that makes it possible for the gospel to advance into regions where Christ has never been preached before (cf. Rom. 15:18–20).

Preaching/Teaching Idea

The church advances when God's power accompanies gospel proclamation.

Contemporary Connections

What does it mean?

Acts 19 is the fifth passage in Acts explicitly demonstrating the power of God through miracles punctuating faithful gospel preaching. It is a supernatural combination of irresistible grace. Paul prioritizes preaching the gospel. He speaks to disciples, he speaks to the synagogue, and he speaks in the hall of Tyrannus. He speaks boldly, he speaks with reasoning, and he speaks to persuade. He uses words—he speaks for years about the "kingdom of God" (19:8) and "the name of the Lord Jesus" (19:17). These words are the Lord's (19:10), living words, with power to save. They need no adornment. Words alone in God's hands spread like wildfire in Asia (19:10).

Even so, God adds "extraordinary" miraculous power to preaching. He does so especially where the gospel crosses into new, unreached cultural or geographical spaces. Signs accompanied the apostles at Pentecost, Stephen with Hellenistic Jews, Philip with Samaritans, and Paul and Barnabas with Greeks. Now as the gospel crossed into the Asian province's capital of Ephesus, God chose to punctuate preaching with power. The net effect was that the church entered a season of deep, abiding repentance (19:18–19) and "the Word of the Lord continued to increase and prevail mightily" (19:20).

Is it true?

It might seem as though Acts is full of signs, dropping anywhere at any time by anyone. Of course, upon closer reading, there is a method to miracles. God places them where they punctuate the preached word, typically in a new field. There were no recorded miracles in Corinth in the previous chapter, nor at Paul's first visit to Ephesus, nor in Achaia. No recorded miracles happened by the hands of Priscilla, or Aquila, or Apollos, or the new believers in Corinth or Ephesus. God chose Ephesus as the place, this second visit as the time, and Paul as the man to display miraculous power.

Although Luke records no powers during Paul's previous time in Corinth, his ministry in that city was in "demonstration of the Spirit and of power" (1 Cor. 2:4). Whether or not miracles were present, God's power was. The sons of Sceva provided the perfect foil for God's power. They peddled false words and fake power. The spirit's attack dramatically and embarrassingly exposed them, so that true word and power prevailed mightily.

Now what?

Today, we are called to be faithful with gospel words by the Spirit's help. If we are faithful, God will choose how to bring power to punctuate his Word whether by miracles in Ephesus or impressions in Corinth. We cannot summon miracles by our own authority. Sceva's sons learned that lesson the hard way. Simon the Magician could have told them so. Instead, we trust God to bring the appropriate power to every situation.

Where we bring weakness, and fear, and trembling, and unimpressive speech that is centered on Jesus and him crucified, God can do extraordinary things (1 Cor. 2:1–5). There is another gospel proclamation in this passage that is not as popular or safe as preaching. The believers here, struck by God's power, entered an extended season of confessing sins in detail and taking steps to change. It is one thing to speak a gospel of repentance and faith. It is another thing for the church today to act upon this gospel of ongoing repentance and faith, of putting off syncretistic sinful indulgences at great cost to ourselves, and putting on Jesus alone. The mighty prevailing of the Lord's Word, then, works in two directions—inward into the heart of the church and outward into the world.

Creativity in Presentation

There are some things that just go together—peanut butter and jelly, front porches and sweet tea, state fairs and fried food. It is impossible have one without the other and not notice that something is missing. Gospel proclamation and power are such a combination. God uses them to create faith that does not "rest in the wisdom of men but in the power of God" (1 Cor. 2:5).

It is no coincidence that when God's power punctuated gospel proclamation, the church experienced a revival of deep repentance. This process has happened many times in many places in church history. One memorable account was in Korea in 1907. During a Bible conference attended by some fifteen hundred people, God began to move dramatically. The conference organizers gathered to discuss and pray over what was happening. William Blair, a first-term missionary at the time, described that meeting in his book *The Korean Pentecost and the Sufferings Which Followed*, "Then began a meeting the like of which I had never seen before, nor wish to see again unless in God's sight it is absolutely necessary. Every sin a human being can commit was publicly confessed that night. . . . We may have our theories of the desirability or undesirability of public confession of sin. I have had mine; but I know now that when the Spirit of God falls upon guilty souls, there will be confession, and no power on earth can stop it." (1977).

That experience sounds like Ephesus. There is no quaint, comfortable, soft move of the Spirit here. It is dramatic and embarrassing. Imagine watching new Christian leaders you respected bringing out dark magic books they had kept hidden all this time to be burned once and for all. As Blair said so honestly, it is not something anyone would wish to see again if possible. Then again, neither is it something any power on earth could stop. God's power punctuates his gospel to advance his church. The church advances when God's power accompanies gospel proclamation.

- Gospel proclamation instructs about the kingdom of God (19:1–10).

- Gospel power shows forth the kingdom of God (19:11–22).

DISCUSSION QUESTIONS

1. What was missing from the theological understanding of the twelve "disciples" Paul encountered upon his arrival in Ephesus? What distinguished them from Apollos, whom Priscilla and Aquila had encountered previously in the same city (cf. 18:24–28)?

2. What approaches characterized Paul's teaching in the synagogue and in the hall of Tyrannus? How might he have varied his approach depending on his audiences?

3. How would you evaluate the response of the citizens of Ephesus to the miraculous works God did through Paul and to the incident involving the sons of Sceva?

4. How did power and proclamation complement one another during Paul's ministry in Ephesus? What role did each play in the advance of the gospel and the growth of the church?

5. Why did Paul plan to travel through Macedonia and Achaia on his way to Jerusalem? How did that plan align with his practice of strengthening the churches he had planted?

Acts 19:23–40

EXEGETICAL IDEA

As Paul prepares to leave for Macedonia, an angry crowd gathers in the city's amphitheater to protest the impact of his ministry on the economy, prestige, and religion of Ephesus.

THEOLOGICAL FOCUS

Although the gospel challenges multiple aspects of a culture, it poses no threat to public order.

PREACHING IDEA

Law-abiding witness can capture a city for Christ.

PREACHING POINTERS

What impact does the peaceful proclamation of the gospel have on the life of a city? Does the gospel pose a threat to the local economy, to local religion, or to the local civic life? What can we learn about those questions from the events that occurred near the close of Paul's ministry in Ephesus? Luke's account of those events sheds light on the way in which opportunists can turn personal interests into public protest, uninformed bystanders can become an irrational mob, innocent parties can be falsely accused, and well-reasoned counsel can defuse a potentially dangerous situation. It also establishes the truth that although Christianity challenges multiple aspects of culture, it poses no threat to established civil law and order. The objective in communicating the passage should be to help listeners understand that ministering peacefully within the established civil order allows Jesus's followers to make a multidimensional impact on a city and its surrounding region.

People today should be able to relate to the emotional response that results when something they hold dear is threatened, whether it is their financial livelihood, their public reputation, or their cherished beliefs. They might well have observed or experienced the confusion that can result when a public demonstration goes out of control. They should also be able to relate to the fear of official intervention or retaliation that widespread public disorder might provoke. This passage corrects the ideas that extralegal action is an appropriate response to an area of concern or that unthinking participation in public protest is wise. It also corrects any suggestion that Christianity is a threat to public order. In fact, the passage teaches the opposite: Christianity might threaten financial and/or religious special interests, but it does not threaten the established civil order. The passage commends discerning assessment of inflammatory claims, prudent restraint in volatile situations, and proper respect for the judicial process. It suggests that persuasion is more effective than protest.

TROUBLE IN EPHESUS (19:23–40)

LITERARY STRUCTURE AND THEMES (19:23–40)

The passage divides naturally into three sections. The first recounts Demetrius's speech before the guild of silversmiths, in which he sets out the perceived threat Paul's ministry posed to the economic, civic, and religious life of the city (19:23–27). The second describes the city-wide uproar that resulted (19:28–34). The third recounts the city clerk's speech, by which he defused the situation and dismissed the crowd (19:35–40).

- ***The Silversmith's Complaint (19:23–27)***
- ***The Crowd's Clamor (19:28–34)***
- ***The Clerk's Counsel (19:35–40)***

EXPOSITION (19:23–40)

Acts 19:23–40 completes Luke's account of Paul's extended ministry in Ephesus. Through Ananias, Paul had learned not only that he would bear Jesus's name before Gentiles, kings, and Jews (9:15), but also that he would suffer for Jesus's sake (9:16). In Acts 19:1–22, Luke described the first aspect of Paul's calling; in Acts 19:23–40, he describes the second. Although Luke includes no account of Paul suffering physically, Paul himself refers to "fighting with wild beasts in Ephesus" (1 Cor. 15:32), and he avoided being drawn into the chaos in the city's amphitheater only because he listened to the advice of local disciples and friendly Asiarchs (19:30–31). As Paul had taught the churches in South Galatia, it would be through many tribulations that Jesus's followers would enter the kingdom of God (14:22).

As was the case in Philippi (16:19–22), the source of opposition in Ephesus was first economic, then civil. As was the case in Corinth (18:12–17), a respected government official in Ephesus declared that the gospel was no threat to the local cult and that the Christians had broken no Roman laws. As Marshall notes, the narrative "expresses the wide effects of the Christian mission . . . brings out the arbitrariness and confusion of the opposition . . . made clear that those who were in positions of authority were opposed to action against the missionaries . . . [and] is in effect a statement that Christians do not constitute a danger to the state" (1980, 314). With the preceding passage, Acts 19:23–40 forms a fitting climax to Paul's Aegean mission and prepares the way for the next phase of his witness for the Lord Jesus.

The Silversmith's Complaint (19:23–27)

Demetrius, the silversmith, gathers other craftsmen and raises concerns about the impact of Paul's ministry on their business.

19:23–25a. As Paul was preparing to leave Ephesus, "serious trouble" (NLT) arose in the city concerning the Christian movement (περὶ τῆς ὁδοῦ). The source of the trouble was Demetrius, a silversmith (ἀργυροκόπος), who made silver shrines (ποιῶν ναοὺς ἀργυροῦς) to the local goddess, Artemis. Since that industry was providing (παρείχετο) "a great deal of employment" (NEB) for him and workmen of similar trades (τοὺς περὶ τὰ τοιαῦτα ἐργάτας), Demetrius gathered them together (συναθροίσας) to air his concerns.

"About that time" (κατὰ τὸν καιρὸν ἐκεῖνον) connects the subsequent events to Paul's plans to depart for Macedonia and Achaia (19:21–22). See 9:2 for "the Way" (16:17; 18:25–26; 19:9). "No small disturbance" (τάραχος οὐκ ὀλίγος) and "no little business" (οὐκ ὀλίγην ἐργασίαν) are both instances of litotes. The former phrase also occurs in 12:18. The imperfect tense of παρείχετο indicates sustained profit over time. Schnabel concludes that Demetrius was either the most prominent silversmith in the city or the master of the guild of silversmiths (2012, 802). Although Longenecker suggests that the phrase ναοὺς ἀργυροῦς Ἀρτέμιδος (NASB, "silver shrines of Artemis") refers to silver statuettes of the goddess (1981, 503), the more likely reference is to silver replicas of her temple (Bock 2007, 607), or possibly, to silver relief plaques of the goddess within her temple (Larkin 1995, 280). Regardless, the production of the artifacts was a major source of income.

> **Artemis and Her Temple in Ephesus**
> The Greek goddess Artemis was the daughter of Zeus, the sister of Apollo, and the virgin goddess of the hunt (Barrett 1998, 922). The comparable Roman goddess was Diana. When Greeks colonized Asia Minor, the indigenous population assimilated Artemis to the mother goddess of Asia Minor, who was the patroness of nature and fertility (Bruce 1988, 373) and to whom they ascribed "unsurpassed cosmic powers" (Larkin 1995, 281). Strabo notes that there were thirty-three sites dedicated to the worship of Artemis/Diana across the empire, ranging from Spain to Syria (*Geogr.* 4.1.5). The most impressive worship site was the temple in Ephesus, which was the largest building in the Greek world (Bock 2002, 608) and was considered one of the seven wonders of the ancient world. The temple covered four times the area of the Parthenon in Athens and had 127 pillars that were sixty feet tall (Bruce 1988, 374). The month-long Artemis festival in March/April drew pilgrims to Ephesus from across the empire.

19:25b–26. After addressing his fellow craftsmen (ἄνδρες), Demetrius reminded them of the economic prosperity they derived from their work (ἐκ ταύτης τῆς ἐργασίας ἡ εὐπορία ἡμῖν ἐστιν) and pointed out the impact Paul's ministry was having, not only in Ephesus (οὐ μόνον Ἐφέσου) but in the entire province of Asia (ἀλλὰ σχεδὸν πάσης τῆς Ἀσίας). The problem was that Paul was persuading "a large crowd" (NET, ἱκανὸν ὄχλον) to turn away (μετέστησεν) from the traditional Greco-Roman religions by teaching that "gods made by hands are not gods at all" (NASB, οὐκ εἰσὶν θεοὶ οἱ διὰ χειρῶν γινόμενοι). The noun εὐπορία points to the prosperity the silversmiths enjoyed (BDAG s.v. "εὐπορία" 410). The verb μεθίστημι carries the sense of bringing someone to a different point of view; here it has a negative nuance (BDAG s.v. "μεθίστημι" 2, 625). Paul uses it with a positive nuance in Colossians 1:13. The constative aorist summarizes the impact of Paul's ministry viewed as a whole.

19:27. The potential danger (κινδυνεύει) was threefold. On the economic front, their business would come under public criticism (τοῦτο . . . ἡμῖν τὸ μέρος εἰς ἀπελεγμὸν ἐλθεῖν). On the civic front, the temple of Artemis would lose its prestige (τὸ τῆς μεγάλης θεᾶς Ἀρτέμιδος ἱερὸν εἰς οὐθὲν λογισθῆναι). On the religious front, the goddess herself would lose her greatness (μέλλειν καθαιρεῖσθαι τῆς μεγαλειότητος αὐτῆς). The verb κινδυνεύω describes the state of being in danger or running a risk (BDAG s.v. "κινδυνεύω" 544). The present tense highlights what Demetrius saw as the immediate urgency of the situation. The noun ἀπελεγμός can carry the sense of criticism relating to questionable conduct or of coming into discredit or disrepute (BDAG s.v. "ἀπελεγμός" 101). The infinitival phrase εἰς οὐθὲν λογισθῆναι describes a lowering of respect (Bock 2007, 609).

The Crowd's Clamor (19:28–34)

An outraged crowd gathers in the city's amphitheater and for two hours shouts down attempts to speak to them.

19:28–29. Becoming outraged (γενόμενοι πλήρεις θυμοῦ) at what they had heard (ἀκούσαντες), Demetrius's listeners began crying out (ἔκραζον), "Great is Artemis of the Ephesians!"—a rhythmic chant the crowd later resumed for two hours (19:34). As a result, the city was filled with confusion (ἐπλήσθη ἡ πόλις τῆς συγχύσεως); and the residents, moved by a shared hostile impulse (ὁμοθυμαδὸν), rushed into the city's amphitheater (ὥρμησάν εἰς τὸ θέατρον), dragging with them (συναρπάσαντες) two of Paul's traveling companions (συνεκδήμους Παύλου).

The Western text adds "and running into the street" (καὶ δράμοντες εἰς τὸ ἄμφοδον) after πλήρεις θυμοῦ and before ἔκραζον. "Confusion" (συγχύσεως) describes "disorderly mob action, with special implications of uproar and disturbance" (L&N §39.43). In the LXX, the word describes the confusing of languages at Babel (Gen. 11:9) and widespread civil confusion (1 Sam. 5:11; 14:20). The adverb ὁμοθυμαδόν suggests that Demetrius's speech provoked a shared reaction of hostility (*TDNT* 5:186). Luke describes both Gaius and Aristarchus as "Macedonians" (Μακεδόνας), which suggests that Aristarchus is the same individual mentioned in 20:4 and 27:2 (cf. Col. 4:10; Philem. 24). The Gaius mentioned in 20:4, however, is from Derbe. The amphitheater in Ephesus could accommodate at least twenty-four thousand people (Barrett 1998, 928).

19:30–31. Although Paul wanted go before the assembled citizens (Παύλου βουλομένου εἰσελθεῖν εἰς τὸν δῆμον), two groups dissuaded him. First, the disciples in the city would not permit him (οὐκ εἴων αὐτὸν οἱ μαθηταί). Second, a group of officials who were "kindly disposed" (φίλοι; cf. BDAG s.v. "φίλος" 1, 1058–59) toward Paul sent word to him (πέμψαντες πρὸς αὐτόν) and strongly urged (παρεκάλουν) him not to go into the amphitheater (μὴ δοῦναι ἑαυτὸν εἰς τὸ θέατρον). The Asiarchs (τινὲς τῶν Ἀσιαρχῶν) were "holders of high office in the Greek cities in the Roman province" (Dunn 1996, 263), and Schnabel notes that one hundred such officials have been attested in forty different cities (2012, 806). Luke's note that these particular officials were kindly disposed toward Paul adds them to the list that includes Sergius Paulus as being receptive to Paul's message (13:6–12) and Gallio as viewing the gospel as no threat to Roman authority (18:12–17).

19:32–34. The confusion in the assembly was so great (ἦν ἡ ἐκκλησία συγκεχυμένη) that some of the citizens were shouting one thing, while others were shouting something else (ἄλλοι ἄλλο τι ἔκραζον). In fact, most of those assembled (οἱ πλείους) did not know (οὐκ ᾔδεισαν) why they had come together (τίνος ἕνεκα συνεληλύθεισαν). The perfect tense of συγκεχυμένη suggests a prolonged state of confusion; the imperfect tense of ἔκραζον highlights the crowd's sustained uproar (Schnabel 2012, 807). When the Jews who were present put him forward (προβαλόντων αὐτὸν τῶν Ἰουδαίων), some from the crowd instructed Alexander about the cause of the uproar (ἐκ τοῦ ὄχλου συνεβίβασαν Ἀλέξανδρον), and he attempted to offer a defense (ἤθελεν ἀπολογεῖσθαι). Luke gives no insight into what Alexander intended to say, but Bock suggests that he wanted to "quell the reaction against Paul, fearing that it will spill over to a blaming of all Jews" (2007, 611). The idea backfired, however, when the crowd recognized that Alexander was a Jew (ἐπιγνόντες ὅτι Ἰουδαῖός ἐστιν). All of them (ἐκ πάντων) in unison (φωνὴ μία) kept on shouting (κραζόντων) the rhythmic chant the silversmiths had begun (19:28): "Great is Artemis of the Ephesians!" Schnabel notes, "public feeling was often expressed during religious festivals and in political assemblies with rhythmic acclamations" (2012, 808). Their shouting continued for about two hours (ὡς ἐπὶ ὥρας δύο), until the city clerk was able to quiet them.

TEXTUAL ANALYSIS: Alexander's Attempt at a Defense
The syntax of verse 33 is difficult. The participial phrase προβαλόντων αὐτὸν τῶν Ἰουδαίων is best understood as a genitive absolute of antecedent time. The verb συμβιβάζω could indicate that the crowd "concluded" (L&N §30.82) that Alexander was the cause of the uproar, or that they "instructed" (L&N §33.298) him about the cause. The latter seems more likely (Culy and Parsons 2003, 377). The sequence of events appears to be: Jews put Alexander forward to find out the cause of the commotion, some in the crowd informed him about what was happening, he attempted to speak to the crowd, and the crowd shouted him down (Larkin 1995, 285).

The Clerk's Counsel (19:35–40)
The clerk of the city addresses the crowd, warns them of the potential consequences of their actions, and sends them home.

19:35–36. Finally, the city clerk (ὁ γραμματεύς) quieted the crowd (καταστείλας … τὸν ὄχλον) and spoke to them. The clerk was "the city official with responsibility for the records of a town or city and . . . for maintaining law and order" (L&N §37.94). His speech is an example of deliberative rhetoric intended to dissuade his listeners from a course of action. It consisted of four parts (Schnabel 2012, 782; Witherington 1998, 598): an *exordium* provided context (19:35), a *propositio* introduced his thesis (19:36), a *probatio* set out three arguments in support of his thesis (19:37–39), and a *peroratio* warned of the potential consequences of their actions (19:40). See 5:35–39 for a similar speech by Gamaliel.

Following an address (ἄνδρες Ἐφέσιοι), the clerk used a rhetorical question to affirm for his listeners what was "undeniable" (ἀναντιρρήτων) regarding Ephesus: the city was the guardian (νεωκόρον) of both the great Artemis (τῆς μεγάλης Ἀρτέμιδος) and of the object that had fallen from heaven (τοῦ

διοπετοῦς). On the basis of these well-known facts, he then introduced his thesis: it was necessary (δέον ἐστίν) for the crowd to "stay calm" (κατεσταλμένους ὑπάρχειν) and "do nothing reckless" (μηδὲν προπετὲς πράσσειν).

Schnabel notes that by framing his exordium as a rhetorical question, the clerk "reinforces the general knowledge as regards the fame of the temple" (2012, 809). The adverb ἀναντίρρητος describes something that cannot be disputed (BDAG s.v. "ἀναντίρρητος" 68–69). The noun νεωκόρος refers to someone who is responsible for the maintenance and security of a temple (BDAG s.v. "νεωκόρος" 670). The adjective διοπετής describes something that has fallen from heaven (BDAG s.v. "διοπετής" 250–51) and most likely referred to a meteorite (Barrett 1998, 936) that was connected with the image of Artemis in the temple, either as inspiration for the image or as a sign of divine approval of the image. The adjective προπετής pertains to impetuous and reckless behavior (L&N §88.98).

19:37–39. Three proofs supported his thesis. First, the men who stood before the crowd were innocent—they had committed neither sacrilege against the temple (οὔτε ἱεροσύλους) nor blasphemy against the goddess (οὔτε βλασφημοῦντας τὴν θεὸν ἡμῶν). A ἱερόσυλος was an individual who committed sacrilege by desecrating or robbing a temple (BDAG s.v. "ἱερόσυλος" 1, 471); a βλασφημῶν was an individual who spoke disparagingly against a god (BDAG s.v. "βλασφημέω" b, 178). The clerk's comments were particularly pertinent, since Larkin notes that the temple in Ephesus was not only "the foremost worship center of Asia" but also "a world-renowned bank" (1995, 282).

Second, if Demetrius and the other craftsmen had a complaint against anyone (εἰ . . . ἔχουσι πρός τινα λόγον), they had access to normal legal channels (ἀγοραῖοι ἄγονται καὶ ἀνθύπατοί εἰσιν) that would have permitted them to bring the appropriate charges (ἐγκαλείτωσαν). Αἱ ἀγοραῖοι refers to court days (BDAG s.v. "ἀγοραῖος" 15), and NASB translates ἀγοραῖοι ἄγονται as "the courts are in session." The plural of ἀνθύπατοι ("proconsuls") is generic, and Bock suggests that clerk's meaning was, "there are such people as proconsuls to appeal to for justice" (Bock 2007, 613). The verb ἐγκαλέω describes the act of bringing a charge against someone (BDAG s.v. "ἐγκαλέω" 273; cf. Rom. 8:33).

Third, if the citizens had a strong desire to pursue the issue further (εἰ τι περαιτέρω ἐπιζητεῖτε), they should seek resolution of it (ἐπιλυθήσεται) in one of the official meetings of the city's assembly (ἐν τῇ ἐννόμῳ ἐκκλησίᾳ). Although Marshall suggests that the gathering described here was an official meeting of the citizen body (1980, 318), the clerk's mention of "in the lawful assembly" (NASB, ἐν τῇ ἐννόμῳ ἐκκλησίᾳ) suggests otherwise (cf. L&N §33.336). The NET notes that such meetings took place three times a year. Ἐπιλύω describes the act of resolving a dispute (BDAG s.v. "ἐπιλύω" 2, 375).

19:40–41. The clerk closed his address by warning the crowd of the potential consequences if they were to continue their course of action. Demetrius had failed to bring charges against Paul's companions, but the crowd was in danger (κινδυνεύομεν) of being charged (ἐγκαλεῖσθαι) with rioting (στάσεως) and sedition (συστροφῆς) concerning the day's events (περὶ τῆς σήμερον). If the Roman authorities were to demand an explanation, the crowd would have no answer (περὶ οὗ δυνησόμεθα ἀποδοῦναι λόγον), because there was no reason for their actions (μηδενὸς αἰτίου ὑπάρχοντος). His carefully reasoned counsel defused the situation, and he dismissed the assembly (ἀπέλυσεν τὴν ἐκκλησίαν).

The verb "we are being in danger" (κινδυνεύομεν) echoes Demetrius's words in 19:27. For Demetrius, the danger was that he and his fellow silversmiths were losing their profit; for the clerk, the danger was that Ephesus and its citizens could lose their status as a free city. The verb "to be charged" (ἐγκαλεῖσθαι) echoes the clerk's own words in 19:38. The noun στάσις denotes an uprising, riot, revolt, or rebellion and describes a state of affairs that is the opposite of civil harmony and peaceful conduct (BDAG s.v. "στάσις" 940). Bock notes that the phrase ἐγκαλεῖσθαι στάσεως carries the sense of "to be accused of a riot" (2007, 613). The noun συστροφή describes a disorderly or seditious gathering or commotion (BDAG s.v. "συστροφή" 1, 979); in Acts 23:12, the word describes a conspiracy or plot.

THEOLOGICAL FOCUS

The narratival function of Acts 19:23–40 is to conclude the account of Paul's ministry in Ephesus and to capture the impact of that ministry on the city and its surrounding region. To the previous account of the impact on the spiritual lives of individuals in the city and province (19:11–20), the passage adds the economic, civic, and religious impact on the city along with the opposition that arose as a result. With the first half of the chapter, the passage serves as an exclamation point at the end of Paul's missionary activity. Much as Acts 12:1–24 illustrated the advance of the gospel in Palestine despite intense civil opposition, so 19:1–40 illustrates the advance of the gospel in Europe and Asia despite intense civil opposition. It also adds another important civil official who affirms that Christianity is no threat to Roman authority of civil order.

Theologically, Acts 19:23–40 highlights three important truths. First, the gospel challenges every aspect of culture—economic, civil, and spiritual. Demetrius made that fact clear as his speech moved from the potential danger to the silversmith's business, to the possibility that the temple of Artemis—and also the city—would lose its prestige, to the possibility that the goddess herself would lost her greatness (19:27). As Larkin writes, "Any Christianity worth its salt will be a challenge to the pocketbook, the flag, and the shrine" (1995, 283). Second, it does so without threatening the established civil order. The city clerk made that fact clear as he moved through the three proofs that supported his thesis. The disciples whom the crowd dragged into the amphitheater had neither desecrated the temple nor blasphemed the goddess (19:37). Demetrius and the other craftsmen had brought no formal charges against the accused men (19:38). The proper time to address issues of civil concern was at official meetings of the citizen body (19:39). Third, any civil disruption connected with the gospel originates with the movement's opponents rather than with the followers of "the Way." As had been true in Pisidian Antioch (13:44–51), Iconium (14:5–7), Lystra (14:19), Philippi (16:19–22), Thessalonica (17:5–9), Berea (17:13), and Corinth (18:12–17), the cause of the uproar in Ephesus was the result of agitation by citizens of the city, not of any seditious behavior by Paul or his followers (19:28–29). Although the gospel challenges multiple aspects of a culture, it does so peacefully and poses no threat to the established civil order.

PREACHING AND TEACHING STRATEGIES

Exegetical/Theological Synthesis

After reading about the spiritual impact of Paul's ministry on the citizens of Ephesus, knowing about the opposition that had arisen in other cities, and perhaps having heard about the public uproar in Ephesus, Luke's first-century readers would have wanted to know whether the gospel affected other aspects of the city's life and culture as well as whether charges that Christianity violated Roman law and disrupted public order had any validity. How serious was the uproar in the city? What caused it? What role did followers of Christ have in it? How was it resolved? What was the outcome? Luke's account of the trouble that arose

in Ephesus addresses each of these questions and leads to a clear conclusion about the gospel and civil order. With his original readers, the twenty-first-century audience shares the need to know that although the gospel challenges multiple aspects of a culture, it poses no threat to public order. If Jesus's witnesses understand that truth, they will work within the established civil order to allow the gospel to transform lives and make the greatest impact for Christ. As leaven added to dough transforms everything with which it comes into contact (Matt. 13:33), when the gospel invades a city, it affects every aspect of that city's life and culture.

Preaching/Teaching Idea

Law-abiding witness can capture a city for Christ.

Contemporary Connections

What does it mean?

Indeed, the gospel challenges every aspect of culture. "The pocketbook, the flag, the shrine" all fall under the lordship of Jesus, and submission to him in salvation will rearrange each. Money and magic took a dramatic hit in the passage's preceding paragraph. The events surrounding Paul's ministry put Demetrius and his guild on notice. They provided product for one of the most substantial institutions in the Roman Empire. The temple of Artemis in Ephesus was one of the seven wonders of the ancient world. It dwarfed the Parthenon and served citizens across the known world. Yet it was no match for the gospel and its transforming message that leaned into Ephesian culture. Nonetheless, the ambassadors who brought the message were committed to peaceful, law-abiding witness. In stark contrast to Demetrius and friends' riotous resistance, the gospel proceeded in word and divine power. Where law prohibits witness and gospel transformation, it is resisted (4:19–20; 5:29). Where it does not, it is respected and upheld (19:37).

Is it true?

There is a delicate irony here. Paul's enemy, Demetrius, complained that Paul was turning people away from Artemis when he taught that handmade gods are not gods. If this thinking were to grow, the cult of Artemis would be in serious trouble (19:26–27). He was *right*. His intuition of where this process was headed was spot on. Technically, Paul's advocate, the town clerk, was *wrong*. He said that Paul was neither sacrilegious nor a blasphemer of Artemis (19:37). Paul was certainly both, but he was respectfully so.

The true problem was that these men were missing each other. Demetrius saw the side of the coin that the gospel challenges every aspect of the culture. The clerk saw the side that Christianity does so as peacefully as possible. To Demetrius, the glass was half empty and leaking as his worshipper-customers rapidly changed their allegiance. To the clerk, the glass was half full of a peaceable exchange of ideas. In the clerk's mind, Demetrius was the offender in Ephesus, not Paul or the gospel. Demetrius sought quick, riotous, definitive change. He received a public reprimand. Paul and friends prayed for deep, abiding, transformative change. It was a change in Christ that would not be counted in days or decisions but in years of repentance, faith, and new life. Paul received public exoneration.

Now what?

These scenes are strikingly relevant for Christianity in the West today. Jesus is unwanted and unwelcome in the public square, in education, in the medical field, and beyond. Allegiance to Christ enjoys no reprieve. The temptations might be to water down the radical cost of following Jesus by making it palatable to our peers on the one hand or by picking aggressive and needless battles with the civic order as it stands. It will take prayer and wisdom to move forward as a church challenging a culture while doing so

as peacefully as possible. By all means, culture should feel the radical, life-altering, culture-transforming message of the kingdom. The church's allegiance to Jesus should give the culture's allegiance to itself something to fear. Demetrius and others who peddle and profit in injustice, idolatry, or sex should feel the pinch of the church's presence. Converted and transforming friends should drain the customer bases of a lot of places. The gospel challenges everything.

Creativity in Presentation

The idea that the gospel challenges every aspect of culture not aligned to Christ can be illustrated worldwide, locally, or even down to a single family or individual. Examples abound. Christianity has had a profound impact on the West. The gospel has altered politics, sex, abortion, slavery, justice, hospitals, orphanages, law, medicine, education, universities, art, philosophy, and more. Those world changes are felt locally, of course. There are communities that have felt the blessing of churches fostering and adopting, bridging racial tensions, or standing against injustice. There are countless stories of individual families who have seen the gospel break alcoholism or generational sins. Indeed, Ephesus stands in a long line of places where the gospel goes to work for change—never perfectly, but in many places, breathtakingly beautifully.

Where the gospel changes and challenges, it does so as peacefully as possible. It would be possible to illustrate this truth by seeing Luke's efforts in this passage much like a resume, a reference, or a testimonial. It reads like an endorsement of the missionary movement to the Roman Empire. It highlights the peace of the church and exposes the riotous rage of certain persons in the culture. One way to illustrate the message of this passage would be to write a modern-day endorsement of missionaries addressed to the mayor of their city, explaining exactly what they are coming to do and why it will be a blessing to the community. Lawful witness can capture a city for Christ.

- Faithful witness can affect an entire city for Christ (19:23–34).

- Lawful witness can honor Christ before an entire city (19:35–40).

DISCUSSION QUESTIONS

1. What new perspectives does the uproar in Ephesus add to previous accounts of opposition to the gospel?

2. How might the gospel pose a perceived threat—whether economic, civil, or religious—to contemporary life and culture? Why might people be particularly sensitive about those areas?

3. What does the way in which Demetrius addressed the crowd and the effect his address had on the crowd suggest how opponents might enflame latent hostility toward the gospel?

4. What does Luke's note that some of the Asiarchs were kindly disposed toward Paul (19:31) suggest about the scope and impact of his ministry?

5. Why is the way in which the city clerk quieted, spoke to, and dismissed the crowd significant with respect to the advance of the gospel?

Acts 20:1–12

EXEGETICAL IDEA

Paul concludes his missionary work in Europe by revisiting and encouraging the churches in Macedonia, Achaia, and Troas.

THEOLOGICAL FOCUS

Local bodies of believers require regular care and support.

PREACHING IDEA

Local congregations need loving care.

PREACHING POINTERS

What do young children and new churches have in common? They both need loving care if they are to develop according to God's design. If parents fail to care for their children well, those children will, in all probability, fail to develop physically, mentally, and/or emotionally. In the same way, if a new church is neglected, it will fail to develop into the sort of body Paul describes in Ephesians 4:1–16: united, speaking the truth in love, maturing, functioning according to the giftedness of its members, growing both spiritually and numerically. Paul understood that the new churches he planted needed regular care and support. Accordingly, his established practice was to revisit those churches and encourage them to persevere in their faith. Acts 20:1–12 describes one of those return trips—this time to visit the churches he had planted in Europe—and underscores the importance of and the means for providing ongoing support and care for believers in local congregations. The objective in communicating the passage should be to help listeners understand that local bodies of believers require regular care and support, so that they will intentionally invest themselves in encouraging other believers through their time, teaching, conversation, and compassion.

People today should be able to relate to visiting churches to which they have previous connections, house group meetings, and people who have the gift of encouragement. They can most likely also relate to listening to long-winded speakers and the experience of getting drowsy while listening to those speakers. The passage, like others before it, both corrects the idea that it is possible to engage in "lone ranger" ministry and commends the value of a working with a team in ministry. Similarly, it both corrects any suggestion that local congregations can stand entirely on their own and commends interdependence among congregations. It also commends the ministry of encouragement and trust in God to do "the impossible." It reinforces the importance of the continuing care and support of congregations and the members of those congregations.

CONCLUDING THE MISSION IN EUROPE (20:1–12)

LITERARY STRUCTURE AND THEMES (20:1–12)

The passage divides naturally into two sections. The first recounts Paul's travels from Ephesus through Macedonia and Achaia to Troas (20:1–6). The second describes the events on the last night of Paul's seven-day stay in Troas (20:7–12). Occurrences of the verb παρακαλέω frame the section (20:1, 2, 12), as do the cognates θόρυβος (20:1) and θορυβέω (20:10).

- ***Travel from Ephesus to Troas (20:1–6)***
- ***Farewell Visit in Troas (20:7–12)***

EXPOSITION (20:1–12)

As Peterson notes, this passage is the first of three in which a travel narrative leads to a scene of Christian community life (2009, 553). This first passage includes an evening gathering of the church in Troas (20:1–12). The second includes Paul's extended farewell to the Ephesian elders, whom he called to Miletus (20:13–38). The third includes a gathering of the church in Caesarea (21:1–14). Beverly Gaventa suggests that the series is intended to draw the churches of Paul's Aegean mission into a fellowship that parallels the fellowship of the church in Palestine (2004, 37). In this passage, the triple occurrence of παρακαλέω (20:1, 2, 12; cf. 14:22; 16:40) suggests that Luke's focus is on Paul's ministry of encouragement among the churches he had planted in Europe (Larkin 1995, 287).

Travel from Ephesus to Troas (20:1–6)

After leaving Ephesus, Paul visits and encourages the churches in Macedonia and Achaia.

20:1–3a. After the public disturbance in Ephesus ended (μετὰ τὸ παύσασθαι τὸν θόρυβον), Paul sent for (μεταπεμψάμενος) the disciples, encouraged (παρακαλέσας) them, and said goodbye (ἀσπασάμενος) to them. He then left the city in order to travel to Macedonia (ἐξῆλθεν πορεύεσθαι εἰς Μακεδονίαν). Once he reached the region (τὰ μέρη ἐκεῖνα), he traveled through (διελθών) it, encouraging (παρακαλέσας) the disciples there "at length" (LEB, λόγῳ πολλῷ). Eventually, he arrived in Greece (ἦλθεν εἰς τὴν Ἑλλάδα), where he spent three months (ποιήσας τε μῆνας τρεῖς). Luke refers to the events recorded in the second half of chapter 19 as a "riot" (NASB, θόρυβος), which describes the noise and confusion of an excited crowd (BDAG s.v. "θόρυβος" 3b, 458; cf. 17:5).

The narrative does not record how Paul reached Macedonia, but 2 Corinthians 2:12–13 suggests that he followed a land route north from Ephesus to Troas. During his travel through Macedonia, he followed his regular practice of visiting the churches he had planted in Philippi (16:11–40), Thessalonica (17:1–9), and Berea (17:10–15). Paul refers to the early part of his Macedonian travels in 2 Corinthians 7:5–16. Many commentators suggest that Paul also evangelized Illyricum (Rom. 15:19) during this period (Bruce 1988, 381; Longenecker 1981, 506; Marshall 1980, 323; Schnabel 2012, 832). Ἑλλάς refers to the region of Achaia, where there were churches in Athens (17:32–34), Corinth (18:1–22), and Cenchrea (Rom. 16:1). In Romans 16:23, Paul mentions writing to the church in Rome from Corinth.

20:3b–4. When Paul was about to set sail for Syria (μέλλοντι ἀνάγεσθαι εἰς τὴν Συρίαν), he became aware of a Jewish plot against him (ἐπιβουλῆς αὐτῷ ὑπὸ τῶν Ἰουδαίων) and made the decision (ἐγένετο γνώμης) to travel back through Macedonia (τοῦ ὑποστρέφειν διὰ Μακεδονίας). Elsewhere, ἐπιβουλή ("plot") occurs in 9:24 and 23:30, also related to Jewish attempts against Paul's life. A literal translation of ἐγένετο γνώμης would be "he was of a mind" (Culy and Parsons 2003, 383). Luke notes that seven men were traveling with (συνείπετο) Paul.

His traveling companions represented the churches of Macedonia, South Galatia, and Asia. Sopater (Rom 16:21) was from Berea; Aristarchus (19:29; Col. 4:10; Philem. 24) and Secundus were from Thessalonica. Gaius was from Derbe; Timothy was from Derbe or Lystra (16:1–3). Tychicus (Eph. 6:21; Col. 4:7; 2 Tim. 4:12; Titus 3:12) and Trophimus (2 Tim. 4:20) were from Asia. Commentators find it noteworthy that the list does not mention representatives from either Philippi or Corinth and have offered a variety of suggestions to fill those gaps (Bock 2007, 618). The most common are that Paul himself represented Corinth and Luke represented Philippi.

20:5–6. Paul sent his companions ahead (προελθόντες) to Troas, where they waited (ἔμενον) for him to arrive. Paul himself traveled overland from Corinth to Philippi, a trip that Schnabel suggests would have taken about five weeks (2012, 834). He sailed (ἐξεπλεύσαμεν) from that city with Luke after the days of Unleavened Bread (μετὰ τὰς ἡμέρας τῶν ἀζύμων). Their voyage against the wind to Troas took five days (ἄχρι ἡμερῶν πέντε), and they remained in that city for seven days (οὗ διετρίψαμεν ἡμέρας ἑπτά). Acts 20:5 begins the second "we" passage (20:5–15), when Luke apparently rejoined Paul in Philippi after remaining in that city for the intervening years (16:10–17). The Days of Unleavened Bread were part of the Feast of the Passover, which Schnabel dates to April 7 in A.D. 57. He further notes that

Paul had five additional weeks after leaving Philippi to reach Jerusalem in time for Pentecost (2012, 834).

> **Troas**
> Although located in Asia Minor, Troas was originally a Greek colony founded in 310 B.C. and later named Alexandria Troas to honor Alexander the Great and distinguish it from Troy, which was about fifteen miles farther north along the coast. It came under Roman rule in 133 B.C., and Caesar Augustus gave it the status of a Roman colony. Troas was the primary seaport in northwestern Asia Minor and the nearest point of departure for travel to Europe. Peterson writes that Troas "was clearly an important place in Luke's experience" (2009, 557). Bruce suggests that Luke had studied at the medical school in Philippi and then practiced as a physician in Troas (1988, 308). Paul had sailed from Troas in response to his Macedonian call (16:6–10) and had found an "open door" for ministry in the city on his return visit seven years later (2 Cor. 2:12–13). Most likely, Paul considered the church in Troas to be within the scope of his mission in Europe.

Farewell Visit in Troas (20:7–12)

On the night before he leaves Troas, Paul encourages the church at length and brings a young boy back to life.

20:7–9. On the eve of their departure (μέλλων ἐξιέναι τῇ ἐπαύριον), while the disciples were gathered together (συνηγμένων ἡμῶν, genitive absolute of time), Paul began speaking (διελέγετο, inceptive imperfect) to them and extended (παρέτεινεν, progressive imperfect) his message (τὸν λόγον) until midnight (μέχρι μεσονυκτίου). Among the group was a young man named Eutychus, who was sitting by the open window (καθεζόμενος . . . ἐπὶ τῆς θυρίδος). Most likely, "the atmosphere became stuffy and oily" (Stott 1990, 320) because of the many lamps (λαμπάδες ἱκαναί) that were in the upper room where they were meeting (ἐν τῷ ὑπερῴῳ οὗ ἦμεν συνηγμένοι). Certainly, the late hour and the fact that "Paul talked on and on" (διαλεγομένου τοῦ Παύλου ἐπὶ πλεῖον; cf. Longenecker 1981, 509) contributed to the situation. Regardless, Eutychus "became very drowsy" (NLT, καταφερόμενος ὕπνῳ βαθεῖ), "sank into a deep sleep" (ESV, κατενεχθεὶς ἀπὸ τοῦ ὕπνου), fell down from the third story (ἔπεσεν ἀπὸ τοῦ τριστέγου κάτω), and was taken up dead (ἤρθη νεκρός).

Dunn notes the echoes of early church life elsewhere in the book (1996, 266), including the pattern of meeting together (συνάγω; cf. 4:31; 11:26; 14:27), the use of upper rooms for the meetings (ἐν τῷ ὑπερῴῳ; cf. Luke 22:12; Acts 1:13; 9:37, 39), and the practice of breaking bread with one another (κλάσαι ἄρτον; cf. Luke 22:19; 24:30–35; Acts 2:42). Commentators differ on whether the reference to "breaking bread" refers to the celebration of the Lord's Supper (Marshall 1980, 325), to a church fellowship meal (Barrett 1998, 950; Peterson 2009, 557), or to both (Bruce 1988, 384; Dunn 1996, 268; Schnabel 2012, 835). Paul's instruction in 1 Corinthians 11:17–34 suggests the third understanding.

Larkin notes that the reference to "on the first day after the sabbath" (ἐν τῇ μιᾷ τῶν σαββάτων; cf. Bruce 1990, 425) is "the earliest unambiguous reference to early church practice concerning Sunday worship" (1995, 288). Other early references include 1 Corinthians 16:2, Revelation 1:10, Didache 14:1, and Epistle of Barnabas 15:9. In verse 9, Luke initially describes Eutychus as a "young man" (νεανίας), which designates a male under the age of forty. Later (20:12), he describes him as "the boy" (τὸν παῖδα), which places his age more precisely as between eight and twelve years old. Barrett writes that the sequence κατενεχθεὶς ἀπὸ τοῦ ὕπνου … καταφερόμενος ὕπνῳ βαθεῖ

"brings out vividly the gradually increasing drowsiness and its climax at the point where Eutychus finally falls asleep" (1998, 953).

20:10. Paul went down (καταβάς), "threw himself upon him" (ἐπέπεσεν αὐτῷ; cf. BDAG s.v. "ἐπιπίπτω" 1b, 377), put his arms around him (συμπεριλαβών), and assured the other disciples that the boy was alive (ἡ ψυχὴ αὐτοῦ ἐν αὐτῷ ἐστιν). The command μὴ θορυβεῖσθε ("do not be disturbed") echoes θόρυβος in 20:1, although in this context, it refers to emotional rather than civil disturbance. This miracle is reminiscent of Elijah raising the widow of Zarephath's son (1 Kings 17:17–24), Elisha raising the Shunammite woman's son (2 Kings 4:18–37), Jesus raising the widow of Nain's son (Luke 7:11–15) and Jairus's daughter (Luke 8:49–56), and Peter raising Dorcas in Joppa (Acts 9:36–43).

Textual Analysis: "His life is in him."
Paul's declaration that "[the boy's] life is in him" (ἡ ψυχὴ αὐτοῦ ἐν αὐτῷ ἐστιν) has raised questions for some about whether the boy was dead or simply mortally wounded (Bauer 2021, 221). Larkin, however, notes two important considerations (1995, 290). First, the boy "was taken up dead" (ἤρθη νεκρός) rather than "was taken up *as* dead." Second, Paul said that the boy's life is "is in him" (ἐν αὐτῷ ἐστιν) not "is *still* in him." Barrett suggests that Paul's statement is best understood as saying, "his life is now, by virtue of my action, within him" (1998, 955; cf. Schnabel 2012, 836).

20:11–12. After he restored the boy to life, Paul went upstairs (ἀναβάς), broke bread (κλάσας τὸν ἄρτον), ate (γευσάμενος) with the other disciples, and continued talking with them until daybreak (ἐφ' ἱκανόν ὁμιλήσας ἄχρι αὐγῆς). After he left (ἐξῆλθεν), the disciples took the boy home alive (ἤγαγον τὸν παῖδα ζῶντα) and were greatly encouraged (παρεκλήθησαν οὐ μετρίως) as a result of Paul's ministry among them. Although the verb γεύομαι can mean "to taste" (Matt. 27:34;

Col. 2:21), the basic sense is "to partake of something by mouth" (BDAG s.v. "γεύομαι" 1, 195) and in Luke 14:24 has the nuance "to take part in a meal." The verb ὁμιλέω denotes the activity of conversing with a group (BDAG s.v. "ὁμιλέω" 705; cf. Luke 24:14). The phrases ἐφ᾽ ἱκανόν (NASB, "a long while") and ἄχρι αὐγῆς ("until daybreak") highlight the extended nature of their conversation. The phrase οὐ μετρίως ("not to a moderate degree") is another instance of litotes. The repetition of παρεκλήθησαν underlines Paul's activity of encouragement both in word (20:2) and in deed (20:12).

THEOLOGICAL FOCUS

The narratival function of Acts 20:1–12 is to bring Paul's missionary work in Europe to a conclusion. The passage marks his departure from Ephesus (20:1) and underscores his established pattern of revisiting mission churches he had planted (20:2–6; cf. 14:21–25; 15:36–16:5; 18:23). The account of the night-long meeting in Troas (20:7–12) provides a glimpse into early church life outside Palestine and Syria and serves as a prelude to Paul's farewell to the Ephesian elders when they meet him in Miletus (20:17–38). The passage as a whole illustrates Paul's concern and care for the congregations that had been entrusted to his care.

Theologically, Acts 20:1–12 reviews key elements of early church life, while also highlighting the importance of providing ongoing support for new congregations and the role of encouragement in the life of the church. The all-night meeting of the church in Troas is reminiscent of the life of the early church in Jerusalem (2:40–47) as well as the life of the early church in Antioch (11:19–30). From that brief vignette, Stott suggests three principles for public worship: Jesus's followers met on the Lord's Day, their time included a fellowship meal and the Lord's Supper, and they gave prominence to the exposition and application of God's Word (1990, 321; cf. Larkin 1995, 289).

The same vignette also provides a glimpse into the way in which Paul sought to strengthen and encourage the churches he had planted when he revisited them. Luke had previously characterized Paul's intent on similar visits as "strengthening and encouraging" the disciples (14:22; cf. 15:41; 16:5; 18:23), and he frames this passage with occurrences of the verb παρακαλέω (20:2, 12). Larkin brings the ideas of encouraging and strengthening together when he writes, "exhortation/encouragement is verbal ministry that by the Spirit's power seeks to strengthen Christians to persevere in the faith in the face of trials, especially persecution" (1995, 287).

Paul's ministry of encouragement as pictured in this passage extended beyond verbal ministry alone. Certainly, the fact that he prolonged his message until midnight and then continued talking with the disciples until daybreak emphasizes the verbal aspect of Paul's ministry of encouragement and suggests that it included both teaching (διαλέγομαι) and conversation (ὁμιλέω). The time Paul invested in the churches, however, extended beyond that all-night session. Bruce and others suggest that Paul spent up to eighteen months visiting the churches in Macedonia (1988, 381), and Luke specifically notes that Paul stayed in Achaia—most likely with the churches in Corinth and Cenchrea—for three months (20:3). Although he was hurrying to be in Jerusalem by the day of Pentecost (20:16), Paul stayed with the disciples in Troas for seven days, perhaps so that he could celebrate the Lord's Day with them (Dunn 1996, 268). He also encouraged the disciples in Troas with his compassion toward Eutychus and his confirmation that God was powerfully at work in their midst (Barrett 1998, 950). The ministry of encouragement is essential to both the health of local churches and the believers in them; it is also multifaceted.

PREACHING AND TEACHING STRATEGIES

Exegetical/Theological Synthesis

Paul had concluded three years of ministry in Ephesus. During that time people throughout the province of Asia had heard the gospel (19:10). Now, with churches planted and stabilized, it was time for him to move on. The Holy Spirit had laid it on his heart to visit Jerusalem and, then, to see Rome (19:21). Luke's first-century readers would have wanted to know why, with that long-term goal in mind, Paul would choose to head in the opposite direction to Macedonia after sending Timothy and Erastus ahead of him (19:22). What was his purpose in traveling northward instead of southward? Where would he go? What would he do? Who would accompany him? The narrative of 20:1–12 makes it clear that Paul viewed this trip as concluding his missionary work in Europe. He wanted to spend time with the churches he had planted there and encourage them to stand firmly for the gospel. With his original readers, the twenty-first-century audience shares the need to understand the importance of, and the means for, providing ongoing support and care for believers in local congregations. That support includes the elements of time, teaching, conversation, and compassion. Luke's account of Paul's final evening in Troas depicts Paul and the disciples in that congregation, as they learned from God's Word, shared in community life together, and experienced God's powerful working in their midst.

Preaching/Teaching Idea

Local congregations need loving care.

Contemporary Connections

What does it mean?

Local congregations are fledgling, embryonic seedlings struggling for survival against forces of flesh and evil power. It is not a foregone conclusion that a planted church is a staying church, just as it is not certain that every seed will grow to become a tree. Like Jesus's parable of the seed on different soils to describe a soul receiving or rejecting his gospel, so a church where two or three such souls are gathered is threatened by the same elements of Satan, shallow soil, or choking weeds. Paul and his team knew well the need to follow up with each local work for care and support. Paul spent much time working back through Philippi, Thessalonica, Berea, Athens, Corinth, and Cenchrea. He picked up additional workers in each place to build his international mission team. As the account focuses in on Troas, the means Paul and his team used to care for congregations emerges. That care intentionally employed key means of grace. The church body gathered for Sunday worship, enjoyed the Word and the sacraments together, and did so in the context of mission.

Is it true?

The pastoral care Paul and his team offered the church in Troas matched the enormous odds that confronted this little body of believers. Troas was an important seaport in northwest Asia Minor, a key city in Europe, with all the influences and vices a Roman international city would have experienced in those days. In her midst, a tiny house church began to grow, hardly causing a ripple in the city. Believers there would have been sorely tempted to slip away from their new faith and the allegiance to Jesus it demanded, and to return to the comfortable and socially acceptable routine from which they came.

The great refuge Paul gave them was so simple, yet so powerful, that it was hiding in plain sight. In essence, he gave them more Jesus. He gave them Jesus in gathering for Sunday worship. He gave them Jesus in preaching and speaking the Word in teaching and conversations. He gave them Jesus in the breaking of bread to proclaim his death until he comes. He gave them Jesus in mutual fellowship with one another. He gave them Jesus in exposing them to the growing international missionary team they hosted. He gave them Jesus in the living power of a resurrection before their eyes. Soon, when Paul would meet with the Ephesian elders, he would explicitly explain his strategy. He would tell them, "I did not shrink from declaring to you anything that was profitable . . . testifying both to Jews and to Greeks of repentance toward God and of faith in our Lord Jesus Christ" (20:20–21).

Now what?

Surely our local congregations today are no less fragile, no less pressured by forces of evil without or tempting forces of the flesh from within, and no less weary of doing good. In fact, in this emerging twenty-first-century find-your-authentic-self culture, stories of deconversion or deconstructing faith are all too common. We are in the "last days" full of those inside and outside the church who have become "lovers of self" (2 Tim. 3:1).

Our help is as simple and profound today as it was for Troas in Paul's day. We are desperate for more of Jesus. We need him in weekly gathering for Sunday worship that stands against the press and pull of a culture alien and hostile to him. We need Jesus, the Word made flesh, in the Word open in our laps. We need Jesus in the table he sets before us in communion, in fellowship with each other, in radical trust for him to lead us in the Great Commission. We need Jesus in his miracles and healings and conquest over death and darkness. A local church that returns to a focus on the means of grace will seem radical in a Christendom racing to ride trends. Nevertheless, it has been and will be the means God uses to care for his local body.

Creativity in Presentation

A 2013 book title made me chuckle. Gary Miller and Phil Campbell wrote a preaching book titled, *Saving Eutychus: How to Preach God's Word and Keep People Awake.* The back blurb reads, "It's humbling to notice that what took Paul many hours of preaching to achieve—near-fatal napping of one of his listeners—takes most preachers only a few minutes on a Sunday. *Saving Eutychus* will help you save your listeners from such a fate."

Poor Eutychus will forever be recognized for this fate. At probably only eight to twelve years of age, after a full day of play, school, or chores, he simply could not make it past midnight in a warm, stuffy, lamplit room listening to Paul preach for hours on end. This experience sounds entirely understandable, but it creates a living metaphor of sorts in the passage. Scripture repeatedly calls the church from sleepiness to wakefulness to follow Christ (Rom. 13:11; 1 Cor. 15:34; Eph. 5:14; Rev. 3:2–3). Eutychus was sleeping physically, and he experienced physical death. The church is sleeping spiritually and sorely needs to wake up. Otherwise, some in her midst will experience spiritual death.

Paul's approach, which should be ours in teaching this passage, is not shaming or browbeating. Instead, he lovingly gives space and time and his very self to show this small, sleepy church her Savior. We preach the importance of gathering around Jesus in Sunday worship, the power of preaching and speaking the Word, the grace of the Lord's Supper and mutual fellowship, and the fire of mission. We preach the One who is the resurrection and the life, raising the physically dead and the spiritually dead until he comes again. In doing so, we give local congregations the loving care they need.

- Concern for the church (20:1–6)

- Care for the church (20:7–12)

DISCUSSION QUESTIONS

1. Why did Paul send Timothy and Erastus ahead of him into Macedonia (19:22)? What do Paul's comments on

2 Corinthians 8–9 suggest was part of his reason?

2. What does the list of Paul's traveling companions (20:4) imply about the nature and extent of Paul's missionary work in Europe and Asia?

3. Why do you think Luke chose to include the events in Troas as part of his narrative rather than events related to other churches Paul visited?

4. What principles about early church life can you derive from Luke's account of the all-night meeting in Troas (20:7–12)?

5. What elements about a biblical ministry of encouragement can you draw from this comparatively brief account of Paul's travels?

Acts 20:13–38

EXEGETICAL IDEA

In his farewell to the Ephesian elders, Paul reminds them of his past ministry among them and prepares them for his future ministry without him.

THEOLOGICAL FOCUS

Responsible leaders learn from the example of those who ministered to them, pay close attention to themselves and their flock, and rely on the God who gives his word of grace to them all.

PREACHING IDEA

Responsible leaders learn from the past and look to the future.

PREACHING POINTERS

What qualities should characterize responsible leaders? How should they view those who have gone before them? How should they view themselves and those they are leading? Where should they turn for the resources they need as they engage in their work? Those questions become particularly acute when a group faces a transition in leadership. During his three years in Ephesus, Paul had invested himself deeply in the new church—working night and day, facing trials and tribulations, teaching the gospel comprehensively. Now, he was on his way to Jerusalem and fully expected that he would never see the disciples or their leaders again. What could he tell them that would prepare them for their work in his absence? In his farewell speech in Miletus, he spoke to the elders to remind them (and us) of his past ministry among them and to instruct them (and us) about the role and responsibility of leaders as they face both external and internal threats to the well-being of the congregation.

People today should be able to relate to transitions in leadership, tearful farewells that include parting words, role models, internal and external threats, and the desire to finish a task well. The passage corrects any suggestion that leadership is easy or a potential source of material gain. It also corrects the idea that it is possible to take time off from the responsibilities of being a leader or that personal well-being provides an "out" from those responsibilities. The passage commends both the example a leader sets for others and the benefits of paying attention to that example. It also commends the qualities of humility, care for others, perseverance, alertness, courage, and commitment. The objective in communicating the passage should be to help listeners understand the role and responsibility of congregational leaders, so that leaders will fulfill their appointed ministry and members of the congregation will give them the respect they deserve (1 Tim. 5:17–20).

CONCLUDING THE MISSION IN ASIA (20:13–38)

LITERARY STRUCTURE AND THEMES (20:13–38)

The passage divides into three sections. The first is an account of Paul's travel from Troas to Miletus (20:13–16), and the third is an account of Paul's departure from Miletus (20:36–38). The center of the passage is Paul's farewell speech to the elders from the church in Ephesus, whom he had asked to come to Miletus (20:17–35).

Reviewing Paul's past presence in Ephesus	**20:18b–21**
ὑμεῖς ἐπίστασθε, ἀπὸ πρώτης ἡμέρας ἀφ' ἧς ἐπέβην εἰς τὴν Ἀσίαν	20:18a
Previewing Paul's future absence from Ephesus	**20:22–24**
καὶ νῦν ἰδοὺ δεδεμένος ἐγὼ τῷ πνεύματι πορεύομαι εἰς Ἰερουσαλήμ	20:22
Instructing the elders for their ministry in Paul's absence	**20:25–31**
καὶ νῦν ἰδού ἐγὼ οἶδα ὅτι οὐκέτι ὄψεσθε τὸ πρόσωπόν μου . . . προσέχετε ἑαυτοῖς καὶ παντὶ τῷ ποιμνίῳ . . . ἐγὼ οἶδα ὅτι εἰσελεύσονται μετὰ τὴν ἄφιξίν μου λύκοι βαρεῖς . . . γρηγορεῖτε	20:25 20:25 20:28 20:29 20:31
Commending the elders to God for their ministry	**20:32–35**
καὶ τὰ νῦν παρατίθεμαι ὑμᾶς τῷ θεῷ καὶ τῷ λόγῳ τῆς χάριτος αὐτοῦ	20:32

The speech begins in 20:18b and divides into four parts, three introduced by καὶ νῦν (20:22, 25, 32). First, Paul reviews his past ministry in Ephesus (20:18b–21). He then explains that he is going to Jerusalem and his future is uncertain (20:22–24). The longest part of the speech provides instructions for the elders to follow in Paul's absence (20:25–31). Those instructions include two commands: they are to watch out for themselves and their flock (20:28), and they are to be on the alert against false teachers (20:31). In the concluding section, Paul commends the elders to God and his grace as they seek to obey his instructions and follow his example (20:32–35). If the speech is deliberative as Schnabel suggests (2012, 829), the four sections potentially correspond to the *narratio*, the *propositio*, the *probatio*, and the *peroratio*.

- *Travel from Troas to Miletus (20:13–16)*
- *Farewell to the Ephesian Elders (20:17–35)*
- *Departure from Miletus (20:36–38)*

EXPOSITION (20:13–38)

Luke has recorded multiple visits Paul made to the churches he had planted (14:22; 15:41; 16:5; 18:23; 20:2–3), and the immediately preceding account of the all-night meeting in Troas gave his readers a glimpse of Paul's ministry on such visits. On that night, Paul spoke to the disciples at length, but Luke recorded none of the content. By including Paul's farewell speech to the elders from the church in Ephesus, Luke provides an example of that content (Bauer 2021, 222). Previous speeches highlighted Paul's ministry as an evangelist (13:16–41) and his ministry as an apologist (17:22–31). His speech in Miletus highlights his ministry as a pastor. Schnabel provides a list of similarities to Paul's letters (2012, 828).

Paul had invested himself for three years in the church in Ephesus. Now, he was concluding his mission in Asia and expected that he would not return to the city. In his absence, the care of the flock would rest with the elders whom he had asked to join him one last time. He had given them a model of humble ministry in the face of opposition. Now, they must follow his example. He had cared for the flock by declaring the whole counsel of God. Now, they must shepherd the church that Jesus had purchased with his blood. He had admonished them night and day for three years. Now, they must be on constant alert for savage wolves who would not spare the flock. He had not relied on material resources of silver, gold, or clothing. Now, they must rely on the spiritual resources of God and the word of his grace. His pastoral care for this group of elders provides timeless spiritual guidance for leaders of every congregation.

Travel from Troas to Miletus (20:13–16)
Paul travels by land and sea from Troas to Miletus.

20:13–16. As Paul moved quickly toward Jerusalem, Luke moves quickly through the next stops on the itinerary—from Troas to Assos to Mitylene to Chios to Samos to Miletus. In Troas, the rest of the team set sail (ἀνήχθημεν) for Assos, while Paul had arranged (διατεταγμένος) to travel over land (πεζεύειν). Luke provides no explanation for the reason Paul chose to go by land, but he met (συνέβαλεν) the team at Assos, where they took him aboard (ἀναλαβόντες). Four days later, they arrived in Miletus. Barrett notes that they sailed past (παραπλεῦσαι) Ephesus on the day when they went from Chios to Samos (1998, 958). Because he was hurrying (ἔσπευδεν) to Jerusalem, Paul had determined (κεκρίκει) that he would not spend time (μὴ γένηται αὐτῷ χρονοτριβῆσαι) in the province of Asia. His hope was that it might be possible (εἰ δυνατὸν εἴη) for him to be in Jerusalem on the day of Pentecost, although the optative εἴη "indicates Paul's awareness of the fact that not all plans can be carried out with certainty" (Schnabel 2012, 838).

The ancient theatre of Miletus. Public domain.

Farewell to the Ephesian Elders (20:17–35)
After asking the elders from the church in Ephesus to come to Miletus, Paul reminds them of his ministry among them, gives them instructions for their own ministries, and commits them to God's grace.

20:17–18a. Peterson summarizes suggested reasons that Paul chose to stop at Miletus (2009, 563). The simplest explanation might have been that the boat carrying Paul and his companions docked there rather than at Ephesus. From Miletus, he sent one or more messengers to Ephesus asking the elders of the church (τοὺς πρεσβυτέρους τῆς ἐκκλησίας) to make the trip, so that he could say farewell to them. Commentators differ on the distance between the two cities, but Wilson's suggestion that the land route would have taken "two long days of travel" to cover approximately forty-five miles appears to be reasonable (2013, 6). If so, Paul's stay in Miletus probably lasted five or six days (Barrett 1998, 960). At some point during that period, the elders arrived (παρεγένοντο), and he spoke to them.

20:18b–19. Paul began by telling the elders that they knew (ὑμεῖς ἐπίστασθε) about his life and witness in Asia (εἰς τὴν Ἀσίαν), from the first day he arrived in the province (ἀπὸ πρώτης ἡμέρας ἀφ' ἧς ἐπέβην). Two salient facts stood out. First, Paul was constantly present with them (μεθ' ὑμῶν τὸν πάντα χρόνον ἐγενόμην). His life among them was characterized by his service (δουλεύων), his humility (πάσης ταπεινοφροσύνης), his caring (δακρύων), and his perseverance in the face of trials (πειρασμῶν). The verb ἐπιβαίνω can have the idiomatic sense of "to set foot in" a locale (BDAG s.v. "ἐπιβαίνω" 2, 367). Δουλεύω includes the idea of total service to another (BDAG s.v. "δουλεύω" 2, 259)—in this instance, total service to the Lord (τῷ κυρίῳ). The source of Paul's trials was the plots of the Jews (ταῖς ἐπιβουλαῖς τῶν Ἰουδαίων). See 9:24, 20:3, and 22:30 for Jewish plots against his life.

20:20–21. Second, Paul held back nothing that would be profitable for them (οὐδὲν ὑπεστειλάμην τῶν συμφερόντων). The methods he used included proclaiming (ἀναγγεῖλαι), teaching (διδάξαι), and testifying (διαμαρτυρόμενος). He employed those methods in both public (δημοσίᾳ) and private venues (κατ' οἴκους). His audience included both Jews (Ἰουδαίοις) and Greeks (Ἕλλησιν). The content of his message consisted of repentance toward God (τὴν εἰς θεὸν μετάνοιαν) and faith in Jesus (πίστιν

εἰς τὸν κύριον ἡμῶν Ἰησοῦν). His ministry was both comprehensive and Christ-centered (Larkin 1995, 293).

Ὑποστέλλω denotes "to hold back from doing something, with the implication of some fearful concern" (L&N §13.160). Schnabel suggests that Paul's declaration implies both boldness and completeness (2012, 840). Συμφέρω describes something that advances the best interests of another (BDAG s.v. "συμφέρω" 2b, 960; cf. 1 Cor. 6:12; 10:23; 12:7). Ἀναγγέλλω suggests a focus on the source of the detailed information communicated (L&N §33.198); διδάσκω suggests a focus on the learning that results (L&N §33.224). Διαμαρτύρομαι, which suggests a focus on the truth of the information communicated (BDAG s.v. "διαμαρτύρομαι" 1, 233), occurs three times in this speech (20:21, 23, 24), and occurs six other times in Acts (2:40; 8:25; 10:42; 18:5; 23:11; 28:23). Schnabel identifies the "public" venues (δημοσίᾳ) as "in the synagogues, in the lecture hall of Tyrannus, and in the agora" (2102, 840). Acts 19:8–10 mentions the first two in Ephesus; Acts 17:17 mentions the first and third in Athens. "From house to house" (κατ' οἴκους) is a variation of κατ' οἶκον in Acts 2:46 and most likely refers to the homes of disciples. When he wrote to the Corinthians, Paul included greetings from a church that met in the Ephesian home of Priscilla and Aquila (1 Cor. 16:19).

"Repentance" and "faith" are not the individual responses of the Greeks and the Jews as some suggest; they are "two sides of the same coin" (Bock 2007, 627). Schnabel writes, "repentance before God involves coming to faith in Jesus, and believing in Jesus involves turning away from everything that displeases God" (2012, 841). The gospel requires both Jews and Greeks to repent of their sins and place their faith in Christ (1 Thess. 1:9–10). For repentance in Paul's letters, see Romans 2:4 and 2 Timothy 2:25; for faith, see Romans 3:22 and Galatians 2:16.

20:22–24. The first of three occurrences of καὶ νῦν (καὶ νῦν ἰδού) introduces the second section of Paul's speech (cf. 20:25, 32). As the first section had reviewed Paul's past presence in Ephesus, the second section previewed his future absence from Ephesus. That absence was related to his travel to Jerusalem (πορεύομαι εἰς Ἰερουσαλήμ). He was bound by the Holy Spirit (δεδεμένος τῷ πνεύματι) to make the trip even though he did not know what would happen to him in that city (τὰ ἐν αὐτῇ συναντήσοντά μοι μὴ εἰδώς). Nevertheless (πλήν), the Spirit was warning (διαμαρτύρεται) him that chains and tribulations (δεσμὰ καὶ θλίψεις) were waiting for him. Whatever it might cost (οὐδενὸς λόγου ποιοῦμαι τὴν ψυχὴν τιμίαν ἐμαυτῷ), though, he was determined to complete (τελειώσω) the ministry he received from the Lord Jesus (τὴν διακονίαν ἣν ἔλαβον παρὰ τοῦ κυρίου Ἰησοῦ)— to bear witness (διαμαρτύρασθαι) to the good news about God's grace (τὸ εὐαγγέλιον τῆς χάριτος τοῦ θεοῦ).

The perfect passive participle δεδεμένος points to the fixed nature of the divine necessity (δεῖ) of Paul's travel to Jerusalem (1:16, 21; 3:21; 4:12; 9:6, 16; 14:22; 17:3). His statement here is a restatement of his plans in 19:21 and reinforces the Holy Spirit's role (τῷ πνεύματι) in his life and ministry. The participle μὴ εἰδώς is adverbial of concession (Culy and Parsons 2003, 394); κατὰ πόλιν is distributive ("in every city"). In verse 23, διαμαρτύρομαι has the sense of "warn" (cf. Luke 16:28). Luke will provide a specific example of the Holy Spirit's warning when Agabus acts out his prophecy in Caesarea (cf. 21:11–12). At the close of his ministry, Paul would affirm that he had fulfilled his desire that "I will complete my course" (τελειώσω τὸν δρόμον μου; cf. τὸν δρόμον τετέλεκα in 2 Tim. 4:7). He received his ministry from the Lord Jesus through Ananias in Damascus (9:10–19; 22:12–16) and had it confirmed through a vision in Jerusalem (22:17–21). In verse 24, διαμαρτύρομαι again describes the solemn declaration of truth (20:21), specifically truth about the gospel. Τῆς χάριτος is an objective genitive; τοῦ θεοῦ is a possesive genitive.

TEXTUAL ANALYSIS: "I do not place any value on my own life."
The grammar of the first clause in 20:24 (οὐδενὸς λόγου ποιοῦμαι τὴν ψυχὴν τιμίαν ἐμαυτῷ) is complex. Culy and Parsons suggest that the phrase οὐδενὸς λόγου is an adverbial genitive of respect, "meaning something like 'on no account'" (2003, 394). The verb ποιοῦμαι with the double accusative carries the sense of "to behave or act in a particular way toward something" (L&N §41.7). In the noun phrase τὴν ψυχήν ("the soul") is a synecdoche for "life," and the article functions as a possessive pronoun. The adjective τίμιος describes something of exceptional value (BDAG s.v. "τίμιος" 1, 1005). The resulting sense is "On no account am I acting as though my life is something of exceptional value to me."

20:25–27. The key phrase καὶ νῦν ἰδοὺ marks the beginning of the third section of the speech and introduces Paul's instructions for the elders. Those instructions divide into two parts, each beginning with ἐγὼ οἶδα ὅτι ("I know that") and concluding with a command. First, because Paul expected that they would not see him again (οὐκέτι ὄψεσθε τὸ πρόσωπόν μου ὑμεῖς πάντες), they needed to assume the responsibility of caring for themselves and for the congregation. While he went about among them (ἐν οἷς διῆλθον), Paul had cared for the disciples in Ephesus by preaching the kingdom (κηρύσσων τὴν βασιλείαν) and fearlessly (οὐ ὑπεστειλάμην) announcing the whole plan of God (τοῦ μὴ ἀναγγεῖλαι πᾶσαν τὴν βουλὴν τοῦ θεοῦ). He could, therefore (διότι), solemnly testify (μαρτύρομαι) that he considered himself to be innocent with regard to anyone's life (καθαρός εἰμι ἀπὸ τοῦ αἵματος πάντων).

Although 1 Timothy 1:3 suggests that Paul later returned to Ephesus, at this point in his ministry his focus was on Jerusalem,

Rome, and Spain, and he considered his work in the eastern empire to be at an end (Rom. 15:22–29). It was logical, therefore, for him to declare that the elders would no longer see him. Τὸ πρόσωπόν μου ("my face") is a synecdoche for Paul (Culy and Parsons 2003, 395). In this context, διέρχομαι carries the sense of "going from place to place" rather than of engaging in missionary travel. "The kingdom" (τὴν βασιλείαν) figured significantly in Paul's preaching in Ephesus (19:8) and elsewhere (14:22; 28:23). The verb μαρτύρομαι describes the act of affirming something with solemnity (BDAG s.v. "μαρτύρομαι" 1, 619; cf. Acts 26:22; Gal. 5:3). The addition of ἐν τῇ σήμερον ἡμέρᾳ ("on this very day," LEB) reinforces the solemnity of Paul's affirmation. See verse 20 for ὑποστέλλω. "The whole plan of God" (πᾶσαν τὴν βουλὴν τοῦ θεοῦ) refers to the divine will (BDAG s.v. "βουλή" 2b, 182), and NLT translates the phrase as "all that God wants you to know" (Eph. 1:11). Peterson writes, "Paul gave them a comprehensive view of the will of God, which included the promise of salvation for people of every race, together with an appeal for individuals to repent and believe the gospel promises" (2009, 568).

Commentators agree that the background for Paul's statement in 20:26 that "I am clean from the blood of all" (καθαρός εἰμι ἀπὸ τοῦ αἵματος πάντων) was God's act of appointing Ezekiel as a watchman over Israel (Ezek. 3:16–21; 33:1–10). If Ezekiel failed to warn Israel and they persisted in their wicked ways, God would require their blood at the prophet's hand. On the other hand, if Ezekiel warned them and they persisted in their wicked ways, God would clear him of any guilt. Paul made a similar declaration to the resistant Jews in Corinth (18:6), and in both instances, αἷμα ("blood") was a synecdoche for life (Lev. 17:11). Paul was declaring, therefore, that he had fulfilled his reponsibility as a faithful watchman,

and no lives would be lost because he had failed to warn them about impending judgment. The NLT translates Paul's statement, "If anyone suffers eternal death, it's not my fault."

20:28. A common approach to Paul's command in verse 28 views it as the beginning of a new section. The repetition of ἐγὼ οἶδα ὅτι in verse 29, however, suggests that the command functions as the ending of verses 25–28 rather than the beginning of verses 28–31. Paul's second command in verse 31 supports that conclusion. After reminding the elders of how he had cared for them while he was present in Ephesus, he challenged them to assume responsibility for themselves and for the congregation now that he would be absent. Specifically, they were to pay close attention (προσέχετε) to themselves (ἑαυτοῖς) and to all the disciples in Ephesus as the flock of God (παντὶ τῷ ποιμνίῳ). The Holy Spirit had placed (ἔθετο) them as overseers (ἐπισκόπους) for the purpose of shepherding the church of God (ποιμαίνειν τὴν ἐκκλησίαν τοῦ θεοῦ). As David Bauer writes, the elders must take "great care . . . for this is God's church and is therefore dear to God . . . [who] has made the church his own possession by acquiring it through the act of redemption" (2021, 224).

The present tense imperative προσέχετε ("keep on paying attention") highlights the elders' continuing responsibility. Although the noun ἐπίσκοπος later came to designate the ecclesial office of "bishop," the basic sense is "one who has the responsibility of safeguarding or seeing to it that something is done in the correct way" (BDAG s.v. "ἐπίσκοπος" 1, 379; cf. Phil. 1:1; 1 Tim. 3:2; Titus 1:7; 1 Peter 2:25). Bock suggests "guardian" as a possible translation (2007, 629), and Barrett suggests a connection to ἐπισκέπτομαι as denoting divine oversight (1998, 975). Another intriguing possible connection is to the word the LXX uses to designate a "watchman" (σκοπός). Although σκοπός appears in the NT only in Philippians 3:14 to denote a "goal," in the LXX it describes "one who directs a watchful glance on someone/something" (*TDNT* 7:414). It occurs with that sense repeatedly (1 Sam. 14:16; Isa. 21:6; Jer. 6:17), including the "watchman" passages in Ezekiel (Ezek. 3:17; 33:2, 6, 7), which lends further support to the suggestion that Ezekiel's book provides background for Paul's understanding of spiritual leadership (20:26).

Similarly, the elders' role of "shepherding" suggests a connection to Ezekiel 34:1–10, where the prophet rebukes the shepherds of Israel for failing to care for the flock of God's people. The combination of ποιμαίνω ("to shepherd") and ποίμνιον ("flock") also occurs in Peter's instructions to elders (1 Peter 5:2–3; cf. John 21:16); the present tense infinitive (ποιμαίνειν) highlights the continuing nature of their task. The Ephesian elders' flock was "the church of God" (τὴν ἐκκλησίαν τοῦ θεοῦ), a phrase that occurs eleven times in Paul's letters (1 Cor. 1:2; 10:32; 11:16, 22; 15:9; 2 Cor. 1:1; Gal. 1:13; 1 Thess. 2:14; 2 Thess. 1:4; 1 Tim. 3:5, 15). Metzger notes that it is the more difficult reading than the variant reading "the church of the Lord" (τὴν ἐκκλησίαν τοῦ κυρίου), which occurs nowhere in the NT, although it occurs seven times in the LXX (*TCGNT*, 425). The middle voice of περιεποιήσατο highlights the personal interest God took in his church. The verb itself describes the act of acquiring possession of something (BDAG s.v. "περιποιέω" 2, 804); the cognate noun (περιποίησις) occurs in 1 Peter 2:9. The purchase price of the acquisition was the "blood" of God's own [Son] (Rom. 8:3, 32). See 20:26 on αἷμα as a synecdoche for life.

TEXTUAL ANALYSIS: "which he purchased through the blood of his own"
Dunn describes the relative clause ἣν περιεποιήσατο διὰ τοῦ αἵματος τοῦ ἰδίου as "the chief difficulty" in "one of the most difficult verses in Acts" (1996, 272). The difficulty arises from what Larkin describes as "an anthropomorphic misunderstanding: how can God who

is spirit have blood?" (1995, 296). That misunderstanding led to two textual variants. The first was to describe the church as τὴν ἐκκλησίαν τοῦ κυρίου ("the church of the Lord"); the second was to assimilate the prepositional phrase to Hebrews 9:12 and 13:12 so that it read διὰ τοῦ ἰδίου αἵματος ("through his own blood"). Schnabel sets out six suggested solutions and concludes that τοῦ ἰδίου is best understood as a christological title referring to Jesus (2012, 846–47; cf. Bock 2007, 630; Marshall 1980, 334). Although that solution involves a title found nowhere else in the NT, the natural Pauline reference is to Jesus's blood as the instrument that secures propitiation (Rom. 3:25), justification (Rom. 5:9), redemption (Eph. 1:7), and reconciliation (Col. 1:20).

20:29–30. The second part of Paul's instructions also begins with ἐγὼ οἶδα ὅτι. Because he knew the dangers that would threaten the flock in Ephesus, the elders would need to be alert and follow his example of unceasing personal care for the members of the church. The dangers would be both external and internal. After Paul's departure (μετὰ τὴν ἄφιξίν μου), "fierce wolves" (λύκοι βαρεῖς) who would not spare the flock (μὴ φειδόμενοι τοῦ ποιμνίου) would infiltrate the congregation (εἰσελεύσονται . . . εἰς ὑμᾶς). In addition (καί), men from among these very elders (ἐξ ὑμῶν αὐτῶν) would arise (ἀναστήσονται) with the purpose of drawing away (τοῦ ἀποσπᾶν) disciples to follow them (ὀπίσω αὐτῶν) rather than Christ.

The external threat would come from "wolves" (λύκοι), who would not protect the flock as good shepherds should. The verb φείδομαι describes saving someone or something from loss or discomfort (BDAG s.v. "φείδομαι" 1, 1051), and the negative μὴ φειδόμενοι ("not sparing") implies the opposite result of inflicting pain and/or loss. On the one hand, this external threat is why it was important for them to pay close attention to the congregation (20:28). On the other hand, the internal threat would come from within the leadership, which is why it was important for them to pay close attention to themselves (20:28). The pronoun αὐτῶν in the prepositional phrase ἐξ ὑμῶν αὐτῶν is intensive ("from among you yourselves"). The verb διαστρέφω describes the act of causing to depart from an accepted standard (BDAG s.v. "διαστρέφω" 2, 237). The ESV translates the participle διεστραμμένα as "twisted things," and NASB translates it as "perverse things." The verb ἀποσπάω carries the sense of drawing away or attracting someone from something, perhaps with the idea of making proselytes (BDAG s.v. "ἀποσπάω" 2, 120).

20:31. They should, therefore (διό), be alert and keep on remembering (μνημονεύοντες) the example he had set for them, as he did not cease (οὐκ ἐπαυσάμην) to admonish (νουθετῶν) each of them (ἕνα ἕκαστον). As in verse 28, the present tense imperative γρηγορεῖτε ("keep on being alert") highlights the elders' continuing responsibility. The verb νουθετέω describes the act of providing instruction about correct behavior and belief (L&N §33.231). Bock suggests that Paul's "continual goal was to urge faithfulness to the living God" (2007, 631). The iterative present tense of the participle (νουθετῶν) highlights Paul's repeated instruction over time. Four qualities characterized his care for the flock. It was long-term, extending over the course of three years (τριετίαν). It was constant, taking place both day and night (νύκτα καὶ ἡμέραν). It was personal, sometimes involving deep emotion (μετὰ δακρύων). It was individual, giving attention to every member of the congregation (ἕνα ἕκαστον). Although "night and day" (νύκτα καὶ ἡμέραν) is hyperbolic, the figure of speech emphasizes Paul's constant activity among the Ephesians (cf. 1 Thess. 2:9).

20:32. Καὶ τὰ νῦν marks the beginning of the fourth and final section of the speech (cf. 20:22, 25). If the elders were going to fulfill their responsibilities as watchmen and shepherds, they would need the resources only God could provide. So, Paul added his third important word for them: he presented (παρατίθεμαι) them to God (τῷ θεῷ) and the message about his grace (τῷ λόγῳ τῆς χάριτος αὐτοῦ). That message was able (τῷ δυναμένῳ) to help them grow spiritually (οἰκοδομῆσαι) and persevere until they obtained the inheritance (δοῦναι τὴν κληρονομίαν) God promises to all those whom he has set apart for himself (ἐν τοῖς ἡγιασμένοις πᾶσιν). Larkin's comment is apt: "More important than the leaders' commitment to their charge is God's faithfulness to his. For by it the leaders receive the ability to keep theirs" (1995, 299).

The middle voice of παρατίθεμαι emphasizes Paul's personal interest in committing the elders to God. The verb itself describes the act of entrusting someone to the care or protection of another (BDAG s.v. "παρατίθημι" 3b, 772), in this case with the aim of divine protection (14:23; 1 Peter 4:19). Barrett identifies τῷ θεῷ καὶ τῷ λόγῳ as an instance of hendiadys, in which two nouns connected by "and" express a single idea (1998, 980). The genitive τῆς χάριτος αὐτοῦ is objective. In this context, the idea might be expressed as "God's message about his grace." The verb οἰκοδομέω ("build up") denotes helping to improve the ability to function in living responsibly and effectively (BDAG s.v. "οἰκοδομέω" 3, 696), with a focus upon the process involved (L&N §74:15). The "inheritance" (τὴν κληρονομίαν) Paul mentions is the eternal reward (Col. 3:24) that God promises (Heb. 9:15) and grants (Eph. 1:18) and that consists of an imperishable (1 Peter 1:14) sharing in the kingdom of God (Eph. 5:5). The verb ἁγιάζω denotes setting apart in an inner circle that is holy (BDAG s.v. "ἁγιάζω" 2, 10). The perfect passive participle ἡγιασμένοις describes "a present reality that has been granted to [believers]" (Peterson 2009, 752; cf. Rom. 15:26; 1 Cor. 1:2; 1 Tim. 4:5; 2 Tim. 2:21).

20:33–35. If they would rely on the spiritual resources God and his Word provided, the elders would have no need to accumulate material resources for themselves. They would follow Paul's example of coveting (ἐπεθύμησα) no one's silver, gold, or clothing (ἀργυρίου ἢ χρυσίου ἢ ἱματισμοῦ οὐδενός). As he worked with his own hands (αἱ χεῖρες αὗται) to provide for (ὑπηρέτησαν) his own needs (ταῖς χρείαις μου) as well as the needs of others (τοῖς οὖσιν μετ' ἐμοῦ), they would work in the same way (οὕτως κοπιῶντας) to assist the weak (ἀντιλαμβάνεσθαι τῶν ἀσθενούντων). If they needed incentive beyond Paul's example, they should continue remembering (μνημονεύειν) Jesus's words that "It is more blessed to give than to receive."

Ἐπιθυμέω describes a strong desire or longing for something (BDAG s.v. "ἐπιθυμέω" 1, 371). Ὑπηρετέω describes the activity of providing continuous and prolonged assistance and help that supplies the needs of someone (L&N §35.32). The combination ταῖς χρείαις μου . . . αἱ χεῖρες αὗται is an instance of wordplay. The verb κοπιάω denotes physical, mental, or spiritual exertion (BDAG s.v. "κοπιάω" 2, 558), often to the point of becoming weary (L&N §23.78). See 20:22 for δεῖ as an indicator of divine necessity. Ἀντιλαμβάνω denotes taking someone's part by assisting them or coming to their aid (BDAG s.v. "ἀντιλαμβάνω" 1, 89). In addition to describing sickness or weakness, ἀσθενέω can denote the lack of material necessities (BDAG s.v. "ἀσθενέω" 3, 142). The present tense of the infinitives ἀντιλαμβάνεσθαι and μνημονεύειν highlights the continuing responsibility followers of Jesus have to come to the aid of those in needs and to remember his instructions. The middle voice of ἀντιλαμβάνεσθαι highlights the personal interest involved in assisting others.

 Gospels, but "the command to give is found in Luke 6:30, 38; 11:41; 12:33; 18:22" (2009, 573). Marshall notes, "Paul quotes the words of Jesus only rarely; when he does so, it is to back up some ethical instruction" (1980, 336; cf. 1 Cor. 7:10; 9:14: 1 Tim. 5:18). Dunn suggests that Paul alluded to or echoed Jesus's teaching in multiple places (Rom. 12:14, 17; 13:7; 14:13–14; 1 Cor. 13:2; 1 Thess. 5:2, 13, 15). He summarizes, "So, we can well imagine that the first Christian churches had a common store of Jesus tradition, which was passed on to them when they were founded, which was preserved and rehearsed by the communities' teachers, and to which preachers could alude with confidence that their congregations would recognize the allusion" (1996, 275).

Departure from Miletus (20:36–38)

After his speech, Paul prays with and takes his leave from the elders.

20:36–38. After he had finished speaking (ταῦτα εἰπών, adverbial participle of time), Paul knelt (θεὶς τὰ γόνατα αὐτοῦ) and prayed with all of the elders (σὺν πᾶσιν αὐτοῖς προσηύξατο). They responded by weeping greatly (ἱκανὸς κλαυθμός), embracing him (ἐπιπεσόντες ἐπὶ τὸν τράχηλον), and kissing him farewell (κατεφίλουν αὐτόν). They were especially distressed (ὀδυνώμενοι μάλιστα) by his statement that they would no longer see him (οὐκέτι μέλλουσιν τὸ πρόσωπον αὐτοῦ θεωρεῖν; cf. 20:25). Then, they accompanied (προέπεμπον) him to the ship.

The phrase θεὶς τὰ γόνατα ("placing the knees") is idiomatic for kneeling as a posture in prayer (BDAG s.v. "γόνυ" 205; cf. Luke 22:41; Acts 9:40; 21:5). The noun κλαυθμός describes weeping or crying; Danker translates the phrase ἱκανὸς δὲ κλαυθμὸς ἐγένετο πάντων as "they all began to weep loudly" (BDAG s.v. "κλαυθμός" 546). To "fall upon someone's neck" (ἐπιπεσόντες ἐπὶ τὸν τράχηλον) is to embrace that person (BDAG s.v. "ἐπιπίπτω"1b, 377; cf.

Luke 15:20). The verb ὀδυνάω denotes mental and spiritual distress (BDAG s.v. "ὀδυνάω" 2, 692). The phrase τὸ πρόσωπον αὐτοῦ ("his face") is a synecdoche for Paul himself (Culy and Parsons 2003, 400). The verb προπέμπω can describe accompanying someone to a destination or assisting someone in making a journey by providing food or money (BDAG s.v. "προπέμπω" 2, 873; cf. 15:3; 21:5; Rom. 15:24; 1 Cor. 16:6, 11; 2 Cor. 1:16).

THEOLOGICAL FOCUS

The narratival function of Acts 20:13–38 is to continue Luke's account of Paul's travel to Jerusalem. It is the second of three passages in which a brief travel narrative leads to a scene of Christian community life. The first scene in Troas highlighted Paul's continuing ministry of encouragement to the churches he had planted. This second scene in Miletus closes the missionary phase of Paul's ministry by allowing him to speak to the leaders of the Ephesian church, and by extension to its members and to Luke's readers. The extended farewell to the elders not only provides an example of the content of Paul's encouragement to the churches, it also provides a model of personal conduct and public ministry that faithful followers of Jesus should follow.

Theologically, Acts 20:13–38 brings together key aspects of Paul's life and teaching to inform a pastoral theology of congregational leadership. Each section of his speech highlights an aspect of the role and responsibility of pastoral leadership. In the first section (20:18b–21), Paul's account of his three-year ministry in Ephesus highlights his exemplary conduct and his comprehensive instruction. Humble, caring service and perseverance in the face of trials characterized his conduct while he lived among them. His comprehensive instruction included proclaiming, teaching, and testifying in both public and private venues to both Jews and Greek with a focus on repentance and faith. In the second section (20:22–24), Paul's

explanation of his travel plans highlights his selfless commitment to follow the Spirit's direction and to complete the ministry he had received from the Lord Jesus.

In the third section (20:25–31), Paul's instruction for the elders highlights the pastoral care and constant alertness they would need to exercise in his absence. As responsible watchmen and shepherds, they needed to pay close attention to themselves and to the congregation, and they needed to be alert to external and internal dangers to the congregation. In the fourth section (20:32–35), Paul's act of committing the elders to God highlights the nature and source of the resources available to them. If they would rely on the spiritual resources God and his Word provided, the elders would have no need to accumulate material resources for themselves. Larkin concludes, "The one who is in line with Paul's charges and exercises leadership graciously, eagerly, and humbly will manifest a kind of leadership that the world—with its concern for money, prestige, and power—does not know but desperately needs to know" (Larkin 1995, 300).

PREACHING AND TEACHING STRATEGIES

Exegetical/Theological Synthesis

Luke had documented Paul's consistent practice of revisiting the churches he had planted to encourage and strengthen them. In his account of Paul's stop in Troas on his way to Jerusalem, he had recorded the fact that Paul spoke at length to the disciples in his all-night meeting with the congregation, but he did not include any details of what Paul had said. Luke's first-century readers would have wanted to know what Paul said to encourage and strengthen the congregations he had planted when he revisited them. How could they continue to remain faithful to their origins? What could they learn from Paul's example of life and ministry? What dangers might they face in his absence? Where should the leaders entrusted with the care of the congregation focus their efforts? What resources would be available to the leaders as they sought to fulfill the ministry to which the Holy Spirit had appointed them? Paul's farewell address to the Ephesian elders addresses each of these issues. With the original readers, the twenty-first-century audience shares the need to understand the role and responsibility of leaders as they care for and instruct their congregations in the face of external and internal threats. As the Ephesian elders did, leaders today need to learn from the example of those who ministered to them, pay close attention to themselves and those entrusted to them, and rely on the God who gives his word of grace to them.

Preaching/Teaching Idea

Responsible leaders learn from the past and look to the future.

Contemporary Connections

What does it mean?

In one of the most moving scenes in the book of Acts, Paul gathered the Ephesian elders and gave them a final exhortation before he departed for good. His words were careful, passionate, and thorough. First, he reminded them of his own ministry among them. With his own life on full display, Paul humbly pointed all to Christ through much suffering. Second, Paul shared his next leg of ministry. The Spirit was leading him to Jerusalem to do much of the same—boldly declare Christ at great expense to himself. Third, he charged these elders to take up the mantle of his work among them, chiefly watching themselves and their hearers. These blood-bought souls were the entrusted responsibility of overseers. Fourth, he commended his hearers to God and his grace. They were going to sorely need it.

Is it true?

Paul, his team, these overseers, the church in Ephesus, and the global church never graduate from the living, breathing, supernatural, Trinitarian grace of God to us in Christ. This theme thunders in each of the four sections of Paul's parting words. When he talks about his previous ministry among them, Paul centers it on declaring repentance and faith in Christ in public and in private, in tears and in joy, in suffering and in health (20:19–21). When he tells the church leaders of his future plans, it is all about completing what Jesus has given him to do, testifying to the grace of God (20:24). When Paul gives these overseers their marching orders, they are much the same. They are to rely on the Spirit to care for God's church, bought with Christ's blood. When Paul commends these men to God, it is into God's grace. From start to finish, Paul's ministry and now the Ephesian elders' ministry was to give their flock what they themselves so desperately depend on, the grace of God in Christ sealed by the Spirit.

Now what?

Although Paul speaks to elders in this passage, his words also apply to the church. Just as apostles hold a unique office that still has parallels to lay members of the church, so elders and overseers hold a unique role with elements that should be true for all of us. Elders shepherd the entire church in their care. All lay believers have a hand in teaching, shepherding, and exhorting the sheep in our spheres of influence, whether it is our family, children, small group members, or ministry efforts. Nevertheless, there is something special and particular in Paul's instructions for ordained elders. There is also something universal in Paul's instructions for all of us in the church who seek to be faithful to the Great Commission of making disciples by faithfully presenting Christ. That realization makes verse 28 important, life-giving news. We must pay careful attention to our own walk not just for ourselves but for others. Our sanctification is for our community's benefit. It points them to Jesus. Since we are not capable of mustering the obedience and fruit our church needs, our commendation to God and his care is sweet balm to our souls. He gives us what we need for our role. We will not be alone in our efforts to draw each other toward the Lord.

Creativity in Presentation

French author Antoine de Saint-Exupéry wrote, "If you want to build a ship, don't drum up the men to gather wood, divide the work, and give orders. Instead, teach them to yearn for the vast and endless sea." He had a point. Handing a person an instruction manual before she knows what she is doing will hardly generate enthusiasm. Dumping a pile of kid's bike parts in front of her, though, while her son's friends whiz around the cul-de-sac will immediately sharpen what is at stake. The goal makes us eager for any help we can get.

Verse 28 is this yearning "for the vast and endless sea." Leaders—lay and elder—are entrusted with their local flock. We are tasked with caring for the priceless, blood-bought church of God. Such a monumental responsibility gets us running toward God's grace for ourselves and for our church. The stakes could not be higher and more glorious. Leaders could not be more in need of help. Wise leaders happily entrust their flock to God's grace as they themselves are entrusted to that same grace.

Greed for God's grace marks the four natural parts of the passage. In the first section, Paul's ministry among them was all about this grace found in God (20:19–21). In the second, his future plans were all about testifying to the grace of God (20:22–24). Third, God's grace is implied in Paul's declaration his has given them the full counsel of God that they will sorely need for the work ahead (20:25–31).

Fourth, Paul commends these leaders to God's grace (20:32–35).

Responsible leaders learn from the past and look to the future.

- God's past grace among his people (20:19–21)

- God's future grace among his people (20:22–24)

- God's full counsel of grace (20:25–31)

- God's hands of grace (20:32–35)

DISCUSSION QUESTIONS

1. Why did Paul decide to bypass Ephesus when he had devoted so much time and energy to the church in that city?

2. How did Paul's three years in Ephesus provide a model of life, ministry, obedience, and a clear conscience?

3. How was Paul able to face with confidence the potential difficulties he expected to encounter when he arrived in Jerusalem?

4. What implications did Paul's future absence from Ephesus have for the church's elders? How did his instructions to the elders address those issues?

5. What does the elders' emotional distress at the thought of never seeing Paul again suggest about their relationship with him?

JERUSALEM AND CAESAREA (ACTS 21:1–26:32)

Having concluded his role in the missions in Europe (20:1–12) and Asia (20:13–38), Paul continued his journey to Jerusalem. As Peterson notes, the pace of the narrative that has moved rapidly through his travels from Corinth to Caesarea (20:1–21:14) "slows considerably" once Paul reaches Jerusalem (2009, 574). Paul was fully aware that jail and suffering awaited him in the Jewish capital (20:22), but he also knew that the commission Jesus had given him included both suffering and bearing Jesus's name before the Gentiles, kings, and the sons of Israel (9:15–16). The two years Paul would spend in Jerusalem and Caesarea would give him ample opportunity to fulfill both aspects of his commission. During his time in those cities, he would face a Jewish riot in the temple (21:27–36), he would narrowly avoid Roman flogging (22:24–29), he would escape yet another Jewish plot to kill him (23:12–22), and he would languish in prison for two years because the Roman governor wanted to do the Jews a favor (24:27). Yet he would also have opportunities to bear witness for Jesus before the sons of Israel (22:1–22; 23:1–10), two Gentile governors (24:1–21; 25:1–15), and the Jewish king (26:1–32). Running throughout Paul's experiences in Jerusalem and Caesarea are the themes of Jewish opposition and Roman justice (Stott 1990, 336–39), unjust suffering (Peterson 2009, 575), and God's providential care (Bauer 2021, 226). The events Luke reports most likely cover the time period from the spring of A.D. 57 to the summer of A.D. 59.

57	Spring	Jerusalem (21:1–23:11)	Jerusalem vision (23:11)
	Summer		Defense before Felix (24:1–27)
	Fall		
58	Winter		
	Spring		
	Summer	Caesarea (23:12–26:32)	
	Fall		
59	Winter		
	Spring		Defenses before Festus (25:1–12) and Agrippa (26:1–32)
	Summer		

Homiletically, the sixth division of Acts consists of eight sections. The first records the final stage of Paul's journey to Jerusalem, with stops in Tyre, Ptolemais, and Caesarea (21:1–14). The second recounts his arrival in Jerusalem and his meeting with the Jerusalem elders (21:15–26). The third describes a riot in the temple, Paul's defense before the assembled mob, and his arrest by the Romans (21:27–22:29). The fourth recounts his defense before the Sanhedrin (22:30–23:11). The fifth describes a Jewish plot against Paul's life and his transfer under Roman custody from Jerusalem to Caesarea (23:12–35). The sixth, seventh, and eighth recount Paul's defenses in Caesarea before Felix (24:1–27), Festus (25:1–12), and Herod Agrippa II (25:13–26:32).

Acts 21:1–14

EXEGETICAL IDEA
As he travels from Miletus to Caesarea, Paul affirms his commitment to follow the Spirit's leading despite repeated attempts to dissuade him from going to Jerusalem.

THEOLOGICAL FOCUS
Following God's will involves remaining steadfast in the face of potentially dangerous circumstances.

PREACHING IDEA
Our commitment to Jesus determines our course of action.

PREACHING POINTERS
How do you respond when you are convinced that you understand the direction in which God is leading you, and everyone else disagrees? How do you evaluate apparently contradictory advice? Do you continue when you know for certain there is danger ahead, or do you let self-interest determine your direction? Paul had to wrestle with those and other questions as he traveled from Europe to Jerusalem. He heard the Holy Spirit speak to him repeatedly about his destination and what awaited him there. His traveling companions, however, interpreted the information differently and did their best to dissuade him from going to Jerusalem. What kept Paul going? How did he remain steadfast in the face of potentially dangerous circumstances? He knew the mission to which Jesus had called him, and like Jesus, he was willing to submit to the task God had for him regardless of the consequences. His commitment to Jesus determined his course of action.

People today should be able to relate to being committed to completing a task—perhaps despite the consequences—and attempts to dissuade someone from a course of action. They should also be able to relate to traveling, visiting friends, and saying farewell to others. The passage corrects any suggestion that majority opinion is always correct or that self-interest should determine a person's actions. It commends discernment of and commitment to God's will; obedience to and alignment with divine guidance; and fellowship, love, and hospitality among Jesus's disciples. The objective in communicating the passage should be to help listeners understand the importance of discerning and submitting to God's will regardless of the consequences, so that they will follow it steadfastly in the face of well-intentioned counsel, opposition, and potential danger.

JOURNEY TO JERUSALEM (21:1–14)

LITERARY STRUCTURE AND THEMES (21:1–14)

The passage consists of two major sections. The first describes Paul's travel from Miletus to Tyre (21:1–6); the second describes his farewell visit with the church in Caesarea (21:7–14). As was the case in the two preceding passages (cf. 20:1–12; 20:13–38), travel narratives alternate with snapshots of church life, as the following table shows.

	Locale	Travel	Distance	Time
21:1	Miletus to Patara	Coastal vessel	190 miles	3 days
21:2–3	Patara to Tyre	Ocean vessel	400 miles	5 days
21:4–6	Tyre			7 days
21:7a	Tyre to Ptolemais	Coastal vessel	25 miles	1 day
21:7b	Ptolemais			1 day
21:8a	Ptolemais to Caesarea	Coastal vessel	40 miles	1 day
21:8b–14	Caesarea			"many days"

- ***Travel from Miletus to Tyre (21:1–6)***
- ***Farewell Visit in Caesarea (21:7–14)***

EXPOSITION (21:1–14)

Acts 21:1–14 both comprises the third "we-passage" in Acts (16:10–17; 20:5–15) and recounts the third stage of Paul's journey to Jerusalem (20:1–12; 20:13–38). Having brought his missionary work in Europe and Asia to a close, Paul continued to follow the Spirit's direction (19:21; 20:22–24) despite progressive prophetic unfolding of what awaited him in the Jewish capital, while his companions and friends grappled with the new information (20:23; 21:4, 11–14). Commentators have long noted the parallels between Paul's and Jesus's journeys to Jerusalem. Longenecker lists five parallels, four of which occur in this passage (1981, 515; cf. Stott 1990, 315). They include plots by the Jews (20:3, 19; cf. Luke 6:7, 11; 11:53–54; 22:1–2), three predictions of impending suffering (20:22–24; 21:4, 10–11; cf. Luke 9:22, 44; 18:31–34), prediction of being handed over to the Gentiles (21:11; cf. Luke 18:32), resolution to complete the journey (20:24; 21:13; cf. Luke 9:51), and commitment to obeying God's will (21:14; cf. Luke 22:42). As Stott notes, the fellowship, hospitality, and support he experienced along the way "fortified Paul in his journey" (1990, 333). In this passage, that support occurred in Tyre (21:4–6), Ptolemais (21:7), and Caesarea (21:8–14). Paul had experienced it previously in Greece (20:3), Troas (20:7–12), and Miletus (20:36–38). It would continue in Jerusalem (21:16).

Travel from Miletus to Tyre (21:1–6)

Paul travels by sea from Miletus in Asia to Tyre in Syria, where he stays for seven days.

21:1–3. Leaving the elders in Miletus (ἀποσπασθέντας ἀπ᾽ αὐτῶν), Paul and his companions set sail (ἀναχθῆναι ἡμᾶς) for Syria. They continued along the coast of Asia Minor with overnight stops in Cos and Rhodes before they reached Patara, a port frequented by grain ships sailing between Egypt and Italy (Schnabel 2102, 854). In Patara, they found (εὑρόντες) a ship that was bound for Phoenicia (πλοῖον διαπερῶν εἰς Φοινίκην), went on board (ἐπιβάντες), and set sail (ἀνήχθημεν). Passing south of Cyprus (καταλιπόντες . . . εὐώνυμον), they sailed to Syria (ἐπλέομεν εἰς Συρίαν) and arrived in Tyre (κατήλθομεν εἰς Τύρον), where the boat unloaded its cargo (τὸ πλοῖον ἦν ἀποφορτιζόμενον τὸν γόμον).

Bruce suggests "we tore ourselves away from them" as a translation for ἀποσπασθέντας ἀπ᾽ αὐτῶν (1988, 397). Barrett writes that the verb in the middle voice describes "a separation made with difficulty" but suggests that Bruce's translation might be too strong (1998, 987). The verb διαπεράω describes moving from one side to another of some geographical object, in this instance a body of water (L&N §15.31; cf. Luke 16:26). The change to a larger vessel at Patara allowed the team to travel directly to Phoenicia rather than continuing the slower route along the coast. John Chrysostom writes that the four-hundred-mile ocean route took five days (*Hom. Act.* 45). Marshall notes, "Luke speaks indifferently of Phoenicia, Syria, and Tyre as [Paul's] destination" and explains, "Tyre was the chief town in Phoenicia which in turn was a region in Syria" (1980, 338).

21:4. In Tyre, the travelers sought out (ἀνευρόντες) other disciples with whom they stayed (ἐπεμείναμεν) for seven days (ἡμέρας ἑπτά). During the stay, the disciples kept on urging (ἔλεγον) Paul not to continue his journey to Jerusalem (μὴ ἐπιβαίνειν εἰς Ἱεροσόλυμα). The verb ἀνευρίσκω denotes intentional searching (L&N §27.28; cf. Luke 2:16). Larkin suggests that Paul might possibly have visited Tyre twice previously (12:25; 15:3) and, therefore, knew about the church in the city (1995, 301). The church was most likely planted through the witness of Hellenistic Jewish disciples who left Jerusalem after Stephen's martyrdom (11:19). Marshall offers three possible explanations for the seven-day stay: they had made good progress and now had time to spare; they had to wait until the same ship departed again; or they had to find another ship (1980, 338). The imperfect tense of ἔλεγον highlights the disciples' repeated urgings (iterative imperfect). Longenecker concludes that διὰ τοῦ πνεύματος ("through the Spirit") indicates "that the Spirit's message was the occasion for the believers' concern rather than that their trying to dissuade Paul was directly inspired by the Spirit" (1981, 516).

21:5–6. When they ended their seven-day stay (ὅτε ἐγένετο ἡμᾶς ἐξαρτίσαι τὰς ἡμέρας), Paul and his companions experienced a farewell similar to their parting from the Ephesian elders in Miletus (20:36–38). All the disciples (πάντων)—including the women and children (σὺν γυναιξὶ καὶ τέκνοις)—accompanied (προπεμπόντων) them outside the city (ἔξω τῆς πόλεως) to the beach (ἐπὶ τὸν αἰγιαλόν), where they prayed together (προσευξάμενοι). After they said farewell (ἀπησπασάμεθα ἀλλήλους), Paul and his companions went aboard the ship (ἐνέβημεν εἰς τὸ πλοῖον), while the disciples returned to their homes (ἐκεῖνοι ὑπέστρεψαν εἰς τὰ ἴδια).

The verb ἐξαρτίζω is causative and describes the act of bringing something to an end (BDAG s.v. "ἐξαρτίζω" 1, 346; cf. L&N §67.71). See 20:38 for προπέμπω ("accompany") and 20:36 for θεὶς τὰ γόνατα ("placing the knees"). Hemer notes that αἰγιαλός "describes correctly the smooth beach at Tyre, as opposed to ἀκτή, used of a rocky shore" (1989, 125). See 21:1 for ἀποσπάω in the middle voice; the reciprocal pronoun ἀλλήλους highlights the mutuality of the emotions involved (Barrett 1998, 991). Robertson notes that τὰ ἴδια carries the sense of "to their own homes" (1934, 691).

Farewell Visit in Caesarea (21:7–14)

From Tyre, Paul travels to Caesarea, where the prophet Agabus foretells what Paul will experience in Jerusalem.

21:7–9. From Tyre, the team continued their journey (τὸν πλοῦν διανύσαντες) and arrived in Ptolemais (κατηντήσαμεν εἰς Πτολεμαΐδα), where they greeted the Christians (ἀσπασάμενοι τοὺς ἀδελφούς) in the city and stayed with them for one day (ἐμείναμεν ἡμέραν μίαν παρ' αὐτοῖς). On the next day (τῇ ἐπαύριον), they left Ptolemais (ἐξελθόντες) and went on to Caesarea (ἤλθομεν εἰς Καισάρειαν), where they entered the house of Philip (εἰς τὸν οἶκον Φιλίππου). The verb διανύω refers to continuing, with the implication of movement (L&N §68.18). As Schnabel notes, τοὺς ἀδελφούς ("the brothers") "is a standard designation for members of the community of Jesus's followers" (2012, 855; e.g., 1:15; 6:3; 9:30; 11:29). Paul had made two previous visits to the port city (9:30; 18:22) and most likely was acquainted with the disciples there.

Luke describes Philip in three ways: he was "the evangelist," "one of the Seven," and the father of four daughters. The first designation (τοῦ εὐαγγελιστοῦ) describes his giftedness in sharing the gospel effectively (8:4–40; Eph. 4:11) rather than referring to a formal office. Either Caesarea was the base for his ministry, or he had ended his itinerant evangelistic work. The second designation (ἐκ τῶν ἑπτά) distinguishes him from Philip the apostle (6:5–6). Luke expands the third designation (τούτῳ ἦσαν θυγατέρες τέσσαρες) to note that the daughters were παρθένοι—young women of marriageable age (BDAG s.v. "παρθένος" a, 777)—and that they prophesied (προφητεύουσαι). Bock suggests that παρθένοι highlights the daughters' pious social status (2007, 637). See 11:27 for the role of NT prophets, who could be either resident or itinerant, sometimes encouraged and strengthened the church, and other times foretold the future. Paul refers to women who prophesied in the Corinthian house churches (1 Cor. 11:5). Schnabel notes that the present tense participle προφητεύουσαι "implies the habitual character of their exercise of the gift of prophecy" (2012, 856). Following Gaventa, Peterson suggests that Luke's mentioning Philip as an evangelist and his daughters as prophetesses highlights "the strength of the community in Caesarea" (2009, 579).

21:10–12. The team remained (ἐπιμενόντων) in Caesarea for "many days" (ἡμέρας πλείους). During their time in the city, the prophet Agabus arrived from Judea and acted out a prophecy. He took Paul's belt (ἄρας τὴν ζώνην τοῦ Παύλου) and bound his own feet and hands (δήσας ἑαυτοῦ τοὺς πόδας καὶ τὰς χεῖρας). He then declared that "in the same way" (οὕτως), the Jews in Jerusalem (ἐν Ἰερουσαλὴμ οἱ Ἰουδαῖοι) would bind (δήσουσιν) the belt's owner (τὸν ἄνδρα οὗ ἐστιν ἡ ζώνη αὕτη) and would hand him over into the hands of the Gentiles (παραδώσουσιν εἰς χεῖρας ἐθνῶν). When Paul's companions and the local disciples (οἱ ἐντόπιοι) heard the prophecy (ἠκούσαμεν ταῦτα), they kept on urging (παρεκαλοῦμεν, iterative imperfect) Paul not to continue his journey to Jerusalem (τοῦ μὴ ἀναβαίνειν αὐτὸν εἰς Ἰερουσαλήμ).

From a Jewish perspective, Caesarea was part of Samaria rather than Judea, which is why Agabus "came down from Judea" (κατῆλθέν ἀπὸ τῆς Ἰουδαίας; cf. Barrett 1998, 995). As part of his itinerant ministry, the prophet had visited Antioch in A.D. 44 and warned the church about the coming worldwide famine. His prophecy at that time prompted the church to send a financial gift to Jerusalem (11:27–30). His visit to Caesarea most likely took place thirteen years later in A.D. 57. His acted prophecy was similar to those of OT prophets (1 Kings 11:27–31; Isa. 8:1–4; Ezek. 4:1–8). Peterson notes that it "illustrated and confirmed the seriousness of the message" (2009, 580). The introductory formula "This is what the Holy Spirit says" (Τάδε λέγει τὸ πνεῦμα τὸ ἅγιον) "asserts divine authority for the prediction" and is comparable to the phrase "thus says the Lord" that occurs 322 times in the OT (Schnabel 2012, 857). The prophecy of binding and handing over to the Gentiles echoes Jesus's predictions on his journey to Jerusalem (Luke 9:22, 44; 18:32; 24:17).

21:13–14. Paul's response was immediate (τότε) and emphatic. It included a question and a declaration. His question—"What are you doing, weeping and breaking my heart?"—reflected the emotional impact the disciples' repeated pleading had on Paul. The declaration that he was willing (ἑτοίμως ἔχω) not only to be bound (οὐ μόνον δεθῆναι) but also to die (ἀλλὰ καὶ ἀποθανεῖν) in Jerusalem on behalf of Jesus's name (ὑπὲρ τοῦ ὀνόματος τοῦ κυρίου Ἰησοῦ) reflected the depth of Paul's commitment to finishing the task Jesus had given him (20:24). After repeated futile attempts to dissuade him (μὴ πειθομένου αὐτοῦ), the others "fell silent" (ἡσυχάσαμεν) and affirmed their willingness to accept the Lord's will (τοῦ κυρίου τὸ θέλημα γινέσθω).

Literally, the verb συνθρύπτω describes breaking something into pieces (BDAG s.v. "συνθρύπτω" 972); figuratively, it describes causing great sorrow; idiomatically, it carries the sense of "to break the heart" (L&N §25.282). Bock suggests that the disciples were "pounding on Paul's emotions" (2007, 639). The pronoun ἐγώ that begins Paul's declaration is emphatic and sets his perspective in sharp contrast to that of the disciples. The combination ἑτοίμως ἔχω describes a state of readiness (L&N §77.2).

References to Jesus's name (τοῦ ὀνόματος τοῦ κυρίου Ἰησοῦ) occur twenty-six times in Acts, including other instances related to opposition and suffering (4:17, 18; 5:28, 40, 41; 9:16; 13:26). See 3:6 for the name of Jesus. The genitive absolute μὴ πειθομένου αὐτοῦ can be either temporal (e.g., NIV, NKJV, NLT, RSV) or causal (e.g., ESV, LEB, NASB, NET, NRSV). The present tense of the participle emphasizes continuing attempts at persuasion. See 11:18 for ἡσυχάζω. Of the disciples' response, Marshall writes, "Their words resemble those of Jesus in Gethsemane (Luke 22:42) and express a readiness for whatever God may will, even if they conceal the hope that God's will may turn out to be different from what they fear" (1980, 341).

THEOLOGICAL FOCUS

The narratival function of Acts 21:1–14 is to bring Paul to Caesarea, his last stop before he reaches Jerusalem. Paul's visits with the churches in Tyre, Ptolemais, and Caesarea highlight the love that existed among the disciples, the hospitality that characterized the early Christian communities, and the Holy Spirit's activity in the life of those communities. Paul himself provides a model of what it means to follow Jesus, even in the face of potential suffering. He was committed to following the Spirit's leading despite repeated attempts by his traveling companions and others to dissuade him from going to Jerusalem. In his responses to the concerns of others, Paul not only affirms his own readiness to follow the Lord's will but also helps them gain a more accurate perspective on what it means to do so. In response, they declare, "The will of the Lord be done."

Theologically, Acts 21:1–14 reinforces several truths. The warmth with which the disciples in Syria received Paul—even though they were outside the scope of his missionary activity—highlights the fellowship, hospitality, and support that characterized the early Christian communities. The repeated references to the work of the Holy Spirit as well as the mention of Philip's four daughters who prophesied highlights the charismatic quality of early church life. Paul's fixed focus on Jerusalem highlights the response Jesus expects from his followers. In the latter regard, the bottom-line principle stands at the end of the passage in Paul's response to the repeated pleas of his companions and the disciples in Caesarea: he was ready to be bound and to die, if necessary, for the name of Jesus, his Lord. For the faithful follower of Jesus, commitment to God's will overrules self-interest, the well-meaning counsel of others, and any dangers that might arise. Like Jesus in the garden of Gethsemane, the proper response to divine leading is "Not my will, but yours be done" (Luke 22:42).

PREACHING AND TEACHING STRATEGIES

Exegetical/Theological Synthesis
Initially, Paul knew only that the Holy Spirit was directing him to travel to Jerusalem (19:21–22). Then, the Spirit repeatedly let him know that bonds and afflictions awaited him (20:22–23). As his companions became aware of the details, they began urging Paul not to set foot in Jerusalem (21:4). Finally, when Agabus acted out his prophecy that the Jews would bind Paul and hand him over to the Gentiles, the disciples in Caesarea begged him not to continue his journey (21:11–12). Throughout his travels, like Jesus, Paul "resolutely set his face to go to Jerusalem" (Luke 9:51). Luke's first-century readers would have wanted to know why Paul was so intent on reaching Jerusalem despite the potential dangers that awaited him and the repeated warnings from other Christians.

The disciples in Tyre, Ptolemais, and Caesarea had embraced Paul as their own, had shown him loving hospitality, and had sent him on his way with their prayers. Yet he refused to accept their well-intentioned counsel. He fixed his focus on Jerusalem because the Spirit had consistently made it clear that Jerusalem was

his destination while also progressively adding details about what he would encounter. The potential dangers that awaited him did not change Paul's objective, but they concerned his companions. When he declared that he was "ready not only to be bound, but to die at Jerusalem for the name of the Lord Jesus" (21:13), Paul made it clear that he was committed to following God's will regardless of the consequences, and his faithful obedience ultimately brought the other disciples into agreement with the Spirit's leading (21:14). Like the disciples in Tyre and Caesarea, the twenty-first-century audience shares the need to understand that following God's will involves remaining steadfast in the face of potentially dangerous consequences.

Preaching/Teaching Idea
Our commitment to Jesus determines our course of action.

Contemporary Connections

What does it mean?
The Spirit's leading made Paul steadfast in suffering. Twice Luke reports the Holy Spirit directed Paul to Jerusalem. After the harrowing events in Ephesus, Paul resolved in the Spirit to go to Jerusalem (19:21). While revisiting the Ephesian elders later on, Paul shared with them, "I am going to Jerusalem, constrained by the Spirit" (20:22), knowing full well "imprisonment and afflictions await me" (20:23). There was no mistake here as to the impetus for Paul's travel plans. His decision was not impulsive, a grasp for attention, or a masochistic resolve. Paul was in step with the Spirit and was committed to following God's will for him. This Spirit-leading made Paul ready for heartfelt opposition from friends. In Tyre and again in Caesarea, believers he knew well begged him not to go. The Spirit had told them essentially what he had told Paul—that prison and affliction lay ahead. Agabus went as far as prophetically acting out his arrest and deliverance to Gentiles who would

have no love for his troublesome mission. Even so, Paul stood fast in the Spirit. When pleading failed, the believers, including Luke himself, gathered and resolved movingly, "Let the will of the Lord be done" (21:14).

Is it true?

Paul's walking in step with the Spirit toward what seems like certain death in Jerusalem looks like Jesus's walking in step with the Spirit toward what seemed like certain death in Jerusalem. Others plotted against both of them. Both shared a triple prediction of suffering. Both were to be handed over to Gentiles. Yet both resolved to continue in obedience to God's will. Paul already considered himself "crucified with Christ" and no longer living his own life but Christ's life in him (Gal. 2:20). Paul did not ultimately fear death. He had already died. Once the sting of that grave force was gone, Paul could hold his new resurrection life with open hands. He could declare readiness for prison or death (21:13).

Other truths emerge on this journey toward persecution in Jesus's name. The church surrounding Paul is deeply affectionate, Spirit-filled, and ultimately, committed to the will of God. Paul had just been on his knees with the Ephesian elders as they commended themselves to God. Now he was in Tyre doing the same thing. He would go on to Caesarea and find similar hearts there. In every place, the Spirit is present and speaking. In every place, there is willingness to let the Spirit's will trump the church's will. Although Paul alone would face suffering in Jerusalem, Paul was not alone. He was surrounded by Spirit-filled friends.

Now what?

Allegiance to Jesus over all comforts, cares, idols, popular opinions, pandering for praise, reputations for reasonableness, and life itself is a desperately high call none of us can do in our own strength. We pray, "Thy kingdom come, Thy will be done," but we harbor a long list of caveats, exceptions, and qualifications. *Total* allegiance sounds terrifying. *Majority* allegiance seems practical. Jesus, however, will not share us with another. The strength we lack to be directed wholly by him, he gives in his Spirit and his church. The Holy Spirit works within us as he did in Paul and speaks to our hearts, "This is the way—walk in it." The church works from without, prayerfully wrestling together with his call on our lives. The best of Christian friends say to us with Luke and friends, "Let the will of the Lord be done." These gifts strengthen us to be steadfast in the suffering that comes with following Jesus.

Creativity in Presentation

I recently met a woman in the Middle East whose story is not uncommon among those brothers and sisters who share the gospel in volatile places. Her evangelism got her in trouble with local authorities. She had already been arrested. Now they were threatening worse. Everything in my flesh wanted to tell this precious saint to run and hide, but that call was not mine to make. Instead, we gathered believers and prayed earnestly for clarity. Through that time, she resolved to continue doing what she had been doing. The Lord's will be done.

A long time ago, I heard a speaker describe our relationship with God like a contract. We would like to fill the contract with nonnegotiable details over health, safety, family, marriage, success, and all else. We are perfectly happy to do the Lord's will inasmuch as it coincides with our will. That life would be easy. Of course, *we* do not write the contract, and *God* certainly does not sign it. Becoming crucified with Christ means signing a blank contract in obedience to God and waiting for him to unfold its details over the course of our lives.

A creative presentation of this message might be to start with the challenge of what lies ahead—certain suffering. What might that knowledge be doing to Paul's mind and heart the closer he gets to Jerusalem? What does knowing the cost of following Jesus do to our minds and hearts? The Lord then graciously answers those fears in this text. He gives us his Spirit to guide us over and against the noise around us. He gives us the local church to walk alongside of us and commend us to his will. God is faithful to give us exactly what we need in that moment. Because we are in gracious hands, our commitment to Jesus determines our course of action.

- Our first commitment is to Jesus above all else (21:13–14).

- This commitment to Jesus will lead us into places we might not have chosen for ourselves (21:1–12).

DISCUSSION QUESTIONS

1. What parallels do you see between Paul's journey to Jerusalem in Acts and Jesus's journey to Jerusalem in the gospel of Luke?

2. How do you reconcile the Spirit's directing Paul to travel to Jerusalem (19:22–23) with Agabus's prophecy about what Paul would encounter in Jerusalem (21:11)?

3. Were Paul's companions wrong to attempt to dissuade Paul from continuing his journey to Jerusalem (21:4, 12)? Why or why not?

4. What principles about knowing and following divine guidance can you draw from Paul's example?

5. What do you learn about the life of the early Christian communities from Paul's stops in Tyre, Ptolemais, and Caesarea?

Acts 21:15–26

EXEGETICAL IDEA
Upon arriving in Jerusalem, Paul received a warm welcome, reported on his ministry activities, and agreed to a proposal from the elders in the hope of alleviating the tension his arrival might cause.

THEOLOGICAL FOCUS
The peace of the church rests on the willingness to accept others with different values and forego personal liberty without compromising the truth of the gospel.

PREACHING IDEA
The pursuit of peace in Christ's church requires flexibility without compromise.

PREACHING POINTERS
One of the ministerial vows in a certain denomination calls the candidate for ordination to "maintain the truths of the gospel and the purity and peace and unity of the church" (PCA *Book of Church Order* 21-5). Did you catch the two guardrails in that vow? On one side of the road are the truths of the gospel and the purity of the church. On the other side of the road are the peace and unity of the church. It can be challenging to stay between those guardrails, can't it? If we go too far in the pursuit of peace, we run the risk of compromising the truth. If we insist on certain nonessential practices as the primary means of preserving the purity of the church, we run the risk of destroying the unity of the body. How do we maintain the proper balance? Paul and the Jerusalem elders faced precisely that challenge in Acts 21:15–26. On the one hand, Paul was known to preach a law-free gospel to the Gentiles. On the other hand, Jewish believers in the Jerusalem church were zealous to uphold the law. How did Paul and the Jerusalem elders resolve the tension?

People today should be able to relate to hearing reports about what God is doing in the ministries of others, to being zealous about something they consider important, or to being concerned about potential differences among friends and/or colleagues. The passage corrects the ideas that certain ways of expressing personal piety are absolute, that individual liberty is more important than the common good, or that accepting unsubstantiated reports about other believers is appropriate. It commends the importance of being committed to unity, being willing to be flexible on nonessentials, and being intentional about resolving conflict within the body of Christ. The objective should be to help listeners understand that the truth of the gospel and the peace of the church are more important than personal preferences, so they will accept others who hold values different from their own and commit to acting in ways that will promote the edification of other believers, the progress of the gospel, and the glory of God.

PAUL'S ARRIVAL IN JERUSALEM AND THE ELDERS' PROPOSAL (21:15–26)

LITERARY STRUCTURE AND THEMES (21:15–26)

The passage consists of two sections. The first narrates Paul's arrival in Jerusalem, his welcome by the church, and his report to the elders (21:15–19). In the second, the elders express their concern about the possible trouble that might arise and make a proposal to Paul that they hope will allow Paul to demonstrate that reports about his ministry are false (21:20–26). The elders' proposal consists of four parts: a description of the current situation in the Jerusalem church (21:20), a synopsis of reports that were circulating about Paul's ministry (21:21), a suggested course of action (21:22–24), and an affirmation that their proposal did not change the previous decision of the Jerusalem Council (21:25).

- ***Paul's Arrival and Report (21:15–19)***
- ***The Elders' Response, Concern, and Proposal (21:20–26)***

EXPOSITION (21:15–26)

Barrett describes Acts 21:15–26 as "the occasion that leads to all the events of the rest of the book, up to and including Paul's arrival in Rome as a prisoner" (1998, 1000). From the time he left Ephesus, Paul was intent on reaching Jerusalem, and then Rome (19:21; 20:23; 21:13). Instead of the hostile reception he expected (Rom. 15:31), the church welcomed him warmly and rejoiced over what God had been doing through him. There were storm clouds on the horizon, however, because of reports about Paul's ministry that had reached a portion of the Jerusalem church. In an effort to disprove those reports,

the elders proposed a plan of action, and Paul readily agreed. Ironically, as a result of his attempt to demonstrate his loyalty to his Jewish heritage, Paul would find himself attacked by the Jews and taken into Roman custody for the next five years. As Bauer notes, "From this point on, Paul will be a prisoner" (2021, 229). He would not be a prisoner, however, because of anything he had done wrong. Rather, it was his desire to do the right thing for the good of the gospel and the peace of the church that led to his bonds and imprisonment. As he had told the disciples in Caesarea, he was ready "not only to be imprisoned but even to die in Jerusalem for the name of the Lord Jesus" (21:14). This passage recounts the events that followed Paul's departure from Caesarea and preceded his arrest in the temple.

Paul's Arrival and Report (21:15–19)

Paul travels from Caesarea to Jerusalem, where he receives a warm welcome from the disciples and reports to the church about his ministry among the Gentiles.

21:15–17. When their stay in Caesarea came to an end (μετὰ δὲ τὰς ἡμέρας ταύτας), Paul and his companions completed their travel preparations (ἐπισκευασάμενοι) and made the trip to Jerusalem (ἀνεβαίνομεν εἰς Ἱεροσόλυμα). Some of the disciples from Caesarea (τῶν μαθητῶν ἀπὸ Καισαρείας) accompanied them (συνῆλθον . . . σὺν ἡμῖν) and brought (ἄγοντες) them to the home of Mnason, with whom they stayed as guests (παρ' ᾧ ξενισθῶμεν). Upon their arrival in Jerusalem (γενομένων ἡμῶν εἰς Ἱεροσόλυμα), members of the church welcomed them "warmly" (ἀσμένως ἀπεδέξαντο ἡμᾶς).

The verb ἐπισκευάζομαι denotes to "pack in readiness for travel" (Barrett 1998, 1002; cf. Chrysostom, *Hom. Act.* 45), but it can also refer to equipping horses (Xenophon, *Hell.* 5.3.1). The distance from Caesarea to Jerusalem was between sixty and sixty-five miles, which would have required four days of travel on foot (Schnabel 2012, 859) or two days by horse or mule (Bruce 1990, 443). Although the Western text suggests that Mnason lived in a village between Caesarea and Jerusalem where Paul and his traveling companions stopped overnight on their trip (*TCGNT*, 428), manuscript evidence does not support that reading, and it seems more likely that Mnason's home was in Jerusalem itself (Marshall 1980, 341).

Luke calls Mnason "an early disciple" (ἀρχαίῳ μαθητῇ), a description that Bruce concludes makes him "a disciple from the beginning" (1988, 402; cf. Longenecker 1981, 517). Larkin suggests he was one of the original 120 disciples (1995, 306). Mnason's Cypriot background (Κυπρίῳ) suggests that he was one of the Hellenistic Jews in the Jerusalem congregation (Peterson 2009, 582). "The brothers" (οἱ ἀδελφοί) who welcomed Paul might have been members of Mnason's household (Marshall 1980, 342), but the more natural reference is to members of the Jerusalem church (Larkin 1995, 307).

21:18–19. Paul wasted no time before meeting with the leaders of the Jerusalem church. On the day after his arrival (τῇ ἐπιούσῃ), he met with James and the Jerusalem elders, greeted them (ἀσπασάμενος αὐτούς), and reported to them in detail (ἐξηγεῖτο καθ' ἓν ἕκαστον) everything that God did (ὧν ἐποίησεν ὁ θεὸς) among the Gentiles (ἐν τοῖς ἔθνεσιν) through his ministry (διὰ τῆς διακονίας αὐτοῦ). Barrett suggests that εἴσειμι "conveys a hint of entering the presence of a great person . . . or coming into a law court" (1998, 1005). Peterson suggests "the rather solemn language . . . suggests a more formal scene" (2009, 584). See 15:13 for James, and 11:30 for the Jerusalem elders.

The verb ἐξηγέομαι carries the sense of describing something in detail (BDAG s.v. "ἐξηγέομαι" 2, 349). Schnabel suggests that it denotes the activity of narrating with interpretive comment (2012, 892). The imperfect tense suggests that the report took some time. For καθ' ἓν ἕκαστον, Culy and Parson suggest "one by one" (2003, 410); Larkin suggests "one item after another" (1995, 304). Paul had made similar reports to the churches in Antioch (14:27; 18:22) and Jerusalem (15:12), and Peter had made a report to the Jerusalem church after the conversion of Cornelius (11:1–17). In each report, the emphasis was on what God was doing rather than on what the witness had done. Dunn notes "that God was the initiator and actor in mission and its developments was . . . Luke's particular emphasis" (1996, 285). Paul's perspective was similar (Rom. 15:17–21).

What About the Collection?

The fact that Luke makes no mention of the collection Paul had gathered among the Gentile churches and delivered to Jerusalem raises questions for most commentators. In fact, except for a passing mention in 24:17, Luke does not refer to the collection anywhere in his narrative of Paul's fifth and final visit to Jerusalem. Barrett suggests that the mention of διακονία in 21:19 might be an allusion to the collection (1998, 1001), but Bock rejects that understanding in favor of a reference to Paul's ministry in general (2007, 646). All the details related to the collection come from Paul's letters (Rom. 15:14–32; 1 Cor. 16:1–4; 2 Cor. 8:1–9:15), and it was clearly an important project for him. Luke writes selectively, however, and his focus is on Paul's submission to God's will as he follows the Holy Spirit's leading—first to Jerusalem, then to Rome (19:21). His arrival in Jerusalem is the beginning of "the final act in [Luke's] drama of Christian beginnings" (Dunn 1996, 278). The delivery of the collection is less important to that drama than the events that set Paul on his next journey that takes him to Rome.

The Elders' Response, Concern, and Proposal (21:20–26)

When the elders hear Paul's report, they glorify God, inform him of negative reports about his ministry, and propose a solution to disprove those reports.

21:20–21. When the elders heard Paul's report (ἀκούσαντες), they began glorifying God (ἐδόξαζον τὸν θεόν), before turning to concerns arising out of other reports about Paul's ministry. The Jerusalem church had grown to the point where there were thousands of Jewish believers (μυριάδες εἰσὶν ἐν τοῖς Ἰουδαίοις τῶν πεπιστευκότων). All of them were "zealous for the law" (ESV, ζηλωταὶ τοῦ νόμου), and they had been informed (κατηχήθησαν) that Paul was teaching Jews to turn away from observing the law. Specifically, the reports said that Paul taught apostasy from the Mosaic Law (ἀποστασίαν ἀπὸ Μωϋσέως), abolishing circumcision (μὴ περιτέμνειν αὐτοὺς τὰ τέκνα), and abandoning Jewish customs (μηδὲ τοῖς ἔθεσιν περιπατεῖν).

Luke passes quickly over the elders' response to Paul's report, but the inceptive imperfect of ἐδόξαζον marks the beginning of an extended time of praising God. Their response, in conjunction with the warm welcome Paul received in Jerusalem (21:17) and the elders' act of addressing Paul as "brother" (ἀδελφέ), highlights what Bauer describes as "the complete concord between Paul and the leadership of the Jerusalem church" (2021, 228). Although some commentators view the report of "thousands" as hyperbole (Dunn 1996, 285), it aligns well with previous reports of the growth of the Jerusalem church (2:41; 4:4; 5:14; 6:7). The perfect tense of the participle πεπιστευκότων highlights the enduring nature of the Jewish disciples' faith. The NLT translates ζηλωταὶ τοῦ νόμου as "they all follow the law of Moses seriously," while NET translates the phrase as "they are ardent observers of the law." Peterson suggests that the phrase indicates zeal for observance of the law, jealousy for the honor of the law, and hostility toward any perceived devaluing of the law (2009, 585). He also suggests that κατηχήθησαν "implies false instruction . . . not just hearsay or rumor" (2009, 585).

> ### What Did Paul Teach and Practice?
>
> The reports about Paul's ministry revolved around what he supposedly taught "all the Jews who are among the Gentiles" (τοὺς κατὰ τὰ ἔθνη πάντας Ἰουδαίους)—that is, Jews in the Diaspora. Essentially, the charge was that Paul was teaching Jews to live like Gentiles. Based on what he taught the Gentiles, it would have been possible to reach the conclusion that Paul minimized the law (Rom. 3:21–31; Gal. 3:1–25) and circumcision (Rom. 2:25–30; Gal. 5:6; 6:15). Based on his practice among the Jews, however, "the report is utterly false" (Bauer 2021, 228). He had circumcised Timothy to avoid offending Jews in South Galatia (16:1–3), and he had undertaken a Nazarite vow at the time of his fourth visit to Jerusalem (18:18). The reports circulating in Jerusalem, therefore, confused Paul's approach to his different audiences.

21:22–24. In light of the fact that everyone in Jerusalem would soon hear about his arrival (πάντως ἀκούσονται ὅτι ἐλήλυθας), the elders made a proposal to address the problem (τοῦτο ποίησον ὅ σοι λέγομεν). There were four men in the community who had placed themselves under a Nazarite vow (εὐχὴν ἔχοντες ἐφ᾽ ἑαυτῶν), and that situation provided an opportunity for the elders to set out a three-part proposal for Paul. First, he should associate with the four men (τούτους παραλαβών) as they completed the period of their vow. Second, he should undergo a purification process with them (ἁγνίσθητι σὺν αὐτοῖς). Third, he should pay the four men's expenses (δαπάνησον ἐπ᾽ αὐτοῖς) to make it possible for them to complete their vow by shaving their heads (ἵνα ξυρήσονται τὴν κεφαλήν). As a result, all the Jewish Christians would know (γνώσονται πάντες) that what they had been told about Paul amounted to nothing (ὧν κατήχηνται περὶ σοῦ οὐδέν ἐστιν) and that Paul actually conformed his conduct to the standard of the law (στοιχεῖς καὶ αὐτὸς φυλάσσων τὸν νόμον).

The verb παραλαμβάνω describes the act of joining someone in close association (BDAG s.v. "παραλαμβάνω" 1, 767). With the middle voice, the passive imperative ἁγνίσθητι carries the sense of purifying or dedicating oneself (BDAG s.v. "ἁγνίζω" 3, 12), and the LXX uses the verb in connection with the Nazirite oath (Num. 6:3). The occurrence of ἁγνίζω in this passage, in conjunction with the four men having their heads shaved, points to their vow as being Nazirite. Δαπανάω denotes paying someone's expenses, with a nuance of doing it freely and lavishly (BDAG s.v. "δαπανάω" 1, 212). Bruce notes, "Another Israelite might associate himself with Nazirites by defraying the cost of the offering; this was regarded as a pious and charitable action" (1988, 406). Longenecker describes it as "an act of piety and a symbol of identification with the Jewish people" and notes a similar action by Herod Agrippa I (1981, 520; cf. Josephus, *A.J.* 19.6.1). The expense of the sacrifice would have involved paying for a male lamb, a female lamb, a ram, a cereal offering, and a drink offering (Num. 6:14–15). The basic sense of ξυράω is to scrape; the middle voice ξυρήσονται carries the sense of having oneself shaved (BDAG s.v. "ξυράω" 686). See 21:21 for κατήχηνται. The verb στοιχέω describes being in line with a standard of conduct (BDAG s.v. "στοιχέω" 946; cf. Gal. 6:16).

To What Did Paul Commit Himself?

Luke's account of the elders' proposal has raised questions about the exact nature of what they intended. Commentators have suggested four possible answers: (1) the elders asked Paul to join the four men in their Nazirite vow (Witherington 1998, 649); (2) they asked Paul to join the four men in a purification ritual because the men had contracted uncleanness during the period of their vow (Bruce 1988, 407); (3) they asked Paul to complete his own vow that Luke had described in 18:18 (Jervell 1998, 526); (4) they asked Paul to purify himself after returning from his time of travel in Gentile territory (Larkin 1995, 308). The shaving of the four men's heads points to a Nazirite vow for them, but such a vow usually lasted for at least thirty days (m. Naz. 6:3). Bruce's suggestion has no evidence to support it, and nearly five years had passed since Paul's own vow. The period of seven days mentioned in 21:27 aligns with the OT requirement for purification from ritual uncleanness (Num. 19:11–13; m. Ohol. 2:3). The most likely explanation is that Paul committed himself both to observing ritual cleansing related to his travel abroad and to paying the expenses related to the four men completing their Nazirite vow. Both acts would demonstrate that Paul still observed both the Mosaic Law and Jewish customs (cf. 21:24).

21:25. The elders' proposal, however, did not change what they had already written (ἡμεῖς ἐπεστείλαμεν) concerning believing Gentiles (περὶ τῶν πεπιστευκότων ἐθνῶν). The prior decision (κρίναντες), articulated in the Jerusalem decree, was that Gentile disciples were to keep themselves (φυλάσσεσθαι αὐτούς) from participating in activities connect with idolatry (εἰδωλόθυτον), consuming blood (αἷμα), eating the meat of animals that had been killed by strangled (πνικτόν), and engaging in sexual immorality (πορνείαν). The pronoun ἡμεῖς is emphatic (Barrett 1998, 1014) and reinforces the elders' commitment to their previous decision. The perfect tense of the participle πεπιστευκότων highlights the enduring nature of the Gentile disciples' faith and places them on equal footing with the Jewish disciples (21:20). See 15:20 for the Jerusalem decree; the wording and order of the stipulations in this verse correspond to that of the earlier letter (15:29). Barrett finds the inclusion of the stipulations of the degree somewhat puzzling (1998, 1015), and Marshall offers several possible explanations for the inclusion (1980, 346). Since Paul and Barnabas had carried the letter back to Antioch (15:30), the information was not new to him. Dunn suggests, "the repetition increases the sense that a formal statement was being made" (1996, 287).

21:26. Again, Paul acted immediately. On the next day (τῇ ἐχομένῃ ἡμέρᾳ), he joined the men (παραλαβὼν τοὺς ἄνδρας), was purified with them (σὺν αὐτοῖς ἁγνισθείς), entered the temple (εἰσῄει εἰς τὸ ἱερόν), and gave notice of when the men's vow would be fulfilled (διαγγέλλων τὴν ἐκπλήρωσιν τῶν ἡμερῶν τοῦ ἁγνισμοῦ). At that time (ἕως οὗ), he would present the required offering for each of them (προσηνέχθη ὑπὲρ ἑνὸς ἑκάστου αὐτῶν ἡ προσφορά). Longenecker summarizes, "What Paul did was to report to the priest at the start of his seven days of purification, inform him that he was providing the funds for the offerings of the four men who had taken Nazirite vows, and return to the temple [on the third and seventh days] during the week for the appropriate rites. He would have also informed the priest of the date when the Nazirite vows of the four would be completed" (1981, 520).

THEOLOGICAL FOCUS

The narratival function of Acts 21:15–26 is to bring Paul's journey to Jerusalem to a close. It marks the transition from Paul's work as a missionary to his confinement as a prisoner and, so, introduces the section of Acts that Dunn calls "the passion of Paul" (1996, 277). As the preceding passages concluded Luke's accounts of missions in Europe (20:1–12), Asia (20:13–38), and Syria (21:1–13), so this passage concludes his account of the mission in Palestine. As Dunn notes parenthetically, "we hear no more of the Jerusalem church/believers/disciples hereafter in Acts" (1996, 284). Subsequent to this meeting with the Jerusalem church, Paul interacts solely with non-Christian Jews and with Romans. The passage, therefore, functions as a hinge between different phases of Paul's ministry in the same way that 15:36–16:10 and 18:18–28 did earlier in the narrative.

Theologically, Acts 21:15–26 provides a model of how believers should live together in the diverse body of Christ when dealing with differences related to nonessentials. As Stott notes, "The issue between them concerned culture, ceremony, and tradition. The solution to which they came was not a compromise, in the sense of sacrificing a doctrinal or moral principle, but a concession in the area of practice" (1990, 342). The Jerusalem Council had previously endorsed Peter's argument that both Jews and Gentiles were saved through faith in Jesus (15:6–11) and had asked the Gentiles to refrain from four practices that their Jewish brothers found objectionable (15:13–21). Now, the Jerusalem elders reaffirmed those essential parameters while also asking Paul to be flexible by practicing particularly Jewish acts of piety.

Paul's willingness to follow the elders' proposal demonstrated his commitment to living out the personal ethic he articulated in his letters. When dealing with differences on nonessentials, followers of Christ are to pursue the unity and peace of the body (Rom. 12:18; 14:19) by applying four principles. They are to avoid acting in ways that might cause others to stumble (Rom. 14:13, 21; 1 Cor. 8:13). They are to seek to edify their brothers and sisters (Rom. 14:19; 15:2; 1 Cor. 8:1; 10:23). They are to promote the spread of the gospel (Rom. 15:8; 1 Cor. 9:12, 23). They are to seek to bring glory to God (Rom. 15:7; 1 Cor. 10:31). Bock concludes, "What we see here is Paul being asked to act with cultural sensitivity to the Jewish context he finds himself in, without compromising the gospel" (2007, 648). In so doing, he pursued the unity and peace of the church by being flexible on nonessentials of practice while being firm on essentials of doctrine.

PREACHING AND TEACHING STRATEGIES

Exegetical/Theological Synthesis

Paul's ministry among the Gentiles in diaspora lands had been immensely successful. He and Barnabas had visited Jerusalem previously and reported on what God was doing through them (15:12). Paul and Silas had visited the city five years later so that Paul could fulfill a Nazirite vow (18:18, 22). After another five-year absence, Paul was intent on reaching Jerusalem in time to celebrate the feast of Pentecost (20:16), and representatives of the Gentile churches in Galatia, Greece, and Asia accompanied him (20:4). At other times and in other contexts, Paul's reports had been the occasion for both joy and concern (15:3–5).

Because Luke had provided repeated warnings that imprisonment and suffering awaited Paul in Jerusalem at the end of his trip, his first-century readers would have wanted to know how the Jerusalem church would receive Paul when he arrived in the city. They would have also wanted to know how Paul would conduct himself in the strongly Jewish context as well as how he and the congregational leaders would resolve any tensions that might arise. Along with the original audience, the twenty-first-century audience shares the need to understand how to address tensions that arise within the body of Christ. What principles can they draw from the account of Paul's arrival in Jerusalem and the elders' proposal? Luke's account suggests four. First, unity is paramount. Second, essentials are nonnegotiable. Third, nonessentials are of secondary importance. Fourth, believers must be willing to forego their personal liberty in order to maintain the peace of the church.

Preaching/Teaching Idea

The pursuit of peace in Christ's church requires flexibility without compromise.

Contemporary Connections

What does it mean?

After much anticipation, Paul touched down in the tinderbox situation that was Jerusalem. He quickly learned that he was pressed on both sides, between fidelity to the gospel of grace he preached to Jew and Gentile alike and great care for Jewish believers in Jerusalem sorely confused by what they have heard about him. Paul could not flinch on doctrine. Christ came to save sinners by grace, through faith, apart from the law. The Jerusalem Council itself had agreed on this truth and had warned about adding undue burdens of the law to Gentile converts (15:10–11). This gospel liberty, however, was never intended to hinder the faith of Jewish converts steeped in tradition and ceremony. This situation is serious and has major consequences.

Fortunately, Paul was not alone. The Jerusalem elders were eager to help find a solution that promoted unity without compromising truth. The elders wisely suggested that Paul show himself publicly in solidarity with Jewish believers, most likely by observing ritual cleansing and by generously providing for men performing a vow. Such a course of action did not fudge the gospel of grace in the slightest but paved the way for true unity with the Jerusalem church.

Is it true?

There is a tender care in these elders for the local flock that reflects the tender care of God for his global flock. God is perfect truth within himself. He cannot lie. He does not compromise. His way of salvation is narrow and exclusive, because his way of salvation leads directly to himself and his finished work through his Son alone. Yet this exclusive gospel of the true God goes forth across nations, languages, and cultures, looking the same but different wherever it flourishes. The gospel does not bowl over culture, tradition, or ceremony. It grows within these deeply human realms, never changing at its core, but taking on the flavors of human place and time, while subverting whatever is out of alignment with allegiance to Jesus.

When the gospel went out from Jerusalem to the Gentiles, it did not force Jerusalem Christianity onto Gentiles. Now as the missionary to Gentiles returns, the leaders of the movement will not force Gentile Christianity on Jerusalem. The Gentile and Jewish church will grow up, sometimes in different places and sometimes under one roof, navigating this beautiful complexity as she does now in this text. In this way, we have the chance to share with one another the kindness of God to us in Christ.

Now what?

Our secular culture and our church culture have not always prepared us well for unity in diversity, to put it as generously as possible. It is scary to realize the little things that can create big problems. We are all for unity, comradery, friendship, togetherness—when we do things our way. When your contour of Christianity looks different from mine, though, look out. We are losing the "meekness and gentleness of Christ" in our dealings with one another (2 Cor. 10:1). We are losing our "obligation to bear with the failings of the weak" (Rom. 15:1). Instead, we are quick to draw battle lines, push opinions, take sides, create strawman arguments, and then attack those arguments. Watching Paul humbly hear from the elders and take their advice should give us pause. Rather than demanding his right to not be responsible for bowing to the opinions of Jewish believers, Paul absorbed the cost of unity and gladly came to Jerusalem to serve and not to be served. His approach sounds like Jesus. May it sound like us, too.

Creativity in Presentation

Truth versus preference can be a fine line to draw, with major consequences. The more time I have spent within one strand of global Christianity—my country, my denomination, my local church, my group within my church—the more foreign other perfectly true expressions of Christianity will look to me. This human tendency puts me at risk of demanding my preference over actual truth.

Take coffee, for example. There are many factors that affect the taste of coffee. Which coffee plant is chosen, where it is grown, how it is processed, how it is harvested, and how it is roasted will all change the flavor profile. I might be dedicated to Brazilian high-altitude coffee, slow maturity, and sweet complex flavor. My preference, however, does not make your low-altitude, mass-produced and processed burnt black watery liquid any less coffee. I might never touch the stuff on my own, but I had better receive it with gratitude in your home. My preference does not make your coffee non-coffee, and it surely should not create division.

That silly illustration makes a serious point. In God's marvelous providence, his gospel grows up with the flavor of the community. We have much to learn from each other if we will humble ourselves. Our text binds Jew and Gentile together under that great gospel word of grace in Acts: "believed" (21:20, 25). Faith is the core, because Jesus is the core. Gentile Christians will not be circumcising themselves or following Jerusalem's customs. Jewish Christians will not be shoving Gentile freedom in each other's faces. If Jesus is the core, all will be well. Whoever joins Paul on the potential fault line of these differences, however, will need great grace from that same Jesus to live with deference toward one another.

A message design could begin with what these believers have in common in Christ, describe the serious differences they have with each other, and conclude with the example from Paul to fight for essentials over peripherals and truth over preferences all for the sake of unity in that same Christ. This pursuit of peace in Christ's church will require flexibility without compromise.

- Different expressions of faith can threaten to disrupt the peace of Christ's church (21:15–22).

- Together the church finds a solution that is flexible on peripherals while remaining committed to essentials (21:23–26).

DISCUSSION QUESTIONS

1. What does the welcome Paul received in Jerusalem suggest about the early disciples' attitude toward one another?

2. How did the reports about Paul that were circulating in Jerusalem misunderstand and/or misrepresent his ministry outside Palestine?

3. Was Paul wrong to agree to the elders' proposal? Did his agreement represent a compromise of this beliefs? Why or why not?

4. How did Paul's actions demonstrate his faithfulness to the Mosaic Law and to Jewish customs?

5. What principles about dealing with different approaches to practicing your piety can you draw from this passage?

Acts 21:27–22:29

EXEGETICAL IDEA

Learning of an uproar in the temple precincts, a Roman commander acts to restore order and, as a result, delivers Paul from a violent death at the hands of a Jewish mob.

THEOLOGICAL FOCUS

God sometimes uses unexpected means to protect his witnesses in the face of injustice.

PREACHING IDEA

God can open doors of deliverance in unexpected directions.

PREACHING POINTERS

There is a story about a man who is trapped on the roof of his house during a flood. Because he is waiting for God to rescue him, he declines help from someone in a rowboat, someone in a motorboat, and someone in a helicopter. Eventually, the waters rise over his head, and he drowns. When the man gets to heaven and asks God why he did not rescue him, God reminds the man that he had sent two boats and a helicopter to rescue him! What's the point? Sometimes God's deliverance can come from sources other than those we might expect. That was Paul's experience when a Jewish mob attacked him in the temple and tried to kill him. In the middle of the uproar, a Roman commander and his soldiers intervened to restore order and, in so doing, delivered Paul from a violent death. The events Luke narrates in Acts 21:27–22:29 remind us that God can open doors of deliverance in unexpected directions.

People today should be able to relate to large group gatherings that turn violent, confusion over the causes of public unrest, or intervention by government authorities to address civil disorder. They should also be able to relate to potential miscarriages of justice and individuals attempting to defend themselves against legal charges. The passage corrects any attitude that gives preference to traditionalism over truth, that believes violence is an appropriate solution to a problem, or that views properly constituted authorities as always hostile to Christianity. It commends willingness to accept truth, trust in God's working to protect his people, and readiness "always to make a defense to everyone who asks you to give an account for the hope that is in you" (1 Peter 3:15). The objective in communicating the passage should be to help listeners understand that God can use secular authorities to protect his witnesses, so that they will be alert to doors of deliverance that God might open for them and will trust him to protect them from persecution by whatever means he might choose.

DEFENSE BEFORE THE MOB (21:27–22:29)

LITERARY STRUCTURE AND THEMES (21:27–22:29)

The passage consists of five sections. The first section describes the riot that followed Paul's appearance in the temple (21:27–32). The second recounts the Roman commander's intervention in an attempt to restore order (21:33–36). In the third section, Paul asks the commander for permission to speak to the assembled crowd (21:37–40). The fourth section records Paul's defense (*apologia*) before the mob (22:1–21). His speech ends abruptly and, therefore, consists only of an *exordium* (22:1–2) and a *narratio* (22:3–21) that covers Paul's life before his conversion (22:3–5), his experience on the Damascus road (22:6–11), his encounter with Ananias (22:12–16), and his vision in the Jerusalem temple (22:17–21). In the fifth section, the Roman commander questions Paul a second time and discovers that he is a Roman citizen.

- ***The Jews' Riot (21:27–32)***
- ***The Commander's Intervention (21:33–36)***
- ***Paul's Request (21:37–40)***
- ***Paul's Defense (22:1–21)***
- ***The Commander's Interrogation (22:22–29)***

EXPOSITION (21:27–22:29)

The pace of Luke's narrative slows even more as he recounts in detail the events of the day that resulted in Paul being taken into Roman custody. A week had passed since Paul and the Jerusalem elders had agreed on their plan to lessen the tensions that might result from Paul's presence in the city. Now, ironically, Paul's arrival to complete the rites to ensure that he did not defile the temple became the trigger for accusations that he had done so. Incited by Jews from Asia, the temple worshippers assaulted Paul and attempted to kill him. Only the intervention of the commander of the cohort of Roman soldiers stationed in the Antonia Fortress saved Paul.

Granted an opportunity by the commander, Paul addressed the assembled crowd in an effort to answer the charges against him that he taught Jews to abandon the Mosaic Law and Jewish tradition and that he had defiled the temple by bringing Greeks into the inner courts. He presented the facts of the case (the *narratio*), including his credentials as a persecutor of the church, the events of his conversion to become a follower of Jesus, and the vision by which Jesus directed him to go far away to the Gentiles. Although the details of 22:6–16 parallel the account of Paul's conversion in 9:3–18, that account is in the third person, while this one is in the first person, and Paul tailors his presentation for this Jewish audience. See 9:1–19a for a comparison of the two accounts.

Paul's Jewish listeners, however, considered the idea of going to the Gentiles so outrageous that they stopped listening to him. He was, therefore, unable to present his own proofs (*probatio*), formally answer the charges against him (*refutatio*), or summarize his case (*peroratio*). When the crowd refused to listen to Paul any longer, the Roman commander ordered him taken to the barracks of the Antonia Fortress in order to determine the cause of their outrage against him. Initially ordering a centurion to interrogate Paul by flogging, the commander stopped the interrogation when the centurion discovered that Paul was a Roman citizen. Troubled by the news about Paul's citizenship, the commander nevertheless continued holding

Paul until he could learn the facts of the case more accurately.

Luke's narrative connects this passage to other features of Acts. As he has drawn parallels between Paul and Peter, he now draws parallels between Paul and Stephen. Bauer summarizes those parallels and observes that Luke presents Paul as "virtually alone and largely abandoned like Jesus" (2021, 229–30). The passage provides a further contrast "between Jewish hostility and Roman justice" (Stott 1990, 345). It also marks what Larkin describes as "the last major spiritual and geographical turning point in Acts." He continues, "Never again will Paul return to Jerusalem for worship or witness" (1995, 313). From this point, Paul is in the hands of the Roman authorities and is on the journey to Rome that will occupy the remainder of the book.

The Jews' Riot (21:27–32)

When Paul enters the temple to complete his purification rites, Jews from Asia stir up the crowd against him, prompting the Roman garrison to respond to the riot.

21:27–29. Seven days later, when Paul was about to complete his purification rites (ὡς ἔμελλον αἱ ἑπτὰ ἡμέραι συντελεῖσθαι), Jews from Asia saw him in the temple (οἱ ἀπὸ τῆς Ἀσίας Ἰουδαῖοι θεασάμενοι αὐτὸν ἐν τῷ ἱερῷ), stirred up other worshippers (συνέχεον πάντα τὸν ὄχλον), seized him (ἐπέβαλον ἐπ᾽ αὐτὸν τὰς χεῖρας), and asked for help against him (κράζοντες, ἄνδρες Ἰσραηλῖται, βοηθεῖτε). The Jews leveled two accusations against Paul. First, they claimed that he taught "everyone everywhere" (πάντας πανταχῆ) against the people, the law, and the temple (κατὰ τοῦ λαοῦ καὶ τοῦ νόμου καὶ τοῦ τόπου τούτου). Second, they claimed that he had defiled the temple (κεκοίνωκεν τὸν ἅγιον τόπον τοῦτον) by bringing Gentiles into it (Ἕλληνας εἰσήγαγεν εἰς τὸ ἱερόν). They had previously seen Trophimus with Paul in the city (ἦσαν προεωρακότες Τρόφιμον τὸν Ἐφέσιον ἐν τῇ πόλει σὺν αὐτῷ) and concluded (ἐνόμιζον) that Paul had also brought him into the temple (εἰς τὸ ἱερὸν εἰσήγαγεν ὁ Παῦλος).

The purification process to which had Paul agreed included washings on the third and seventh days (Num. 19:12). It is unclear whether the "Jews from Asia" were specifically from the city of Ephesus or from the province of Asia in general (Dunn 1996, 288). Regardless, Paul's ministry in Ephesus had made an impact on the entire province (19:10) and, no doubt, explained their outrage. The verb συνέχω denotes causing dismay or confusion and echoes the noun συγχύσεως in 19:29 that described a similar uproar in Ephesus. Schnabel suggests that the imperfect tense of συνέχεον "places the emphasis on the process of the deliberate fomentation of trouble" (2012, 890).

The first charge against Paul was parallel to charges leveled against Stephen (6:11–14) and, before him, Jesus (Matt. 26:60–61; Luke 6:1–11; 13:10–17; 14:1–6). The second charge was an incorrect inference, as Luke makes clear by using the verb νομίζω, which carries the sense of regarding something as presumably true, but without particular certainty (L&N §31.29). The verb κεκοίνωκεν carries the sense of to profane or defile (BDAG s.v. "κοινέω" 2b, 552); the perfect tense is intensive and highlights the charge that "the effect of [Paul's] action is that the sacred space stands desecrated" (Bock 2007, 651). As Stott notes, the first charge was a half-truth, and the second charge was an untruth (1990, 344).

21:30–32. As a result of the Jews' actions, the whole city was aroused (ἐκινήθη ἡ πόλις ὅλη) and rushed to the temple precincts (ἐγένετο συνδρομὴ τοῦ λαοῦ). They seized Paul (ἐπιλαβόμενοι τοῦ Παύλου) and dragged him outside the temple (εἷλκον αὐτὸν ἔξω τοῦ ἱεροῦ), and the temple police immediately closed the gates (εὐθέως ἐκλείσθησαν αἱ θύραι). While the mob was seeking to kill Paul (ζητούντων αὐτὸν ἀπο κτεῖναι), the commander of the cohort stationed in the adjacent Antonia Fortress received a report (ἀνέβη φάσις τῷ χιλιάρχῳ τῆς σπείρης) that all of Jerusalem was in an uproar (ὅλη συγχύννεται Ἰερουσαλήμ). The commander immediately (ἐξαυτῆς) took solders and centurions (παραλαβὼν στρατιώτας καὶ ἑκατοντάρχας) and rushed down to the mob (κατέδραμεν ἐπ' αὐτούς), who stopped beating Paul (ἐπαύσαντο τύπτοντες τὸν Παῦλον) when they saw the commander and the solders (οἱ ἰδόντες τὸν χιλίαρχον καὶ τοὺς στρατιώτας).

The basic sense of the verb κινέω is "to set in motion" (BDAG s.v. "κινέω" 545). In this context, it should be translated as "to stir up against," "to start a riot," or "to cause an uproar" (L&N §39.44). Bock views "the whole city" (ἡ πόλις ὅλη) as hyperbole for "widespread" (2007, 652), although Schnabel disagrees that it is a Lukan exaggeration (2012, 894). The noun συνδρομή describes the action of assembling quickly (L&N §15.133). In this context, it carries the sense of "the formation of a mob by persons running together" (BDAG s.v. "συνδρομή" 967). When the mob dragged Paul "outside the temple" (ἔξω τοῦ ἱεροῦ), it was most likely into the Court of the Gentiles. The gates (αἱ θύραι) were most likely the gates that separated the inner court from the outer court. Schnabel suggests that the captain of the temple guard ordered the closing (2012, 894). Συγχύννω is an alternate form of συνέχω; see 21:27.

Luke portrays the violence of the crowd (21:35) vividly by recording that they seized Paul (21:30), dragged him outside the inner court (21:30), beat him repeatedly (21:32), and sought to kill him (21:31). Roman soldiers in the Antonia Fortress were responsible for maintaining order in the city. A χιλίαρχος was a military tribune who commanded one thousand soldiers. Those soldiers comprised a cohort (σπεῖρα), the tenth part of a legion. A centurion (ἑκατοντάρχης) commanded one hundred men, or the tenth part of a cohort. The fact that the commander recruited more than one centurion (ἑκατοντάρχας) might suggest that at least two hundred soldiers were involved (Bock 2007, 652), although Barrett is more cautious about the precise number (1998, 1022).

> **Courts of the Temple and the Antonia Fortress**
> The precincts of Herod's Temple encompassed a total area of twenty-six acres and included four courts. The outermost court was the Court of the Gentiles, which non-Jews could enter since it was not holy ground. Within the Court of the Gentiles, a wall with stone tablets at regular intervals prohibited foreigners from entering the inner court on penalty of death (cf. Josephus, *A.J.* 15.11.5). The smaller eastern portion of the inner court was the Court of the Women; the larger western portion was the Court of Israel. Within the Court of Israel was the Court of the Priests, where the sanctuary stood and where only priests could enter. The Antonia Fortress stood adjacent to the northwest corner of the outer court with two stairways leading to the Court of the Gentiles (cf. Josephus, *B.J.* 5.5.8). The fortress housed a garrison of one thousand Roman soldiers, led by a tribune, who could deal quickly with trouble in the temple, particularly during festivals. The Roman commander and soldiers who rescued Paul from the mob entered the Court of the Gentiles by one of the stairways from the Antonia Fortress.

The Commander's Intervention (21:33–36)

When the Roman commander is unable to determine the reason for the uproar, he orders the soldiers to take Paul into the barracks for safety.

21:33–34. The Roman commander had taken immediate action by gathering soldiers and centurions and rushing down one of the stairways that led to the Court of the Gentiles in order to restore order (21:32). Next, he approached (ἐγγίσας) Paul, arrested him (ἐπελάβετο αὐτοῦ), and ordered the solders to bind him with two chains (ἐκέλευσεν δεθῆναι ἁλύσεσι δυσί). When he began asking who Paul was (ἐπυνθάνετο τίς εἴη, inceptive imperfect) and what had happened (τί ἐστιν πεποιηκώς), some in the crowd kept on shouting one thing, while others were shouting something else (ἄλλοι δὲ ἄλλο τι ἐπεφώνουν ἐν τῷ ὄχλῳ). Because of the confusion (διὰ τὸν θόρυβον), the commander was not able to know for certain (μὴ δυναμένου δὲ αὐτοῦ γνῶναι τὸ ἀσφαλές) what was happening. So, he commanded the soldiers to lead Paul back to the barracks (ἐκέλευσεν ἄγεσθαι αὐτὸν εἰς τὴν παρεμβολήν).

When the commander ordered the soldiers to bind Paul, he fulfilled part of what the Spirit had told Paul awaited him (20:23). The two chains were most likely placed on each of Paul's hands and attached to a soldier on either side of him (Barrett 1998, 1022). The confusion Luke calls an "uproar" (τὸν θόρυβον) in which "some shouted one thing and some another" (ἄλλοι ἄλλο τι ἐπεφώνουν) echoes his description of the riot in Ephesus (19:32; 20:1). As Peterson notes, in Ephesus, Gentiles caused the uproar; in Jerusalem, Jews were the instigators (2009, 590). Many versions translate τὸ ἀσφαλές as "the truth" (e.g., ESV, NIV). The substantival adjective is "an expression that ensures certainty about something" with the nuance of digging out the facts (BDAG s.v. "ἀσφαλής" 2, 147; cf. 25:26). The "barracks" (παρεμβολή) were the headquarters of the Roman troops in the Antonia Fortress (21:37; 22:24; 23:10, 16, 32).

21:35–36. Because the crowd was acting so violently (διὰ τὴν βίαν τοῦ ὄχλου), the soldiers had to carry Paul (συνέβη βαστάζεσθαι αὐτὸν ὑπὸ τῶν στρατιωτῶν) when they reached the stairs to the barracks (ὅτε ἐγένετο ἐπὶ τοὺς ἀναβαθμούς). Meanwhile, the crowd kept on following (ἠκολούθει) and demanding that the soldiers remove Paul from the temple precincts (κράζοντες, αἶρε αὐτόν). The noun βία denotes a strong, destructive force (L&N §20.1).

It can describe violent natural forces that can destroy a ship (27:41), or it can describe the violence of a mob pressing forward, as is the case in this context (BDAG s.v. "βία" b, 175). The combination συνέβη βαστάζεσθαι is best translated as something like "it happened that he had to be carried" (LEB). The imperfect tense of ἠκολούθει highlights the persistence of the mob. Their cry "Away with him!" echoes the crowd's cries in response to Pilate's offer to release Jesus (Luke 23:18).

Paul's Request (21:37–40)

As he is being taken to the barracks, Paul asks the Roman commander for permission to address the people.

21:37–38. When the soldiers were about to lead him into the barracks (μέλλων τε εἰσάγεσθαι εἰς τὴν παρεμβολήν), Paul asked the commander whether he might be permitted to say something to him (εἰ ἔξεστίν μοι εἰπεῖν τι πρὸς σέ). Apparently surprised by Paul's question, the commander asked about Paul's ability to speak to him in Greek (Ἑλληνιστὶ γινώσκεις;). The commander thought that Paul might be an Egyptian revolutionary who had caused trouble in the city three years previously.

> ### The Commander's Question About Paul's Identity
> Since the uproar was created by Jews in the temple precincts, the commander naturally expected Paul to speak Aramaic. When Paul spoke to him in Greek, the commander reached a different conclusion. Since Egyptians regularly spoke Greek, and since Paul was the apparent focus of the disorder, the commander asked Paul whether he was an Egyptian insurrectionist who had caused trouble several years previously. Josephus reports that the individual in question had appeared in Jerusalem around A.D. 54–55, claimed to be a prophet, and led thirty thousand followers from the wilderness to the Mount of Olives in preparation for taking

Jerusalem by force. The Egyptian fled when Felix led Roman soldiers in defeating the uprising (*B.J.* 2.13.5; *A.J.* 20.8.6). The commander was, in effect, asking whether Paul had returned to cause more trouble. Marshall notes that Josephus's tendency to exaggerate explains the difference between thirty thousand and four thousand followers (1980, 351). Longenecker offers the alternate explanation of Josephus misreading Δ, which equals four thousand, for Λ, which equals thirty thousand (1981, 527).

21:39. In response to the commander's questions, Paul identified himself as a Jew (εἰμι Ἰουδαῖος) and a citizen (πολίτης) of Tarsus (Ταρσεύς), an important city of the province of Cilicia (τῆς Κιλικίας, οὐκ ἀσήμου πόλεως). He then asked for permission to speak to the crowd (ἐπίτρεψόν μοι λαλῆσαι πρὸς τὸν λαόν). "A not insignificant city" (οὐκ ἀσήμου πόλεως) is litotes (Culy and Parsons 2003, 420). Longenecker notes that similar phrases occur elsewhere—dating back to ancient Athens—to publicize a city's greatness (1981, 524).

21:40. When the commander gave him permission (ἐπιτρέψαντος αὐτοῦ), Paul stood on the stairs (ὁ Παῦλος ἑστὼς ἐπὶ τῶν ἀναβαθμῶν), motioned to the people with his hand, and in the resulting silence (πολλῆς δὲ σιγῆς γενομένης), began speaking (προσεφώνησεν, inceptive aorist). "Motioning with the hand" (κατέσεισεν τῇ χειρί) was a standard gesture of an orator (12:17; 13:16; 19:33; 26:1). Schnabel writes that "in the Hebrew dialect" (τῇ Ἑβραΐδι διαλέκτῳ) refers to Aramaic, which was "the main language spoken by the Jews of Palestine" (2012, 898). Buth and Pierce, however, argue at length that "Ἑβραΐς means Hebrew" (2014, 67). Regardless, Bauer correctly notes that Paul's ability to speak in the crowd's language gave him an initial hearing with them (2021, 230).

Paul's Defense (22:1–21)

Paul refutes the charges against him by recounting his life as a zealous Jew, his encounters with Jesus and Ananias, and the divine vision that sent him to the Gentiles.

22:1–2. Luke records Paul's brief introduction and then interrupts his account with a parenthetical comment that Paul's decision to speak in Aramaic (τῇ Ἑβραΐδι διαλέκτῳ) led the crowd to adopt an attitude of respectful quiet (μᾶλλον παρέσχον ἡσυχίαν). Paul used a formal Jewish address (ἄνδρες ἀδελφοὶ καὶ πατέρες) that echoes Stephen's in 7:2 (Longenecker 1981, 524). The NLT translates it as "brothers and esteemed fathers." In so doing, he demonstrated respect for his audience and identified himself as one of them. An ἀπολογία is a speech of defense (BDAG s.v. "ἀπολογία" 1, 117) in which the speaker "makes the case for what [he or she] is doing or believing" (Bock 2007, 659). The noun occurs again in 25:16; the cognate verb (ἀπολογέομαι) occurs in 24:10; 25:8; 26:1–2, 24. See 21:40 on "the Hebrew dialect." The combination παρέχειν ἡσυχίαν carries the sense of "quiet down" or "give a hearing," with a possible nuance of reverence, devotion, or respect. (BDAG s.v. "ἡσυχία" 2, 440).

22:3–5. Paul introduced himself using five descriptors. First, he was a Jew (Ἰουδαῖος). Second, he had been born in Tarsus of Cilicia (γεγεννημένος ἐν Ταρσῷ τῆς Κιλικίας). Third, although he was born in a city of the Diaspora, he had been nurtured spiritually and mentally (ἀνατεθραμμένος) in Jerusalem (ἐν τῇ πόλει ταύτῃ) under the guidance of the well-known rabbi Gamaliel (παρὰ τοὺς πόδας Γαμαλιήλ). Fourth, he had been instructed in living responsibly (πεπαιδευμένος) according to the strictness of the ancestral law (κατὰ ἀκρίβειαν τοῦ πατρῴου νόμου). Fifth, he was zealous for God (ζηλωτὴς ὑπάρχων τοῦ θεοῦ), just as all of them were (καθὼς πάντες ὑμεῖς ἐστε).

Paul's zeal for God was evident from his deeds. He persecuted (ἐδίωξα) members of "the Way" to the point of death (ἄχρι θανάτου). He arrested (δεσμεύων) both men and women (ἄνδρας τε καὶ γυναῖκας) and handed them over for imprisonment (παραδιδοὺς εἰς φυλακάς)—as both the high priest (ὁ ἀρχιερεύς) and the whole body of elders (πᾶν τὸ πρεσβυτέριον) could bear witness. He went so far as to secure letters to the Jews in Damascus (ἐπιστολὰς δεξάμενος πρὸς τοὺς ἀδελφοὺς εἰς Δαμασκόν) so that he could go there (ἐπορευόμην) and bring prisoners back to Jerusalem (ἄξων καὶ τοὺς ἐκεῖσε ὄντας δεδεμένους εἰς Ἰερουσαλὴμ) in order to have them punished (ἵνα τιμωρηθῶσιν).

Paul's point, as Bock suggests, was to make it clear to his audience that "I was where you are" (2007, 659). He was a faithful Jew, "standing well within the traditions of his people" (Dunn 1996, 291), who "was familiar with, and had access to, the highest levels of Jewish officialdom, probably being a member of the Sanhedrin himself, enjoying their confidence and securing their permission for his activities" (Peterson 2009, 598). Rather than teaching against the people and the law (21:28), he was, in fact, a zealous member of the Jewish people who had learned and upheld Jewish law and tradition and had previously enjoyed the support of the religious leadership in Jerusalem.

TEXTUAL ANALYSIS: The Syntax of Acts 22:3
Paul's description of his early life follows the three stages of a notable person: born (γεγεννημένος), brought up (ἀνατεθραμμένος), and educated (πεπαιδευμένος). The question that arises is how the modifying phrases relate to the adjectival participles. Does παρὰ τοὺς πόδας Γαμαλιήλ ("at the feet of Gamaliel") modify ἀνατεθραμμένος, which precedes it, or πεπαιδευμένος, which follows it? Does κατὰ ἀκρίβειαν τοῦ πατρῴου νόμου ("according to the strictness of the ancestral law") modify πεπαιδευμένος, which precedes it, or

ζηλωτὴς ὑπάρχων, which follows it? Scholars have suggested three primary combinations, but Longenecker's conclusion that the participles mark the heads of each segment seems most natural (1981, 525; cf. ASV, GNB, LEB, NKJV, NLT, NRSV). The resulting syntactical layout is:

I am a Jew,
> who has been born in Tarsus of Cilicia,
> who has been brought up in this city at the feet of Gamaliel,
> who has been instructed according to the ancestral law,
> who is zealous for God just as all of you are today.

22:6–11. Next, Paul moved to his heavenly vision on the Damascus road. His account paralleled Luke's narrative in 9:3–8 and was rich in OT overtones. The voice that spoke to him and the great light that flashed at noon (περὶ μεσημβρίαν) on the Damascus road had their sources in heaven (ἐκ τοῦ οὐρανοῦ), which served to highlight their divine origin. The glory of the light (ἀπὸ τῆς δόξης τοῦ φωτὸς ἐκείνου) was blinding (οὐκ ἐνέβλεπον) and it flashed around him (περιαστράψαι φῶς ἱκανὸν περὶ ἐμέ) in the same way that lightning accompanied God's OT presence (Exod. 19:16; Ezek. 1:14). Paul most likely understood it to be God's shekinah glory (Bock 2007, 661). Falling to the ground (ἔπεσά εἰς τὸ ἔδαφος) was a common OT response to a divine visitation (Ezek. 1:28; Dan. 8:17; 10:9). When he addressed Paul, Jesus repeated his name (Σαοὺλ Σαούλ) in the same way that God addressed prominent individuals in the OT (Gen. 22:11; 46:2; Exod. 3:4; 1 Sam. 3:4, 6). In response, Paul addressed the voice as "Lord" (κύριε), which was the Greek word the LXX used 6,156 times to translate the proper name יהוה (*TDNT* 3:1059). The verb τέτακται is a divine passive, and the perfect tense "shows that the order [is rooted in] the eternal thought of God" (Barrett 1998, 1039). Although Jesus identified himself as "Jesus the Nazarene"

('Ιησοῦς ὁ Ναζωραῖος), Paul clearly recognized that the one speaking to him was the one true God of Israel.

TEXTUAL ANALYSIS: "They saw the light, but they did not hear the voice."
One of the apparent discrepancies between Paul's accounts in chapter 9 and chapter 22 is the nature of what his companions did/did not see and what they did/did not hear. In 9:7, Luke records, "On the one hand, they heard the voice; on the other hand, they saw nothing." In 22:9, Paul says, "On the one hand, they saw the light; on the other hand, they did not hear the voice of the one who was speaking to me." As Peterson notes, in both passages, "Paul's companions shared the experience, while not enjoying the full revelation granted to Paul" (2009, 599). His companions saw the light (22:9) but did not see Jesus (9:7); they heard the sound of the voice (9:7) but did not understand the words it spoke. Since he was to be a witness to all people of what he had seen and heard (22:15), however, it was imperative that Paul both see the risen Christ and hear what he had to say.

22:12–16. Paul next recounted his meeting with Ananias after he entered the city. His account omitted Jesus's appearance to Ananias (9:10–16) and focused instead on Ananias's visit to the Damascus street called "Straight" (9:17–18). It was Ananias who informed Paul of his calling to be God's witness (ἔσῃ μάρτυς αὐτῷ) "to all men" (πρὸς πάντας ἀνθρώπους). Ananias was "devout according to the law" (εὐλαβὴς κατὰ τὸν νόμον), was respected by all the Jews in Damascus (μαρτυρούμενος ὑπὸ πάντων τῶν κατοικούντων Ἰουδαίων), and recognized Paul as a "brother" (Σαοὺλ ἀδελφέ), that is, as a member of God's covenant people. So, the individual through whom Jesus chose to communicate Paul's commission was "a respected, devout, law-abiding Jew" (Bruce 1988, 417).

The commission itself came from "the God of our fathers" (ὁ θεὸς τῶν πατέρων ἡμῶν),

who chose (προεχειρίσατο) Paul to know the divine will (γνῶναι τὸ θέλημα αὐτοῦ) and to hear and see "the Righteous One" (ἰδεῖν τὸν δίκαιον καὶ ἀκοῦσαι). See 3:14 for righteousness as a characteristic of Messiah. Peterson notes, "The fact that Paul recovered his sight (κἀγὼ αὐτῇ τῇ ὥρᾳ ἀνέβλεψα εἰς αὐτόν) acted as divine confirmation that what Ananias had to say to him was indeed a message from the Lord" (2009, 601). Calling on God's name (ἐπικαλεσάμενος τὸ ὄνομα αὐτοῦ) was an OT response of faith (Ps. 50:15; 91:15; Isa. 55:6; Jer. 29:12; 33:3; Joel 2:32). God had previously commissioned Israel to be his witnesses (Isa. 43:10; 44:8) and a light to the nations (Isa. 41:2; 42:6). So, Paul's commission came directly from the God of Israel and was fully aligned with his revealed will for his people.

22:17–21. Subsequently, Paul returned to Jerusalem (ὑποστρέψαντι εἰς Ἰερουσαλήμ). While he was praying in the temple (προσευχομένου μου ἐν τῷ ἱερῷ), he "fell into a trance" (γενέσθαι με ἐν ἐκστάσει; cf. BDAG. s.v. "ἔκστασις" 2, 309). In that trance, Paul saw the one who was speaking to him (ἰδεῖν αὐτὸν λέγοντά μοι), who commanded him to leave Jerusalem quickly (σπεῦσον καὶ ἔξελθε ἐν τάχει ἐξ Ἰερουσαλήμ) because the people would not accept his testimony (διότι οὐ παραδέξονταί σου μαρτυρίαν). Paul responded that the people knew his activities well, including imprisoning and beating Jesus's followers (ἐγὼ ἤμην φυλακίζων καὶ δέρων κατὰ τὰς συναγωγὰς τοὺς πιστεύοντας) and approving of Stephen's stoning (αὐτὸς ἤμην ἐφεστὼς καὶ συνευδοκῶν καὶ φυλάσσων τὰ ἱμάτια τῶν ἀναιρούντων αὐτόν). Jesus's instructions, however, were unequivocal. Paul was to leave (πορεύου), because the Lord was sending him "far away to the Gentiles" (ἐγὼ εἰς ἔθνη μακρὰν ἐξαποστελῶ σε).

As Dunn notes, this paragraph provides new information that is absent from both 9:3–18 and 26:12–18 (1996, 296). Most likely, the vision occurred during Paul's initial visit to Jerusalem after his conversion and contributed to his hurried departure for Tarsus (9:26–30).

The fact that Paul was praying in the temple both confirmed his practice of Jewish piety and refuted the charge that he spoke against the temple (21:28). Peterson notes that the vision in the temple also marked Paul as a prophet of the Lord (2009, 604; cf. 1 Sam. 3:1–18; Isa. 6:1–9). Paul's two visions—the first on the Damascus road, the second in the Jerusalem temple—echo the double instructions to Philip (8:26, 29) and the double instructions to Peter (10:10, 19).

Paul did not identify the speaker, but he again addressed him as "Lord" (κύριε), as on the Damascus road when he spoke with Jesus (9:5). His response suggests that he expected to make Jerusalem the venue for his ministry and that he expected the Jews to be the audience to whom he ministered (Longenecker 1981, 526), perhaps continuing the ministry Stephen had begun (Bauer 2021, 229). The doubled command to leave Jerusalem, however, makes it clear that God had other plans for him. Paul's point was that it was God himself who commanded him to leave Jerusalem and go far away to the Gentiles. As Stott writes, "those features of [Paul's] faith which had changed, especially his acknowledgment of Jesus and his Gentile mission, were not his own eccentric ideas. They had been directly revealed to him from heaven, the one truth in Damascus and the other in Jerusalem" (1990, 348).

The Commander's Interrogation (22:22–29)

When the commander orders the soldiers to interrogate him, Paul reveals his Roman citizenship and averts a flogging.

22:22–24. The Jewish crowd continued listening to Paul (ἤκουον αὐτοῦ) until he reported Jesus's instructions for him to go to the Gentiles (ἄχρι τούτου τοῦ λόγου; cf. 22:21). At that point, they began shouting again (ἐπῆραν τὴν φωνὴν αὐτῶν) and calling for Paul's death (οὐ καθῆκεν αὐτὸν ζῆν). Because they were shouting (κραυγαζόντων), throwing their garments (καὶ ῥιπτούντων τὰ ἱμάτια), and throwing dust into the air (κονιορτὸν βαλλόντων εἰς τὸν ἀέρα), the Roman commander intervened again. He commanded (ἐκέλευσεν) the soldiers to take Paul into the barracks (εἰσάγεσθαι αὐτὸν εἰς τὴν παρεμβολήν) and interrogate him by flogging (μάστιξιν ἀνετάζεσθαι αὐτόν).

The phrase οὐ καθῆκεν ("it is not fitting") carries the sense of something that is not right and has the implication of a moral judgment (L&N §66.1). The LEB translates the clause as "he should not be allowed to live." The three participles (κραυγαζόντων . . . ῥιπτούντων . . . βαλλόντων) are genitive absolutes of cause (Culy and Parsons 2003, 433). The present tense of the participles highlights the extended duration of the mob's action, as does the imperfect tense of ἐπεφώνουν. Bruce describes flogging as "a murderous instrument of torture" (1990, 460). See Josephus for details (*A.J.* 15.8.4; 16.8.1, 4). Barrett notes that it was "the recognized way of 'interviewing' a slave or other lower classes and possibly reluctant witnesses and finding out the truth" (1998, 1047). Most likely, the commander had not understood what Paul had said in Aramaic and was still unclear about the reason for the crowd's rage.

TEXTUAL ANALYSIS: "throwing their cloaks and flinging dust in the air"
The crowd's actions are somewhat unusual. More common would be "tearing their garments" (14:14) and "shaking off the dust of their feet" (13:51; 18:6). The verb ῥιπτέω (elsewhere ῥίπτω) can mean to wave or throw (L&N §16.10). In this context, the sense is most likely throwing something away forcefully (BDAG s.v. "ῥίπτω" 1, 906). In the OT, throwing dust was a gesture that accompanied cursing (2 Sam. 16:13) or a sense of dismay (Job 2:12). Bock concludes that the actions "symbolize waving away the sound of the words" (2007, 664); Larkin writes that to

the crowd "[Paul] is as repulsive as an unclean Gentile" (1995, 324). Regardless, the mob was expressing their anger and rejection of Paul and his words.

22:25–26. As the soldiers were tying him in preparation for flogging (ὡς προέτειναν αὐτὸν τοῖς ἱμᾶσιν), Paul asked the centurion in charge of the interrogation whether it was lawful to flog a Roman citizen who had not been charged with a crime (εἰ ἄνθρωπον Ῥωμαῖον καὶ ἀκατάκριτον ἔξεστιν ὑμῖν μαστίζειν;). As a result, the centurion reported Paul's status to the commander (ὁ ἄνθρωπος οὗτος Ῥωμαῖός ἐστιν) and asked whether he was certain of what he was about to do (τί μέλλεις ποιεῖν;). The verb προτείνω describes the act of stretching out someone who is about to be flogged (BDAG s.v. "προτείνω" 888); Louw and Nida suggest "tied in a stretched-out position" (L&N §16.21). The noun ἱμάς refers to a leather strap or thong (L&N §6.20). It could refer to straps of sandals or straps of a whip. The dative τοῖς ἱμᾶσιν could refer to means ("with straps") or purpose ("for straps") with the latter referring to the act of flogging. Barrett views the second understanding as "probably correct" (1998, 1047).

See 16:37 on Roman citizenship. The proper judicial process for Roman citizens included the formulation of charges and penalties, a formal accusation, and a hearing before a magistrate (Longenecker 1981, 528). When he asked whether it was permitted to flog a Roman citizen who was ἀκατάκριτον ("uncondemned"), Paul was pointing out that the soldiers had not followed proper judicial procedure. Furthermore, Roman citizens were exempt from flogging (Bruce 1988, 420). Cicero wrote, "To bind a Roman is a crime; to flog him is an abomination; to slay him is almost an act of murder" (*Verr.* 2.5.66). The commander was about to perpetrate a serious injustice against Paul.

22:27–29. In response to the centurion's report, the commander approached (προσελθών) Paul and asked him for confirmation of his status (λέγε μοι, σὺ Ῥωμαῖος εἶ;). When Paul responded positively (ναί), the commander asked him how he had obtained his citizenship. As soon as the commander understood Paul's status (εὐθέως), the soldiers who were about to flog him (οἱ μέλλοντες αὐτὸν ἀνετάζειν) withdrew (ἀπέστησαν ἀπ᾽ αὐτοῦ). The commander then found himself in the unenviable position of having bound a Roman citizen without a trial (ὁ χιλίαρχος ἐφοβήθη ἐπιγνοὺς ὅτι Ῥωμαῖός ἐστιν καὶ ὅτι αὐτὸν ἦν δεδεκώς) and still without an answer as to why the crowd was demanding Paul's death (22:24). His solution was to keep Paul in custody until the Jewish Sanhedrin could examine him.

Longenecker notes that there were three ways to obtain Roman citizenship: to be someone of high social or governmental status, to perform some exceptional service for the empire, or to bribe a governmental official (1981, 528). The commander had clearly secured his citizenship through the third means (ἐγὼ πολλοῦ κεφαλαίου τὴν πολιτείαν ταύτην ἐκτησάμην). Paul, on the other hand, was born a citizen (ἐγὼ γεγέννημαι), which actually placed him on a higher social level than the commander (Schnabel 2012, 924). Although commentators have offered several explanations for how Paul's parents secured their citizenship (Dunn 1996, 299), Marshall concludes, "speculation is idle" (1980, 339).

THEOLOGICAL FOCUS

Acts 21:27–22:29 serves several functions in Luke's narrative. First, the passage explains how Paul came to be in Roman custody. How was it that an itinerant Jewish evangelist/missionary from Tarsus in Cilicia ended up under house arrest in rented quarters in Rome, awaiting an audience with the emperor? The answer to that question began with the riot in the Jerusalem temple. Second, the passage depicts the ultimate Jewish rejection of Paul and his message. His life was fully in line with his Jewish heritage, and his ministry was fully in line with God's will. Yet, the mob in the Court of the Gentiles refused to accept his testimony of divine call, commission, and vision. Third, in the metanarrative of Luke-Acts, that Jewish rejection culminates Paul's own journey to Jerusalem, just as Jewish rejection culminated the journey to Jerusalem of Jesus, who had told Paul that he not only would bear his name before both Jews and Gentiles but also would suffer many things for his name's sake.

Theologically, Acts 21:27–22:29 reinforces the continuity between the Christian faith and its Jewish origins. Bock writes, "the 'new' faith has 'old' roots" (2007, 655). Paul's heritage, upbringing, and education were Jewish to the core, as was his respect for the Jewish people, the Mosaic Law, and the Jerusalem temple. His call and commission followed the pattern of the visionary calling of the OT prophets. As Barrett notes, "[Paul's] conversion was within and not from Judaism" (1998, 1031). Even his vision of Jesus's command to go to the Gentiles was in line with God's mission for Israel. Dunn writes, "Paul's new direction in mission is in full accord with the will of Israel's God" (1996, 295).

Paul understood that continuity even if his accusers did not. Instead, they viewed his ministry as a threat. As was true in Philippi, Corinth, and Ephesus, although Christianity might be a threat to special interest groups, it did not threaten the public order and stability of the empire. As Bock notes, "Paul is not the problem . . . zealous Jews unjustly disturbed the peace" (2007, 650). Consequently, the Roman authorities—acting to restore the peace—delivered Paul from injustice and so demonstrated the protection and justice that should characterize God-appointed governing authorities (Rom. 13:1–7). They also provided an unexpected source of deliverance for God's suffering witness.

PREACHING AND TEACHING STRATEGIES

Exegetical/Theological Synthesis

Luke's first-century readers would have wanted to know how the Jews in Jerusalem would respond to Paul and his mission among the Gentiles. He had met opposition from the beginning of his ministry—Gentile opposition in Europe and Asia; Jewish opposition in Syria, South Galatia, Macedonia, and Achaia. Would he meet similar opposition in the religious center of Judaism? Would his former reputation as a persecutor of the Christian movement, including his work under the auspices of the recognized religious authorities, make any difference in how the non-Christian Jews in Jerusalem received him? If not, would God protect Paul as he had elsewhere, and how would he do it? Luke's account of Paul's assault by the Jewish mob and his deliverance by the Roman authorities provides answers to those questions and sharply contrasts Jewish injustice with Roman justice. Ultimately, it is Roman soldiers who deliver Paul from the violent intentions of his own people. The twenty-first-century audience shares the need to understand that God can and does use human authorities to protect his witnesses in the face of injustice. That audience needs to believe that God can open doors of deliverance in unexpected directions. In Paul's case, the doorkeeper was a Roman commander, who was acting to restore public order, was ignorant of the reason for the uproar, and narrowly avoided a miscarriage of Roman justice. Yet, God used that commander to deliver Paul from a violent death.

Preaching/Teaching Idea

God can open doors of deliverance in unexpected directions.

Contemporary Connections

What does it mean?

There is a double deliverance in this passage. Both are unexpected, and both are in God's providential hands. In the first, Paul faced certain death from an aggressive mob on the temple grounds ready to kill him. By an ironic twist, pagan Romans intervene to deliver God's servant Paul from God's chosen people Israel. No one could have anticipated that turn of events. Back at Caesarea, Paul proclaimed with great emotion he was prepared for imprisonment and even death (cf. 21:13). His friends responded, "Let the will of the Lord be done" (21:14). It was. God chose imprisonment for Paul this day, not death. Paul was delivered.

Paul's second deliverance preceded the first—it was his testimony of God's deliverance of him from darkness to light, from eternal death to glorious salvation. Paul loved to tell this story and readily shared it with the crowd. Paul was well established in Judaism and a persecutor of the Way and was surely the world's least likely convert. Even so, this God of providential surprises and infinite means, a God who could receive Stephen into glory but spare Paul another day, this God delivered Paul's soul. After that, these "little" deliverances like the one in Jerusalem seem easy.

Is it true?

There are multiple layers of parallels in this passage that make these scenes masterful. When Paul is charged with shirking law and temple, he shares that muddled accusation with Stephen. Both share it with Jesus. Unlike Stephen, for whose martyrdom Paul played a large role, Paul is spared death by a mob whose hands might have had Stephen's blood on them. Unlike Jesus, Paul's birthright as a Roman citizen affords him a higher earthly status than his Savior. Rome crucified Jesus, and Jerusalem Jews martyred Stephen. Rome, however, spares Paul from Jerusalem Jews. Paul is following in the footsteps of Jesus alongside Stephen, but with a different fate for now, because all are in the hands of the Lord who orchestrates all things.

Paul famously and beautifully declared, "If God is for us, who can be against us? He who did not spare his own Son but gave him up for us all, how will he not also with him graciously give us all things?" (Rom. 8:31–32). Paul's testimony of God's salvation in 22:3–21 is that "he who did not spare his own Son but gave him up for us all." Once that deliverance is secure, all others pale in comparison. The remarkable story of Roman soldiers saving Paul from certain death becomes one of many examples of "how will he not also with him graciously give us all things." God's great deliverance in his Son opens the way for all God's lesser, unexpected, gracious deliverances. Happy is the heart that experiences them all.

Now what?

God can deliver his people in unexpected ways. He did it for Paul; he does it for us today. Paul was ready in Christ to face the worst possible outcome (21:13). Are we? Have we counted the cost of following Jesus and acknowledging what it might mean for us? With an acceptance of God's sovereignty, Job challenged his wife: "Shall we receive good from God, and shall we not receive evil" (Job 2:10)? The church similarly acknowledged God's will to be done in Paul's situation (Acts 21:14).

Psalm 34:19 reminds us that "Many are the afflictions of the righteous, but the Lord delivers him out of them all." Afflictions can and do come to us. They are not rare; they come in multiples ("*many* are the afflictions"). As believers, we stand with Job, Paul, and a cloud of witnesses to embrace this reality. We do so with absolute faith that God delivers, in his unexpected ways and in his unexpected timing. It looked different for Stephen and Paul, for James and Peter. Whatever the ways and means and whenever the times, though, God's deliverance is sure and perfect.

Creativity in Presentation

I heard an excellent sermon years ago on the way the Bible often makes the case for trusting God "from the greater to the lesser." In other words, if God is able to do the greater (X), surely he is able to do the lesser (Y). For example, Jesus uses this approach in the Sermon on the Mount when he tells us that if God is able to do the greater far-reaching work of feeding every bird on the planet, surely he is able to do the lesser work of caring for his people who are far more valuable to him (Matt. 6:25–34).

New research estimates there are at least fifty billion birds worldwide and maybe as many as 430 billion. Compare that colossal number to the fractional number of not quite eight billion humans alive today. There are at least six birds for every person and up to fifty or more. Not a single bird on record has sown seed, reaped a harvest, or stored crops in a barn. Yet God feeds each one. That operation of foresight and planning hurts our brains when we try to imagine it. Jesus's point is that if God is able to orchestrate that provision for birds, tending to the fraction of people in his care is much easier to believe.

Making the case in this text from the greater to the lesser starts with Paul's great deliverance from sin and self in his salvation (22:1–21) and ends with his lesser deliverance from the mob bent on killing him (21:27–40) and his captors bent on torturing him (22:22–29). If God has done the greater work of sending his Son and securing our eternal deliverance, he is both able and willing to do the lesser work of a myriad of deliverances in our lives. They will not always look as dramatic and immediate as Paul's in this text. Remember, his life is spared, but he is still under captivity. God's deliverance, however, is always assured, in his way—in this life or in the life to come—and it often comes from unexpected places.

- Like Paul, we also face trouble and suffering relationally, physically, and spiritually (21:27–40; 22:22–29).

- God's big deliverance happens at our salvation (22:1–21).

- God's small-by-comparison deliverances may come to us from unexpected places (21:31–35; 22:22–29).

DISCUSSION QUESTIONS

1. How are the mob's charges and actions against Paul parallel to charges and action against Stephen and Jesus? What conclusions would you draw from the three episodes?

2. What was the commander's motive for rushing Romans soldiers into an uproar in the Jewish temple? What are some of the ways in which God can use current events to further his purposes?

3. What did Paul hope to accomplish by making his defense before the mob? Was it to change their minds, to defend the gospel, or to accomplish some other objective?

4. Why was the Jewish mob infuriated by Paul's account of his call, commission, and vision? Why was the idea of his going to the Gentiles such a flashpoint with them?

5. Why did Paul wait until what seems like the last minute to disclose his Roman citizenship? How might disclosing his status sooner have made the situation better or worse?

EXEGETICAL IDEA

Paul's defense before the Sanhedrin responded to the charges against him, defined the central theological issue of the gospel, and resulted in assurance from the Lord Jesus.

THEOLOGICAL FOCUS

Remaining faithful to the task God has assigned honors him and results in his assurance.

PREACHING IDEA

If you take a stand for Jesus by his power, he will stand by you.

PREACHING POINTERS

How do you know when you have effectively accomplished an assigned task? Do you measure success by faithfulness, completion, or positive results? What measure does God use? Can failure in our eyes be success in God's eyes? Paul's experience before the Sanhedrin suggests that the answer to the last question is a resounding "yes." On the face of it, Paul's defense before the council was a failure. The high priest ordered him punished. The members of the council rebuked him for losing his temper. The council discussion deteriorated into a theological free-for-all. The Roman commander ordered him returned to custody in the Antonia Fortress. Had he failed in the task assigned to him? If he had any doubts, Jesus's appearance and words put them to rest. As he had been faithful to the task God had assigned to him in Jerusalem, God would be faithful to enable Paul to fulfill the same task when he reached Rome.

People today should be able to relate to fact-finding investigations that sometimes involve emergency meetings, divisions over religious beliefs, and legal irregularities. The passage corrects hypocritical behavior or suggestions that it is acceptable to act contrary to established legal standards. It also corrects the belief that it is always possible to receive a fair hearing and the idea that a negative response is necessarily failure. It commends remaining faithful in difficult circumstances, discernment to know what topics to pursue with an audience, and trust in God's sovereign working. The objective in communicating the passage should be to help listeners understand that although telling the truth might not persuade opponents, it honors Jesus and results in his approval, so that they will remain steadfast in their testimony for him and trust in his sovereign care.

DEFENSE BEFORE THE SANHEDRIN (22:30–23:11)

LITERARY STRUCTURE AND THEMES (22:30–23:11)

Luke frames the passage with the circumstances that led to Paul's appearance before the Sanhedrin (22:30) and the vision that followed his appearance (23:11). The account of the appearance consists of five parts: Paul's opening statement that he is a law-abiding Jew (23:1), the high priest's reaction (23:2–6), Paul's declaration that he is on trial for his belief in the resurrection (23:6), the council's reaction (23:7–9), and the commander's decision to return Paul to the Antonia Fortress (23:10). There are no verbal parallels that mark the passage as an intentionally concentric structure, although Paul's declaration about the resurrection stands at the center of the paragraph. Since Paul was interrupted twice, his "defense" actually consisted of two key statements. The first "is a direct response to the charges that he teaches everyone everywhere against the people, against the law, and against the temple" (Schnabel 2012, 926; cf. 21:28). The second "changes[s] the focus . . . to the fundamental theological issue at stake" (Peterson 2009, 616).

- *The Circumstances (22:30)*
- *Paul's Opening Statement and the High Priest's Reaction (23:1–5)*
- *Paul's Declaration and the Council's Reaction (23:6–10)*
- *The Aftermath (23:11)*

EXPOSITION (22:30–23:11)

Rescued by the Romans from a violent Jewish mob, Paul found himself standing before the Jewish high council, exactly as Jesus (Luke 22:66–71), the Jerusalem apostles (4:5–23; 5:27–42), and Stephen (6:12–7:60) had. Although it was an informal meeting intended to gather information that the commander could use to determine the nature of the charges against him, Paul used it as an opportunity both to address those charges and, for the last time, to bear witness to the name of Jesus before the sons of Israel. Interrupted twice—once by the high priest and once by the members of the council—his comments divided the council to such a degree that the commander again feared for Paul's life and returned him to the Antonia Fortress. Lest Paul fear that his efforts in Jerusalem had been a failure or that being in Roman custody would somehow hinder him from visiting Rome as the Spirit has repeatedly testified, Jesus himself appeared and assured him not only that he had accomplished his task in Jerusalem but also that he would do the same in Rome. The passage concludes the church's witness in Jerusalem with Paul being rejected by the Jews but protected by the Romans.

The Circumstances (22:30)

In an attempt to determine the Jewish accusations against Paul, the Roman commander arranges for the Sanhedrin to examine him.

22:30. The Roman commander was still at a loss about the reasons for the uproar in the temple, and so acted the next day (τῇ ἐπαύριον) to determine the precise nature (γνῶναι τὸ ἀσφαλές) of the reasons the Jews were accusing Paul (τὸ τί κατηγορεῖται ὑπὸ τῶν Ἰουδαίων). He ordered the chief priests and the entire Sanhedrin to convene (συνελθεῖν τοὺς ἀρχιερεῖς καὶ πᾶν τὸ συνέδριον), released (ἔλυσεν) Paul, and ordered him brought down (καταγαγών) from the Antonia Fortress to stand before the council (ἔστησεν εἰς αὐτούς).

The present tense of the participle βουλόμενος highlights the commander's continued confusion, and the imperfect tense of the verb κατηγορεῖται highlights his expectation that the Jews would bring charges against Paul (Schnabel 2012, 924). See 21:34 for ἀσφαλές. Κατηγορέω is a technical term for bringing charges in court (BDAG s.v. "κατηγορέω" 1, 533). Bruce argues that in the procurator's absence, the commander of the Roman cohort could convene a meeting of the Sanhedrin (1988, 422). Barrett disagrees, but allows for the possibility that he could ask the group to serve as an informal fact-finding body (1998, 1056). The commander's act of "releasing" (ἔλυσεν) Paul reflects the law that protected a citizen from the disgrace of appearing publicly in bonds (Peterson 2009, 609). Schnabel notes that handing Paul over to the Jewish authorities "would be a violation of his status as a Roman citizen" (2021, 924). The meeting, therefore, is best understood as an unofficial, preliminary hearing to determine the charges against Paul for violating Roman law (Bock 2007, 668).

Paul's Opening Statement and the High Priest's Reaction (23:1–5)

When he declares that he has lived with a good conscience before God, the high priest's order to strike him leads Paul to invoke God's judgment and then explain his words.

23:1. As Peter did with the lame man in the temple (3:4) and as Stephen did with Jesus standing at God's right hand (7:55), Paul "fixed his gaze" (ἀτενίσας) on the members of the council (τῷ συνεδρίῳ) and made his opening statement. In response to the suggestion that he taught against the Jewish people, the Mosaic Law, and the Jerusalem temple (cf. 21:28), Paul declared that "with all good conscience" (πάσῃ συνειδήσει ἀγαθῇ) he continued to live as a law-abiding Jew (πεπολίτευμαι τῷ θεῷ ἄχρι ταύτης τῆς ἡμέρας). See 10:4 for ἀτενίζω and 4:5 for συνέδριον. With the phrase ἄνδρες ἀδελφοί (1:16; 2:29, 37; 7:2, 26; 13:15, 26, 38; 15:7, 13; 22:1), Paul "addressed the the members of the council . . . as a Jew speaking to fellow Jews" (Peterson 2009, 612).

Johnson notes that συνείδησις is "a thoroughly Pauline word" (1992, 396; cf. Rom. 2:15; 9:1; 13:5; 1 Cor. 8:7, 10, 12; 10:25–29; 2 Cor. 1:12; 4:2; 5:11; 1 Tim. 1:5, 19; 3;9; 4:2; 2 Tim. 1:4; Titus 1:15). Paul uses it here with the same sense as in Romans 2:15, "their conscience and thoughts either accuse them or tell them they are doing right" (NLT). Although the verb πολιτεύομαι can have the specific sense of "to be a citizen" (BDAG s.v. "πολιτεύομαι" 1, 846; cf. Phil. 1:27), more generally, it can denote "to conduct one's life in relation to others" (L&N §41.34; cf. 2 Macc. 26:1; 3 Macc. 3:4; 4 Macc. 5:16). The dative τῷ θεῷ denotes either reference ("with reference to God") or rule ("in conformity with God's standard"). "Until this day" (ἄχρι ταύτης τῆς ἡμέρας) makes it clear that Paul still considered himself to be living in conformity with God's standards for his people.

23:2–3. The high priest reacted to Paul's statement by ordering (ἐπέταξεν) those who were standing near Paul (τοῖς παρεστῶσιν αὐτῷ) to strike his mouth (τύπτειν αὐτοῦ τὸ στόμα). In turn, Paul invoked divine judgment on the high priest, because although he was supposedly judging Paul according to the standard of the law (σὺ κάθῃ κρίνων με κατὰ τὸν νόμον), he had ordered an action that was contrary to the law (παρανομῶν κελεύεις με τύπτεσθαι). To punish someone before a verdict was rendered was to judge unjustly (Lev. 19:15; cf. Larkin 1995, 327). As Dunn notes, "Paul is more law-abiding than the high priest" (1996, 304).

Ananias was a notoriously unscrupulous high priest (Barrett 1998, 1058; cf. Josephus, *A.J.* 20.9.1–4). Commentators have suggested several motives for his order to strike Paul (Larkin 1995, 326), although Luke provides no explanation. Paul's response—"God is going to strike you, you whitewashed wall!" (ESV)—invokes divine judgment on Ananias for disobeying God's command. The idea of God striking someone for disobedience (τύπτειν σε μέλλει ὁ θεός) echoes Deuteronomy 28:22 (LXX), and the description "whitewashed wall" (τοῖχε κεκονιαμένε) echoes Ezekiel 13:8–16. Peterson suggests, however, that the latter idea is closer to Jesus's denunciation of the religious leaders' hypocrisy in Matthew 23:27–28 (2009, 613). Josephus records Ananias's subsequent death at the hands of revolutionaries early in the uprising against Rome (*B.J.* 20.19.6–9). Was that death God's execution of the judgment Paul had invoked?

23:4–5. When they heard Paul's words, the members of the council who were standing near Paul (οἱ παρεστῶτες)—and who had probably just struck him—charged Paul with speaking to the Ananias in a highly insulting manner (τὸν ἀρχιερέα τοῦ θεοῦ λοιδορεῖς; cf. L&N §33.393). Paul explained that he did not know that the speaker was the high priest (οὐκ ᾔδειν . . . ὅτι ἐστὶν ἀρχιερεύς) and immediately placed himself under the authority of Exodus 22:28, which prohibited the people from speaking evil against their leaders (ἄρχοντα τοῦ λαοῦ σου οὐκ ἐρεῖς κακῶς).

When members of the council rebuked him, Paul explained, "I did not know that he was the high priest" (ESV), which raises the question of how he could have made such a statement. The four primary suggestions are that Paul's poor eyesight prevented him from seeing clearly who had made the statement (Stott 1990, 352), that Paul spoke in irony because the high priest had not acted in line with OT law (Dunn 1996, 304; Marshall 1980, 364), that Paul did not know the high priest by sight because he had not recently been in Jerusalem (Bruce 1988, 427; Longenecker 1981, 531; Schnabel 2012, 927), or that Paul had not taken into account Ananias's position as high priest when he spoke (Larkin 1995, 328; Polhill 1992, 419). Regardless, when rebuked, Paul immediately acknowledged that he had broken the apodictic law against cursing a ruler of the people (Exod. 22:28).

Paul's Declaration and The Council's Reaction (23:6–10)

When Paul declares that he is on trial because of his belief in the resurrection, the Pharisees and Sadducees engage in a heated debate, and the commander returns Paul to the barracks.

23:6–8. As a Pharisee, Paul knew (γνούς) that the council included both Sadducees (τὸ ἓν μέρος ἐστὶν Σαδδουκαίων) and Pharisees (τὸ ἕτερον Φαρισαίων). His declaration that he was a Pharisee (ἐγὼ Φαρισαῖός εἰμι) and that he stood before the council because of his belief in the resurrection (περὶ ἐλπίδος καὶ ἀναστάσεως νεκρῶν ἐγὼ κρίνομαι) placed the central theological issue of Jesus's resurrection before the council, split his audience (ἐσχίσθη τὸ πλῆθος), and ignited a theological dispute between the two parties (ἐγένετο στάσις τῶν Φαρισαίων καὶ Σαδδουκαίων).

Paul's letters bear witness to his background as a Pharisee (Phil. 3:5). His statement that he was "a son of Pharisees" (υἱὸς

Φαρισαίων) could refer to a line of ancestors or to his upbringing and education under Gamaliel (22:3). Peterson views the latter as more likely (2009, 616). The phrase "hope and resurrection" (ἐλπίδος καὶ ἀναστάσεως) is either an instance of hendiadys ("hope in the resurrection"; cf. Bruce 1988, 465), or the conjunction is epexegetical ("hope that is the resurrection"; cf. Larkin 1995, 328). Although the meeting of the council was an informal hearing, Paul characterized his appearance before the council as "being judged" (ἐγὼ κρίνομαι). See Wallace for the use of the genitives in the phrase στάσις τῶν Φαρισαίων καὶ Σαδδουκαίων (GGBB, 139). Τὰ ἀμφότερα commonly refers to two ("both") as in Luke 5:38 and 6:39 (BDAG s.v. "ἀμφότεροι" 1, 55), although it can also refer three or more ("all") as in Acts 19:16 (L&N §59.26).

Division over the Resurrection

The dispute that erupted between the Pharisees and the Sadducees was over theology. According to Josephus, the Pharisees believed in fate, human free will, the immortality of souls, the eternal punishment of the wicked, and the resurrection of the righteous (*A.J.* 18.1.3; *B.J.* 2.8.14). The Sadducees believed that the soul died with the body, that the written law alone was valid, that acts of good and evil were the result of human choice, and that there was neither eternal reward nor eternal punishment (Josephus, *A.J.* 18.1.4; *B.J.* 2.8.14). See Bock for an extended discussion of Luke's comment that the Sadducees denied the existence of angels and spirits (2007, 671–72). Dunn suggests that Paul made his declaration because he saw "that no useful exchange is in prospect and no realistic defense can hope to succeed" (1996, 302). Peterson, however, points out that the "definition of the main question" was part of the *narratio* in a forensic address and that the theme of the resurrection runs throughout Paul's defense speeches (2009, 615, 619; cf. 24:14–16, 21; 26:6–8, 22–23; 28:20).

23:9–10. As the commotion increased (ἐγένετο κραυγὴ μεγάλη), some of the scribes from the party of the Pharisees (τινὲς τῶν γραμματέων τοῦ μέρους τῶν Φαρισαίων) stood up (ἀναστάντες), protested strongly (διεμάχοντο) that they found nothing wrong in what Paul had said (οὐδὲν κακὸν εὑρίσκομεν ἐν τῷ ἀνθρώπῳ τούτῳ), and raised the possibility that a spirit or an angel might have spoken to him (εἰ πνεῦμα ἐλάλησεν αὐτῷ ἢ ἄγγελος;). The intensity of the dispute (πολλῆς γινομένης στάσεως) led the Roman commander to fear (φοβηθείς) that the council members might tear Paul apart (μὴ διασπασθῇ ὁ Παῦλος ὑπ' αὐτῶν). In response, he commanded the soldiers (ἐκέλευσεν τὸ στράτευμα) to remove Paul from the meeting (ἁρπάσαι αὐτὸν ἐκ μέσου αὐτῶν) and return him to the barracks (ἄγειν εἰς τὴν παρεμβολήν). Once again, Luke highlights Paul's innocence (cf. 16:37–39; 18:12–17; 19:37–38), and the Roman authorities act as his protectors in the face of Jewish violence and injustice.

The Aftermath (23:11)

On the following night, the Lord appears to Paul in a vision, affirms his witness in Jerusalem, and confirms that he will also bear witness in Rome.

23:11. It was not a spirit or an angel who had spoken to Paul previously; it was the risen Lord Jesus (9:3–6; 22:6–10, 17–21). Now, on the night following (τῇ ἐπιούσῃ νυκτὶ) his defense before the Sanhedrin, the Lord again stood at Paul's side (ἐπιστὰς αὐτῷ ὁ κύριος) and spoke words of encouragement. As Paul had testified regarding Jesus in Jerusalem (ὡς διεμαρτύρω τὰ περὶ ἐμοῦ εἰς Ἰερουσαλήμ), he would do the same in Rome (οὕτω σε δεῖ καὶ εἰς Ῥώμην μαρτυρῆσαι).

The verb θαρσέω ("take courage," ESV) denotes the quality of being firm or resolute in the face of danger or adverse circumstances (BDAG s.v. "θαρσέω" 444). See 20:21, 24 for the seriousness and solemnity implicit in διαμαρτύρομαι.

See 19:21 for δεῖ as pointing to the divine necessity of Paul bearing witness both in Jerusalem and in Rome. Barrett writes, "Paul did not use a clever trick in the Sanhedrin to get out of trouble, but he has borne the witness he was intended to bear" (1998, 1068). As he had been faithful to Jesus in the past, Paul could believe that Jesus would be faithful to sustain his witness in whatever events might come his way in the future.

THEOLOGICAL FOCUS

Acts 22:30–23:11 serves two narratival functions. First, the passage closes the door on Paul's—and the church's—witness to Israel. Like the Jerusalem apostles and Stephen before him, he stood on trial before the Sanhedrin. Like Jesus, he experienced rejection not only by the Jewish people but also by their religious leaders. Also like Jesus, the judicial process demonstrated his innocence. From this point forward, Jerusalem and the Jewish people exit the narrative as the action moves to Caesarea, Malta, and Rome. Second, the passage continues Paul's protection by the Roman authorities. As a result of the council's divided reaction, he returns to Roman custody, where he remains for the remainder of the book. As he has experienced violence and injustice at the hands of the Jews, he experiences protection and justice at the hands of the Romans. The commander's continuing search for the exact nature of the Jewish accusations against Paul demonstrates that the issues are theological and no threat to Roman law or authority.

Theologically, Acts 22:30–23:11 highlights the continuity of Christianity with Judaism, both in Paul's testimony that he lived with a good conscience before God and in his declaration that he was on trial for the hope of the resurrection. Although Paul's belief was specifically in Jesus's resurrection, that belief was the logical extension of the OT testimony and a tenet of faith for at least a segment of the Jews. The passage also continues the theme of faithful witness in the face of opponents who are unwilling to consider the facts but are perfectly willing to resort to violence to suppress alternate views. Finally, the passage continues the theme of God's divine guidance and assurance to his witnesses in general—the Jerusalem apostles (5:19–20), Stephen (7:55–56), Philip (8:26–29), and Peter (10:9–20; 12:7–11)—and Paul in particular (9:3–6; 16:6–10; 18:9–10; 20:22–23; 22:17–21).

PREACHING AND TEACHING STRATEGIES

Exegetical/Theological Synthesis

The members of the mob had been confused about the reason for the riot in the Court of the Gentiles (21:33–36). Although Roman law had prevented him from interrogating Paul about the charges against him (22:22–29), the commander still needed to know the facts of the case. Since the riot had occurred in the temple precincts, it was only logical to seek additional information from the Sanhedrin—the body responsible for religious, civil, and noncriminal matters related to the Jewish people. The council chamber outside the western wall of the temple, therefore, would be the next venue in which Paul would have the opportunity to defend himself. Luke's first-century readers would have wanted to know both about Paul's reception by the Jewish leadership and about how he would defend himself before that leadership. He had been rejected by the Jewish populace. Would he fare any better before the Jewish leadership? How would they respond? How would he defend himself? Would his strategy be effective? In fact, Paul was only able to speak two sentences as part of his defense. His opening statement spoke to the idea that he taught against the law, the people, and the temple by asserting that he continued to live as a law-abiding Jew. Interrupted by the high priest, he continued by declaring his belief in the resurrection, which brought the main theological issue to the forefront. Although the members of the council rejected his testimony,

Jesus appeared to Paul in a vision to affirm his witness and confirm that he would do the same in Rome. The twenty-first-century audience shares the need to know that although telling the truth in the face of opposition might not persuade their opponents, remaining faithful to the task Jesus has assigned honors him and results in his approval.

Preaching/Teaching Idea

If you take a stand for Jesus by his power, he will stand by you.

Contemporary Connections

What does it mean?
Opposition creates chaos. Paul's time in Jerusalem has been memorable. He was nearly beaten to death by a mob in our previous preaching section, only to be saved at the last minute by Roman soldiers. He was nearly tortured by flogging by these same soldiers. Now this preliminary hearing started with a punch in the mouth and ended with a violent argument that threatened to tear Paul apart once again. The whole scene was loud and chaotic and vehemently hostile to truth. All the while, there was One who was not clamoring, arguing, having an outburst of anger, divided over theology, or jealous and grasping for his way, his word, his turn to speak. Jesus is Lord of all and Lord of Acts. He breaks no reeds nor snuffs any wicks at the council itself. He does not need to. Rather, he appears glorious and stable and constant to Paul the following night. Jesus was orchestrating all events from Jerusalem on to Rome and he would have his way. He stood by Paul throughout the chaos and appeared in a vision to assure him.

Is it true?
The chaos caused by opposition touches every person in this scene, because sin touches every person in this scene. The high priest Ananias breaks the law in supposed pursuit of upholding the law, by ordering others to strike Paul before

the preliminary hearing got underway. The Sadducees and Pharisees make a pitiful display of hostility toward one another, letting Paul's single statement spark deep-seated anger between the groups. They bubble over uncontrollably. Even Paul seems to lose his temper in anger, sharply rebuking Ananias. When opposition comes, its chaos includes sinful responses from persecutor and persecuted alike.

The chaos makes the beauty of Jesus's faithfulness all the more precious. He embodies the trustworthy statement Paul quotes in his second letter to Timothy, "If we are faithless, he remains faithful, for he cannot deny himself" (2 Tim. 2:13). Three aspects of his faithfulness stand out in our passage. First, God has been faithful to all he promised Israel. Paul is able to report that he followed God's will "up to this day" (23:1). From persecutor to born-again believer, Paul has walked in step with God's plan of salvation from Israel to new Israel. Second, and central to the text, God has been faithful in raising Jesus from the dead. Paul's statement gets the Pharisees thinking that Paul might have heard from a spirit or angel (23:9). Even better, Paul saw Jesus. Third, God has been faithful to Paul (23:11). Faithful in fulfilling God's promises to Israel and faithful in following God's will for him, Jesus now faithfully stands by Paul, who has faithfully stood up for him.

Now what?
By now in Acts we have revisited the theme of persecution often and for good reason. Violent opposition is real in Acts and real in our world today. Yet there are many places and seasons where the church is not actively persecuted. Even so, opposition to faith exists and threatens to wreak chaos. Peter says that the desires of our flesh "wage war against your soul" (1 Peter 2:11). This struggle makes Jesus's faithfulness in our turmoil a precious gift to us now. We need all the ways Jesus is faithful in our text as we engage in our fight of faith. Jesus as the culmination of a salvation plan that has never wavered since

creation locates us and our hardships squarely within his millennia-old story of victory. Jesus, who has risen from the dead, has broken the bonds of our greatest enemy, and has made all lesser enemies tremble. Now this same Jesus, who stood with Paul in assurance, stands with us to give us courage in the fight.

Creativity in Presentation

To illustrate Jesus's stability, think of examples where chaos rages but something remains constant—an anchored ship in a storm, a calm general under attack, an athlete stepping into the arena for a championship game. Jesus himself used the illustration of a house built on rock; the house withstood torrential rain, flooding, and winds. Were the same house built on sand and not rock, it would have collapsed against those elements (Matt. 7:24–27). It was not the house's strength but the rock's that made it stand. An informal teaching venue might even have hearers attempt to build something to test its stability.

A lesson or sermon falls into two parts. First, set the stage of chaos from within and without. Show the opposition to Christ and Christians from without at the hands of the high priest, Pharisees, and Sadducees. Show opposition from within as persecutor and persecuted give in to what appears to be sin. Relate these dynamics to our own struggle for faith with our own opposition from outside ourselves in other people or circumstances and opposition from within in our sinful desires. The second part is Jesus's help to Paul and us from being "tossed to and fro by the waves and carried about by every wind of doctrine, by human cunning, by craftiness in deceitful schemes" (Eph. 4:14). Relate the three aspects of Jesus's faithfulness in the text—his fulfillment and continuation of the story of God in the world, his death and resurrection, and his present and active assurance and comfort of believers. He is faithful in the midst of the chaos that rages against us. As we stand in Jesus by his power, he graciously stands by us.

- Believers are called to stand firm in the face of serious opposition (22:30–23:10).

- Jesus stands faithfully by us giving us the strength we need (23:11).

DISCUSSION QUESTIONS

1. How did Paul's opening statement address the charges against him? Why did the high priest react to the statement as he did?

2. How did Paul's response compare with Jesus's response in similar circumstances? Was it appropriate? Why or why not?

3. Calvin writes that Paul's declaration about the resurrection "was not far from lying," and a later commentator views it a "a tactic not worthy of an apostle." How would you respond to those evaluations? Why?

4. Why did Paul's declaration create such a division in the council? Was the commander's concern about Paul's safety legitimate? Why or why not?

5. Why did Jesus appear to Paul after his meeting with the Sanhedrin? How would his words have been both a confirmation and an encouragement?

Acts 23:12–35

EXEGETICAL IDEA
When he receives a report about a Jewish conspiracy to kill Paul, the Roman commander transfers him to the governor's custody in Caesarea.

THEOLOGICAL FOCUS
God can and will use human agency to protect his people, but they must act wisely in response to the opportunities he provides.

PREACHING IDEA
Trust God's providential working, but act wisely while he works.

PREACHING POINTERS
Alexander Graham Bell said, "When one door closes, another opens." It is important to remember that God closes doors and opens windows to establish his purposes. The theological idea that lies behind the saying is the doctrine of God's providence, which the Westminster Shorter Catechism defines as "his most wise, and powerful preserving and governing of all his creatures, and all their actions." That is, God is continually at work to accomplish his purposes in the world. The version of the saying that applies most directly to Paul's situation in Acts 23:12–35, though, comes from Jeannette Walls: "When God closes a door, he opens a window . . . but it is up to you to find it." Jesus had promised Paul that he would reach Rome, but he was in custody in Jerusalem. The door that led to Rome seemed shut. Then, his nephew became aware of a Jewish plot to kill Paul. Paul found an open window in that news as he connected his nephew with the Roman commander, who arranged for his transfer to Caesarea. Paul's experience reminds us that God can and will use human agency to protect his people, but they must act wisely in response to the opportunities he provides.

People today should be able to relate to multiple details from the passage, including conspiracies among religious extremists, potential ambushes that call for protective details, insider information that comes from confidential sources, reports to superiors or supervisors, and spinning information to put yourself in the best possible light. The passage corrects using violence to solve problems, thinking that human actions can upset God's plans, and taking no action in the face of trouble. It commends using discernment in asking for help, being concerned for those in your care, acting promptly on information, and being faithful in acting on orders and information. The objective in communicating the passage should be to help listeners understand, on the one hand, that God can and will use human agency as part of his providential working, and on the other hand, that he expects his people to act wisely when he opens windows for them to ask for help.

TRANSFER TO CAESAREA MARITIMA (23:12–35)

LITERARY STRUCTURE AND THEMES (23:12–35)

The passage consists of four sections. The first section recounts the origin of a Jewish conspiracy to kill Paul (23:12–15). The second section describes how Paul's nephew became aware of the plot and reported it to the Roman commander (23:16–22). The third section records the commander's actions in responding to the news of the plot (23:23–30), including the letter he wrote to Felix, the procurator (23:26–30). The fourth section documents the events that led to Paul's lengthy imprisonment in Caesarea (23:31–35).

- ***The Jews' Conspiracy to Kill Paul (23:12–15)***
- ***Paul's Nephew's Report to the Commander (23:16–22)***
- ***The Commander's Response to the Plot (23:23–30)***
- ***Paul's Arrival in Caesarea (23:31–35)***

EXPOSITION (23:12–35)

Acts 23:12–35 is a transitional passage that records the circumstances of Paul's departure from Jerusalem and his arrival in Caesarea during the spring of A.D. 57. The events followed immediately upon Jesus's appearance to Paul (23:11), took place over two or three days (depending on the understanding of verses 31–32), and represented the first stage of Paul's journey to Rome. The inciting event in the narrative was a fourth plot against Paul (9:23–25; 9:29–30; 20:3). As Gaventa notes, this passage includes the most detailed account of the four (2003, 317) and so highlights the danger to Paul (Peterson 2009, 621). Once again, the events contrast Jewish opposition with Roman protection. At the center of the passage is the Roman commander's letter, which provides the "official Roman version" of the recent events in Jerusalem (Dunn 1996, 307). His assessment of the situation (23:29) echoes the previous declaration of Paul's innocence (23:9) and provides the fifth instance in which Luke makes it clear that the gospel is not a threat to public order or Roman law (16:35–40; 18:12–17; 19:35–41; 21:27–36).

The Jews' Conspiracy to Kill Paul (23:12–15)

More than forty Jews conspire to kill Paul and approach the leaders of the council with their plot.

23:12–13. The next day (γενομένης ἡμέρας), a group of more than forty (πλείους τεσσαράκοντα) Jews conspired (ποιήσαντες συστροφήν) against Paul. They placed themselves under a curse (ἀνεθεμάτισαν ἑαυτούς) that they would neither eat nor drink (μήτε φαγεῖν μήτε πίειν) until they had killed Paul (ἕως οὗ ἀποκτείνωσιν τὸν Παῦλον). Although συστροφή describes a "commotion" in 19:40, in this context it is synonymous with συνωμοσία and describes a "conspiracy" that is the product of a clandestine gathering (BDAG s.v. "συστροφή" 2, 979). The verb ἀναθεματίζω denotes the act of invoking divine harm if what is said is not true or if one does not carry out what has been promised (L&N §33.472). The LEB translates ἀνεθεμάτισαν ἑαυτούς as "bound themselves under a curse." In verse 14, ἀναθέματι ἀνεθεματίσαμεν includes a cognate dative emphasizing "the speaker's view that this was a very serious oath" (Culy and Parsons 2003, 446). Ἀναιρέω refers to killing by violence (BDAG s.v. "ἀναιρέω" 2, 64; cf. 10:39).

23:14–15. Next, the conspirators approached the chief priests and the elders (προσελθόντες τοῖς ἀρχιερεῦσιν καὶ τοῖς πρεσβυτέροις) and explained both their oath and their plan. They recommended that the leaders inform (ἐμφανίσατε) the commander and the council that they wanted to "make a more thorough examination of [Paul's] case" (NRSV, διαγινώσκειν ἀκριβέστερον). When the soldiers would bring Paul down to the council (καταγάγῃ αὐτὸν εἰς ὑμᾶς) but before he arrived (πρὸ τοῦ ἐγγίσαι αὐτόν), they would be prepared to kill him (ἕτοιμοί ἐσμεν τοῦ ἀνελεῖν αὐτόν). Διαγινώσκειν describes giving careful attention to facts or a subject as a basis for forming a judgment (BDAG s.v. "διαγινώσκω" 1, 227). Ἀκριβέστερον is a Lukan favorite in judicial settings (18:25–26; 23:20; 24:22) and connects to his stated purpose in writing his first volume (Luke 1:3).

Paul's Nephew's Report to the Commander (23:16–22)

When his nephew informs him about the planned Jewish ambush, Paul requests that the young man report the information to the Roman commander.

23:16–19. Paul's nephew (ὁ υἱὸς τῆς ἀδελφῆς Παύλου) somehow heard about the planned ambush (ἀκούσας . . . ἐνέδραν), entered the barracks (εἰσελθὼν εἰς τὴν παρεμβολήν), and reported (ἀπήγγειλεν) the plot to Paul. Paul then summoned one of the centurions (προσκαλεσάμενος...ἕνα τῶν ἑκατονταρχῶν), explained that the young man had something to report (ἔχει ἀπαγγεῖλαί τι), and requested that the centurion lead him to the commander (ἀπάγαγε πρὸς τὸν χιλίαρχον). The centurion responded by doing as Paul requested. In turn, the commander took the young man by the hand (ἐπιλαβόμενος δὲ τῆς χειρὸς αὐτοῦ), withdrew with him for a private conversation (ἀναχωρήσας κατ᾿ ἰδίαν), and began to inquire (ἐπυνθάνετο) what he had to report (τί ἐστιν

ὃ ἔχεις ἀπαγγεῖλαί μοι;). A νεανίας was a young man between the ages of twenty-four and forty (BDAG s.v. "νεανίας" 667). Bock suggests that the use of the diminutive νεανίσκος in verses 18 and 22 places Paul's nephew in his twenties (2007, 678).

23:20–22. The young man told the commander that the Jews had agreed (συνέθεντο) to ask him to bring Paul to the council on the next day for further examination. The commander, however, should not be persuaded (σὺ μὴ πεισθῇς) because a group of conspirators had concealed themselves in a suitable position for a surprise attack (ἐνεδρεύουσιν; cf. BDAG s.v. "ἐνεδρεύω" 1, 334). He repeated their vow not to eat or drink until they killed Paul and informed the commander that they were waiting for him to agree with the request by the Jewish leaders (εἰσιν ἕτοιμοι προσδεχόμενοι τὴν ἀπὸ σοῦ ἐπαγγελίαν). In response, the commander dismissed the young man (ἀπέλυσε τὸν νεανίσκον) after he had commanded (παραγγείλας) him to tell no one what he had reported (μηδενὶ ἐκλαλῆσαι ὅτι ταῦτα ἐνεφάνισας πρός με). Peterson notes that by repeating the plot and adding details Luke "effectively heightens the sense of danger for Paul" (2009, 621). Dunn observes that the young man turned to the Romans because he could expect no help from any of the Jews in Jerusalem (1996, 307).

The Commander's Response to the Plot (23:23–30)

In response to the young man's report, the commander arranges for Roman soldiers to bring Paul safely to Caesarea.

23:23–25. The commander instructed two centurions to deliver Paul safely (διασώσωσι) to Felix, the governor, in Caesarea. They were to prepare (ἑτοιμάσατε) a horse for Paul to ride (κτήνη παραστῆσαι ἵνα ἐπιβιβάσαντες τὸν Παῦλον) and assign a force to guard him. The force consisted of two hundred soldiers (στρατιώτας διακοσίους), seventy horsemen (ἱππεῖς ἑβδομήκοντα), and two hundred spearmen (δεξιολάβους διακοσίους). The party was to be ready to depart "by the third hour of the night" (ἀπὸ τρίτης ὥρας τῆς νυκτός), which Larkin places between 9:00 and 9:30 p.m. (1995, 333). The commander also composed a letter of explanation (γράψας ἐπιστολήν) to accompany Paul.

The verb διασῴζω denotes the act of rescuing or delivering from a hazard or danger (BDAG s.v. "διασῴζω" 237). The meaning of δεξιολάβος is uncertain (BDAG s.v. "δεξιολάβος" 217). Larkin suggests "holding in the right hand" as a literal translation (1995, 332; cf. Bruce 1990, 470). The association with the right hand might have led to the Vulgate's translation as "spearmen" (Barrett 1998, 1078) and Louw and Nida's definition as "soldiers armed with spears" (L&N §55.22). Another possibility is that the noun refers to individuals who led additional horses for the calvary (Peterson 2009, 623). Schnabel suggests "bowmen" or "archers" (2012, 936). On the size of the guard, Bock writes, "the number seems large, but the extent of the threat is something the tribune does not know, and the trip to Caesarea is filled with the possibility of attacks from other zealots" (2007, 681).

TEXTUAL ANALYSIS: "a letter having this form" Luke introduces the commander's letter with the phrase "a letter having this form" (ἐπιστολὴν ἔχουσαν τὸν τύπον τοῦτον). Marshall and Dunn conclude that Luke composed the letter following the form that was common at that time and summarized the probable content (Dunn 1996, 308; Marshall 1980, 308). Following Judge, Bruce, Larkin, and Schnabel argue that, in the papyri, the phrase refers to a verbatim account (Bruce 1990, 471; Larkin 1995, 335; Schnabel 2012, 936). Bock views it as a translation from an original in Latin (2007, 682). Peterson suggests that the letter was "the sort of document that would be preserved for the trial of Paul" (2009, 624). The verbatim understanding is probably best, and NLT reflects that understanding when it translates the phrase as "he wrote this letter."

23:26–30. The opening of the commander's letter (23:26) followed the standard form of sender (Κλαύδιος Λυσίας), recipient (τῷ κρατίστῳ ἡγεμόνι Φήλικι), and greeting (χαίρειν). The commander addressed Felix as "most excellent" (κρατίστῳ; cf. 24:3), which was an honorary form (BDAG s.v. "κράτιστος" 565) used to address a governor of a third-class province (Bruce 1990, 472). See uses of the same title to address Theophilus (Luke 1:1) and Festus (Acts 26:25). The body of the letter (23:27–30) summarized the events that led the commander to send Paul to Caesarea as well as his assessment of the Jews' accusations against Paul. The commander's account generally followed the narrative account of the events of 21:27–23:30, although with three omissions and a variation that placed him in a good light. The letter lacked the usual closing.

It was natural for the commander to omit Paul's defense before the mob, since what Paul said was not germane to the case. The commander was not present when Jesus appeared to Paul, and omitting that event was also understandable. The commander adjusted his account of the events surrounding his discovering Paul's citizenship, however, to his own advantage. He omitted the fact that he ordered an interrogation by flogging in violation of Roman law, and he connected his act of rescuing Paul to the knowledge that Paul was a Roman citizen. The participle μαθών is best understood as adverbial to ἐξειλάμην, expressing either time ("when I learned") or cause ("because I learned"). On either understanding, "the tribune is improving on the facts for the benefit of his superior" (Barrett 1998, 1083).

Central to the commander's letter (23:28–29) was his succinct statement that when he brought Paul to the Sanhedrin to determine the reason the Jews were accusing him (ἐπιγνῶναι τὴν αἰτίαν δι' ἣν ἐνεκάλουν αὐτῷ), he found (εὗρον) that the members repeatedly raised accusations (ἐγκαλούμενον, iterative imperfect) related to controversial questions about Jewish law (περὶ ζητημάτων τοῦ νόμου αὐτῶν). According to Roman law, therefore, Paul had done nothing that deserved either death or imprisonment (μηδὲν ἄξιον θανάτου ἢ δεσμῶν ἔχοντα ἔγκλημα). His assessment added yet another witness to Luke's argument that Christianity was no threat to Roman law or to public order (16:35–40; 18:12–17; 19:35–41; 21:27–36).

Letter	Event	Narrative
23:27a	The Jews seized Paul. (συλλημφθέντα ὑπὸ τῶν Ἰουδαίων)	21:27–30
23:27b	The Jews sought to kill Paul. (μέλλοντα ἀναιρεῖσθαι ὑπ' αὐτῶν)	21:31
23:27c	The commander rescued Paul. (ἐπιστὰς σὺν τῷ στρατεύματι ἐξειλάμην)	21:32–36
--	Paul spoke to the mob.	21:37–22:21
--	The commander ordered an interrogation by flogging.	22:22–24
23:27d	The commander learned that Paul was a Roman citizen. (μαθὼν ὅτι Ῥωμαῖός ἐστιν)	22:25–29
23:28	The commander brought Paul to the council. (κατήγαγον εἰς τὸ συνέδριον αὐτῶν)	22:30
23:29	The council presented no actionable charge. (μηδὲν ἄξιον θανάτου ἢ δεσμῶν ἔχοντα ἔγκλημα)	23:1–10
--	Jesus appeared to Paul.	23:11
23:30a	The commander learned about a plot against Paul. (μηνυθείσης μοι ἐπιβουλῆς εἰς τὸν ἄνδρα ἔσεσθαι)	23:12–22
23:30b	The commander sent Paul to Felix. (ἔπεμψα πρὸς σέ)	23:23–30

Paul's Arrival in Caesarea (23:30–35)
When the soldiers deliver Paul to the governor, he agrees to hear the case as soon as Paul's accusers arrive.

23:31–33. Following their orders (κατὰ τὸ διατεταγμένον αὐτοῖς), the soldiers took (ἀναλαβόντες) Paul and led (ἤγαγον) him to Antipatris, where the party split. The foot soldiers returned to the barracks (ὑπέστρεψαν εἰς τὴν παρεμβολήν) in Jerusalem, while the horsemen continued with Paul (ἐάσαντες τοὺς ἱππεῖς ἀπέρχεσθαι σὺν αὐτῷ). When they arrived in Caesarea (εἰσελθόντες εἰς τὴν

Καισάρειαν), they delivered the letter to the governor (ἀναδόντες τὴν ἐπιστολὴν τῷ ἡγεμόνι) and presented Paul to him (παρέστησαν τὸν Παῦλον αὐτῷ).

Antipatris was thirty-five to forty miles from Jerusalem and thirty to thirty-five miles from Caesarea; see Barrett for different estimates of the distances (1998, 1086). Since the city was on the coastal plain in predominantly Gentile territory, the dangerous part of the journey was behind the travelers (Schnabel 2012, 939). It is unlikely that the foot soldiers were able to cover the entire distance from Jerusalem to Antipatris in one night. It is probably best, therefore, to understand διὰ νυκτός as "overnight into the next day" (Bock 2007, 683) and τῇ ἐπαύριον ("on the next day") as referring to the day after

they arrived in Antipatris (contra Barrett 1998, 1086).

23:34–35. The governor read the letter (ἀναγνούς) and asked Paul about his province of origin (ἐπερωτήσας ἐκ ποίας ἐπαρχείας ἐστίν). When he learned that it was Cilicia (πυθόμενος ὅτι ἀπὸ Κιλικίας), he agreed to hear the case (διακούσομαί σου) as soon as Paul's accusers arrived in Caesarea (ὅταν καὶ οἱ κατήγοροί σου παραγένωνται). Until that time, he ordered Paul to be placed under guard in Herod's Praetorium (κελεύσας ἐν τῷ πραιτωρίῳ τοῦ Ἡρῴδου φυλάσσεσθαι αὐτόν). Πυνθάνομαι denotes the process of acquiring information by questioning (4:7; 10:18; 23:19, 20). The information concerning Paul's home province was important for determining where

The historic archways of the aqueduct at Caesarea along the coast of Israel. Public domain.

the Roman authorities would hear his case. At that time, Cilicia was part of the province of Syria, and it was not necessary to return its citizens there for trial (Sherwin-White 1963, 56). Herod the Great built the Praetorium, and the Romans made it their administrative headquarters for the province (Barrett 1998, 1088).

Felix

Felix was a freed slave, whom Claudius promoted to procurator of Judea in A.D. 52–53 (Josephus, *A.J.* 20.7.1; *B.J.* 2.12.8; cf. Bruce 1990, 470). He subsequently married Drusilla, the daughter of Herod Agrippa I and the sister of Herod Agrippa II (Barrett 1998, 1080; Acts 24:24). His term in office was a period of civil upheaval, and his attempts to maintain public order alienated the Jewish people (Josephus, *A.J.* 20.8.5–8). Nero recalled him in A.D. 58–59 (Josephus, *A.J.* 20.8.9; cf. Bruce 1990, 484; contra Barrett 1998, 1117) and replaced him with Festus. Tacitus characterized Felix as "a master of cruelty and lust who exercised the powers of a king with the spirit of a slave" (Tacitus, *Hist.* 5.9). Marshall suggests that his decision to hear the case in Caesarea rather than returning Paul to his home province of Cicilia would gain favor with the Jews by reducing the distance they needed to travel to present their accusations and would relieve the governor of Syria of having to deal with a comparatively minor case (1980, 373).

THEOLOGICAL FOCUS

Acts 23:12–35 is a transitional passage in multiple ways. Geographically, Paul moved from Jerusalem to Caesarea. Culturally, Paul moved from the Jewish world to the Roman world. Judicially, Paul moved from the sphere of religious authority to the sphere of civil authority. Narratively, Paul's transfer to Caesarea marked the first stage of his journey to Rome in fulfillment of Jesus's reassurance (23:11). Apologetically, the commander's letter that accompanied Paul during the transfer provided the official Roman version of the events in Jerusalem; set the stage for Paul's hearings before Felix, Festus, and Herod Agrippa II; and affirmed his status as having done nothing worthy of death or imprisonment (23:29).

Theologically, Acts 23:12–35 again contrasts Jewish opposition and danger with Roman protection and safety and provides insight into the Christian's relationship with governing authorities. The Jews stand as negative examples of authoritarian religious intolerance and extremism that is willing to resort to violence to further its aims. The Roman commander stands as a positive example of reputable civil authority that deals justly with the citizens under its jurisdiction. He heard Paul's nephew's concerns respectfully and held those concerns in confidence (23:19–22). He acted promptly to protect Paul (23:23–24). He understood that he was not competent to judge Paul in matters related to religion (23:28). He evaluated Paul's civil case impartially (23:29). Special interest groups did not manipulate him (23:20–21). Instead, he respected and followed standard civil procedure by referring Paul's case to the governor (23:30).

Although Paul is a minor actor in the passage, he understood, respected, and appealed to the civil authorities as God providentially opened the window for him to do so (23:16–17). As God used human agency to protect him, Paul acted wisely to work within the established civil order and guard himself from injustice. Acts 23:12–35 is the third of four instances in which Paul appealed to civil authorities to protect the church or himself. In Philippi, he appealed to his Roman citizenship to protect the new church (16:37–39). In Jerusalem, he again appealed to his Roman citizenship to avoid potential death (22:24–26). In this passage, by requesting that the centurion present his nephew to the commander, he avoided the ambush the Jews had planned (23:17–22). Later in Caesarea, he would again appeal to his Roman citizenship to avoid being returned to Jewish custody (25:8–12).

PREACHING AND TEACHING STRATEGIES

Exegetical/Theological Synthesis

Following his lively but inconclusive hearing before the Sanhedrin, Paul's case remained unresolved. The commander had returned him to the safety of the Antonia Fortress, but what would the next steps be? Would the Romans continue to protect Paul? In the meantime, Jesus had appeared to him and reassured him that he would bear witness in Rome as he had in Jerusalem. Under current circumstances, however, that possibility seemed remote. How would Jesus fulfill that promise? Luke's first-century readers would have wanted to know the answers to these questions and more. The account of the events that resulted in Paul's transfer to Caesarea answers them and demonstrates how God works providentially to protect his people and accomplish his purposes. The Jews set out to kill Paul. Instead, they began a chain reaction that made him even more secure. Paul's nephew learned of the plot and reported it to the Roman commander. The commander mobilized 470 foot and horse soldiers to make certain Paul would arrive safely in Caesarea. The soldiers delivered Paul to the Roman governor, who agreed to hear Paul's case and placed him in protective custody in the administrative headquarters for the province. All were agents whom God used to ensure that Paul would escape Jerusalem and arrive safely at the first stop on his journey to Rome. Paul had his own part to play as he worked within the Roman authority structure to alert the commander to the increased danger he faced. Luke's account of Paul's transfer to Caesarea instructs his twenty-first-century audience, who shares the need to understand that God can and will use human agency to protect his people, but they must act wisely in response to the windows God opens for them to work within the established judicial system.

Preaching/Teaching Idea

Trust God's providential working, but act wisely while he works.

Contemporary Connections

What does it mean?

No sooner did Jesus appear to Paul and encourage him than the Jews concocted a serious plot against his life. If Paul was ever going to make it to Rome as Jesus had promised, something miraculous must happen to stop forty conspirators, bound by an oath, collaborating with the highest powers in Jerusalem, literally dead set on killing Paul. Something miraculous was precisely what happened. Jesus was not guessing that Paul would make it to Rome and have more work to do (23:11). Jesus was promising. God's providence works on promises, not guesses. He will achieve his ends. Unlike Peter's miraculous deliverance from death row under Herod in Acts 12, however, God's providential working looked different in Paul's case. There were no bright lights, no angels, and no unlocked prison doors. This time it was something that was almost too coincidental to believe. Providentially, Paul's own nephew heard about the Jewish plot. Paul did not have the luxury of passivity under God's sovereignty. He acted quickly, he put his nephew in touch with the tribune, and God delivered him.

Is it true?

This passage displays the dance of divine sovereignty and human responsibility. Ephesians 1:11 says that God "works all things according to the counsel of his will." That is *what* God does. Just *how* God does it has taken on all shapes and sizes in the book of Acts alone. According to Peter's sermon at Pentecost, God used "the hands of lawless men" to achieve his "definite plan" of the death of his son (2:23). God was sovereign over his plan. Wicked men were responsible for innocent blood. In another place, God told Paul at Corinth, "I have many in this city who are my people" (18:10). God sovereignly chose those who would believe. Paul was responsible to reach them with the good news. Those dances of sovereignty and responsibility match our passage. God makes a definite plan. Paul is responsible to act within that God-directed plan. When Paul does, God provides tremendous help. In the face of forty untrained men hoping to ambush Paul, the tribune provides two hundred soldiers, two hundred spearmen, and seventy horsemen. It is not a fair fight. It never was. Jesus declared Paul's safety and achieved it in an overwhelming display.

Now what?
We live out our Christian life in this dance of divine sovereignty and human responsibility. We trust and we obey. We believe and we act. We lay hold of God's promises and live out of them. We are like the early church praying for God's gift of boldness (4:29), only to act out of God's answer to our prayer by speaking boldly (4:31). Like Paul, we find ourselves listening intently to Jesus and then preparing to be surprised at the way he fulfills his purposes as we put one foot in front of the other in faith. If we neglect sovereignty and responsibility, we harm our Christian walk. If we live with all sovereignty and no responsibility, passivity sets in. We can so presume on God's sovereignty that we shrug off our God-given responsibility to pray, trust, and act. If we live with all responsibility and no sovereignty, we throw ourselves into an anxious frenzy of activity. We act as if our walk and work depend on us, and we lose the divine power readily available to us. Instead, we are to trust that God will work—and then get busy in this God-dependent work.

Creativity in Presentation
Luke's narrative does not mention God, Jesus, the Holy Spirit, or the church. Paul's world is shifting, and no doubt he is feeling anxious. Surely our hearers can relate to such seasons in their own lives. We wonder whether God is near, whether he hears, or whether he cares. We join the psalmists with more questions than answers.

After such a bleak introduction, we move to the verse that precedes our section: Acts 23:11. The Lord tells Paul to "take courage," presumably because he lacked courage. He then tells Paul that he will protect him. So, we already know the end of the story before it really gets underway. I had an annoying friend in middle school who loved spoiling endings. He would see a movie opening night and blab about it the next day. He would grab an assigned book, read the last few pages, and blurt out the key climax. It was irritating. Here in our text, knowing the ending is life-giving.

The message unfolds in its key movements of the story under the banner of God's providential plan: there is a conspiracy that seems like it cannot fail (23:12–15), a surprise discovery by Paul's very own nephew (23:16–22), and a safe resolution (23:23–35). There is danger, discovery, and deliverance. The danger of the conspirators echoes the many ways we today face danger. The discovery is a beautiful provision of God's orchestrating and Paul's acting on that help. The deliverance is God's answer to his own promise. As we trust in God's providential working, we walk wisely in the paths he provides.

- Believers often face danger (23:12–15).

- Believers are eager to discover God's providential working (23:16–22).

- Believers enjoy God's deliverance (23:23–35).

DISCUSSION QUESTIONS

1. What do the conspirators' plans suggest about the depth of the Jewish opposition to Paul and the lengths to which they were willing to go to eliminate him?

2. Why do you think the commander was willing to listen to Paul's nephew and give credence to what he had to say?

3. Were the commander's arrangements in response to hearing about the plot excessive? Why or why not?

4. Was the commander's report to the governor accurate? How did he shape his report to place himself in the best light?

5. How would you evaluate the governor's actions when the soldiers delivered the commander's letter and Paul to him? How do those actions anticipate his later actions (cf. 24:22–27)?

Acts 24:1–27

EXEGETICAL IDEA
During his two years of imprisonment in Caesarea, Paul defended himself against Jewish accusations while also declaring the gospel to the Roman governor.

THEOLOGICAL FOCUS
Jesus's faithful witnesses are able not only to refute false charges effectively but also to present the gospel boldly before whatever audience they might face.

PREACHING IDEA
The best defense is a good offense.

PREACHING POINTERS
"The best defense is a good offense" is an axiom that applies to multiple areas of human endeavor, including sports, military combat, and business. In law, it refers to defense counsel's strategy of attacking the prosecution's case to persuade the jury that there is reasonable doubt about the defendant's guilt. It can also apply to the defense of the gospel, as Paul's appearance before Felix, the Roman governor of Judea, demonstrates. Facing formal legal accusations presented before the governor by a polished professional advocate, Paul effectively refuted those accusations, proved that there was no legal case against him, and boldly proclaimed the gospel to the governor, both during the legal proceedings and during frequent personal conversations with Felix and his wife, Drusilla. He turned the defense of his activities on behalf of Jesus into a proclamation of the good news about Jesus by applying the axiom that the best defense is a good offense.

People today can relate to various aspects of judicial proceedings, including prosecutors, defendants, adjourning the proceedings while waiting for additional evidence or witnesses, and delayed verdicts. They should also relate to trying to decide between two choices, attempting to gain favor with others, and the potential for securing financial gain through unscrupulous means. The passage corrects attempts to manipulate the judicial process for personal gain, any tendency to think that Christians must passively accept false charges against them, and the idea that it is possible to accept only part of the gospel message. It commends holding fast to the truth in the face of lies, making an active defense against false charges, seizing the opportunities God provides to present the gospel, and maintaining a faithful witness in the face of difficult circumstances. The objective in communicating the passage should be to help listeners understand that it is possible both to refute false charges effectively and to present the gospel boldly before authority figures, so that they will stand boldly for truth and the gospel regardless of the audiences they might face.

DEFENSE BEFORE FELIX (24:1–27)

LITERARY STRUCTURE AND THEMES (24:1–27)

The passage consists of three sections. In the first, the advocate Tertullus appears before Felix, the Roman governor, to present the Jews' accusations against Paul (24:1–9). Most early manuscripts do not include verse 7 as originally part of the section. In the second, Paul refutes the charges, and Felix defers a decision on the case (24:10–23). The third describes Paul's subsequent appearances before Felix in which he presents the gospel to the governor (24:24–27).

Schnabel provides an analysis of the two embedded speeches (2012, 948). Tertullus's brief speech before Felix (24:2b–8) consists of an *exordium* (24:2b–4), a *narratio* (24:5), a *probatio* (24:6), and a *peroratio* (24:8). Paul's longer defense speech (24:10–21) consists of an *exordium* (24:10), a *narratio* (24:11), a *probatio* (24:12–13), a *refutatio* (24:14–18), and a *peroratio* (24:19–21). Dunn notes the legal terminology that runs throughout the passage (1996, 310).

- ***The Jews' Accusations (24:1–9)***
- ***Paul's Defense (24:10–23)***
- ***Felix's Delay (24:24–27)***

EXPOSITION (24:1–27)

Acts 24:1–23 narrates the first of three appearances Paul made before Roman governmental authorities during his imprisonment in Caesarea. The hearing before Felix includes a presentation on behalf of his Jewish accusers (24:1–9), Paul's defense in response to the charges against him (24:10–21), and Felix's decision to defer a verdict (24:22–23) despite the fact that Paul refuted each of the charges and demonstrated that there was no case against him.

Tertullus's Prosecution (24:2–8)	Paul's Defense (24:10–21)
Felix is qualified to judge the case (24:2–4). Maintained law and order (24:2b) Instituted many reforms (24:2c)	Felix is qualified to judge the case (24:10–11). Judged for many years (24:10) Knew the timing of events (24:11)
Paul stirs up trouble throughout the empire (24:5a).	There was no trouble (24:12–13). No dispute (24:12a) No agitation (24:12b) No venue (21:12c) No proof (24:13)
Pauls leads a dangerous new movement (24:5b).	There is no danger (24:14–16). Same worship (24:14a) Same truth (24:14b) Same hope (24:15) Same ambition (24:16)

Tertullus's Prosecution (24:2–8)	Paul's Defense (24:10–21)
Paul even tried to desecrate the temple (24:6).	There was no desecration (24:17–18). Presented alms (24:17a) Presented offerings (24:17b) Completed purification (24:18a) Caused no uproar (24:18b)
Paul will confirm his guilt under cross-examination (24:8).	There is no case (24:19–21). No eyewitnesses (24:19) No unrighteous act (24:20) No legal issue (24:21)

The passage concludes with a brief description of Paul's continued interaction with Felix during the remaining two years of the latter's time in office (24:24–27). Paul had incorporated a summary of the gospel into his defense speech (24:14–16), but subsequent conversations with Felix gave him repeated opportunities to speak more fully with the governor and his wife about "faith in Messiah Jesus . . . righteousness and self-control and future judgment" (24:24–25). The closing section contrasts Felix's character with Roman justice in the preceding sections and highlights the fact that Paul's time in Roman custody "operates as the continuation of his missionary work, not the end or suspension of it" (Skinner 2003, 138).

The Jews' Accusations (24:1–9)

Serving as a legal advocate for the Jewish religious leaders, Tertullus presents their case against Paul before Felix, the Roman governor.

24:1–2a. Five days (πέντε ἡμέρας) after Paul's arrival in Caesarea (23:32–35), Ananias and a group of Jewish elders (μετὰ πρεσβυτέρων τινῶν) arrived. Since a group of people needed a representative to speak on their behalf (Marshall 1980, 376), "a certain Tertullus" (Τερτύλλου τινός) accompanied them. As their legal advocate (ῥήτορος), it was his task to present their case against Paul to the governor (ἐνεφάνισαν τῷ ἡγεμόνι κατὰ τοῦ Παύλου), which he began to do (ἤρξατο κατηγορεῖν) after the governor summoned Paul (κληθέντος αὐτοῦ).

Longenecker counts the five days from Paul's arrest in the temple (1981, 539), but five days from Paul's arrival in Caesarea is a more natural understanding (Schnabel 2012, 951). Although there is some discussion about Tertullus's background (Barrett 1998, 1093; Bruce 1990, 475), as Peterson notes, "The evidence is insufficient to be convincing either way" (2009, 630). Bock suggests that the best translation for ῥήτορος is "legal advocate" (2007, 689). Barrett suggests that the presence of Tertullus "implies that the High Priest and his colleagues could not use Greek well enough to use it in court" (1998, 1094). The verb ἐμφανίζω denotes the act of making a formal report before authorities on a judicial matter (L&N §56.8). The present tense of κατηγορεῖν suggests an extended discourse, although the content Luke includes is brief and, most likely, a summary. Schnabel provides helpful information on the process used for recording summaries of court proceedings (2012, 949).

24:2b–4. Tertullus began his speech by setting out Felix's credentials to hear the case. He cited the "great peace" and "reforms" the nation had experienced through the governor's "foresight." As a result, "in every way and everywhere" (πάντη καὶ πανταχοῦ) the group he represented welcomed (ἀποδεχόμεθα) those benefits "with all thanksgiving" (μετὰ πάσης εὐχαριστίας). He then promised that his remarks would be brief (παρακαλῶ ἀκοῦσαί σε ἡμῶν συντόμως) to avoid troubling the governor (ἵνα μὴ ἐπὶ πλεῖόν σε ἐγκόπτω; cf. L&N §25.185) in his kindness (τῇ σῇ ἐπιεικείᾳ).

Peterson notes links between the credentials Tertullus cited and the charges he would bring (2009, 631). Felix's thoughtful planning and management (προνοίας) had brought widespread (πανταχοῦ) peace (εἰρήνη) and reforms (διορθωμάτα) to the people he governed. Paul's history of stirring up rebellion across the empire (24:5) would threaten that happy state of affairs. Felix would, therefore, need to demonstrate kindness (ἐπιείκεια)—the quality of "reasonableness, fairness, in general and especially perhaps in a judge who is prepared not to break the laws but to give them an understanding, non-legalist interpretation" (Barrett 1998, 1096)—as he considered the case before him. Larkin notes the contrast between the portrait Tertullus paints and historical reality, "In fact, the governor's rule brought anything but a long period of peace, and there is no record of many improvements" (1995, 337).

24:5–6. Tertullus leveled three charges against Paul. First, he was a "public menace" (λοιμός; cf. BDAG s.v. "λοιμός II" 2, 602), who stirred up rebellion (κινοῦντα στάσεις) among all the Jews (πᾶσιν τοῖς Ἰουδαίοις) across the empire (τοῖς κατὰ τὴν οἰκουμένην). Second, he was the leader (πρωτοστάτην) of the sect of the Nazarenes (τῆς τῶν Ναζωραίων αἱρέσεως). Third, he had tried to desecrate the temple (τὸ ἱερὸν ἐπείρασεν βεβηλῶσαι). The third offense had initially led the Jews to seize Paul (ἐκρατήσαμεν).

The charges were a mixture of truth and misrepresentation. Paul's ministry in Ephesus had, indeed, led to a public disturbance (στάσις), but he had no part in inciting the mob (19:23–41). Paul was, indeed, a prominent figure in the Christian movement. The fact that the Romans had crucified the founder of that movement for claiming to be a king (Luke 23:2, 38) and "stirring up people all over Judea" (Luke 23:5) added seriousness to the charge, because Felix had recently put down another messianic movement led by an Egyptian perpetrator (21:38). The charge of trying to desecrate the temple was a restatement of the claim the Jews from Asia had made (21:28), but it had no basis in fact. It was, however, a serious charge in that the Romans had granted the Jews the right to execute the death penalty on anyone who defiled the temple (Josephus, *B.J.* 6.2.4). Paul would refute each of the charges in short order.

TEXTUAL ANALYSIS: The Textual Variant in 24:6–8

Western and Byzantine manuscripts include an extended variant after ὃς καὶ τὸ ἱερὸν ἐπείρασεν βεβηλῶσαι, ὃν καὶ ἐκρατήσαμεν in 24:6 that comprises verses 6b–8a. The addition reads "and we wanted to judge him according to our Law. 7 But Lysias the commander came along and with much violence took him out of our hands, 8 ordering his accusers to come before you" (NASB). Although the variant provides a Jewish argument that they had the right to judge the case, there is no apparent transcriptional reason for omitting it, and earlier manuscript evidence (P74, ℵ, A, B) supports the shorter reading.

24:8–9. Tertullus brought his speech to a close by declaring that when Felix cross-examined Paul concerning these matters (ἀνακρίνας περὶ πάντων τούτων), he would be able to learn for himself (δυνήσῃ . . . ἐπιγνῶναι) about the accusations they were making (ὧν ἡμεῖς κατηγοροῦμεν αὐτοῦ). Marshall suggests that Tertullus was indicating that Paul would incriminate himself under cross-examination (1980, 376). When their spokesperson concluded, the high priest and elders joined (συνεπέθεντο) in affirming (φάσκοντες; cf. BDAG s.v. "φάσκω" 1050) the claims he had made.

Paul's Defense (24:10–23)

Although Paul effectively refutes the Jewish charges and demonstrates that there is no case against him, the governor decides to delay a verdict.

24:10–11. Paul also noted Felix's credentials for hearing the case, although he cited different factors. The first factor was that Paul knew Felix had been a judge of Jewish affairs for many years (ἐκ πολλῶν ἐτῶν ὄντα σε κριτὴν τῷ ἔθνει τούτῳ). Felix would, therefore, be able to evaluate the charges against him objectively. The second factor was that Felix had the sources to confirm that the events in question had occurred within the space of twelve days (οὐ πλείους εἰσίν μοι ἡμέραι δώδεκα ἀφ᾽ ἧς ἀνέβην προσκυνήσων εἰς Ἰερουσαλήμ). Felix would, therefore, understand that twelve days was too short a time for Paul to organize a revolt, especially after he had been absent from the city for several years (24:17).

Νεύσαντος αὐτῷ τοῦ ἡγεμόνος is a genitive absolute of antecedent time. Νεύω denotes the act of signaling to someone by means of part of the body, especially by means of the head or hands (L&N §33.485). Some English versions translate the verb as "to nod" (e.g., ESV). The "many years" most likely included the years Felix had served as an aide to Cumanus, the previous governor (Barrett 1998, 1101). Ἐπιστάμενος is adverbial of cause. Εὐθύμως refers to being encouraged (L&N §25.147). See 22:1 for ἀπολογέομαι and the cognate noun ἀπολογία. Προσκυνήσων indicates the purpose for which Paul had originally come to Jerusalem.

TEXTUAL ANALYSIS: "It is not more than twelve days"

Commentators have calculated the "twelve days" Paul mentions in 24:11 in different ways. Marshall (1980, 376) and Witherington (1998, 710) conclude that the time frame began with Paul's arrival in Jerusalem and ended with his arrest in the temple. Bruce (1988, 443) and Larkin (1995, 339), however, conclude that the phrase describes the length of time from Paul's arrival in Jerusalem and until his arrival in Caesarea. The latter approach adopts the following timeline.

Day	Scripture	Event
1	21:17	Arrival in Jerusalem
2	21:18–25	Meeting with James and the elders
3	21:26	Visit to the temple (first day of purification)
9	21:27–22:29	Riot in the temple (seventh day of purification)
10	22:30–23:11	Hearing before the Sanhedrin
11	23:12–30	Discovery of the plot against Paul
12	23:31–35	Arrival in Caesarea

24:12–13. Paul opened his defense by presenting four pieces of evidence to address the charge that he was a troublemaker. First, he was not the source of any dispute, because he did not argue with anyone (πρός τινα διαλεγόμενον). Second, he was not the cause of any agitation, because he did not stir up a crowd (ἐπίστασιν ποιοῦντα ὄχλου). Third, he had caused no trouble in the temple (οὔτε ἐν τῷ ἱερῷ), in the local synagogues (οὔτε ἐν ταῖς συναγωγαῖς), or in the city at large (οὔτε κατὰ τὴν πόλιν). Fourth, his accusers were not able to present any proof of their allegations against him (παραστῆσαι δύνανταί σοι περὶ ὧν νυνὶ κατηγοροῦσίν μου).

24:14–16. Paul continued by acknowledging (ὁμολογῶ) that he followed the way that was being called a "party" (τὴν ὁδὸν ἣν λέγουσιν αἵρεσιν)—in this case, the party of the Nazarenes (τῶν Ναζωραίων; cf. 24:6). Although that movement was relatively new, at least compared to other groups such as the party of the Sadducees (cf. 5:17) and the party of the Pharisees (cf. 15:5), it was just as Jewish. First, the members worshipped the ancestral God of the Jews (λατρεύω τῷ πατρῴῳ θεῷ). Second, they believed everything that had been written in the OT law and prophets (πιστεύων πᾶσι τοῖς κατὰ τὸν νόμον καὶ τοῖς ἐν τοῖς προφήταις γεγραμμένοις). Third, they looked forward to the future hope in God (ἐλπίδα ἔχων εἰς τὸν θεόν) that there would be a resurrection of both the righteous and the unrighteous (ἀνάστασιν μέλλειν ἔσεσθαι δικαίων τε καὶ ἀδίκων). Fourth, they did their best (ἀσκῶ) to have a good conscience before God and men (ἀπρόσκοπον συνείδησιν ἔχειν πρὸς τὸν θεὸν καὶ τοὺς ἀνθρώπους). As Stott writes, Paul "worshipped the same God . . . believed the same truths . . . shared the same hope . . . and cherished the same ambition" as mainstream Judaism (1990, 361). Since the Romans recognized Judaism as a legal religion, and since the movement of which Paul was a part was Jewish in its worship, theology, eschatology, and ethics, neither that movement nor Paul posed any threat to Roman law or government.

24:17–18. The third charge against Paul was that he had desecrated the temple. That charge was patently false. Paul explained that he came (παρεγενόμην) to Jerusalem to present alms and offerings (ἐλεημοσύνας ποιήσων . . . καὶ προσφοράς) as an observant Jew. Further, he had faithfully completed the purification process (ἡγνισμένον) that was necessary for him to be present in the temple after his time in Gentile lands (21:24). Finally, he was present in the temple "without a crowd or a disturbance" (NET, οὐ μετὰ ὄχλου οὐδὲ μετὰ θορύβου)

when the Jews seized him. The NIV translates ἐλεημοσύνας ποιήσων εἰς τὸ ἔθνος μου as "to bring my people gifts for the poor." The phrase most likely refers to the money from the Gentile churches that Paul brought with him to Jerusalem (Rom. 15:26). If so, it is the only reference to the collection in Acts (Marshall 1980, 379).

24:19–21. Paul concluded his defense with a summary of the reasons there was no case against him. First, his accusers had called no eyewitnesses against him. Certain Jews from Asia (τινὲς ἀπὸ τῆς Ἀσίας Ἰουδαῖοι) had originally accused him of bringing Gentiles into the temple (21:27–28), and they should have been present before Felix (οὓς ἔδει ἐπὶ σοῦ παρεῖναι) if they had any proof of their accusations against him (εἴ τι ἔχοιεν πρὸς ἐμέ). Second, none of his accusers were able to say that they found him guilty of an unrighteous act (εἰπάτωσαν τί εὗρον ἀδίκημα) when he stood before the Sanhedrin (στάντος μου ἐπὶ τοῦ συνεδρίου). Third, the true issue was theological, not civil—he was being judged concerning the resurrection of the dead (περὶ ἀναστάσεως νεκρῶν ἐγὼ κρίνομαι). With no witnesses, no charges, and no civil offense, it should have been clear to Felix that there was no case under Roman law against Paul.

24:22–23. Although there was no case against Paul, Felix adjourned (ἀνεβάλετο) the hearing without issuing a ruling. His explanation was that he would hear the evidence Lysias, the Roman commander, would provide before deciding the case. In the meantime, he instructed a centurion (διαταξάμενος τῷ ἑκατοντάρχῃ) to hold Paul under custody (τηρεῖσθαι αὐτόν), but with liberty (ἔχειν ἄνεσιν) for his companions to care for him (μηδένα κωλύειν τῶν ἰδίων αὐτοῦ ὑπηρετεῖν αὐτῷ).

Ἀναβάλλω is a technical term for adjourning a trial (BDAG s.v. "ἀναβάλλω" 58–59). Felix did not dismiss the case; he simply delayed a ruling. In 23:15 διαγινώσκω denotes giving careful attention to facts as a basis for forming a judgment (BDAG s.v. "διαγινώσκω" 1, 227). In this context it might well refer to the act of making a judicial decision based on the facts presented. Ἄνεσις denotes a relaxation of custodial control (BDAG s.v. "ἄνεσιν" 1, 77); NASB translates the phrase ἔχειν ἄνεσιν as "to have some freedom."

> *TEXTUAL ANALYSIS: "knowing more accurately"*
> See 23:15 for other occurrences of ἀκριβέστερον in Luke-Acts. Culy and Parsons note that in this context the adverb could mean either "more accurately" or "rather well" (2003, 469). The LEB, NASB, NET, and NKJV choose the former; ESV, NIV, NLT, and NRSV choose the latter. The participle εἰδώς could be either causal (e.g., LEB, "because he knew") or adjectival (e.g., NIV, "who knew"). In any of the four possible combinations, the unresolved question is whether Felix already possessed his knowledge of "the Way" before the hearing (Peterson 2009, 639) or acquired it as a result of the hearing (Culy and Parsons 2003, 469). Most commentators suggest that the former understanding is more likely, either because of Felix's marriage to Drusilla (Bruce 1988, 446) or because of his extended service in Palestine (Dunn 1996, 314).

Felix's Delay (24:24–27)

Hoping he will receive money to release Paul, Felix keeps him in custody for two years, during which time Paul shares the gospel with the governor and his wife.

24:24–25. After an unspecified period of time (μετὰ ἡμέρας τινάς), Felix and his wife Drusilla summoned (μετεπέμψατο) Paul and listened to him (ἤκουσεν αὐτοῦ) as he spoke concerning faith in Christ Jesus (περὶ τῆς εἰς Χριστὸν Ἰησοῦν πίστεως). Specifically, Paul discussed three topics with them: righteousness, self-control, and impending judgment. Felix was sufficiently disturbed (ἔμφοβος γενόμενος) by the

conversation that he dismissed Paul but promised to meet with him again (μετακαλέσομαι), when he had an opportunity to do so (καιρὸν μεταλαβών).

Drusilla was Felix's third wife and the sister of Herod Agrippa II. Luke writes that the couple "arrived" (παραγενόμενος), which might mean that they had been away from Caesarea and returned, that they arrived at the specific room where Paul was held in custody, or that they came to the Praetorium from elsewhere in the city (Barrett 1998, 1113). "Faith in Christ Jesus" highlights the messianic theme of Paul's message. In this context, "righteousness" (δικαιοσύνη) is an ethical concept referring to the act of doing what God requires (L&N §88.13). "Self-control" (ἐγκράτεια) denotes exercising control over desires and actions (L&N §88.83). "Judgment" (κρίμα) refers to God's ultimate act of evaluating the ethical conduct of all human beings. The combination most likely alludes to the circumstances of Felix's marriage to Drusilla (Bock 2007, 695), highlights their need for the forgiveness and deliverance available through faith in Messiah Jesus, and explains Felix's strong reaction to Paul's message. As Larkin writes, "judicial delay leads to gospel declaration" (1995, 342).

24:26. Felix's motives, however, were not altogether pure. Luke notes that "at the same time" (ἅμα) the governor was also hoping (καὶ ἐλπίζων) Paul would give him money (χρήματα δοθήσεται αὐτῷ ὑπὸ τοῦ Παύλου). Commentators offer several suggestions as to why Felix might have expected that Paul would have the financial means to offer a bribe, although Luke provides no information that would make one explanation more likely than another. The governor frequently (πυκνότερον, perhaps with the ellative sense of "very often"; cf. BDAG s.v. "πυκνός" 897) summoned (μεταπεμπόμενος) Paul and "used to talk with him" (ὡμίλει; cf. BDAG s.v. "ὁμιλέω" 705). Luke does not record whether their conversations were about Messiah or money. Peterson concludes that Luke presents Felix "as a confused and divided man, with some understanding of the great issues at stake, but unwilling to take the steps required of him by the challenge of Paul's gospel" (2009, 642).

24:27. Finally, after two years (διετίας πληρωθείσης) of delay and dishonesty, Felix's term in office ended, and Porcius Festus replaced him (ἔλαβεν διάδοχον; literally, "he received a successor"). His final act was to leave Paul behind as a prisoner (κατέλιπε τὸν Παῦλον δεδεμένον; cf. BDAG s.v. "δέω" 1b, 221), because he wanted to grant a favor to the Jews (θέλων χάριτα καταθέσθαι τοῖς Ἰουδαίοις; cf. BDAG s.v. "κατατίθημι" 2, 528). Felix's term most likely ended in A.D. 58–59 (Peterson 2009, 642). Little historical information exists regarding Festus, although Josephus records that he caught and executed many of the robbers who were disturbing the province (Josephus, *A.J.* 20.8.10; *B.J.* 2.14.1). He died in office in A.D. 60, and Albinus replaced him (Peterson 2009, 643; contra Longenecker, who dates his time in office as A.D. 60–62; cf. Longenecker 1981, 544).

THEOLOGICAL FOCUS

The narratival function of Acts 24:1–27 is to document the events of Paul's two-year imprisonment in Caesarea, including the reason for its extended duration. The passage records the continuing Jewish attempts to do away with Paul, in this instance by secular judicial means. It also continues the theme of the interaction between Christianity and governmental authorities, reinforcing Luke's contention that the movement poses no threat to civil order or Roman law. Further, it juxtaposes Roman justice with human corruption as Felix chooses to keep Paul imprisoned in the hope of receiving financial gain and currying favor with the Jews. Finally, the passage fulfills one of the aspects of Paul's mission as set out in 9:15. He had declared Jesus before the Jewish people (22:1–21) and leaders (23:1–10).

He would soon do the same before a king (26:1–29). In this passage he bears Jesus's name before Felix, the Roman governor, as a representative of Gentile authority.

Theologically, Acts 24:1–27 provides the most complete account of a Christian defense of the gospel before the Roman civil authorities, including a representative of judicial authority, a formal presentation of accusations, and a defense refuting those accusations. Paul will present two more defenses, one before Festus (25:1–22) and one before Herod Agrippa II (25:23–26:32). Yet at this point, it is possible to compare five interactions between Christian witnesses and civil authorities and draw some conclusions. In Philippi, a slave girl's masters, motivated by economic concerns, charged Paul and Silas with proclaiming un-Roman customs, and the magistrates had them beaten and imprisoned. When the missionaries appealed to their Roman citizenship, the magistrates reversed their verdict and released them (16:19–40). In Corinth, unbelieving Jews, motivated by jealousy, charged Paul with unlawful worship. The Roman proconsul responded with indifference, declared that Paul had committed no crime, and yet allowed the Jews to beat Sosthenes (18:1–17).

In Ephesus, Demetrius and his fellow silversmiths, motivated by economic concerns, charged Paul and his companions with turning "all Asia" away from the worship of Artemis. The town clerk quelled the public protest, made it clear that nothing illegal had transpired, and released Gaius and Aristarchus, whom the protestors had dragged into the theater (19:23–41). In Jerusalem, the Jews, motivated by religious concerns, charged Paul with bringing Gentiles into the temple. In an attempt to determine the nature of the charges, the Roman commander ordered Paul flogged contrary to Roman law. When Paul appealed to his Roman citizenship, the commander concluded that Paul had done nothing deserving death or imprisonment (21:27–23:30). In Caesarea, the Jews, again motivated by religious concerns, charged Paul with dissension and desecration. Despite Paul's defense that refuted in detail all the accusations against him, Felix delayed a decision, sought personal financial gain, resorted to political expediency, and left Paul in custody for two years (24:1–27).

Taken together, these experiences suggest that the system of civil authority is imperfect. It can be abused, manipulated, and misapplied. It can be indifferent and it can reach erroneous verdicts. Nevertheless, Christians should respect that system. It can be equitable, impartial, and objective. It can reach correct verdicts and it can reverse unjust verdicts. As Paul wrote to the Romans, "There is no authority except from God, and those which exist are established by God" (Rom. 13:1). To whatever extent might be possible, therefore, Jesus's followers should be subject to the civil authorities and render to those authorities the honor that is due them (Rom. 13:5, 7). They should also make use of the legal options available to them, defend themselves actively against any false charges they might face, and present the gospel boldly to the authorities before whom they might appear.

PREACHING AND TEACHING STRATEGIES

Exegetical/Theological Synthesis

With his transfer from Jerusalem to Caesarea and from a Jewish religious context to a Roman secular context, Paul had new opportunities to bear witness for Jesus, now before important governmental officials. His defense before Felix in 24:10–21 is the fifth major Pauline speech that Luke includes in his narrative. The previous four speeches highlighted Paul's ministry as an evangelist (13:16–41), an apologist (17:22–31), a pastor (20:18–35), and a witness to the Jewish people (22:1–21). Now, Paul would stand before the Roman governor to defend himself and Christianity. Luke's first-century readers would

have wanted to know how Paul would defend himself in a secular judicial hearing. How would he address the charges leveled against him? How would he maintain a faithful witness for Jesus and the gospel? What would the results be?

Luke's account records how Paul effectively refuted the charges against him by demonstrating that he caused no public disturbance, posed no political threat, and committed no religious vandalism. There was, in fact, no legal issue for the Roman governor to decide. As had been true in Philippi, Corinth, Ephesus, and Jerusalem, the gospel and its representatives might pose an economic or religious threat to special interest groups, but they did not pose a threat to established authority. Before Felix, however, Paul not only defended the gospel; he also proclaimed it. He took advantage of his initial audience before Felix to include a synopsis of his views on worship, theology, eschatology, and ethics—all of which sprang from the fact of Jesus's resurrection. In subsequent conversations he presented the message of faith in Messiah Jesus and explained how that message addressed the issues of righteous living, self-control, and coming judgment. With his original readers, Luke's twenty-first-century audience shares the need to know that Jesus's faithful witnesses are able not only to refute false charges effectively but also to present the gospel boldly before whatever audience they might face.

Preaching/Teaching Idea

The best defense is a good offense.

Contemporary Connections

What does it mean?

Paul was experiencing a grave miscarriage of justice. He had been falsely accused, violently apprehended, nearly tortured by Roman soldiers, nearly torn apart by the Jewish council, plotted against, and now held in delayed custody without credible charges. Paul would spend two years here. Tertullus's carefully crafted prosecution failed to stick. He accused Paul of stirring up riots, of being the ringleader of a new and foreign movement, and of trying to profane the temple. Paul, however, had a convincing defense against each accusation. Claudius Lysias was right: there was nothing here deserving imprisonment or death (23:29). Luke further underscores the injustice in two closing scenes. It became clear that Felix was hoping for a bribe (24:26) and that he was willing to leave a falsely accused man in prison to "do the Jews a favor" (24:27). In response, Paul changed from his angry outburst earlier into confident self-control. Taking comfort in the Lord's promise that he has work in Rome to do (23:11), he offered a careful defense in court and continued to witness while he was in custody. His public and private ministry could continue because he was confident that God is the ultimate judge of the living and the dead (24:21, 25).

Is it true?

Paul's experience of false accusations and fumbling injustice sounds like Jesus's similar experience. Hasty hearings with muddled allegations and the death penalty in view join Savior and servant. Jesus knew his trial would lead to death, and he made little defense. Paul knew he would travel to Rome, and so made a credible defense. Either way, both men knew that their immediate future was not their ultimate destiny. God's will is ultimate.

Paul returns to this confidence in God's justice twice in the passage. He concludes his defense in court by repeating what he testified before the Jewish council, that there is a resurrection of the dead (24:21). If that belief is true, those present in the room are not rendering a final judgment in the matter. They might render a temporary judgment, but they will soon face God and his judgment. Paul tells Felix plainly in private that the divine judge would judge the human judge (24:25).

Jesus made the same point before the Jewish council. He would endure their injustice, but he reminded them of an ultimate justice in the resurrection. At that time, he sat in the defendant's seat subjecting himself to the unjust whims of the council. At the resurrection, however, Jesus assumes a different seat, one "at the right hand of the power of God" (Luke 22:69). Injustice might have its way today, but justice will reign forever.

Now what?

It is painful to face any kind of injustice, whether civic or personal. To sit in Paul's seat as the defendant and endure mistreatment, false accusations, jockeying for civic favor, and hyperbole could infuriate the tamest individual among us. All of us have experienced wrong. All of us are sorely tempted to repay evil for evil. That is why the Lord speaks so emphatically against trying to assume his role as judge who executes justice (Deut. 32:35). That is why Paul later devotes a huge portion of his community exhortations to forgiveness and trust in God's justice (Rom. 12:14–21). That is why Jesus teaches a countercultural ethic of loving enemies and enduring injustice (Matt. 5:38–48). The fruit of following God's way of abundant living is the difference between Paul rebuking the high priest in chapter 23 and Paul patiently defending himself in chapter 24. Raging outwardly or inwardly never makes us happy. It cannot. Only entrusting ourselves to God can make us truly happy and confident in him.

Creativity in Presentation

We love a good story with a satisfying ending. If you think about it, much of that satisfaction comes from a *just* ending. To the degree the bad guys are punished and the good guys live happily ever after, we are pleased. To the degree that bad guys get away with bad things, we are incensed. Movies like *There Will Be Blood* or *No Country for Old Men* really bother us. That is why stories that end with blatant injustice are few and far between. We struggle with swallowing such a bitter pill. Our text will test our sense of justice.

A message could bring out this tension by beginning with human injustice and ending with God's justice. Human injustice includes Tertullus's false accusations (24:2–8) that have ready answers by Paul (24:2–21), Felix's questionable integrity (24:26–27), and the stunning final verse of the passage that leaves Paul in prison *for two years and counting* (24:27). Fill in the feelings behind the blunt reporting of this timeline. What would it feel like to experience such unfairness? What does it feel like in our lives today?

There is no civic justice found here. It must be sought in God. We do not get the inner working of Paul's mind and heart. We hear the overflow. Paul believes emphatically in God's justice that can come now but will certainly come at the resurrection (24:21, 25). His response to human injustice is to believe and preach divine justice. Paul's best defense was a good offense.

- We will experience injustice in our lives and in our world at the hands of men (24:1–8, 22–27).

- We must rely on God to bring his perfect justice (22:9–21).

DISCUSSION QUESTIONS

1. Where were the holes in Tertullus's presentation of the case against Paul? Where did he stretch or misrepresent the facts?

2. How did Paul refute each of the charges against him? How did he incorporate gospel witness into his presentation?

3. What do you think Luke means when he writes that Felix "had a more exact understanding of the way"? Do you think that he already possessed that understanding, or did Paul's speech enhance his understanding?

4. Why did Paul's conversations with Felix evoke such a strong reaction from the governor? How might his marital history have contributed to his reaction?

5. How did Felix's actions represent both the best features of Roman justice and the worst features of human depravity?

Acts 25:1–12

EXEGETICAL IDEA

After the new Roman governor denies a Jewish request for a change of venue to Jerusalem, Paul appears before Festus in Caesarea, defends himself against Jewish charges, and appeals to his right as a Roman citizen to present his case before Caesar in Rome.

THEOLOGICAL FOCUS

Wise witnesses use every legitimate means available to them to meet the challenges before them and fulfill the mission entrusted to them.

PREACHING IDEA

Trust God's providential means to accomplish his providential purposes.

PREACHING POINTERS

"Desperate times call for desperate measures." That saying traces its roots to the ancient Greek physician Hippocrates, who originally wrote that "extreme diseases must have extreme remedies." What he meant was that, sometimes, what might seem to be the last resort is the right one for the circumstances you are facing. You can see that idea at work in Paul's defense speeches in Acts 22–25. Before the Jewish mob in the temple, Paul emphasized his continuity with his Jewish heritage. Before the Sanhedrin, he focused on a point of doctrine. Before Felix, he refuted, point by point, the Jewish charges and demonstrated that there was no case against him. Before Festus—facing a choice between Roman execution or Jewish assassination—he appealed to Caesar as a last resort that stopped the judicial process, protected him from a Jewish ambush, and ensured that he would travel to Rome. He understood that desperate times call for desperate measures, and by appealing to Caesar he relied on the rule of civil law as one of the means God has ordained to accomplish his purposes.

People today should be able to relate to the judicial aspects of the passage—following legal procedures, requests to change the venue of trials, hung juries that cannot decide whether to convict or acquit, and appealing a verdict. They should also be able to relate both to political intrigue and favors and to using the legal system to gain an advantage. The passage corrects the practice of seeking to manipulate the judicial system and trading impartial decisions for political expediency. It commends knowing and making wise use of legal rights, relying on the rule of law, and being committed to the task God has assigned. The objective in communicating the passage should be to help listeners understand that God expects his witnesses to use every legitimate means available to them to meet the challenges before them, including trusting in his providential means to accomplish his providential purposes.

DEFENSE BEFORE FESTUS (25:1–12)

LITERARY STRUCTURE AND THEMES (25:1–12)

The passage consists of three sections. The first section takes place in Jerusalem and records the Jewish leaders' request to the governor that he return Paul to Jerusalem, as well as the governor's denial of that request (25:1–5). The second section moves the action to Caesarea and summarizes both the Jews' accusations and Paul's defense (25:6–8). The third section documents the occasion, content, and outcome of Paul's appeal that Festus transfer his case to Caesar's tribunal (25:9–12). Festus's question (25:9) and decision (25:12) frame the third section. Within that section, Larkin suggests a concentric structure for Paul's answer (25:10–11) that highlights his statement of integrity at the center (1995, 348). The repetition of Καῖσαρ in the first and fifth lines and the repetition of οὐδέν in the second and fourth lines support his analysis.

> A ἐπὶ τοῦ βήματος Καίσαρός ἐστὼς
> εἰμι, οὗ με δεῖ κρίνεσθαι.
> B Ἰουδαίους οὐδὲν ἠδίκησα, ὡς καὶ
> σὺ κάλλιον ἐπιγινώσκεις.
> C εἰ μὲν οὖν ἀδικῶ καὶ ἄξιον θανάτου
> πέπραχά τι, οὐ παραιτοῦμαι τὸ
> ἀποθανεῖν·
> B′ εἰ δὲ οὐδέν ἐστιν ὧν οὗτοι
> κατηγοροῦσίν μου, οὐδείς με
> δύναται αὐτοῖς χαρίσασθαι·
> A′ Καίσαρα ἐπικαλοῦμαι.

The passage concludes with Festus's famous statement in verse 12: "You have appealed to Caesar. To Caesar you will go!"

- *Decision on Venue (25:1–5)*
- *Hearing Before Festus (25:6–8)*
- *Appeal to Caesar (25:9–12)*

EXPOSITION (25:1–12)

When Festus replaced Felix as the governor of Judea, he made an initial visit to Jerusalem. While he was in that city, the Jewish leaders renewed their case against Paul and asked that the governor return Paul to Jerusalem, hoping to kill him before he arrived. Since he was returning to Caesarea soon, Festus denied the request for a change of venue and invited the Jewish leaders to accompany him to Caesarea if they had any charges to bring against Paul. In Caesarea, the Jewish leaders restated their charges, and Paul refuted them. When Festus gave him the option of returning to Jerusalem for another hearing, Paul appealed to his right as a Roman citizen that he be allowed to defend himself before the emperor.

Luke recounts the events in Jerusalem (25:1–5) and the hearing in Caesarea (25:6–8) briefly in order to highlight the new feature of Paul's defense: his appeal to Caesar (25:9–12). As a Roman citizen, Paul had certain legal rights, including the right of protection from being punished before being convicted, the right of protection from being punished in public using a disgraceful method, and the right of appeal to Caesar as the court of final redress. He had invoked the first right in Philippi for the sake of the new church (16:37–39) and the second right in Jerusalem to avoid potential death by flogging (22:24–46). He invoked the third right in Caesarea both to avoid potential death at the hands of the Jews and, more importantly, to secure a way to travel to Rome and fulfill the promise

Jesus had given him in a vision after his hearing before the Sanhedrin (23:11). As Bock writes, "in a sense, Paul sends himself to Rome through his own actions in appealing to Roman law" (2007, 703). Festus's only option was to grant Paul's appeal.

Decision on Venue (25:1–5)
While Festus is on a brief initial visit to Jerusalem, the Jews ask him to return Paul to Jerusalem for trial, but the governor denies their request and invites them to Caesarea if they have any legal issues to present.

25:1–3. Three days after Festus arrived in Judea (ἐπιβὰς τῇ ἐπαρχείᾳ μετὰ τρεῖς ἡμέρας), he traveled from Caesarea to Jerusalem for what Marshall calls "a courtesy visit" to become familiar with any matters that might have concerned the Jewish authorities (1980, 383). During his time in the city, the Jewish religious leaders renewed their charges against Paul and urged the governor to grant them a favor directed specifically against him (αἰτούμενοι χάριν κατ' αὐτοῦ; cf. BDAG s.v. "αἰτέω" 30). They also asked that Festus return Paul to Jerusalem (μεταπέμψηται αὐτὸν εἰς Ἰερουσαλήμ), because they were preparing an ambush to kill him while he was en route (κατὰ τὴν ὁδόν).

Barrett notes that although Judea was technically a department of the province of Syria rather than a separate province, the term ἐπαρχεία was used somewhat loosely (1998, 1123). The wording that describes the Jews bringing charges (ἐνεφάνισάν . . . κατὰ τοῦ Παύλου) echoes 24:1. Josephus writes that Herod Agrippa II appointed Ishmael ben Phabi to succeed Ananias toward the end of Felix's tenure (Josephus, *A.J.* 20.8.8–11). The plural οἱ ἀρχιερεῖς most likely reflects Ananias's continuing influence (Longenecker 1981, 544). Οἱ πρῶτοι describes persons who were "first, foremost, most important, or most prominent" (BDAG s.v. "πρῶτος" 2aβ, 894; cf. Luke 19:47; Acts 28:17). The NASB translates

the phrase οἱ πρῶτοι τῶν Ἰουδαίων as "the leading men of the Jews." Bock notes that the imperfect tense of παρεκάλουν suggests that the Jews were making an ongoing request, perhaps accompanied by pressure (2007, 700). The wording that describes the Jews' planned ambush (ἐνέδραν ποιοῦντες ἀνελεῖν αὐτὸν κατὰ τὴν ὁδόν) echoes 23:15.

25:4–5. The governor's response was that Paul was already in custody in Caesarea (τηρεῖσθαι τὸν Παῦλον εἰς Καισάρειαν), and he was about to return there soon (ἑαυτὸν μέλλειν ἐν τάχει ἐκπορεύεσθαι). He invited the leaders to accompany (συγκαταβάντες) him. If Paul had done anything improper (εἴ τί ἐστιν ἐν τῷ ἀνδρὶ ἄτοπον), they could continue presenting their charges (κατηγορείτωσαν) there. Οἱ δυνατοί ("the prominent people"; cf. BDAG s.v. "δυνατός" 1aβ, 264) in verse 5 refers to the same group as οἱ πρῶτοι ("the leading men") in verse 2. Schnabel suggests that the first class condition (εἴ) "allows for the possibility that the Jewish leaders may yet want to decide whether they are convinced that Paul has done something improper or wrong that demands official accusations in a trial" (2012, 987). The adjective ἄτοπος denotes something that is "behaviorally out of place" (BDAG s.v. "ἄτοπος" 2, 149) or "that which is unusual . . . generally with the implication of harmful or dangerous" (L&N §58.54). Barrett describes it as "a mild word for a crime (1998, 1125); Bock calls it "a soft legal word" (2007, 700). The implication is that Festus would not judge Paul's guilt or innocence until he heard heard all the evidence in the case.

Hearing Before Festus (25:6–8)
In Caesarea, the Jewish leaders renew their unproven charges against Paul, and he refutes those charges in a formal hearing before the governor.

25:6. The governor's stay in Jerusalem lasted no longer than eight or ten days (ἡμέρας οὐ πλείους ὀκτὼ ἢ δέκα) before he returned to Caesarea (καταβὰς εἰς Καισάρειαν). The day after he arrived (τῇ ἐπαύριον), he took his seat on the judicial bench (καθίσας ἐπὶ τοῦ βήματος) and ordered that Paul be brought (ἐκέλευσεν τὸν Παῦλον ἀχθῆναι) before him for a hearing. Bruce notes that Festus's act of taking his seat on the judicial bench was "a formality [that] was necessary for his decision to have legal validity" (1988, 451).

25:7. When Paul arrived (παραγενομένου αὐτοῦ), the Jews who had come down from Jerusalem (οἱ ἀπὸ Ἱεροσολύμων καταβεβηκότες Ἰουδαῖοι) surrounded him (περιέστησαν αὐτόν) and repeatedly brought (καταφέροντες) "many serious charges" (πολλὰ καὶ βαρέα αἰτιώματα) against him. They were not, however, able to prove those charges (ἃ οὐκ ἴσχυον ἀποδεῖξαι). Culy and Parsons conclude that the conjunction in the phrase πολλὰ καὶ βαρέα is epexegetical and intensifies the expression (2003, 476). The participle καταφέροντες describes "causing something adverse to happen to someone" (L&N §13.133). In 26:10, when Paul says that "[he] cast [his] vote against them" (NLT), he uses the same verb. The iterative present highlights the bringing of repeated accusations. Barrett writes that the imperfect tense of ἴσχυον has the sense of "continual but unsuccessful attempts" and suggests the translation "They could not prove, however hard they tried" (1998, 1126).

25:8. Luke does not record the Jews' charges, but it is possible to infer them from Paul's defense (τοῦ Παύλου ἀπολογουμένου). He declared that he committed no sin (τι ἥμαρτον) against the Jewish law (οὔτε εἰς τὸν νόμον τῶν Ἰουδαίων), against the temple (οὔτε εἰς τὸ ἱερόν), or against Caesar (οὔτε εἰς Καίσαρά). The charges combined the original accusations by the Jerusalem mob (law and temple in 21:28) and the later accusations by Tertullus (rebellion and temple in 24:5–6). Paul had already refuted the charges at length before Felix (24:12–21), and he would do the same more concisely before Festus (25:10–11).

Appeal to Caesar (25:9–12)

When Festus offers him the option of returning to Jerusalem for another hearing, Paul chooses to exercise his right as a Roman citizen and appeal to Caesar as the court of final redress.

25:9. Like Felix, Festus wanted to do the Jews a favor. So, he asked Paul whether he wanted to travel to Jerusalem (θέλεις εἰς Ἱεροσόλυμα ἀναβάς) to be judged on the charges there (ἐκεῖ περὶ τούτων κριθῆναι). The wording of doing the Jews a favor (θέλων τοῖς Ἰουδαίοις χάριν καταθέσθαι) echoes 24:27. Since Festus could only transfer Paul to the Sanhedrin's jurisdiction if he dismissed the political charges (Schnabel 2012, 990), his question offered a change in venue rather than a change in jurisdiction. The phrase ἐπ᾽ ἐμοῦ points to a legal tribunal (BDAG s.v. "ἐπί" 3, 363–64; cf 23:30; 24:20; 1 Cor. 6:1; 1 Tim. 6:13). Barrett suggests "in my presence" (1998, 1127). The phrase might also denote "under my authority or control" (Harris 2011, 137). Regardless, the hearing would have taken place with Festus, not the Sanhedrin, as the judicial authority. It is ironic that if Paul had agreed with Festus's proposed action, the result would have been exactly what the Jews had originally requested (25:3).

25:10–11. Paul's response was the climax of the narrative. As a Roman citizen, he had the right to be judged (με δεῖ κρίνεσθαι) before the emperor's judicial bench (ἐπὶ τοῦ βήματος Καίσαρος). He had not harmed the Jews (Ἰουδαίους οὐδὲν ἠδίκησα), as Festus understood very well. The impersonal verb δεῖ refers to Paul's legal right, but it also echoes the "divine necessity" about which Jesus had informed him in 23:11. Robertson classifies the adverb κάλλιον is an elative comparative ("very well") and notes, "Paul hints that Festus knows his innocence better than he is willing to admit" (1934, 665).

Paul made it clear that he was not trying to avoid death (οὐ παραιτοῦμαι τὸ ἀποθανεῖν), if he had done anything worthy of death (εἰ ἀδικῶ καὶ ἄξιον θανάτου πέπραχά τι). If, however, there was no truth to the charges against him (εἰ οὐδέν ἐστιν ὧν οὗτοι κατηγοροῦσίν μου), Festus could not hand him over to the Jews' control (οὐδείς με δύναται αὐτοῖς χαρίσασθαι; cf. L&N §37.30). He concluded his response as he began it: by appealing to Caesar (Καίσαρα ἐπικαλοῦμαι). Schnabel suggests three possible reasons for Paul's decision—the Jews' ongoing efforts against him, the possibility that he had information about the renewed plans for an ambush, and/or suspicion that the governor wanted to hand him over to the Jews (2012, 990). As Bock notes, a fourth reason was that "Paul's greater concern is to take the gospel to Rome, and this appeal is an easy way to do so" (2007, 704).

25:12. Festus found himself in a difficult political position. On the one hand, he could offend the Jewish leaders by releasing Paul and, as a result, threaten the stability of the province. On the other hand, he could ignore Roman law by convicting Paul or handing him over to the Jews and, as a result, threaten his own appointment as governor. Paul's appeal to Caesar allowed Festus to resolve his predicament by transferring jurisdiction for the case to Rome. Since he was not required to grant Paul's appeal (Schnabel 2012, 993), he conferred with his council of advisors (συλλαλήσας μετὰ τοῦ συμβουλίου; cf. BDAG s.v. "συμβούλιον" 4, 957) before granting Paul's appeal by declaring, "You have appealed to Caesar. To Caesar you will go" (Καίσαρα ἐπικέκλησαι, ἐπὶ Καίσαρα πορεύσῃ).

THEOLOGICAL FOCUS

The narratival function of Acts 25:1–12 is to recount both the circumstances that led to Paul's decision to appeal to Caesar and the result of that appeal. In order to escape once and for all ongoing Jewish attempts to kill him and in order to overcome Roman judicial inaction, Paul claimed his right as a Roman citizen to have Caesar hear his case. His appeal was a crucial step on the road to Rome. Although Festus was not required to grant Paul's appeal, he would have subverted Roman justice to deny it. By making his appeal, Paul cut through the tangled knot of Judean religion and politics, made his journey to the capital of the empire inevitable, and facilitated the fulfillment of Jesus's promise that Paul would be his witness in Rome. By granting the appeal, the governor resolved a sticky political situation, implicitly affirmed Paul's innocence, and committed the empire to transporting Paul to Rome.

Theologically, Acts 25:1–12 presents Paul as an example of a Christian who was both faithful to his religious convictions and knowledgeable about his constitutional rights. As Bock writes, "[Paul] is a good Jew and a good citizen" (2007, 701). Luke effectively contrasts Festus, who was willing to compromise and place political expediency ahead of judicial impartiality (Peterson 2009, 650), with Paul, who was willing to trust in the integrity of Roman law and seek the progress of the gospel. As Bauer comments, "Luke portrays Paul as a better Roman than the Roman officials with whom he . . . has to do" (2021, 237). In his dual role as Roman citizen and gospel witness, Paul was willing to make wise use of the tactical options available to him. He used his rights as a Roman citizen sparingly but strategically throughout his ministry (16:37–39; 22:24–46; 25:10–11). In his defense before Festus, the governor's equivocation prompted Paul's decision. In appealing to Caesar, he relied on the rule of civil law as one of the providential means God has ordained to govern his creation and advance his kingdom purposes.

PREACHING AND TEACHING STRATEGIES

Exegetical/Theological Synthesis

Paul had languished in Roman custody for two years while Felix pursued personal profit. Then, Festus replaced him. Luke's first-century readers would have wanted to know whether Paul's prospects changed with the change in governors. Would the new governor approach the case in the same way Felix had? Would the Jewish leaders continue their efforts to do away with Paul? Would Paul find a way out of the religious and political intrigue that surrounded him and finally begin his travel to Rome as Jesus had promised? Luke's narrative answers those questions by recording a mixture of positive and negative results.

Festus proved to be a mixed blessing for Paul. He began his term in office as an impartial administrator who adhered to the technicalities of Roman jurisprudence and rejected the Jewish request for a change of venue. Yet, like Felix, he wanted to do the Jews a favor and kept Paul in custody when he should have released him. The Jews remained constant—repeating the same unproven accusations against Paul and renewing their plot to ambush and kill him. Paul remained faithful in defense of his innocence, declared his willingness to face death if he had committed any offense worthy of it, and appealed to his right as a Roman citizen to present his case before the emperor. Facing the danger of Roman execution on the one hand and the danger of Jewish assassination on the other hand, he exercised wisdom in choosing the solution that would protect him from death and deliver him to Rome.

With his original readers, Luke's twenty-first-century audience shares the need to know that, sometimes, what seems to be the last resort is the right solution. Wise witnesses use every legitimate means available to them to meet the challenges before them and fulfill the mission entrusted to them. They must act wisely when facing dangerous situations and trust that God can use their decision as part of his providential work in fulfilling his purposes.

Preaching/Teaching Idea

Trust God's providential means to accomplish his providential purposes.

Contemporary Connections

What does it mean?

Paul found himself backed into a legal corner for a third or fourth time now, depending on who is counting. He has stood before the Roman tribune, the Jewish council, Felix, and now Festus. Once again, unjust punishment seemed inevitable. Jerusalem's leaders had held a two-year grudge against Paul while he was in custody in Caesarea, and they were determined to claim his life either by trial, ambush, execution, or assassination. Against such persistent vehemence, despair could have easily set in. Yet God surprises. Once again, God provided a providential solution. Paul made his defense in court. When legal argument did not work, he appealed to the highest court in the land, Caesar. Truly, he trusted in God's hand to hold him in life and in death, in justice and injustice, to fulfill God's plan for his life.

Is it true?

Was the Lord's promise so long ago that the testimony of him in Rome (23:11) was starting to feel a bit distant and foggy to Paul? Did he mishear? Did the Lord mean for him to testify or someone else? Was God changing his mind? What was spoken as encouragement to be brave and stand firmly is taking time to play out. Paul has now languished in the muddled vortex between Jerusalem and Caesarea. God promised him Rome, but he is no closer to that city and call than he was two years prior. Felix and Festus would rather to hand out favors than a favorable legal ruling. We have no indication that Paul was sensing the Lord's specific leading in each step, only that after two years of waiting and standing before another indecisive judge, he now appeals to Caesar. He uses the natural and legal means before him as God's providential path to lead him toward God's providential end.

Now what?

Paul's long story to get from Jerusalem to Rome mirrors our own stories well. Canaan's fair and happy land of God's promises seems an alien world when we are standing on Jordan's stormy banks. Waiting for God to act is hard. Waiting for God to do what he says he is going to do is harder. When we know his promises but do not experience them, we are tempted to doubt or despair, which is right where the enemy wants us. In our passage, the Jewish leaders, who harbor murderous intent, and Festus, who is stuck between legal responsibility and approval ratings, are really hurting. They are unsteady. Paul is stable in their midst. The Lord's call for courage is a gift to him. May it be to us as well. May we trust his providential means to accomplish his providential plans—that wherever he leads, he also makes a way.

Creativity in Presentation

Whitewater rafting is a thrilling if sometimes terrifying adventure. Obviously, most commercial rides are harmless, and the worst that can happen is that we bounce out of the raft and rattle down the river until the guide can pull us back in again. The real danger is where there is what the experts call a *hole* or *hydraulic*. This river feature forms beyond an obstacle and

recirculates water with tremendous force. It pulls whatever is on top of the river down to the bottom and pins it there in a vortex. Strong swimmers can be churned under water until they drown.

That experience is dramatic, and it feels like Paul's situation here. He is stuck. He knows that he is bound for Rome, but he cannot get out of the churning vortex between Jerusalem and Caesarea. He is pinned under water by an infuriating and unjust system of favors passing between Roman and Jewish leaders. After two years under water, it would seem that despair is not far behind. The churning vortex illustrates the first part of the message, a dangerous situation. Paul does not even know the entirety of what transpires against him, but it is formidable.

Against the backdrop of the Jewish leaders' appeal (25:1–5) and the hearing before Festus (25:6–8), Paul reaches out for the second part of the message, a providential solution. His Roman citizenship is no accident. It has been the Lord's means for his protection in past situations. Here God's providence provides once again a way of escape. Paul appeals to Caesar, and like a swimmer moving with the whitewater out of the hydraulic trap, the Lord lifts him outward and onward into his promises. Once again, God's providential means accomplish his purposes.

- Trust in God in the face of opposition (25:1–11).

- God will accomplish his purposes (25:12).

DISCUSSION QUESTIONS

1. What positive administrative qualities does Festus exhibit as he begins his term in office as the governor of Judea?

2. How is Paul's defense before Festus similar to and/or different from his previous defense before Felix?

3. How does Festus's position change after hearing from both the Jews and Paul? What do you think motivates his reversal on the possibility of a change of venue from Caesarea to Jerusalem?

4. How would you evaluate Barrett's suggestion that "Paul had as much to fear from acquittal as from condemnation" (1998, 1121)? Why?

5. How does Paul's appeal to Caesar resolve the difficult situation in which Festus finds himself? How does his appeal advance God's purposes for him?

Acts 25:13–26:32

EXEGETICAL IDEA

Paul's defense before King Herod Agrippa II had the goal of helping Festus determine what to write to Caesar, focused on Jesus as the fulfillment of the OT promise of the resurrection, and convinced the king that Paul was innocent of all charges.

THEOLOGICAL FOCUS

The gospel message fulfills the OT promises, focuses on the risen Jesus, offers universal blessing, is true and reasonable, and poses no threat to civil authority.

PREACHING IDEA

The gospel proclaims Messiah, not madness or mayhem.

PREACHING POINTERS

Do some people who hear the message of the gospel consider it madness? Or is the message that Jesus rose from the dead true and reasonable? The answer to all three of those questions is a resounding "Yes!" It is entirely possible that at some point in our lives each of us has encountered someone who has considered incredible the basic message of the gospel that Jesus died, was buried, rose after three days, and appeared to his followers (1 Cor. 15:3–8). The idea of someone rising from the dead differs so drastically from our normal way of thinking that some people might consider it to be insane. Festus, the Roman governor of Judea, certainly did. When Paul concluded the account of his life, conversion, commission, and ministry in Acts 26, Festus responded in a loud voice, "Paul, you are out of your mind! Your great learning is driving you mad." Paul's response was, "I am not out of my mind, but I am speaking words that are true and reasonable." Paul's experience on the road to Damascus changed his thinking, his theology, and his life's work. He had met the risen Jesus and he knew that the gospel proclaims Messiah, not madness or mayhem.

People today should be able to relate to making a presentation, having others challenge their thinking or beliefs, and seeking to be faithful in completing a task assigned to them. The passage corrects the idea that the gospel is foolish or accepted only by ignorant people, the idea that the ministry of the gospel oversteps established legal boundaries, and the idea that the state has jurisdiction over matters of faith or religious practice. It commends bold proclamation of the gospel in the face of potentially intimidating or hostile audiences, faithful obedience to an assigned task regardless of the personal consequences, and willingness to accept the truth, even if doing so involves changing beliefs or practices. The objective in communicating the passage should be to help listeners accurately understand the nature and message of the gospel so that they will proclaim it boldly before whatever audience God gives them.

DEFENSE BEFORE HEROD AGRIPPA II (25:13–26:32)

LITERARY STRUCTURE AND THEMES (25:13–26:32)

The passage consists of five sections. Paul's speech before King Herod Agrippa II is the longest section and the focal point of the passage. In the first section, Festus introduces the king to the circumstances that have led him to keep Paul in custody, and the king expresses his interest in hearing what Paul has to say (25:13–22). In the second section, with Agrippa, his sister, the Roman military leaders, and the prominent citizens of the city assembled, Festus explains the background that has led him to bring Paul before the assembly (25:23–27). In the third section, after the king gives him permission to speak for himself, Paul explains his background, his Damascus road vision, his commission, and his ministry (26:1–23). In the fourth section, the governor and king react to Paul's speech (26:24–29). In the fifth section, the king states his verdict that Paul would have been set free if he had not appealed to Caesar (26:30–32).

- *Festus's Dilemma (25:13–22)*
- *Festus's Preamble (25:23–27)*
- *Paul's Defense (26:1–23)*
- *Paul's Interaction with Festus and Agrippa (26:24–29)*
- *Agrippa's Verdict (26:30–32)*

EXPOSITION (25:13–26:32)

Paul's appeal to Caesar ensured that he would travel to Rome, but it left Festus with the problem of formulating the charges he would send with the prisoner, since he had concluded that the Jews "had certain disagreements with [Paul] about their own religion and about a man named Jesus who had died, whom Paul claimed to be alive" (25:19). In other words, Paul had done nothing worthy of death or imprisonment under Roman law (cf. 23:29), but Festus was now obliged to follow the judicial process and send Paul to Rome. So, the governor took advantage of the opportunity that arose when King Herod Agrippa II and his sister, Bernice, arrived at Caesarea for a visit and asked the king for his advice. The result was a public hearing before the king, the military leaders, and the prominent citizens of Caesarea, in which Paul had another opportunity to bear witness for Jesus in fulfillment of the commission he had received in Damascus (cf. 9:15). After Paul completed his speech, the king confirmed his innocence with the final verdict that closed Paul's lengthy imprisonment at the hands of the Romans, first in Jerusalem, then in Caesarea (26:30–32).

Paul's speech before the king is the focal point of the passage. Bruce Winter (1993, 229–31) analyzes the structure as *exordium* (26:2–3), *narratio* (26:4–18), *probatio* (26:19–20), *refutatio* (26:21), and *peroratio* (26:22–23); Bock (2007, 713) and Schnabel (2012, 983) adopt a similar analysis. Other commentators suggest different arrangements (Larkin 1995, 357; Witherington 1998, 737–38). If the *narratio* in a forensic address explains the nature of the case, another option would be to understand 26:4–8 as the *narratio*, in which Paul established his lifelong hope in the promise of the resurrection as the heart of his case. The proofs of his case (the *probatio* or *confirmatio*) explained why he now proclaimed Jesus as the fulfillment of that hope, and the conclusion of his speech (*peroratio*) summarized the essential elements of that hope.

<table>
<tr><td colspan="2">Introduction (exordium) 26:2–3</td></tr>
<tr><td colspan="2">Agrippa is an expert in Jewish customs and disputes.</td></tr>
<tr><td>Nature of the Case (narratio)</td><td>26:4–8</td></tr>
<tr><td colspan="2">Paul is on trial because of his lifelong hope in the promise of the resurrection.</td></tr>
<tr><td colspan="2">Proofs in the Case (confirmatio) 26:9–20</td></tr>
<tr><td colspan="2">Paul opposed the name of Jesus. (26:9–11)
Jesus appeared to Paul on his way to Damascus. (26:12–16a)
Jesus commissioned Paul to be his witness. (26:16b–18)
Paul is obedient to his commission from Jesus. (26:19–20)</td></tr>
<tr><td>Answer to the Charges in the Case (refutatio)</td><td>26:21</td></tr>
<tr><td colspan="2">The Jews oppose Paul because he declares the hope to both Jews and Gentiles.</td></tr>
<tr><td colspan="2">Conclusion (peroratio) 26:22–23</td></tr>
<tr><td colspan="2">The prophets and Moses predicted these events. (26:22)
Messiah Jesus was destined to suffer. (26:23a)
Messiah Jesus was the first to rise from the dead. (26:23b)
Messiah Jesus proclaims light to both Jews and Gentiles. (26:23c)</td></tr>
</table>

As the preceding table demonstrates, the conclusion of Paul's speech includes four of the six essentials of the gospel: the salvation plan set out in Scripture (26:22), the salvation events of Jesus's death (26:23a) and resurrection (26:23b), and the universal scope of the salvation offer (26:23c). The other two essentials are also present: the salvation call to repentance (26:18a, 20b) and the salvation promise of forgiveness of sins (26:18b). As Shawn Redford notes, the gospel focus of the speech makes it clear that "Although Paul is in prison, this discussion is not about securing his release. . . . Paul is primarily concerned about sharing his faith with the rulers that surround him and sending a record of his faith before he arrives in Rome" (2004, 291).

Festus's Dilemma (25:13–22)

Festus explains the circumstances that have led him to keep Paul in custody to King Herod Agrippa II, who expresses his interest in hearing what Paul has to say.

25:13–16. When Herod Agrippa II and his sister Bernice arrived in Caesarea (κατήντησαν εἰς Καισάρειαν) for an extended visit with Festus (ὡς πλείους ἡμέρας διέτριβον ἐκεῖ), the governor took the opportunity to present Paul's case to the king (ὁ Φῆστος τῷ βασιλεῖ ἀνέθετο τὰ κατὰ τὸν Παῦλον). He began by noting that Felix had left Paul in custody (ἀνήρ τίς ἐστιν καταλελειμμένος ὑπὸ Φήλικος δέσμιος). He then briefly summarized the attempt by the Jewish religious leaders to secure a guilty verdict against Paul (αἰτούμενοι κατ᾽ αὐτοῦ καταδίκην) and reported that he had carefully adhered to Roman judicial procedure.

The verb ἀνατίθημι denotes the act of laying something before someone for consideration (BDAG s.v. "ἀνατίθημι" 2, 74; cf. Gal. 2:2). See 25:15, 22 for ἐμφανίζω. The noun καταδίκη refers to a sentence of condemnation or a guilty verdict (BDAG s.v. "καταδίκη" 516). Festus's denial of the Jews' request for a change of venue (25:2–5) was based on two points of Roman law. First, the accused had the right to face his accusers (ὁ κατηγορούμενος κατὰ πρόσωπον ἔχοι τοὺς κατηγόρους); see Appian, *Bell. civ.* 3.1.3. Second, the accused had the right to answer the charge against him (τόπον ἀπολογίας λάβοι περὶ τοῦ ἐγκλήματος); see Appian, *Bell. civ.* 3.54.222. Barrett notes that the optatives (ἔχοι … λάβοι) replace the subjunctives of direct speech (1998, 1137).

25:17–19. Next, Festus summarized the hearing before him in Caesarea. When the Jewish accusers assembled (συνελθόντων), he did not delay (ἀναβολὴν μηδεμίαν ποιησάμενος) arranging for the judicial hearing. The accusers, however, were not able to bring any charges (οἱ κατήγοροι οὐδεμίαν αἰτίαν ἔφερον) that he considered serious (ὧν ἐγὼ ὑπενόουν πονηρῶν). Instead, the hearing devolved into certain disagreements about the Jewish religion (ζητήματα τινα περὶ τῆς ἰδίας δεισιδαιμονίας). In particular, the dispute focused on "a certain Jesus who had died, whom Paul claimed to be alive" (περί τινος Ἰησοῦ τεθνηκότος, ὃν ἔφασκεν ὁ Παῦλος ζῆν).

The imperfect tense of ἔφερον suggests repeated efforts by the accusers to find charges that the governor would find worthy of a guilty verdict. Αἰτία is a technical term that denotes "the basis for legal action" (BDAG s.v. "αἰτία" 2, 31); it suggests a "ground for complaint" of the sort that a Roman governor would usually handle (Schnabel 2012, 996). Ὑπονοέω denotes having an opinion based on scant evidence; in this context, it is best translated as "imagine" or "suspect" (L&N §31.32). A literal translation of πονηρῶν would be "evil deeds" with the sense of serious crimes worthy of death. The noun ζήτημα describes a "controversial question" (BDAG s.v. "ζήτημα"

428). Δεισιδαιμονία describes a set of beliefs concerning deity, with the implication of corresponding behavior (L&N §53.2); Schnabel suggests "'religion' in terms of a particular set of cultic beliefs and practices" (2012, 997). The word also occurs in 17:22 to describe the Athenians' interest in spiritual things. Although the account of 25:1–12 did not specifically mention Jesus's resurrection, it is clear from Festus's comments that he recognized the theological focal point of Paul's defense (cf. 23:6, 8; 24:15, 21; 26:23).

25:20–22. Festus concluded his account by describing Paul's appeal to Caesar. Because he found himself "at a loss" (ἀπορούμενος) concerning these theological questions (τὴν περὶ τούτων ζήτησιν), he asked Paul whether he wanted to go to Jerusalem (εἰ βούλοιτο πορεύεσθαι εἰς Ἱεροσόλυμα) for a further hearing there (κἀκεῖ κρίνεσθαι) concerning these religious questions (περὶ τούτων). Paul chose, however, to be held for the emperor's decision (εἰς τὴν τοῦ Σεβαστοῦ διάγνωσιν). Festus, therefore, commanded that Paul be kept in custody (ἐκέλευσα τηρεῖσθαι αὐτόν) until he was able to send him to Caesar (ἕως οὗ ἀναπέμψω αὐτὸν πρὸς Καίσαρα). When Festus completed his explanation, Agrippa expressed his interest in hearing from Paul also, and Festus agreed to make the arrangements.

The verb ἀπορέω describes being uncertain or in doubt (BDAG s.v. "ἀπορέω" 119); the NLT translates the participial phrase as "I was at a loss to know how to investigate these things." Διάγνωσις refers to a judicial inquiry or investigation that culminates in a decision (BDAG s.v. "διάγνωσις" 227). The adjective σεβαστός denotes something that is "worthy of reverence." The noun ὁ Σεβαστός was a translation of the Latin title Augustus, first conferred on Julius Caesar and subsequently used as a title for his successors. The Greek title came to mean "His Majesty the Emperor" (BDAG s.v. "σεβαστός" 917; cf. Schnabel 2012,

998). Larkin notes that ἀναπέμπω denotes "transfer to a superior tribunal" (1995, 352; cf. Josephus, *B.J.* 2.20.5). The imperfect tense of ἐβουλόμην either indicates a longstanding desire to learn more about Paul (Schnabel 2012, 998) or expresses a polite willingness to hear what Paul has to say (Williams 1989, 413).

> ### Herod Agrippa II
>
> Herod Agrippa II (A.D. 27–100) was the son of Herod Agrippa I (cf. 12:1–23). He was educated in Rome, lived a Hellenistic lifestyle, professed adherence to the Jewish religion, collaborated with the Romans, and sided with the Romans during the Jewish revolt that began in A.D. 66. Bernice was his slightly younger sister. In A.D. 53, Claudius installed him as a client king of the region north of Judea (Josephus, *B.J.* 2.12.1, 8; *A.J.* 20.5.2), and Nero later expanded his territory (Josephus, *B.J.* 2.13.2; *A.J.* 20.7.1; 20.8.4). He had authority to appoint and depose the high priests (Josephus, *A.J.* 20.5.2; 20.9.4) and had authority over the temple and its treasury (Josephus, *A.J.* 20.9.7). He was a logical source for Festus to consult on matters related to the Jewish religion.

Festus's Preamble (25:23–27)

Festus explains to the king and those assembled that he has brought Paul before them to determine the charges he should write to Caesar against Paul.

25:23. On the next day (τῇ ἐπαύριον), Agrippa, Bernice, Festus, the Roman military officers (χιλιάρχοις), and the prominent men of the city (ἀνδράσιν τοῖς κατ᾽ ἐξοχὴν τῆς πόλεως) processed into the audience hall (εἰσελθόντων εἰς τὸ ἀκροατήριον), and Festus commanded that Paul appear before the assembly (κελεύσαντος τοῦ Φήστου ἤχθη ὁ Παῦλος). "With great pageantry" (μετὰ πολλῆς φαντασίας) reflects that fact that "the Romans always knew how to process well" (Longnecker 1981, 551). The "audience hall" (τὸ ἀκροατήριον) was the auditorium in the governor's praetorium, where he held hearings and dispensed justice privately (BDAG s.v. "ἀκροατήριον" 39). The military officers (χιλιάρχοις) were leaders of cohorts (six hundred to one thousand men) equivalent in rank to majors or colonels (BDAG s.v. "χιλιάρχοις" 1084). Bock suggests that there were most likely five of them stationed in Caesarea (2007, 712; cf. Josephus, *A.J.* 19.9.2). "The prominent men of the city" (ἀνδράσιν τοῖς κατ᾽ ἐξοχὴν τῆς πόλεως; cf. BDAG s.v. "ἐξοχή" 354) would have been members of the city's aristocracy. Schnabel writes, "The time and effort Luke spends on this scene serves to highlight the innocence of Paul and confirms the relevance of the gospel of Jesus, Israel's Messiah and Savior, for both Jews and Gentiles" (2012, 999).

25:24–25. Festus addressed the king and everyone present (πάντες οἱ συμπαρόντες ἡμῖν) and briefly summarized Paul's situation. "The whole population of the Jews" (LEB, ἅπαν τὸ πλῆθος τῶν Ἰουδαίων) repeatedly petitioned (ἐνέτυχόν, iterative imperfect) Festus about Paul—both in Jerusalem and in Caesarea (ἔν τε Ἱεροσολύμοις καὶ ἐνθάδε)—while they kept on shouting loudly (βοῶντες) that Paul should not live any longer (μὴ δεῖν αὐτὸν ζῆν μηκέτι). Festus's assessment (ἐγὼ κατελαβόμην) was that Paul had done nothing worthy of death (μηδὲν ἄξιον αὐτὸν θανάτου πεπραχέναι). When Paul appealed to the emperor (αὐτοῦ δὲ τούτου ἐπικαλεσαμένου τὸν Σεβαστόν), however, the governor reached the decision that he should send him (ἔκρινα πέμπειν) to stand before Caesar.

Ἐντυγχάνω describes the Jews as asking for something with urgency and intensity (L&N §33.169). Βοάω also described the shouts of the excited crowd in Thessalonica (17:6) and most likely reflected what Festus had heard about the mob in the temple (22:22–24). Larkin notes that μὴ δεῖν "stood in direct opposition to the divine δεῖ of Paul's mission to Rome" (1995, 353). Καταλαμβάνω describes the process of reaching a conclusion about something through a process of inquiry (BDAG s.v. "καταλαμβάνω" 4, 520). See verse 21 for ὁ Σεβαστός. Festus's summary was the second time a Roman official had declared Paul innocent (23:29).

25:26–27. Festus had determined that Paul should go to Rome, but he needed to have something definite to write to Caesar (ἀσφαλές τι γράψαι τῷ κυρίῳ). At this point, however, he had nothing (οὐκ ἔχω). For that reason (διό), he had brought Paul before the assembled group (προήγαγον αὐτὸν ἐφ' ὑμῶν), so that after the investigation he might have something to write (σχῶ τί γράψω). To send Paul to Rome without indicating the charges against him would be "absurd" (NASB, ἄλογον). Ἀνάκρισις describes a preliminary examination that would assist in preparing a matter for trial (LSJ s.v. "ἀνάκρισις II" 109). Τῆς ἀνακρίσεως γενομένης is a genitive absolute of time. The adjective ἄλογος describes something that is contrary to reason (BDAG s.v. "ἄλογος" 2, 48). The verb σημαίνω describes the act of making something both specific and clear (L&N §33.153). The NET translates the infinitival phrase μὴ καὶ τὰς κατ' αὐτοῦ αἰτίας σημᾶναι as "without clearly indicating the charges against him."

Paul's Defense (26:1–23)
Paul declares that he is on trial because he proclaims Jesus as the fulfillment of his lifelong hope in the OT promise of the resurrection.

26:1–3. Although Festus arranged the hearing and briefed the participants, Agrippa led the proceedings and gave Paul permission to speak for himself (ἐπιτρέπεταί σοι περὶ σεαυτοῦ λέγειν). In response, Paul extended his hand (ἐκτείνας τὴν χεῖρα) in a typical rhetorical gesture (Marshall 1980, 390) and began his defense (ἀπελογεῖτο, inceptive imperfect; cf. 19:33; 24:10; 25:8) against all the Jewish charges

(περὶ πάντων ὧν ἐγκαλοῦμαι ὑπὸ Ἰουδαίων). He opened his speech by telling the king that he "considered himself fortunate" (ἥγημαι ἐμαυτὸν μακάριον) to be appearing before Agrippa, because the king was "especially knowledgeable" (μάλιστα γνώστην) about "all Jewish customs and controversies" (NLT, πάντων τῶν κατὰ Ἰουδαίους ἐθῶν τε καὶ ζητημάτων). Bock comments, "Agrippa was known for being pious, so the compliment fits" (2007, 713). Paul's request (δέομαι) was that Agrippa would hear him patiently (μακροθύμως ἀκοῦσαί μου).

26:4–8. From Paul's perspective, the central issue for which he was on trial was his lifelong hope in the promise of the resurrection. If they were willing to testify to it (ἐὰν θέλωσι μαρτυρεῖν), all the Jews knew (ἴσασι πάντες Ἰουδαῖοι) his background (τὴν βίωσίν μου). Paul chose to highlight three key points related to that background. First, his commitment to his Jewish heritage was lifelong. He emphasized the length of that commitment with three temporal phrases: "from my youth" (ἐκ νεότητος), "from the beginning" (ἀπ' ἀρχῆς), and "for a long time" (ἄνωθεν; cf. BDAG s.v. "ἄνωθεν" 3, 92). Second, he had lived his life to this point (ἔζησα, culminative aorist; cf. Larkin 1995, 355) in conformity with the standard of the strictest Jewish religious party (κατὰ τὴν ἀκριβεστάτην αἵρεσιν τῆς ἡμετέρας θρησκείας)—the Pharisees.

Paul's reference to his association with the Pharisees made a logical transition to his third and most important point: he was on trial for his hope in the promise of the resurrection (cf. 23:6–10). That hope was also integral to his background as a Jew. God made the promise to their fathers (ἐπ' ἐλπίδι τῆς εἰς τοὺς πατέρας ἡμῶν ἐπαγγελίας γενομένης ὑπὸ τοῦ θεοῦ), and their twelve tribes (τὸ δωδεκάφυλον ἡμῶν) were hoping to arrive at that objective (ἐλπίζει καταντῆσαι) by earnestly serving God night and day (ἐν ἐκτενείᾳ νύκτα καὶ ἡμέραν λατρεῦον). Yet, it was precisely concerning that hope (περὶ ἧς ἐλπίδος) that the Jews were accusing him (ἐγκαλοῦμαι ὑπὸ ᾿Ιουδαίων). The rhetorical question with which Paul closed this part of his speech (τί ἄπιστον κρίνεται παρ᾽ ὑμῖν εἰ ὁ θεὸς νεκροὺς ἐγείρει;) made it clear that such a hope was entirely credible (Bock 2007, 714). So far, Paul had left unstated the truth that the risen Jesus was the fulfillment of that resurrection hope. His subsequent proofs would make that truth increasingly clear.

26:9–11. Although he was fully committed to the Jewish hope of an end-time resurrection, Paul did not initially accept the early church's claims that Jesus had risen. In fact, he convinced himself (ἔδοξα ἐμαυτῷ) that it was necessary (δεῖν) "to do everything [he] could to oppose the very name of Jesus the Nazarene" (NLT, πρὸς τὸ ὄνομα ᾿Ιησοῦ τοῦ Ναζωραίου . . . πολλὰ ἐναντία πρᾶξαι). He recounted four ways in which he pursued that objective, beginning in Jerusalem. He received authority from the high priests (τὴν παρὰ τῶν ἀρχιερέων ἐξουσίαν λαβών) to lock up (κατέκλεισα) many of the saints in prison (πολλούς τῶν ἁγίων ἐγὼ ἐν φυλακαῖς). He cast his vote against them (κατήνεγκα ψῆφον) when they were executed (ἀναιρουμένων αὐτῶν). Many times, he punished them in the synagogues (πάσας τὰς συναγωγὰς πολλάκις τιμωρῶν αὐτούς) and tried to compel them to blaspheme (ἠνάγκαζον βλασφημεῖν). Because he was enraged with them beyond measure (περισσῶς ἐμμαινόμενος αὐτοῖς), he began persecuting them (ἐδίωκον, inceptive imperfect) even in the cities outside (καὶ εἰς τὰς ἔξω πόλεις) Palestine.

It is most natural to understand "casting his vote" against those who were executed as an allusion to Paul's support for the stoning of Stephen (7:58) and perhaps others like him. For "in all the synagogues," NIV suggests "I went from one synagogue to another." In this context, to "blaspheme" would be to "deny their faith" (GNB) or to "curse Jesus" (NLT). Schnabel concludes that the tendential imperfect of ἠνάγκαζον "denotes a consistent effort that did not succeed" (2012, 1006). The verb ἐμμαίνομαι describes the mental state of "being so furiously angry with someone as to be almost out of one's mind" (L&N §88.182). The reference to cities outside Palestine sets the stage for Paul's description of his encounter with the risen Jesus.

26:12–15. Paul's perspective changed radically, however, when the risen Jesus appeared to him on the road to Damascus. This description of Paul's Damascus road vision repeats information that is present in previous accounts (9:1–5; 22:5–8). Paul was traveling to Damascus with authority from the high priests (μετ᾽ ἐξουσίας καὶ ἐπιτροπῆς τῆς τῶν ἀρχιερέων), when a heavenly light shone around the travelers (οὐρανόθεν . . . λαμπρότητα τοῦ ἡλίου περιλάμψαν με φῶς καὶ τοὺς σὺν ἐμοὶ πορευομένους). In response, they all fell to the ground (πάντων καταπεσόντων ἡμῶν εἰς τὴν γῆν). Then, Paul heard a voice asking why he was persecuting the speaker (Σαοὺλ Σαούλ, τί με διώκεις;). When Paul asked who the speaker was (Τίς εἶ, κύριε;), the speaker identified himself as the very Jesus whom Paul had been opposing (ἐγώ εἰμι ᾿Ιησοῦς ὃν σὺ διώκεις).

The account also includes three new pieces of information. First, Paul described the light that shone around the party as "brighter than the sun" (ὑπὲρ τὴν λαμπρότητα τοῦ ἡλίου). Second, he noted that Jesus spoke to him "in the Hebrew dialect" (τῇ ῾Εβραΐδι διαλέκτῳ). Third, he added Jesus's statement, "It is difficult for you to kick against the goads" (σκληρόν σοι πρὸς κέντρα λακτίζειν). The brightness of the light highlights the divine glory of the risen Jesus, and as Larkin notes, in the next section of Paul's speech, light becomes a metaphor for revelation and salvation (1995, 359). See 21:40 on "the Hebrew dialect." Lothar Schmid suggests that Jesus's statement about the difficulty of kicking against the goads echoed a common Greek and Roman saying that was "an expression of futile and detrimental resistance to a stronger power, whether it be that of a god, of destiny, or of man" (*TDNT* 3:664). Redford views the saying as one that would have captured Agrippa's attention as a client king who was subject to Roman authority (2004, 292). For Paul, it would have emphasized Jesus's divine authority. When the risen Jesus appeared to Paul, it was as one with divine glory and authority, a combination that radically altered his understanding of who Jesus was.

26:16–18. Not only did the risen Jesus appear to Paul, but he also explained the reason for appearing (εἰς τοῦτο γὰρ ὤφθην σοι): to commission Paul for ministry. As Larkin notes, the account of Jesus commissioning Paul on the Damascus road is "unparalleled in chapters 9 and 26" (1995, 360), where Ananias confirms the commission. Bock concludes, however, that the information "is supplied here for its dramatic effect . . . giving details held back until now" (2007, 717). Peterson notes the echoes of OT prophetic calls in Ezekiel 2:1–10, Jeremiah 1:1–10, and Isaiah 42:1–9 (2009, 668). Paul's account includes six elements: call, role, assurance, audience, mission, and message.

Call (26:16a)	Rise and stand	ἀνάστηθι καὶ στῆθι ἐπὶ τοὺς πόδας σου
Role (26:16b)	Chosen as a servant and witness of things seen	προχειρίσασθαί σε ὑπηρέτην καὶ μάρτυρα ὧν τε εἶδές ὧν τε ὀφθήσομαί σοι
Assurance (26:17a)	Protection from Jews and Gentiles	ἐξαιρούμενός σε ἐκ τοῦ λαοῦ καὶ ἐκ τῶν ἐθνῶν
Audience (26:17b)	Sent to Jews and Gentiles	εἰς οὓς ἐγὼ ἀποστέλλω σε
Mission (26:18a)	To open eyes in order to turn from darkness to light and from Satan to God	ἀνοῖξαι ὀφθαλμοὺς αὐτῶν, τοῦ ἐπιστρέψαι ἀπὸ σκότους εἰς φῶς καὶ τῆς ἐξουσίας τοῦ Σατανᾶ ἐπὶ τὸν θεόν
Message (26:18b)	Resulting in forgiveness of sins and a share among the saints by faith in Jesus	τοῦ λαβεῖν αὐτοὺς ἄφεσιν ἁμαρτιῶν καὶ κλῆρον ἐν τοῖς ἡγιασμένοις πίστει τῇ εἰς ἐμέ

Jesus's command for Paul to rise and stand echoes God's command to Ezekiel (Ezek. 2:1). The idea of God choosing him is present in both 9:15 (σκεῦος ἐκλογῆς ἐστίν μοι) and 22:14 (προεχειρίσατό σε), as is his role as a witness, although it is articulated differently in 9:15 (τοῦ βαστάσαι τὸ ὄνομά μου). The assurance of protection echoes a similar promise to Jeremiah (Jer. 1:8). That protection is from both Jews (ἐκ τοῦ λαοῦ) and Gentiles (ἐκ τῶν ἐθνῶν), who are the audience to whom Jesus sent Paul (9:15; 22:15). Opening the eyes of the blind was part of the mission of the servant of the Lord (Isa. 42:7), as was bringing light to the Gentiles (Isa. 42:6; 49:6). "Turning" (ἐπιστρέφω) was a key aspect of the early church's message (9:35; 11:21; 14:15; cf. 1 Thess. 1:9), while both repentance and the forgiveness of sins were essentials of the gospel (Luke 24:47; Acts 2:38). Werner Foerster concludes that κλῆρος ("share" or "portion") in this passage "denotes the heavenly gift which God has allotted to each called believer in fellowship with all the saints, not so much as a 'lot,' but as a present benefit which God apportions to each, thus giving him a share, his individual share, in that which is prepared for the community" (*TDNT* 3:764; cf. 8:21; Col. 1:12). Schnabel suggests that verse 18 sets out three parts of the process of conversion: understand, change direction, and receive (2012, 1012).

TEXTUAL ANALYSIS: "to open . . . to turn . . . to receive"
The function of the three infinitives in verse 18 is debated (Barrett 1998, 1161; Culy and Parsons 2003, 498). The absence of conjunctions suggests that the most likely understanding is to take ἀνοῖξαι as the purpose of ἀποστέλλω, τοῦ ἐπιστρέψαι as the purpose of ἀνοῖξαι, and τοῦ λαβεῖν as the result of τοῦ ἐπιστρέψαι. In other words, God sends his witness with the purpose of opening the eyes of the audience, which in turn, has the purpose of the audience turning from darkness to light, with the result that they receive forgiveness of sins and a share among the saints by means of their faith (πίστει, dative of means) in Jesus.

26:19–20. Confronted and commissioned by the risen Jesus (τῇ οὐρανίῳ ὀπτασίᾳ) whom he had been persecuting, Paul responded obediently (οὐκ ἐγενόμη ἀπειθής) by proclaiming (ἀπήγγελλον) the message Jesus gave him—first in Damascus (ἐν Δαμασκῷ πρῶτόν), then in Jerusalem (Ἱεροσολύμοις), then throughout Judea (πᾶσάν τε τὴν χώραν τῆς Ἰουδαίας), and finally to the Gentiles (τοῖς ἔθνεσιν). Barrett notes οὐκ ἐγενόμην ἀπειθής ("I was not disobedient") as an instance of litotes (1998, 1161), and Bock translates Paul's statement as "[I] was fully obedient" (2007, 719). The geographical progress corresponds to Luke's narrative in 9:20–23 (Damascus), 9:26–29 (Jerusalem), 15:3 (Judea), and 15:36–20:38 (the Gentiles). The progressive imperfect tense of ἀπήγγελλον highlights the extended and ongoing nature of Paul's obedience. Paul's message was congruent

with Jesus's commission and the preaching of the early church—repentance (μετανοεῖν), turning to God (ἐπιστρέφειν ἐπὶ τὸν θεόν), and a changed life (ἄξια τῆς μετανοίας ἔργα πράσσοντας).

26:21–23. Paul's obedience in proclaiming to both Jew and Gentile that the risen Jesus was the fulfillment of the OT promise of the resurrection (ἕνεκα τούτων) began the process that brought him to stand before the king in the audience hall of the governor's praetorium in Caesarea. Despite the Jews seizing him while he was in the Jerusalem temple (συλλαβόμενοι [ὄντα] ἐν τῷ ἱερῷ) and repeatedly trying to kill him (ἐπειρῶντο διαχειρίσασθαι), Paul remained obedient to his commission. The help he received from God (ἐπικουρίας τυχὼν τῆς ἀπὸ τοῦ θεοῦ) sustained him "until this day" (ἄχρι τῆς ἡμέρας ταύτης), so that he now stood (ἕστηκα) before Agrippa and the assembly and continued bearing witness (μαρτυρόμενος) "to both small and great" (μικρῷ τε καὶ μεγάλῳ). The imperfect tense of ἐπειρῶντο reflects the Jews' repeated attempts on Paul's life. Διαχειρίζω denotes taking hold of someone forcibly with malicious intent and frequently ending in the taking of life (BDAG s.v. "διαχειρίζω" 240). Τυχών is an adverbial participle of cause. Culy and Parsons suggest that the genitive article in the phrase τῆς ἀπὸ τοῦ θεοῦ "adds force to the expression," and the suggest the translation "the kind of help that only comes from God" (2003, 500).

Paul's message was nothing other (οὐδὲν ἐκτός) than what both the prophets and Moses said was about to happen (ὧν . . . ἐλάλησαν μελλόντων γίνεσθαι) and included three events. First, the Messiah would be subject to suffering (εἰ παθητὸς ὁ Χριστός). Second, the Messiah would be the first to rise from the dead (εἰ πρῶτος ἐξ ἀναστάσεως νεκρῶν). Third, light would be proclaimed (φῶς μέλλει καταγγέλλειν) both to the Jews and to the Gentiles (τῷ τε λαῷ καὶ τοῖς ἔθνεσιν). Culy and Parsons conclude that the two occurrences of εἰ at the beginning of verse 23 introduce questions ("Was Christ destined to suffer? Was he the first to rise from the dead?) leading to the logical conclusion that "Then of course he is going to proclaim light" (2003, 489). The adjective παθητός denotes "being subject to suffering" (L&N §24.85). The phrase πρῶτος ἐξ ἀναστάσεως νεκρῶν ("first out of the resurrection of the dead") echoes the language of Paul's letters where he writes that Jesus is "the firstborn from the dead" (1 Cor. 15:20; Col. 1:18). The reference to light (φῶς) forms an *inclusio* around verses 12–23 and connects the light of Jesus's glory to the light of salvation he offers.

Paul's testimony of his witness to both small and great was a synopsis of the gospel message that runs throughout Luke's narrative, including the salvation plan set out in Scripture (26:22), the salvation events of Jesus's death (26:23a) and resurrection (26:23b), and the universal scope of the salvation offer (26:23c). Central to that message was Jesus's resurrection. Larkin writes, "Without the resurrection of Christ, the defining moment in human history, there is no future hope for anyone. But when we let Christ's resurrection be our defining moment, the lights come on for our past, present and future" (1995, 363).

Paul's Interaction with Festus and Agrippa (26:24–29)

Paul assures Festus that he is not insane and invites Agrippa to believe the message he has delivered.

26:24–25. Paul's theological explanation was so far outside Festus's frame of reference that the governor considered it irrational. While he was still making his defense (ταῦτα αὐτοῦ ἀπολογουμένου), the governor interrupted loudly (μεγάλῃ τῇ φωνῇ φησιν), accused Paul of being out of his mind (μαίνῃ, Παῦλε), and declared "Too much study has made you crazy!" (NLT, τὰ πολλά σε γράμματα εἰς μανίαν περιτρέπει). In response, Paul assured Festus he was not insane (οὐ μαίνομαι); rather, what he was saying was both true and reasonable (ἀληθείας καὶ σωφροσύνης ῥήματα). The verb μαίνομαι describes thinking or reasoning in a completely irrational manner (L&N §30.24), and the noun μανία denotes madness, frenzy, or delirium (BDAG s.v. "μανία" 615). In contrast, σωφροσύνη denotes soundness of mind, reasonableness, and rationality (BDAG s.v. "σωφροσύνη" 1, 987).

26:26–27. Paul's primary audience, however, was Agrippa, who knew about these matters (ἐπίσταται περὶ τούτων ὁ βασιλεύς) and to whom he was speaking boldly (πρὸς ὃν παρρησιαζόμενος λαλῶ). Since the events surrounding the beginning of the Christian movement had not happened "in a corner" (οὐ ἐστιν ἐν γωνίᾳ πεπραγμένον τοῦτο), Paul could not bring himself to believe (οὐ πείθομαι) that any of those events had escaped the king's notice (λανθάνειν αὐτὸν τούτων . . . οὐθέν; cf. BDAG s.v. "λανθάνω" 586). So, he spoke directly to Agrippa and asked whether the king believed the prophets (πιστεύεις . . . τοῖς προφήταις;).

"This" (τοῦτο) and "these things" (τούτων) point back to the messianic events Paul described in verse 23. Πείθομαι is a reflexive middle, with the sense of "I am persuading myself," although most English versions translate the phrase οὐ πείθομαι as "I am convinced" (e.g., NIV) or "I cannot believe" (e.g., NET). Culy and Parsons conclude that it is best to take οὐθέν with λανθάνειν αὐτὸν τούτων (2003, 503). The resulting translation would be "he is aware of none of these things." Bock notes that the idea of something done "in a corner" (ἐν γωνίᾳ) was a metaphor describing "hidden events tucked away somewhere . . . out of public sight" (2007, 722). Schnabel writes that Paul used the proverb "to emphasize that the event connected with Jesus of Nazareth and the activities of his followers were common knowledge and part of the historical record" (2012, 1016).

26:28–29. Agrippa found himself in danger of being caught in a logical trap (Marshall 1980, 400). On the one hand, he was not prepared to deny that he believed the prophets. On the other hand, he was not prepared to affirm that Jesus was the fulfillment of what the prophets taught. So, he temporized with a rhetorical question: "Do you think that in such a short time you can persuade me to be a Christian?" (NIV, ἐν ὀλίγῳ με πείθεις Χριστιανὸν ποιῆσαι;). Paul, however, continued by challenging the king and all those who were listening to him that day (πάντας τοὺς ἀκούοντάς μου σήμερον) to become as he was (γενέσθαι τοιούτους ὁποῖος καὶ ἐγώ εἰμι)—with the exception of his chains (παρεκτὸς τῶν δεσμῶν τούτων).

TEXTUAL ANALYSIS: Agrippa's Response to Paul

Commentators raise multiple questions about Agrippa's response to Paul's question about whether he believed the prophets (Barrett 1998, 1170–71). Was his response a statement or a question? Was he being serious or ironic? Does the phrase ἐν ὀλίγῳ refer to time ("in a little time") or to degree ("with a little effort")? Was the original reading με πείθεις Χριστιανὸν ποιῆσαι ("you think to make me a Christian," RSV) or με πείθεις Χριστιανὸν γενέσθαι ("you are persuading me to become a Christian," NET)? Ποιῆσαι has stronger manuscript support (P[74], ℵ, A, B). Ἐν ὀλίγῳ is most likely temporal (Schnabel 2012, 1017). If so, the corresponding phrase in Paul's counterresponse (καὶ ἐν ὀλίγῳ καὶ ἐν μεγάλῳ) is also temporal ("in a short time or in a long time," LEB). The use of Χριστιανός (cf. 11:26) suggests that Agrippa was being ironic rather than serious (Bock 2007, 723). If Agrippa's response was a question (Peterson 2009, 676), he asked, "In this short time do you think you will make me a Christian?" (GNB).

Agrippa's Verdict (26:30–32)

Agrippa declares that Paul has done nothing worthy of death or imprisonment and could have been set free if he had not appealed to Caesar.

26:30–32. With the hearing at an end, the action reached "the judicial climax of Luke's narrative since 21:27" (Schnabel 2012, 1018), and King Agrippa became the third high-ranking official to declare that Paul was not guilty of doing anything contrary to Roman law (cf. 23:29; 25:25). Agrippa, Festus, Bernice, and the other assembled participants (οἱ συγκαθήμενοι αὐτοῖς) arose (ἀνέστη) withdrew (ἀναχωρήσαντες) and began discussing together (ἐλάλουν πρὸς ἀλλήλους, inceptive imperfect) what they had heard. Their conclusion was that Paul had done nothing worthy of death or imprisonment (οὐδὲν θανάτου ἢ δεσμῶν ἄξιον πράσσει ὁ ἄνθρωπος οὗτος). Agrippa's verdict was the final word on the matter: It would have been possible to release Paul (ἀπολελύσθαι ἐδύνατο ὁ ἄνθρωπος οὗτος) if he had not appealed to Caesar (εἰ μὴ ἐπεκέκλητο Καίσαρα). As Bock writes, "the speech is a legal success, but it changes nothing" (2007, 725), because "to acquit Paul now would be to short-circuit his appeal, and so to invade the Emperor's territory" (Stott 1990, 377). Paul's time in Caesarea was at an end. His next journey would take him to Rome.

THEOLOGICAL FOCUS

Acts 25:13–26:32 serves several narratival functions. It closes the period of Paul's extended imprisonment in Caesarea and climaxes the series of five defense speeches in chapters 22–26. It includes the third account of Paul's conversion that, with the account in chapter 9, "brackets the main body of Paul's missionary work" (Dunn 1996, 324). It incorporates a gospel presentation before high government officials that, most likely, previews Paul's future defense before the emperor. It fulfills Jesus's statement to Ananias that Paul would bear his name "before the Gentiles, kings, and the sons of Israel" (9:15). It concludes with the third declaration of Paul's innocence (23:29; 25:25; 26:32) and confirms that Christianity poses no threat to Roman civil authority.

The theological heart of Acts 25:13–26:32 is the account of Paul's speech and his interaction with Festus and Agrippa that follows the speech (26:2–29). In that section, he provides a clear response to Jewish critics and a clear appeal to Roman seekers. In responding to Jewish critics, Paul makes it clear that the Christian movement rests on divine revelation and authority (26:12–15), affirms the messianic promises of the OT (26:22), and fulfills Israel's responsibility to bring the light of salvation to the nations (26:23). In appealing to Roman seekers, Paul makes it clear that his message is true and reasonable (26:25); that the events surrounding Jesus's life, death, and resurrection are matters of public record (26:26); that the gospel offers light, forgiveness of sins, and a place among God's people to both Jew and Gentile (26:16–18); and that neither his ministry nor the Christian movement is a threat to Roman law or public order (26:21).

PREACHING AND TEACHING STRATEGIES

Exegetical/Theological Synthesis
Festus had made the decision to send Paul to Rome in response to his appeal to Caesar, but the governor was still at a loss as to the charges that should accompany the prisoner. Luke's first-century readers would have wanted to know how Festus would go about solving his problem. What process would he use? Would he consult anyone outside his council of advisors? What conclusion would he reach? When the governor consulted King Herod Agrippa II, the king gave Paul one final opportunity to address the question of why Festus was sending him to Rome. His answer was simple: he was going to Rome because he was an obedient witness in response to the commission that the risen Jesus had given him.

In his appearance before Agrippa and other assembled dignitaries, Paul made a formal speech in polished, literary Greek (Bruce 1988, 461) that summarized his own life and ministry, incorporated the essentials of the gospel message, and concluded with an evangelistic invitation. In so doing, he provided Luke's readers with a preview of his presentation before Caesar and a model of how to present the gospel faithfully before a distinguished non-Jewish audience. With his original readers, Luke's twenty-first-century audience shares the need to understand the nature of the gospel and how to present its message effectively. Paul's speech makes it clear that the gospel is the product of divine revelation, is the fulfillment of the OT promises, focuses on Jesus and his resurrection, has universal scope, is true and reasonable, expects a response of obedient commitment, and poses no threat to the state.

Preaching/Teaching Idea
The gospel proclaims Messiah, not madness or mayhem.

Contemporary Connections

What does it mean?
The gospel is not madness or mayhem. This legal proceeding against Paul has spanned six chapters now and counting. He has stood before a crowd, a Roman tribune, the Jewish council, governors Felix and Festus, and now King Herod Agrippa II. This latest and highest hearing declared Paul to be innocent of wrongdoing and deserving no punishment (26:31–32). Paul's message was not mayhem, and it was not anarchy. Where Caesar sticks to the things that are Caesar's, the church can freely attend to the things of God (Matt. 22:21). Nor is the gospel the madness with which Festus charged Paul (26:24). The good news is girded in "true and rational words" (26:25).

Over against those charges, the gospel is the pronouncement of the risen Messiah in accordance with Moses. Festus himself even understood the heart of the matter in his fumbling explanation to Agrippa (25:19). Paul once thought as the court did, that Jesus died and stayed dead. Upon his encounter with the very living and breathing, once dead now alive Jesus, however, he did what he would go on to tell Gentiles to do: "repent and turn to God, performing deeds in keeping with their repentance" (26:20). Paul's entire testimony aligned exactly "with what the prophets and Moses said would come to pass" (26:22).

Is it true?

As Paul speaks his final lines on the stage of God's providence, we lean in to listen well. Clearly Luke is taking his time to linger over this trial to give full weight to the Spirit speaking through Paul. As noted above, it is no coincidence that all the essential elements of the gospel are here on full display—a gospel that has been preached, prayed, and defended, even to the point of martyrdom. This gospel that proclaims a risen Messiah was always God's plan according to the Scriptures. Moses and all the prophets pointed to him. This long-promised Messiah has finally come in the person of Jesus, who lived, died, and rose from the dead to offer salvation to all, Jew and Gentile alike. The person who repents and believes will receive forgiveness of sins. Yet Festus and Agrippa take turns mocking this winsome gospel presentation. Festus calls Paul mad. Agrippa seems to tease sarcastically that Paul could possibly talk him into faith. They cannot see the plain truth sitting in front of their noses for what it is.

Now what?

The world seeks to pigeonhole the gospel. In our passage, madness and mayhem are the charges. In our day and age, it is considered quaint, archaic, a feel-good chicken soup for the sickly souls in our midst. Others view the gospel as narrow-minded, exclusive, and bigoted. Whatever the presupposition, putting God and his gospel in a box frees an audience to stand in judgment over its validity.

Festus and Agrippa did just that. Our friends and neighbors do it too. The need of the hour, however, is to silence the outside noise belittling this message and to hold fast to the good news of great joy for all people. Find space to savor the essentials of the gospel listed above: promised in Scripture, Jesus's death and resurrection, salvation offered to all, repentance, and the forgiveness of sins. Each is a treasure trove to study and value for this lifetime and for an eternal life to come. No worldly derision can take it from a believer.

Creativity in Presentation

The 2003 film *Luther* depicts the incredible drama of the German reformer Martin Luther before the Diet of Worms in 1521. It has a bit of an Acts 26 ring to it. Luther stands alone before the pomp and power of Rome. He is being pressed to recant his views, but against that pressure, Luther declares, "My conscience is captive to the Word of God. I cannot and I will not recant anything, for to go against conscience is neither right nor safe. God help me. Amen." Luther sounds a lot like Paul, who doubled down on the truth of Scripture at the risk of whatever punishment and prolonged imprisonment lay ahead.

A sermon or lesson from this passage starts with an accusation of madness and mayhem (25:13–27; 26:24). The Jews petition for death, accusing Paul of blasphemy and stirring up trouble in Jerusalem. Festus chalks Paul's teaching up to madness. Agrippa is hard to read and uses sarcasm well to hide his true feelings. In response, Paul lays out a defense of the gospel of the Messiah according to Moses (26:1–29). All the elements of the gospel are here to expound and savor. Paul can testify to them from Scripture and from personal experience. They are "true and rational words" (26:25). They do more than merely inform an audience; they appeal for a response (26:27–29). In a stroke of irony, Agrippa delivers his personal verdict with no legal bearing to the case. He thinks Paul does not deserve death and could have been set free (26:30–32). The irony is that his verdict is also the gospel. Paul has been declaring the same truth all along. In the Messiah, Paul has crossed from death to life, from chains to freedom. God has rendered that very verdict, and it is his verdict that matters most.

The gospel proclaims Messiah, not madness or mayhem.

- The gospel is not the madness or mayhem it is often occused of being (25:13–27; 26:24).

- The gospel is the proclamation of the Messiah (26:1–29).

DISCUSSION QUESTIONS

1. Why did Festus bring Paul's situation to Agrippa's attention? What insight did he hope Agrippa would be able to provide?

2. What does Paul's account of his upbringing and opposition to Christianity contribute to the account of his life and ministry?

3. How does the third account of Paul's encounter with Jesus compare with the previous two accounts (9:1–19a; 22:1–21)? Which elements are similar? Which are different?

4. Why would Festus have considered Paul's presentation to be "madness"? What elements would he have had difficulty understanding or accepting?

5. How would you evaluate Agrippa's answer to Paul's appeal (26:28)? Was he being serious or evasive? Why?

MALTA AND ROME (ACTS 27:1–28:31)

Agrippa's verdict (26:32) confirmed Festus's declaration to Paul, "You have appealed to Caesar; to Caesar you shall go" (25:12). All that remains for Luke to narrate is Paul's travel to Rome so that he could bear witness in that city as Jesus had promised (23:11). That travel would involve storm (27:13–38), shipwreck (27:39–44), and snakebite (28:1–6), and would once again demonstrate God's divine protection and control over Paul's life and ministry. Along the way, Paul would have the opportunity to minister encouragement to his fellow travelers (27:21–26, 33–38) and healing to the residents of Malta (28:7–10). After completing his travel to Rome (28:11–15), Paul followed his proven ministry practice of preaching the gospel to the Jews first and then—when they rejected his message—turning to the Gentiles (28:16–28). While he waited for his appearance before Caesar, Paul openly and freely preached the Lord Jesus Christ to anyone who would listen for two full years (28:30–31). The events Luke reports most likely cover the time period from the fall of A.D. 59 to the spring of A.D. 62.

59	Fall	Caesarea to Malta (27:1–44)	
60	Winter	Malta (28:1–10)	
	Spring	Malta to Rome (28:11–15)	
	Summer		
	Fall		
61	Winter		
	Spring	Rome (28:16–31)	Colossians and Philemon
	Summer		Ephesians
	Fall		
62	Winter		Philippians
	Spring		

Homiletically, the seventh division of Acts consists of three sections. The first section narrates the first phase of Paul's journey to Rome, as a violent storm propelled the ship on which he was traveling across the Mediterranean and wrecked that ship on the island of Malta (27:1–44). The second section describes Paul's three-month ministry on Malta while he waited for sea travel to resume (28:1–10). The third section closes the book by recounting Paul's arrival in Rome and summarizing his ministry in the capital of the empire (28:11–31).

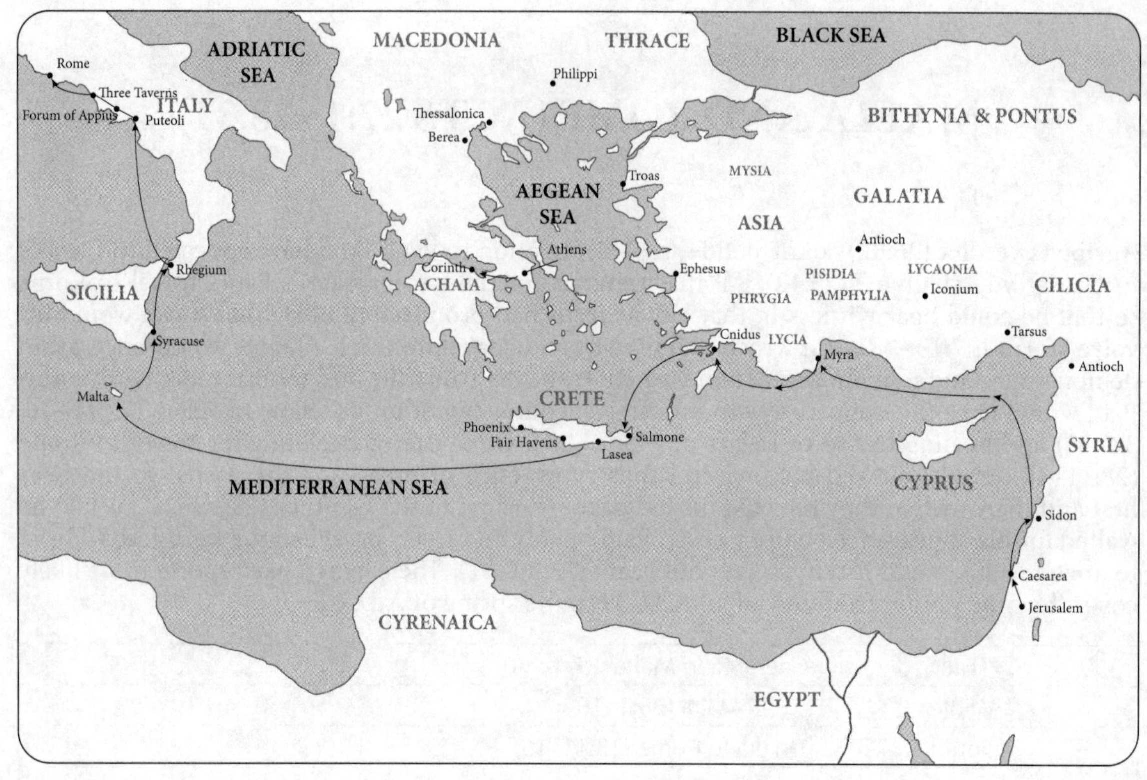

Paul's Journey to Rome

Acts 27:1–44

EXEGETICAL IDEA
Paul's sea voyage to Rome began with travel against contrary winds, continued with a violent storm, ended in a shipwreck, and gave Paul opportunities to speak words of encouragement to his fellow travelers based on God's promise of deliverance.

THEOLOGICAL FOCUS
God's protection from danger provides opportunities to point others to him.

PREACHING IDEA
God's protection should prompt our proclamation.

PREACHING POINTERS
"God moves in a mysterious way, his wonders to perform. He plants his footsteps in the sea, and rides upon the storm." Was William Cowper (1731–1800) thinking of Acts 27 when he wrote that hymn? One thing is certain: we can all relate to the power of God that storms reveal. Some people might talk about the power of "Mother Nature," but God is the true power behind any storm. In fact, storms are simply one facet of God's providential governing of his creation. Storms—natural or spiritual— are also one of the means God uses to accomplish his purposes in and for his people. The divine reassurance he offers in the midst of those storms is another. When a violent storm swept down from the mountains of Crete and blew Paul and his traveling companions across the Mediterranean Sea to run aground fourteen days later on the island of Malta, they were never outside God's will or outside his protection. The angelic reassurance Paul received in the midst of the storm led him to encourage the crew and other passengers to trust in God's protection and deliverance. Confidence in God's protection from danger prompted Paul to point others to him as well.

People today should be able to relate to travel and decisions related to travel, as well as to severe weather and storms. They should also be able to relate to anxiety created by danger, seemingly hopeless circumstances, and the positive effects of encouragement in those circumstances. The passage corrects putting profit ahead of prudence, thinking that a majority opinion is necessarily always the best one, viewing any situation as hopeless in God's providential control, and failing to look for the potentially positive side of dangerous situations. The passage commends trusting in God's protection, heeding wise counsel, caring about the safety of others, encouraging others in dangerous situations, and speaking up for God in those situations. The objective in communicating the passage should be to help listeners understand that they can trust God to protect them from danger, so that they will look for opportunities to share their trust in him with others.

STORM AND SHIPWRECK (27:1–44)

LITERARY STRUCTURE AND THEMES (27:1–44)

The passage is a continuous travel narrative describing a sea voyage. The voyage proceeds in three stages: from Caesarea in Palestine to Myra in Lycia (27:1–5), from Myra to Fair Havens on the island of Crete (27:6–12), and from Crete to the island of Malta (27:13–44). The third stage divides into five sections that follow an A-B-A-B-A pattern, alternating between the desperate actions of the crew and passengers as they face a violent storm (A) and two brief speeches by Paul as he seeks to assure them of God's deliverance (B).

A   The first thirteen days of the storm (27:13–20)

B   Paul's encouragement to trust God (27:21–26)

A   The fourteenth night of the storm (27:27–32)

B   Paul's encouragement to take food (27:33–38)

A   The shipwreck on the fourteenth day (27:39–44)

The interplay of storm, speeches, and shipwreck highlights Paul's trust in God and his care for his fellow travelers. Peterson suggests that the passage "portray[s] human beings in a desperate situation, in need of God's help . . . shows the importance of believing his word and relying on his power for deliverance . . . [and] demonstrates the opportunity that the believer has in such a situation to draw attention to the character of God and to encourage unbelievers to turn to him for mercy" (2009, 680).

- ***Travel from Caesarea to Myra (27:1–5)***
- ***Travel from Myra to Crete (27:6–12)***
- ***The Storm at Sea (27:13–20)***
- ***Paul's First Word of Encouragement (27:21–26)***
- ***Approaching Land (27:27–32)***
- ***Paul's Second Word of Encouragement (27:33–38)***
- ***Shipwreck on Malta (27:39–44)***

EXPOSITION (27:1–44)

Bruce writes, "Luke's narrative of the voyage and shipwreck of Paul on his way to Italy is a small classic in its own right" (1988, 474). Longenecker calls the passage "one of the most vivid pieces of descriptive writing in the whole Bible" (1981, 556). Bruce and others note echoes in Luke's account of sea voyages found in the writings of Homer and the OT book of Jonah (Bruce 1998, 474). The first-person narrative that begins in 27:1 adds vividness to the passage. Because first-person narrative occurred frequently in ancient literary accounts of long sea voyages, however, some scholars suggest that its use in this passage is a literary convention. It is more natural, however, to view its use in this narrative as Luke recording his eyewitness account of events. See the introduction for a discussion of the "we" passages. As a whole, the voyage narrated in Acts 27 divides into three stages, with the third as the longest and most dangerous.

Stage	Approximate Distance	Duration
Caesarea to Myra (27:1–5)	450 miles	15 days (27:5 textual variant)
Myra to Fair Havens (27:6–12)	370 miles	many days (27:7)
Fair Havens to Malta (27:13–44)	500 miles	14 days (27:27)

To say that Paul had faced danger during his ministry would be an understatement. The dangers he enumerated when he wrote to the Corinthians included "three times I was shipwrecked," "a night and a day I have spent in the deep," and "[I have been in] dangers on the sea" (2 Cor. 11:25–26). During this voyage, Paul and his fellow travelers found themselves facing dangers on the sea because others had ignored his sound advice (27:10). Travelers on the Mediterranean were well acquainted with four periods of sea travel (Hesiod, *Op.* 663–68):

Dangerous travel	March 11 through May 14
Optimum travel	May 15 through September 15
Dangerous travel	September 16 through November 10
No travel	November 11 through March 10

In A.D. 59, the Jewish fast days began on October 5 (Bock 2007, 733), and Luke notes that "the fast was already over" (27:9). Despite Paul's advice to spend the winter in Fair Havens, the ship most likely left that harbor around the end of October or the beginning of November,

which would have been approaching the end of the dangerous fall travel period.

As Paul was no stranger to storms and shipwreck, he was also no stranger to God's protection in and deliverance from danger. This passage highlights four dynamics that were at work as Paul faced this particular storm and shipwreck. First, God's providential protection brought him through the dangers created by the poor decisions of others and the powerful forces of nature. Second, God's faithfulness to his promises included angelic reassurance that Paul would reach Rome regardless of the dangers before him. Third, his confidence that he would survive those dangers rested on his faith in God's promises. Fourth, his faith also led him to encourage those around him to follow his example of turning to God as they faced danger.

Travel from Caesarea to Myra (27:1–5)

The centurion who is delivering Paul to Rome arranges passage on a ship that sails along the coast from Caesarea to Myra.

27:1–2. Perhaps because Luke describes Paul's transfer for the voyage to Italy so succinctly, the Western text expands verse 1 to read "So then the governor decided to send him to Caesar; and the next day he called a centurion named Julius of the Augustan Cohort, and delivered to him Paul with the other prisoners" (*TCGNT*, 439). Julius was able to arrange passage on a ship that was about to sail (μέλλοντι πλεῖν) for its home port of Adramyttium and was stopping at places along the coast of Asia (εἰς τοὺς κατὰ τὴν Ἀσίαν τόπους). When the ship put out to sea (ἀνήχθημεν), Paul's companions included Luke and Aristarchus from the church in Thessalonica.

The Augustan Cohort was based in Syria (Barrett 1998, 1181). Bruce suggests that Julius was an officer charged with supervising the transport of grain to Rome (1988, 477), but others disagree (Rapske 1994, 274). Adramyttium was on the western coast of the province of Asia, not far from Troas (Marshall 1980, 403). The fourth and final "we" passage begins in 27:1 and continues through Paul's arrival in Rome (28:16). The natural reading is that Luke accompanied Paul on the trip. Both Luke (Acts 19:29; 20:4) and Paul (Col. 4:10, 14; Philem. 24) mention Aristarchus in connection with Paul's travels and his imprisonment in Rome.

27:3–5. The ship made its first stop in Sidon, where the centurion treated Paul with consideration (φιλανθρώπως) and permitted him to visit friends in the city (ἐπέτρεψεν πρὸς τοὺς φίλους πορευθέντι) who cared for him (ἐπιμελείας τυχεῖν). From Sidon, the ship sailed north of Cyprus (ὑπεπλεύσαμεν τὴν Κύπρον) in order to deal with headwinds that hindered its progress (διὰ τὸ τοὺς ἀνέμους εἶναι ἐναντίους) as it crossed the open sea (τό πέλαγος . . . διαπλεύσαντες) parallel with the regions of Cilicia and Pamphylia. It finally arrived (κατήλθομεν) at the port of Myra in Lycia. The Western text notes that the travel time from Caesarea to Myra was fifteen days (27:5).

It is possible that Paul might have visited Sidon three times previously (11:30; 12:25; 15:3). The adverb φιλανθρώπως describes the act of treating someone in a kindly fashion (BDAG s.v. "φιλανθρώπως" 1056); ἐπιμελείας denotes care, diligent concern, or provision of whatever might be needed (L&N §35.44). The nautical term ὑπεπλεύσαμεν describes sailing under the lee of an island in such a way that the island protects the ship from the wind (BDAG s.v. "ὑποπλέω" 1040). Διαπλεύσαντες denotes sailing through an area from one side to the other (L&N §54.11); πέλαγος describes a relatively deep area of the ocean sufficiently far from land as to be beyond the range of any protection from the seacoast (L&N §1.73). Myra was a port along the southern coast of Asia Minor that was due north of Alexandria and a regular stop for ships carrying grain from Egypt to Italy. In Myra, the ships could take on provisions for the next stage of their journey (Schnabel 2012, 1035). It was a port in which the centurion could be reasonably certain of finding a ship bound for Italy,

Travel from Myra to Crete (27:6–12)

The centurion arranges passage on a ship sailing for Italy that travels along the southern coast of Asia Minor, crosses open water to Crete, and travels along the southern coast of the island to Fair Havens, where Paul advises the centurion and the boat's captain to spend the winter months.

27:6–8. When he found a ship from Alexandria that was sailing for Italy, the centurion booked passage on it and put the travelers aboard (ἐνεβίβασεν). The ship continued sailing slowly (βραδυπλοοῦντες) for many days (ἐν ἱκαναῖς ἡμέραις) until it reached the island of Cnidus. When the wind prevented them (μὴ προσεῶντος ἡμᾶς τοῦ ἀνέμου) from continuing directly west to Achaia, they traveled southwest to Salmone on Crete, where they could sail under lee of that island (ὑπεπλεύσαμεν). With difficulty (μόλις), they then sailed along the south coast (παραλεγόμενοι) until they reached Fair Havens, near the city of Lasea.

The prefix βραδυ- in βραδυπλοέω pertains to an extended period of time, with the implication of being slow to do something (L&N §67.123). See 27:4 for ὑπεπλεύσαμεν. The adverb μόλις describes something that is difficult to accomplish (BDAG s.v. "μόλις" 1, 657); παραλέγομαι is another nautical term that describes sailing along the coast of a place (L&N §54.8). Cnidus was an island at the extreme southwestern corner of Asia Minor, approximately 150 miles west of Myra. Salmone was located on the easternmost tip of Crete, approximately 110 miles southwest of Cnidus. Fair Havens lay approximately one hundred miles farther west on the southern coast of the island.

27:9–10. Because a considerable time had passed (ἱκανοῦ χρόνου διαγενομένου) and the Jewish fast days had already come and gone (τὴν νηστείαν ἤδη παρεληλυθέναι), travel had become dangerous (ὄντος ἤδη ἐπισφαλοῦς τοῦ πλοός). Those circumstances led Paul to begin advising strongly (παρῄνει, inceptive imperfect) those responsible for the ship that further travel would lead to damage and considerable loss (μετὰ ὕβρεως καὶ πολλῆς ζημίας) of cargo (τοῦ φορτίου), ship (τοῦ πλοίου), and life (τῶν ψυχῶν).

27:11–12. The centurion, however, was more persuaded (μᾶλλον ἐπείθετο) by the ship's master (τῷ κυβερνήτῃ) and the shipping agent (τῷ ναυκλήρῳ) than by what Paul was saying (ἢ τοῖς ὑπὸ Παύλου λεγομένοις). Together, they concluded that Fair Havens was not a suitable harbor in which to spend the winter months (ἀνευθέτου τοῦ λιμένος ὑπάρχοντος πρὸς παραχειμασίαν) and therefore made the decision to set sail (ἔθεντο βουλὴν ἀναχθῆναι), hoping that it might be possible to reach Phoenix (εἴ πως δύναιντο καταντήσαντες εἰς Φοίνικα), which lay farther west along the coast and was more favorably situated for spending the winter.

The κυβερνήτης was the individual who managed the operation of the ship (BDAG s.v. "κυβερνήτης" 1, 573–74); the ναύκληρος was the individual who chartered the ship to carry the cargo (BDAG s.v. "ναύκληρος" 667). Sea travel on the Mediterranean ceased entirely for the winter from mid-November until mid-March. "The majority" (οἱ πλείονες) most likely includes the centurion, the ship's master, and the shipping agent. Phoenix lay approximately fifty miles farther west along the coast of Crete and, according to Hemer, had "two recessed beaches on the western flank of the headland facing northwest and southwest respectively" (1989, 139). The fact that the violent wind the travelers soon encountered came from the northeast (27:14) explains why they considered the harbor at Phoenix to be preferable, since it was sheltered by land on the eastern side.

The Storm at Sea (27:13–20)
When a violent storm drives the ship into the open sea, the passengers and crew begin to jettison cargo and gear as they lose hope of surviving.

27:13–15. When a south wind began blowing gently (ὑποπνεύσαντος νότου), they viewed it as confirmation of their decision (δόξαντες τῆς προθέσεως κεκρατηκέναι), raised the anchor (ἄραντες ἆσσον), and resumed their travel along the southern coast of Crete (παρελέγοντο τὴν Κρήτην). They had not gone far (μετ' οὐ πολύ), however, before a hurricane-force wind known as Euraquilo rushed down on them from the island (ἔβαλεν κατ' αὐτῆς ἄνεμος). The wind seized the ship forcibly (συναρπασθέντος τοῦ πλοίου) and, because they were not able to keep the bow pointed into the wind (μὴ δυναμένου ἀντοφθαλμεῖν τῷ ἀνέμῳ), they allowed themselves to be carried along (ἐπιδόντες ἐφερόμεθα) by it.

See 27:8 for παραλέγομαι. The phrase ἔβαλεν κατ' αὐτῆς is an intransitive use of βάλλω (BDAG s.v. "βάλλω" 6, 164). Barrett suggests, "the wind rushed down [the island]" (1998, 1194). Larkin describes the wind as "blowing down from 8,056-foot Mount Ida" (1995, 370). Luke writes that the wind was "like a whirlwind" (τυφωνικός; cf. BDAG s.v. "τυφωνικός" 1021) and calls it Εὐρακύλων, a hybrid formation of Latin-Greek sailor's language, made from Greek εὖρος (east wind) and Latin *aquilo* (north wind), or a "northeaster" (BDAG s.v. "εὐρακύλων" 411). The verb ἀντοφθαλμέω describes facing straight ahead (L&N §8.29). In this case, the ship was not able to keep its bow facing into the wind and resulting waves (BDAG s.v. "ἀντοφθαλμέω" 91).

27:16–17. The northeast wind blew the ship southwest approximately twenty-five miles where the crew could take advantage of sailing under the lee (ὑποδραμόντες) of the small island (νησίον) of Cauda to take three safety measures. First, with difficulty (μόλις), they gained control of the ship's rowboat (περικρατεῖς γενέσθαι τῆς σκάφης) and hoisted it aboard (ἣν ἄραντες). Second, they used cables (βοηθείαις ἐχρῶντο) to strengthen the ship's hull (ὑποζωννύντες τὸ πλοῖον). Third, because they were afraid they would drift far enough to run aground in the Gulf of Sidra (φοβούμενοί τε μὴ εἰς τὴν Σύρτιν ἐκπέσωσιν), they lowered the sea anchor (χαλάσαντες τὸ σκεῦος) to slow their progress. With those measures in place, they let themselves be carried along (ἐφέροντο, permissive middle).

Culy and Parsons suggest that ὑποτρέχω, in contrast with ὑποπλέω in verse 4, suggests a lack of control (2003, 516). The basic meaning of βοήθεια is "material things that help" (BDAG s.v. "βοήθεια" 2, 180); in this context, it most likely denotes ropes or cables. Marshall suggests four possible options for ὑποζωννύντες τὸ πλοῖον: (1) ropes tied vertically under the ship's hull, (2) ropes tied horizontally around the ship's hull, (3) ropes tied laterally across the ship's hold, or (4) ropes tied longitudinally across the ship's deck (1980, 409). The Syrtis (ἡ Σύρτις) lay in the Gulf of Sidra off the northern coast of modern Libya. Sailors feared the area for its quickly shifting sandbars that produced unpredictable shoals, hazardous tides, and dangerous currents. (*TBD*, 1232).

27:18–20. On the next day (τῇ ἑξῆς), while they were being tossed about violently by the storm (σφοδρῶς χειμαζομένων ἡμῶν), they began throwing some of the cargo overboard (ἐκβολὴν ἐποιοῦντο, inceptive imperfect). On the third day (τῇ τρίτῃ), with their own hands (αὐτόχειρες), they threw some of the ship's equipment (τὴν σκευὴν τοῦ πλοίου ἔρριψαν) into the sea. For many days (ἐπὶ πλείονας ἡμέρας), neither the sun nor the stars appeared (μήτε ἡλίου μήτε ἄστρων ἐπιφαινόντων), and

they continued being battered by a severe storm (χειμῶνός οὐκ ὀλίγου ἐπικειμένου). Finally (λοιπόν), they reached a point where they abandoned (περιῃρεῖτο) all hope of being rescued (ἐλπὶς πᾶσα τοῦ σῴζεσθαι ἡμᾶς).

The phrase σκευή τοῦ πλοίου refers to the nonessential equipment of the ship (BDAG s.v. "σκευή" 927). The phrase χειμῶνός οὐκ ὀλίγου ("not a little storm") is another instance of litotes. When the verb ἐπίκειμαι occurs with an impersonal force, it has the sense of "confront" or "lie upon" (BDAG s.v. "ἐπίκειμαι" 2b, 373); the present tense participle highlights the ongoing nature of the experience. English versions render the idea in various ways; NIV translates it as "the storm continued raging." Περιαιρέω carries the implication of complete cessation (L&N §68.43); the imperfect tense suggests a process over time. A translation that reflects the passive voice of περιῃρεῖτο would be "all hope was abandoned." Verse 20 is the first occurrence of "salvation" language (τοῦ σῴζεσθαι ἡμᾶς) in the passage (cf. 27:31, 34, 43, 44).

Paul's First Word of Encouragement (27:21–26)

Paul encourages his fellow travelers to keep up their courage, because an angel has assured him that there will be no loss of life.

27:21–22. After they had gone a long time without food, Paul stood and spoke to them. He began by reminding them that his previous advice (27:10) had been sound, and they should have accepted it (ἔδει … πειθαρχήσαντάς μοι). If they had not sailed from Crete (μὴ ἀνάγεσθαι ἀπὸ τῆς Κρήτης), they would have been able to avoid (κερδῆσαι) the damage and loss (τὴν ὕβριν ταύτην καὶ τὴν ζημίαν) they were facing. Now (τὰ νῦν), he had more advice (παραινῶ). They should be encouraged (ὑμᾶς εὐθυμεῖν), because he could assure them that although they would lose the ship, they would not lose their lives (ἀποβολὴ ψυχῆς οὐδεμία ἔσται ἐξ ὑμῶν πλὴν τοῦ πλοίου).

The noun ἀσιτία describes a state of having been without food, frequently with the implication of being caused by a lack of appetite (L&N §23.32). Schnabel translates the genitive absolute πολλῆς ἀσιτίας ὑπαρχούσης as "since almost nobody wanted to eat" and ascribes the lack of appetite to "anxiety, seasickness, and the impossibility of cooking" (2012, 1041). The verb πειθαρχέω denotes submitting to authority or reason by obeying (L&N §36.12); παραινέω describes the act of advising strongly, recommending, or urging (BDAG s.v. "παραινέω" 764); εὐθυμέω carries the sense of being or becoming encouraged and, therefore, cheerful (L&N §25.146).

27:23–26. Paul's encouragement rested on (γάρ) angelic assurance he had received. That very night (ταύτῃ τῇ νυκτί), an angel from the God whom he served stood before (παρέστη) him, told him not to be afraid (μὴ φοβοῦ), and gave him two words of encouragement—one for Paul and one for his fellow travelers. First, it was necessary for Paul to stand before Caesar (Καίσαρί σε δεῖ παραστῆναι). Second, God had graciously given Paul (κεχάρισταί σοι ὁ θεός) the assurance that his fellow travelers would also escape with him. The crew and passengers, therefore (διό), should be encouraged (εὐθυμεῖτε), because (γάρ) Paul believed God (πιστεύω τῷ θεῷ) that everything would turn out in the manner that the angel had told him (οὕτως ἔσται καθ' ὃν τρόπον λελάληταί μοι). In God's plan (δεῖ), they would run aground (ἡμᾶς ἐκπεσεῖν) on an unspecified island (εἰς νῆσον τινα).

Angels previously appeared at key points in the narrative: to the apostles as a group (5:19), to Philip (8:26), to Cornelius (10:3), and to Peter (12:7). See 5:19 for "Angel of the Lord." Jesus had previously told Paul not to be afraid (μὴ φοβοῦ) in the vision that instructed him to remain in Corinth (18:9). The impersonal verb δεῖ is yet another reference to divine necessity, particularly as it relates to Paul's life and ministry (9:6,

16; 19:21; 23:11; 27:24, 26). The verb χαρίζομαι can denote giving graciously and generously, with the implication of good will on the part of the giver (L&N §57.102) or handing someone over into the control of another person (L&N §37.30). Peterson suggests that the use of the verb in this context indicates that God has answered Paul's prayers "for deliverance on behalf of the whole ship's company" (2009, 690). Schnabel comments, "there is no doubt that the rescue of crew and passengers is due to the presence of Paul, whose protection by God is the cause of their deliverance" (2012, 1043). Although he did not know all the details of the way in which God would deliver them, Paul believed that the God whom he served would keep his promise, and he called his fellow travelers and to put their trust in his God as well.

Approaching Land (27:27–32)
When they realize that the ship is approaching land, the sailors let down anchors in order to avoid running aground on rocks.

27:27–29. On the fourteenth night (τεσσαρεσκαιδεκάτη νύξ), as the ship was being carried about in the Sea of Adria (διαφερομένων ἡμῶν ἐν τῷ Ἀδρίᾳ), in the middle of the night (κατὰ μέσον τῆς νυκτός), the sailors began to suspect (ὑπενόουν, inceptive imperfect) that they were coming near land (προσάγειν τινὰ αὐτοῖς χώραν). So, they used a weighted line to determine the depth of the water (βολίσαντες) and found it to be 120 feet. After a short time passed (βραχὺ διαστήσαντες), they repeated the process and found the depth to be 90 feet. Because they were afraid the ship might run aground on a rocky coast (φοβούμενοί μή που κατὰ τραχεῖς τόπους ἐκπέσωμεν), they lowered four anchors (ῥίψαντες ἀγκύρας τέσσαρας) from the stern of the ship (ἐκ πρύμνης) and prayed for daylight to come (ηὔχοντο ἡμέραν γενέσθαι).

The Sea of Adria (ὁ Ἀδρίας) was the central portion of the Mediterranean bounded by Italy, Malta, Crete, and Greece (Dunn 1996, 340). The verb βολίζω describes using a weighted line to determine depth (BDAG s.v. "βολίζω" 180); Schnabel describes the equipment used in the process (2012, 1044). Ὀργυιὰς εἴκοσι was a depth of twenty fathoms, or 120 feet; ὀργυιὰς δεκαπέντε was a depth of fifteen fathoms, or ninety feet. The adjective τραχύς describes a place that is rough and uneven (BDAG s.v. "τραχύς" 1014); NET translates κατὰ τραχεῖς τόπους as "on the rocky coast." Schnabel describes lowering four anchors from the stern (ἐκ πρύμνης ῥίψαντες ἀγκύρας τέσσαρας) as "an exceptional emergency measure," since anchors were usually lowered from the bow (2012, 1044). The intent was to stop the ship's progress, while keeping its bow pointed toward the land they were approaching in order to avoid having the waves swamp them by hitting the ship broadside (Larkin 1995, 374). The iterative imperfect of ηὔχοντο highlights the repeated prayers for the day to dawn.

27:30–32. The crew tried to escape (τῶν ναυτῶν ζητούντων φυγεῖν) by lowering the ship's rowboat (χαλασάντων τὴν σκάφην) under the pretext (προφάσει) of dropping an anchor from the bow (ἐκ πρῴρης ἀγκύρας μελλόντων ἐκτείνειν). Paul, however, warned the centurion and the soldiers that if the sailors did not remain in the ship (ἐὰν μὴ οὗτοι μείνωσιν ἐν τῷ πλοίῳ) it would not be possible for everyone to be delivered (ὑμεῖς σωθῆναι οὐ δύνασθε). The soldiers then cut the ropes to the rowboat (ἀπέκοψαν οἱ στρατιῶται τὰ σχοινία τῆς σκάφης) and let it drift away (εἴασαν αὐτὴν ἐκπεσεῖν). Would the crew have made it safely to shore in the rowboat? Would the ship have made it safely to shore without the crew? Should the soldiers have set the rowboat adrift? Could they have used the rowboat to ferry groups ashore after the ship ran aground on the reef? What the reader knows for certain is that Paul was convinced that if everyone stayed together,

no one would be lost, and the centurion trusted Paul's judgment this time.

Paul's Second Word of Encouragement (27:33–38)

As they wait for dawn, Paul encourages his fellow travelers to eat and trust that God will deliver them.

27:33–34. When day was about to dawn (ἄχρι οὗ ἡμέρα ἤμελλεν γίνεσθαι), Paul repeatedly encouraged (παρεκάλει, iterative imperfect) all of his fellow travelers to share in some food (μεταλαβεῖν τροφῆς). For fourteen nights, they had been waiting with anxiety (προσδοκῶντες), had gone without food (ἄσιτοι διατελεῖτε), and had eaten nothing (μηθὲν προσλαβόμενοι). They should, therefore (διό), take some food (μεταλαβεῖν τροφῆς), because (γάρ) it was important to their survival (τοῦτο πρὸς τῆς ὑμετέρας σωτηρίας ὑπάρχει; cf. L&N §21.18). As further encouragement, Paul declared that not one of them would lose a hair from his head (οὐδενὸς ὑμῶν θρὶξ ἀπὸ τῆς κεφαλῆς ἀπολεῖται).

Although ἄχρι οὗ usually carries the sense of "until," Culy and Parsons note that in the initial position, it can mean "when" (2003, 123). Barrett calls τεσσαρεσκαιδεκάτην σήμερον ἡμέραν ("today is the fourteenth day") a "curious expression of time" that reflects the practice of counting night before day and suggests the translation "today, you are looking at the fourteenth day" (1998, 1176, 1207). Elsewhere ἡ σήμερον ἡμέρα carries the sense of "this very day" (BDAG s.v. "σήμερον" 921). Μεταλαμβάνω denotes the act of receiving a share in something (L&N §57.129). Culy and Parsons note that προσδοκάω describes "apprehension and worry with regard to the outcome" (2003, 525). The present tense of the verb in the phrase ἄσιτοι διατελεῖτε highlights their ongoing lack of food (cf. BDAG s.v. "διατελέω" 238).

27:35–38. After he spoke these words of encouragement (εἴπας ταῦτα) to the crew and passengers, Paul followed his own advice. He took bread (λαβὼν ἄρτον), gave thanks to God before all of them (εὐχαρίστησεν τῷ θεῷ ἐνώπιον πάντων), broke (κλάσας) the bread, and began eating (ἤρξατο ἐσθίειν) it. His words encouraged everyone (εὔθυμοι γενόμενοι πάντες), and his actions prompted them to follow his example of eating (αὐτοὶ προσελάβοντο τροφῆς). When the 276 people on board had eaten all the food they needed (κορεσθέντες τροφῆς), they began the final step of lightening the ship (ἐκούφιζον τὸ πλοῖον) by throwing the cargo of wheat into the sea (ἐκβαλλόμενοι τὸν σῖτον εἰς τὴν θάλασσαν).

Was the Shipboard Meal a Celebration of the Eucharist?

Similarities in wording between Luke 22:19 and Acts 27:35 raise the natural question of whether Luke understands the shipboard meal as eucharistic. The parallels actually extend beyond Acts 27 to Jesus's feeding of the five thousand in Luke 9 and his meal with the two disciples on the Emmaus Road in Luke 24.

Luke 22:19	λαβὼν	ἄρτον	εὐχαριστήσας	ἔκλασεν	ἔδωκεν
Acts 27:35	λαβὼν	ἄρτον	εὐχαρίστησεν	κλάσας	
Luke 9:16	λαβὼν	τοὺς πέντε ἄρτους	[εὐλόγησεν]	κατέκλασεν	ἐδίδου
Luke 24:30	λαβὼν	τὸν ἄρτον	[εὐλόγησεν]	κλάσας	ἐπεδίδου

Barrett writes, "the coincidence in language with that of the Last Supper . . . can hardly be accidental" (1998, 1209); and Bruce concludes, "to the majority it was an ordinary meal . . . for those who ate with eucharistic intention . . . it was a valid eucharist" (1998, 492). Marshall (1980, 414), Stott (1990, 392), Dunn (1996, 341), and Schnabel (2012, 1046), however, all view the experience in Acts as an ordinary meal that reflected a normal Jewish/Christian meal and included the common elements of breaking bread and saying grace (Peterson 2009, 693). Witherington has a detailed critique (1998, 772–73). With Bock, it is probably best to understand the shipboard meal as "a sacred moment because God would deliver them" with "echoes" of the Lord's Supper (2007, 740).

Shipwreck on Malta (27:39–44)

When day comes, the ship runs aground on a reef, the passengers and crew jump overboard, and all make their way safely to land.

27:39–41. When daybreak came (ὅτε ἡμέρα ἐγένετο), they realized that they were not familiar with the land (τὴν γῆν οὐκ ἐπεγίνωσκον), but they observed a bay that had a sandy beach (κόλπον τινα κατενόουν ἔχοντα αἰγιαλόν) and they determined (ἐβουλεύοντο)—if possible (εἰ δύναιντο, conditional optative)—to run the ship ashore (ἐξῶσαι τὸ πλοῖον) on it. So, they cast off the anchors (τὰς ἀγκύρας περιελόντες), left them in the sea (εἴων εἰς τὴν θάλασσαν), unfastened the ropes that had secured the rudders (ἀνέντες τὰς ζευκτηρίας τῶν πηδαλίων), hoisted the foresail to the wind (ἐπάραντες τὸν ἀρτέμωνα τῇ πνεούσῃ), and held course for the beach (κατεῖχον εἰς τὸν αἰγιαλόν). Unfortunately, when they struck a reef (περιπεσόντες εἰς τόπον διθάλασσον), they ran the ship aground (ἐπέκειλαν τὴν ναῦν), so that the bow stuck fast and remained immovable (ἡ πρῷρα ἐρείσασα ἔμεινεν ἀσάλευτος), and the stern began to be destroyed by the waves that were crashing against it (ἡ πρύμνα ἐλύετο ὑπὸ τῆς βίας τῶν κυμάτων).

Bock notes that the sailors did not know this part of the island, because it was not on the normal sea route to Malta (2007, 741). The basic sense of κόλπος is the hollow formed by a curve; in this context it denotes an indentation or bay in the shoreline (BDAG s.v. "κόλπος" 3, 557). See 21:5 for αἰγιαλός. Lowering the anchors had stopped the ship's progress (cf. 27:29); casting them loose allowed to ship to head for shore. Most ships had two rudders (πηδαλίων) connected by a crossbar and operated by one man (BDAG s.v. "πηδάλιον" 811). Larkin concludes that the crew had secured the rudders during the storm and now lowered them into the sea to steer the ship (1995, 377). The ἀρτέμωνα ("foresail") was a relatively small sail toward the prow of the ship that helped in steering (L&N §6.49). In this context, κατέχω is a nautical term for holding a course (BDAG s.v. "κατέχω" 7, 533). The phrase τόπον διθάλασσον ("a place of two seas") can denote a place where two currents come together or a bar or reef created by those currents (L&N §1.68). It seems unlikely that the ship would become stuck fast between two currents.

27:42–44. The soldiers' plan was to kill the prisoners (τῶν στρατιωτῶν βουλὴ ἐγένετο ἵνα τοὺς δεσμώτας ἀποκτείνωσιν), so that none of them would escape by swimming away (μή τις ἐκκολυμβήσας διαφύγῃ) and hiding on the island. The centurion, however, wanted to save Paul's life (ὁ ἑκατοντάρχης βουλόμενος διασῶσαι τὸν Παῦλον) and prevented them from carrying out their plan (ἐκώλυσεν αὐτοὺς τοῦ βουλήματος). He then commanded those who were able to swim (ἐκέλευσέν τε τοὺς δυναμένους κολυμβᾶν) to jump in (ἀπορίψαντας) and get to land (ἐπὶ τὴν γῆν ἐξιέναι). The rest (τοὺς λοιπούς) made their way to land on whatever would float—some on planks (οὓς μὲν ἐπὶ σανίσιν) and some on other pieces from the ship (οὓς δὲ ἐπί τινων τῶν ἀπὸ τοῦ πλοίου). In this way (οὕτως), everyone arrived safely on shore (ἐγένετο πάντας διασωθῆναι ἐπὶ τὴν γῆν). Schnabel writes, "it was as a result of God's providence that despite the violent storm, despite the planned flight of the crew, and despite the soldiers' intention to kill the prisoners, all [the travelers] were saved" (2012, 1049).

THEOLOGICAL FOCUS

The narratival function of Acts 27:1–28:16 is to recount Paul's travel from Caesarea to Rome. Within that longer account, 27:1–44 describes the first thirteen hundred miles of his journey as well as God's protection in the face of storm and shipwreck. It also portrays Paul as a man of wisdom, faith, and concern for others. Stott calls Paul "a man of God and of action, a man of the Spirit and of common sense" (1990, 392). Larkin describes him as "an 'impractical' holy man, a Christian apostle who receives messages from angels, that he can be an encouragement in the fury of the storm" and concludes "such faith is the foundation for a life of encouragement" (1995, 373).

Theologically, Acts 27:1–44 continues the themes of divine necessity, divine reassurance, and divine protection that have run throughout Luke's account of Paul's ministry. As it was "necessary" (δεῖ) for Paul to suffer for Jesus's name (9:16), to see Rome (19:21), and to witness in Rome (23:11), it was also necessary that the ship carrying him would run aground on an island and survive the storm (27:26). As an angel had reassured Paul that he should remain in Corinth (18:9–10), and as Jesus himself had reassured Paul that he would bear witness in Rome (23:11), in the middle of the storm an angel also reassured Paul that he would reach

Rome and that his fellow travelers would survive (27:23–24). As God had protected Paul from a violent Jewish mob (21:32–36), from an enraged Sanhedrin (23:10), from Jewish assassination plots (23:12–15; 25:2–3), and from Roman political expediency (24:27; 25:9), he also protected Paul from "the treachery of the sea" (Bauer 2021, 241).

To those themes, the passage adds the theme of divine deliverance. Although the travelers gradually lost hope of being saved (περιηρεῖτο ἐλπὶς πᾶσα τοῦ σῴζεσθαι ἡμᾶς; cf. 27:20), if they remained in the ship, they would be saved (ἐὰν μὴ οὗτοι μείνωσιν ἐν τῷ πλοίῳ, ὑμεῖς σωθῆναι οὐ δύνασθε; cf. 27:31). Following Paul's encouragement to eat was important to their salvation (τοῦτο γὰρ πρὸς τῆς ὑμετέρας σωτηρίας ὑπάρχει; cf. 27:34), and the centurion's determination to save Paul from danger (ὁ ἑκατοντάρχης βουλόμενος διασῶσαι τὸν Παῦλον; cf. 27:43) resulted in everyone being saved from danger on Malta (οὕτως ἐγένετο πάντας διασωθῆναι ἐπὶ τὴν γῆν; cf. 27:44). The convergence of these four themes in the account of Paul's sea voyage, along with his act of encouraging his fellow travelers, suggest that divine necessity leads to divine reassurance—which, in turn, encourages trust in divine protection and deliverance.

PREACHING AND TEACHING STRATEGIES

Exegetical/Theological Synthesis

After two years of being held in Roman custody in Caesarea, Paul would soon travel to Rome. Luke's first-century readers would have wanted to know the details of that journey. Since God had reassured Paul that he would reach Rome, did God keep his promise? How did Paul travel? Who went with him? How long did the journey take? What dangers did he face? How did God protect him? Did his status as a Roman citizen make any difference in his treatment? What impact did his presence have on his fellow passengers? As Luke's narrative unfolds, his readers would discover the answers to those questions. They would also learn that God's power prevails over the forces of nature, that God protects his people in line with his purposes, that God's care of his people has an impact on those around them, and that dangerous circumstances can provide opportunities for ministry. With Luke's original readers, his twenty-first-century audience shares the need to understand that God's purposes lead to his reassurance which, in turn, strengthens trust in his protection and allows his people to point others to him for deliverance.

Preaching/Teaching Idea

God's protection should prompt our proclamation.

Contemporary Connections

What does it mean?

Against all odds, God protects Paul and the 275 other souls on board in a remarkable display of sovereign power. God spared every life and even every hair on every head (27:34) from a violent whirlwind of a storm. Indeed, even the wind and the waves obey him (Matt. 8:27). God spared the lives of the passengers when the crew attempted to abandon ship without them. Just as Paul miraculously became aware of a plot on his life earlier (23:16), so Paul became aware of this plan. Finally, God spared all the lives of the prisoners when the centurion resisted the soldiers' plan to kill them all to keep them from escaping. God's hand was guiding every turn, protecting Paul and those around him from storms, from sailors, and from soldiers.

All this protection prompted Paul's proclamation. God delivered him, and Paul could not stop talking about it. Early in the voyage, Paul was vocal about his advice (27:10). That changed in the face of danger. He now shared God's promises. As God spoke to Paul through an angel, he was bold to relate that message to his fellow travelers. He testified that he served and worshipped the God who was able to save from storms and from sin. As God continued to protect them, Paul gave thanks to God "in the presence of all" (27:35). Not a person on that ship was without a witness that the one true God delivers.

Is it true?

Paul wrote to one of his churches that God "works all things according to the counsel of his will" (Eph. 1:11). God has a sovereign will. That will cannot be thwarted. It will come to pass. God has been expressing that perfect, unbreakable will to Paul since Paul's conversion. More recently, he has told Paul that he would witness in Rome before Caesar (19:21; 23:11; 27:24). It is spoken; it must come to pass. This Word of God is surer than the ground beneath our feet. It is surer than the wind and waves that buffet our lives.

Paul celebrated this sure word aboard the ship in a meal oozing with symbolism. He urged all to eat, taking bread, giving thanks, breaking it, and serving it. It sounds like the Last Supper, the feeding of the five thousand, or the meal with the disciples walking to Emmaus. If it was an ordinary meal, it was one packed with meaning. At the very least, Paul would enjoy this communing (if not communion meal) in the presence of Jesus, under the call of Jesus, in the footsteps of Jesus, as a proclamation of Jesus. His great Shepherd had prepared "a table before [him] in the presence of [his] enemies" and dangers (Ps. 23:5).

Now what?

Celebrating and proclaiming God's protection and provision begins with having eyes to see it. We cannot give thanks for what we do not think comes from God. A million provisions slip through distracted hands that easily forget that without him we cannot "live and move and have our being" (17:28). We ask for daily bread with cupboards already full of it. We offer up a prayer for traveling mercies, never doubting that we will arrive at our destination. Proclaiming God's protection starts with seeing God's protection.

Once we start to see God's hand everywhere in our physical and spiritual lives, may he so fill our hearts with thanksgiving and our mouths with praise, that we cannot help but share it. This praise does not have to be obnoxious, but it must be prayerful and intentional. When Paul saw God's provision for the ship, he was bold to share it. When Paul offered food to the hungry crew, he gave thanks to God for it and for protection. We too can find these daily, moment-by-moment ways to speak, pray, give thanks for what God has done in Christ and in our lives to those around us.

Creativity in Presentation

My children love this riddle: A ship sank and forty heads from forty souls onboard splashed into the water. Forty-four heads came out. How can this be? It was forty foreheads. Forty heads went in and forty foreheads came out; all heads and foreheads were accounted for. So it is with the miracle in our text. Only the riddle does not work with 276 heads.

A message from this passage finds its rhythm between God's protection during the storm and shipwreck (27:13–20, 27–32, 39–44) punctuated by Paul's proclamation of all that God is doing (27:21–26, 33–38). Paul's first address is rich. He tells a ship full of hardened sailors and soldiers about the God "to whom I belong and whom I worship" and in whom he "has faith." The one true God is personal (belong to), worthy (to worship), and trustworthy (to believe in). Paul's second proclamation is all thanksgiving to God for his protection. The one true God is also sovereign, so holding events in his hands that when they come to pass, Paul can rightly give thanks.

Paul covers a lot of proclamation ground around God's protection. Without ever giving a formal sermon or physically opening up Scripture, Paul was able to speak to his fellow travelers about a personal, worthy, trustworthy, sovereign God whom those around him did not know but would now be intrigued to know. May God's protection also prompt our proclamation. so use us too.

- God provides miraculous protection (27:1–20, 27–32, 39–44)

- God's protection prompts happy proclamation (27:21–26, 33–38)

DISCUSSION QUESTIONS

1. What themes have you seen in previous passages that are also present in this passage? Why are they significant?

2. Did Paul's status as a Roman citizen influence the centurion's treatment of him? What evidence would you offer for your answer?

3. What led to the centurion changing his attitude toward Paul's advice after he initially rejected the suggestion that the ship should spend the winter at Fair Havens?

4. How did God protect Paul not only from the dangers of the storm but also from the dangers posed by the actions of the crew and the soldiers?

5. How did Paul view his responsibility to his fellow travelers? What does his example suggest about how we should relate to those around us who are not Jesus's disciples?

Acts 28:1–10

EXEGETICAL IDEA

Paul's ministry on Malta included humble service to his fellow travelers, divine protection from snakebite, and compassionate healing of those who were ill.

THEOLOGICAL FOCUS

God's providence opens doors for ministry to those in need.

PREACHING IDEA

We should seize the opportunity to serve those who suffer.

PREACHING POINTERS

Carpe diem! The admonition of the ancient Roman poet Horace to "seize the day" has found its way into popular culture at various times, including the title of Saul Bellow's 1956 novel *Seize the Day*, and Robin Williams's exhortation to his students in the 1989 movie *Dead Poets Society*. The apostle Paul articulated the same idea in Colossians 4:5. The KJV translated his words in that verse as "redeeming the time," which sounds a bit like time management. The NASB and other versions capture the sense more clearly as "making the most of the opportunity," which fits well in the immediate context of Paul's prayer request that he would know how to share the gospel while he was in Roman custody. Making the most of the opportunity must have been a ministry axiom for Paul. Wherever he was, whoever was around, whatever the circumstances might be, he looked for the opportunities he could seize to minister to others. You can see him implementing that axiom during his brief period of ministry on the island of Malta in Acts 28:1–10. Through shipwreck, snakebite, and a father's sickness, God providentially opened the doors for Paul to minister to those in need. When God opened the doors, Paul walked through them and engaged in a ministry of service to his fellow travelers and a ministry of healing to the Maltese people.

In this passage, people today should be able to relate to the discomfort caused by rain and cold as well as the relief gathering around a warm fire gives. The passage corrects a fatalistic view of divine judgment for wrongdoing, the idea that people will necessarily interpret the miraculous correctly, and the idea that the agent God chooses to use is the true source of the healing. The passage commends trust in God's protection, trust in God to heal, and trust in God to open doors for ministry. It also commends an attitude that is alert to those in need and is willing to serve those in need humbly. The objective in communicating the passage should be to help listeners understand that wherever God's providence places them, there are opportunities to minister for him, so that they will seize the opportunities before them to serve others who are in need.

WITNESS ON MALTA (28:1–10)

LITERARY STRUCTURE AND THEMES (28:1–10)

The passage consists of two paragraphs that describe two episodes during Paul's three-month stay on the island of Malta (28:11). In the first, he ministered to his fellow travelers by gathering fuel for a fire to warm them (28:1–6). In the second, he ministered to the residents of the island by curing those who were sick (28:7–10).

- *Ministry of Service (28:1–6)*
- *Ministry of Healing (28:7–10)*

EXPOSITION

The shipwreck on Malta provides an interlude in Paul's journey to Rome, and Luke records two vignettes from that time. In both, Paul "continues to appear in the story as one who helps his friends and rescues them from danger" (Marshall 1980, 418). Longenecker suggests that "God seems, through the experiences at Malta, to have been refreshing Paul's spirit after the two relatively bleak years at Caesarea and the disastrous time at sea and preparing him for his witness in Rome" (1981, 565). Having protected Paul from storm and shipwreck, God now protects him from snakebite as he serves his fellow travelers by gathering fuel for a fire. Although the islanders misinterpret the divine protection, the subsequent divine healing of Publius's father opened the door for Paul to engage in a healing ministry that paralleled Peter's ministry of healing in Lydda and Joppa (9:32–43). During his three-month stay among a new people group, these events once again validated Paul as God's authorized witness, whose powerful ministry led the islanders to hold him in the same high esteem that the ministry of the twelve apostles generated among the residents of Jerusalem (5:12–16).

Ministry of Service (28:1–6)

Safely ashore on the island, Paul gathers fuel for a fire to warm his fellow travelers and suffers no ill effects when a snake bites him.

28:1. After the travelers made it ashore safely (διασωθέντες), they learned (ἐπέγνωμεν) that the island was called Malta. Some scholars have suggested that Μελίτη refers to the island of Mljet in the Adriatic Sea at about the same latitude as Rome. That location, however, would have required a wind from the southeast rather than the northeast and would have made travel to Rome via Sicily extremely roundabout. The traditional site of their landing is called St. Paul's Bay and is located on the northeastern shore of the island. Most likely, they did not initially recognize the island (27:39) because they were some distance from the main harbor of Valletta (Bruce 1988, 494). The use of διασώζω in 28:1 links this paragraph to the preceding section (cf. 27:44).

28:2. The islanders (οἱ βάρβαροι) showed the refugees extraordinary kindness by lighting a fire (ἄψαντες πυράν) and welcoming them to warm themselves against the rain and the cold. Βάρβαρος was a standard designation for someone who did not speak Greek (Culy and Parsons 2003, 1220). The residents of Malta spoke a Punic dialect that was a development of the language of the Phoenicians who originally colonized the island (Schnabel 2012, 1049). The phrase οὐ τὴν τυχοῦσαν φιλανθρωπίαν ("not the usual kindness") is another occurrence of litotes. Whether all 276 travelers gathered around a single large bonfire or several smaller fires is impossible to determine.

28:3–4. After Paul had gathered a bundle of sticks (συστρέψαντος τοῦ Παύλου φρυγάνων τι πλῆθος) and added them to the fire (ἐπιθέντος ἐπὶ τὴν πυράν), a snake came out because of the heat (ἔχιδνα ἀπὸ τῆς θέρμης ἐξελθοῦσα) and fastened on Paul's hand (καθῆψεν τῆς χειρὸς αὐτοῦ). When the islanders saw the snake hanging from his hand (ὡς εἶδον οἱ βάρβαροι κρεμάμενον τὸ θηρίον ἐκ τῆς χειρὸς αὐτοῦ), they concluded that Paul was certainly a murderer (πάντως φονεύς ἐστιν ὁ ἄνθρωπος οὗτος) and that, although he had escaped death by drowning (διασωθέντα ἐκ τῆς θαλάσσης), the goddess Justice was not permitting him to live (ἡ δίκη ζῆν οὐκ εἴασεν). Danker writes, "our texts do not permit identification of species, but the term ordinarily suggests a poisonous [snake] . . . commonly known as sandviper" (BDAG s.v. "ἔχιδνα" 419). The fact that there are no poisonous snakes on Malta in the twenty-first century does not preclude their presence on the island in the first century. Larkin notes, "The Greeks viewed Justice as the virgin daughter of Zeus who kept watch for any injustice done on earth and reported it to her father who then dispensed retributive justice to make it right" (1995, 380).

28:5–6. Paul, however, shook the snake off into the fire (ὁ ἀποτινάξας τὸ θηρίον εἰς τὸ πῦρ) and suffered no ill effects (ἔπαθεν οὐδὲν κακόν). The islanders were expecting (προσεδόκων) him to swell up (αὐτὸν μέλλειν πίμπρασθαι) or fall dead suddenly (καταπίπτειν ἄφνω νεκρόν). They waited expectantly for a long time (ἐπὶ πολὺ αὐτῶν προσδοκώντων) and saw that nothing unusual happened to him (θεωρούντων μηδὲν ἄτοπον εἰς αὐτὸν γινόμενον). They then changed their way of thinking (μεταβαλόμενοι) and began to say that Paul was a god (ἔλεγον αὐτὸν εἶναι θεόν). The verb προσδοκάω suggests anticipation (L&N §30.55). The present

tense of the participles προσδοκώντων and θεωρούντων suggests an extended period of time. The imperfect tense of ἔλεγον is inceptive.

Ministry of Healing (21:7–10)

After he healed the father of the leading citizen of the island, the other residents of Malta came to Paul, who healed their diseases.

28:7–8. There were cultivated lands (χωρία) in the area where they landed that belonged to Publius, the most prominent person on the island (τῷ πρώτῳ τῆς νήσου). He welcomed Paul and his companions (ἀναδεξάμενος ἡμᾶς) and for three days kindly opened his home to them (φιλοφρόνως ἐξένισεν). When Publius's father was lying in bed (κατακεῖσθαι), seriously ill with fever and dysentery (πυρετοῖς καὶ δυσεντερίῳ συνεχόμενον), Paul went into his room (εἰσελθών), prayed (προσευξάμενος), laid hands on him (ἐπιθεὶς τὰς χεῖρας αὐτῷ), and healed him (ἰάσατο αὐτόν). The adjective πρῶτος describes the most prominent person on the island (BDAG s.v. "πρῶτος" 2aβ, 894). Publius might have been the Roman governor, the Maltese representative of the Roman government, or simply the wealthiest person on the island (Peterson 2009, 710). The verb ξενίζω describes the act of receiving a stranger as a guest (BDAG s.v. "ξενίζω" 1, 683). It is likely that Publius extended hospitality to Paul because of his status as a Roman citizen. Dysentery (δυσεντέριον) is an infection of the intestines that causes diarrhea and causes painful stomach cramps, vomiting, and a high temperature. Larkin notes that Paul's act of praying clarifies the means and source of the healing (1995, 382).

28:9–10. After the healing took place (τούτου γενομένου), the rest of the islanders who were sick (οἱ λοιποὶ οἱ ἐν τῇ νήσῳ ἔχοντες ἀσθενείας) began coming to Paul (προσήρχοντο) and were being healed (ἐθεραπεύοντο). As a result, they "showered" Paul and his companion with honors (NLT, οἳ καὶ πολλαῖς τιμαῖς ἐτίμησαν ἡμᾶς) and supplied them with everything they needed (ἐπέθεντο τὰ πρὸς τὰς χρείας) when they set sail (ἀναγομένοις) at the end of their time on the island. The imperfect tenses of προσήρχοντο and ἐθεραπεύοντο point to an extended period of time during which the healings took place. A literal translation of the clause οἳ πολλαῖς τιμαῖς ἐτίμησαν ἡμᾶς would be "they honored us with many honors."

THEOLOGICAL FOCUS

The narratival function of Acts 28:1–10 is to continue the account of Paul's final journey to Rome while providing a brief breather between the high drama of the storm at sea and the climax of Paul's successful arrival in Rome. The passage further demonstrates God's care of Paul, including the warm reception by the islanders, the deliverance from snakebite, the hospitality provided by Publius, and the honor and provision afforded to Paul by the islanders. It draws parallels between Paul's ministry and that of the twelve apostles in general (5:12–16) and of Peter in particular (9:32–43) as the gospel expanded into new territories. It also reinforces Paul's innocence, authenticates him as God's witness, and highlights the positive reception of his ministry by members of a new people group.

Theologically, Acts 28:1–10 continues to demonstrate God's providential hand on his witness through protection, hospitality, opportunity for ministry, and provision for travel. Rescue from shipwreck leads to the opportunity for Paul to minister to his fellow travelers. Publius's hospitality leads to the opportunity for Paul to minister to the prominent man's father. The combination of suffering no harm from snakebite and healing Publius's father leads to the opportunity for Paul to engage in a widespread healing ministry. That healing ministry leads to the opportunity for Paul to receive practical provision from the islanders for the next stage of his journey to Rome. On Malta, God leads Paul from opportunity to opportunity as he serves those in need and penetrates new territory for the gospel.

PREACHING AND TEACHING STRATEGIES

Exegetical/Theological Synthesis

At certain points in a well-told story, readers find themselves asking, "What happened next?" At this point in Luke's narrative, that question would have been at the forefront of his first-century readers' minds. Paul and his fellow travelers had survived the storm at sea and had made it safely to shore—somewhere—but what happened next? Where were they? How did the inhabitants receive them? How long did they stay there? What did they do during their stay? How did they secure the resources to continue their journey? Luke's brief account of Paul and his companions' three months on the island of Malta provides two vignettes from their stay that highlight God's provision for Paul and Paul's ministry to those in need. God provided protection, hospitality, opportunity for ministry, and provision for travel. In turn, Paul ministered to his fellow travelers, his host's father, and large numbers of islanders who were sick and suffering. With Luke's original readers, his twenty-first-century audience shares the need to understand that suffering comes in many forms—including destitution and disease—and that, in God's providence, opportunities are everywhere to serve those who are suffering. Their response should be to seize those opportunities for God's glory.

Preaching/Teaching Idea

We should seize the opportunity to serve those who suffer.

Contemporary Connections

What does it mean?
That Paul *gives* kindness to the island inhabitants is not surprising at all. He had reminded

the Ephesian elders that Jesus taught us, "It is more blessed to give than to receive" (Acts 20:35). Paul crash-lands on Malta and immediately begins serving. While his co-travelers are warming themselves by the fire, Paul jumps up to gather wood. When he visits Publius, he prays for his father's healing. When the islanders come with their sick, he heals in Jesus's name. Paul gives kindness, and God is glorified. Paul also *receives* a lot of kindness. While certainly not looking to be served, Paul is cold, wet, hungry, and far from home. The text makes much of others making much of Paul. The inhabitants show "unusual kindness" preparing a fire to warm the crew. The chief of the area, Publius, receives and entertains the group comfortably for three days. After healing many, the people of the island honor the team and provide them with all they need for the journey to Rome. Paul gave great kindness, but he also received great kindness. God is glorified in the giving and receiving.

Is it true?

There is something deeply Christlike and communal about giving and receiving kindness. Jesus served with a gospel love that becomes paradigmatic for the church. As he himself made clear, "the Son of Man came not to be served but to serve" (Matt. 20:28). Jesus traded his wealth for poverty and our well-being (2 Cor. 8:9). For believers to "have this mind among yourselves, which is yours in Christ Jesus" is to follow his road of exchanging wealth and privilege for the sake of serving another (Phil. 2:5–8).

Others also served Jesus. He did not seek it, but it came to him, and he welcomed others' kindness as a means of sharing himself and his kingdom proclamation. Jesus received invitations to parties, to wedding(s), to synagogues, to meals, and to homes. In fact, he allowed others to serve him so much food and drink that he began to get a reputation (Luke 7:34). He asked for favors, like a place on a boat to preach, a drink from a well, a colt, an upper room, and

care for his mother. Others supported his ministry financially with generous gifts (Luke 8:3). Jesus received kindness, and the kindness others showed to him endeared him in many cases to the ones who showed it.

Now what?

We as the church follow Paul as he follows Christ. It is better to give than to receive. We come to serve rather than be served. Our lives of generosity will feel the pinch of cruciformity. We strive to be so filled to overflowing with God's grace to us that we are lavish with grace to others. May our reputation be that of cross-carrying kindness, and may such a reputation cause friends and neighbors to see such good deeds and seek to glorify our heavenly Father (Matt. 5:16). There is also gospel proclamation power in receiving kindness. Opening hands and hearts and letting others serve us is a kind of vulnerability and transparency that can start friendships and steer conversations. As we look for ways to serve, we are also sensitive to ways others might be trying to serve us. In receiving that kindness, we have an opportunity for a relationship that leads to the message of the greatest kindness shown: Jesus himself.

Creativity in Presentation

Almost any cross-cultural missionary will tell you that behind every sane and safe "expat" worker is a host of kind, gracious, hospitable, longsuffering nationals. Stories of my family's time in South Asia needing help abound. It took my toddler locking himself in his bedroom for me to meet everyone on our apartment floor. It took having my cell phone stolen by the honey dealer to meet everyone in the entire apartment complex. Our family had come to serve to be sure, but we received much more serving from others. Those moments, mini-crises, and happy times of being hosted built long-lasting friendships and opened doors to share the gospel.

The passage presents itself in two parts: God opens doors for Paul to give kindness for the sake of his name, and God opens doors so that he can receive it in return. The first point is familiar; the second might be surprising. One way to structure a sermon would be to begin by outlining the examples of Paul serving at the fire, with Publius, and on the island. Trace these examples to Christ himself, his grace to serve us in the gospel and make this possible, and his power to give us the example and means to serve others against our natural inclination. In fact, Jesus said a few words about how unimpressive it is to serve as the world does (Matt. 5:43–48). The second point could draw out the examples of "unusual kindness" shown to Paul in the fire, the hospitality, the honor, and the sailing provisions. Again, connect these acts to Paul's example in Christ himself. Talk about how being served when we might least expect it has a way of building relationships and opening doors to speak Christ's name. God truly opens doors to give and receive kindness for the sake of his name, so that we can serve those who suffer.

- Paul receives God's kindness from others in the midst of suffering (28:1–6).

- Paul shares God's kindness to others in the midst of suffering (28:7–10).

DISCUSSION QUESTIONS

1. What similarities do you see between Paul's ministry on Malta and the ministries of other witnesses earlier in Acts?

2. How is the islanders' response to the miraculous similar to the responses of people in other passages where the gospel entered new territory? What is the role of the miraculous in this and similar passages?

3. Paul's healing of Publius's father is the only place in Acts where prayer accompanies healing. What conclusion(s) do you draw from the combination in this passage? Is it normative or exceptional? Why?

4. Is it significant that Luke does not record Paul preaching during his stay on Malta? Why or why not? How would you explain that omission?

5. What is the significance of the islanders' honoring Paul and his companions and providing support for the next stage of their travels?

Acts 28:11–31

EXEGETICAL IDEA

Paul's witness in Rome began with a warm welcome by Christians, included two meetings with the members of the Jewish community, and continued for two years during which he preached the kingdom of God and taught about Jesus to anyone who visited him in his rented quarters.

THEOLOGICAL FOCUS

God continues to extend his mission to all who seek him, regardless of locale, listeners, or apparent limitations.

PREACHING IDEA

The end of the book is not the end of the story.

PREACHING POINTERS

"Are we there yet?" Have you ever been on a long trip and heard this plaintive question come from the back seat of the car: "Are we there yet?" Although we might agree intellectually with musician Michael Card that there is "joy in the journey," most of us are far more focused on the destination; and when the journey gets long, we wonder when we will ever arrive. Perhaps Luke's original readers were wondering whether Paul would ever reach Rome. After all, he had been talking about it for at least three years. Imprisonment, judicial trials, storm at sea, shipwreck, snakebite, three months on Malta—he had endured all of those experiences since Jesus told him that he would bear witness in Rome. In Acts 28, Paul reached the capital of the empire. He was finally there! Yet Luke leaves his readers hanging about what ultimately happened to Paul, because the end of the book is not the end of the story. His account of Paul's witness in Rome reminds us that God continues to extend his mission to all who seek him, regardless of locale, listeners, or apparent limitations. Acts is not a biography of the apostle Paul; it is an account of Jesus's faithful followers, whom he commissioned and empowered to be his witnesses to the ends of the earth. Are we there yet?

People today should be able to relate to people who are spiritually blind, deaf, or hard-hearted; to meeting with civic leaders; and to someone being placed under house arrest. The passage corrects the attitudes of giving credence to unsubstantiated reports or prejudging new ideas uncritically. It also commends being open to the truth, trusting God to open doors for witness, and being willing to engage others with the gospel as long as they are willing to listen. The objective in communicating the passage should be to help listeners understand that God is in charge of his ongoing mission and its progress, so that they will be faithful in carrying out the commission he has given them.

WITNESS IN ROME (28:11–31)

LITERARY STRUCTURE AND THEMES (28:11–31)

The passage consists of four sections. The first traces the final stage of Paul's journey to Rome, following his three months in Malta (28:11–16). The second and third sections describe Paul's meetings with the Jews in Rome—the first meeting with a group of leaders to whom he explained his arrived in the city in Roman custody (28:17–22) and the second with a larger group whom he sought to persuade concerning Jesus (28:23–28). The fourth section provides a brief summary of Paul's subsequent two-year ministry in Rome (28:30–31). The Western text includes verse 29, which reads, "And when he had said these words, the Jews departed, and had great reasoning among themselves." Although the verse provides a smoother transition between verse 28 and verse 30, it is most likely a secondary addition.

- ***Welcome by the Roman Christians (28:11–16)***
- ***Meeting with the Jewish Leaders (28:17–22)***
- ***Witness to the Jewish Community (28:23–28)***
- ***Unhindered Witness to All (28:30–31)***

EXPOSITION (28:11–31)

After three months on the island of Malta, Paul and his companions embarked on what Bruce calls "the last lap" of his journey to Rome (1990, 534). He had already traveled more than thirteen hundred miles, and he had another five hundred miles to go.

Stage	Approximate Distance	Duration
Malta to Syracuse (28:11–12)	90 miles	1 day of travel + 3-day stay
Syracuse to Rhegium (28:13a)	75 miles	1 day of travel + 1-day stay
Rhegium to Puteoli (28:13b–14)	200 miles	2 days of travel + 7-day stay
Puteoli to Three Taverns (28:15)	120 miles	4 days of travel
Three Taverns to Rome (28:16)	30 miles	1 day of travel

Luke passes over Paul's travels briefly, highlights his warm welcome by fellow Christians in Rome, and focuses on his two meetings with the Jews in the city. His first meeting was with leaders of the Jewish community to whom he explained his arrived in the city in Roman custody. Paul's speech during the meeting is his twelfth in the book. Schnabel describes it as an abbreviated forensic speech that consists of a *narratio* setting out the background of the case followed by a *propositio* introducing the topic on which Paul wanted to address the Jewish leaders (2012, 1064). The *narratio* forms a five-part concentric structure (Larkin 1995, 386).

Background of the Case (narratio)		28:17b–19
A	Paul had done nothing against the people or the patriarchal customs.	(28:17b)
B	The Jews handed Paul over to the Romans as a prisoner.	(28:17c)
C	The Romans were willing to release Paul.	(28:18)
B′	The Jews opposed Paul's release.	(28:19a)
A′	Paul appealed to Caesar although there were no accusations against him.	(28:19b)

Introduction of the Topic (propositio)		28:20
Paul is in chains for the sake of the hope of Israel.		(28:20)

His second meeting was with a large number of visitors from the entire Jewish community, whom he sought to persuade concerning Jesus. Luke's account of that meeting summarizes Paul's day-long witness briefly, focuses on the way in which the response of the listeners echoes that of Isaiah's OT audience, and concludes with the declaration that God has extended salvation to the Gentiles as well as to the Jews. Paul's preaching and the response of his Jewish listeners echo previous experiences throughout his missionary work (13:13–52; 14:1–7; 17:1–9, 10–15; 18:1–17; 19:8–10) and effectively create a bookend with his first ministry to the Jews in Pisidian Antioch.

As is the case in other portions of Acts (6:7; 9:31; 12:24; 16:5; 19:20), both the passage and the book conclude with a summary statement describing Paul as preaching "boldly and without hindrance" to "all who came to see him" for two years. Stott writes, "Just as Luke's gospel ended with the prospect of a mission to the nations, so the Acts ends with the prospect of a mission radiating from Rome to the world" (1990, 405).

Welcome by the Roman Christians (28:11–16)

After three months, Paul leaves Malta and travels to Rome, where Christian brothers welcome and encourage him.

28:11. Three months later (μετὰ δὲ τρεῖς μῆνας), the centurion was able to secure passage on an Alexandrian ship that had spent the winter in the island's harbor (παρακεχειμακότι ἐν τῇ νήσῳ). This particular ship had a figurehead or insignia (παρασήμῳ) designating it as "Heavenly Twins" (Διοσκούροις), which referred to the two sons of Zeus, Castor and Pollux, who were the patron gods of navigation, and whose constellation was Gemini (Bruce 1988, 501). The Alexandrian ship was most likely part of the wheat fleet. If the shipwreck occurred in early or mid-November, Paul and his companions' date of departure was most likely in mid-February, since the west winds began in early February and would facilitate coastal travel (Longenecker 1981, 566).

28:12–14. The ship's first stop was Syracuse on the island of Sicily, where they stayed for three days (ἐπεμείναμεν ἡμέρας τρεῖς). From Syracuse, they sailed to Rhegium at the extreme southwestern tip of Italy. After a one-day stay (μετὰ μίαν ἡμέραν), a south wind (νότου) allowed them to sail northward along the coast to Puteoli, which was the main port in southern Italy for the wheat trade and approximately five days' travel from Rome on foot. In Puteoli, they found a Christian community (εὑρόντες ἀδελφούς), who invited them to stay with them for seven days (παρεκλήθημεν παρ' αὐτοῖς ἐπιμεῖναι ἡμέρας ἑπτά). Larkin notes that the statement "And so we came to Rome" (καὶ οὕτως εἰς τὴν Ῥώμην ἤλθαμεν) "points forward, telling the reader to note the way in which Paul and his party came to Rome: in the company of Roman Christians who came to give them the kind of welcome reserved for dignitaries" (1995, 384).

28:15. From Rome (κἀκεῖθεν), Christian brothers, who had heard the news about Paul and his companions' arrival (οἱ ἀδελφοὶ ἀκούσαντες τὰ περὶ ἡμῶν), traveled south approximately thirty miles on the Appian Way as far as Three Taverns. Some of the party went ten miles farther to the Forum of Appius, where they met Paul and his companions who had traveled north on the same road more than one hundred miles in four days. When Paul saw them, he gave thanks (εὐχαριστήσας) and gained confidence for the challenges that awaited him. The phrase λαμβάνω θάρσος is an idiom that describes "becoming confident or courageous in the face of real or possible danger" (L&N §25.157). Luke's mention of the Christians who met Paul makes it clear that others had planted the church in the city.

28:16. When the party arrived in Rome (ὅτε εἰσήλθομεν εἰς Ῥώμην), Paul received permission to stay by himself (ἐπετράπη τῷ Παύλῳ μένειν καθ' ἑαυτόν) with the soldier who was guarding him (σὺν τῷ φυλάσσοντι αὐτὸν στρατιώτῃ). The Western text expands the details of the custodial arrangement to read "When we arrived in Rome, the centurion delivered the prisoners to the captain of the guard, but Paul was allowed to live by himself outside the camp" (Marshall 1980, 420). Larkin writes, "Paul the imperial prisoner makes a triumphal procession to the capital of the empire" (1995, 385). Luke's narrative of Paul's travel from Malta to Rome is also reminiscent of the narrative describing his travel from Miletus to Jerusalem, including the warm reception and hospitality of Christian communities in Tyre, Caesarea, and the Jewish capital (21:1–17).

Meeting with the Jewish Leaders (28:17–22)

In his initial meeting with Jewish leaders in the city, Paul explains his circumstances, and they express a willingness to hear from him at greater length.

21:17–19. Three days after his arrival (μετὰ ἡμέρας τρεῖς), Paul called together (συγκαλέσασθαι) the most prominent representatives of the Jews in Rome (τοὺς ὄντας τῶν Ἰουδαίων πρώτους). After they gathered (συνελθόντων αὐτῶν), he offered a five-part summary of the events in Palestine that preceded his journey to Italy. First, Paul did nothing contrary to the Jewish people or to their ancestral customs (οὐδὲν ἐναντίον ποιήσας τῷ λαῷ ἢ τοῖς ἔθεσι τοῖς πατρῴοις). Second, from Jerusalem, the Jews delivered him into Roman custody (δέσμιος ἐξ Ἱεροσολύμων παρεδόθην εἰς τὰς χεῖρας τῶν Ῥωμαίων). Third, the Romans examined him and wanted to release him (ἀνακρίναντές με ἐβούλοντο ἀπολῦσαι), because they found no grounds for putting him to death (διὰ τὸ μηδεμίαν αἰτίαν θανάτου ὑπάρχειν ἐν ἐμοί). Fourth, the Jews opposed his release (ἀντιλεγόντων τῶν Ἰουδαίων). Fifth, Paul found it necessary to call upon Caesar (ἠναγκάσθην ἐπικαλέσασθαι Καίσαρα), although he had no grievance against his own people (οὐχ ὡς τοῦ ἔθνους μου ἔχων τι κατηγορεῖν).

See 28:7 for πρῶτος. In this passage, it most likely refers to the leaders of the various synagogues in the city. Barrett notes that there were eleven synagogues known by name (1998, 1238). By addressing the leaders as "brothers" (ἀδελφοί), Paul identified himself with the Jewish community (Bock 2007, 752). He continued to maintain that his conduct conformed to Jewish customs (28:17b) and that, despite their opposition, he did not hold the actions of the Jewish people against them (28:19b). His presence in Rome, therefore, had nothing to do with a departure from Judaism; it was the result of the working of the Roman judicial system.

Paul's summary of the judicial process in Caesarea is complete, although "radically abbreviated" (Barrett 1998, 1238). Being "handed over" (παρεδόθην) to the Romans might refer to the Roman commander rescuing him from the Jewish mob in the temple (21:32–33), or more likely, it referred to his transfer "out of Jerusalem" to Caesarea (23:23–35). The Roman "examination" (ἀνακρίναντες) involved three different sessions—before Felix (24:1–21), before Festus (25:6–12), and before Agrippa (26:1–29). Despite the consistent verdict that Paul had done nothing contrary to Roman law (23:28–29; 25:25; 26:30–31), both Felix and Festus kept him in custody because they wanted to do a favor for the Jews (24:27; 25:9), who "opposed" (ἀντιλεγόντων τῶν Ἰουδαίων) his release and had plotted to kill him while he was in Roman custody (23:12–23; 25:1–5). Paul, therefore, felt compelled (ἠναγκάσθην) to appeal to Caesar, as was his right as a Roman citizen (25:10–12).

28:20–22. He had asked to see and speak to them (παρεκάλεσα ὑμᾶς ἰδεῖν καὶ προσλαλῆσαι) to explain that he wore his chain (τὴν ἅλυσιν ταύτην περίκειμαι) for the sake of the promised OT hope of Israel (ἕνεκεν τῆς ἐλπίδος τοῦ Ἰσραήλ). They responded with four assertions of their own. First, they had received no letter from Judea concerning Paul (ἡμεῖς γράμματα περὶ σοῦ ἐδεξάμεθα ἀπὸ τῆς Ἰουδαίας). Second, no one had arrived (παραγενόμενός τις τῶν ἀδελφῶν) to report or speak anything bad about Paul himself (ἀπήγγειλεν ἢ ἐλάλησέν τι περὶ σοῦ πονηρόν). Third, they were interested in hearing his views (ἀξιοῦμεν δὲ παρὰ σοῦ ἀκοῦσαι ἃ φρονεῖς). Fourth, they knew that people everywhere (πανταχοῦ) opposed the movement he represented.

Paul consistently connected "the hope of Israel" (τῆς ἐλπίδος τοῦ Ἰσραήλ) with Jesus's resurrection (23:6; 24:15; 26:6–7). The leaders' mention of a letter or report from Judea suggests that there was regular communication between Jerusalem and Rome. The absence of either might reflect slower travel from Palestine or a decision by the Jewish authorities in Jerusalem to abandon the case (Schnabel 2012, 1069). The combination of ἀπήγγειλεν and ἐλάλησεν "emphasizes the fact that no news whatsoever about Paul had reached them" (Culy and Parsons 2003, 543). The verb ἀξιόω denotes a desire to hear what Paul had to say on the basis of its worth or value (L&N §25.5), and in this context, the verb φρονέω describes holding a view about something (L&N §31.1). The leaders' phrase τῆς αἱρέσεως ταύτης follows the consistent use in Acts to refer to a religious party or movement within Judaism (5:17; 15:5; 24:5, 14; 26:5), potentially with the sense of "this heretical sect" (BDAG s.v. "αἵρεσις" 1b, 28) in this context. The leaders' use of ἀντιλέγω to describe opposition to the Christian movement (28:22) echoes Paul's description of the Jews' opposition to his release (28:19).

Witness to the Jewish Community (28:23–28)

In a second meeting, Paul proclaims Jesus to a larger gathering of Jews with mixed results and declares that God has sent him to the Gentiles.

28:23–24. After they had appointed a day (ταξάμενοι ἡμέραν), even more (πλείονες)

Jews came to Paul's rented quarters (εἰς τὴν ξενίαν). He then spent the entire day (ἀπὸ πρωῒ ἕως ἑσπέρας) talking with them about the kingdom of God (τὴν βασιλείαν τοῦ θεοῦ) and Jesus (περὶ τοῦ Ἰησοῦ) from both the Law and the Prophets (ἀπό τε τοῦ νόμου Μωϋσέως καὶ τῶν προφητῶν). At the end of the day, some of his listeners were persuaded (οἱ μὲν ἐπείθοντο) by what he was saying (τοῖς λεγομένοις), while others refused to believe (οἱ δὲ ἠπίστουν).

Πλείονες can be either comparative "in greater numbers" (e.g., ESV) or ellative "in great numbers" (e.g., NRSV); Barrett prefers the latter (1998, 1243). The main verb Luke uses to describe Paul's activity is ἐκτίθημι, which denotes conveying information by careful elaboration (BDAG s.v. "ἐκτίθημι" 2, 310). The participles διαμαρτυρόμενος and πείθων are adverbial of means. See 20:21 for διαμαρτυρόμενος; πείθων is a conative present. See 14:22 on the kingdom of God (cf. 28:31). Paul's persuasion "concerning Jesus" (περὶ τοῦ Ἰησοῦ) undoubtedly included the essentials of the gospel (cf. 3:1–26). Larkin notes that teaching about Jesus must always accompany preaching about the kingdom (1995, 392). The phrase ἀπὸ πρωῒ ἕως ἑσπέρας combines πρωῒ (the early part of the day; L&N §67.187) and ἑσπέρα (the period from late afternoon until darkness; L&N §67.191) to denote "from morning until evening" (e.g., NET).

28:25–28. The mixed response of Paul's audience in Rome was characteristic of Jewish responses to his preaching throughout his ministry (13:13–52; 14:1–7; 17:1–9, 10–15; 18:1–17; 19:8–10). After this second meeting, Luke describes the Jews as "being in disagreement with one another" (ἀσύμφωνοι ὄντες πρὸς ἀλλήλους). In that divided manner, they departed (ἀπελύοντο), but not before Paul shared with them one final word (εἰπόντος τοῦ Παύλου ῥῆμα ἓν) from the prophet Isaiah (Isa. 6:9–10).

The Holy Spirit's words to their fathers through the OT prophet applied to Paul's audience, just as they had applied to Jesus's generation (Matt. 13:14–15; Mark 4:11–12; Luke 8:9–10; John 12:27–40). They might see and hear, but they had dull hearts (ἐπαχύνθη ἡ καρδία), slow ears (τοῖς ὠσὶν βαρέως ἤκουσαν), and closed eyes (τοὺς ὀφθαλμοὺς αὐτῶν ἐκάμμυσαν). As a result, they could not see (ἴδωσιν τοῖς ὀφθαλμοῖς), hear (τοῖς ὠσὶν ἀκούσωσιν), understand (τῇ καρδίᾳ συνῶσιν), or change their ways (ἐπιστρέψωσιν). As a result, God could not heal them (ἰάσομαι αὐτούς). They should know (γνωστὸν ἔστω ὑμῖν), therefore, that God had also sent salvation to the Gentiles (τοῖς ἔθνεσιν ἀπεστάλη τοῦτο τὸ σωτήριον τοῦ θεοῦ), who would listen (αὐτοὶ ἀκούσονται).

Following Larkin, Bock sets out four suggestions of the significance of this passage for the church's mission to Israel: (1) the Gentiles replace Israel, (2) a Jewish remnant is included with the Gentiles, (3) the Jewish leaders reject the gospel but individual Jews do not, and (4) the mission continues despite Jewish rebelliousness (2007, 756). Four pieces of evidence support the last suggestion. First, in contrast to 13:46 and 18:7, Paul did not say that he was turning from the Jews to the Gentiles. Second, Paul stated that God had already sent salvation to the Gentiles, not that he was doing so at that time. Third, during his ministry in Rome, Paul welcomed "all who came to him," which most likely included both Jews and Gentiles (28:30). Fourth, when writing to the Romans, Paul also used the image of blind eyes and deaf ears in his explanation that God has not rejected Israel (Rom. 11:8), but instead has a future for them (Rom. 11:25–32).

Unhindered Witness to All (28:30–31)

Paul continues his ministry in Rome for two years, preaching boldly to all who visit him in rented quarters.

28:30–31. Luke's closing summary statement provides specific details about Paul's witness in Rome. The duration was two full years. The venue was his own rented quarters. His audience included anyone who visited him. His activities consisted of preaching the kingdom of God and teaching about Jesus. Boldness characterized his ministry. The scope of his ministry had no restrictions.

Paul's two years (διετίαν ὅλην) in Rome most likely began in the spring of A.D. 60 and extended through the spring of A.D. 62. The phrase ἐν ἰδίῳ μισθώματι can carry the sense of "at his own expense" or "in his own rented quarters" (BDAG s.v. "μίσθωμα" 654). The latter is more likely, and Peterson suggests that Paul "lived in a room or rooms in one of the many thousands of tenement buildings in Rome" (2009, 721). Whether Paul had sufficient financial resources to pay rent for the two full years himself, plied his trade as a leatherworker, or received support from other Christians is unknown. His visitors (τοὺς εἰσπορευομένους πρὸς αὐτόν) most likely included both Jews and Gentiles.

Larkin notes that preaching (κηρύσσων) and teaching (διδάσκων) are different activities: "preaching appeals to the will, calling for a decision, while teaching informs the mind, requiring growth in knowledge and understanding" (1995, 392). There are only eight references to the kingdom of God (τὴν βασιλείαν τοῦ θεοῦ) in Acts, but four of them form an *inclusio* around the book as a whole (1:3, 6; 28:23, 31). The Lord Jesus Christ (τοῦ κυρίου Ἰησοῦ Χριστοῦ) is both the "Lord Jesus" whom the early church preached to the Gentiles (e.g., 11:20–21) and the "Messiah Jesus" whom they preached to the Jews (e.g., 3:20). For "boldness" (παρρησία) see 4:13. The adverb ἀκωλύτως denotes "freely" or "without restrictions" (L&N §13.151). Schnabel suggests that "the general tolerance of Paul's activities in Rome was proof that Paul was innocent of the charges brought against him" (2012, 1078).

The Ending of Acts

Marshall describes the picture at the end of Acts as "ambiguous" (1980, 426), and Peterson writes that scholars have been discussing "the incompleteness of [the] narrative" since Luke wrote it (2009, 723). Commentators have suggested three broad categories of reasons that Luke ended the book as he did. Historical suggestions include that Luke described events that had happened until the time when he wrote, that Luke planned to write a third volume that was lost or never completed, or that Paul's Jewish accusers never came to Rome. Literary suggestions revolve around the idea that an account of Paul's trial and execution would not have been edifying, possibly promoting a piety of martyrdom. The most likely explanation is that Luke was writing a history of the Christian mission rather than a biography of Paul. For that reason, the arrival of Jesus's witness in the capital of the empire in fulfillment of God's promise was more important than his final fate, and the open-endedness of the narrative reminds Luke's readers that the proclamation of the gospel continues beyond Rome to the ends of the earth by the power of the Holy Spirit and in obedience to Jesus's promise-command.

THEOLOGICAL FOCUS

The immediate narratival function of Acts 28:11–31 is to bring Paul's journey to Rome to a close. The passage pulls together multiple facets of the early church's mission that run throughout the book, and so echoes not only Paul's own ministry but also the ministries of the Jerusalem apostles: Peter, Stephen, Philip, and Barnabas. The broader function is to close the book as a whole and, with Acts 1, to bookend the narrative with references to the kingdom of God as the message to proclaim and the Holy Spirit who is the agent who empowers that proclamation.

The end of the book, however, is not the end of the story. Luke 24 brought an end to

Jesus's ministry but not to the promised proclamation that would extend to all the nations. Similarly, Acts 28 brings an end to Paul's ministry but not to the promised witness that would extend to the ends of the earth. What Jesus had begun to do and teach in Luke's first volume, the early church continued to do and teach in his second volume as they carried the gospel across cultural thresholds to Hebrew-speaking Jews, to Greek-speaking Jews, to Samaritans, to an Ethiopian proselyte, to a Gentile Godfearer, to pagan Gentiles, to Greeks, to Maltese islanders, and to Romans. Luke leaves Acts open-ended because it falls to his readers to write the third volume—as they continue Jesus's commission to carry the gospel onward from the capital of the empire to the ends of the earth.

Theologically, Acts 28:11–31 portrays God as the one who is in charge of his ongoing mission and its progress. He keeps his promises by bringing Paul safely to Rome. He provides encouragement and support through the Christians in Rome who welcome Paul warmly. He provides a venue for Paul to preach the gospel by allowing him to stay in rented quarters where the public is free to visit him. He gives Paul an initial audience with the Jewish leadership in the city as well as the opportunity to speak at length to the Jewish community at large. He gives Paul insight through the Holy Spirit to apply Scripture to his listeners'` responses. He uses their unresponsiveness to extend salvation to Jew and Gentile alike. He gives Paul a two-year period in which to minister in the capital of the empire. In turn, he expects his witnesses to be faithful in proclaiming the message of the kingdom and the truth about Jesus to all who will listen, regardless of locale, listeners, or apparent limitations.

PREACHING AND TEACHING STRATEGIES

Exegetical/Theological Synthesis

Paul had traveled more than thirteen hundred miles from Caesarea to Malta, where he spent three months until sea travel resumed. He had five hundred miles of sea and land travel left before he reached Rome. Luke's first-century readers would have wanted to know the details of Paul's travel, arrival, and ministry in the capital of the empire. How did the Roman Christians respond to his arrival? How did the Jews in Rome respond to his arrival? How did the Roman authorities respond to his arrival? What was the outcome of his appearance before Caesar? Luke leaves that final question unanswered, but his narrative answers the others, and those answers are consistent with what the reader has seen throughout the book. The Roman Christians welcomed Paul as warmly as the Christians in Tyre, Caesarea, and Jerusalem had. The mixed response of the Jews in Rome corresponded to the Jewish responses in Pisidian Antioch, Iconium, Thessalonica, Berea, Corinth, and Ephesus. The Roman authorities acknowledged Paul's innocence by allowing him to stay in rented quarters rather than in prison. Paul's ministry in Rome was simply the next step on the road to the ends of the earth as Jesus had commanded. The mission that Jesus began, the early church continued as God kept his promises, provided support and encouragement, and opened doors for witness. With Luke's original readers, his twenty-first-century audience shares the need to understand that God continues to extend his mission through his faithful witnesses to all who seek him, regardless of locale, listeners, or apparent limitations.

Preaching/Teaching Idea

The end of the book is not the end of the story.

Contemporary Connections

What does it mean?
In Acts 23:11, Jesus told Paul, "Take courage, for as you have testified to the facts about me in Jerusalem, so you must also testify in Rome." It took three years, eighteen hundred miles of travel, and near-death dangers to fulfill God's

promise to Paul. We watch the last third of those events in Acts 28, as Paul travels from Malta to Rome to arrive sovereignly by the skin of his teeth to testify in Rome, and God accomplishes his divine purpose.

Jesus's promise to Paul in Acts 23 is both an echo of the Great Commission and a pregnant promise to the whole church. What Jesus "began to do and teach" (Acts 1:1) in the gospel of Luke, his disciples continued to do and teach by his Spirit in the Acts of the Apostles. Paul's great ministry is just a chapter in the greater story of the kingdom of God, proclaimed in the Lord Jesus Christ by his witnesses, until it reaches the capital of the Roman Empire. Luke's second volume might end, but God's work does not, because the Holy Spirit is still writing the story through the church today. That story will not end until the gospel reaches the ends of the earth as Jesus promised (Acts 1:8).

Is it true?
Acts might have started to feel like a biography of Paul. After all, Paul looms large for more than half of the book. God's hand is clearly on him, but Acts is not his biography. Luke would be appalled by the inference. His second volume is an account of Jesus's continued work by his Spirit through the church (Acts 1:1). The clues abound in our text. First, the Jews in Rome had not even heard of Paul, but they had definitely heard about Jesus (28:21–22). Second, the emphasis of their time together is not about Paul and his ministry but about Jesus and his presence on every page of Scripture (28:23). Third, Paul counters unbelief with a declaration that "this salvation of God has been sent to the Gentiles" (28:28). It is not *Paul* whom God has sent but *this salvation*. The message will go on with or without Paul. Fourth, and most strikingly, is the way Luke ends his second volume. It feels abrupt because there is much more to tell about Paul, his trial, his martyrdom. Luke is not writing a story about Paul, though, and these details do not drive his structure. Instead,

he ends the book with God's gospel going forth "without hindrance" (28:31)—a not-so-subtle nod to the church to take up that baton and run with it by the power of God.

Now what?
There is a global church-planting organization today aptly named Acts 29. That name is fitting for the church, because we are the next chapter. Luke can only follow the story so far. He takes us from Jesus's ascension to Paul's house arrest in Rome. He packs a lot into those thirty years, but there is more to tell. As the curtain closes on the apostles, it opens on the next act of the Great Commission. We imitate Paul as he imitated Christ (1 Cor. 11:1). We take the message of salvation to the next place, the next people group, the next generation. The end of Acts is not the end of the story. It is the beginning of God's next chapter of his Spirit working through his church.

If Luke is our foundation and Acts is our guide, the church's third volume will share in the echoes of our passage. Our message will still and always be the good news about the kingdom of God, focused on the Lord Jesus Christ and received by repentance and faith (28:31). Our efforts will still and always meet resistance wherever we go (28:22, 26–27). Despite the opposition, though, God will still and always guard his Word, and it will go and grow unhindered (28:31). He will bless our efforts today and use us for this spreading kingdom.

Creativity in Presentation
One of my favorite feelings is starting to read a novel I already love. The whole story is in front of me to savor and enjoy. One of my least favorite feelings is coming to the end of a novel I have loved. I slow down, knowing those few pages pinched in my right hand are all that is left of a world to which I have become attached. Unless I stop reading, the story must end. In the case of a stand-alone novel, the end is the *end*. Acts, however, is different. Unlike most books

we read, Acts is not information but an invitation. It is a book with blank pages pasted in the back—not in the sense of adding new revelation to Scripture but in the sense of adding new stories that tell of the continuing progress of God's Great Commission.

A creative presentation of the passage can clarify what the chapter is *not* and what the chapter *is*. The chapter is *not* a biography of Paul. For all the attention given to Paul, this story is not his. The clues are there in the text. The Jews are more interested in Paul's message than in Paul. His message passes to the Gentiles, and the book ends abruptly for Paul but aptly for the gospel. Instead, the chapter *is* the beginning of God's next chapter of his Spirit working through his church. The church today shares the same *message* that we have heard throughout the book and in this chapter. We share the same *opposition* we have seen and still see in Acts, and we share in the same *victory* the early church tasted. God will have his way. What he began to do and to teach, what he continued to do and to teach, he still does and teaches among us and through us as the church today. His gospel is unhindered. *Soli Deo gloria!*

The end of the book is not the end of the story.

- Acts ends where it began, with Jesus continuing to do and to teach through the church (28:11–28).

- Believers today take up this hopeful expectation to continue to see what Jesus will do and teach through the church unhindered (28:30–31).

DISCUSSION QUESTIONS

1. Why do you think Luke omits any mention of the church in Rome after he records the Christians' welcome when Paul arrives?

2. Why do you think Paul wanted to meet with the Jewish leadership in Rome so soon after he arrived? What do you think he wanted to accomplish in that meeting?

3. How does Paul's message in his second meeting with the Jews in Rome summarize his evangelistic preaching across the empire?

4. Why was Isaiah's prophecy particularly relevant for Paul's Jewish audience in Rome? What parallels are there to Jesus's use of the same prophecy?

5. Why do you think Luke left the ending of Acts as ambiguous as he did? What impact does that ambiguity have on his readers?

REFERENCES

Allen, Roland. 1977. *Missionary Methods: St. Paul's or Ours?* Grand Rapids: Eerdmans.

Archer, Gleason L., and Gregory C. Chirichigno. 1983. *Old Testament Quotations in the New Testament*. Chicago: Moody.

Ascough, R. 1998. "Civic Pride at Philippi: The Textual Critical Problem of Acts 16:12." *NTS* 44:93–103.

Aune, David E. 1987. *The New Testament in Its Literary Environment*. LEC 8. Philadelphia: Westminster.

Barnes, Timothy D. 1969. "An Apostle on Trial." *JTS* 20:407–19.

Barrett, C. K. 1994. *A Critical and Exegetical Commentary on the Acts of the Apostles*. Vol. 1: *Preliminary Introduction and Commentary on Acts I–XIV*. ICC. Edinburgh: T&T Clark.

______. 1998. *A Critical and Exegetical Commentary on the Acts of the Apostles*. Vol. 2: *Introduction and Commentary on Acts XV–XXVIII*. ICC. Edinburgh: T&T Clark.

Bauer, David R. 2021. *The Book of Acts as Story: A Narrative-Critical Study*. Grand Rapids: Baker Academic.

Beale, Gregory K., and D. A. Carson, eds. 2007. *Commentary on the New Testament Use of the Old Testament*. Grand Rapids: Baker.

Blair, William Newton. 1977. *The Korean Pentecost and the Sufferings Which Followed*. Edinburgh: Banner of Truth Trust.

Bock, Darrell. L. 2007. *Acts*. BECNT. Grand Rapids: Baker Academic.

Bonz, Marianne Palmer. 2000. *The Past as Legacy: Luke-Acts and Ancient Epic*. Minneapolis: Fortress.

Bruce, F. F. 1988. *The Book of the Acts*. Rev. ed. NICNT 13. Grand Rapids: Eerdmans.

______. 1990. *The Acts of the Apostles: Greek Text with Introduction and Commentary*. 3rd ed. Grand Rapids: Eerdmans.

Buth, Randall, and Chad Pierce. 2014. "Hebraisti in Ancient Texts: Does Ἑβραϊστί Ever Mean 'Aramaic'?" In *The Language Environment of First Century Judea*. Vol. 2. Edited by Randall Buth and R. Steven Notley, 66–109. Leiden: Brill.

Clinton, Hillary. 1996. *It Takes a Village: And Other Lessons Children Teach Us*. New York: Simon & Schuster.

Conzelmann, H. 1987. *Acts of the Apostles: A Commentary on the Acts of the Apostles*. Hermeneia. Philadelphia: Fortress.

Culy, Martin M., and Mikeal C. Parsons. 2003. *Acts: A Handbook on the Greek Text*. BHGNT. Waco, TX: Baylor University Press.

Daube, David. 1956. *The New Testament and Rabbinic Judaism*. London: Athlone.

Davids, Peter H. 1982. *The Epistle of James*. NIGTC. Grand Rapids: Eerdmans.

Davis, Thomas W., and Mark W. Wilson. 2016. "The Destination of Paul's First Journey: Asia Minor or Africa." *PJT* 97:1–14.

Derrett, J. Duncan M. 1988. "Clean and Unclean Animals (Acts 10:15; 11:9): Peter's Pronouncing Power Observed." *Heythrop Journal* 29:205–21.

Dupont, Jacques. 1964. *The Sources of Acts: The Present Position*. Translated by Kathleen Pond. London: Darton, Longman & Todd.

Dunn, James D. G. 1996. *The Acts of the Apostles*. Grand Rapids: Eerdmans.

Estrada, Nelson P. 2004. *From Followers to Leaders: The Apostles in the Ritual Status Transformation in Acts 1–2*. JSNTSup 255. London: Continuum.

Fitzmyer, Joseph A. 1998. *The Acts of the Apostles: A New Translation with Introduction and Commentary*. AB 31. New York: Doubleday.

Friesen, Garry. 1980. *Decision-Making and the Will of God*. Portland: Multnomah.

Gärtner, Bertil. 1955. *The Areopagus Speech and Natural Revelation*. Acta Seminarii Neotestamentici Upsaliensis 21. Lund: Gleerup.

Gaventa, Beverly R. 2003. *The Acts of the Apostles*. ANTC. Nashville: Abingdon.

______. 2004. "Theology and Ecclesiology in the Miletus Speech: Reflections on Content and Context." *NTS* 50:36–52.

Green, Joel B. 1995. *The Theology of the Gospel of Luke*. Cambridge: Cambridge University Press.

Haenchen, Ernst. 1971. *The Acts of the Apostles: A Commentary*. Translated by Bernard Noble and Gerald Schinn. Oxford: Blackwell.

Hansen, R. P. C. 1967. *The Acts in the Revised Standard Version*. New Clarendon Bible. Oxford: Clarendon.

Harris, Murray J. 2011. *Prepositions and Theology in the Greek New Testament: An Essential Reference Resource for Exegesis*. Grand Rapids: Zondervan Academic.

Harvey, John D. 1998. *Listening to the Text. Oral Patterning in Paul's Letters*. Grand Rapids: Baker.

______. 2008. *Anointed with Spirit and Power. The Holy Spirit's Empowering Presence*. Explorations in Biblical Theology. Phillipsburg, NJ: P&R Publishing.

______. 2012. *Interpreting the Pauline Letters: An Exegetical Handbook*. HNTE. Grand Rapids: Kregel.

______. 2015. "Recognizing Normative Content in New Testament Narrative, with Special Attention Given to Luke-Acts." In *Transformed from Glory to Glory: Celebrating the Legacy of J. Robertson McQuilkin*, edited by Christopher R. Little, 79–96. Fort Washington, PA: CLC.

Hemer, Colin J. 1985. "First Person Narrative in Acts 27–28." *TynBul* 36:79–109.

______. 1987. "The Name of Felix Again." *JSNT* 31:45–49.

______. 1989. *The Book of Acts in the Setting of Hellenistic History*, edited by Conrad H. Gempf. WUNT 49. Tübingen: Mohr Siebeck.

Hertig, P. 2004. "The Magical Mystery Tour: Philip Encounters Magic and Materialism in Samaria." In *Mission in Acts: Ancient Narratives in Contemporary Context*, edited by Robert L. Gallagher and Paul Hertig, 103–13. American Society of Missiology Series 34. Maryknoll, NY: Orbis.

Hurtado, Larry W. 2003. *Lord Jesus Christ: Devotion to Jesus in Earliest Christianity*. Grand Rapids: Eerdmans.

Ice, Thomas D. 1994. "Dispensational Hermeneutics." In *Issues in Dispensationalism*, edited by Wesley R. Willis and John R. Master, 29–49. Chicago: Moody.

Jervell, Jacob. 1998. *Die Apostelgeschichte*. 17th ed. 3 vols. Kritisch-exegetischer Kommentar über das Neue Testament. Göttingen: Vandenhoeck & Ruprecht.

Johnson, Luke Timothy. 1992. *The Acts of the Apostles*. SP 5. Collegeville, MN: Liturgical Press.

Kaiser, Walter C., Jr. 1989. *Back toward the Future: Hints for Interpreting Biblical Prophecy*. Grand Rapids: Baker.

Keener, Craig S. 2012. *Acts: An Exegetical Commentary*. Vol. 1: *Introduction and 1:1–2:47*. Grand Rapids: Baker Academic.

Kistemaker, Simon. 1991. *Exposition of the Acts of the Apostles*. Grand Rapids: Baker.

Klauck, Hans-Josef. 2000. *The Religious Context of Early Christianity: A Guide to Graeco-Roman Religions*. Translated by Brian McNeil. SNTW. Edinburgh: T&T Clark.

Knox, John. 2000. *Chapters in a Life of Paul*. Rev. ed. Macon, GA: Mercer University Press.

Knox, Wilfred L. 1948. *The Acts of the Apostles*. Cambridge: Cambridge University Press.

Köstenberger, Andreas J., L. Scott Kellum, and Charles L. Quarles. 2016. *The Cradle, the Cross, and the Crown: An Introduction to the New Testament*. 2nd ed. Nashville: B&H Academic.

Larkin, William J., Jr. 1995. *Acts*. IVPNTC 5. Downers Grove, IL: InterVarsity Press.

Longenecker, Richard N. 1981. "The Acts of the Apostles: Introduction, Text and Exposition." In *The Expositor's Bible Commentary*, edited by Frank E. Gaebelein, 9:207–573. Grand Rapids: Eerdmans.

Losie, Lynn Allan. 2004. "Paul's Speech on the Areopagus: A Model of Cross-Cultural Evangelism." In *Mission in Acts: Ancient Narratives in Contemporary Context*, edited by Robert L. Gallagher and Paul Hertig, 221–38. American Society of Missiology Series 34. Maryknoll, NY: Orbis.

Marshall, I. Howard. 1980. *Acts*. TNTC. Grand Rapids: Eerdmans.

Marshall, I. Howard, and David Peterson. 1998. *Witness to the Gospel: The Theology of Acts*. Grand Rapids: Eerdmans.

Mason, Steve. 2003. *Josephus and the New Testament*. 2nd ed. Grand Rapids: Baker Academic.

McQuilkin, J. Robertson. 2009. *Understanding and Applying the Bible*. Rev. and expanded ed. Chicago: Moody.

Miller, Gary, and Phil Campbell. 2013. *Saving Eutychus: How to Preach God's Word and Keep People Awake*. Kingsford, NSW: Matthias Media.

Mitchell, Scott. 1980. "Population and Land in Roman Galatia." In *Augstieg und Niedergang dor Roemischen Welt*, II.7.2, 1074 n. 134. Berlin/New York.

Moule, C. F. D. 1953. *An Idiom Book of New Testament Greek*. Cambridge: Cambridge University Press.

Neudorfer, Heinz-Werner. 1998. "The Speech of Stephen." In *Witness to the Gospel: The Theology of Acts*, edited by I. Howard Marshall and David Peterson, 275–94. Grand Rapids: Eerdmans.

Palmer, Darryl W. 1993. "Acts and the Ancient Historical Monograph." In *The Book of Acts in its Ancient Literary Setting*. Edited by Bruce W. Winter and Andrew D. Clarke, 1–29. Grand Rapids: Eerdmans.

Pao, David W. 2000. *Acts and the Isaianic New Exodus*. WUNT 2/130. Tübingen: Mohr Siebeck.

Pervo, Richard I. 1987. *Profit with Delight: The Literary Genre of the Acts of the Apostles*. Philadelphia: Fortress.

Peterson. David G. 2009. *The Acts of the Apostles*. PNTC. Grand Rapids: Eerdmans.

Phillips, J. B. 1961. *Your God Is Too Small*. New York: Macmillan.

Polhill, John B. 1992. *Acts*. NAC 26. Nashville: Broadman.

Ramsay, Sir William M. 1895. *St. Paul the Traveller and the Roman Citizen*. London: Hodder & Stoughton.

Rapske, Brian. 1994. *The Book of Acts and Paul in Roman Custody*. Vol. 3 of *The Book of Acts in Its First Century Setting*. Edited by Bruce W. Winter. Grand Rapids: Eerdmans.

Redford, Shawn B. 2004. "The Contextualization and Translation of Christianity: Acts 9:1–9; 22:3–33; 26:2–33." In *Mission in Acts: Ancient Narratives in Contemporary Context*, edited by Robert L. Gallagher and Paul Hertig, 283–96. American Society of Missiology Series 34. Maryknoll, NY: Orbis.

Reeves, Keith H. 2004. "The Ethiopian Eunuch: A Key Transition from Hellenist to Gentile Mission, Acts 8:26–40." In *Mission in Acts: Ancient Narratives in Contemporary Context*, edited by Robert L. Gallagher and Paul Hertig, 114–22. American Society of Missiology Series 34. Maryknoll, NY: Orbis.

Robbins, Vernon K. 1978. "By Land and by Sea: The We-Passages and Ancient Sea Voyages." In *Perspectives on Luke-Acts*, edited by Charles H. Talbert, 215–42. Edinburgh: T&T Clark.

Robertson, A. T. 1934. *A Grammar of the Greek New Testament in the Light of Historical Research*. Nashville: Broadman.

Robinson, Barbara. 1972. *The Best Christmas Pagaent Ever*. New York: Scholastic.

Schmithals, Walter. 1982. *Die Apostelgeschichte des Lukas*. ZBKNT 3.2. Zurich: TVZ.

Schnabel, Eckhard J. 2004. *Early Christian Mission*. 2 vols. Downers Grove, IL: InterVarsity Press.

______. 2012. *Acts*. ZECNT 5. Grand Rapids: Zondervan.

Schwartz, Joshua. 1991. "Once More on the Nicanor Gate." *HUCA* 62:245–83.

Sherwin-White, A. N. 1963. *Roman Society and Roman Law in the New Testament*. Sarum Lectures. Oxford: Clarendon.

Skinner, Matthew I. 2003. *Locating Paul: Places of Custody as Narrative Settings in Acts 21–28*. AcBib 13. Atlanta: Society of Biblical Literature.

Sterling, George E. 1992. *Historiography and Self-Definition: Josephus, Luke-Acts, and Apologetic Historiography*. NovTSup 64. Leiden: Brill.

Stott, John R. W. 1990. *The Spirit, the Church, and the World: The Message of Acts*. Downers Grove, IL: InterVarsity Press.

Tajra, Harry R. 1989. *The Trial of St. Paul: A Juridical Exegesis of the Second Half of the Acts of the Apostles*. WUNT 2/35. Tübingen: Mohr Siebeck.

Talbert, Charles H. 1974. *Literary Patterns, Themes, and the Genre of Luke-Acts*. SBLMS 20. Missoula, MT: Scholars Press.

______. 1984. *Acts*. Knox Preaching Guides. Atlanta: John Knox.

______. 2005. *Reading Acts: A Literary and Theological Commentary on the Acts of the Apostles*. Rev. ed. Reading the New Testament. Macon, GA: Smyth & Helwys.

Tannehill, Robert C. 1994. *The Acts of the Apostles*. Vol. 2 of *The Narrative Unity of Luke-Acts: A Literary Interpretation*. Minneapolis: Fortress.

Towner, Philip H. 1998. "Mission Practice and Theology under Construction (Acts 18–20)." In *Witness to the Gospel: The Theology of Acts*, edited by I. H. Marshall and David Peterson, 417–36. Grand Rapids: Eerdmans.

Treier, Daniel J. 1997. "The Fulfillment of Joel 2:28–32: A Multiple-Lens Approach." *JETS* 40:13–26.

Turner, David L. 2019. *Interpreting the Gospels and Acts: An Exegetical Handbook*. HNTE. Grand Rapids: Kregel.

Valdez, Erbey Galvan. 2020. *On the Shores of Perga: How John Mark's Departure from the First Pauline Missionary Journey Changed the Gentile World*. Bloomington, IN: Westbow.

Weiser, Alfons. 1985. *Die Apostelgeschichte Kapital 13–28*. Gütersloh: Mohn.

Williams, David J. 1989. *Acts*. NIBC. Peabody, MA: Hendrickson.

Wilson, Mark W. 2009. "The Route of Paul's First Journey to Pisidian Antioch." *NTS* 55:471–83.

______. 2013. "The Ephesians Elders Come to Miletus: An Annaliste Reading of Acts 20:15–18a." *VE* 34:1–9.

______. 2016. "Saint Paul in Pamphylia: Intention, Arrival, Departure." *Adayla* 19:229–50.

Wimber, John. 1985. *Power Evangelism: Signs and Wonders Today*. London: Hodder.

Winter, Bruce W. 1993. *The Book of Acts in Its Ancient Literary Setting*. Vol. 1 of *The Book of Acts in Its First Century Setting*. Edited by Bruce W. Winter. Grand Rapids: Eerdmans.

Witherington, Ben, III. 1998. *The Acts of the Apostles: A Socio-Rhetorical Commentary*. Grand Rapids: Eerdmans.

KERUX COMMENTARY SERIES

---

1 & 2 Kings: A Commentary for Biblical Preaching and Teaching
David B. Schreiner & Lee Compson

Psalms, Volume 1: The Wisdom Psalms: A Commentary for Biblical Preaching and Teaching
W. Creighton Marlowe & Charles H. Savelle Jr.

Jeremiah and Lamentations: A Commentary for Biblical Preaching and Teaching
Duane Garrett & Calvin F. Pearson

Zephaniah–Malachi: A Commentary for Biblical Preaching and Teaching
Gary V. Smith & Timothy D. Sprankle

Acts: A Commentary for Biblical Preaching and Teaching
John D. Harvey & David Gentino

Ephesians: A Commentary for Biblical Preaching and Teaching
Gregory S. MaGee & Jeffrey D. Arthurs

Philippians: A Commentary for Biblical Preaching and Teaching
Thomas S. Moore & Timothy D. Sprankle

Colossians and Philemon: A Commentary for Biblical Preaching and Teaching
Adam Copenhaver & Jeffrey D. Arthurs

Hebrews: A Commentary for Biblical Preaching and Teaching
Herbert W. Bateman IV & Steven Smith

1 Peter: A Commentary for Biblical Preaching and Teaching
Timothy E. Miller & Bryan Murawski